Includes Exercise Files and De[mo...]

MACROMEDIA®

Flash™ MX 2004

Beyond the Basics

Hands-On Training

lynda.com/books

Shane Rebenschied | with Lynda Weinman

Macromedia Flash MX 2004 Beyond the Basics | H•O•T Hands-On Training

By Shane Rebenschied
Developed with Lynda Weinman

lynda.com/books | Peachpit Press
1249 Eighth Street • Berkeley, California • 94710
800.283.9444 • 510.524.2178
510.524.2221 (fax)
http://www.lynda.com/books
http://www.peachpit.com

lynda.com/books is published
in association with Peachpit Press,
a division of Pearson Education

ISBN: 0-321-22853-7

0 9 8 7 6 5 4 3 2

Printed and bound in the
United States of America

H•O•T | Credits

Original Design: Ali Karp, Alink Newmedia *(alink@earthlink.net)*

Editor: Jennifer Eberhardt

Copyeditor: Darren Meiss

Compositors: Rick Gordon, Deborah Roberti

Technical Editor: Ron Haberle

Beta Testers: Snow Dowd, Bill Perry

Cover Illustration: Bruce Heavin *(bruce@stink.com)*

Indexer: Larry Sweazy

H•O•T | Colophon

The original design for *Macromedia Flash MX 2004 Beyond the Basics HOT* was sketched on paper. The layout was heavily influenced by online communication–merging a traditional book format with a modern Web aesthetic.

The text in *Macromedia Flash MX 2004 Beyond the Basics HOT* was set in Akzidenz Grotesk from Adobe and Triplex from Emigré. The cover illustration was painted in Adobe Photoshop and Adobe Illustrator.

This book was created using QuarkXPress 4.1, Adobe Photoshop, Microsoft Office 2003, and OS X Panther on a Macintosh G4, running Mac OS X (10.3). It was printed on 50 lb. Utopia Filmcoat at Phoenix Color, Book Tech Park.

Dedication

What is a dedication anyway? I'd always skimmed over them in books. They were always ramblings about people I didn't know or inside jokes I didn't get. When you write a book, you essentially dedicate a portion of your *life* to accomplishing that specific task. A book dedication, therefore, is a statement that dedicates part of your *life* to someone or something. It's hard to fathom something more amazing than that idea.

Having said that, I dedicate this book–a moment in my life–once again to my wife, Marla, and my son and daughter, Ethan and Eva. You lived for five months without a husband and a father. It's good to finally be home.

Alright...enough of the gushy stuff...

Macromedia Flash MX 2004 Beyond the Basics | H•O•T — Table of Contents

Introduction

H•O•T

Macromedia Flash MX 2004
Beyond the Basics

A Note from Lynda Weinman

It has always been my opinion that most people buy computer books in order to learn, yet it is amazing how few of these books are actually written by teachers. In this book, you will find carefully developed lessons and exercises to help you learn intermediate-level Macromedia Flash MX 2004 skills. This book was written by one of lynda.com's most popular instructors, Shane Rebenschied, who not only works professionally as a digital illustrator/artist, but has years of teaching experience with lynda.com through classes, books, and movie-based instruction. Shane is a respected teacher for a reason–he knows his stuff, he has patience and respect for his students, he makes you laugh, and he teaches you really cool stuff.

This book is written for Macromedia Flash designers and developers who want to go beyond the basics of simple animations and button programming. It walks you through the creation of a real-world project that includes modular ActionScript code, video, sound, and interactivity. The premise of the hands-on exercise approach is to "learn by doing." It's one thing to read about a product and another experience entirely to try the product and get measurable results. Our motto is, "Read the book, follow the exercises, and you will know the product." We have received countless testimonials to this fact, and it is our goal to make sure it remains true for all of our Hands-On Training books.

Many exercise-based books take a paint-by-numbers approach to teaching. Although this approach works, it's often difficult to figure out how to apply those lessons to a real-world situation, or to understand why or when you would use the technique again. What sets this book apart is that the lessons contain lots of background information, advice, and insights into each given subject, designed to help you understand the process as well as the exercise.

At times, pictures are worth a lot more than words, and moving pictures are even better! When necessary, we have also included short QuickTime movies to show processes that are difficult to explain with words. These files are located on the **H•O•T CD-ROM** inside a folder called **movies**. It's our style to approach teaching from many different angles, because we know that some people are visual learners, others like to read, and still others like to get out there and try things. This book combines a lot of teaching approaches so that you can learn Macromedia Flash as thoroughly as you want to.

In this book, we didn't set out to cover every single aspect of Macromedia Flash MX 2004. The manual and many other reference books are great for that! What we saw missing from the bookshelves was a process-oriented tutorial that taught readers core principles, techniques, and tips in a hands-on training format.

We welcome your comments at **fl04btbhot@lynda.com**. Please visit our Web site at **http://www.lynda.com.** The support URL for this book is **http://www.lynda.com/products/books/fl04btbhot/**.

–Lynda Weinman

About the Author

Shane Rebenschied graduated from the Art Center College of Design in 1998 with an emphasis on traditional and digital media. Since then his work has appeared in the Society of Illustrators Los Angeles and New York annuals, as well as numerous national and international publications and advertising campaigns. He is a fan of old paper and stains, and he can often be found staring at pieces of corroded, rusted metal. Shane is a professional freelance illustrator, Macromedia Flash designer/developer/consultant, and author living somewhere in the Arizona desert. Shane is currently the "Photoshop Guide" at InformIT.com and is also the author of *Photoshop Elements 2 Hands-On Training*. He maintains an online illustration portfolio at **www.blot.com** and is a partner in the interactive design firm Cloudforge (**www.cloudforge.com**).

Past clients include BBC, *Maxim* Magazine, Scholastic, D'Arcy Masius Benton & Bowles, Tor, Harper Collins, Harlequin, Hodder Headline Plc, Summertime Publishing, Harcourt Brace, Ziff Davis, Hanley-Wood LLC, Spirit IC, *Backpacker* Magazine, *X-Files* Magazine, McGraw-Hill, Vanderbilt University, Flashforward, *Phoenix New Times*, *Miami New Times*, *San Francisco Weekly*, and *Cleveland Scene*.

Snapshot

Shane Rebenschied when he's semi-conscious.

Acknowledgments from Shane

What are you doing reading these acknowledgments? Shouldn't you be building something in Macromedia Flash MX 2004 instead? ;-)

My deepest gratitude and admiration goes to the following people:

Lynda Weinman, for giving me the opportunity to write this book. While I haven't always expressed it (I'm kinda bad at that emotional expressing myself thing), you've continually been a kind and influential force in my life and the life of my family. You have my sincerest appreciation for everything you've done.

Garo Green. What is there, really, to say about Garo Green? Like a solar flare, you're a force unto your own. Seriously, you're an awesome person to work with, and a great and valued friend. Thank you for letting me bother you with petty questions when you were sick, tired, and just sick and tired.

Darren Meiss, the copy editor for this book, for–once again–somehow finding meaning and clarity in the ramblings and scribblings I send you. Your ability to turn a muddled sentence into a statement of genius amazes me. Thank you for your hard and detailed work on this book.

Ron Haberle, the technical editor for this book. You have my eternal appreciation for your hard work, your attention to detail, and for making sure I didn't make myself sound like a complete moron. You write ActionScript like an artist creates a sculpture out of clay. You're truly a master at your craft.

Snow Dowd and **Bill Perry**, the beta testers for this book. What can I say? You both did an exceedingly awesome job and are fantastic Macromedia Flash designers and developers yourselves. Thank you for slogging through page after page of exercises, ramblings, and screenshots while at the same time maintaining a keen eye and an attention to detail. Your comments, suggestions, and criticisms have made this a far better book than I could have written alone. Be sure to check out Snow Dowd's work at **http://www.theMAKERS.com** and Bill Perry's work at **http://www.pocketpcflash.net/** and **http://www.flashdevices.net**.

Robert Hoekman, Jr., the consultant for this book. You were instrumental in shaping what this book is and, ultimately, what the reader learns from it. Thank you greatly for your thoughts and opinions. Check out Robert's work at **http://www.loveandrage.net**.

Peachpit Press and **Jennifer Eberhardt**, for letting me do my thing. You are remarkably open to the individuality of the author and maintaining their unique voice. I thank you for that and for sending me boxes of tissues to quell my sobbing when I thought I just couldn't go on. ;-)

Apple Computer, for making the coolest computers and most stable OS in the known universe.

Macromedia, for developing an incredible and revolutionary piece of software called Macromedia Flash.

The Universe, for existing. Is this place cool or what?

Ryan Conlan, for doing the majority of the incredible design work for the L.A. Eyeworks Web site that is built throughout this book. Ryan, if I were to die and come back as someone else, I'd come back as you… you swank, slick guy, you. Check out Ryan's über design goodness at **http://www.angelplasma.net** and **http://www.cloudforge.com**.

My mother, Adele Earnshaw (**http://www.adeleearnshaw.com**), for working your fingers to the bone so you could see me graduate from college. In appreciation, I'd be happy to leave your grandchildren with you for a whole week for some "quality time at Nana's house."

My wife, Marla Ferguson. While I wrote this book, you handled the kids, Thanksgiving, Christmas, New Years, two birthdays, the flu, snotty noses, soiled diapers, midnight feedings, and every other small thing that makes up "life" in-between. Remind me to buy you flowers more often.

My kids, Eva and Ethan, the "fantastic E's." I'd wither away and die without you both. Thank you for simply being alive.

And last, but certainly not least, **you, the reader**, for buying this book. Congratulations for wanting to further yourself and your knowledge. Keep learning!

How To Use This Book

Please read this section–it contains important information that's going to help you as you use this book. The following list outlines the information that is covered:

- The Formatting in This Book
- Interface Screen Captures
- Mac and Windows System Differences
- Opening Windows Files on a Mac
- A Note to Windows Users
- Making Exercise Files Editable on Windows Systems
- Making File Extensions Visible on Windows Systems
- Flash System Requirements–Authoring and Playback
- H•O•T CD-ROM Contents

The Formatting in This Book

This book has several components, including step-by-step exercises, commentary, notes, tips, warnings, and movies. Step-by-step exercises are numbered, and file names and command keys are bolded so they pop out more easily.

Captions and commentary are in italicized text: *This is a commentary*. File names/folders, command keys, menu commands, and URLs are bolded: **images** folder, **Ctrl+click**, **File > Open**, and **http://www.cloudforge.com**.

Interface Screen Captures

Most of the screen captures in the book were taken on a Windows machine using the XP operating system. The only time Macintosh shots were taken was when the interface differed from the Windows interface. I also own and use numerous Macintosh systems, so I noted important differences when they occurred and took screen captures accordingly.

Mac and Windows System Differences

Macromedia did a great job of ensuring that Macromedia Flash MX 2004 looks and works the same between the Macintosh and Windows operating systems. However, some differences do exist. If you are using this book with one of the Windows operating systems, please be sure to read the section below titled "A Note to Windows Users" carefully.

Opening Windows Files on a Mac

As you work with Macromedia Flash MX 2004, you might need to open a PC-created file on a Macintosh. Because of this, I wanted to make sure you were aware of a little glitch that could cause you some confusion. The Macintosh has difficulty recognizing FLA files that were created on a PC. This means that when using a Mac, you may not be able to simply double-click the FLA file that was created on a PC to open it. Instead, you will need to open Flash and then choose **File > Open**. At this point, you still may not see some of the FLA files when you use the Browse dialog box. You can get around this by changing the **Enable** option to **All Files**. This will display all files in the folder. You can then save the file on your Mac, and it should then open normally when double-clicked.

A Note to Windows Users

This section contains essential information about making your exercise folders editable and making file extensions visible.

Making Exercise Files Editable on Windows Systems

By default, when you copy files from a CD-ROM to your Windows 98/2000/XP hard drive, they are set to read-only (write protected). This causes a problem with the exercise files, because you need to write over some of them. To remove this setting and make the files editable, use the following procedures:

1. Copy the **la_eyeworks** folder from the **H•O•T CD-ROM** to your hard drive.

2. Right-click the **la_eyeworks** folder and choose **Properties**.

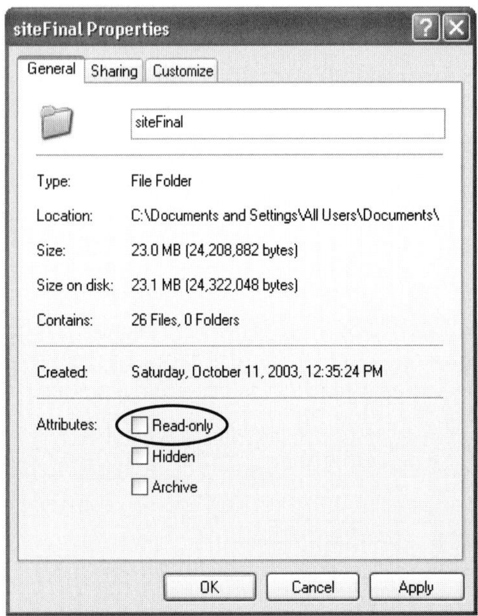

3. In the **General** tab, uncheck the **Read-only** check box. This will change the setting for all of the files that were selected. If **Archive** is selected, you can remove that check as well.

4. Click **OK**.

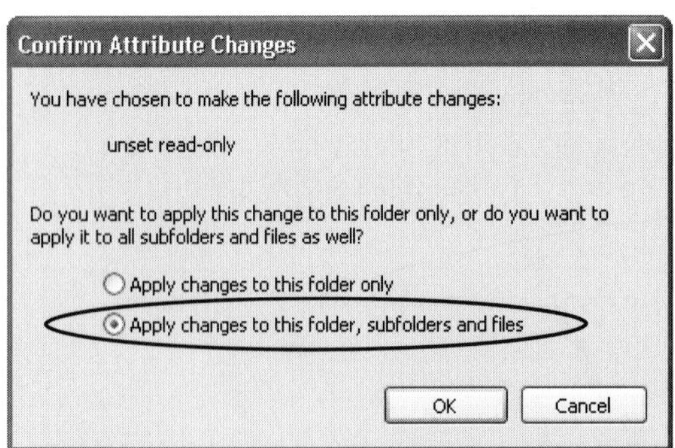

Note: *If there are other folders inside the **la_eyeworks** folder, change the attributes of those folders as well by selecting **Apply changes to this folder, subfolders and files** when the dialog box shown here appears.*

Making File Extensions Visible on Windows Systems

In this section, you'll learn how to turn on file extensions for the Windows operating system. By default, Windows 98/2000 users cannot see file extensions, such as SWF, FLA, JPG and so forth. Fortunately, you can change this setting!

1. Double-click on the **My Computer** icon on your desktop. **Note:** If you (or someone else) has changed the name, it will not say **My Computer**.

2. Select **View > Folder Options** (or **Tools > Folder Options** in Windows 2000/XP). This opens the **Folder Options** dialog box.

3. Click on the **View** tab at the top. This opens the **View** options screen so you can change the view settings for Windows.

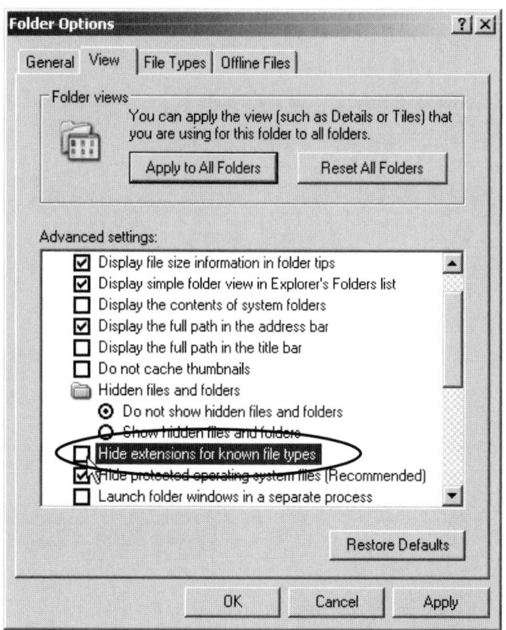

4. Uncheck the **Hide file extensions for known file types** check box and click **Apply**. This makes all of the file extensions visible.

Macromedia Flash MX 2004 System Requirements

This book requires that you use either a Macintosh operating system (Power Macintosh G3 running System 10.2.6 or later) or Windows 98, Windows 2000, or Windows NT 4.0, Windows ME, or Windows XP. You also will need a color monitor capable of 1024 x 768 resolution and a CD-ROM drive. I suggest that you have at least 256 MB of RAM in your system, because that way you can open Macromedia Flash MX 2004 and a Web browser at the same time. More RAM than that is even better. The following chart cites Macromedia's system requirements.

Macromedia Flash MX 2004 System Requirements

AUTHORING **Windows**	**Macintosh**
600 MHz Intel Pentium III processor or equivalent	500 MHz PowerPC G3 processor
Windows 98 SE, Windows 2000, or Windows XP	Mac OS X 10.2.6 or higher
128 MB RAM (256 MB recommended)	128 MB RAM (256 MB recommended)
275 MB available disk space	215 MB available disk space
1024 × 768, 16-bit (thousands of colors) color display or better	1024 × 768, 16-bit (thousands of colors) color display or better
CD-ROM drive	CD-ROM drive

PLAYBACK **Platform**	**Browser**
Windows 98	Microsoft Internet Explorer 5.x, Netscape 4.7, Netscape 7.*x*, Mozilla 1.*x*, AOL 8, and Opera 7.11
Windows ME	Microsoft Internet Explorer 5.5, Netscape 4.7, Netscape 7.*x*, Mozilla 1.*x*, AOL 8, and Opera 7.11
Windows 2000	Microsoft Internet Explorer 5.*x*, Netscape 4.7, Netscape 7.*x*, Mozilla 1.*x*, CompuServe 7, AOL 8, and Opera 7.11
Windows XP	Microsoft Internet Explorer 6.0, Netscape 7.*x*, Mozilla 1.*x*, CompuServe 7, AOL 8, and Opera 7.11
Mac OS 9.x	Microsoft Internet Explorer 5.1, Netscape 4.8, Netscape 7.*x*, Mozilla 1.*x*, and Opera 6
Mac OS X 10.1.x or Mac OS X 10.2.x	Microsoft Internet Explorer 5.2, Netscape 7.*x*, Mozilla 1.*x*, AOL 7, Opera 6, and Safari 1.0 (Mac OS X 10.2.*x* only)

What's on the CD-ROM?

Exercise Files and the H•O•T CD-ROM

Your exercise files are located inside a folder called **la_eyeworks** on the **H•O•T CD-ROM**. In Chapter 3, you will be instructed to copy the exercise files to your hard drive. You will be using those exercise files to complete the various exercises throughout the book. Unfortunately, when files originate from a CD-ROM, the Windows operating system defaults to making them write-protected, meaning that you cannot alter them. You will need to alter them to follow the exercises, so please read the section titled "A Note to Windows Users" earlier in this Introduction for instructions on how to convert them to read-and-write formatting.

QuickTime Files on the H•O•T CD-ROM

There is a folder on the **H•O•T CD-ROM** called **movies** that contains several QuickTime tutorial movies for some of the exercises in this book. It's my hope that these movies will help you understand some of the more difficult exercises in this book by watching me perform them myself. If you like these movies, you should definitely check out the *Learning Macromedia Flash MX 2004 CD-ROM* by me, Shane Rebenschied at **http://www.lynda.com**, which contains several hours' worth of QuickTime movies on Flash MX 2004. If you find that you enjoy watching Macromedia Flash instruction in video format, be sure to also check out *Learning Intermediate Flash MX 2004*, also by me, at **http://www.lynda.com**. These videos are, in essence, this entire book but in video format.

Demo Files on the CD-ROM

In addition to the exercise files, the **H•O•T CD-ROM** also contains a free 30-day trial version of Macromedia Flash MX 2004 for Mac or Windows. All software is located inside the **software** folder on the **H•O•T CD-ROM**. I have included trial versions of the following:

- Macromedia Flash MX 2004
- QuickTime 6
- Sorenson Squeeze

I also have included several players on the **H•O•T CD-ROM**. If you don't have these players installed already, you should install them before working with any exercise in this book that calls for one of them. All of the players are located inside the **software** folder. I have included the following:

- Flash Player 7 (Windows only)
- Shockwave Player 8 (Windows only)
- QuickTime Player 6

Background

What Is This Book?	What Is "Beyond the Basics"?
Modular, Modular, Modular	What's New in Flash MX 2004
Upgrading?	What Am I Building?
Updates	Finished Site Files

H•O•T

Macromedia Flash MX 2004
Beyond the Basics

Right now, you're probably standing in a small, cramped bookstore aisle, trying to decide whether or not you should buy this book. You're probably thinking to yourself, "What is this book going to teach me? Do I *want* to learn what this book is teaching? *Can* I learn what's in this book? How much of Flash do I really want or need to know?" These are all perfectly valid questions. Questions which I most assuredly can't answer in this first paragraph. So bear with me, and read a little more of this first chapter as I outline the topics this book will cover, what you will be learning, and how you will go about doing it. You may want to go find a place to sit down first, though. ;-)

What Is This Book?

In its barest essence, the goal of this book is to teach you intermediate-level Flash. (See the next section, "What Is 'Beyond the Basics?'," for more about what the definition of "intermediate" is.) Expanding upon that goal, this book aims to teach you intermediate-level Flash in the context of building *things*. In this book, you will learn how to use Flash MX 2004 (you can use Flash MX Professional 2004 as well) to construct the following (partial list):

- Scrolling text (text that is loaded into Flash from an external text file and has its appearance modified using **C**ascading **S**tyle **S**heets [CSS])
- Dynamic slideshow (from external JPG files that are loaded into your Flash movie)
- Feedback form
- MP3 jukebox
- Streaming video player
- Navigation menu
- Preloader
- Macromedia Flash Player 7 detector
- Much, much, more

To learn how to build these things, you should already be very comfortable and familiar with basic Flash concepts such as the tools, animation techniques of motion and shape tweening, various types of symbols and what their differences are, *at least* basic ActionScript knowledge such as **`stop`**, **`play`**, **`goto`**, and **`loadMovie`**, what variables are, and so forth. For a good idea of what this book assumes that your Flash MX 2004 knowledge base is, see the lynda.com H•O•T book, *Macromedia Flash MX 2004 Hands-On-Training*. Scan through the table of contents of that book and make sure that you are very familiar with the topics that book covers. From a skill-level perspective, this book starts where that book leaves off, and it ends where an "advanced" Flash MX 2004 book would pick up.

By the end of this book, you will have covered how to take all these separate pieces (MP3 jukebox, streaming video player, and so forth) and integrate them into a unified, cohesive Web site. This book focuses on "modular" Flash MX 2004 construction–that is, I emphasize constructing your Flash MX 2004 content in a way where you can treat the separate pieces of a Web site as individual modules. A module can play and function by itself, or it can easily be plugged into a Web site for added functionality. As I'll describe later in this chapter, this gives you–a Flash MX 2004 designer/developer–great freedom when creating your content because it can be used and reused for multiple purposes.

What Is "Beyond the Basics"?

The term "beyond the basics" applies to the next level of education after the basic "Hands-On Training" series. What does that mean? Essentially, "Beyond the Basics" is intermediate-level, whereas the basic "Hands-On Training" series is beginner-level. To get the most out of this book, you should have a firm grasp of beginner-level Flash development. You should already know the Flash interface including:

- How to access the various panels
- How to use the different drawing tools
- How to animate using motion and shape tweens
- How to work with and create the different types of symbols, as well as how the symbols differ from each other
- How to import assets (vectors, bitmaps, and so forth) into your project
- How to work with text and the different types of text fields
- Basic ActionScript such as **stop**, **play**, **goto**, and **loadMovie**
- Variables
- Working with sound and video
- Publishing your movies

Having a solid grasp of these beginner-level Flash MX 2004 concepts will allow you to absorb the information in this book, as best as possible.

One of the most overlooked areas of Flash MX 2004 training is the intermediate-level. If you look around on the bookshelves for other Flash MX 2004 training books, you'll see a plethora of material that covers beginner-level and advanced-level Flash MX 2004 learning, but a vast desert exists where the "intermediate" Flash MX 2004 training should be. Did I say desert? Heck, I meant Death Valley. There is very, very little material that allows the average Flash MX 2004 student to gracefully navigate the chasm that exists between intro- and advanced-level Flash MX 2004. This book is designed specifically to bridge that gap by teaching you not only intermediate-level Flash MX 2004 content, but best development practices, thinking modularly, and site development as well.

So if you're not quite ready to enter the "advanced" Flash MX 2004 realm where you learn about arrays, data binding, and the like, but you're ready to move past the basics and into more challenging Flash MX 2004 design and development, calmly rise from your seat and advance slowly (walk, don't run) to the checkout counter with this book in hand.

Modular, Modular, Modular

Picture this. You design and build a Web site for a client. You build for them a slideshow to show off their products, create some scrolling text about the company and the products they sell, develop a video player, make a menu system so the viewer can navigate around the site, and even add a little music player. Then, a month later, imagine you're contacted by a company who saw the previous site you did and wants you to build a site for them. This potential client would also like similar features–slideshow, video player, menu, music, and so forth–but they're in a real hurry, and they need the site done yesterday. Taking a deep breath, you calmly explain to the client that Flash sites are complex, can't be done overnight, and require lots of ActionScript programming to customize their features. You thank the client for complimenting you on the site you previously built but clarify to them that to build a new Web site–even though the features are similar–would still take a lot of time to construct because everything needs to be customized. Or does it?

In this book, the focus is not only to show you intermediate-level ActionScript and how to build a Flash MX 2004–based Web site, but how to do it in a **modular** fashion. Instead of building a customized Web site where everything is tied together and reliant upon each other, you'll learn how to break the Web site up into logical, stand-alone modules. These modules will work the same in one site as they could in another, or even be removed from a Web site completely and played by themselves (like on a PDA [Personal Data Assistant] device such as a Pocket PC or even burned onto a CD-ROM or attached to an e-mail). This provides you with an *extraordinary* amount of freedom because it allows you to **design a module once, then reuse it for multiple purposes**. This comes at a price, however. To construct a modular Web site takes a little extra pre-planning when building those modules, so that they will function the same *in* a Web site as they would *outside* of it. But in exchange for extra pre-planning, you gain–in return–the satisfaction of turning to the aforementioned hypothetical client, and saying, "Sure, I can have something for you by tomorrow." ;-)

What's New in Flash MX 2004

As with any product upgrade, Flash MX 2004 introduced a huge list of improvements, modifications, and additions. Probably the biggest change is that Macromedia split Flash into two "flavors": Flash MX 2004 and Flash MX Professional 2004. In essence, they are the same product. (Even when you purchase Flash, everyone gets the same program shipped to them. But if you purchased and thereby enter a "Professional" serial number, it then "unlocks" the professional features.) The following table describes a few of the new features, and whether those features are only available in the "Professional" version.

New Features			
Feature	**Description**	**Flash MX 2004**	**Flash MX Professional 2004**
Timeline effects	Allows you to easily create standard animations in a "wizard" interface. Easily create animations such as "Blur," "Drop Shadow," and "Explode."	√	√
Behaviors	Easily add some common actions with one click. Behaviors allows you to apply prebuilt ActionScript functionality to keyframes, button symbols, or movie clips symbols.	√	√
PDF & EPS file support	Easily import and integrate content into your Flash MX 2004 movies with support for high-quality PDF and EPS files from such programs as Adobe Acrobat and Adobe Illustrator.	√	√
Integrated Help	Help is now built into Flash MX 2004 in its own panel! By simply pressing **F1** on your keyboard, you can open the Help panel. From there, you can search through the Help documentation, or by clicking on the **How Do I** tab, you can read step-by-step instructions for completing common tasks. The Help documentation is also frequently updated by Macromedia. Click the **Update** button at the top of the Help panel to download the latest Help documentation from Macromedia's servers!	√	√
Spell checking and search/replace	Yes. It's finally here. You can now spell check the text in your Flash MX 2004 movie! The *extremely* powerful search and replace feature allows you to perform search and replace across actions, the Library, the Stage, layers, fonts, text fields...the list goes on and on. A *very* powerful new addition and a real butt-saver.	√	√
Video Import Wizard	Provides you with a "wizard" interface when importing video. The Video Import Wizard allows you to edit your video by clipping out unwanted segments, change the hue and value of the video, and set up preset encoding and processing settings so the same settings can be easily applied to other videos that you import into your Flash projects.	√	√

continues on next page

New Features *continued*			
Feature	**Description**	**Flash MX 2004**	**Flash MX Professional 2004**
External FLV support	Macromedia Flash Player 7 now supports progressive downloading (via an HTTP Web server) of external FLV files, using ActionScript, into your Flash MX 2004 projects! A similar feature was also available for Macromedia Flash Player 6, but it supported FLV streaming only if the project was served from the Macromedia Flash Communication Server. Now, in Macromedia Flash Player 7, a FLV can be progressively downloaded from a standard Web server without requiring any extra server software. The neat thing about this is that the video will actually start playing while it is still downloading. Although this may sound like a small detail, it's actually a **big** deal because you can now have video in your Flash project that is not limited to file size, or video length, and has a better video playback quality/speed, too!	√	√
Aliased text	This is a biggie for Flash designers of the past. Flash MX 2004 now has an **Alias Text** button in the Properties inspector that allows you to, of course, alias (remove the smoothing [anti-aliasing]) around text. This allows you to have small text point sizes while still maintaining readability. The aliasing of your text is assured if you use the Alias Text feature in conjunction with **View > Snapping > Snap to Pixels.** This will prevent all fonts, even the traditionally troublesome bitmap fonts, from becoming blurry on playback.	√	√
Improved performance	Macromedia touts a performance increase of two to eight times that of Flash MX, for projects that are created in Flash MX 2004 and viewed in Macromedia Flash Player 7. This includes Flash playback performance as well as faster video performance at full frame rates. Huzzah!	√	√

continues on next page

New Features *continued*

Feature	Description	Flash MX 2004	Flash MX Professional 2004
ActionScript 2.0	ActionScript now more closely adheres to ECMA (**E**uropean **C**omputer **M**anufacturers **A**ssociation) standards with the introduction of AS 2.0. AS 2.0 allows experienced programmers to more easily create robust code using object-oriented programming. You'll see some examples of AS 2.0 being used in this book.	√	√
Flash video exporter plug-in	A separate plug-in that allows you to give FLV export functionality to third-party video editing/ compression applications such as Apple Final Cut Pro, Discreet Cleaner, Avid Xpress/Media Composer, and so forth. This FLV exporter plug-in also allows you to have higher-quality video in your Flash MX 2004 projects.		√
Advanced components	Use advanced components such as media components for audio and video playback, as well as data components for easily integrating data-driven content into your Flash MX 2004 projects.		√
History panel/ commands	Flash MX 2004 now has a History panel! The History panel keeps track of the previous 100 changes (by default—but you can change this in the preferences) you've made to a project. You can easily move back and forth between modifications by clicking on a change in the panel. As if that wasn't enough, you can also select a series of changes in the History panel and convert it into a reusable command, easily accessible from the **Commands** menu. Wowzers!	√	√
CSS support in HTML text fields	Text fields with HTML support enabled can now utilize Cascading Style Sheet (CSS) styles! This provides you with even *more* options when styling your text and also allows you the added benefit of sharing external CSS files with the HTML and Flash MX 2004 portions of a Web site.	√	√

These are just a *few* of the new features that have been added to both Flash MX 2004 and Flash MX Professional 2004. For a list of many more additions and improvements, visit Macromedia's Flash MX 2004 Features page here:

http://www.macromedia.com/software/flash/productinfo/features/

This book does *not* cover any of the features that are specific to the Flash MX Professional 2004 version. As you can see in the previous table, many of the specialized features found in the Professional version truly are professional. Don't worry, though–there are more than enough capabilities in the "standard" version of Flash to enable you build even the most complex of Web sites.

Upgrading from MX to MX 2004?

Sometimes, upgrading your software from an old version to a newer one can be a steep, slippery slope. Fortunately, that really isn't the case if you're upgrading from Flash MX to Flash MX 2004. Oh, sure there are new features and additions (as I mentioned in the last section) that you need to learn, but in terms of "gotchas" or caveats, there aren't that many. Obviously, not *all* differences are listed here, but here are a few items that you need to be aware of if you're upgrading from Flash MX:

- **Insert > Convert to Symbol** is now located at **Modify > Convert to Symbol.** In fact, quite a few items have been reorganized in the main menu structure, many of which have been nested in sub-menus within the main menu. These changes were introduced by Macromedia to help increase the usability of navigating around the plethora of features.
- When you launch Flash MX 2004, you'll immediately recognize the newly added "Start Page." The **Start Page** is a window that opens when you launch Flash MX 2004, and it allows you to quickly perform a variety of common tasks. From the Start Page, you can create a new blank FLA, create a FLA based on a template, open a previously opened FLA, and more. Depending on whom you talk to, the Start Page is either a great new addition or an annoyance. Give it a try yourself and see what you think.
- The Show Streaming feature is now called **Simulate Download**. This will allow you to test your Flash MX 2004 movie to see how it would appear if accessed using various connection speeds. However, in Flash MX, show streaming would not work if using **`loadMovie`**. All assets loaded using **`loadMovie`** would ignore show streaming and you therefore would have no idea how your Flash movie would play if accessed using different connection speeds. In Flash MX 2004, Simulate Download now will accurately simulate the download of assets that are loaded using **`loadMovie`** (and its replacement, the MovieClipLoader). Yayy!

- Some of you might have wrestled with a bug in Flash MX that caused bitmap graphics to shift, split, or wiggle if you animated other graphics on top of them. This bug has now been fixed in Flash MX 2004 when publishing for Macromedia Flash Player 7.
- The Scrollbar component has been removed from Flash MX 2004. Instead it has been replaced by its successor, the **TextArea** component.
- Components have been reworked in Flash MX 2004. They are now referred to as **V2 components**. Because of the new component framework, when you add a component to your project, it can easily–and instantly–increase the file size of your movie by *at least* 40 kilobytes. The idea behind that is that even though the initial increase in file size may be drastic, adding more components should only increase the file size by small amounts. It's one of those "better in the long run" arrangements.
- When working in the Actions panel, the ActionScript Normal mode has been removed. Instead, the Actions panel is now permanently set in **Expert mode**, meaning that you just manually type the actions in the Actions panel, or just double-click an action from the Actions toolbox.
- ActionScript is now case-sensitive. In other words if, in Flash MX, you defined a variable **`myVar`**, you could later refer to that variable as **`myvar`** (notice the lack of capitalization of the letter "v") and everything would still work. However, because Flash MX 2004 is case-sensitive, Flash would see those as two *different* variables, and the script would break. When writing ActionScript, be aware of how you use capitalization in your scripts.

To see a complete list of the new additions to both Flash MX 2004 and Flash MX Professional 2004, point your Web browser to the following URL:

http://www.macromedia.com/software/flash/productinfo/upgrade_center/extended_list.html

You can also read a great article on Macromedia's Web site about migrating from Flash MX to Flash MX 2004 here:

http://www.macromedia.com/devnet/mx/flash/articles/migrate_flashmx2004_print.html

I. What Am I Building?

In this opening exercise, you will examine the online L.A. Eyeworks Web site, which is the culminating project that you will build at the end of this book. At the beginning of each chapter, you will get to see the finished result of what you're building *before* you actually start building it. That way, as you're assembling a module, you'll already have a clear understanding of what the final result looks like and how it behaves.

First you need to make sure you have the latest version of the Macromedia Flash Player.

1. Open your preferred browser and type in this URL:

http://www.macromedia.com/go/getflashplayer

---

2. Follow the instructions to download and install the latest version of the Macromedia Flash Player. This will ensure that you're using an up-to-date version of the Macromedia Flash plug-in.

---

3. After you've finished installing the Macromedia Flash Player 7, enter this URL in your preferred Web browser:

http://www.lynda.com/flashbtb/laeyeworks/

As you can see, when the site finishes loading, there are quite a few things going on. You'll see the main menu navigation bar at the top of the page, a splash graphic in the middle, and a music player at the bottom of the page. The music is turned off by default so that viewers aren't inundated with sound as soon as they visit the Web site. If you want to listen to music as you browse through the site, click the Play button in the lower-left corner of the site.

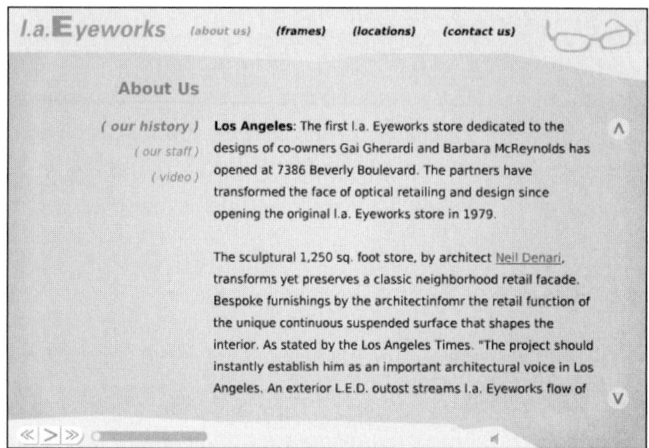

4. Click the **(about us)** button at the top of the page in the navigation bar. This will load the **About Us** section. Notice that the **About Us** section has a submenu and is divided up into three subsections: **our history**, **our staff**, and **video**.

*The **our history** and **our staff** subsections both contain scrolling text. (You can scroll the text up or down by clicking on the up and down arrow buttons at the right side of the page.) One of the interesting things about this text, however, is that it is styled using Cascading Style Sheets (CSS)! This is a new feature in Flash MX 2004. Cascading Style Sheets have traditionally been a way to define the style and layout of "standard" HTML-based Web pages. But now, Flash can use CSS to style text as well! You'll learn more about this feature in later chapters.*

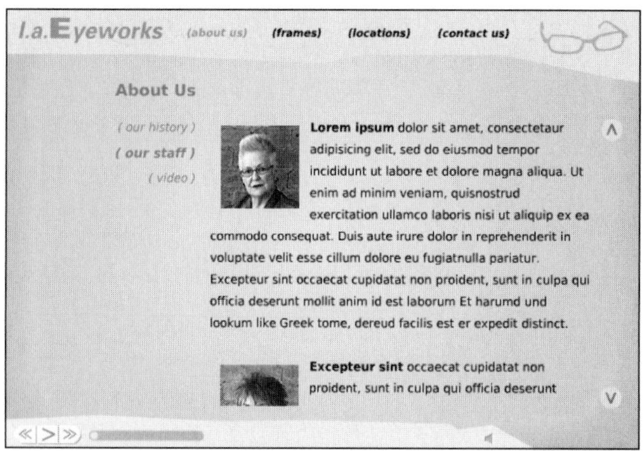

5. Click the **(our staff)** subsection. Notice how, integrated into the text, are two animated images. This demonstrates another new Flash MX 2004 feature: inline JPG or SWF files. You can now integrate into the text (inline) within a dynamic (HTML-enabled) text field, JPG or SWF graphics. Neat!

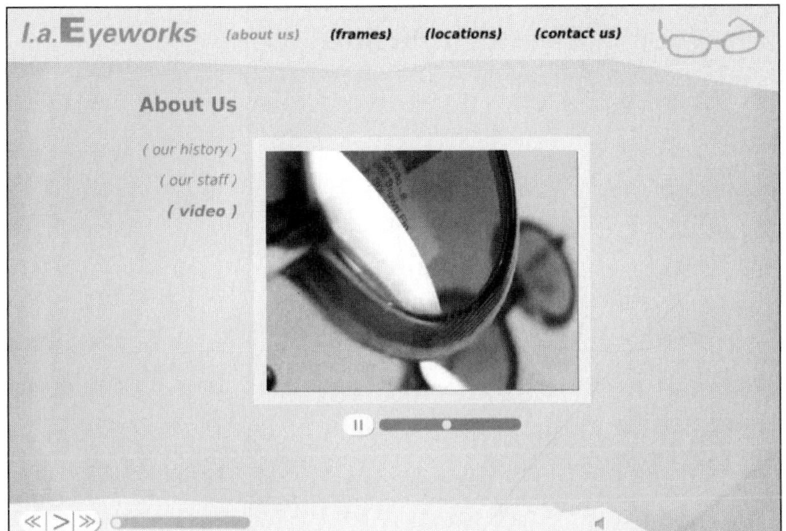

6. Click the **(video)** subsection button. Here you will see a video that will start playing. (**Note:** If you have a slow Internet connection, it will take longer for the video to start playing.)

This is actually an external FLV file (meaning, it wasn't placed in the Flash MX 2004 movie; it's a separate FLV file that exists apart from the other files) that is being streamed off of a Web server (no fancy server software required), using ActionScript, into the About Us section. This is also a new feature to Macromedia Flash Player 7. (I'll talk all about this new feature, and its advantages, in Chapter 11, "Building a Video Player."*) Notice that below the video has a pause button so that the viewer can pause/play the streaming video. Next to that is a progress slider that displays the playback progress of the playing video.*

Next, you're going to explore some of the other sections.

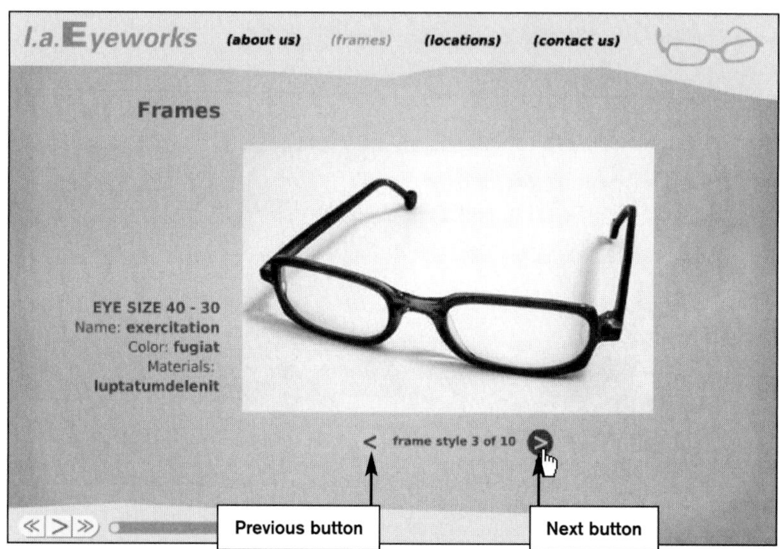

7. Click the **(frames)** button in the navigation bar at the top. This will load in the **frames** section, which is an interactive slideshow that allows you to view a sampling of 10 frames. Click the **Next** button to advance to the next image, or choose the **Previous** button to go back to the previous image.

Notice that to the left of each of the images is an updated description of each pair of frames. Below the frames' images are buttons to navigate backward and forward through the slideshow. Between the buttons is a bit of text that informs you–out of how many frames total–which frame you're currently viewing. The interesting thing about this slideshow is that each frame image is an external JPG file, and each text description is an external TXT file (that also gets styled using CSS). These files are dynamically loaded into the Macromedia Flash SWF file and displayed as the user clicks through the slideshow. You will learn how to build this slideshow, as well as why it is constructed in this manner, in Chapter 7, "Building a Slideshow."

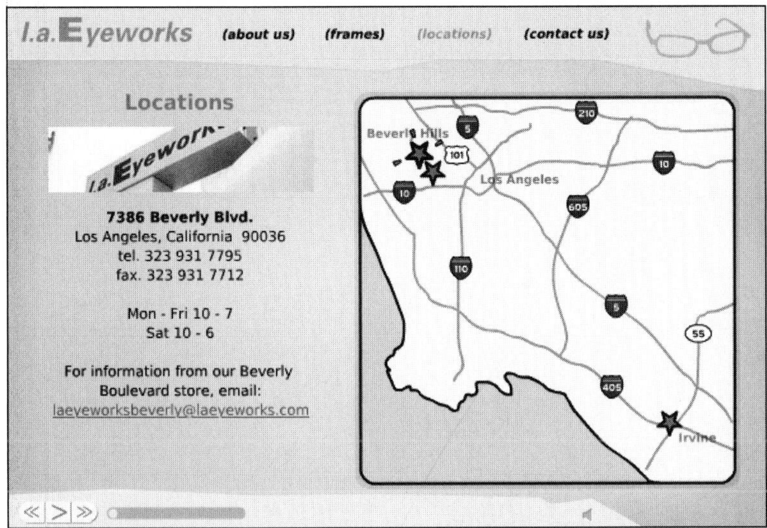

8. Next, click the **(locations)** button from the navigation bar. This will load an interactive map. Clicking on one of the stars on the map of Los Angeles (and surrounding areas) will load more information about that particular L.A. Eyeworks location. Similar to the **Our Staff** subsection in **About Us**, the location detail displays an inline, animated SWF file, accompanied by CSS-styled text.

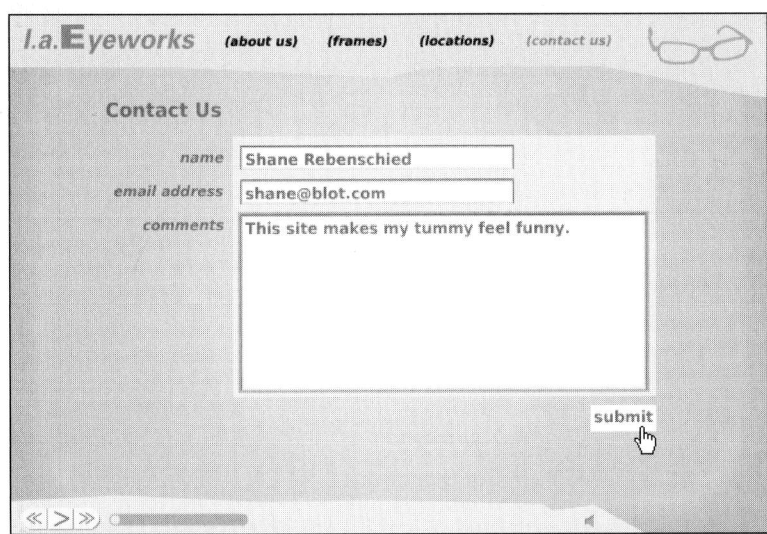

9. From the main menu navigation bar, click the **(contact us)** button. This will load a feedback form where you can enter your **name**, **email address**, and **comments**. Once you have entered your information in this form, click the **submit** button.

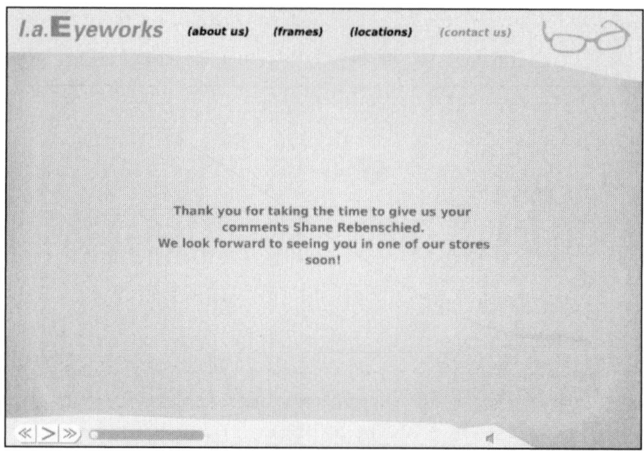

If you entered information in each field, when you click the submit button you will be presented with this "thank you" message. Notice how your name (or whatever you entered in the name field) has been inserted into this message. When you get to this part, you'll be surprised how easy it is to do this. :-) If you didn't enter information in each field, when you clicked the submit button you would have been presented with an error message. This error message would politely inform you that you forgot to fill out each field and would provide you with a back button so you could fix the error of your ways.

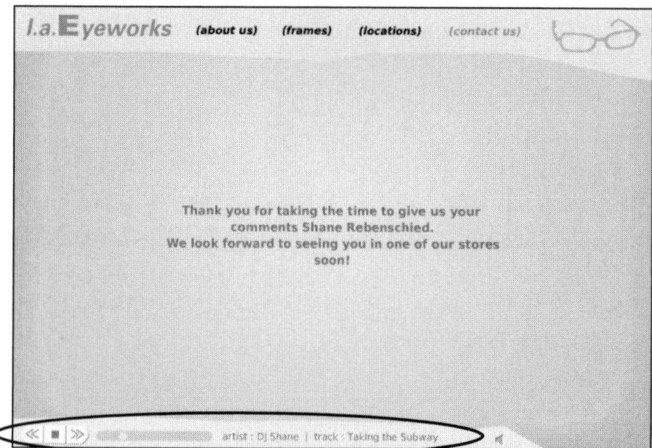

10. Lastly, click the **play** button down at the lower-left corner of the site window. This will begin downloading and playing an MP3. Like the video player module, this MP3 player progressively downloads an MP3 from the Web server. Not only that, but this MP3 player also displays the artist and track name of the currently playing MP3. (This information is retrieved from the MP3's ID3 tags [more on that later].) It also allows you to change the currently playing music track by clicking on the **next track** and **previous track** buttons, and adjust the volume of the playing music by dragging the **volume** slider. It's one sexy bit of Flash MX 2004 ActionScript that will wow your neighbors and amaze your friends.

So as you can see in this brief site tour, there's a lot going on in this site. During the construction of this Web site, you'll be introduced to a wide array of topics and ideas. Everything ranging from site development techniques, to workflow suggestions, to a multitude of ActionScript objects (classes), variables (properties) and functions (methods). As you begin to learn these new techniques and ActionScript, each step will be explained in detail.

Updates

At the time of this book's publication, there is only one update for Flash MX 2004. Update 7.0.1, available for both Macintosh and Windows operating systems, is for users of both Flash MX 2004 and Flash MX Professional 2004. The 7.0.1 update addresses many items, but I can safely say, **go download it now!** You can easily download the 7.0.1 update by pointing your preferred Web browser to the following URL:

http://www.macromedia.com/support/flash/downloads.html

If you would like to see a list of the items affected by the 7.0.1 updater, point your Web browser to this URL:

http://www.macromedia.com/support/documentation/en/flash/mx2004/releasenotes.html#Update

Finished Site Files

Located at **http://www.lynda.com/books/hot/fl04btbhot/** are all of the finished FLAs that make up the completed L.A. Eyeworks site. If you ever need to refer to the completed site files as you're working through the exercises–for whatever reason–feel free to refer to those completed files. As is noted in a few places throughout this book, there are a few minor differences when authoring this site on Windows or on a Macintosh. The finished site files are the completed site files for Windows users. For us Mac users, there will only be a few minor differences–that are, again, outlined throughout this book–that mostly have to do with creating shared fonts, using those shared fonts, and referencing them within CSS files. So if you're referring to the completed site files on a Macintosh, please note that there will be some minor discrepancies with some of the files. These discrepancies are mentioned in this book. Mac users can ensure the synchronicity between the completed site files and the steps in the book by applying those platform-specific changes to the completed files as they are reached.

In the next chapter, you will begin to learn about Web site development/construction techniques, as well as which file formats work best when importing graphics from a separate image-editing program.

---

2. Where Do I Start?

| What Is the Site Construction Process? |

| What Program Do I Start In? |

| Integration | Workflow Suggestions |

H•O•T

Macromedia Flash MX 2004
Beyond the Basics

As a Flash instructor–teaching at lynda.com's training center in Ojai, California, for three years, teaching at numerous corporations, and speaking at three FlashForward conferences in San Francisco and New York–there is one question that follows me no matter where I go. That question is, "How do I take all of this piecemeal knowledge and build a site? Where do I start? Where does it all begin?" Okay, okay... so that's three questions...but they all really fall under one question: **Where Do I Start?**

This chapter attempts to answer that question. Keep in mind that there are many different approaches to this process. I will outline one way to go about constructing a site, show how to integrate all sorts of files into Flash, and offer some workflow suggestions that should make your life a little easier as you begin the process of building modules and–in the end–a Web site, all inside of Flash MX 2004.

What Is the Site Construction Process?

The site construction process is a very unique thing. What follows is a general guideline of steps that, when followed, should help to ease any bumps and bruises that might occur as you transition from the idea of the Web site in your head, to working on actual designs, to bringing those designs into Flash, to building the finished Web site. I would expect that, over time as you gain more experience and know-how in Flash, you will modify these steps so they are geared more towards your workflow and technique. Without further ado, here is my suggested three-part process for constructing a Flash–based Web site:

1. Content and Target Audience

a. What Is the Content?

Before you even start *thinking* about design, sit down and come up with a solid plan of what you want to say or present, and how you're going to go about doing it. What are you going to be putting online for the world to see? What's the subject matter?

For the L.A. Eyeworks site, the content of the Web site revolves around the company–the glasses, their history, their staff, their culture, their love of art, and so forth. L.A. Eyeworks, as a company, gives design a high priority. Everything from the frames they sell to the stores they sell them in. In preparing to design the site, I knew the same emphasis in design had to be carried over into the Web site. I also knew that I had the following material to integrate into the site design:

- Text about the history of L.A. Eyeworks
- Staff information
- Video about L.A. Eyeworks
- Pictures and information about the glasses
- Where the L.A. Eyeworks stores could be located
- A form where a visitor to the Web site could send feedback
- Music

This was the material that I had to work with and had to take into consideration as I began thinking about the construction of the Web site.

b. Who Is the Target Audience?

After you've determined what the content is going to be, you next need to determine who is going to be interested in this content. Your content consumer is called your "target audience." For example, if you're designing a Web site for a villa in France, your target audience is most likely going to be 1) wealthy, and 2) have "refined" tastes. Once you can identify what the target audience is, you will then have a head-start on how the site is going to be presented. Using the aforementioned villa as an example, you probably would choose a color palette that is similar to the landscape of the area and of the villa itself (ask the client to fly you out there so you can "gather reference" ;-)), choose script fonts for decorative type and easily readable sans-serif font faces for body text, and simple (yet elegant) navigation. As you can see, determining your target audience defines the *entire design* of the Web site and, as such, should be decided early on in the site development process.

For the L.A. Eyeworks Web site, the target audience–generally–is the urban, young, hip L.A. crowd. This information is gathered by the type of person that purchases glasses from L.A. Eyeworks as well as the type of person that L.A. Eyeworks caters to. Because of that target audience, I can ascertain that using Flash MX 2004 to build the Web site is certainly warranted, and that I can "get away with" more in terms of design. I can legally (in a design sense) use more garish colors, louder music, and a less traditional user interface if I so choose. By clearly defining who the target audience is, I know specifically what I can and cannot use in the construction of the Web site. And yes, even whether I should use Flash MX 2004 or not is also determined by who my target audience is.

2. Layout and Design

a. Flowchart

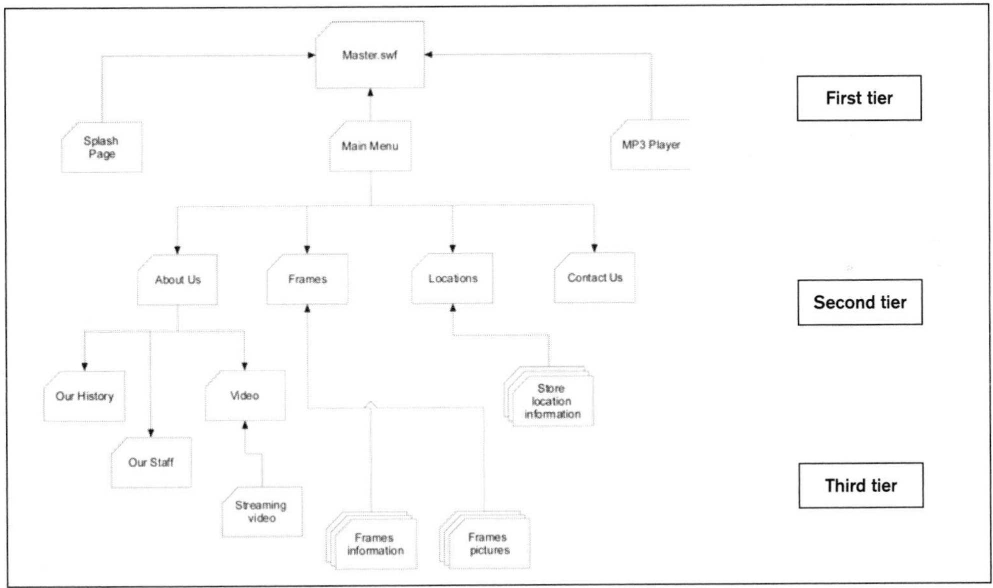

Now that you've figured out your content and who the target audience for that content is, you're ready to start creating a flowchart. A flowchart, as its name implies, is built so you can see the "flow" of your Web site (see the screen shot above for an example of a flowchart). A flowchart allows you to define the overall structure of the site and helps you to begin thinking about the navigation and how the viewer is going to traverse through your site. It also helps you to locate and remove any possible road blocks in the navigation; that is, being able to navigate to one section of your Web site but then not having a way to navigate *away* from that page and getting stuck there. The structure of your Web site, as laid out in the flowchart, is also commonly referred to as "tiers." The fist tier of the site is often the main page and navigation bar. The second tier is any page that is linked to from the first tier, and so on and so forth.

The screen shot above is the flowchart for the L.A. Eyeworks Web site. As you can see, the first tier is the main "master" SWF where the splash page, main menu, and MP3 player initially load. From the main menu, the viewer can navigate to the second tier, which includes the About Us, Frames, Locations, and Contact Us sections. In the screen shot above, the third tier is really a pseudo tier because it doesn't represent a separate "page" of information, just information that is being loaded into the second tier. But from this flowchart you can easily and quickly see how the viewer will navigate through the L.A. Eyeworks site. This gives you a very good idea how the navigation bar needs to be constructed and the options that will comprise it.

b. Storyboard

After the flowchart comes the storyboard. The storyboard is, essentially, an evolvement of the flowchart. Similar to the storyboards that are created for film and television, your storyboard would be a small sketch (you can whip out the ol' pen and paper if you'd like) that would define where the main design elements would be, as well as a general estimate of the physical size of the movie. Is it going to be wide? Tall? Small? You should start to think, in general terms, how big the movie is going to be. For instance, here's a storyboard sketch for the main L.A. Eyeworks page:

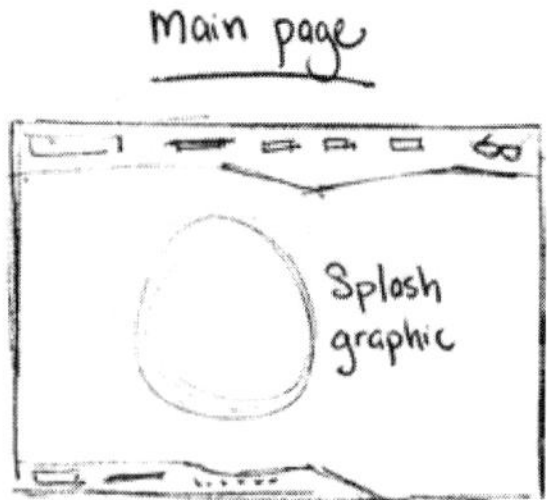

So as you can see, the storyboard would be just a collection of quick sketches that very generally begins to block in the graphic elements of your Web site. The storyboard is where you first begin to think about the overall design of the site. From this sketch of the main L.A. Eyeworks page, you can begin to see where the main menu is located (and some of the elements contained within it), the music player, and the main splash graphic. Oftentimes the client will want to sign off on the storyboard sketches, so you might want to consider "formalizing" them (a fancy word for makin' them look purty) by creating them in another graphics program like Macromedia FreeHand, Macromedia Fireworks, Adobe Illustrator, or any other graphics-editing program that you're familiar working with. There are also many programs out there that are used *specifically* for creating flowcharts and diagrams. Although there will be more recommendations in Appendix A at the end of this book, a couple of quick recommendations would be Graffle (**http://www.omnigroup.com/**) for Mac users or Microsoft's Visio (**http://office.microsoft.com/**) for Windows.

c. Static Mockups

To further extend the storyboard, another (optional) step is to take the simple storyboard graphics (or site diagrams) and import them into a new Flash MX 2004 project. You can then quickly add invisible buttons (with simple **gotoAndStop** actions assigned to them) to the navigational elements of the mockup to create a click-through of the entire site. This process is a great way to bring the flowchart and storyboard together to manufacture a quick, clickable mockup of the site navigation. This step allows you to more easily identify navigational bottlenecks as well as gives you a good understanding of the flow of the site as the viewer navigates from page to page. Building a static mockup should minimize the possibility of discovering navigational mistakes *after* the design or construction process has begun.

d. Design

Now that you've done all that prep work, it's time to start working on the design. The design of the site is often the step in the site development process that most of the questions revolve around. Which program should I start working in? Should I start working in Flash? Macromedia Fireworks? Adobe Illustrator? Adobe Photoshop? Ahhhh! Take deep breaths. Yes, there are myriad design programs on the market today, each with their own pros and cons. This question will be answered, in detail, in the section entitled "What Program Do I Start In?" later in this chapter. Until then, just keep in mind that the design of the site comes after the storyboard.

For the L.A. Eyeworks Web site, I constructed some initial design concept graphics in three different programs. I used Adobe Photoshop to plan out some rough designs, decide on the physical size of the site, build the background graphic, and decide on a color scheme. I used Adobe Illustrator to build some vector graphics, such as the vector glasses' shape, and the main menu background shape. I then used Flash MX 2004 to integrate the content, lay it out, and begin to experiment with the animated mask for the main menu, as well as a little of the interactivity. I then contracted the remaining design work out to a designer-friend of mine (Ryan Conlan at cloudforge.com *plug *plug) who worked on the designs in Adobe Photoshop. When he was done with the designs, he gave the Photoshop file to me. I opened his file in Photoshop, exported each section (about us, frames, and so forth) as a JPG graphic, imported each into a new FLA in Flash, and then used it as a template to build the finalized (and slightly modified) work on top of. Although there are many ways to go about integrating graphics that were created in other programs (some of which integrate into Flash MX 2004 easier than others) into a Flash MX 2004 movie (as you'll see later), Adobe Photoshop was the format of choice in this case.

3. Development and Implementation

a. Flash – Step 1: Lay Out the Navigation

Out of all of the steps, these next three are the ones that will differ the most from person to person. When beginning the final design phase, I prefer to get the navigation laid out first. Why? Because the navigation is an *essential* element of the site. It is the main vehicle for the viewer to get the content that they want and then get out of there. Once the design and layout of the navigation has been settled, you will then know *exactly* how much physical space you have left over for the second- and third-level tier content.

When planning out the navigation for the L.A. Eyeworks site, I knew–based on the movie size of 600 pixels wide by 400 pixels high–that whatever navigation layout I came up with, it needed to take up a minimal amount of space to leave enough room for the content. Based on that, I decided to go with a long, skinny, horizontal layout that spanned the length of the Web site. By being loaded into its own level, the navigation bar would be visible throughout the Web site, regardless of whichever section was currently being viewed.

b. *Flash – Step 2: Design and Implement the Main and Tertiary Content*

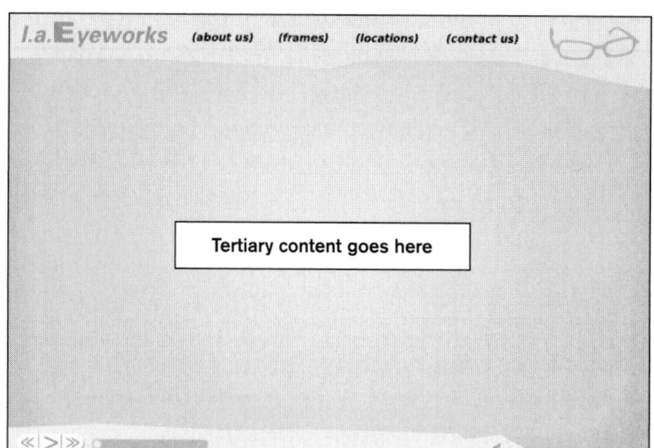

Once I've laid out the navigation, I now know how much available design space is left over for **tertiary content**. Tertiary content refers to layout, designs, and the implementation of those second- and third- (and so forth) tier pages.

c. *Flash – Step 3: Create Navigation Interactivity*

This is the last step in the construction process. By now, the designs are finished, and the content is all laid out and can be viewed and interacted with correctly. All that is left to do is to program the main navigation menu so that when the viewer clicks on a button in the navigation bar, the appropriate section loads and displays. Of course, after you've programmed the navigation bar and the site is working correctly, the very *last* step is to create your Flash plug-in detector, upload your content to a Web site, and begin the testing process.

4. Deployment/Upload and Testing

Lastly, you will–of course–need to deploy (upload) the finished site. Once the completed site has been fully uploaded, then you should begin the process of testing the Web site on a variety of computers using a variety of Internet connections. Your Flash MX 2004 project can become a completely different beast, in the blink of an eye, once it is uploaded to a Web site for testing. Once you start viewing the site as it gets streamed over the Internet, and as it gets played back by fast or slow computers, you may notice many things you didn't notice before. Some content may load before others, some graphics might not appear, and–potentially–some content might not load at all! For the most part, if anything is going to "break" when you test the project on different computers, it's either going to be information (data), or text. There's a variety of ways to deal with text in Flash MX 2004, and because of that, there's more room for compatibility errors, font embedding issues, and the like. Testing remains a vital step in the deployment of *any* Web-based content.

Flash has a built-in Simulate Download feature that allows you to simulate how a SWF will look/perform when downloaded over an Internet connection of various speeds. (You can choose what speed to test it on.) Although this is a great and useful feature (and one that you will be using later in this book), it simulates what a SWF file would look like if downloaded at a *constant* speed. Unfortunately, downloading content on the Internet is rarely constant. Internet traffic, noise in your phone line, and so forth can have drastic effects on *actual* download speeds. Because of that, it's best to test a Web site using "real-world" Internet connections over a period of time. Using the Simulate Download feature also only shows you (of course) how your movie performs on *your* computer. Viewers on faster or slower computers may have a completely different experience when viewing your project. That's why it's always a good idea to view a Flash project on as many different kinds of computers as possible. This testing should–ideally–approximate how an average Internet viewer would see your work. Usually after a round or two of testing, you'll need to make some modifications/adjustments to your site so that it is relatively glitch-free.

When building your site and coding ActionScript, I would first suggest to just get it–whatever "it" is that you're working on–working and then go back and make it pretty. As you are programming your interactivity and fixing the bugs that will inevitably crop up, it'll be easier to track down the source of a bug if you have less going on. That way, if something goes wrong, you can more easily trace a bug because you will know that it could only be one or two things that are causing the problems. After you have the interactivity working correctly, *then* you can go back and slowly start making it pretty and adding on to it, making sure to test it as you modify it. If you build and test in stages, it will greatly help you track down problems before they become buried under lines of code, fonts, and symbols.

For the L.A. Eyeworks Web site, because a lot of attention was given to how (from an ActionScript viewpoint) all the assets (SWFs, JPEGs, variables, and so forth) would be loaded, it's relatively easy to program the navigational interactivity.

Resources on Site Construction

The subjects of Web site construction, usability, and user interface design are hot topics. If you stop by your local bookstore or library, there should be a whole section devoted to these themes. If you want to read up before you begin your Web site planning, here are my book suggestions:

- *Don't Make Me Think: A Common Sense Approach to Web Usability* by Steve Krug. New Riders, 2000.
- *Web Navigation: Designing the User Experience* by Jennifer Fleming. O'Reilly & Associates, 1998.
- *Web Redesign: Workflow that Works* by Kelly Goto and Emily Cotler. New Riders, 2001.

What Program Do I Start In?

So you've got your content, figured out your target audience, created a flowchart, even sketched out storyboards, and now you're ready to start designing your Web site. Should you just open Flash MX 2004 and start drawing, or should you start somewhere else? If somewhere else, where? What program should you start designing in? The answer is, without sounding like a cop-out, whichever program you are most comfortable working in. Yes, yes...I can hear the boos and hisses now, but hear me out.

Sure, each graphics-editing program has its pros and cons. Each graphics-editing program also has *different* pros and cons when it comes to integrating with Flash MX 2004. The question is, are those pros and cons *serious* enough to warrant you switching your graphics-editing program of choice for another one that you're not so familiar with? My answer would be, "No." Now what if you don't really have a "graphics-editing program of choice?" What should you do then? For those of you who aren't attached to a specific graphics-editing program, or who might consider switching for a greater ease of workflow, here's a more detailed breakdown of the different image-editing applications.

There are quite a few image-editing applications currently out on the market. For this example, I'm going to focus only on a few of the "heavy hitters." When beginning to work on your designs, your choices are essentially the following:

- Flash MX 2004
- Macromedia FreeHand
- Macromedia Fireworks
- Adobe Illustrator
- Adobe Photoshop

Separating those into groups, you have Flash MX 2004, Macromedia FreeHand, and Adobe Illustrator that are *exclusively* vector-based image-editing applications. On the other side of the graphics gamut, you have Macromedia Fireworks and Adobe Photoshop which both—primarily—work and output graphics in a bitmap (raster) format. Without getting into the details at this point, here are a few things to keep in mind when choosing one of these programs to create your graphics:

Flash MX 2004, being the Macromedia program that it is, will obviously have slightly stronger integration capabilities with *other* Macromedia applications. When importing Macromedia Fireworks or Macromedia FreeHand graphic files into Flash MX 2004, you will get more options to specify how Flash MX 2004 treats those files when they are imported. Translation? Macromedia products play well with other Macromedia products. That's not to say that you can't correctly import Adobe Photoshop or Adobe Illustrator graphics. In fact, exporting your Adobe Illustrator designs as a SWF file can yield some fantastic results when imported into Flash MX 2004. Now obviously, if you could do all your design work directly inside of Flash MX 2004, it would greatly streamline your workflow. But Flash MX 2004's strength is being an animation, interactivity, and programming application, and not really a graphics-editing application. Chances are, you (or other designers working with you) will need to do a decent portion of your design work elsewhere. In the next exercise, I will show you the different options you're given when importing various graphics from numerous sources.

With Flash MX 2004's improved support for high-quality PDF and EPS importing, coupled with the capability for Adobe Illustrator to export great SWF files, your choice for which image-editing program to do the majority of your design work in should really come down to whichever one you're most comfortable working with. Everything else is just details.

I. Installing the Site Font

In this exercise, you will install the free, cross-platform, open source font *Bitstream Vera* that you will use throughout the creation of the L.A. Eyeworks site content. The font is included on the **H•O•T CD-ROM**, so all you have to do is follow the steps in this exercise to install the font on your computer.

You can also download and read more about the Bitstream Vera font on the GNOME Web at **http://www.gnome.org/fonts/**.

1. Quit Flash MX 2004 if you have it open. When installing fonts, it's best if you have your applications closed first.

---

2. Open the **la_eyeworks** folder on the **H•O•T CD-ROM**, and then navigate through the folders **resources > font > ttf-bitstream-vera-1.10**. Within the **ttf-bitstream-vera-1.10** folder are all the faces of the Vera font. Install all the faces of the Vera font onto your computer. If you need more information about installing fonts for your particular operating system, here are some resources that should help you:

- For Mac OS X v10.2 and earlier:
  http://docs.info.apple.com/article.html?artnum=106417
- For Mac OS X 10.3 (Panther):
  Simply double-click the font faces you want to install. This will launch Font Book and give you the option to install the font at that time.
- For Windows 95/98/2000/NT/ME/XP:
  http://support.microsoft.com/default.aspx?scid=kb;en-us;314960

In the next exercise, you will learn how well a graphic created in another graphics-editing program, such as Macromedia Fireworks or Adobe Illustrator, can be imported into a Flash MX 2004 movie. As a Flash MX 2004 designer or developer, you will most likely be working with graphics provided by co-workers or freelance designers that were created in various programs. You will learn which file formats import into Flash MX 2004 with the least amount of difficulty in the next exercise.

---

2. Integration

It's a rare Flash MX 2004 Web site designer that can create all the graphics needed for a Web site, all using Flash MX 2004. However, as the drawing and typography tools gain more features and flexibility with each release of Flash, you might start to see more designers using Flash more often to create the majority of their graphics. Until then, however, it's actually quite common that as a designer, you will be developing the Web site graphics in *multiple* graphics programs and then assembling them all into one cohesive project–in the end–in Flash. Trying to get programs to play well with each other's files has never been a dauntless task, however.

In this exercise, you're going to learn which file formats can be imported into a Flash MX 2004 movie with the *least* amount of trouble. You're going to start by creating an empty FLA file in Flash MX 2004 and then importing a layout of the navigation menu for the L.A. Eyeworks Web site, all created with different image-editing programs. This will allow you to see the options you're given when importing images of various file types into Flash MX 2004, as well as which file types translate better when imported into Flash MX 2004. By the end of this exercise, you should have a much stronger understanding of which file formats you can rely on and, conversely, which ones you should avoid when building graphics for your Flash MX 2004 Web site.

1. On the **H•O•T CD-ROM** is a folder titled **file_types**. This folder contains the various image files that you will use for this exercise. Copy this folder, and its contents, onto your **Desktop**.

---

2. Open Flash MX 2004 and create a new, blank FLA by pressing **Ctrl+Alt+N** (Windows) or **Cmd+Option+N** (Mac). Or just click **Flash Document** under the **Create New** header in the **Start Page**.

---

3. Change the **Stage** dimensions to better fit the size of the graphics you will be importing by pressing **Ctrl+J** (Windows) or **Cmd+J** (Mac) to open the **Document Properties** dialog box. (You can also open the **Document Properties** dialog box by clicking the **Size** button in the **Properties inspector**).

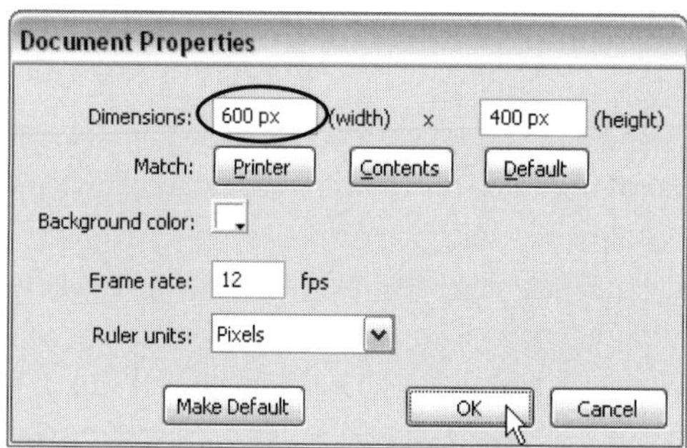

4. Change the **width** to **600 px** and click **OK**.

This will give you more horizontal space to fit the graphics you will be importing.

First, you're going to import the navigation bar graphic that was created with Macromedia Fireworks MX 2004.

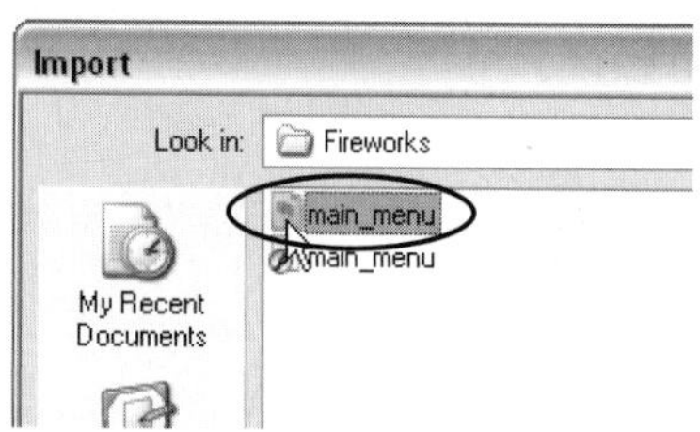

5. Choose **File > Import > Import to Stage**. From the **Import** dialog box, navigate to the **file_types** folder that you copied over earlier. It should be located on your **Desktop**. Then, navigate to the **Fireworks** folder, and double-click the file **main_menu.png**. (Depending on your operating system, you might not see the **.png** extension.) This is a native PNG graphic that was saved from Macromedia Fireworks MX 2004.

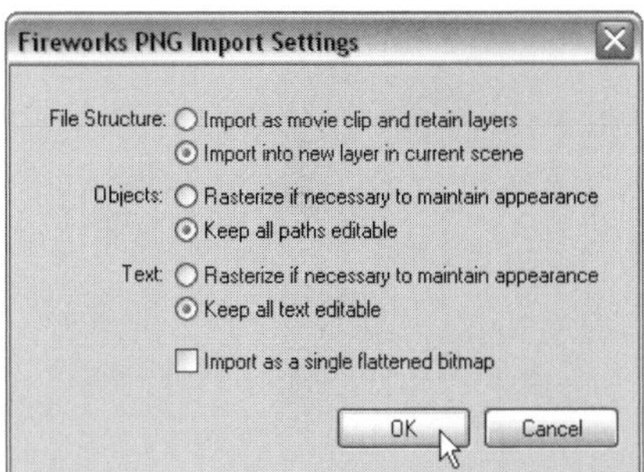

6. Flash MX 2004, recognizing that you're attempting to import a Macromedia Fireworks MX 2004 PNG file, will open the **Fireworks PNG Import Settings** dialog box to allow you to specify *how* you want the graphic to be translated when it's imported into Flash MX 2004. As you can see by looking over the options, you can choose whether or not you want the graphic to be imported into a movie clip symbol or into a new layer. You can also choose whether or not you want the text and objects to remain editable, or–to maintain their closest appearance to the original graphic–to rasterize the images, thereby making them uneditable. Select **Import into new layer in current scene**, **Keep all paths editable**, and **Keep all text editable**. Make sure **Import as a single flattened bitmap** is unchecked, and then click **OK**.

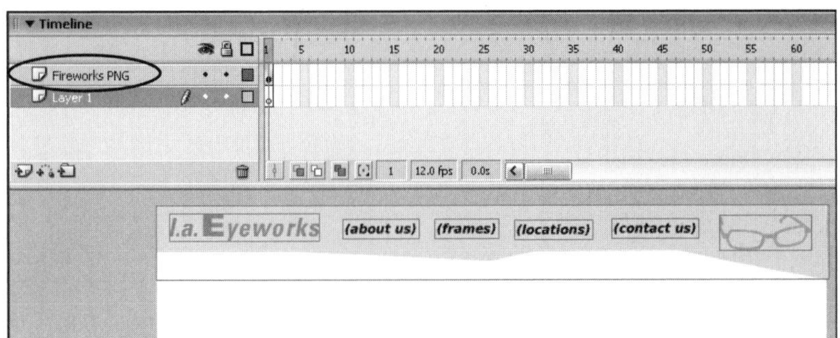

The Macromedia Fireworks MX 2004–created navigation bar will then be imported, complete with graphics and text, into its own new layer titled ***Fireworks PNG****. In Step 6, if you had chosen to* ***Import as movie clip and retain layers****, Flash MX 2004 would have automatically created a movie clip symbol, imported the Macromedia Fireworks MX 2004 PNG into that movie clip, and sorted the various parts of the image into named layers that corresponded to the named layers in the Macromedia Fireworks MX 2004 file. Neat! This has the benefit of 1) retaining the layer naming/separation that you set up in the Macromedia Fireworks MX 2004 file, and 2) because the Macromedia Fireworks MX 2004 graphics are imported into a new movie clip, it keeps the scene Timeline nice and clutter-free. Also, if you had created any symbols in the Macromedia Fireworks MX 2004 file, when you imported the PNG into Flash MX 2004, it would retain those symbols! It unfortunately doesn't keep the symbol names that you defined in Macromedia Fireworks MX 2004, however.*

7. Deselect the selected graphics by pressing **Esc**. Then, double-click the navigation option **(about us)**. Notice how the text is still editable, here inside of Flash MX 2004!

8. Close this FLA, don't save the changes, and create a new, blank FLA. Change the movie dimensions to **600 px** wide.

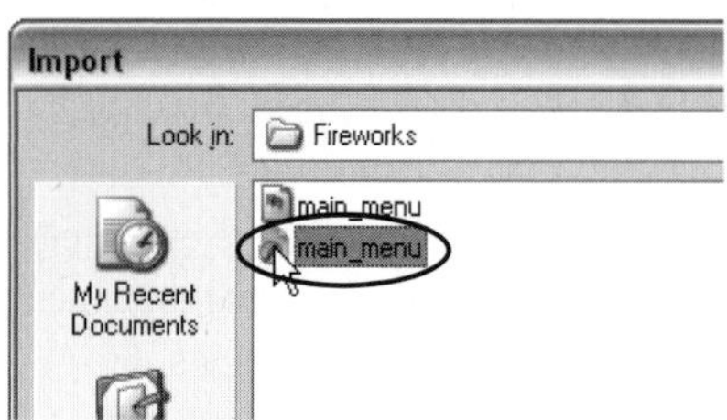

9. Choose **File > Import > Import to Stage**. From the **Import** dialog box, navigate to your **Desktop > file_types > Fireworks** folder and double-click the file **main_menu.swf** file. This is a SWF file that was exported from Macromedia Fireworks MX 2004.

Notice how it looks identical to the Macromedia Fireworks MX 2004 PNG file that you imported previously.

10. Double-click the **(about us)** navigation option. This time, however, notice how the text "(about us)" has been placed within a group. Within the group, however, the text still remains editable. The only difference, in this case, between a Macromedia Fireworks MX 2004–created PNG and exported SWF is that the text is directly editable from the PNG import, but the SWF import groups the editable text. All in all, Flash MX 2004 likes both Macromedia Fireworks MX 2004 PNG and SWF files, with minor differences between the imported graphics and text and the original Macromedia Fireworks MX 2004 graphic.

Next you're going to import a graphic created with Macromedia FreeHand.

---

11. Close this FLA, don't save the changes, and create a new, blank FLA. Change the movie dimensions to **600 px** wide.

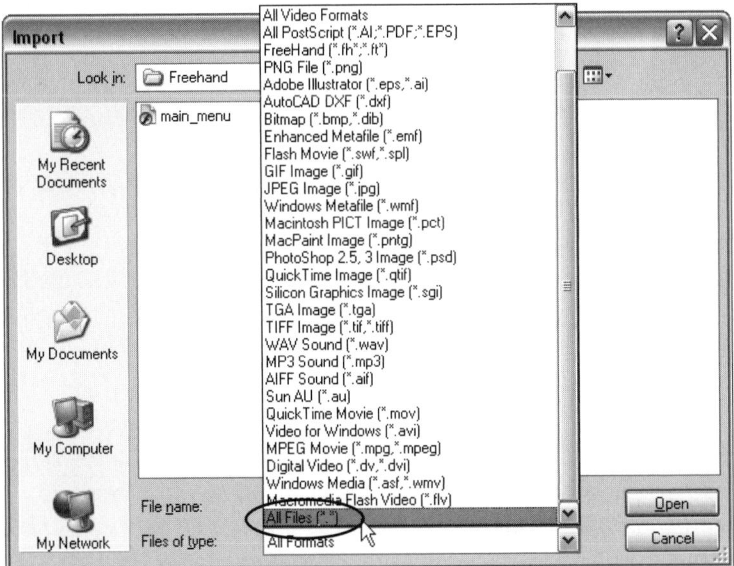

12. Import a file to your **Stage** by pressing **Ctrl+R** (Windows) or **Cmd+R** (Mac). From the **Import** dialog box, navigate to your **Desktop > file_types > Freehand** folder. If you don't have Macromedia FreeHand installed on your computer, you'll most likely only see one file, **main_menu.swf**. If you don't see the FreeHand file **main_menu**, click the **Files of type** pull-down menu and choose **All Files**. This will show you all the files in the current folder, whether Flash MX 2004 thinks it can import them or not.

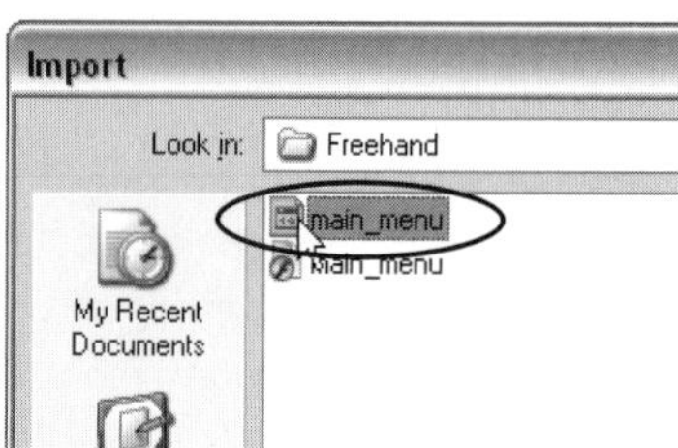

13. Double-click the FreeHand file **main_menu** to import it into your Flash MX 2004 movie.

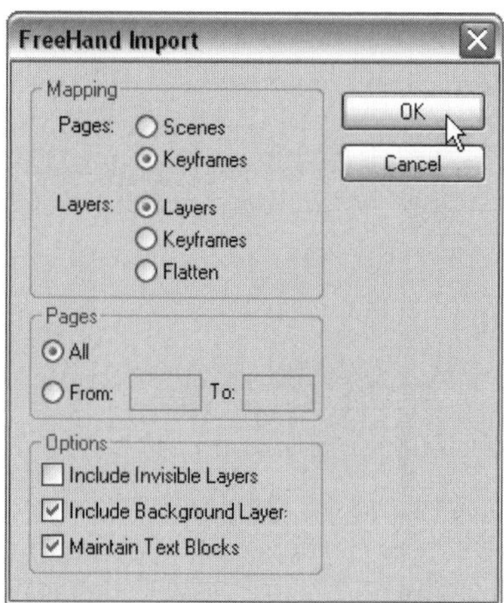

14. Flash MX 2004, understanding that you're importing a Macromedia FreeHand file, opens the **FreeHand Import** dialog box. From here, you can specify a few options to modify how Flash MX 2004 will treat various aspects of this file as it imports it. You can specify what the Macromedia FreeHand pages and layers will be translated to when they are imported, as well as which FreeHand pages you want to import, whether or not invisible and background layers are included, and whether Flash MX 2004 should maintain the editable text blocks.

15. Modify your options so they match the ones in the screen shot above, and then click **OK**.

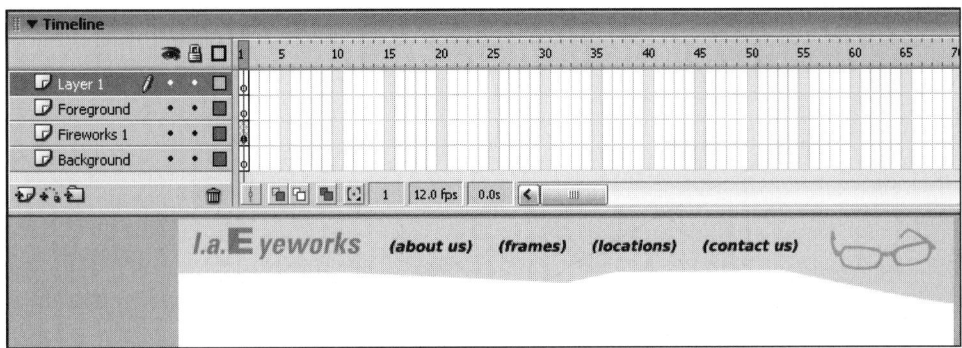

One of the first things you'll notice is that new layers have been automatically created for you. These layers, and their names, correspond to the layering in the original Macromedia FreeHand document! However, because of how the graphics were set up in the original Macromedia FreeHand document, only one of the layers, ***Fireworks 1****, actually contains the graphics.*

16. Double-click the navigation text **(about us)**. You'll notice that, just like the imported Macromedia Fireworks MX 2004 file, the text is editable! Strangely, the text blocks for text imported from a Macromedia FreeHand document are all fixed-size text blocks (as represented by the square at the top-right corner of an editable text block). To convert a fixed-size text block into a "stretchy" text block (one that resizes to fit the text you type within it), double-click the square at the top-right corner of the text block.

Other than that, you'll notice that the Macromedia FreeHand file translates nicely when imported into the Flash MX 2004 movie. The graphics look great, and the text is still editable.

Now that you've seen how the two flagship Macromedia image-creation applications fared–Macromedia FreeHand and Fireworks–it would be irresponsible of me to not show how Adobe's image-creation apps stack up.

17. Close this FLA, don't save the changes, and create a new, blank FLA. Change the movie dimensions to **600 px** wide.

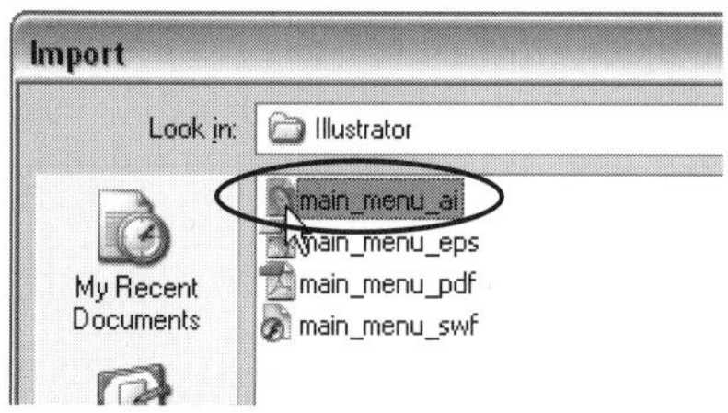

18. Import a file to your **Stage** by pressing **Ctrl+R** (Windows) or **Cmd+R** (Mac). From the **Import** dialog box, navigate to your **Desktop > file_types > Illustrator** folder. Then, locate the file **main_menu_ai.ai** and double-click it.

This is the same navigation layout graphic that you've seen in this exercise, except the graphics were created and saved through Adobe Illustrator CS.

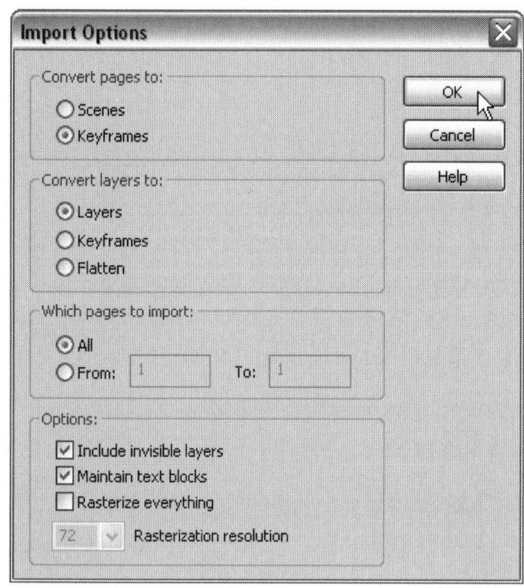

19. The **Import Options** dialog box will display, allowing you to choose how you want Flash MX 2004 to deal with various aspects of importing the Adobe Illustrator file. The options here are nearly identical to those given when importing a Macromedia FreeHand file. Modify your options so they match the ones in the screen shot above, and then click **OK**.

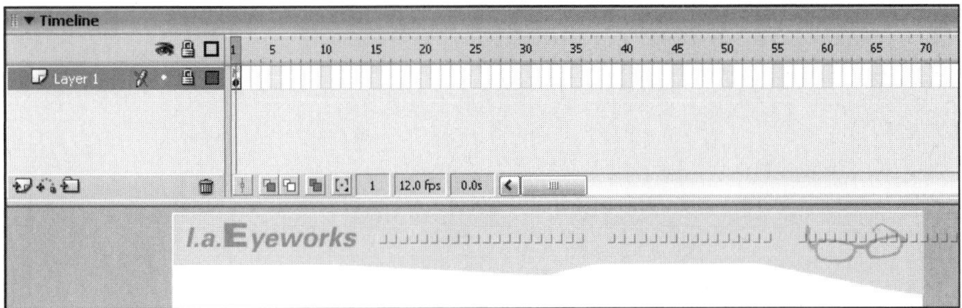

20. As you can see, when the file finishes importing, Flash MX 2004 didn't do the greatest of jobs (in this case) translating the navigation bar text. The green background, the vector L.A. Eyeworks logo, and the vector glasses all translated fine. But the text is a mess. If you take a peek in the **Library**, you'd also notice that Flash MX 2004 created a new folder called **Clip Paths** and inserted a couple of automatically created symbols into it.

So native Adobe Illustrator CS files faired moderately, but what about EPS files created from Adobe Illustrator CS?

---

21. Close this FLA, don't save the changes, and create a new, blank FLA. Change the movie dimensions to **600 px** wide.

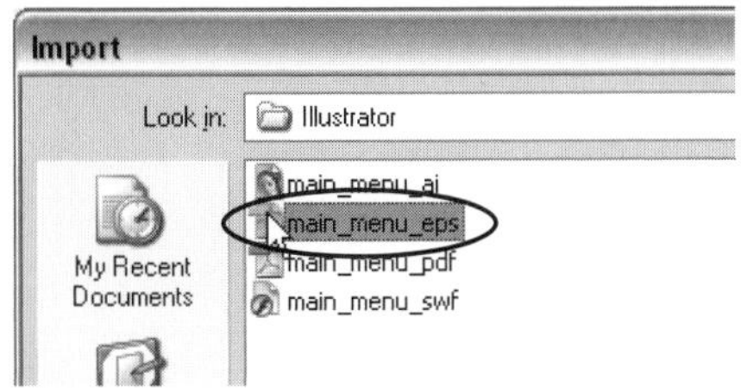

22. Import a file to your **Stage** by pressing **Ctrl+R** (Windows) or **Cmd+R** (Mac). From the **Import** dialog box, navigate to your **Desktop > file_types > Illustrator** folder. Then, locate the file **main_menu_eps.eps** and double-click it.

---

23. The **Import Options** dialog box will appear, as shown in Step 19. Because you're already familiar with the choices it offers, modify your options so they match the ones in the screen shot above, and then click **OK**.

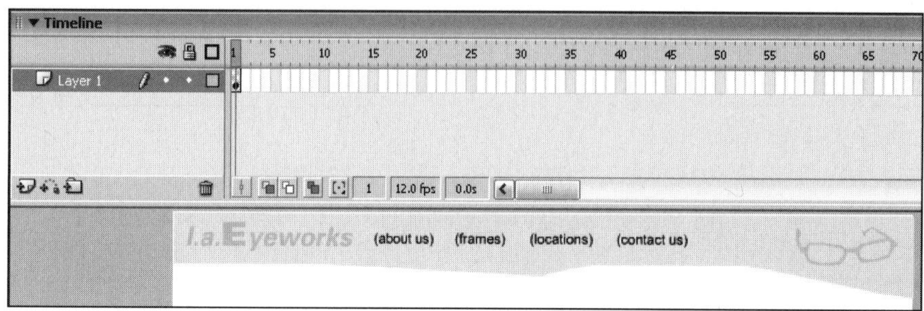

Once the file has finished importing, one of the first things you'll most likely notice is the color shift that has occurred. The L.A. Eyeworks logo, in particular, has shifted to a rather garish, '80s, florescent green. The navigation bar text has also been turned into one, giant text block. Whereas, in the original file, the navigation options were each separate text blocks, now they have been combined into one text block. Barring those inconsistencies, the EPS file created in Adobe Illustrator CS fared better than did the actual Adobe Illustrator file (AI) itself.

You've now seen importing AI and EPS files, but what about PDF files?

---

24. Close this FLA, don't save the changes, and create a new, blank FLA. Change the movie dimensions to **600 px** wide.

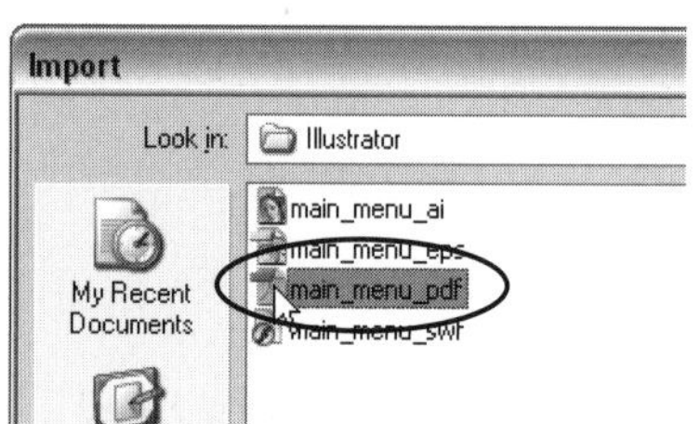

25. Import a file to your **Stage** by pressing **Ctrl+R** (Windows) or **Cmd+R** (Mac). From the **Import** dialog box, navigate to your **Desktop > file_types > Illustrator** folder. Then, locate the file **main_menu_pdf.pdf** and double-click it.

---

26. The **Import Options** dialog box will appear, as shown in Step 19. Because you're already familiar with the choices it offers you, modify your options so they match the ones in the screen shot above, and then click **OK**.

27. Once the file has finished importing, the results you're greeted with are the same as the results you achieved when importing the actual Adobe Illustrator CS file.

Adobe Illustrator can also export its images as Macromedia SWF files. Next, you're going to import a SWF file generated by Adobe Illustrator CS, and observe the results.

---

28. Close this FLA, don't save the changes, and create a new, blank FLA. Change the movie dimensions to **600 px** wide.

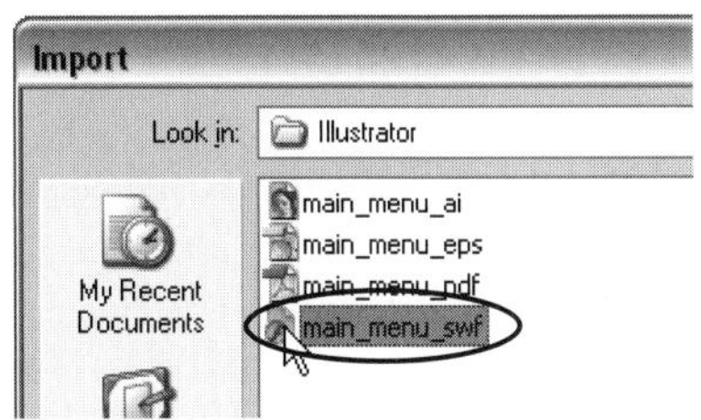

29. Import a file to your **Stage** by pressing **Ctrl+R** (Windows) or **Cmd+R** (Mac). From the **Import** dialog box, navigate to your **Desktop > file_types > Illustrator** folder. Then, locate the file **main_menu_swf.swf** and double-click it.

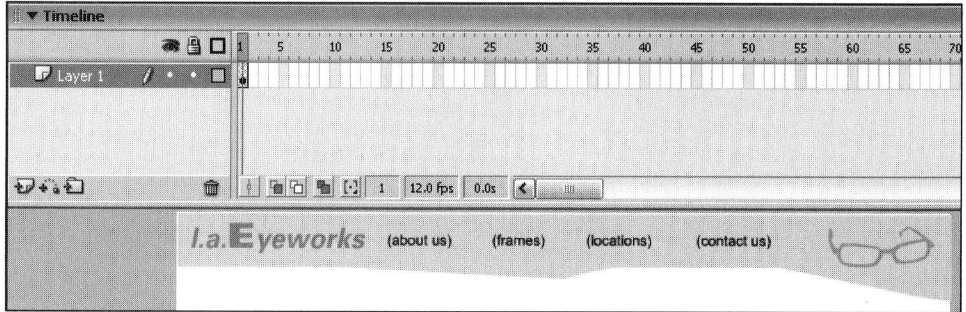

When the file finishes importing, you'll notice that the results you've achieved with this imported SWF is roughly the same as the results that the imported EPS provided. One big difference, however, is evident if you double-click one of the navigation options. You'll see that the navigation option is grouped, but the text within the group is an editable text block. Unlike the imported EPS, the textual navigation options haven't *all been clumped together into one, large text block.*

The final results give the edge to exporting a SWF from an Adobe Illustrator design. The colors, designs, and even the editable type are all translated into Flash MX 2004 with minimal difficulty. However, with complex designs that use Adobe Illustrator–specific techniques, the results might vary. It's best to export/save your Adobe Illustrator designs as a variety of formats, and then import those into Flash, keeping whichever one gives you the best results.

Although Adobe Photoshop is not a vector-editing graphics program like Adobe Illustrator, Macromedia FreeHand, and Macromedia Fireworks are, it still remains the graphics-editing program of choice for a large number of professionals. As such, you should be aware of how to save your Adobe Photoshop designs to achieve the best results for importing them into your Flash MX 2004 projects.

30. Close this FLA, don't save the changes, and create a new, blank FLA. Change the movie dimensions to **600 px** wide.

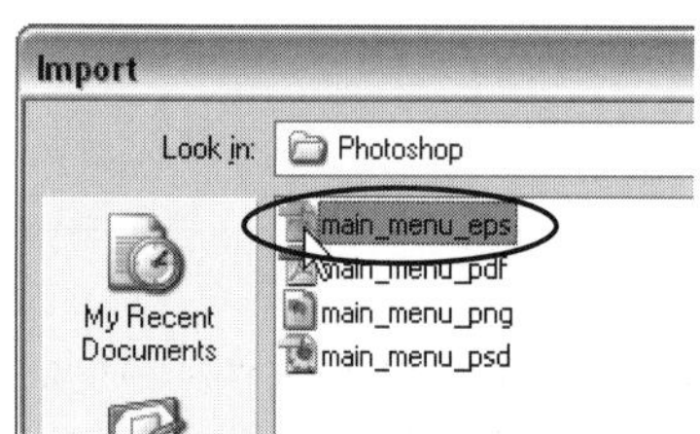

31. Import a file to your **Stage** by pressing **Ctrl+R** (Windows) or **Cmd+R** (Mac). From the **Import** dialog box, navigate to your **Desktop > file_types > Photoshop** folder. Then, locate the file **main_menu_eps.eps** and double-click it. This is an EPS file that was created from an Adobe Photoshop CS layout.

32. The **Import Options** dialog box will appear, as shown in Step 19. Because you're already familiar with the choices it offers you, modify your options so they match the ones in the screen shot above, then click **OK**.

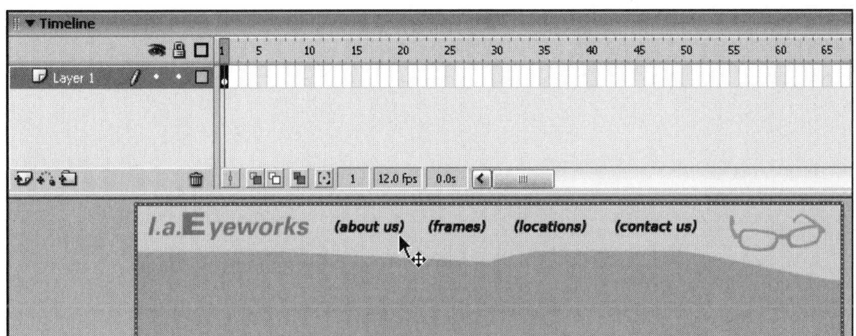

On first glance, the results look very promising. In fact, the layout looks exactly *like the original file. But if you click one of the text navigation options, you'll quickly realize that, essentially, the image has been rasterized, and it's one, big bitmap graphic. Flash MX 2004 did some funny business with making some symbols and masks from the L.A. Eyeworks logo, but you'll notice that it has been converted into a raster graphic as well. If you open the Library for this FLA, you'll also notice that Flash MX 2004 has automatically created some bitmap and graphic symbols that make up the pieces of this graphic. So while the EPS exported from Adobe Photoshop CS does a great job at retaining the image quality, the image has been locked down into an uneditable raster graphic.*

33. Close this FLA, don't save the changes, and create a new, blank FLA. Change the movie dimensions to **600 px** wide.

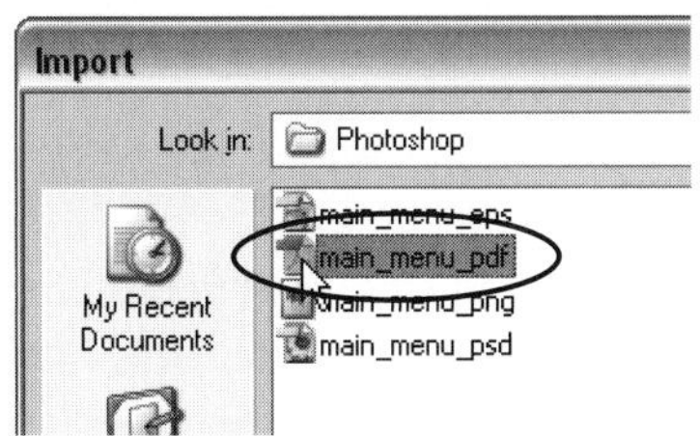

34. Import a file to your **Stage** by pressing **Ctrl+R** (Windows) or **Cmd+R** (Mac). From the **Import** dialog box, navigate to your **Desktop > file_types > Photoshop** folder. Then, locate the file **main_menu_pdf.pdf** and double-click it. This is a PDF file that was created from an Adobe Photoshop CS layout.

35. The **Import Options** dialog box will appear, as shown in Step 19. Because you're already familiar with the choices it offers you, modify your options so they match the ones in the screen shot above, and then click **OK**.

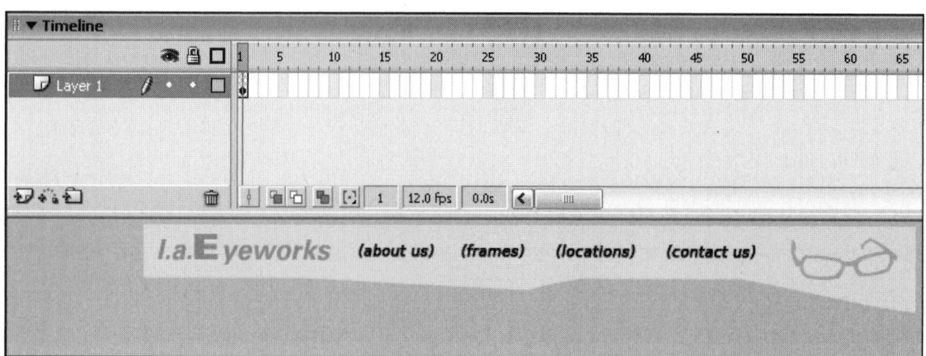

To save you the time and trouble of poking through this imported graphic, I'll let you in on a secret. The results for this imported Adobe Photoshop CS–created PDF is identical *to the results of the imported Adobe Photoshop CS–created EPS. Although the image looks great, it has been flattened into an uneditable raster graphic.*

36. Close this FLA, don't save the changes, and create a new, blank FLA. Change the movie dimensions to **600 px** wide.

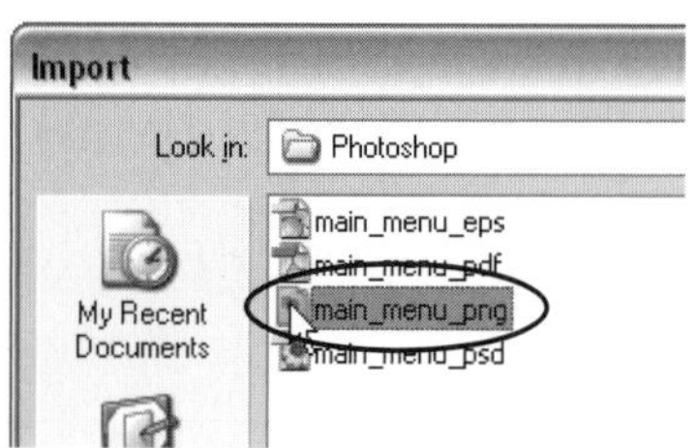

37. Import a file to your **Stage** by pressing **Ctrl+R** (Windows) or **Cmd+R** (Mac). From the **Import** dialog box, navigate to your **Desktop > file_types > Photoshop** folder. Then, locate the file **main_menu_png.png** and double-click it. This is a PNG file that was created from an Adobe Photoshop CS layout.

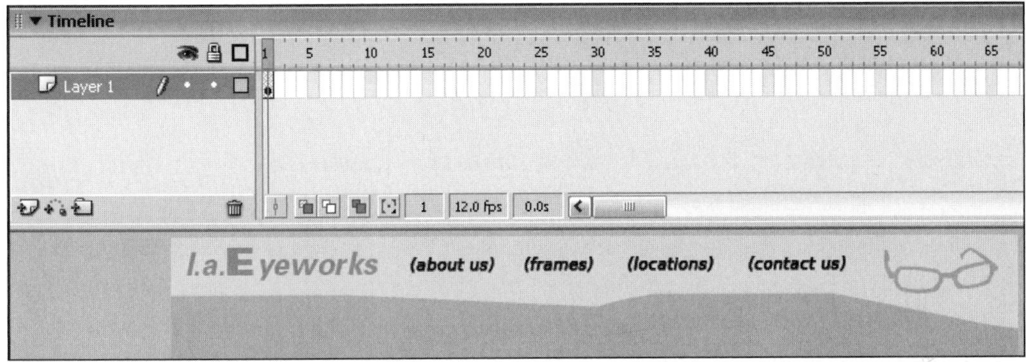

Unlike PNG files created by Macromedia Fireworks MX 2004, PNG files created by Adobe Photoshop do not contain vector information. In other words, when you create a PNG file from Adobe Photoshop, Photoshop is going to output that graphic, whether it contains editable-text or not, as a flattened raster graphic. If you were to open the Library for this FLA, you'd notice that unlike the other Adobe Photoshop formats that you've imported thus far, only one *PNG raster graphic has been imported. Also, like the other Adobe Photoshop formats, the image looks great but is an uneditable raster image. Because of the lack of Library clutter that importing a PNG provides, I recommend exporting a PNG file from an Adobe Photoshop layout when you want to import that graphic into Flash MX 2004.*

What about the Adobe Photoshop file (PSD) itself? Can that be imported into a Flash MX 2004 movie? If you have QuickTime installed, Flash MX 2004 will import the PSD file using QuickTime translation. If you currently have QuickTime installed, give it a try.

---

38. Close this FLA, don't save the changes, and create a new, blank FLA. Change the movie dimensions to **600 px** wide.

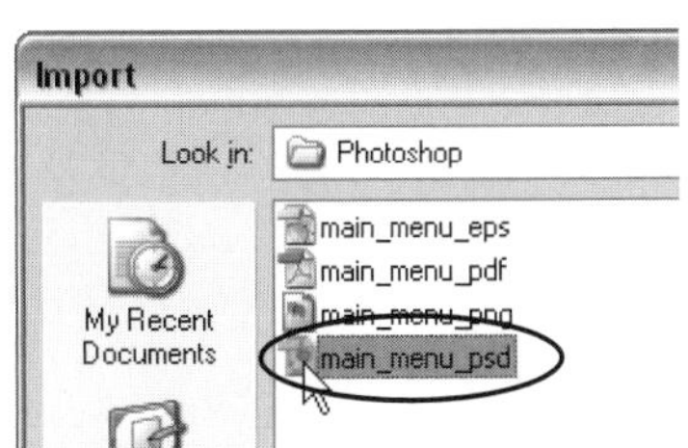

39. Import a file to your **Stage** by pressing **Ctrl+R** (Windows) or **Cmd+R** (Mac). From the **Import** dialog box, navigate to your **Desktop > file_types > Photoshop** folder. Then, locate the file **main_menu_psd.psd** and double-click it. This is the original PSD document natively saved by Adobe Photoshop CS.

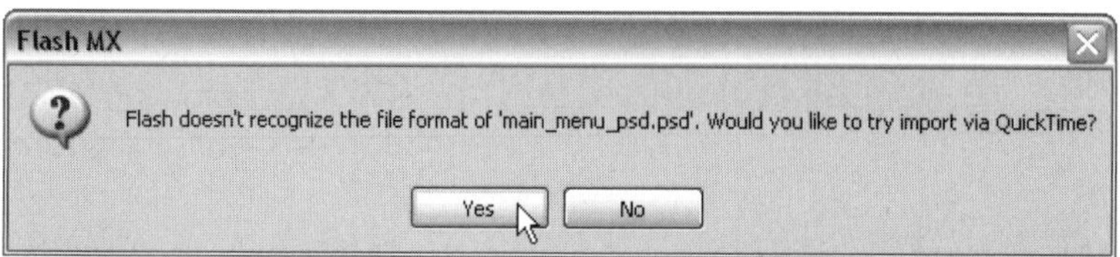

40. If you have QuickTime installed, you'll see this dialog box appear. It informs you that Flash MX 2004 does not recognize this file format but offers to import the file anyway using QuickTime translation. Click **Yes**.

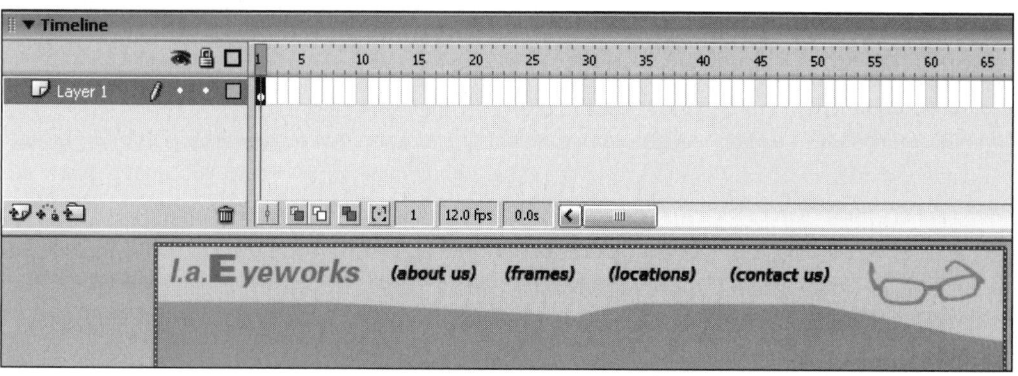

After the file has finished being translated/imported, you'll notice that–as usual–the graphic looks great but it is one, large, uneditable raster graphic. If you open the Library for this FLA, you'll notice that there is just one bitmap graphic: ***main_menu_psd***.

41. Close the FLA (and don't save the changes) that you imported the Adobe Photoshop (PSD) file into. You won't be needing it again in this chapter.

The final word: *In this exercise you've imported quite a few files that were created with a variety of image-editing programs. You've imported files created by Macromedia Fireworks MX 2004, Macromedia FreeHand, Adobe Illustrator CS, and Adobe Photoshop CS. All in all, each program was able to create at least one file format that could be imported into Flash MX 2004 with workable results. Some files, albeit, were more "workable" than others.*

In essence, it comes down to this: If you're in charge of the graphics production, and you want to create the graphics in a way in which they can be imported into Flash MX 2004 and still remain editable, use another Macromedia program such as Fireworks MX 2004 or the Adobe vector program Adobe Illustrator to create those graphics.

As you saw in this exercise, the best results from Adobe Illustrator occurred when the graphics were exported as SWF files. The vector graphics and text remained intact and editable upon importing into a Flash MX 2004 project. If you were hoping to import Adobe Photoshop–created images and keep them editable in Flash MX 2004, I'm sorry to say that you'll be disappointed. Adobe Photoshop–the bitmap-editing program that it is–is simply incompatible (when it comes to retaining the editability of the imported graphic) with how Flash MX 2004 edits images (in a vector format). On the other hand, as you saw, Adobe Photoshop can import some great-looking raster graphics that look just like the original images. As a designer/developer, you can easily import and work with Adobe Photoshop PNG files as long as you understand how and where those images can be used.

Workflow Suggestions

Now that you've seen various ways to import artwork that was created in other graphics-editing programs, here are a few workflow suggestions:

- If you're working in a team, utilize shared libraries. As you'll also see in this book, shared libraries are a great way to share graphics, fonts–and anything else you can import into your Flash MX 2004 library–with the rest of your team. That way, if you need to make a change to an asset, all you have to do is open the shared library FLA, make your changes, and publish the SWF file. Everyone else on your team using that SWF file will now have access to those updated graphics. How about that?!
- Split one project up into multiple pieces (FLAs). If you're working in a team environment, this is a great way to delegate different parts of a single project to different people on your team. You can then bring all the separate pieces back together again by using the **`MovieClipLoader`** (or its predecessor, **`loadMovie`**) to load all the SWF files into one, unified project. I hate to sound like a broken record, but yeah, you'll be doing this in the book as well. ;-)

In the next chapter, you're going to be getting your hands dirty by creating the "master" FLA, which will contain much of the reusable ActionScript that will be used throughout the L.A. Eyeworks Web site. You will also begin to write some of that reusable ActionScript by creating the **`MovieClipLoader`** *script that will control all of the loading of external SWF and JPG files. Lastly, you will create and pre-cache a shared library that will contain elements that you can easily reuse throughout all of the modules in the Web site.*

---

3. Getting Started

"Master" SWF	Classes, Objects, Methods, and Properties
"Strict Typing"	Functions	MovieClipLoader
Shared Libraries	Creating and Precaching the Shared Library

la_eyeworks

Macromedia Flash MX 2004
Beyond the Basics

In the previous two chapters, you learned about the basic concepts behind Flash MX 2004 Web site construction, but here is where you see those concepts begin to be put into practice. In this chapter, you will create the "master" SWF file that will act as the container to hold all the other SWF files for this Web site, as well as where many reusable ActionScripts will be stored. Here you will also write the main script that controls the loading of all of the SWF and JPG files that will be used throughout the entire Web site. You will additionally learn about–and create–a shared library to store assets (such as font faces) that will be reused throughout the site. This is quite a large chapter that covers many new and very important topics, so if you're reading this late at night and thinking, "I'll just finish this chapter before I head to bed," I would strongly suggest waiting until you've had a good night's rest before continuing...unless you want to have really weird dreams of being chased by giant MovieClipLoaders with large, gnashing fangs. ;-)

What Is a "Master" SWF?

Unless you've been living in a cave since 1954, you're probably aware of J.R.R. Tolkien's books, turned three-part movie series, *The Lord of the Rings*. In today's omnipresent media, I'm sure you've heard the movie tagline, "One ring to rule them all," in reference to a magically crafted omnipotent ring that has the power to control the many other magical rings. In the upcoming exercise, you're going to create the "one ring" of this Web site. This master SWF is going to act as the container for all the other SWF files to load into. It is also going to be a container that holds some ActionScripts that you will use and reuse throughout the Web site, such as the ActionScript to load assets (the **`MovieClipLoader`**), the ActionScript to load variables (**`LoadVars`**), and the ActionScript to load and apply cascading style sheets (**`TextField.StyleSheet`**). By creating this master SWF and using it to store ActionScript variables and functions that you will frequently refer to from the other SWF files that comprise this Web site, you are accomplishing two major goals:

- You are keeping your commonly used ActionScript code centralized. This allows you to easily make modifications to your ActionScript code in one, centralized location. Because the other SWF files all refer to this central code, they will automatically utilize any changes you make to that ActionScript. Instead, if you had written this commonly used ActionScript directly into each SWF that needed it, when you wanted to make a change (or fix a mistake) to that script, you would have to make that modification *multiple* times for each SWF file that code resided in. As you will see, keeping your ActionScripts centralized can *greatly* improve your workflow.
- By centralizing your ActionScript, you are reducing the file size of your Web site by keeping the scripts in one location. If you were to insert this repeatedly used ActionScript into each SWF file, you could potentially add quite a lot to the overall file size of the project. But by keeping the common, frequently used code in one place and just *referring* to it from other SWFs whenever you need it, you're cutting down on the overall file size of the Web site by not repeating identical code.

What Are Classes, Objects, Methods, and Properties?

As you begin to write the ActionScript code that will make this Web site functional, you will run into some terminology that you probably won't be familiar with. This section offers a brief description of the ActionScript language definitions for classes, objects, methods, and properties. I'm a big believer in using analogies to help in the learning process. To help you better understand these complex topics, I'm going to use a dog in my explanations. Although some of this terminology may sound confusing to you, you will become much more familiar with these terms as you complete the exercises throughout this book.

- **Classes:** Classes are the blueprint that defines a grouping of objects. For example, if referring to a dog, a dog would fall under a class of animal. All animals have certain characteristics of which a dog shares. A class can be thought of as, simply, a category of objects. From a Flash MX 2004 viewpoint, movie clips and buttons are classes. Both movie clips and buttons have methods and properties that make up their classes and define what they can and cannot do when you use them in your projects.

- **Objects:** An object is, essentially, an instance of a class. Just like you can have an instance of a graphic symbol on your Stage, an object (from an ActionScript standpoint) is an instance of a class. An object, such as a dog, is just a collection of properties and methods (more on properties and methods next) that are inherited from its class. Also, like dogs, objects are unique in that each one can have a distinctive name and can be referred to by that name. Within Flash MX 2004, for example, instances of movie clips and button symbols are objects because they are instances of their respective classes.
- **Methods:** Methods are the behaviors of an object. The behaviors (methods) of a dog object would be that it barks, pants, slobbers, pees on your furniture, and chews up your shoes. In terms of Flash MX 2004 ActionScript, classes have their own built-in methods that you can use, or you can even create your own methods by assigning them to a function (more on functions later in this chapter). This would be analogous to the fact that a dog inherently barks (its built-in method), but if you so desired, you could add a behavior that allowed the dog to levitate cats and fly them around a room (an added method). A movie clip object, for example, has methods such as play, stop, next frame, and so forth.
- **Properties:** Properties are attributes that define an object. For instance, all dogs (well...most anyway) have four legs, two eyes, a tail, a mouth, and bad breath. A movie clip object, for example, has properties such as its visibility (`_visible`), alpha (`_alpha`), rotation (`_rotation`), and so forth.

You'll gain some exposure with a few of these terms in Exercise 1 in this chapter.

NOTE | What Are Variables?

Something you'll see used very frequently throughout this book are variables. A variable, in essence, is a container–that you create with ActionScript–that you can use to store data or references to object instances, or even assign to objects you've created. A variable can be thought of as similar to a symbol; but where a symbol is a container to hold something visual–a graphic, some text, and so forth–a variable is a container to hold data such as a name, some numbers, and so on. In this book, you'll get plenty of exposure and experience creating variables. You'll use variables as containers to hold numbers (such as the running time of your music tracks), as containers to hold strings (such as the name of the visitor who is sending you comments using your feedback form), and as containers to hold ActionScript objects (such as the MovieClipLoader object that you'll be building later in this chapter).

Variables are an invaluable keystone for working inside of Flash MX 2004, and as such, you'll get a ton of experience using variables to accomplish various tasks.

What Is "Strict Typing?"

As you write ActionScript during the course of this book, you'll notice something that you probably haven't seen before. As you are writing your actions and creating variables, you'll include a little extra text that comes after the variable name. This bit of additional text that immediately follows a variable is new to Flash MX 2004 and is called **strict typing**. Strict typing is essentially a bit of text that you write after a variable name that allows you to specify what kind of data type the value of that variable will be. If this initially sounds confusing, keep in mind that you will gain more confidence and experience with strict typing as you use it within the exercises in this, and other, chapters. For your reference, here is a sample of strict typing:

```
var myVar:String= "Here is a string of text.";
var myVar2:Number= 1234;
```

See how after **myVar** it says **:String** and after **myVar2** it says **:Number**? These circled identifiers are two examples of strict typing tags. When adding strict typing into your own actions, you simply write them in immediately following a variable. The purpose of those strict typing tags is to specify that the value of the variable **myVar** contains data of the String type, and **myVar2** contains data of the Number type. There are various advantages of using strict typing when writing your ActionScripts, but as an intermediate-level Flash MX 2004 user, there are two that you should be aware of:

- Strict typing allows you to explicitly state what sort of data is being entered into a variable. Strict typing also allows you to *change* the data type within a variable. In other words, if a number is being entered into a variable, but you want the data type to be a string, you can specify that by using strict typing. *Why* would you want to do something like that? Well, if you were performing some calculations (division, multiplication, and so forth) with numbers, you would want those numbers to be handled as the Number data type, *not* as the String data type. Trying to perform mathematical calculations (as you will be doing to create progress bars and preloaders) on a String data type will only yield errors.
- It's considered good ActionScript 2.0 coding practice to use strictly typed variables and objects. The reason is because by using strict typing, you're explicitly specifying the data type (String, Number, and so forth) of a variable or object. By unequivocally letting Flash MX 2004 know what the data type of a variable is, it helps to cut down on errors that might occur in your movie.
- Also note that because the Actions panel Normal mode was removed in Flash MX 2004, strictly typing variables will help you write ActionScript faster, because the Actions panel will supply code hints and auto-completion for built-in classes (objects) as you're writing them.

It should be said that strict typing is not mandatory when writing your ActionScript, and for that matter, it is only supported when publishing a SWF using ActionScript 2.0 (the default ActionScript version when you create a new FLA in Flash MX 2004). If you don't use strict typing, in most cases your actions will work just fine. I want to point it out early in the book as something new to ActionScript 2.0. As well, my goal in this book is to teach you correct ActionScript practices. Not only that, but to also educate you so that if you choose to learn more about advanced-level Flash MX 2004 ActionScript, you'll already have a good understanding of what some of these terms and practices are. You'll learn how to add your own strict data typing assignments to variables later on in this chapter.

What Is a Function?

A symbol can be thought of as a container that holds graphics. One nice thing about a symbol is that it can be reused multiple times without adding a significant amount to the file size of your SWF file. A function is similar in that respect, but a function doesn't hold graphics, it holds ActionScript. A function can be thought of as a container to hold ActionScript code that can be reused throughout your project. Functions are *extremely* useful when you have a block of ActionScript code that needs to be repeated during your movie.

As an example, say you had a series of buttons, like in the navigation bar on a Web site. And when the viewer clicks any of those buttons, you want an animation in a movie clip to start playing, you want the background music to stop, and you want some text to appear in a dynamic text field on the Stage. Without using a function, you would have to put all those same actions on *each button instance*. Then, when you wanted to make a change to those actions, you would have to make the same ActionScript changes on every button instance! What if you had 50 buttons? That's a recipe for insanity if I've ever seen one. Instead, you could create a function that contained the ActionScript code that performed those same three actions (start movie clip playing, stop background music, display message), and then just add one line of ActionScript code to each button instance that tells the function to execute the actions contained within it. Then, if you ever needed to make any changes to your ActionScript, you wouldn't have to make those changes on each button instance. Instead, you just change the ActionScript in the function, and you're all done. So you can see what a function looks like, here is a sample:

```
function buttonClick () {
     myMC.play();
     myMusic.stop();
     myMessage.text = "You clicked on a button. Congratulations!";
}
```

In this sample, **buttonClick** is the name that this function was given. A function can be any name you want, as long as it doesn't begin with a number, have spaces in the name, or contain any special characters (?, *, %, and so forth). Indented between the brackets ({ }) are the actions that you want to be performed when the function is called. To get the actions contained within that function to execute, you simply type out the function name (making sure you specify the path to that function if it resides on a different Timeline) and add the function's call operator "()" like so:

```
buttonClick();
```

And yes, new to Flash MX 2004, ActionScripts *are* case-sensitive, so if you wrote

```
buttonclick();
```

the function would not be executed.

Another nicety that functions offer is that you can pass parameters to a function. What that means is that you can pass commands to the function from wherever the function is being triggered. (In the aforementioned example, the function is being triggered from a button.) For example, using the same function in the previous sample, what if you wanted the message to be different depending upon which button the viewer clicks. Right now, that message is "hard coded" into the function, meaning that same message will be displayed no matter which button the viewer clicks. In that case, you could assign a parameter to the function, and then from the button that the viewer clicks, send a string of text to that function parameter. If it sounds like I'm speaking Greek, maybe this example will help. Here's what the same function would look like, but with a parameter assigned to the message:

```
function buttonClick (msg) {
     myMC.play();
     myMusic.stop();
     myMessage.text = msg;
}
```

As you can see, the only differences are that now after the **buttonClick** function name, between the parentheses, it now says **msg**. And no, that doesn't refer to the taste-enhancing food additive; it's just a name that I assigned it, and it's short for "message." If you look at the last action within that function, you'll also see the same **msg** parameter repeated after **myMessage.text =**. The parameter **msg** essentially just acts like a placeholder for whatever you send it when you trigger the function. For example, when someone clicks a button in the navigation bar titled Our Products, and you want the aforementioned function to be executed but the message to display "We have lots of stuff. Check it out.", this is the action you would assign to the Our Products button:

```
on (release) {
     buttonClick ("We have lots of stuff. Check it out.");
}
```

That bit of text–"We have lots of stuff. Check it out."–is the function parameter that gets passed to the function when the viewer clicks the button. The message gets inserted where you added the parameter placeholder **msg**, and voilà, your dynamic text field on the Stage will display unique text when the viewer clicks that particular button.

A function parameter is essentially just a local variable. By "local," I mean that as soon as the function is executed, that parameter (local variable) is destroyed to conserve memory. You can even create variables with the same name as the function parameter, and the two will not conflict.

The function used in the previous examples is a function that you create with ActionScript. A function that you create is called a **top-level function**. On the other hand, objects also have built-in functions (as you'll see when you build the MovieClipLoader later in this chapter), and those are called **methods** (as described earlier in the "What Are Classes, Objects, Methods, and Properties?" section.

Although I'm sure you still have many questions about functions and how they can be used, you'll learn plenty more about top-level functions and methods throughout the chapters in this book.

What Is the MovieClipLoader, and How Does it Differ from loadMovie?

loadMovie allows you to load a SWF or JPG file into another SWF file. This is an awesome feature because it allows you to break up one large project into multiple, smaller pieces, thereby allowing you to load those other SWF files whenever the viewer requests them. It's also a great way to reduce the download time of your Flash MX 2004–based Web sites because it allows you to have only the *basic* information (such as the navigation menu) initially be downloaded and displayed on viewers' computers. Then, when the viewer requests it, other sections of the Web site can be downloaded piecemeal.

As nice as that was, there were shortcomings in loadMovie that left many a Flash MX 2004 developer wanting more, such as better procedures for constructing a preloader, for error management, and so forth. Because of these reasons, Macromedia–in Flash MX 2004–introduced a new (and improved) way to load external assets such as SWF and JPG files. This new action is called the MovieClipLoader.

The MovieClipLoader, in effect, does the same thing that loadMovie did–it allows you to load SWF and JPG files into another SWF file (or level). The big difference, however, between loadMovie and the new MovieClipLoader is that the MovieClipLoader is much more sophisticated and offers many more options for loading–and dealing with–SWF and JPG files.

The MovieClipLoader is its own class that you assign **listeners** to. These listeners (as their name implies) simply listen to what the MovieClipLoader is doing. Then, when a particular event occurs, they'll do whatever you tell them to do. For example, if you use the MovieClipLoader to load an external JPG file, and that file doesn't exist, you can have the onLoadError listener return an error to the viewer. In the past, when using loadMovie to load assets, if you wanted to create a preloader to show the preloading progress of that loading file, you would have to create some kind of loop that would continually trigger your preloader ActionScript code. But now, with the MovieClipLoader, it has its own built-in loop capabilities in another listener called onLoadProgress. In many respects, the MovieClipLoader is much easier to work with, and it gives you many more options for handling the loading of external SWF and JPG files. For your reference, the table on the next page describes various MovieClipLoader listeners and what they do.

MovieClipLoader Listeners	
Listener	**Description**
onLoadComplete	This listener is triggered (and all the actions within this listener function) when the loading asset has been completely downloaded.
onLoadError	This listener (and its associated actions) is triggered if the loading asset fails to load for one reason or another.
onLoadInit	Similar to onLoadComplete, this listener (and its associated actions) is triggered when the loading asset has been completely downloaded and the first frame of the loaded clip has been executed. In some ways, this is preferred over onLoadComplete because by the time onLoadInit is triggered, you know the loaded clip is completely loaded and ready to go.
onLoadProgress	This listener (and its associated actions) is triggered every time loaded content is written to disk. This means that every time any bit of information is downloaded from the clip you're loading, the onLoadProgress listener is triggered. onLoadProgress is—essentially—your ActionScript loop that continually gets triggered as your content is downloading. Within the onLoadProgress method is where you'd write your preloader ActionScript code (as you'll see in Chapter 8, "Building a Preloader").
onLoadStart	This listener (and its associated actions) is triggered when your asset begins to download.

As you can see (but probably not fully comprehend just yet), the MovieClipLoader is a very powerful, new addition to Flash MX 2004. You will be writing your first MovieClipLoader later in this chapter.

I. Creating the Master SWF and Setting Up the MovieClipLoader

In this exercise, you will begin the construction of the first piece of the L.A. Eyeworks site by designing the master SWF. As you read in the section "What Is a 'Master' SWF?," the **master.swf** file is going to act as the container for the other SWF modules (music, frames, about us, and so forth) to load into. It's also going to be the container to hold some ActionScript code that you will be reusing frequently. By keeping the frequently used actions in a central location, you cut down on production time because you don't have to repeat the code wherever you need it, and you'll have a *much* easier time making changes to the script later. In this exercise, you will also write the MovieClipLoader script that will do *all* of the loading of SWF and JPG files throughout the entire site.

You're going to be learning quite a lot in this exercise, so if you need to take a break or jog around the block, now's the time to do it. ;-)

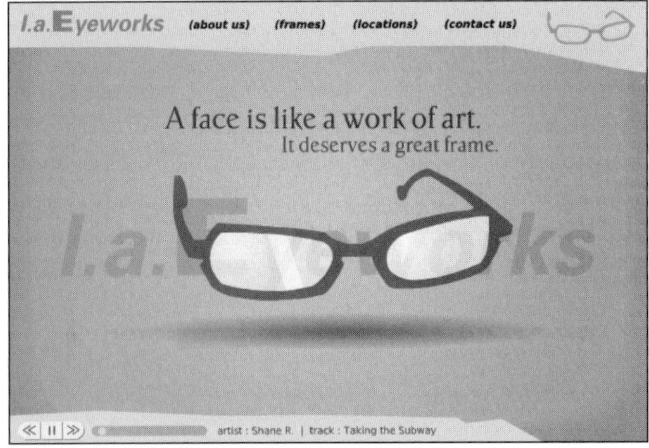

1. Open your preferred Web browser, and enter in this URL:

http://www.lynda.com/flashbtb/laeyeworks/

This will open the completed site in your browser. Depending on the speed of your Internet connection, it may load fast, or it may take a minute. When the completed L.A. Eyeworks Web site first loads, you'll see the navigation bar appear at the top, the music player appear at the bottom, and an animated splash graphic appear in the middle. These three things are actually all separate SWF files, ***main_menu.swf***, ***music.swf***, *and* ***splash.swf***, *respectively. These three SWF files are all automatically loaded into the* ***master.swf*** *container file when the Web site is first loaded.*

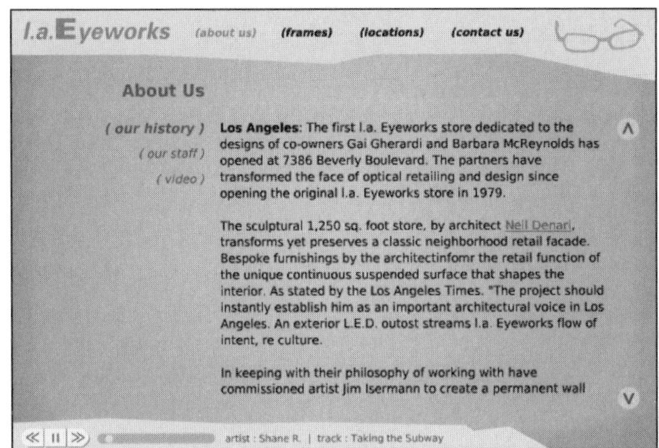

If you click one of the navigation buttons at the top, such as ***about us****, you'll see the splash graphic disappear, and in its place loads the About Us module (another SWF file). The same holds true if you click any of the other navigation buttons. The center content is essentially an interchangeable module that gets swapped out whenever the viewer clicks a navigation button. All of this content is loaded–and contained within–the* ***master.swf*** *file that you will be constructing next. When the viewer clicks one of the navigation buttons, it instructs the MovieClipLoader instance on the* ***master.swf*** *to load a particular SWF or JPG file. Sound pretty simple? Straightforward? In essence, it is. Of course, it takes a bit of elbow grease, hard work, and some well-thought-out ActionScript to make it look this simple, but that's why you're reading this book–to learn how to do all that, right? :-)*

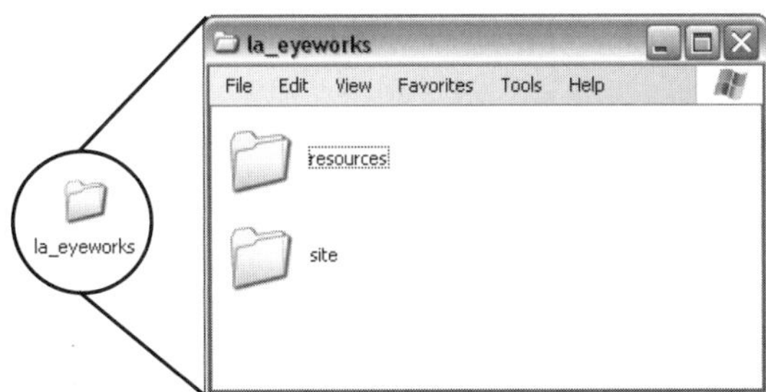

2. On the **H•O•T CD-ROM** is a folder titled **la_eyeworks**. This folder contains all of the files you will be working with throughout the entire book. Copy this folder, and its contents, onto your **Desktop**.

You'll be referring to the files within this folder very frequently, so make sure you know exactly *where that folder resides on your computer. This folder is also going to act as the root site folder for the L.A. Eyeworks site. In other words, the* ***la_eyeworks*** *folder you just copied onto your Desktop is where you will save all the files that you work with throughout this book.*

Note: *If you're currently working on a Windows computer, follow the instructions in the* Introduction *to make the folder and files within it read/writeable.*

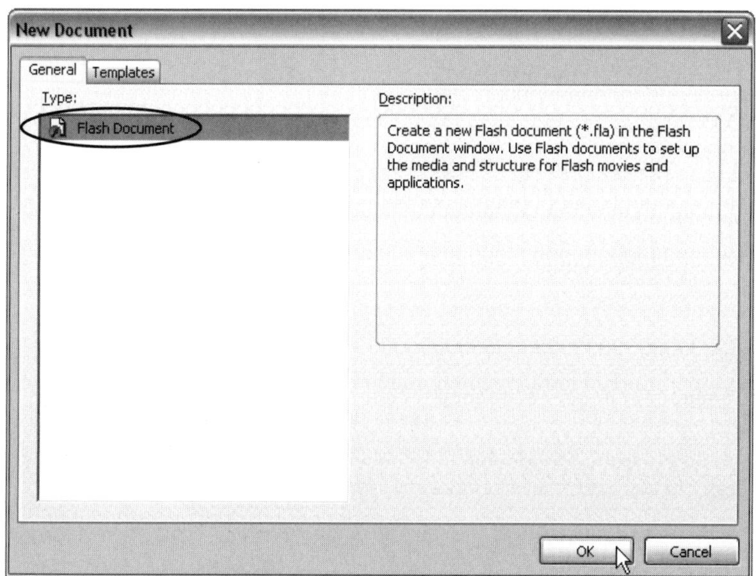

3. Launch Flash MX 2004. Choose **File > New**, and from the **New Document** dialog box, select **Flash Document**. Click **OK**.

Note: *Some windows in Flash MX 2004 will have slightly different appearances depending on whether you're using Flash MX Professional 2004 or Flash MX 2004. For example, the professional version's Start Page is slightly different from the standard version's Start Page. The New Document dialog box (pictured above), is another one of those places. In Flash MX Professional 2004, the General and Templates tabs have more options than are available in the standard version. Although differences occur depending on which version of Flash MX you're using, the exercises in this book cover processes that will work in both versions of the program.*

When one SWF file loads into another, the base SWF file defines the frame rate of all the other SWF files that load into it. This means that the ***master.swf*** *file (which you just created) determines the frame rate for* all *the SWF files that load into it. For the L.A. Eyeworks Web site, so that the splash graphic and main menu animations play smoothly, the frame rate should be set to 21 fps. Although the frame rate one should use is a contentious issue among Flash MX 2004 designers, it's my opinion that 21 fps is a fast enough frame rate to make your animations play back smoothly. (Lower frame rates tend to make animations stutter.) It's also not too taxing on the viewers' computer processors. (The faster the frame rate you set, the harder it is for the viewers' computers to keep up with that frame rate.)*

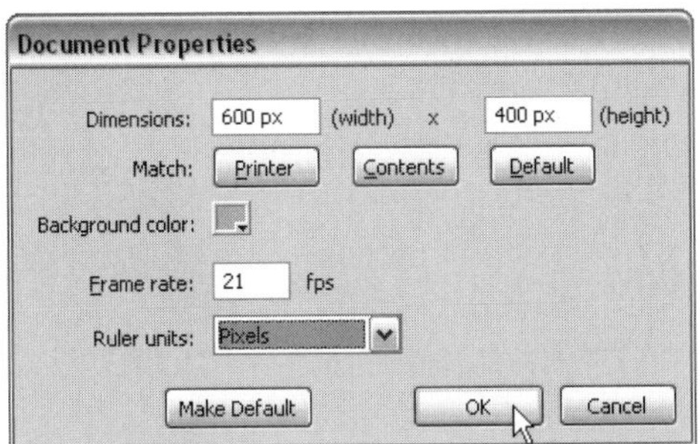

4. Open the **Document Properties** by pressing **Ctrl+J** (Windows) or **Cmd+J** (Mac). Set the **Dimensions** to **600 px** wide by **400 px** high. Set the **Background color** to the hexadecimal color **#B4CCE5**. You can do this by clicking on the **Background color** swatch, and from the color picker that appears, typing in the hexadecimal color value in the field to the right of the color swatch. (This color value was taken from the original Adobe Photoshop site mockup.) Set the **Frame rate** to **21 fps**. Click **OK**.

Tip: *If you click* ***Make Default****, Flash MX 2004 will use the* ***Document Properties*** *settings you've just specified as the base settings for all new documents you create.*

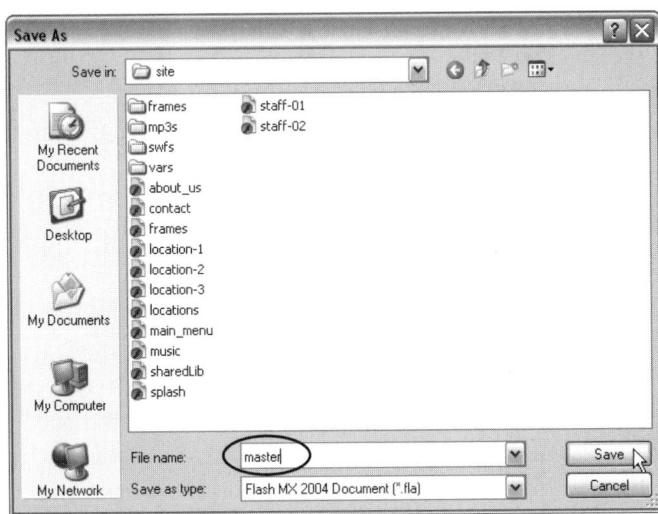

5. Choose **File > Save** to save this FLA. In the **Save As** dialog box, navigate to your **Desktop**, into the **la_eyeworks** folder you copied there at the beginning of this exercise, and then into the **site** folder. Name your file **master**, and click **Save**.

Another element that's common to all the loaded SWF files is the background. The same image is visible in the background, no matter which SWF file the viewer is currently looking at. In the next step, you are going to add that background image to the ***master.fla*** *file.*

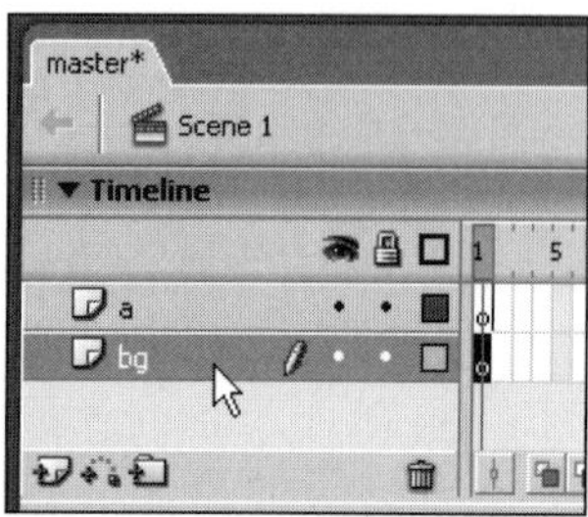

6. Rename **Layer 1** to **bg**, create a new layer, and rename it to **a**. The **a** layer is where you will write your ActionScript code, and the **bg** layer is–yup, you guessed it–where the background image will go. Make sure you have the **bg** layer selected before continuing to the next step.

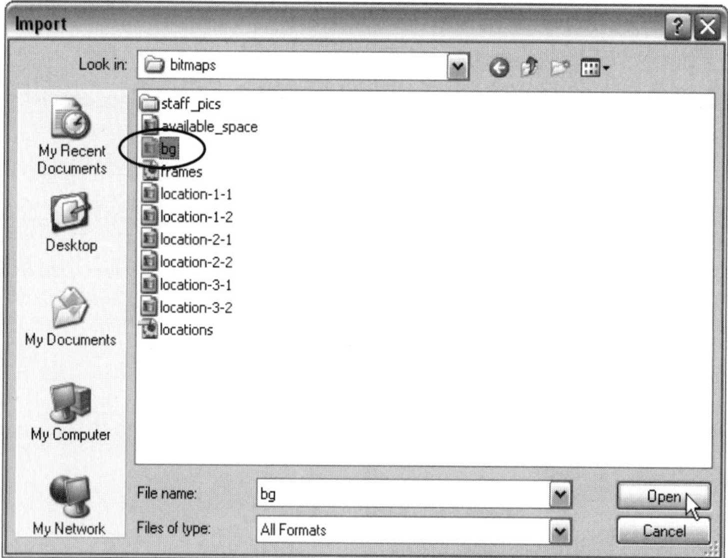

7. Press **Ctrl+R** (Windows) or **Cmd+R** (Mac) to import an item onto the **Stage**. In the **Import** dialog box, navigate to your **Desktop**, into the **la_eyeworks** folder, into the **resources** folder, and then into the **bitmaps** folder. Select the bitmap graphic **bg** and click **Open** (Windows) or **Import** button (Mac) to import the selected bitmap graphic onto the **Stage**.

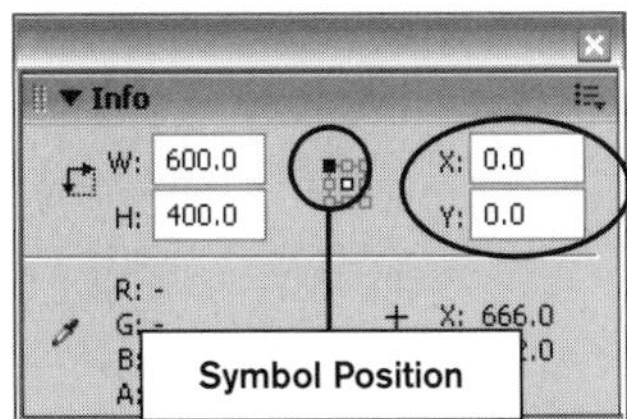

*The **bg** bitmap graphic (which is the same physical size as the Stage—600 x 400) should automatically place itself so that it's aligned right on top of the Stage. You can verify this by opening the **Info** panel (**Ctrl+I** [Windows] or **Cmd+I** [Mac]) and making sure that the **Symbol Position** registration point is set to the top-left point and that the X and Y coordinates are both set to **0**.*

---

8. Lock the **bg** layer and single-click the first keyframe in the **a** (actions) layer. Open the **Actions** panel (**F9**).

Before you can use the MovieClipLoader, you first have to create it with ActionScript. Just like if you wanted to use an image in your Flash MX 2004 movie, you'd first need to create the image, convert it into a symbol, and place it on the Stage. The MovieClipLoader needs to be set up the same way essentially. Using ActionScript, you first need to create an instance (called an object) of the MovieClipLoader class before it can be used. That's what you will be doing next.

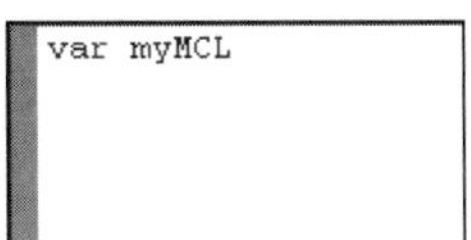

9. In the **Actions** panel, type:

```
var myMCL
```

*In simple English, this instructs Flash MX 2004 to create a variable called **myMCL**. The text "var" in ActionScript is short for "variable." (It also determines something called 'variable scope' as well, which you'll see a little of later in this book.) So when you see "var" preceding a name (in this case, myMCL), it means create a variable and assign the following name to it. Although preceding a variable name with the text "var" isn't required in* all *cases, it is recommended to adhere to good ActionScript practices, and it is needed when assigning a data type to a variable (as you will see next). In the next step, you're going to assign a MovieClipLoader object to that variable. That way, whenever you need to tell the MovieClipLoader object to do anything, you just refer to it by its variable name, **myMCL**.*

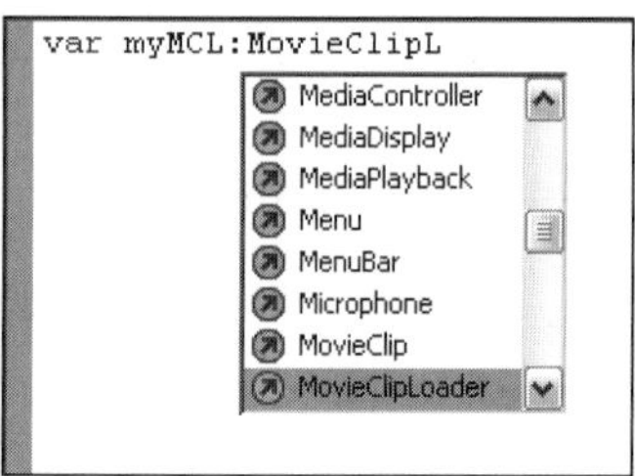

10. After **`var myMCL`**, type:

`:MovieClipLoader`

*As you type out **:MovieClipLoader**, you'll notice a scrollable box appear with different options to choose from. If you'd like, without typing out the rest of **`:MovieClipLoader`**, you can simply select it from this list and then press Enter or Return. Flash MX 2004 will then insert that into your code for you! This scrollable box is one example of **code hinting**–Flash MX 2004's way of trying to be helpful. Based on what you're typing, Flash MX 2004 sees that you're using strict typing (denoted by the colon) to set the data type of the variable you just created, **`myMCL`**. In this case, you're using strict typing to tell Flash MX 2004 that the variable **`myMCL`** is of the type MovieClipLoader. If you left out the strict typing statement, **`:MovieClipLoader`**, your ActionScript would still work. But with the introduction of ActionScript 2.0 in Flash MX 2004, using strict typing is recommended because it complies with ActionScript 2.0 specifications. In other words, using strict typing is recommended by Macromedia because it follows good ActionScript programming practices. That is primarily why you will be using it throughout the exercises this book.*

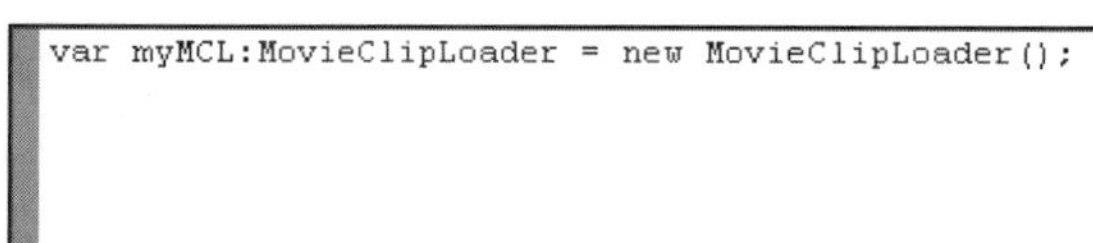

11. After **`var myMCL:MovieClipLoader`**, type:

`= new MovieClipLoader();`

*In essence, this tells Flash MX 2004 to create a new instance of the MovieClipLoader object, and to place it within the variable **myMCL**. In the future, when you want to tell this particular MovieClipLoader instance to do anything, you can simply refer to it by using the variable you assigned the reference to, **myMCL**.*

Congratulations! You've just created a new MovieClipLoader object that you will soon be able to use to load in SWF and JPG files to your heart's content. Without knowing it, you have just also added quite a lot of functionality to your Flash MX 2004 project. Much like adding a movie clip to your project automatically gives you the ability to use ActionScript to modify its methods and properties such as visibility, alpha, rotation, and so forth, adding the MovieClipLoader object to your project also allows you to use its built-in methods and listeners to load SWF and JPG files, get progress reports on their downloading progress, and so forth. Adding just that one line of code actually added a lot more than you realize. You'll begin to see all of the functionality that the MovieClipLoader provides in later exercises.

*Now, even though you've created a new MovieClipLoader object, you still need a few more lines of ActionScript to make it work. Once the MovieClipLoader is complete and fully scripted, you will be able to tell it to do things like load a SWF file. But if you want to find out things about that loading process–like how much of the file has been loaded, what to do after the file has been fully downloaded, and so forth–don't ask the MovieClipLoader, because it doesn't know. To get information about what the MovieClipLoader is doing, you need to assign a **listener** to the MovieClipLoader. The listener will then respond to different events that the MovieClipLoader sends it. For example, when you tell the MovieClipLoader object to load a SWF, the MovieClipLoader begins loading that SWF. When it's finished, it sends a parameter (success) to the onLoadComplete listener (if you added one) assigned to that MovieClipObject. You can then write a script within the onLoadComplete listener that specifies what should happen when that SWF file is completely loaded.*

```
var myMCL:MovieClipLoader = new MovieClipLoader();
var myListener:Object = new Object();
```

12. Click at the end of the first line of code that you just wrote and press **Enter** (Windows) or **Return** (Mac) to create a new line. Then type:

```
var myListener:Object = new Object();
```

*In essence, this tells Flash MX 2004 to create a new variable called **myListener** (which is strict typed to specify that the value of the variable will be an object), and to place a new, generic object within that variable. Up to this point, the variable **myListener** is just a variable with a generic object assigned to it. It is not yet* listening *to the events being passed from the MovieClipLoader. You are going to do that next.*

```
var myMCL:MovieClipLoader = new MovieClipLoader();
var myListener:Object = new Object();

myMCL.addListener(myListener);
```

13. Click after the second line of code, and press **Enter** (Windows) or **Return** (Mac) a couple times. (Flash MX 2004 ignores empty breaks, so you could have one line break or 50; it doesn't matter.) Then type:

myMCL.addListener(myListener);

This takes the generic object that you created, called **myListener***, and assigns it as a listener to the MovieClipLoader object called* **myMCL***. Now, whenever the MovieClipLoader (***myMCL***) sends out an event (when it starts loading a file, when it stops, and so forth), you can assign a listener to perform some script when that event occurs.*

Note: *You can add as many listeners as you want to respond to events fired from this object. You'll see a few of these in this, and upcoming chapters.*

Congratulations! You just created your first MovieClipLoader script! As you will see later, there is so much more that the MovieClipLoader can do. To prevent you from bursting too many brain cells all at once, you're going to add functionality onto the MovieClipLoader piecemeal. In Chapter 8, "Building a Preloader," you will give the MovieClipLoader more functionality by building a preloader into it. But for now, this simple MovieClipLoader will load whichever SWF or JPG file you tell it to. In the next step, you're going to do just that.

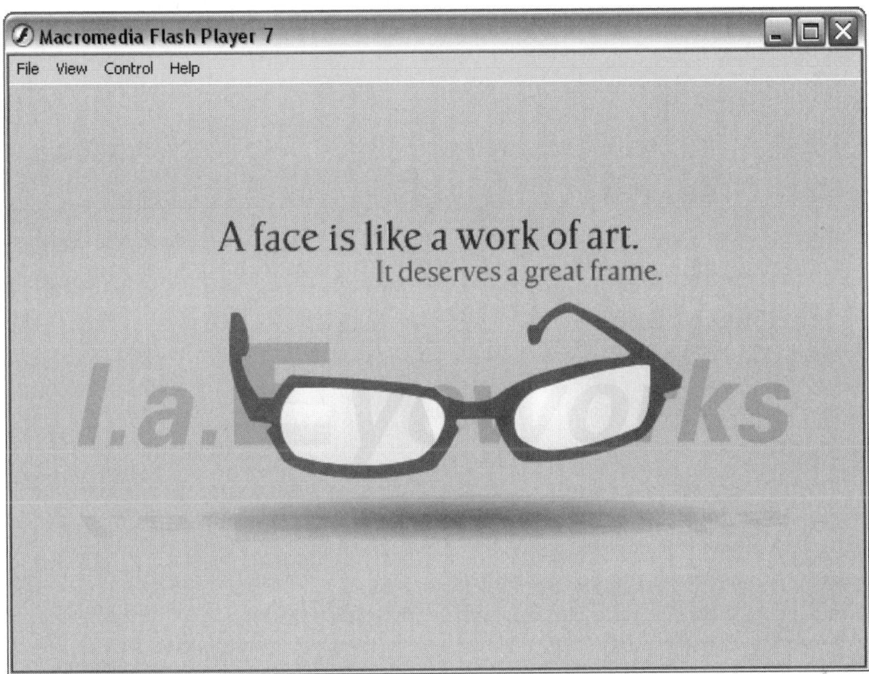

14. Hide or minimize Flash MX 2004. Then, open the **la_eyeworks** folder you copied onto your **Desktop** at the beginning of this exercise. Now, open the **site** folder and double-click the file **splash.swf**. (Your operating system might not show the file extension.) This should automatically open the animated **splash.swf** file in the stand-alone Macromedia Flash Player 7, which is provided with the Flash MX 2004 install. In the next step, you are going to write one line of code that will instruct your new MovieClipLoader in the **master.fla** file to load this **splash.swf** file.

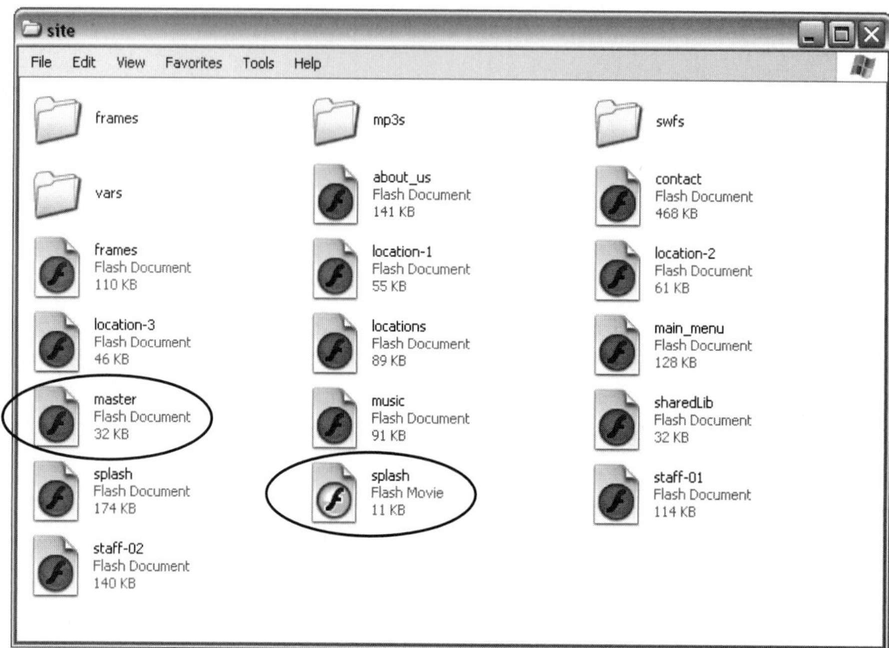

15. Close the **splash.swf** file, and look at the **site** folder again. Notice how the **splash.swf** file is in the same folder that your **master.fla** (where the MovieClipLoader script resides) file is.

When loading assets into Flash MX 2004 projects, it's important that you understand where the assets are located in relation to the file that's doing the loading.

---

16. Back in Flash MX 2004, make sure that you still have Keyframe 1 in the **a** layer selected, and that the **Actions** panel is open (**F9**). Then, click after the last line of code and press **Enter** (Windows) or **Return** (Mac) on your keyboard a couple of times to create a few line breaks. (This just gives you a little visual space between the important parts of your script.)

```
var myMCL:MovieClipLoader = new MovieClipLoader();
var myListener:Object = new Object();

myMCL.addListener(myListener);

myMCL.loadClip("splash.swf", 5);
```

17. Type:

```
myMCL.loadClip("splash.swf", 5);
```

*Simply, this instructs your MovieClipLoader (**myMCL**) to load the SWF file **splash.swf** into Level 5. By this point, you most likely know that you have two choices for a destination when loading one SWF (or JPG) file into another SWF file: You can load the SWF/JPG file into a movie clip, or you can load the SWF/JPG file into a level. A level is essentially an invisible layer that floats above the movie that's doing the loading. Loading content into a level also gives you the ability to set the visual stacking order of that loaded content. In this case, you're loading the **splash.swf** file into Level 5. Level 2 is above Level 1, Level 3 is above Level 2, so on and so forth. The movie that is doing all of the loading (in your case, **master.swf**) is referred to as Level 0 (or, in ActionScript terms, **_level0**).*

***Note:** When loading assets (SWF files, JPGs, and so forth) into a level, you can load them into any level starting with 0, all the way to the incredibly ridiculously high number of 2,130,706,429 (yes, that's two* billion *and change). So as you can see, there's plenty of room to load assets into any level that you choose.*

NOTE | MovieClipLoader Backwards Compatibility

One thing to keep in mind is that the MovieClipLoader you just constructed is *not* backwards compatible with viewers who are looking at your content with version 6 (or prior) of the Flash plug-in. The MovieClipLoader will work correctly *only* for viewers who are using the latest version (version 7) of the Flash Player. Toward the end of this book, you will learn how to create a Flash plug-in detector that will allow you to identify visitors who are using earlier versions of the Flash plug-in. Once those visitors have been identified, they can be redirected to another page–or Web site–of your choosing. This will prevent visitors from entering your site and discovering a Flash MX 2004 movie that isn't compatible with their older plug-ins.

If you (or your client) *requires* backwards compatibility with earlier versions of the Flash plug-in (such as versions 5 or 6), you will need to use the ActionScript command **loadMovie** (or **loadMovieNum**), which *is* compatible with older plug-in versions. Because this book is about learning the latest version of Flash and the features it provides, there are obviously many features used in this book that are for Flash MX 2004 *only* and are not backwards compatible. However, because the MovieClipLoader is such an *integral* part of this method of site construction, I felt you should be aware of its lack of backwards compatibility.

NOTE | New Security Policy

Introduced with the new Macromedia Flash 7 Player is a new security policy that restricts any kind of data (variables, SWF/JPG files, and so forth) from being loading into a SWF file if that data resides outside the exact domain name that the SWF file resides on. In other words, if you have a SWF file located at **http://www.mydomain.com**, and you are attempting to load data that is on another server accessible at **http://www.myotherdomain.com**, it won't work. If you need to load data that is located outside of the exact domain name where your SWF file is located (the SWF file that's doing the loading), you need to create something called a **cross-domain policy file**. A cross-domain policy file is essentially a simple XML file (named **crossdomain.xml**) that is stored at the root level of the server that has the data on it that you want to load. Within that XML file is a list of URLs that are *allowed* to access the data on that server. An example of the **cross-domain.xml** file looks like this:

```
<?xml version="1.0"?>
<!DOCTYPE cross-domain-policy SYSTEM "http://www.macromedia.com/xml/dtds/
   cross-domain-policy.dtd">
<cross-domain-policy>
   <allow-access-from domain="www.company.com" />
</cross-domain-policy>
```

If you are trying to load data into your Flash MX 2004 project that is located under a different domain name and you are *not* using a cross-domain policy file, when visitors view your Flash MX 2004 content, they will be presented with a warning dialog box that will ask them whether or not they are willing to accept the loading of content from another server. Obviously, as a Flash MX 2004 designer/developer, this is not something you would like the viewer of your Web site to see.

For more information about the specifics of the new Macromedia Flash 7 plug-in security policy and the cross-domain policy file, visit Macromedia's Web page on this issue here:

http://www.macromedia.com/support/flash/ts/documents/loadvars_security.htm

Note: With the latest version (at the time of this book's publication) of the Macromedia Flash Player, 7.0.r19, a new action has been added (`System.security.loadPolicyFile`) that allows the cross-domain policy files to be placed in other locations on the hosting Web server. You can read more about these cross-domain policy file changes here:

http://www.macromedia.com/devnet/mx/flash/articles/fplayer_security.html

18. Test your movie by choosing **Control > Test Movie.**

*As you can see, the **splash.swf** file loads perfectly into the **master.swf** file (where your MovieClipLoader script is located). When you load a SWF or JPG file into a level, as you have just done, the top-left corner of the asset (x:0, y:0) is aligned with the top-left of the base SWF file (also x:0, y:0), the **splash.swf** file is positioned perfectly aligned with the **master.swf** file. This is because both the splash and master SWF files were created with the same Stage size. That way, when designing content in the asset files (splash, music, about us, and so forth), you know–relative to the Stage–how everything is going to be positioned when it gets loaded into the container **master.swf**.*

Now, I know that the four lines of ActionScript code that you have written in this exercise may seem somewhat excessive to just load one SWF file into another. Keep in mind, however, that this MovieClipLoader code will be controlling the loading of all *of the SWF and JPG files throughout the* entire *L.A. Eyeworks site. Not to mention all the advantages that the MovieClipLoader has over the quasi-deprecated loadMovie that you should already be familiar with. (See the previous section "What Is the MovieClipLoader, and How Does it Differ From loadMovie?" for more detailed information on the major differences.)*

There you have it, your first, working example of the new MovieClipLoader!

---

19. Save your **master.fla** file by choosing **File > Save**.

*In the next exercise, you are going to learn how to use the incredibly useful, file-saving awesomeness that is the **shared library**. A shared library is essentially a SWF file with a bunch of assets contained within it–symbols, fonts, and so forth–that you can use within* any *of your other SWF files. It's almost the same concept as a symbol (a reusable element), except this is essentially an* entire library *of reusable elements that can be shared across multiple SWF files.*

What Is a Shared Library?

You've seen how you can use symbols (graphic symbols, movie clip symbols, and so forth) to reduce the file size of your Flash MX 2004 movie when reusing identical elements. But what if you've broken your Flash MX 2004–based Web site into multiple pieces, are loading them into another SWF file using loadMovie or the MovieClipLoader (as you are doing in this book), and you have a symbol that you want to use in each of those SWF files? More commonly, what if you had a common font that you were using across all those SWF files as well? Traditionally, you would simply duplicate the symbol within each SWF file, or in the case of fonts, you would just embed the font face in each SWF file where you're using it. This adds to the overall file size of your project because you are causing the user to download the same symbol multiple times for each SWF file where it's used *and* causing them to download the same font multiple times as well! But what can you do? You can't have one symbol or font being used *across* multiple SWF files right? Wrong. By using something called a **shared library**, you can.

A shared library, by itself, is very unglamorous. Essentially, it's just an FLA whose library you populate with symbols, fonts, and so forth. The difference between a plain FLA and a FLA with a shared library starts when you assign a linkage ID name (a unique name, much like an instance name that you assign to a symbol instance) to each of the items that you want to be available for sharing in other SWF files. You'll learn to do this in the upcoming exercise. When you want to share one of those items in another FLA, you simply drag the item from your shared library to the library in another FLA where you want to use that item. Flash MX 2004 automatically makes a link to that shared element (which is essentially just an alias to the item in the shared library), and you can then use it in your project. You can share those elements in as many files as you want.

A shared library element is not actually embedded in the file that you dragged it into. It still resides in the shared library FLA. The shared element in the host FLA file is, for all intents and purposes, an alias to the original item in the shared library! It's just like the concept behind symbols (reusable elements), except taken to the level of being able to reuse items (nearly anything that you can import into a library) *across* SWF files. How incredibly powerful is that?!

2. Creating and Precaching the Shared Library

In this exercise, you will create the shared library. The shared library will contain the shared elements that you will use to complete the exercises throughout this book.

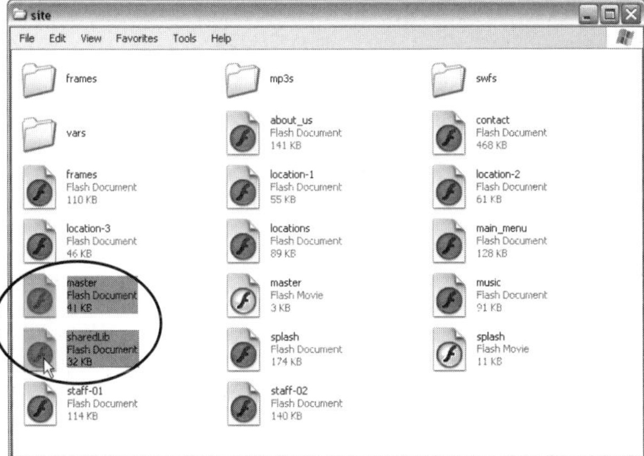

1. Open **master.fla** (which you created in the last exercise) if you accidentally closed it, *and* **sharedLib.fla**. These files are both located in the **site** folder, which is in the **la_eyeworks** folder on your **Desktop**.

2. In the **sharedLib.fla** file, open its library. In there you'll notice only one file, a button symbol called **btn. arrow**. Don't worry, though–you'll flesh out that shared library some more in just a minute.

The intended use of a shared library is to share assets that are used across multiple SWF files. If an asset is being used only once, in one SWF file, there's really no reason to include it in a shared library.

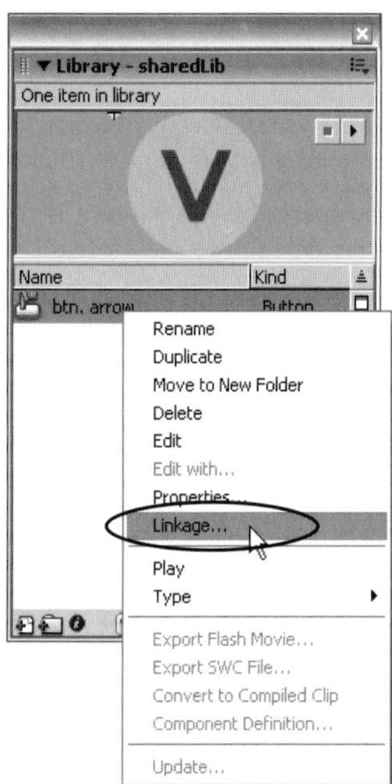

3. Right-click (Windows) or **Ctrl+click** (Mac) on the **btn. arrow** symbol in the **sharedLib** library, and from the contextual menu, choose **Linkage**.

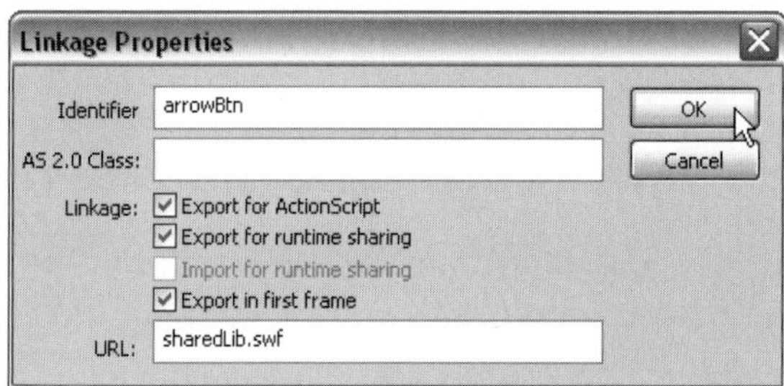

4. This will open the **Linkage Properties** dialog box. Here is where you specify how this library item can be shared and what its name will be. First, click the **Export for ActionScript** check box. This will automatically check the **Export in first frame** check box as well. Then, in the **Identifier** field, type **arrowBtn**. This Identifier name can be anything you'd like. But just like when you give a name to a symbol instance, don't begin the Identifier name with numbers, or use spaces or special characters like ?, *, and so forth. Lastly, click the **Export for runtime sharing** check box. This will also automatically fill in the **URL** field with the name that this SWF file will be when it is published, **sharedLib.swf**.

The table on the next page provides further explanation of what those various fields and check boxes are.

Linkage Properties	
Option	**Description**
Identifier	This is a unique name you need to assign each library element you wish to share. This name can be whatever you'd like, but you should avoid spaces in the name, numbers at the beginning of the name, and special characters such as ?, #, and so forth.
AS 2.0 Class	The name of the ActionScript 2.0 class that you want to assign to this shared library symbol.
Export for ActionScript	Enables this shared library element to be manipulated with ActionScript.
Export for runtime sharing	Enables this shared library element to be used during "runtime." Runtime refers to when the SWF file is playing (running). If you don't check this check box, your shared library element will not appear in its destination document when it is playing.
Import for runtime sharing	This check box is available when choosing Linkage on the shared library item in the *destination* document. Leaving this check box unchecked will disallow that shared library element from being displayed during runtime.
Export in first frame	Exports this shared library element so that it's accessible in the very first frame. If you *don't* check this check box, place an instance of your shared library item on the Stage in the frame where it is first needed.
URL	The URL to where this shared library SWF file will be located. Flash MX 2004 automatically enters in the name of the SWF file that the shared library element resides in, in this case, **sharedLib.swf**.

5. Click **OK**. That symbol is now sharable and can be dragged into the library of other FLA files.

Next, you need to create a new font symbol that you can share in your other SWF files!

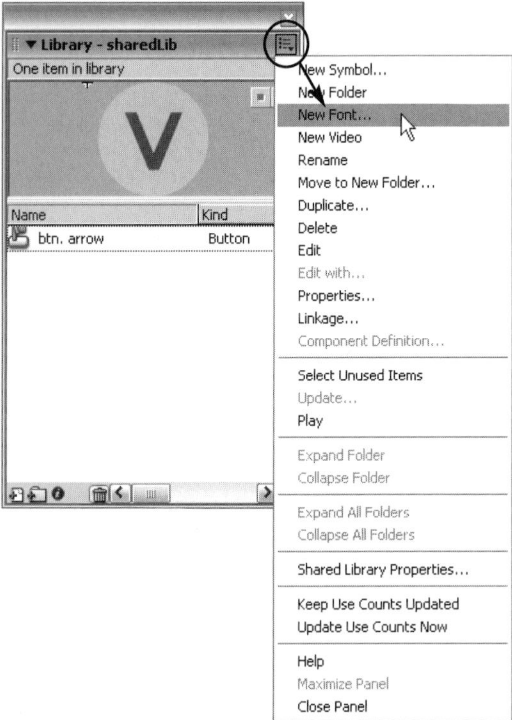

6. Click the **Library Preferences** button, and from the pop-up menu, choose **New Font**.

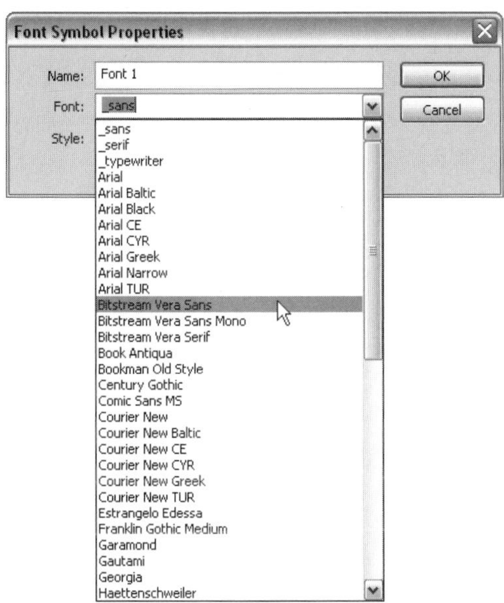

*This will open the **Font Symbol Properties** dialog box. From here, you choose the font symbol you want to create and what name you want to give that symbol (the name that appears in the library). From the **Font** list pull-down menu, you should see the Bitstream fonts you installed in Chapter 2, "Where Do I Start?". On Mac OS X, you should see more Bitstream Vera fonts than the ones listed in the Windows screen shot above. The Windows operating system groups the various font face styles together, whereas the face styles are* not *grouped on the Mac. This means that Windows and Macintosh users will have to follow a slightly different procedure which, you can be sure, I will make note of in the following steps.*

7. On both Macintosh and Windows, choose **Bitstream Vera Sans** from the **Font** pull-down menu. In the **Name** field, type **Vera**. Make sure that **Bold**, **Italic**, and **Alias text** are all unchecked. The **Size** of the text is irrelevant with how you're using fonts in this book, so leave the **Size** value set to whatever it is currently. Click **OK**.

Great! You just created a symbol in your library, except this symbol is an entire font face! Pretty cool. Next you need to add three other Vera faces you will be using throughout the L.A. Eyeworks site.

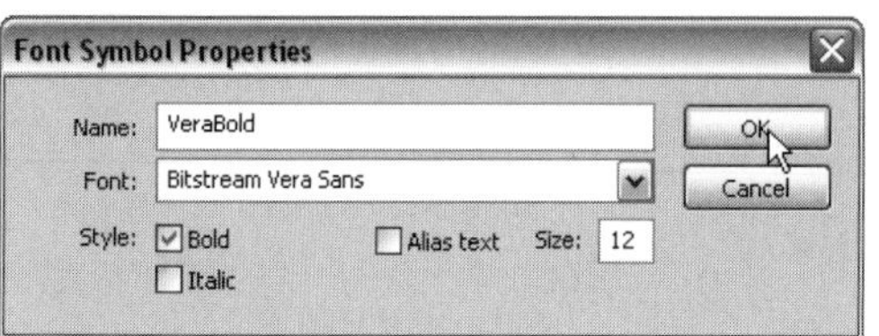

(Windows XP)

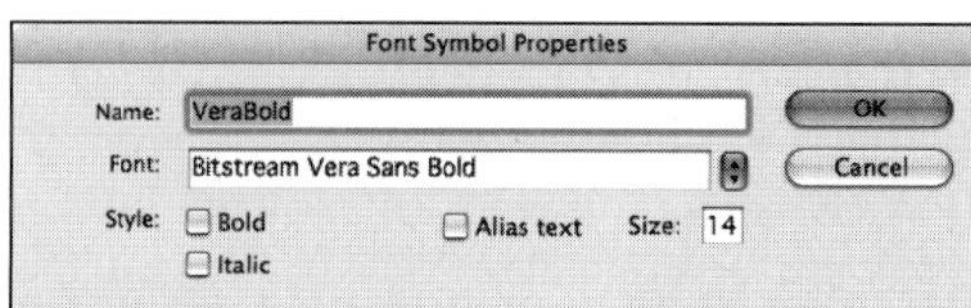

(Mac OS X 10.3)

8. Repeat Step 7, but in Windows, choose the font **Bitstream Vera Sans**, and then click the **Bold** check box. On the Macintosh, choose the font **Bitstream Vera Sans Bold.** On the Macintosh, you *do not* need to check the **Bold** check box. On both Mac and Windows, in the **Name** field type **VeraBold.** Click **OK.**

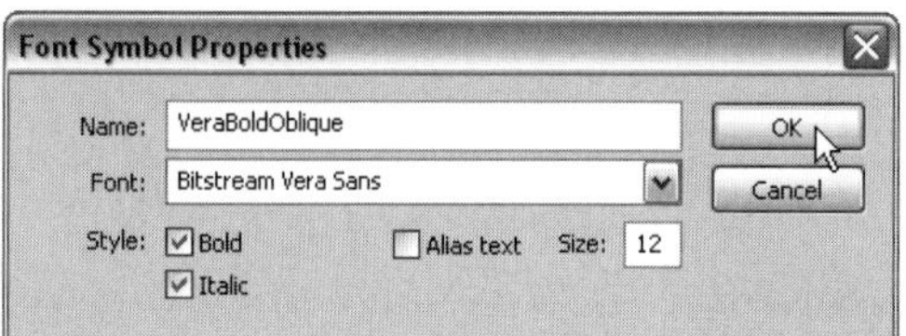

(Windows XP)

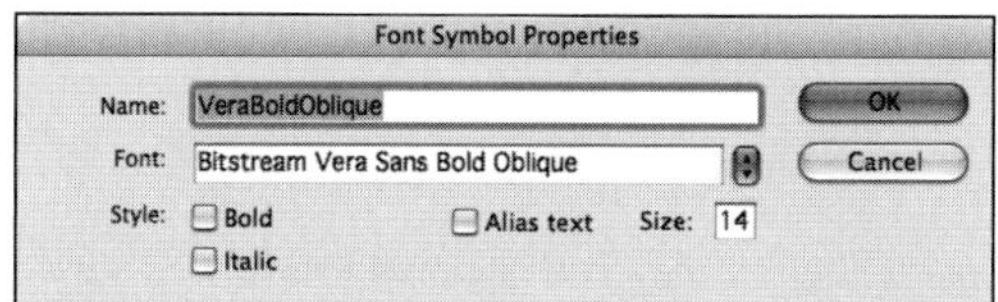

(Mac OS X 10.3)

9. Repeat Step 7 again, but on Windows, choose the font **Bitstream Vera Sans**, and then click the **Bold** and **Italic** check boxes. On the Macintosh, choose the font **Bitstream Vera Sans Bold Oblique.** On the Macintosh, you *do not* need to check the **Bold** and **Italic** check boxes. On both Mac and Windows, in the **Name** field type **VeraBoldOblique.** Click **OK.**

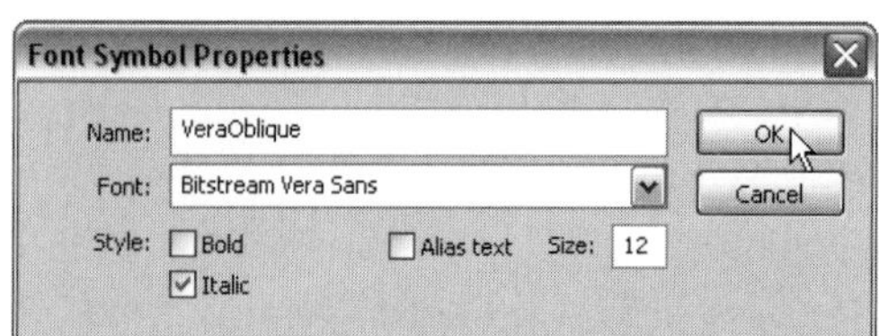

(Windows XP)

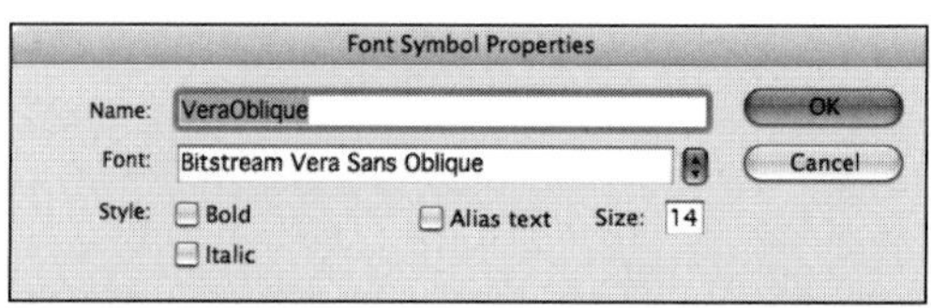

(Mac OS X 10.3)

10. Repeat Step 7 once more, but on Windows, choose the font **Bitstream Vera Sans**, and then click the **Italic** check box. On the Macintosh, choose the font **Bitstream Vera Sans Oblique.** On the Macintosh, you *do not* need to check the **Italic** check box. On both Mac and Windows, in the **Name** field type **VeraOblique.** Click **OK.**

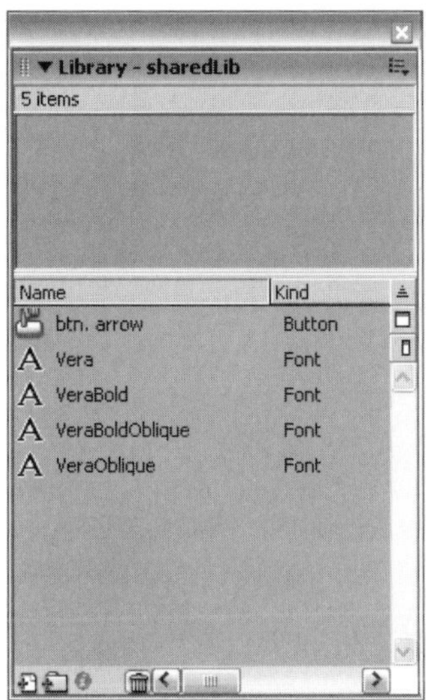

*Fantabuloso! Now, if you look at your **sharedLib.fla** library, you'll notice that you have the original shared button symbol, **btn. arrow**, but now you also have four font symbols in there, too: **Vera**, **VeraBold**, **VeraBoldOblique**, and **VeraOblique**. Next you need to set the linkage options for each of those font symbols (just as you did for the btn. arrow symbol back in Steps 3 and 4) so they can be shared with your other SWF files.*

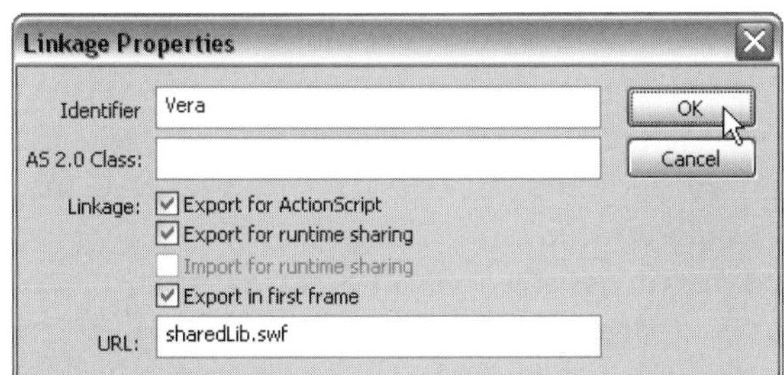

11. In the **sharedLib** library, **right-click** (Windows) or **Ctrl+click** (Mac) on the font symbol **Vera**, and from the contextual menu choose **Linkage**. In the **Linkage Properties** window, check the **Export for ActionScript** check box (which will also automatically check the **Export in first frame** check box), and the **Export for runtime sharing** check box. Also make sure that the **Identifier** field automatically sets itself to **Vera** (the same name you gave the font symbol when you created it) and the **URL** field automatically sets itself to **sharedLib.swf**. Click **OK**.

---

12. Repeat this process for the remaining three font symbols. All the settings should be the same as the settings in Step 11, with the following exceptions: for the font symbol **VeraBold**, make sure the **Identifier** is set to **VeraBold**; for the font symbol **VeraBoldOblique**, make sure the **Identifier** is set to **VeraBoldOblique**; and lastly, for the font symbol **VeraOblique**, make sure the **Identifier** is set to **VeraOblique**. Whew!

Now that you've enabled linkage for those font symbols, you can use them in as many SWF files as you'd like. (You'll see how to do that in the next chapter.) The huge benefit that using a shared library provides is that the font outlines for these four Vera faces are only embedded into this sharedLib SWF file. All the other SWF files that comprise the L.A. Eyeworks site, which also *use these shared Vera font faces, will* not *have the font outlines embedded into their SWF files. They just reference the font faces embedded in this one **sharedLib.swf** file. Using a shared library to share fonts across SWF files (as you just set up in this exercise), can* greatly *reduce the overall size of your Flash MX 2004 project because the same font outlines are not being embedded in every SWF file that they're used in. Huzzah!*

*The last item of business is to perform a little shared library trickery. Before you start, however, you should first understand why you have to perform these extra steps. In the next chapter, you will use some of the shared fonts from the shared library you just created within another SWF file. When a visitor first comes to your Web site and starts viewing your content, the first time a shared library element is requested from another SWF, Flash MX 2004 starts downloading the entire shared library SWF file. Flash MX 2004 will not simply download the one item it needs from the shared library (unfortunately). Instead, when the first item within a shared library is requested, it will trigger the downloading of the entire shared library SWF. Although this is fine and workable, depending on the size of the shared library SWF, it could bring the playback of your Flash MX 2004 movie to a grinding halt. It would, of course, be best to be able to load the **sharedLib.swf** in a controlled manner so that the viewer knows what's going on.*

*The problem, however, is that simply preloading the **sharedLib.swf** file doesn't do the trick. (Even though you'd think that would work, logically.) Flash MX 2004 simply re-downloads the **sharedLib.swf** file when the first shared element is used. Instead, you're going to create a "trigger" SWF whose job it is, essentially, to trigger the downloading of the **sharedLib.swf** at a point in the movie where you can control its downloading. All this "trigger" SWF will be comprised of is one of the shared library elements on its Stage. This **trigger.swf** file will then get loaded (no...not drunk–keep your eye on the ball here folks. Focuss...focuss.) using the MovieClipLoader at the beginning of the project. When the **trigger.swf** loads, since it uses a shared library element, it triggers the loading of the **sharedLib.swf** file, and from that point on, any of the shared library elements can be used–instantly–in any SWF file in the Web site.*

*First, you need to create the trigger man, **trigger.fla**, which will simply use one of the shared library elements and will trigger the downloading of the **sharedLib.swf**.*

---

13. Save your changes to the **sharedLib.fla** file, and then choose **File > Publish** to publish a SWF file into the same directory where the **sharedLib.fla** file resides (**Desktop > la_eyeworks > site**).

---

14. Close the **sharedLib.fla** file.

---

15. Create a new, blank FLA by pressing **Ctrl+Alt+N** (Windows) or **Cmd+Opt+N** (Mac).

*You don't need to be concerned with the dimensions or background color of this FLA because all it's being used for is to trigger the loading of the shared library. The viewer will never even know this file has loaded. Once the shared library loads, the loaded **trigger.swf** will be replaced by the **splash.swf** file.*

---

16. First, save this new FLA by choosing **File > Save As**. Save the file in your **Desktop > la_eyeworks > site** folder, and name it **trigger**. Click **Save**.

---

17. Open the **sharedLib Library** window by choosing **File > Import > Open External Library**. In the **Open as Library** dialog box, double-click **sharedLib**. This will open *just the library* of the **sharedLib.fla** file.

*The trigger file needs only one symbol from the shared library. As soon as the **master.swf** loads the **trigger.swf**, and sees that there's a shared element on the Stage, it will immediately start downloading (and caching) the entire **sharedLib.swf** shared library!*

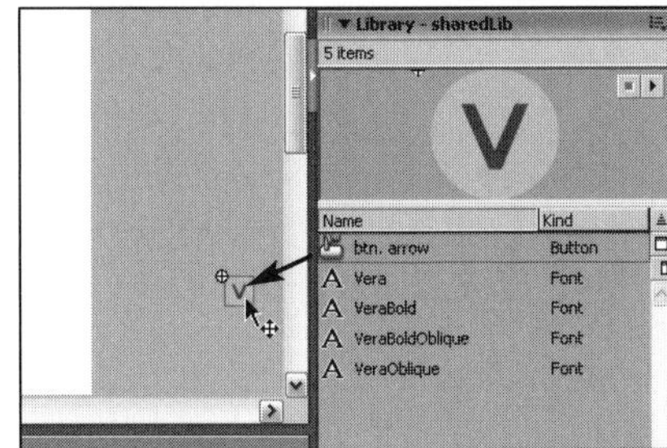

18. Drag **btn. arrow** onto the work area (the gray area around the outside of the white Stage area) of **trigger.fla**. You want this button symbol to be on the work area because you don't want it to be visible on the Stage when the **trigger.swf** file gets loaded into **master.swf**.

*A problem with how the **master.fla** Timeline is currently set up is that the loading of* all *of the SWF files occur on Keyframe 1. Now that you've created a trigger file that will trigger the loading of the shared library SWF, you obviously want that to happen* before *the **splash.swf** file loads. The loading of the shared library, because it's such an essential piece of this Web site (after all, it contains the fonts that will be used throughout nearly all of the SWF files), needs to load* first. *Because of that, you will start spacing out the loading of the various SWF files throughout the **master.swf** Timeline. The initial content (**trigger.swf**, **sharedLib.swf**, and so forth) will load right away on Keyframe 1; then, once that content has been loaded, the playhead will proceed down to Keyframe 10 where the next piece will load, the splash graphic **splash.swf**. For now, however, you need to add an action that triggers the **master.swf** Timeline to start playing once the **trigger.swf** file has been loaded and has also completely loaded the shared library, **sharedLib.swf**.*

19. Rename **Layer 1** to **shared lib asset**. Then create a new layer and rename it **a**.

20. Select the first keyframe in the **a** layer and open the **Actions** panel (**F9**).

```
_level0.play();
```

21. Write an action that instructs the **master.swf Timeline** to play by clicking in the **Actions** panel and typing:

```
_level0.play();
```

*This instructs the **master.swf** Timeline (`_level0`) to play. This action will get triggered, obviously, once **trigger.swf** has been completely downloaded. But because **trigger.swf** also has on its Stage a shared library element, which thereby triggers the downloading of **sharedLib.swf**, the `_level0.play();` action won't be executed until* both ***trigger.swf** and **sharedLib.swf** have been completely downloaded. *whew**

*Now you just need to save the changes to this **trigger.fla** file and publish a SWF.*

To avoid cluttering your site folder, you should instruct this FLA not to create the extraneous HTML file when you publish it.

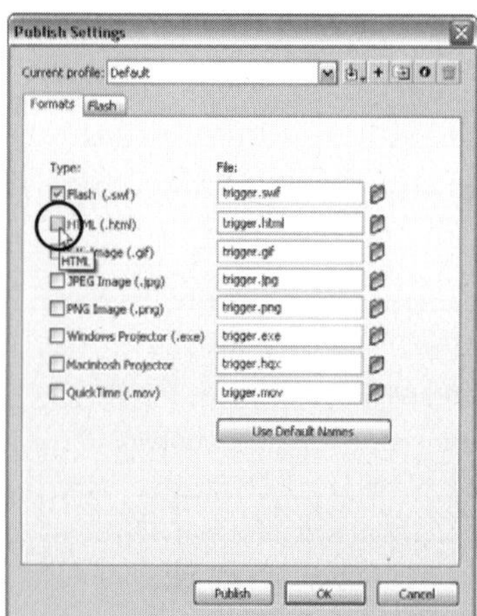

22. Choose **File > Publish Settings**. In the **Publish Settings** dialog box, uncheck **HTML**. This will prevent a **trigger.html** file from being created when you publish this FLA. Because the **trigger.swf** file will get loaded into the **master.swf** file, the html file is unnecessary.

23. Click **Publish**. This will publish a **trigger.swf** file into the **site** folder (the same location where the **trigger.fla** is saved). Then click **OK** to close the **Publish Settings** dialog box.

---

24. Save the changes you've made to **trigger.fla** by choosing **File > Save**. Once you've saved the changes, close **trigger.fla** by choosing **File > Close**. (You can also use the keyboard shortcut **Ctrl+W** [Windows] or **Cmd+W** [Mac] to close a file.)

*Meanwhile, back on the **master.fla** Timeline, all the actions are still all bundled up together on Keyframe 1. In the next few steps, you'll need to move the loading of the **splash.swf** file so that it happens further down the Timeline of **master.swf**. You'll also instruct the MovieClipLoader on **master.fla** to load **trigger.swf**. **Trigger.swf**, of course, will trigger the loading of the shared library because it uses a shared library item on its Stage. Lastly, you'll also need to create some sort of loading message so the viewer isn't just left staring at a blank page while **trigger.swf** and **sharedLib.swf** are downloading behind the scenes.*

---

25. Make sure you are in the **master.fla** file. (If you closed it, you can open it again by navigating to your **Desktop > la_eyeworks > site** folder and double-clicking on **master.fla**.) Select Keyframe 1 in the **a** layer, and open the **Actions** panel.

```
var myMCL:MovieClipLoader = new MovieClipLoader();
var myListener:Object = new Object();

myMCL.addListener(myListener);

myMCL.loadClip("splash.swf", 5);
myMCL.loadClip("trigger.swf", 5);
```

26. Click after the **`myMCL.loadClip("splash.swf", 5);`** line and press **Enter** (Windows) or **Return** (Mac) to create a new line break. Then, load the **trigger.swf** file into Level 5 by typing:

```
myMCL.loadClip("trigger.swf", 5);
```

*Because the **trigger.swf** file doesn't have any items visible on the Stage–only the one shared library button on the work area–you won't see anything visual on the **master.swf** Stage when the **trigger.swf** file gets loaded. Once the **trigger.swf** file is loaded and the Macromedia Flash Player 7 sees that it is referencing a shared library item, it will begin downloading (and caching) all of the items in the shared library (**sharedLib.swf**). Once the **sharedLib.swf** file has been completely downloaded, you will be able to instantly use any shared items from within any loaded SWF file. Neat-o!*

*You probably have also noticed that **trigger.swf** is loading into the same level as **splash.swf**, _level5. This is because all **trigger.swf** is needed for is to (as its name implies) trigger the downloading of the shared library. But once **trigger.swf** has done its job, then it isn't needed any more. Because of that, **splash.swf** will simply load into its place (_level5), kicking **trigger.swf** out in the process. How's that for gratitude? ;-) Although having both **trigger.swf** and **splash.swf** load into the same level is not a problem, having them load into the same level at the* same time, *however, is. With the way the script is currently set up, **splash.swf** will start to load, but will get immediately unloaded and replaced with **trigger.swf**. In this setup, the viewer would never get to see **splash.swf**. Instead, you want **splash.swf** to load* after ***trigger.swf** has loaded and done its job, and* after *the shared library has loaded as well. You will be reorganizing the loading order in the next few steps.*

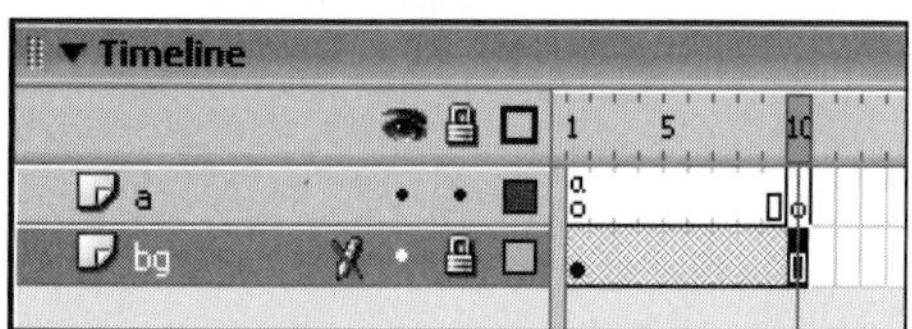

27. Click **Frame 10** in the **a** layer, and add a new keyframe by pressing **F6**. Then, so the **bg** layer is also visible out to Frame 10, select **Frame 10** in the **bg** layer, and add frames out to that point by pressing **F5**.

*On Keyframe 10 in the **a** layer is where you will insert the action that triggers the **splash.swf** file to load. One of the reasons why you're triggering **splash.swf** to load from Frame 10 goes back to the idea that you want **splash.swf** to load* after ***trigger.swf** has been loaded (which occurs on Frame 1) and triggers the downloading of the shared library (**sharedLib.swf**). Once both **trigger.swf** and **sharedLib.swf** have been completely downloaded, the `_level0.play();` action that you assigned to the first keyframe of **trigger.swf** will be executed, and **master.swf** will play on to Frame 10. Of course, you need **master.swf** to be paused on the first keyframe to begin with, so you will be writing a stop action to do just that in the next few steps. In Chapter 12, "The Main Menu," you will see another reason why having the action that triggers the loading of **splash.swf** on Frame 10 is beneficial.*

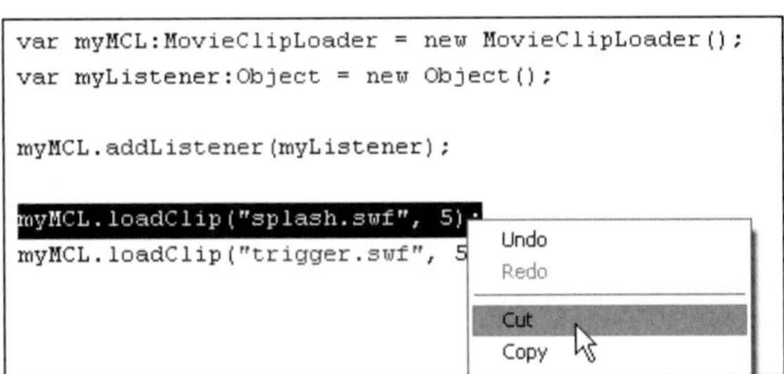

28. Click **Keyframe 1** in the **a** layer, and open the **Actions** panel (**F9**). Then, select the **`myMCL.loadClip("splash.swf", 5);`** line by dragging over it, and **right-clicking** (Windows) or **Ctrl+clicking** (Mac) that selected line. From the contextual menu that appears, choose **Cut**. This will cut the action from **Keyframe 1**, and store it in the computer's clipboard, to be pasted elsewhere.

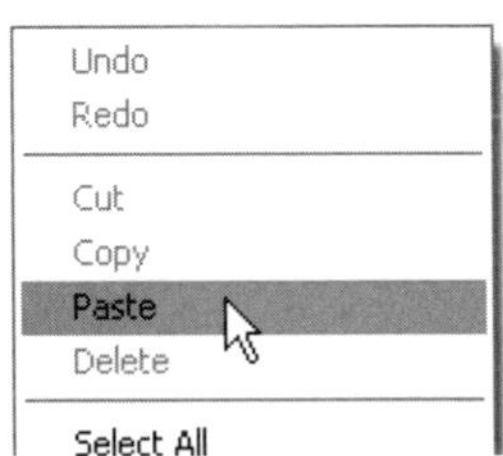

29. Select **Keyframe 10** in the **a** layer (which you added in Step 27), and in the **Actions** panel, **right-click** (Windows) or **Ctrl+click** (Mac). From the contextual menu that appears, choose **Paste**. This will paste the **`myMCL.loadClip("splash.swf", 5);`** action that you cut from **Keyframe 1** into **Keyframe 10**.

Because you don't want these actions to be continually executed as the playhead loops through the Timeline, you need to add a ***`stop()`*** *action to Keyframe 10 as well.*

```
stop();
myMCL.loadClip("splash.swf", 5);
```

30. Click to the left of the **`myMCL.loadClip("splash.swf", 5);`** line, and press **Enter** (Windows) or **Return** (Mac) to create a line break *above* that action. Then, click the top, empty line in the **Actions** panel, and write a **`stop()`** action by typing:

```
stop();
```

When the playhead encounters Keyframe 10, it will stop. The MovieClipLoader will then load ***splash.swf*** *into Level 5, thereby unloading and replacing* ***trigger.swf****, which loaded there in Keyframe 1. So that* ***master.swf*** *doesn't initially start playing by itself (you want it to wait on the first keyframe until* ***trigger.swf*** *and* ***sharedLib.swf*** *have been completely downloaded), you need to add another stop action to Keyframe 1 as well.*

```
stop();
var myMCL:MovieClipLoader = new MovieClipLoader();
var myListener:Object = new Object();

myMCL.addListener(myListener);

myMCL.loadClip("trigger.swf", 5);
```

31. Single-click **Keyframe 1** in the **a** layer. Then, in the **Actions** panel, click before the top line of code, **`var myMCL:MovieClipLoader = new MovieClipLoader();`** and press **Enter** (Windows) or **Return** (Mac) to create a line break. Click the new line break you just created, and add a stop action by typing:

`stop();`

*Now the **master.swf** Timeline will be paused until both **trigger.swf** and **sharedLib.swf** have both been completely downloaded, thereby triggering the action that tells **master.swf** that it's okay to play: **_level0.play();***

Even though you're not quite finished yet, this is a good point to stop and test your work thus far.

---

32. Save the changes you've made to **master.fla** by choosing **File > Save**. Then, test the movie by choosing **Control > Test Movie.**

*When the Preview window appears, you should see (within half a second), the splash graphic appear. Although it's great to see that it, at least, is loading and working correctly, you don't really know if the shared library is loaded correctly and if the **trigger.swf** file did its job properly. To get more information about the loading process, as well as what a viewer on a slow modem would see, you're going to use the **Bandwidth Profiler** in conjunction with a feature called **Simulate Download**. (In prior versions of Flash MX 2004, Simulate Download used to be referred to as **show streaming**.)*

---

33. While you're still viewing the preview of **master.swf**, choose **View > Bandwidth Profiler**. This will divide your **Preview** window in half. The bottom half contains the viewable SWF file, and the top half contains the **Bandwidth Profiler** itself.

The Bandwidth Profiler, as you probably know, tracks how much data would be sent, for each frame, were a SWF being viewed by someone over the Internet. It also allows you to preview how a SWF will perform as it is downloaded using a variety of Internet connection speeds. When using loadMovie or–as in your case–the MovieClipLoader, the Bandwidth Profiler will also show you exactly which assets are being downloaded and will simulate how long those assets will take to download over different Internet connection speeds.

First, you need to give the Bandwidth Profiler pane, which displays the loading information, more room so you can see everything.

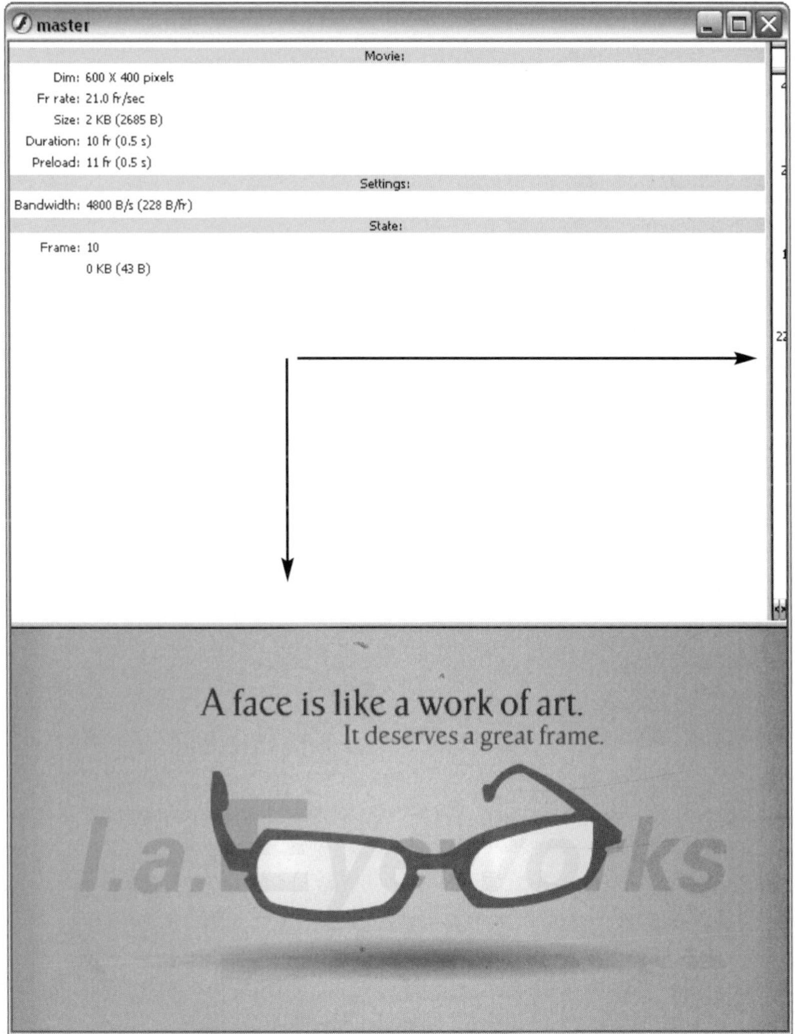

34. First, make the entire **Preview** window as tall as your monitor will allow. Then, drag the moveable horizontal bar down so that you can still see the SWF itself but are using the majority of the space to see what's going on in the **Bandwidth Profiler**. Lastly, drag the moveable vertical bar as far to the right as possible. Essentially, you're reshuffling the three panes of the **Bandwidth Profiler** so that the statistics portion gets the most available space. This area is where you will see which assets are being loaded and their progress as they are being downloaded.

Now that you've set up your Preview window, you next need to choose a modem speed for the test.

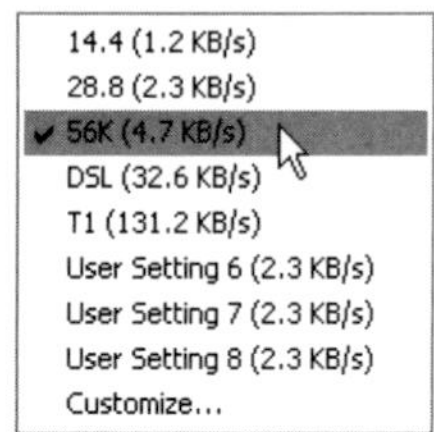

35. Choose **View > Download Settings > 56k (4.7 KB/s)**. As you can see from this list, you can choose from quite a few Internet connection speeds to test, or even create your own by choosing **Customize**. However, you've selected the most common nonbroadband connection speed: a 56k modem. Next, when you tell Flash MX 2004 to play this SWF back, it will play it back as it would if it were being accessed over the Internet using a 56k modem. Neat!

---

36. Choose **View > Simulate Download**.

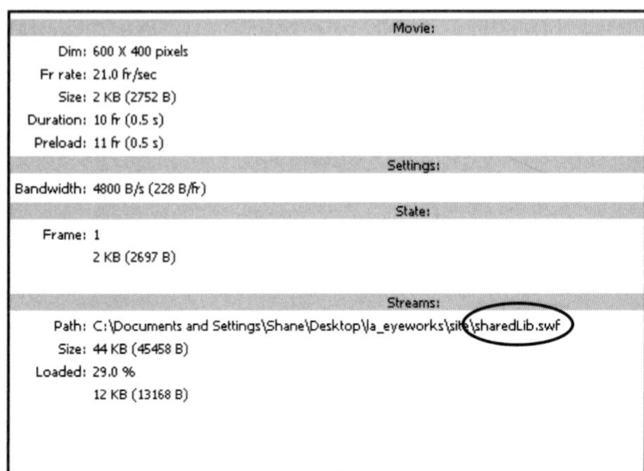

Watch the Bandwidth Profiler as it shows you which assets are loading and their progress. You'll notice how, almost instantly, the ***sharedLib.swf*** *file begins to download. Once it has finished downloading, you'll see–under the State section–the Frame quickly advance to 10, and then the* ***splash.swf*** *file will download and display. Magnifique! The only problem with how this is currently set up is that the viewer gets the unfortunate experience of having to sit there and look at a blank screen while the* ***sharedLib.swf*** *file gets downloaded in the background. In this case, the shared library SWF is relatively small (44 KB), but that's not always the case. So that viewers know what the heck is going on, you should write a short message that informs them that something is actually happening, and no, the Web site isn't broken.*

---

37. Close the **Preview** window.

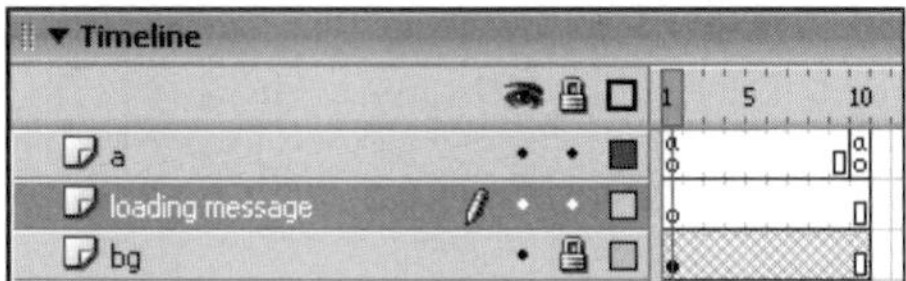

38. Click the bottom-most layer, **bg**, and add a new layer. Rename the new layer **loading message**. This is the layer that will, of course, contain the text message **loading assets** on the **Stage**.

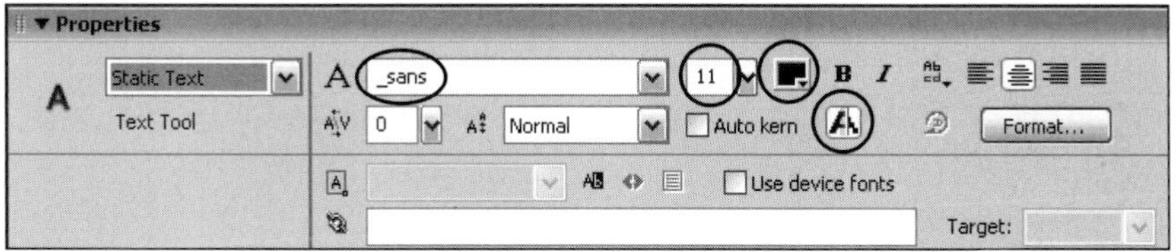

39. With the **loading message** layer still selected, select the **Text** tool. Then, in the **Properties inspector**, choose a **Static Text** type, a **Font** of **_sans** (located at the top of the font list on Windows and at the bottom of the font list on a Mac), a **Font Size** of **11** pt, and a color of **black**. Make sure that **Align center** is selected as well as **Alias Text**. These settings will allow you to type your loading message with the device font **_sans**. A device font, as you probably know, is a font that is not embedded into the published SWF. Instead, it instructs the viewer's computer to use a font already installed on its system to display the text with, much like standard text viewed on an HTML-based Web page does.

Note: *There's a bug in Flash MX 2004 that has to do with the Text tool. Sometimes (and I say "sometimes" because it doesn't happen consistently) when you select the Text tool, the Properties inspector will not update to show you the Text tool options. If you experience this bug, to see the text options in the Properties inspector, click the Text tool, and then click the Stage with the Text tool. Although this will create a text field based on your previous settings, it will also update the Properties inspector to display the text options. You can then simply delete that text field and set the text options in the Properties inspector.*

You want to use a device font for this loading message because you want the text to display instantly, without having to download any font outlines first. That way, from the time this file first loads, the viewer will know exactly what's happening.

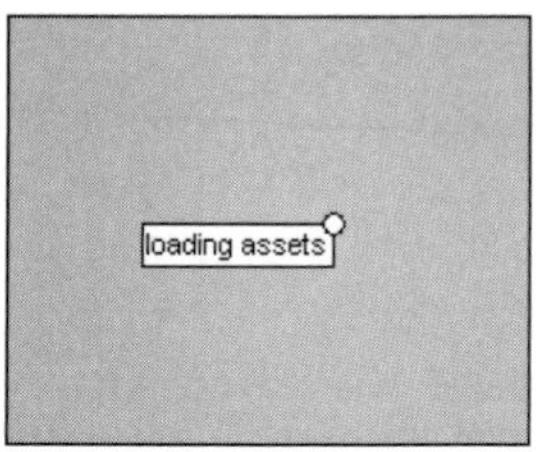

40. Click the **Stage**, and type **loading assets**. This is the brief message viewers will see as they wait for the **sharedLib.swf** file to finish downloading.

41. Press the **Esc** key to exit out of type-editing mode, and open the **Align** panel (**Ctrl+K** [Windows] or **Cmd+K** [Mac]).

42. First making sure the **To Stage** button is selected, click the **Align horizontal center** and then the **Align vertical center** buttons. This will align the text block **loading assets** to the center of the **Stage**.

43. Close the **Align** panel.

*You want the **loading assets** message to be displayed on the Stage only while the playhead is paused on the first keyframe. But after the playhead plays on to Keyframe 10 and loads **splash.swf**, you want the loading assets message to disappear. To accomplish this, all you need to do is insert a blank keyframe on Frame 2 of the **loading message** layer.*

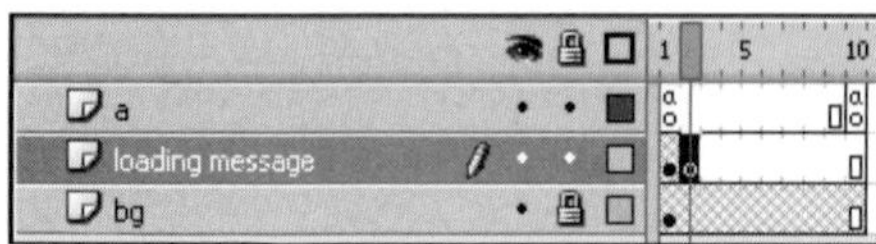

44. Single-click **frame 2** in the **loading message** layer, and then add a blank keyframe there by pressing **F7**. Now, the **loading assets** message is visible only on **Frame 1**.

45. Lock the **loading message** and **a** layers, and then save the changes you've made to **master.fla** by choosing **File > Save**.

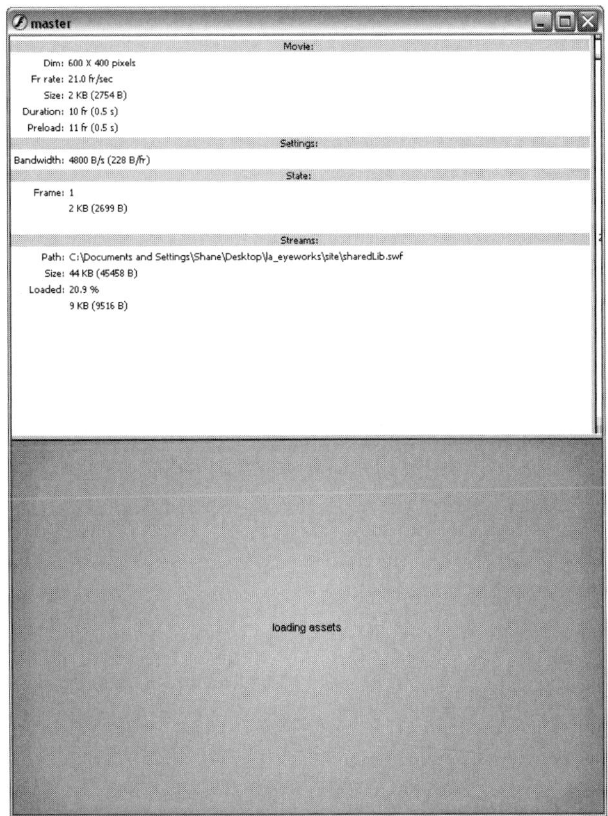

46. Test the movie again by choosing **Control > Test Movie**. Once the **Preview** window opens, choose **View > Simulate Download** to simulate the downloading of **master.swf** and the assets that load into it. You'll see your new message, **loading assets**, appear on the **Stage** while the **sharedLib.swf** file is downloading. Once the shared library SWF file has been completely downloaded, the message will disappear, and in its place will load and display the splash graphic, **splash.swf**.

*Congratulations! You've successfully created, loaded, and provided loading feedback for the shared library. Now that it has been precached, it can be used in any SWF file that is also loaded into the **master.swf** file, instantly.*

In the next chapter, not only will you learn how to utilize those shared library items, but also how to populate a dynamic text field with text from an external TXT file (using the LoadVars class), how to make that text scroll, how to modify that loaded text using a combination of HTML and (a new feature) Cascading Style Sheets (CSS), and lastly, how to add inline SWF files within the scrolling text (another new feature)! There's a ton *of new and very exciting examples in the next chapter, so go lock the door and tell your significant other to go to bed without ya because you have a* different *date tonight! ;-)*

4. LoadVars Class

la_eyeworks

Macromedia Flash MX 2004
Beyond the Basics

In this chapter, you're going to learn how to utilize the **LoadVars** class to dynamically load text–from an external text (TXT) file–into a text field in the About Us module. By using ActionScript to dynamically load external text into your Flash MX 2004 project, you open yourself–and the client–up to new possibilities. Without using dynamically loaded text, when you want to make even a simple change to the text in one of your movies, you (or the client) would have to open the FLA, make the changes to the text, and publish an updated SWF. But if you dynamically load the text into your movie using the **LoadVars** class, when you (or the client) want to make any changes to the text, you can simply open the text file in a simple text editor, make your changes, and save the file. There's no need to open the FLA or to even own a copy of Flash MX 2004! Once you've learned to load the external text into your movie, you will also learn how to make the text scrollable. So as you might suspect, you're going to be introduced to loads of new actions and techniques in this chapter. I'll wait while you go guzzle some coffee and sugar to gear yourself up. ;-)

I. What You Are Building

In this exercise, you will preview exactly what it is that you will be building in this chapter *before* you start building it. That way, as you begin to learn about some of these more advanced topics, the steps will make more sense to you because you will already know how they can be applied to a working Web site.

1. Open your preferred Web browser, and navigate to the following URL:

http://www.lynda.com/flashbtb/laeyeworks/

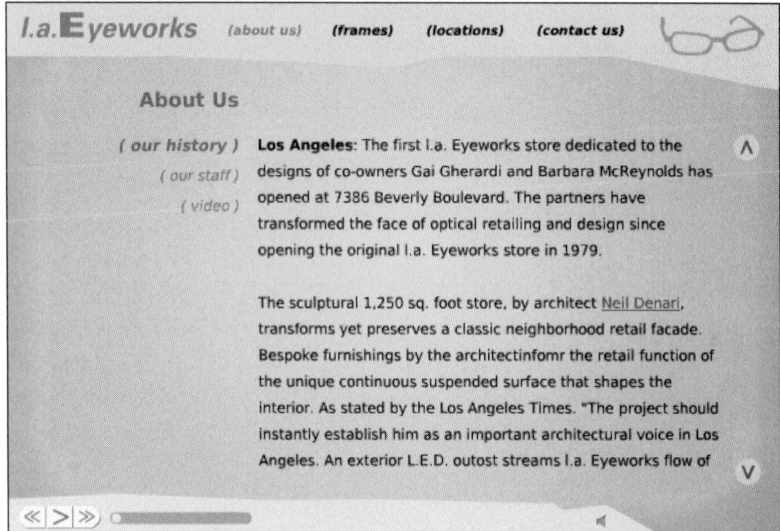

2. Once the L.A. Eyeworks Web site finishes loading, click the **about us** button from the top navigation bar. This will load the **about_us.swf** file into **master.swf**, replacing the splash graphic.

The loaded/scrolling text is what you will be building in this chapter. Notice how, when the about us section loads, the ***our history*** *text is automatically displayed. The our history text is actually from a separate text file (**our_history.txt**) that is loaded into the* ***about_us.swf*** *module using an ActionScript class called* ***LoadVars****. Also notice how some of the text is bolded, there are paragraph breaks, and there is even a hyperlink that changes color when you hover your mouse over it! This text is styled using HTML (to create the bolding, paragraph breaks, and hyperlinks) and further enhanced with Cascading Style Sheets (in this case, to create the hyperlink color change when the mouse hovers over it) that is also loaded in–and applied–from a separate CSS file. You will learn how to style the text using HTML and CSS in the following chapter.*

I'm sure you've started to realize that there's going to be a lot of dynamic text being loaded and styled (using HTML and CSS) in this–and later–chapters. This might make one wonder, "Why go through all the extra effort of dynamically loading in text and styling it with a CSS file? Why not just type the darn text right into Flash MX 2004 and be done with it?!" The main reason why I'm showing you, in this book, how to dynamically load text in from a separate text file, all comes down to one reason: ***Making content easy to update by yourself, or the client****. By loading text that's inside of an external TXT file, it makes it* very *easy to update. The client (or even yourself, for that matter) doesn't even need a copy of Flash MX 2004 to update the Web site. All one would have to do is to open the text file, make any necessary changes, and upload the updated text file back to the server. The next time visitors check out the Web site, the updated content would then be presented to them. How spiffy is that?! So, it may take a little longer to plan and construct, but–as you'll see–it's more than worth the extra time in the long run.*

2. Setting Up the Shared Fonts

In this exercise, you will incorporate the fonts from the shared library. By linking to the shared fonts, you can display text in this About Us module using those shared font outlines. Since the font information will be "borrowed" from the shared library, no font information will need to be embedded in the **about_us.swf**, and the file size of the final SWF file will be greatly reduced.

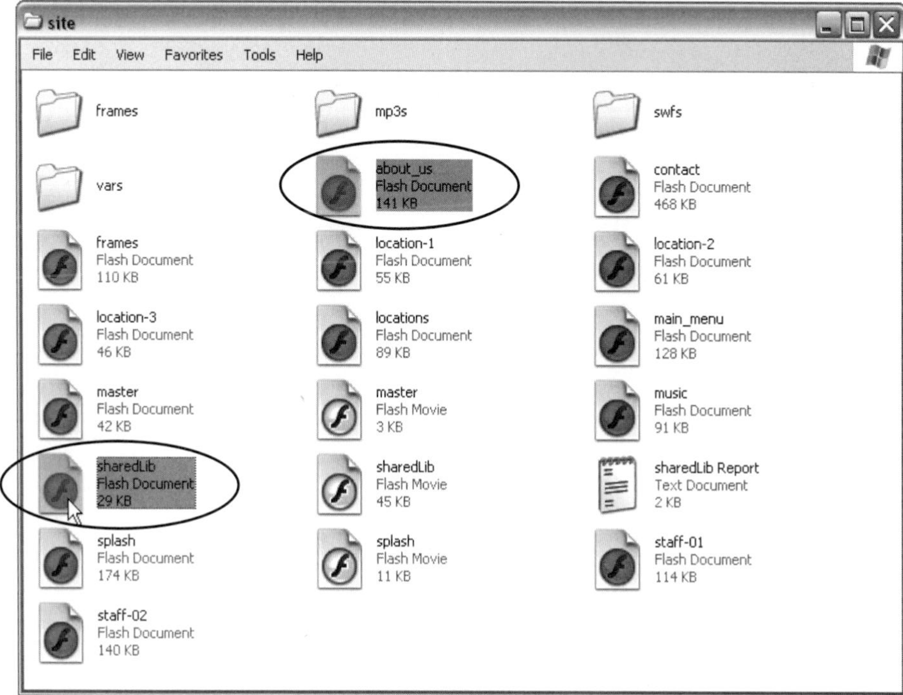

1. Hide Flash MX 2004, and navigate to your **Desktop > la_eyeworks > site** folder. From there, open the two FLAs, **sharedLib** and **about_us**, by double-clicking them.

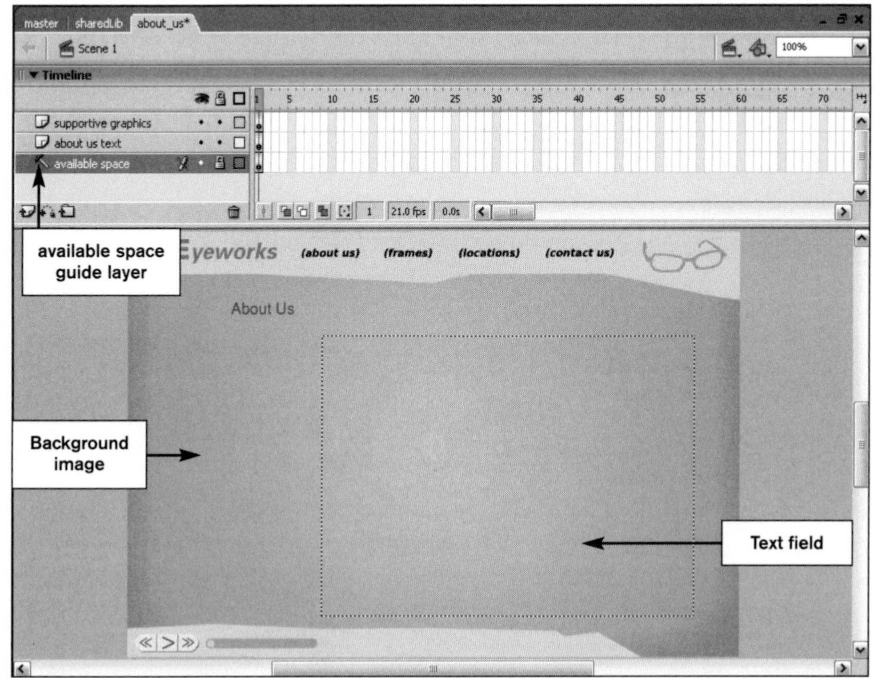

When you open the about_us FLA, you'll notice that there are already a few items in place for you. Probably the first thing you'll notice is the background image. This image was taken from the Web site design mockups that were constructed in Adobe Photoshop, saved as a JPG, and then imported and placed into the ***about_us.fla*** *file. You'll also notice that the layer this image is in,* ***available space****, is set to a guide layer. This means that whatever is in the layer (in this case, the background image) will* not *be in the SWF file when it's published; it's only visible while you're working with the FLA. The background image has been placed inside this FLA so that, as you're building the content for the about us module, you already know* exactly *how much available design space you have to work with. The background image shows you where the main navigation menu is and where the MP3 player is, thereby also revealing to you how much space there is left over to work with. Without this background guide image, you'd be designing blind.*

You'll also notice that this ***about_us.fla*** *already has the dynamic text field drawn out for you (where the content will be loaded), and if you open the Library (****Ctrl+L*** *[Windows] or* ***Cmd+L*** *[Mac]) you'll notice that there are already some prebuilt elements there for you to work with. To conserve time, many of the FLAs and graphical elements that you'll be needing to complete the exercises have already been created for you. You'll also find that the prebuilt items are simple things such as a button, or a movie clip with a text field inside of it–items that you should already know how to build. Adding the ActionScript and fabricating their functionality, however, will be constructed by you as you complete the exercises in this book.*

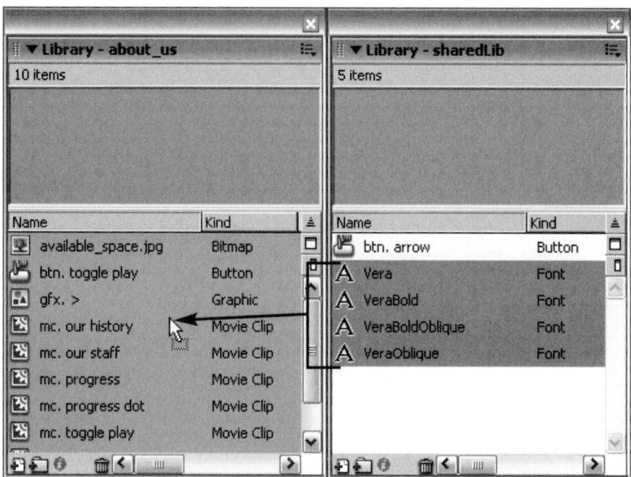

2. Open the libraries of **about_us** and **sharedLib** and undock them so they're positioned side-by-side. Then, in the **sharedLib Library**, select the four, shared **Vera** fonts that you created in the previous chapter by **Shift+clicking** them. After you have the four fonts selected, drag them onto the **about_us Library** window.

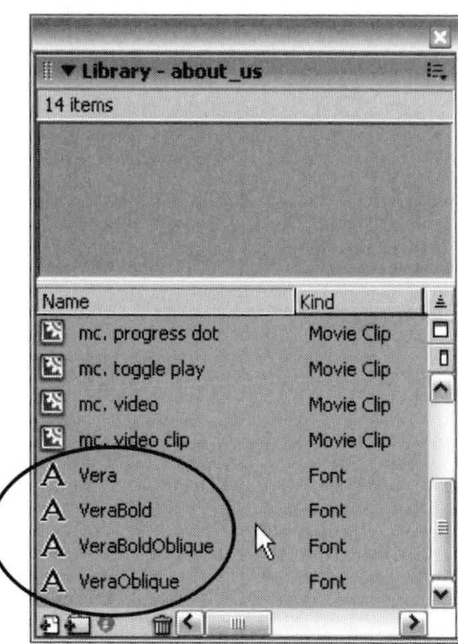

After you've dragged the four fonts into the about_us Library, you should see them appear there. Next, you should verify that the linkage was set correctly when you dragged the shared Vera fonts from the sharedLib Library into the about_us Library.

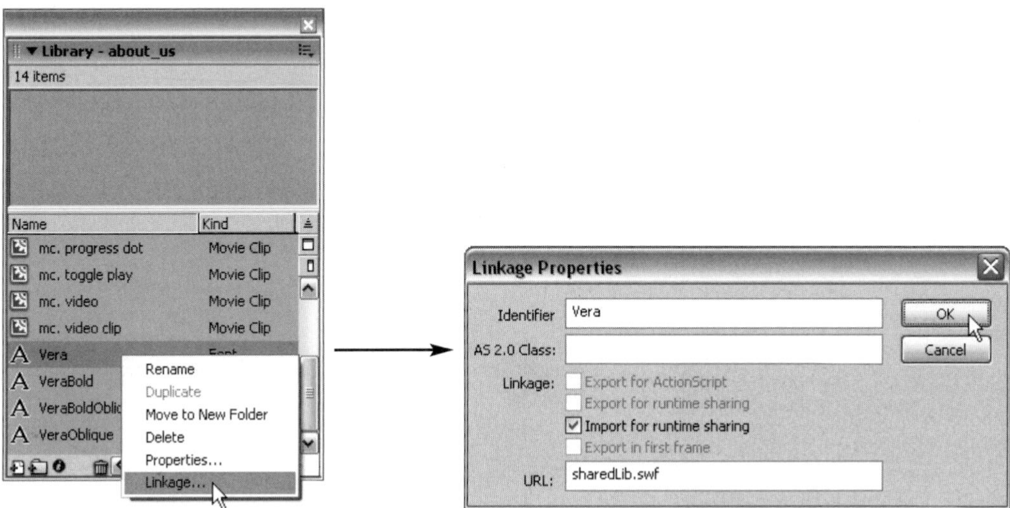

3. In the **about_us Library** window, **right-click** (Windows) or **Ctrl+click** (Mac) the font **Vera**. From the contextual menu that appears, choose **Linkage**. This will open the same **Linkage Properties** dialog box that you saw in Chapter 3, "*Getting Started*," when you assigned the Linkage Properties to the Vera fonts in the **sharedLib Library**. However, in the **about_us** FLA, the **Identifier** field should contain **Vera**, and only the **Import for runtime sharing** check box should be checked. Below that, in the **URL** field, it should also read **sharedLib.swf**.

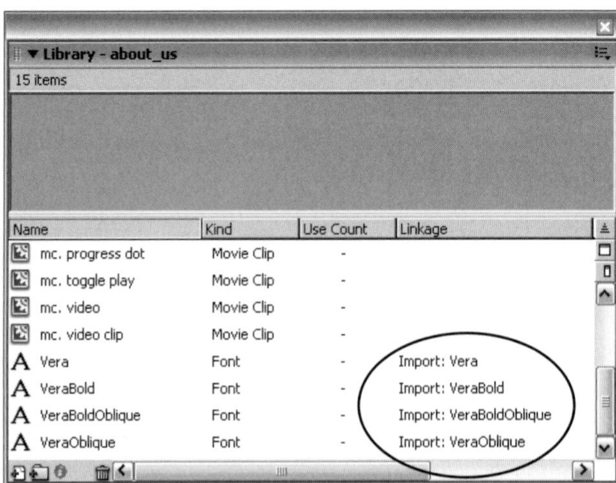

Note: *If you were to expand a library window wide enough, you'd notice that—under the **Linkage** column—it would list which library items are shared (linked) and what the **Identifier** name of that shared item is.*

*These options were set automatically for you by Flash MX 2004 when you dragged the shared fonts from the sharedLib Library into the about_us Library. As its name implies, the **Import for runtime sharing** check box is a sure sign that these shared Vera fonts are being imported (from the **sharedLib.swf** file indicated in the URL field) for runtime sharing, and as such, the fonts outlines will* not *be embedded in the **about_us.swf** file when it is published. Instead, the **about_us.swf** file will simply reference the Vera font outlines in the **sharedLib.swf** file whenever it needs them. Über awesome!*

***Note:** If your Linkage Properties dialog box doesn't look the same as the one in the previous screen shot, you might have incorrectly set the options for the shared Vera fonts when you created them. If your settings differ from the previous screen shot, delete the four shared fonts you just dragged into the about_us Library, open (or bring to the foreground) the sharedLib FLA, and verify that you completed Steps 6 through 14 in the exercise "Creating and Precaching the Shared Library" in Chapter 3,* "Getting Started," *correctly. Once you've verified that those steps were completed correctly, go back through the steps in this exercise again.*

4. Once you've verified that the Linkage Properties are correctly set, click **OK** to close the **Linkage Properties** dialog box.

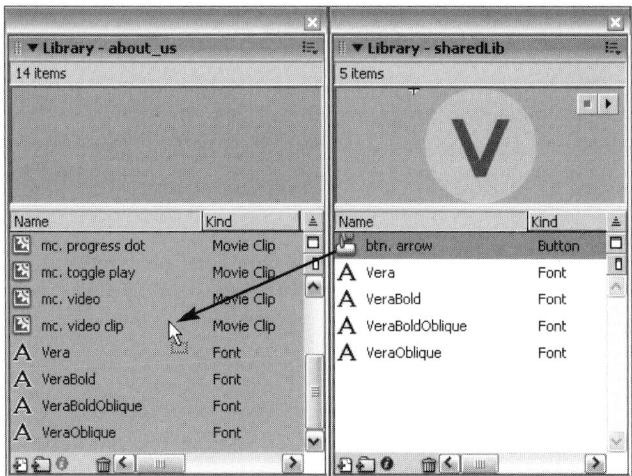

*You'll also be using the shared button **btn. arrow** in the about us module to give the user a button to click to scroll through the loaded text.*

5. In the **sharedLib Library** window, drag the shared button symbol, **btn. arrow**, onto the **about_us Library** window. Just like you did with the shared Vera fonts, this will make a shared link with the **btn. arrow** symbol in the **about_us Library**. You will be utilizing this button in Exercise 3.

6. Close the **sharedLib.fla**–you won't be needing it again in this chapter. Save the changes you've made to the **about_us.fla** file.

*You just created links from the shared library elements in the **sharedLib.fla** file, with the about us module. Now you can use those shared elements (the four Vera fonts and the btn. arrow symbol), knowing that each time you use them, you're not adding* in the least *to the file size of the **about_us.swf** file. Thanks to the precaching of the shared library you constructed in the previous chapter, you can also use those shared elements instantly, in any SWF that's loaded into **master.swf**. Now, if only I could eat that extra slice of pizza without it adding* in the least *to* my *file size! ;-)*

Commenting

When authoring ActionScript, there will be times when you want to prevent a line or a block of code from being performed (when troubleshooting a script, for example). You might also want to insert messages in your ActionScript to make it easier for yourself, or the client, to more easily understand what's going on in a script. Unless you're one of those rare scripting geniuses, it can be difficult to look at 100+ lines of ActionScript code and immediately understand what's doing what. Luckily, there's a way to prevent lines or blocks of actions from being performed on playback and a way to leave messages within the scripting itself. This is done with something called **commenting**, which allows you to leave comments within a script. Commenting also allows you to "comment out," or prevent from being performed on playback, a line or multiple lines of ActionScript code. So you can see what commenting looks like, here is a sample of some comments in a script:

```
// create the new MCL and Listener Objects
var myMCL:MovieClipLoader = new MovieClipLoader();
var myListener:Object = new Object();

// attach the Listener, myListener, to the MCL
myMCL.addListener(myListener);

// load the clips
myMCL.loadClip("splash.swf", 5);
myMCL.loadClip("sharedLib.swf", 1);
```

This code was taken from the **MovieClipLoader** script you wrote in the last chapter, but with comments added so that the main parts of the script are identified with instructions. Adding comments to your scripts is highly encouraged. As you can see, you just need to type two forward slashes (//) before the line you want to comment (or the line of code that you want to comment out). Commenting is recommended for the following reasons:

- Commenting allows you to easily scan through, and identify, the parts of a script. Commenting is especially helpful for longer scripts because the comments can help you see what's going on in a complex script.

- Commenting is not only helpful while you're working on a Flash MX 2004 project, but also after you've completed a project. Take this mini-hypothetical example: you complete a Flash MX 2004-based Web site for a client, and months later, the client returns to you, wanting to update the Web site. If you commented your scripts, you'll be able to more easily jump back in and identify the various pieces of a script after a long hiatus. It's always difficult to understand exactly what a script is doing if you aren't familiar with it or haven't seen it in awhile. Commenting can help ease that transition.
- Clients might sometimes want you (or your company) to design and program the Web site, but then want to do the updating/maintenance of the site themselves. Commenting can help them understand what a script is doing, and even provide them with instructions for updating the actions.
- When troubleshooting buggy scripts, it's sometimes useful to prevent a line or multiple lines of code from performing. By adding a couple forward slashes before a line of code, you can comment that line out and prevent it from being performed on playback.

When attempting to write a large comment, or comment out a large block of ActionScript, it becomes very time consuming (to say the least) to add double forward slashes at the beginning of each line. Luckily, it's extremely easy to comment multiple lines. To mark the beginning of a multi-line comment, simply type /*, and to mark the end of the comment, type */. Here's a sample–using the previous code example–of a multi-line comment:

```
/*
Dynamic slideshow code © 2003 by Shane Rebenschied
Feel free to distrubute and use this code (but do not sell) , but
if any changes or improvements are made, I'd love to hear about them!
comments@blot.com
*/

//// variable initialization

// Specify how many total images there are in the slideshow here:
var totalItems:Number = 5;

// Specify the name of the folder that the images are in here:
var imageFolderName:String = "images/";

// Specify the base name (If your images are all titled
// "slide1.jpg", "slide2.jpg", etc. your "base name" would be "slide") of the images here:
var imageBaseName:String = "image"

var imageNum:Number = 1;
preloader._visible = false;

////
```

So as you can see, it's very easy to comment an entire block of text or ActionScript of any length. Flash MX 2004 will also gray-out commented text or actions to make it clearly evident what in the Actions panel is commented, and what is not. (However, the color that the actions and comments are displayed as can be changed under the **ActionScript** tab in **Preferences**).

In the following steps, you will be adding yet more ActionScript to **master.fla**. To begin to follow good practices and to clearly mark the separate areas and functionality of the script, you will be instructed to add comments to better define those areas.

3. Writing the LoadVars Object

In this exercise, you're going to assign one of those shared Vera fonts to the dynamic text field that's on the **about_us.fla** Stage and start writing the **LoadVars** object that makes this whole thing work. Detailed charts that explain more about the capabilities of the **LoadVars** class are located at the end of this exercise.

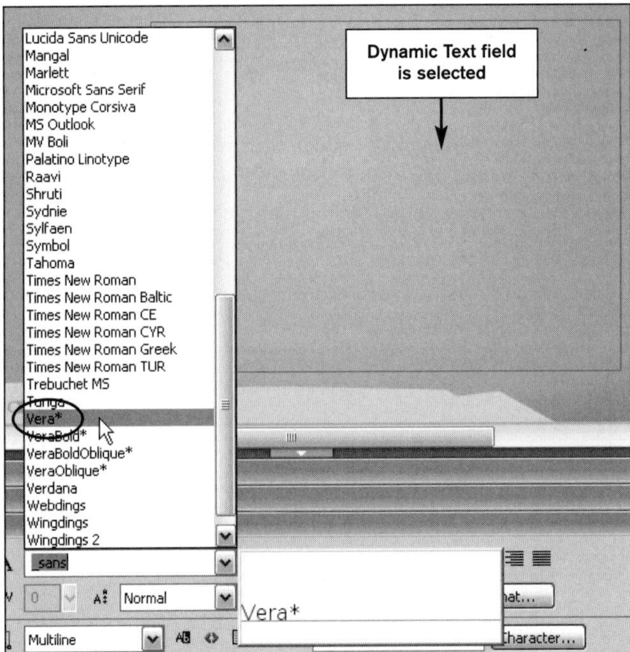

1. Make sure that you're in the **about_us.fla** document, and then single-click the dynamic text field on the **Stage** to select it. Once the text field is selected, click the **Font** pull-down menu in the **Properties inspector**, and from the font list that appears, choose **Vera***. Notice that **Vera** has an asterisk (*) after its name (as do **VeraBold**, **VeraBoldOblique**, and **VeraOblique**, for that matter). This is how Flash MX 2004 lets you know that **Vera** is a font symbol that resides in the library.

Currently, the dynamic text field is set to display Vera at 12 pt black. Although these settings are fine for now, you will actually be using Cascading Style Sheets (CSS) to modify the size and color of the text later in this chapter.

Now that you've imported and linked the shared font Vera to the dynamic text field, it's time to load some text in there. You will be accomplishing this with the **LoadVars** *class. But where should you write this script? Should it be written into the Timeline of* **about_us.fla**, *or somewhere else? The answer mostly depends on how frequently the* **LoadVars** *object will be used. In the context of this book's site construction, the* **LoadVars** *script will actually be used in every module. It will be used in the about us module to load the our history and our staff text, in the frames module to load the descriptive frames text, in the locations module to load information about each store location, and even in the contact module to potentially* send *the form variables to a CGI script that will process the information. So, because of the frequency of which the* **LoadVars** *script will be used, it would make the most sense to write that script in a place where each module can access it, the* **master.fla**.

As with the **MovieClipLoader** *script, care needs to be taken when writing the* **LoadVars** *script so that it doesn't have actions that refer to an individual SWF. Because each module will reference this* **LoadVars** *script, it needs to be written in a way that will work correctly, no matter which module is accessing it. However, as you'll see later in this book, if you need to use a* **LoadVars** *object to perform a task* separate *from the* **LoadVars** *object in* **master.fla**, *you'll need to write a new* **LoadVars** *object wherever it's needed. The overall point is to put commonly used scripts (***LoadVars**, **MovieClipLoader**, *and so forth) in* **master.fla**, *but if you need one of those objects to build separate interactivity, you can easily create a new object for that specific purpose.*

---

2. Save your changes to the **about_us.fla**, and then open (or bring to the foreground) the **master.fla** file. If you accidentally closed the **master.fla** file, you can open it again by hiding Flash MX 2004, and then navigating to your **Desktop > la_eyeworks > site** folder and double-clicking **master.fla**. You can also easily open **master.fla** by choosing it from the **File > Open Recent** menu.

---

3. Single-click the first keyframe in the **master.fla Timeline**, and open the **Actions** panel (**F9**).

```
stop();
//----------------<MCL>-----------------\\
var myMCL:MovieClipLoader = new MovieClipLoader();
var myListener:Object = new Object();

myMCL.addListener(myListener);
//----------------</MCL>-----------------\\

myMCL.loadClip("trigger.swf", 5);
```

4. Add the comment

//------------<MCL>------------

above the **MovieClipLoader** script (and below the **stop** action), and then add the comment

//------------</MCL>------------

below the **myMCL.addListener(myListener);** line of code. (Note the addition of the "/" to the comment.)

These two comments mark the beginning and end of the ***MovieClipLoader*** *(MCL) actions respectively. Later, after more actions have been added to the first keyframe in the* ***master.fla****, the beginning and end of the* ***MovieClipLoader*** *code will be clearly visible, thanks to those comments.*

Note: *Commenting comes in many sizes, shapes, and flavors. All that's really required to make a single-line comment are two forward slashes (//). In the comments you will be making in this exercise and others, you will add two forward slashes at the beginning of the comment, some text (--------<description>---------), and two backslashes at the end. Everything after the two forward slashes is, of course, completely up to you. The comments used throughout this book are written in this manner because it gives a clear, visual separation between scripts, as well as identifying where a particular script starts and ends.*

After you've finished this book, I encourage you to come up with a commenting style that works best for you. My only suggestion would be that whichever style you come up with, use it consistently throughout your projects. That way, when you return to some ActionScript you had written months earlier, everything will still make sense to you. If you're working as part of a team, I'd also encourage you to come up with a commenting style that everyone can understand and work with. Good commenting can make the difference between quickly understanding what's going on in a script and struggling to comprehend what the ActionScript is doing.

```
stop();
//----------------<MCL>-----------------\\
var myMCL:MovieClipLoader = new MovieClipLoader();
var myListener:Object = new Object();

myMCL.addListener(myListener);
//----------------</MCL>-----------------\\

// trigger the MCL to load these assets:
myMCL.loadClip("trigger.swf", 5);
```

5. Add the comment

`// trigger the MCL to load these assets:`

above the **`myMCL.loadClip("trigger.swf", 5);`** line of code. This single-line comment is a note to yourself (or to the client) that the following actions trigger the **`MovieClipLoader`** to load assets. (However, in this case, there's only one action–the **trigger.swf** file that will trigger the downloading [precaching] of the **sharedLib.swf**.)

*Now that you've commented the **MovieClipLoader** ActionScript in the **master.fla** file, you can start adding the **LoadVars** code that will control the loading of variables throughout each module.*

```
// trigger the MCL to load these assets:
myMCL.loadClip("trigger.swf", 5);

//---------------<LoadVars>-----------------\\
```

6. In the first keyframe of the **master.fla** file, with the **Actions** panel open, click at the end of the **`myMCL.loadClip("trigger.swf", 5);`** line, and press **Enter** (Windows) or **Return** (Mac) a couple of times to create some visual space in the **Timeline**. Then, type another comment:

`//------------<LoadVars>------------\\`

*This comment will mark the beginning of the **LoadVars** script.*

```
//----------------<LoadVars>-----------------\\
var myLV:LoadVars = new LoadVars();
```

7. Click at the end of the **LoadVars** comment and press **Enter** (Windows) or **Return** (Mac) to create a line break and type the following:

`var myLV:LoadVars = new LoadVars();`

*Similar to the first line of the **MovieClipLoader** script, the first line of the **LoadVars** script creates a new **LoadVars** object. Another similar item is the use of strict typing. Where the **MovieClipLoader** used the strict typing data type of **MovieClipLoader**, the **LoadVars** object uses a strict typing data type of...yep, you guessed it, **LoadVars**. This becomes evident as you begin to type the script **var myLV:**. As soon as you type the colon (:), Flash MX 2004 will display a code hinting window, allowing you to choose from the different strict typing data types. Because you are creating a new **LoadVars** object, you need to choose* the correct data type, which is ***LoadVars***.

```
//----------------<LoadVars>-----------------\\
var myLV:LoadVars = new LoadVars();

myLV.onLoad = function (success) {
```

8. Click at the end of the **`var myLV:LoadVars = new LoadVars();`** line, and press **Enter** (Windows) or **Return** (Mac) twice to create a couple of line breaks. Then, type the following:

`myLV.onLoad = function (success) {`

*In essence, the **onLoad** event handler function (in this case) gets automatically triggered when, and* only *when, all the variables that have been told to load have actually been* completely *loaded and parsed (ready to be used) by Flash MX 2004. Simply, this line reads, "Tell the **myLV LoadVars** object, that when the loading variables have been completely downloaded...." As you can see, this is only the first part of the script. The **success** parameter in this function is one that gets automatically passed from the **LoadVars** object to let you know if the action was successful or if it failed. The **success** parameter comes back as a Boolean, **true** or **false**. Next, you will learn to tell this **onLoad** event handler what to do when the loading variables have been completely downloaded.*

```
//----------------<LoadVars>-----------------\\
var myLV:LoadVars = new LoadVars();

myLV.onLoad = function (success) {
    if (success){
```

9. Click at the end of the **`myLV.onLoad = function (success) {`** line, press **Enter** (Windows) or **Return** (Mac) once to create a line break, and type the following:

`if (success) {`

*An **if** action is called a **conditional statement**–"conditional" meaning that whether or not the actions placed within the **if** action will be performed are based on whatever condition you specify in the parentheses. In this case, the **if** conditional is the same parameter specified in the **onLoad** function, **success**. As I previously mentioned, **success** is a parameter that is automatically passed from the **LoadVars** object when it is called on to load **data**. Depending on whether or not the data is found, downloaded, and parsed correctly, that **success** parameter can equal either true (if everything was downloaded and parsed correctly) or false (if there was an error). So, when the loading variables have been completely downloaded and parsed, the **LoadVars** object sets the **success** parameter to equal **true**. This parameter is picked up by the **onLoad** event handler, which is then used by the conditional **if** statement to determine the status of the action. Next, you need to tell the **if** statement what to do if the loading variables have been completely downloaded and parsed (**if success = true**, in other words). For further clarification, you'll learn more about the conditional **if** statement–and how it can be used–in Chapter 7, "Building a Slideshow."*

```
//----------------<LoadVars>-----------------\\
var myLV:LoadVars = new LoadVars();

myLV.onLoad = function (success) {
    if (success){
        _level5.loadedInfo.htmlText = myLV.info;
```

10. Click at the end of the **if (success) {** line, press **Enter** (Windows) or **Return** (Mac) once to create a line break, and type the following:

_level5.loadedInfo.htmlText = myLV.info;

*Simply, this line says "Tell the **loadedInfo** text field on the SWF that's loaded into Level 5 to be populated with the value of the variable **info**." At this point, that probably makes absolutely no sense to you. Here's essentially what the different parts of that action mean:*

- ***_level5** If you remember, in the previous chapter after you had constructed the **MovieClipLoader**, you then instructed the **MovieClipLoader** to load the **splash.swf** (the animated splash graphic) file into **_level5**. Level 5 is also the same level where each section module will be loaded. That way, when the viewer clicks on the **frames** button in the nav bar (for example), it will load the **frames.swf** into Level 5, thereby replacing the splash graphic. As each module SWF loads into the same level (Level 5), it will boot out the previous SWF that was loaded there, and will take its place. Voilà! This is a great way to create a section of a Web site that acts as the area where the requested information is displayed. So in the previous script, **_level5** is targeting whichever SWF file happens to be loaded into Level 5 at that time.*

- ***loadedInfo*** *In most of the SWF files that will load into Level 5 (the about us, frames, and locations modules), you will create a dynamic text field where the loaded variable content will be inserted.* ***loadedInfo*** *is the instance name of the text field where the loaded variable content will be placed. Remember, this* ***LoadVars*** *script is potentially going to be used by each module. Because the* ***LoadVars*** *script needs to know the exact name of the text field where the variables (or, more specifically, the value of the variable) will be inserted, you have to pick a name, and then use that same name for the dynamic text field instance names throughout each SWF file.*

- ***htmlText*** *This tells Flash MX 2004 that the value of the variable you're inserting into the* ***loadedInfo*** *text field is going to be HTML formatted text. Later in this chapter, you will insert HTML (and CSS) tags into the text file that will be loaded using this* ***LoadVars*** *script. In place of* ***htmlText****, your other option would be to use, simply,* ***text****. If you use* ***text*** *(and did not set the* ***Render text as HTML*** *option for the text field itself), the loaded text would not be HTML formatted, and you would have limited control over how the text would be displayed.*

- ***myLV*** *This is, of course, the name of the* ***LoadVars*** *object that you created earlier in this exercise. When using* ***LoadVars****, the variables are loaded directly into the* ***LoadVars*** *object that you created. When you want to retrieve those variables to insert into a text field, you first have to tell Flash MX 2004 the name of the* ***LoadVars*** *object that those variables were loaded into. In this case, that* ***LoadVars*** *object is called* ***myLV****.*

- ***info*** *Once you've told Flash MX 2004 the* ***LoadVars*** *object name where the variables were loaded into, you then need to tell it which variable you want the values of. In the next few steps you will add the variable name* ***info*** *to the text file that the* ***LoadVars*** *script will be directed to load.*

- ***;*** *This semicolon (which you'll see at the end of most lines of ActionScript) tells Flash MX 2004 that that is the end of that action. (****Note:*** *Flash MX 2004 will still compile your scripts without them, but it is a good habit to get into since other programming languages you might get into later will not!)*

So, again, this script essentially reads, "On ***Level 5*** *there is a text field called* ***loadedInfo****. I want you to take the value of the variable* ***info*** *(which was loaded into the* ***myLV LoadVars*** *object from the external text file) and insert it as* ***HTML formatted text****." This action will be executed only if the loading variables have been completely downloaded and parsed.*

Keep in mind that because this ***LoadVars*** *script is going to be used by multiple SWF modules, whatever you tell this script to do needs to work properly across all of the modules. Having said that, what should happen when all the variables have been completely downloaded? Well, once the variables have been downloaded, you want to insert them into a text field and display them to the viewer (which is what you just scripted in the last step). However, Flash MX 2004 needs to know the exact instance name of the dynamic text field where these variables are going to be inserted. What this means is that by specifying an exact text field instance name in this script, you will need to make sure that as* *you're constructing the other modules, the text field–where the variables will load into when the* ***LoadVars*** *action is triggered–has to have the same instance name as the name referenced in this script. In other words, the text field–in each module–that the variables are going to load into, needs to have the same name as the one that is referenced in the* ***LoadVars*** *script. Programming ActionScript that can be reused by multiple SWFs takes a little extra preplanning, but as you'll begin to realize as you work through the exercises in this book, it's well worth the effort.*

Later in this exercise, you will write an action that specifies what Flash MX 2004 should do if the loading variables don't *load correctly. For example, maybe the variables file wasn't named correctly, or it wasn't uploaded to the correct location on the server. In that case, the variables file wouldn't load properly. If this were to happen, you would want some kind of error message to appear so the viewer would know something has happened in the loading process. Luckily, the* ***LoadVars*** *object gives you the ability to deal with error management, whereas the older* ***loadVariables*** *action does not. If you used* ***loadVariables****, and there was a problem loading some variables, the viewer would never know it unless you wrote a bunch of extra code.*

In the next step, you need to tell Flash MX 2004 where this ***if*** *statement (which you just wrote the previous action within) ends. If you have experience with writing HTML, you know that when you create a beginning anchor tag,* **<a>***, you also need to specify where that anchor ends by writing* **</a>***. Writing an* ***if*** *statement (and a function, too, for that matter) in Flash MX 2004 is similar, in that you've started the* ***if*** *statement (back in Step 9); now you need to specify where it ends.*

```
//----------------<LoadVars>----------------\\
var myLV:LoadVars = new LoadVars();

myLV.onLoad = function (success) {
     if (success){
          _level5.loadedInfo.htmlText = myLV.info;
     }
```

11. Click at the end of the line **`_level5.loadedInfo.htmlText = myLV.info;`** and press **Enter** (Windows) or **Return** (Mac) once to create a line break. Then, end the conditional **`if`** statement by typing the following:

}

This closed curly brace marks the end of the ***if*** *statement and the action that resides inside of it.*

You should also specify what should happen if there's a problem loading the variables file.

```
//----------------<LoadVars>-----------------\\
var myLV:LoadVars = new LoadVars();

myLV.onLoad = function (success) {
    if (success){
        _level5.loadedInfo.htmlText = myLV.info;
    } else {
```

12. Click after the closed curly brace (}) that you typed in Step 11, and type the following:

else {

*When writing an **if** statement, you specify for certain actions to be executed* if *a statement turns out to be true. In this exercise, you're using **if** to see if some variables have been successfully loaded into the **myLV LoadVars** object. But how do you tell Flash MX 2004 to do something different if that statement is* not *true? The answer is, **else**. In plain English, it would essentially read, "If the variables have been loaded, insert those variables into the **loadedInfo** text field. Otherwise, do something else." That "Otherwise, do something else" part, is **else**. Just like the **if** statement, under **else** you need to specify what should happen if the variables fail to load for one reason or another.*

```
//----------------<LoadVars>-----------------\\
var myLV:LoadVars = new LoadVars();

myLV.onLoad = function (success) {
    if (success){
        _level5.loadedInfo.htmlText = myLV.info;
    } else {
        _level5.loadedInfo.text = "There has been an error loading the requested information.
Please contact the Webmaster and report your error.";
```

13. Click at the end of the **} else {** line, press **Enter** (Windows) or **Return** (Mac) once to create a line break, and type the following:

_level5.loadedInfo.text = "There has been an error loading the requested information. Please contact the Webmaster and report your error.";

What this line (and the line prior to it) essentially says, is "If the loading of the external variable file is not *successful, display an error message in the **loadedInfo** text field on the Stage of the SWF file that is loaded into Level 5." Next, you just need to end **else** and the **onLoad** function actions.*

```
//----------------<LoadVars>-----------------\\
var myLV:LoadVars = new LoadVars();

myLV.onLoad = function (success) {
    if (success){
        _level5.loadedInfo.htmlText = myLV.info;
    } else {
        _level5.loadedInfo.text = "There has been an error loading the requested information.
Please contact the Webmaster and report your error.";
    }
}
```

14. Click at the end of the `_level5.loadedInfo.text = ...;` line, press **Enter** (Windows) or **Return** (Mac) once to create a line break, and then end **else** by typing a closed curly brace (**}**). Close the function action by then pressing **Enter** (Windows) or **Return** (Mac) to create another line break, and then typing another closed curly brace (**}**).

Congratulations! You've just completed your first ***LoadVars*** *script!! Much like the* ***MovieClipLoader*** *script, the* ***LoadVars*** *script doesn't require that much code (only eight lines in this case, including the extra [but not required] error handling), but you get a lot of oomph for that little amount of scripting. This* ***LoadVars*** *script will handle the loading of* all *of the variables that will be used throughout* all *of the modules. Your work is not quite done yet, however. Now that you have written the* ***LoadVars*** *script, you still need to insert the correct variable name* ***(info)*** *into the our history text that you want to load into the about us module, assign an instance name of* ***loadedInfo*** *to the text field that the variables will load into, and you have to write the action that tells that text file to be loaded.*

As a good housekeeping chore, you should write a comment that shows where the ***LoadVars*** *script ends.*

```
//----------------<LoadVars>-----------------\\
var myLV:LoadVars = new LoadVars();

myLV.onLoad = function (success) {
    if (success){
        _level5.loadedInfo.htmlText = myLV.info;
    } else {
        _level5.loadedInfo.text = "There has been an error loading the requested information.
Please contact the Webmaster and report your error.";
    }
}
//----------------</LoadVars>-----------------\\
```

15. Click after the very bottom closed curly brace (which you typed in Step 14), and press **Enter** (Windows) or **Return** (Mac) once to create a line break. Then, select and copy the comment

```
//------------<LoadVars>--------------\\
```

and paste it underneath the bottom curly brace. Once you've pasted the comment, add a forward slash "/" before the word "LoadVars." This symbolizes the end of the **LoadVars** script. When finished, your script should look like the one in the screen shot shown above.

16. Save your changes to the **master.fla** file by choosing **File > Save**.

What Is LoadVars?

Simply put, **LoadVars** is to variables what the **MovieClipLoader** is to SWF and JPG files. The **MovieClipLoader**–which you constructed in the last chapter–allows you to load external SWF or JPG files. Built into the **MovieClipLoader** class are listeners that allow you to monitor the downloading progress of an asset, detect if an error has occurred (like attempting to load a file that doesn't exist), and so forth. Similarly, the **LoadVars** class also allows you to load external assets, as well as provides you with the ability to monitor the downloading progress and detect if any errors occur. The major difference between the **MovieClipLoader** and **LoadVars** class is that **MovieClipLoader** loads external SWF and JPG files, whereas **LoadVars** loads *variables* from external files. Another difference is that **LoadVars** also allows you to *send* variables from your Flash MX 2004 movie to a URL of your choosing. You'll see this feature used in a later chapters for sending the information (variables) the viewer types in the contact form to a CGI that processes and emails the results. For your reference, here is a list of methods, properties, and event handlers for the **LoadVars** class.

Methods, Properties, and Event Handlers for the LoadVars Class

METHODS

Method	Description
addRequestHeader()	Allows you to add or change the HTTP header when you send your variables using POST. An HTTP header is basically a little bit of information that precedes the variable/value pairs that lets the receiving server know how to deal with the information it is receiving.
getBytesLoaded()	Reports the number of bytes that have been downloaded from a file that was triggered using the **load()** method. (See below for more on **load()**.)
getBytesTotal()	Reports the total amount of bytes for a file triggered using the **load()** method.
load()	Downloads a file from a URL of your choosing.
send()	Essentially, the opposite of **load()**, **send()** sends the variables (using POST method) to a URL of your choosing.
sendAndLoad()	Performs a **send()** (sends variables to a URL, such as a CGI), and then downloads the server's response.
toString()	Takes all the variables in a **LoadVars** instance and returns them in a url-encoded format, like so: **myVar1=my%20value1&myVar2=my%20value2**

continues on next page

Methods, Properties, and Event Handlers for the LoadVars Class *continued*

PROPERTIES

Property	Description
contentType	Allows you to modify the MIME type of the data being sent to the server. The default is **application/x-www-form-urlencoded**. The only time you should need to adjust the **contentType** is if the middleware (ASP, PHP, CGI, and so on) is expecting to receive the variables from a different MIME type.
loaded	Querying this property will allow you to determine whether or not variables you're loading using **load()** or **sendAndLoad()** have been fully loaded. This is a Boolean value (meaning, it's either true or false)—true if the variables have been fully loaded, false if they haven't or if there was an error in the loading process.

EVENT HANDLERS

Event Handler	Description
onData	This handler (and any actions you place within it) is triggered when the data you're downloading has been *completely* downloaded from the server *or* if there's an error in the downloading process. What's the difference between the **onData** event handler and the **loaded** property? The **loaded** property will just return a true or false depending on whether the variables have been downloaded or not. The **onData** event handler, on the other hand, is essentially a function you can place actions within (just like a regular function). When the unparsed data has been completely downloaded from the server, the **onData** event handler (and the actions within it) are triggered.
onLoad	Similar to **onData** except that the **onLoad** event handler is triggered *after* **onData** is triggered. Essentially, **onData** is triggered when the unparsed (raw) data has been completely downloaded, and **onLoad** is triggered when the data has been completely downloaded *and* parsed (put in a format that Flash MX 2004 [and you] can use). If you want an action(s) to be performed after all your variables have been downloaded and are ready to use (place in a dynamic text field, for example), use the **onLoad** event handler instead of the **onData** event handler.

As you can see, the **LoadVars** class is a fairly robust method for loading, sending, and handling variables.

4. Loading the "Our History" Text

In this exercise, you will utilize the **LoadVars** script–which you wrote earlier in this chapter–to load text from an external text file into a text field to form the **Our History** subsection in the About Us module. You will learn how to add the proper variable to the text file as well as how to write the action that instructs the **LoadVars** object to load the variables from a particular text file.

1. Hide or minimize Flash MX 2004, and then navigate to your **Desktop > la_eyeworks > site > vars**.

*Inside the **site** folder is a folder titled **vars**. The **vars** folder (short for variables) is where most of the variables files–used throughout the L.A. Eyeworks Web site–will be stored. Because the text files with the variables are stored in a* different *folder within the **site** folder, you need to make sure–when writing the ActionScript–that you tell Flash MX 2004* exactly *which folder the variables are in and the name of the text file that you want to load.*

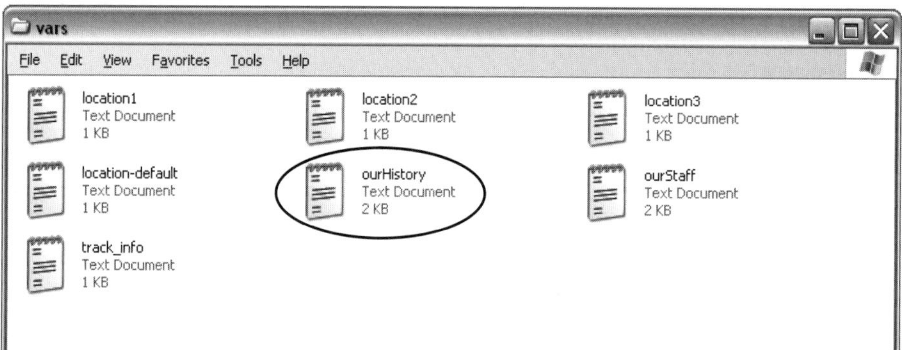

2. Within the **vars** folder, open the file **ourHistory.txt** (some operating systems, such as Windows XP, hide the file name extension) in a simple text editor. (Use Notepad if you're running Windows, or TextEdit or BBEdit if you're running Macintosh.)

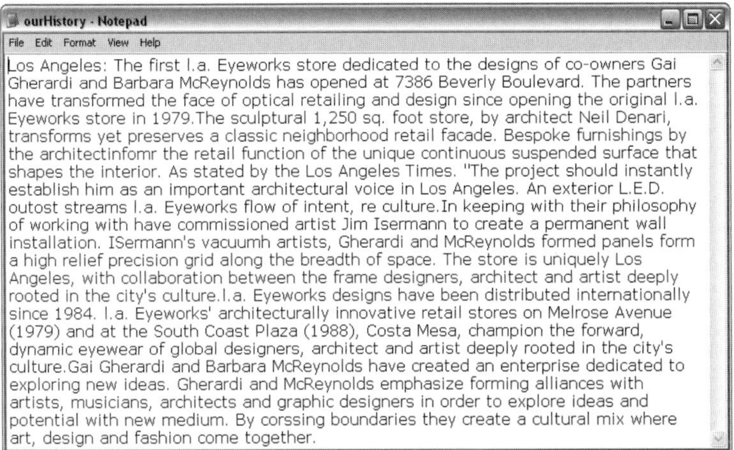

Los Angeles: The first l.a. Eyeworks store dedicated to the designs of co-owners Gai Gherardi and Barbara McReynolds has opened at 7386 Beverly Boulevard. The partners have transformed the face of optical retailing and design since opening the original l.a. Eyeworks store in 1979.The sculptural 1,250 sq. foot store, by architect Neil Denari, transforms yet preserves a classic neighborhood retail facade. Bespoke furnishings by the architectinfomr the retail function of the unique continuous suspended surface that shapes the interior. As stated by the Los Angeles Times. "The project should instantly establish him as an important architectural voice in Los Angeles. An exterior L.E.D. outost streams l.a. Eyeworks flow of intent, re culture.In keeping with their philosophy of working with have commissioned artist Jim Isermann to create a permanent wall installation. ISermann's vacuumh artists, Gherardi and McReynolds formed panels form a high relief precision grid along the breadth of space. The store is uniquely Los Angeles, with collaboration between the frame designers, architect and artist deeply rooted in the city's culture.l.a. Eyeworks designs have been distributed internationally since 1984. l.a. Eyeworks' architecturally innovative retail stores on Melrose Avenue (1979) and at the South Coast Plaza (1988), Costa Mesa, champion the forward, dynamic eyewear of global designers, architect and artist deeply rooted in the city's culture.Gai Gherardi and Barbara McReynolds have created an enterprise dedicated to exploring new ideas. Gherardi and McReynolds emphasize forming alliances with artists, musicians, architects and graphic designers in order to explore ideas and potential with new medium. By corssing boundaries they create a cultural mix where art, design and fashion come together.

As you can see, this file is essentially a large amount of unformatted text. The goal, however, is to take all this text and use ActionScript to insert it into the dynamic text field on the Stage in the about us module. You've already written the **`LoadVars`** *script that, when triggered, will load the value of the variable* **`info`** *from this text file and place it inside a text field with the instance name of* **`loadedInfo`**. *You might also notice that there is no sign of an* **`info`** *variable in this text file. In the next step, that's what you're going to add.*

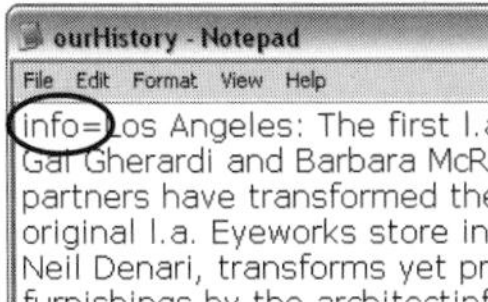

3. At the beginning of the text file, click and type the following:

```
info=
```

Make sure there are no spaces before or after the equals sign. When specifying variable/value pairs (also known as key/value pairs) in a text file that will be loaded into Flash MX 2004 using **`LoadVars.load`** *or* **`MovieClip.loadVariables`**, *the variable (in this case, it's* **`info`**) *is typed, and then immediately followed by an equals sign. Everything after the equals sign is the value of the variable. It's the value of the* **`info`** *variable that will actually be loaded into the* **`loadedInfo`** *text field on the Stage of the about us module. So that you can see a comparison, when you are creating a variable/value pair directly inside of the Actions panel in Flash MX 2004, you would type it as such:*

```
var info:String = "Los Angeles: The first…";
```

As you can see, there are similarities between how variable/value pairs are defined in a text file and how they are defined directly inside of Flash MX 2004.

---

4. Save the **ourHistory.txt** file, and bring Flash MX 2004 into the foreground again.

5. Bring the **about_us.fla** file into the foreground. You should still have the **about_us.fla** file open, but if you accidentally closed it, you can open it up again by navigating to your **Desktop > la_eyeworks > site** folder and double-clicking **about_us.fla**.

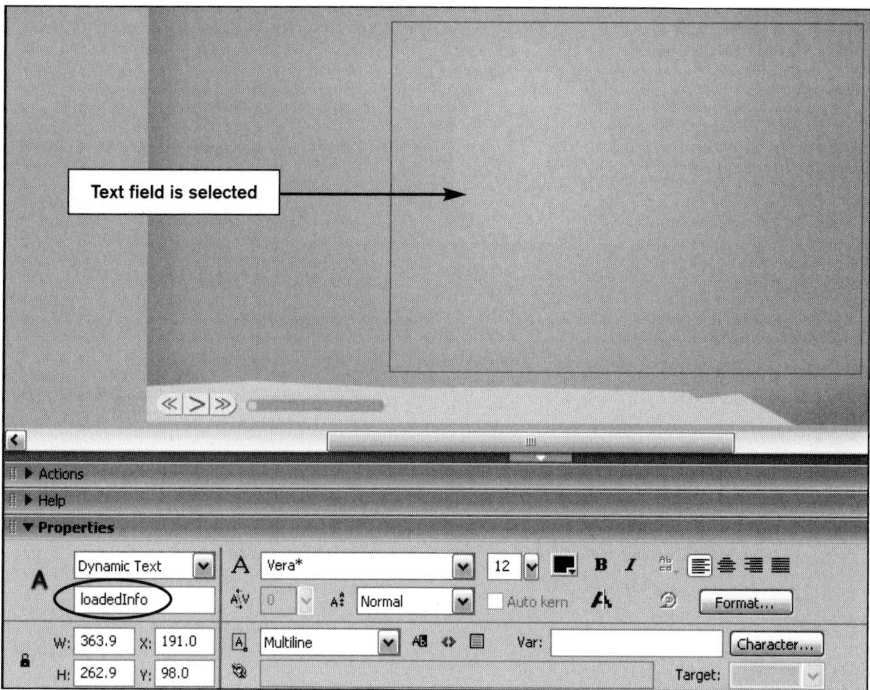

6. Single-click the large dynamic text field on the **about_us.fla Stage** to select it, open the **Properties inspector** (**Ctrl+F3** [Windows] or **Cmd+F3** [Mac]) and type **loadedInfo** in the **Instance Name** field. Make sure that you capitalize the "I" in "Info." Flash MX 2004 is case sensitive, so if you accidentally type a lowercase "i," the loaded variables would *not* load into this text field.

*Now that you have the **LoadVars** script all dressed up with no place to go, the variable specified in the text file, and the instance name specified for the text field the variable's value will load, you need to tell the about us module which text file to load the variables from.*

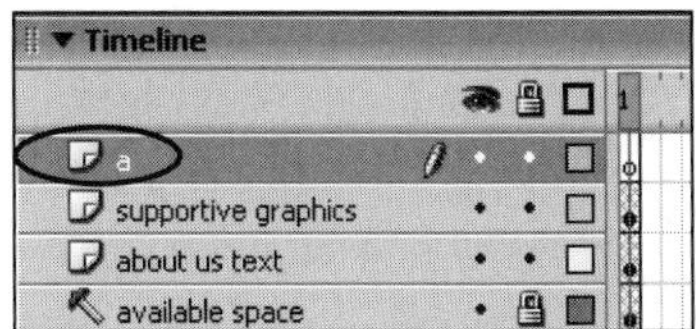

7. In the **about_us.fla**, create a new layer and make sure that layer resides above the other layers. Rename this new layer **a** (for actions).

---

8. Click the first keyframe in the new **a** layer, and open the **Actions** panel (**F9**).

```
_level0.myLV.load("vars/ourHistory.txt");
```

9. In the Actions panel, type the following:

`_level0.myLV.load("vars/ourHistory.txt");`

*In simple terms, this action says "Tell the **myLV LoadVars** object on Level 0 (the **master.swf** file) to load the variables from the text file **ourHistory.txt**, which is located in a folder called **vars**. Remember, the **LoadVars** script, which controls the loading of variables throughout the L.A. Eyeworks site, is located on the **master.fla** Timeline. The **master.fla** file is the container that all the other SWF modules (including **about_us.swf**) will load into. As such, whenever you're writing a script in one of the modules that refers to something in the **master.swf** file (in this case, the **LoadVars** script), you have to tell Flash MX 2004 to look in **_level0**, which refers to the container SWF file, **master.swf**.*

*Eventually, the **_level0.myLV.load("vars/ourHistory.txt");** line will be integrated into other actions you will be creating in the about us module. For now, however, you've added it to check the **LoadVars** script and to make sure that everything works the way it should. This goes back to the idea of building the functionality in pieces. First, build it simply to make sure it works; then build all the bells and whistles on top of that.*

*Because the about us module refers to the master **LoadVars** script located within the **master.fla** Timeline, to test the about us module and make sure that everything works, the **about_us.swf** file must be loaded into the **master.swf** file (so that it can refer to and use the **LoadVars** script). In the following steps, you're going to add the action to make this happen.*

---

10. Save your changes to the **about_us.fla** file by choosing **File > Save**. Then, publish a SWF from the **about_us.fla** file by choosing **File > Publish**. The publish settings for the **about_us.fla** file have already been set up so that when this movie is published, it publishes only a SWF file (instead of the default SWF and HTML combination).

*If you want to see the publish settings that have been specified for this–and the other–modules, choose **File > Publish Settings**.*

---

11. Bring the **master.fla** file to the foreground, or if you accidentally closed the **master.fla** file, hide or minimize Flash MX 2004, navigate to your **Desktop > la_eyeworks > site**, and double-click the **master.fla** file to open it. In the **master.fla** file, single-click **Keyframe 10** in the **a** layer and open the **Actions** panel (**F9**).

```
stop();
// myMCL.loadClip("splash.swf", 5);
```

12. Comment out the **`myMCL.loadClip("splash.swf", 5);`** line by adding two forward slashes at the beginning of the action. As covered in the "Commenting" section earlier in this chapter, adding two forward slashes before a line of code will "comment out" that line and will prevent it from being included when the code is compiled by Flash MX 2004.

*Instead of loading the **splash.swf** file (which is the action you just commented out), you want to load the **about_us.swf** file into the **master.swf** file to make sure that the **LoadVars** script is set up correctly and that everything works.*

```
stop();
// myMCL.loadClip("splash.swf", 5);
myMCL.loadClip("about_us.swf", 5);
```

13. Click at the end of the commented **`// myMCL.loadClip("splash.swf", 5);`** line and press **Enter** (Windows) or **Return** (Mac) once to create a line break. Then, write the action that will load the **about_us.swf** file into the **master.swf** file into **Level 5** (the same level that the splash graphic, and all the other module SWF files, loads into) by typing the following:

`myMCL.loadClip("about_us.swf", 5);`

*Just like the other **myMCL.loadClip** actions that you wrote in the previous chapter to load the splash and trigger SWF files, this action loads the **about_us.swf** file into Level 5.*

---

14. Save the **master.fla** file by choosing **File > Save**, and then test the movie by choosing **Control > Test Movie**.

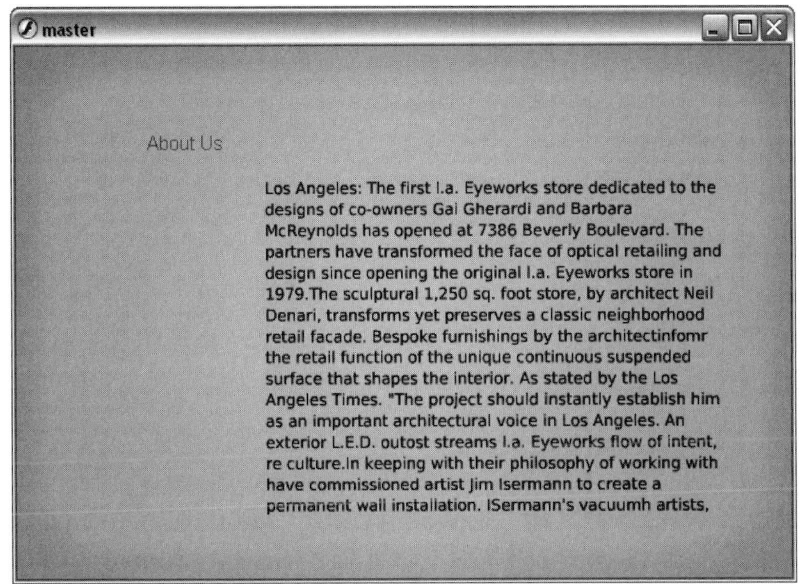

*After you choose **Control > Test Movie**, you should see the about us SWF module loaded, and within it, a large block of text. That block of text is the same text that is in the **ourHistory.txt** file, but it has now been loaded into the **about_us.swf** file, thanks to your new **LoadVars** script! How very cool is that?! Lastly, you need to make sure that the **LoadVars** error handling, which you scripted in the previous exercise, works correctly. To test the error handling, you need to locally simulate an error accessing or loading the variable file by changing the name of the **ourHistory.txt** file that the script is attempting to load.*

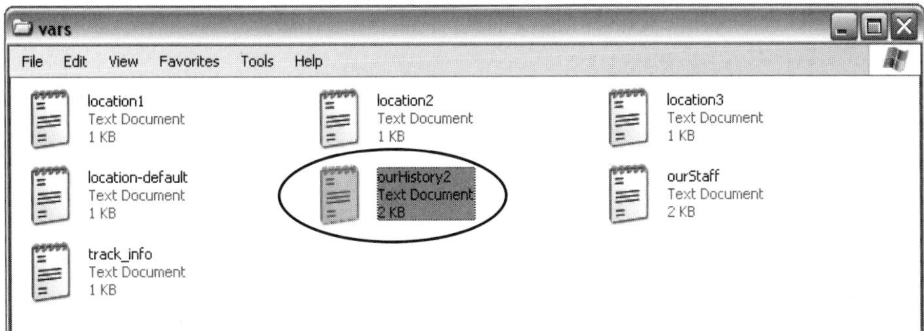

15. Hide or minimize Flash MX 2004, and then access your **Desktop > la_eyeworks > site > vars** folder. Within the **vars** folder, change the name of the **ourHistory.txt** file to something else, like **ourHistory2.txt**.

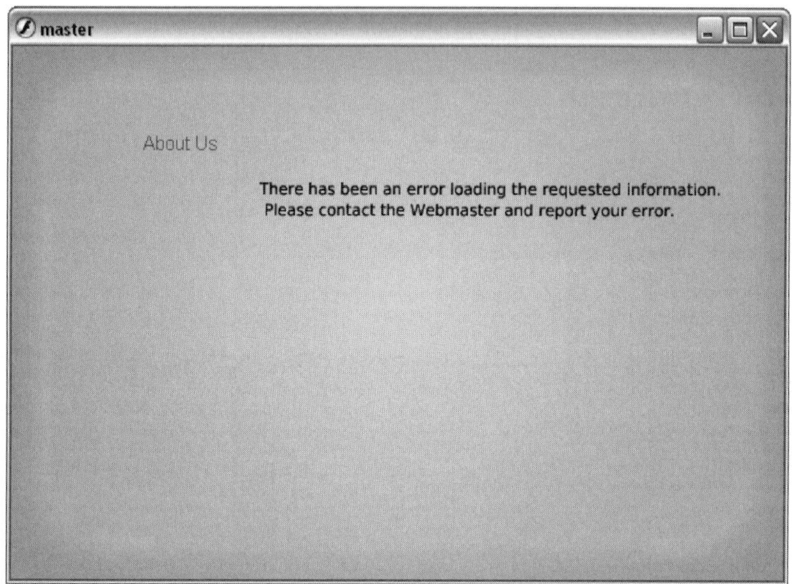

16. After you have changed the name of the **ourHistory.txt** file, return to Flash MX 2004. Make sure that the **master.fla** file is in the foreground, and that you've saved all your changes; then test the movie by choosing **Control > Test Movie**. When the **master.swf** file displays, in place of the our history text, you should now see your error message, "There has been an error loading the requested information. Please contact the Webmaster and report your error." Fantastic!

As you can see, the error handling works like a champ. This is the message the viewer would see if there was a problem accessing or loading the variables file that you're instructing Flash MX 2004 to load. Before you call this exercise done and smack it on the butt, you need to change the ***ourHistory2.txt*** *file back to its previous, correct, name.*

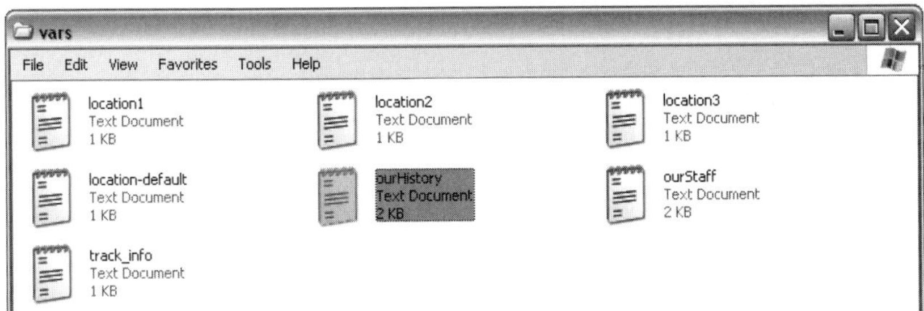

17. Hide or minimize Flash MX 2004, navigate to your **Desktop > la_eyeworks > site > vars** folder, and change the file name **ourHistory2.txt** back to its original name of **ourHistory.txt**.

Undoubtedly, there was a lot of new material you learned in this single exercise. To better drive home the idea behind the ***LoadVars*** *object and how it is integrated with the various SWF files, here's a diagram that visually explains how everything is set up:*

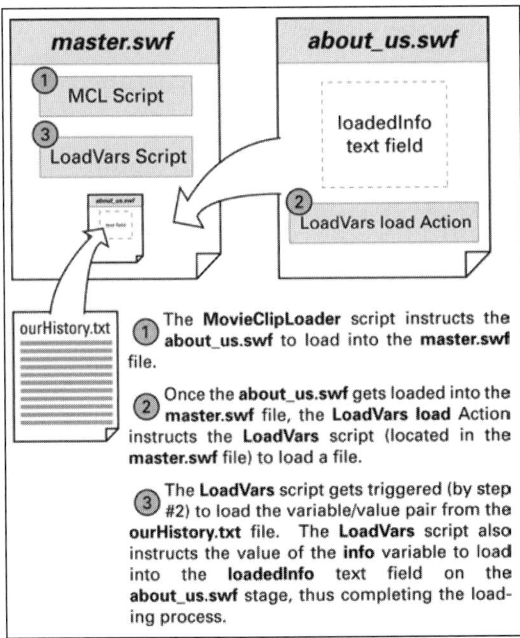

1 The **MovieClipLoader** script instructs the **about_us.swf** to load into the **master.swf** file.

2 Once the **about_us.swf** gets loaded into the **master.swf** file, the **LoadVars load** Action instructs the **LoadVars** script (located in the **master.swf** file) to load a file.

3 The **LoadVars** script gets triggered (by step #2) to load the variable/value pair from the **ourHistory.txt** file. The **LoadVars** script also instructs the value of the **info** variable to load into the **loadedInfo** text field on the **about_us.swf** stage, thus completing the loading process.

In the next exercise, you're going to learn how to add some actions to a couple of buttons that allow the visitor to scroll up or down through the loaded text. Now go take a break before continuing. You deserve it after completing these exercises. ;-)

5. Making the Text Scroll

In this exercise, you are going to add a couple buttons to the about us module that allow the viewer to scroll through the loaded text. As you will see, making text in a text field scroll is actually quite simple.

1. Bring the **about_us** module FLA to the foreground. If you accidentally closed it, you can open it again by navigating to your **Desktop > la_eyeworks > site** folder and double-clicking the **about_us.fla** file to open it.

2. Lock the top-most layer, **a**, and create a new layer. Rename this new layer **scroll buttons** and position it so that it is underneath the **a** layer.

3. With the **scroll buttons** layer selected, open the **about us** module **Library** (**Ctrl+L** [Windows] or **Cmd+L** [Mac]).

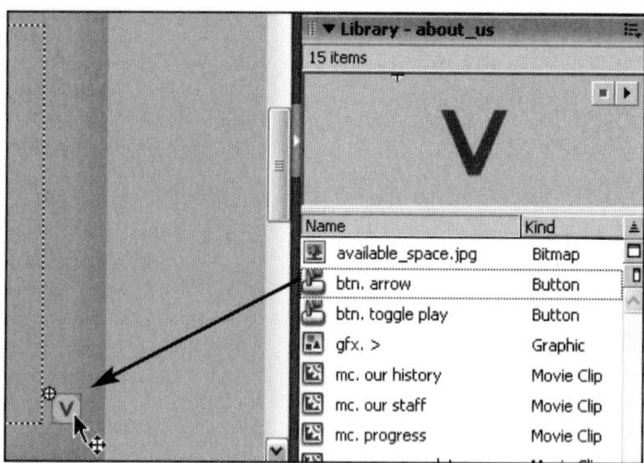

4. Drag the shared **btn. arrow** button symbol from the **about us Library** onto the **Stage**, and position it towards the bottom-right corner of the text field. If you remember, this **btn. arrow** button symbol is a symbol you brought over from the **sharedLib** shared library file. Because of this, adding this button to your movie doesn't add to the file size of the published SWF. Yay for shared libraries!

So now you have a button to allow viewers to scroll down through the text, but what about allowing them to scroll up? Easy enough. All you need to do is copy the downward-facing arrow button and flip it so it's pointing up. Simple!

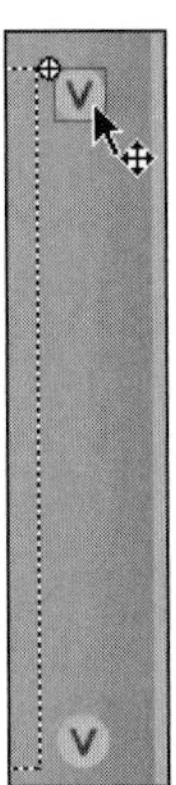

5. While holding down the **Alt** and **Shift** keys (Windows) or the **Option** and **Shift** keys (Mac), drag the **btn. arrow** symbol up so that it's aligned with the top of the text field. The **Alt/Option** key copies the symbol as you drag it, and the **Shift** key constrains the dragging so that you're assured that you're dragging it straight up.

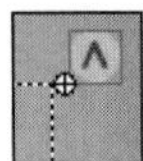

6. With the copied button symbol still selected, choose **Modify > Transform > Flip Vertical.** This will...well...flip the button vertically so that it is facing upward. Doing this will also offset the button alignment with the text field a little, so you'll need to reposition it.

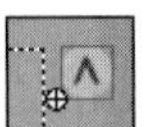

7. Reposition the up-facing button symbol so that it's aligned with the top of the text field. The easiest way to do that is by using the arrow keys on the keyboard. This will allow you to fine-tune the position of whatever you have selected.

I'm sure the majority of you, by the time you've read this book, have added at least a few simple actions to button instances. When you've added actions to buttons, you've probably selected the button symbol instance on the Stage, opened the Actions panel, and began to write actions to add interactivity to the button. Well, starting with this book, you're going to learn to do things a little...differently. And for many of you, this will probably be a major leap in how you think about the relationship between actions and their accompanying symbols. Are you ready? (I can almost hear you holding your breath. ;-))

You're not going to add actions directly to these arrow button symbol instances. In other words, you're not going to select the button symbol on the Stage, open the Actions panel, and add actions to the button symbol in that manner (as you're probably used to doing). Instead, you're going to add your button actions to the first keyframe in the ***about_us.fla****, where all the rest of your actions will also be placed that make up the interactivity for everything (well, nearly everything) that goes on in the about us module. You're probably saying to yourself, "What?! How can I make my buttons interactive by adding actions to a keyframe?" Furthermore, why would I want to do something as daft as that?"*

*You'll learn by doing in this exercise, but essentially, it goes like this: Yes, you can script mouse events (****onRollOver****,* ***onRelease****, and so forth) to button and movie clip symbols from a keyframe action. The mouse event is actually attached to a function, and then the actions within that function are executed when that particular mouse event occurs (when the viewer clicks on the button, for example). The reason why you'd want to do something like this goes back to one of the main points in this book, which is centralization–keeping as much content and ActionScript code as possible centralized in one location. When you attach ActionScript directly to button symbol instances, you're essentially scattering your actions into the wind. Whenever you've needed to modify an action that is attached to a button symbol–that is, nested within a couple of other symbols–you'd have to manually open each symbol nesting until you reach the symbol the actions are attached to. Then you could modify the actions and backtrace your steps to where you were previously.*

After I show you this method of adding actions to symbols, you'll look back at the method of adding actions directly to symbol instances and say to yourself, "Geez. What a pain that was." By keeping all the ActionScript code in one location, it also makes it much easier to see how all the pieces interact. It's difficult to see the interconnectivity of the scripts when you're jumping from symbol to symbol, looking at each script snippet, isolated from all the others. So hop on yer hawg dawg, and ready yourself for the "great awakening". ;-)

The first step in this process is to add instance names to the symbols you want to attach scripts to.

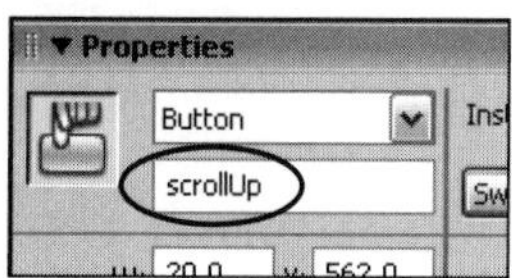

8. With the upward-facing arrow on the **Stage** still selected, open the **Properties inspector**. In the **Instance Name** field, type **scrollUp**. Now that that button symbol has a unique instance name, you can add interactivity to it using ActionScript.

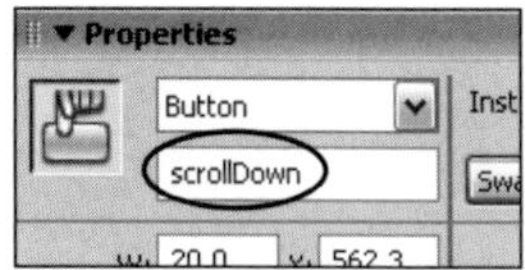

9. Single-click the downward-facing arrow on the **Stage** to select it, then in the **Properties inspector**, name it **scrollDown** in the **Instance Name** field.

Now that both button symbols have instance names, you can attach actions to them from the first keyframe.

---

10. Select the first (and only) keyframe in the **a** layer, and open the **Actions** panel (**F9**).

```
_level0.myLV.load("vars/ourHistory.txt");

//-------------<scroll buttons>--------------\\

//-------------</scroll buttons>--------------\\
```

11. Click at the end of the `_level0.myLV.load("vars/ourHistory.txt");` line, press **Enter** (Windows) or **Return** (Mac) two times to create a couple of line breaks, and add the following comment:

```
//-------------<scroll buttons>-------------\\
```

Then press **Enter** (Windows) or **Return** (Mac) two more times to create some space to add some script, and add the closing comment:

```
//-------------</scroll buttons>-------------\\
```

Now you have your commenting set up, but the actions still need to be placed within them.

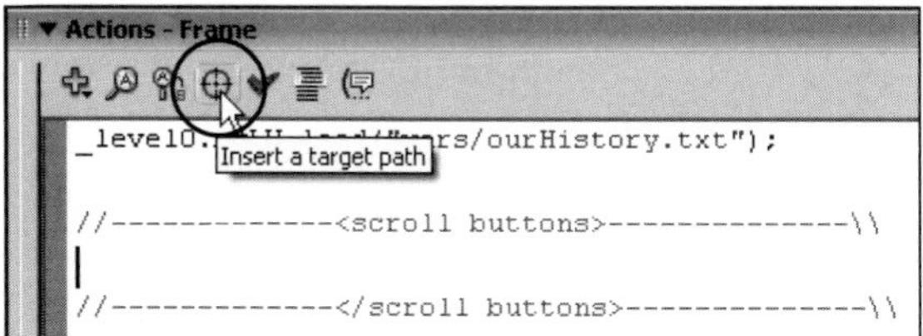

12. Click between the two comment lines, and then click the **Insert Target Path** button (the small target) located at the top of the **Actions** panel.

This button will open the ***Insert Target Path*** *dialog box, which allows you to easily find a "target" to assign ActionScript to. Essentially, any item (movie clip/button symbol, dynamic/input text field, and so forth) that you've given an instance name to will appear in the Insert Target Path dialog box.*

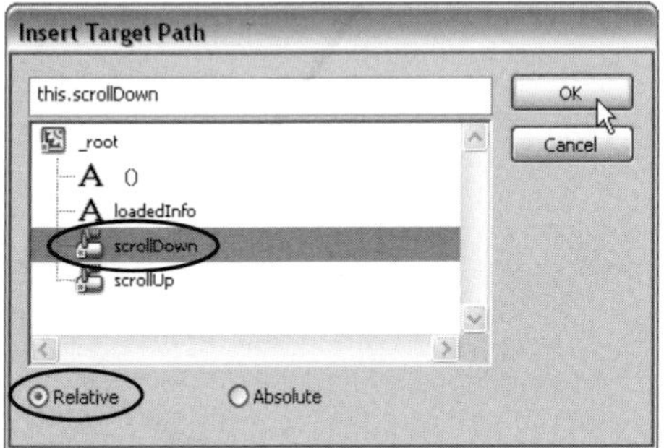

13. Make sure the **Relative** radio button is selected (which means, *relative* to where you're writing this script), and click the button target **scrollDown**. When you select **scrollDown**, you'll notice that the path to that particular symbol instance is inserted in the path field at the top of the dialog box. The "this" that precedes the button instance name **scrollDown** refers to "this" **Timeline** that the action is being triggered from. In this case, "this" refers to the main **Timeline** of the **about_us.fla** file. Once you've selected **scrollDown**, click **OK**.

Note: *If you don't see the* ***scrollDown*** *and* ***scrollUp*** *button symbols listed in the* ***Insert Target Path*** *dialog box, you probably forgot to assign instance names to those button symbols. Return to Steps 8 and 9 and make sure you followed them correctly.*

```
//-------------<scroll buttons>--------------\\
this.scrollDown
//-------------</scroll buttons>-------------\\
```

After you clicked OK in the Insert Target Path dialog box, you'll be returned to the Actions panel, where you should see ***`this.scrollDown`*** *inserted where you had originally clicked, between the comments.*

```
//-------------<scroll buttons>--------------\\
this.scrollDown.onRelease = function () {
//-------------</scroll buttons>-------------\\
```

14. After **`this.scrollDown`**, type the following:

`.onRelease = function () {`

Don't forget to add the dot (.) between ***`scrollDown`*** *and* ***`onRelease`****. Simply, this action reads, "When the* ***`scrollDown`*** *button is clicked...." As yet, this is only the first part of the script. When adding actions to button mouse events (as you're doing here), you must assign it to a function, hence the* ***`= function () {`*** *portion of the action. Then, whatever you want to happen when the viewer clicks on the* ***`scrollDown`*** *button, you add within the function, as you're about to do next. At this point, you might also be wondering what the various mouse events are (****`onRelease`****,* ***`onRollOver`****, and so forth). You can see the mouse events, and read a description of each one, by opening the Help panel (****F1****). In the* ***Help*** *panel sidebar, navigate to* ***ActionScript Dictionary > O*** *and then click* ***on()****.*

```
//-------------<scroll buttons>--------------\\
this.scrollDown.onRelease = function () {
    loadedInfo.scroll += 1;
//-------------</scroll buttons>--------------\\
```

15. Click at the end of the **`this.scrollDown.onRelease = function () {`** line, press **Enter** (Windows) or **Return** (Mac) once to create a line break, and then type the following:

`loadedInfo.scroll += 1;`

A simple explanation of what this line says would be, "Set the ***`scroll`*** *property of the* ***`loadedInfo`*** *text field to be whatever it currently is, but add one onto it."*

`loadedInfo`*, if you remember, was the instance name you gave to the text field on the Stage. It's the one where the variables load into.*

An inherent property of a text field is ***`scroll`****. The* ***`scroll`*** *property is measured in lines. So if you added 5 onto the* ***`scroll`*** *property of a text field that had text inside of it, it would make the text jump up 5 lines.*

The **+=** *is called an "addition assignment." Essentially, all it does is to tell Flash MX 2004 to take the first part of the script,* ***`loadedInfo.scroll`****, and add the value on the right of it (1) and reassign it back to the variable on the left. In other words, when making text in a text field scroll, you essentially want to tell Flash MX 2004, "Take the* ***`scroll`*** *property and add 1 onto whatever the* ***`scroll`*** *property is currently set to." One way of writing that idea in ActionScript would be* ***`loadedInfo.scroll = loadedInfo.scroll + 1;`****. This would simply read, "Take the* ***`scroll`*** *property of the* ***`loadedInfo`*** *text field and set it to whatever the* ***`scroll`*** *property of the* ***`loadedInfo`*** *text field* currently *is, but add 1 onto that." When setting an expression to itself, it's easier and simpler to just write* **+=***, as you used in this script.*

```
//-------------<scroll buttons>--------------\\
this.scrollDown.onRelease = function () {
    loadedInfo.scroll += 1;
}
//-------------</scroll buttons>--------------\\
```

16. Click at the end of the **`loadedInfo.scroll += 1;`** line, press **Enter** (Windows) or **Return** (Mac) to create a line break, and close the function by typing the following:

}

That's it! That's all you need to do to make the text scroll down one line when the viewer clicks on the scroll down button. (It actually moves the text up*, but it makes sense to think of it as scrolling down.) Now you just need to write a similar function to scroll the text up.*

Rather than write all that from scratch again, it will save you a lot of time to copy the script you just wrote and then change the parts that you need.

17. Select the script you just wrote (between the comment lines) by clicking and dragging. Then, **right-click** (Windows) or **Ctrl+click** (Mac) that selected code, and from the contextual menu, choose **Copy**.

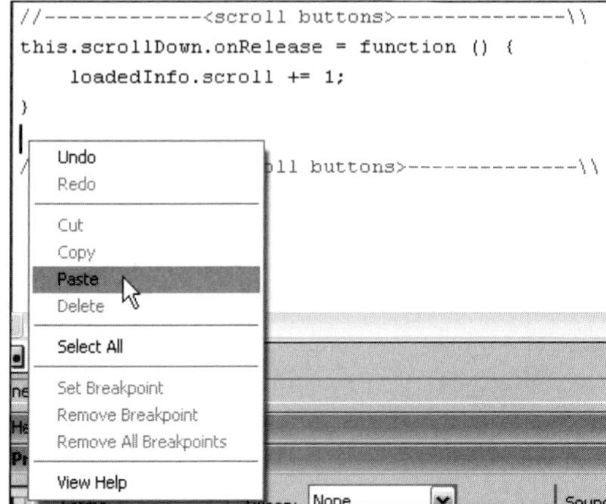

18. Click after the closed curly brace (}), press **Enter** (Windows) or **Return** (Mac) to create a line break, **right-click** (Windows) or **Ctrl+click** (Mac) that new line break and then from the contextual menu that appears, choose **Paste**. This will paste the script you just copied to the new line.

This copied script now needs to be modified to make the text field scroll up when the viewer clicks on the ***`scrollUp`*** *button.*

```
//-------------<scroll buttons>--------------\\
this.scrollDown.onRelease = function () {
    loadedInfo.scroll += 1;
}
this.scrollUp.onRelease = function () {
    loadedInfo.scroll -= 1;
}
//-------------</scroll buttons>--------------\\
```

19. In the copied script, change **scrollDown** to **scrollUp** (the instance name of the scroll up button). If you can't remember the scroll up button instance name, you could always use the **Insert Target Path** button to have Flash MX 2004 insert the name and path for you, just like you did in Steps 12 and 13. Change += to –=. (You want to set the **scroll** property 1 line down [hence, the negative value] not 1 line up.) The finished script should read like this:

```
this.scrollUp.onRelease = function () {
    loadedInfo.scroll -= 1;
}
```

That's it! Six lines of ActionScript later, and you have scrolling text! But before you start breaking out the champagne and caviar, you should test your movie first to make sure everything works. Keep in mind that, as yet, you can only view the about us module when it is loaded into the ***master.swf*** *file. This is because the script needed to load the dynamic text (variables) into the* ***about_us.swf****, which is located within the* ***master.swf*** *file.*

---

20. Save the changes you've made to the **about_us.fla** file by choosing **File > Save**. Then publish an updated SWF from this file by choosing **File > Publish**.

---

21. Bring the **master.fla** file to the foreground, or if you accidentally closed it, open it again by hiding or minimizing Flash MX 2004, navigating to your **Desktop > la_eyeworks > site** folder, and double-clicking the **master.fla** file.

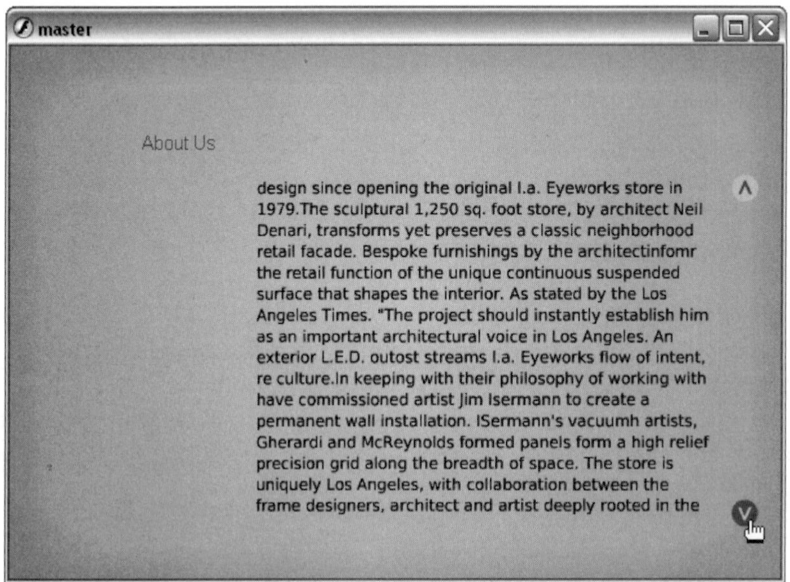

22. Preview the **master.fla** file by choosing **Control > Test Movie**. When the **master.swf** file is displayed, you will see the **about us** module automatically load, and the loaded text will also automatically be displayed. By clicking the scroll down and scroll up buttons, you will be able to make the dynamic text scroll down and up. Sweet! Each time you click the scroll down or scroll up buttons, the text will respectively scroll down or up one line.

MOVIE | Advanced Scroller

Included on the **H•O•T CD-ROM** in the **movies** folder, are two movies titled **adv_scroller.mov** and **adv_scroller_part2.mov**. In this movie, you will learn how to make text scroll (as you just learned) in a more advanced manner. With the scrolling text you just constructed, the text will scroll only if you repeatedly click the scroll up/scroll down buttons. But what if you want the text to *continually* scroll as the viewers hold their mouse button down on the scroll up/scroll down buttons? Creating that kind of functionality requires learning some new actions and requires an additional script. You will learn how to create this advanced scrolling technique in the **adv_scroller.mov** and **adv_scroller_part2.mov** movies.

TIP | Creating Scrolling Text with the TextArea Component

Another way to easily create scrolling text is by using a component that ships with Flash MX 2004. Components are, of course, pre-built widgets that you can easily drag and drop onto your Flash MX 2004 movies to add functionality. Among other things, components were given a major overhaul in Flash MX 2004. One of those components is called the **TextArea** component, and it essentially allows you to quickly and easily add scrollable text to your project.

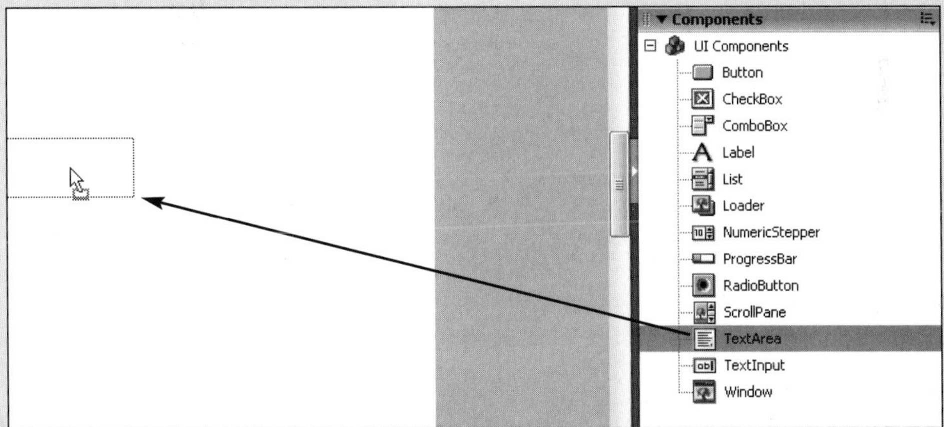

To add the **TextArea** component into your Flash MX 2004 movie, you simply drag it from the **Components** panel and drop it on the **Stage**.

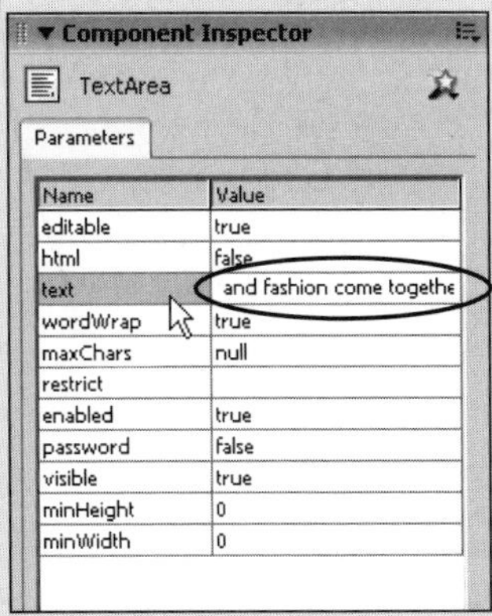

Then, with the **TextArea** component selected on the **Stage**, simply open the **Component Inspector** panel and type (or paste) the text you want to be displayed.

continues on next page

TIP | Creating Scrolling Text with the TextArea Component *continued*

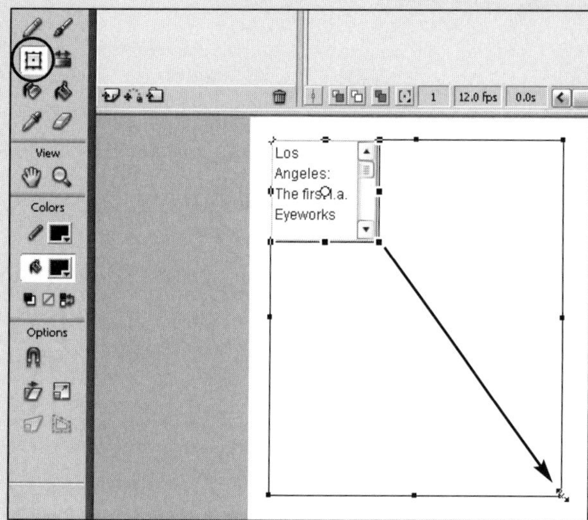

By using the **Free Transform** tool, you can grab one of the **TextArea** component resize handles and resize it so that it's any size you want.

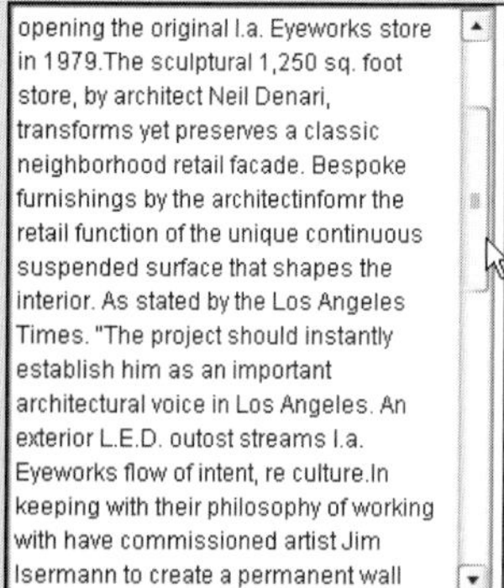

Choose **Control > Test Movie**, and you now have instant scrollable text, complete with a draggable slider! Voilà! Super simple, eh?

However, one of the major differences between the scrolling text you built manually in the last exercise and the scrollable text in the **TextArea** component, is that by using a component, you're *significantly* adding to the overall file size of your project. For instance, just adding the **TextArea** component to your project *immediately* adds a cool 40 K to the file size of a SWF. Although the **TextArea** component provides you with a quick and easy way to add scrolling text (with a draggable scroll bar) to your project, you have to ask yourself if it's worth the additional file size hit.

Once again, congratulations! In this exercise, you not only learned how to make text scroll up and down, but more importantly you learned how to attach actions to a symbol from the Timeline! Again, this is a powerful technique because it allows you to keep your ActionScript centralized for easy modifications, comparisons, and references.

In the next chapter, you will learn how to format and style the loaded text by using a combination of HTML and Cascading Style Sheets (CSS). Being able to control the styling of dynamically loaded text is a very valuable piece of knowledge because it allows you (or the client) to make modifications to the text without having to deal with the FLA or even open Flash MX 2004 itself. Changes can be made quickly and easily by using a simple text editor. You'll learn how to utilize some of that flexibility in the next chapter.

---

5. HTML and CSS

| What You Are Building |

| Modifying the Loaded Text Using HTML |

| About CSS and Flash | Using CSS |

la_eyeworks

Macromedia Flash MX 2004
Beyond the Basics

In the last chapter, you learned how to use the **LoadVars** class to dynamically load text from an external text file and populate a text field with that loaded text. In this chapter, you will learn how to style and modify the appearance of that loaded text using HTML and Cascading Style Sheets (CSS). Not only that, but you will also learn how to use the **TextField.StyleSheet** class to dynamically load an *external* CSS file, much like you learned how to use **LoadVars** to dynamically load text from an external TXT file. By keeping the CSS file *external* to the Flash MX 2004 project, and using ActionScript to load and utilize that file, you gain the same benefits that loading external text provides. It makes it very easy for you, or the client, to modify how the text is styled by simply making modifications to the external CSS file with a simple text editor or even a WYSIWYG HTML editor like Macromedia Dreamweaver MX 2004. If you're designing two versions of a Web site–HTML and Flash MX 2004–they can even *share* the same CSS file. How about that for making life simpler!

I. What You Are Building

In this exercise, you will get to preview exactly *what* it is you are building *before* you start building it. That way, as you're working through the exercises in this chapter, you'll have a better idea of how some of these abstract ActionScript concepts fit together to create a functional piece of the L.A. Eyeworks Web site.

1. Open your preferred Web browser, and navigate to the following URL:

http://www.lynda.com/flashbtb/laeyeworks/

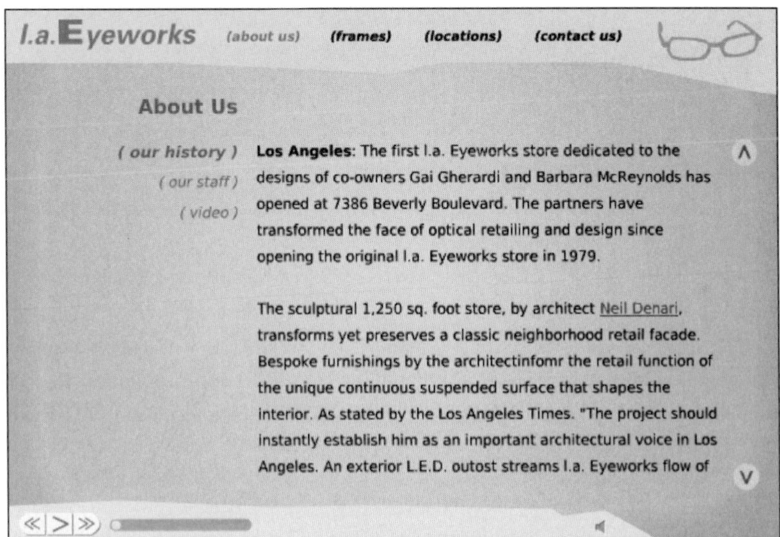

2. Once the L.A. Eyeworks Web site finishes loading, click the **about us** button from the top navigation bar. This will load the **about_us.swf** file, replacing the splash graphic.

Notice how some of the text is bolded, there are paragraph breaks, and there is even a hyperlink that changes color when you hover your mouse over it! This text is styled using HTML (to create the bolding, paragraph breaks, and hyperlinks) and further enhanced with Cascading Style Sheets (in this case, to create the hyperlink color change when the mouse hovers over it). The CSS file is also loaded in–and applied–from a separate CSS file.

3. When you're finished, close your Web browser.

2. Modifying the Loaded Text Using HTML

So you've gotten some text to load into your Flash MX 2004 movie. What now? What about making it pretty? How can you change the font, color, size, and so forth, of text that gets loaded dynamically? Up until this point, you've probably modified the look and feel of your text by selecting it with the Text tool and then changing the text settings in the Properties inspector. But with dynamic text, that text doesn't exist in the text field when you're working in the Flash MX 2004 project. So how do you go about modifying the text styles? Fortunately, Flash MX 2004 allows you to modify the look and feel of the dynamic text by adding HTML tags into the text file where the text resides! Not only that, but as you'll see in the next exercise, Macromedia introduced in Flash MX 2004 the capability to further modify the text by using Cascading Style Sheets (CSS)! In this exercise, you're going to learn how to modify the dynamic text by writing a few, simple HTML tags into the **ourHistory.txt** text file.

Flash MX 2004 supports a few HTML tags that you can apply to your text. These tags, with a short example, are as follows: anchor **<a>**, bold **<b>**, font color **<font color="#FFFFFF">**, font face **<font face="Arial, Helvetica, sans-serif">**, font size **<font size="18">**, image **<img>**, italics **<i>**, list **<li>**, paragraph **<p>** (which you can use the **align** and **class** attributes with), span **<span>** (which you can use the **class** attribute with), line break **
, and underline **<u>. You can also use the following HTML attributes within the tag **<textformat>**: **leftmargin**, **rightmargin**, **blockindent**, **indent**, **tabstops**, and **leading**. So, as you can see, Flash MX 2004 supports only a small subset of the many HTML tags that modern Web browsers support. There's a lot you can do with these available tags, however. For a full description of each HTML tag that Flash MX 2004 supports, open your **Help** panel (**F1**), and from the Help "books" on the left, choose **ActionScript Reference Guide > Working with Text > Using HTML-formatted text > Supported HTML tags**.

Another great advantage of using HTML tags (and later, CSS) to modify the text appearance is that you never need to open Flash MX 2004. All of this work can be done right inside the text file, alongside the text! In this exercise, you will be using a few of these tags to modify the appearance of the dynamic text.

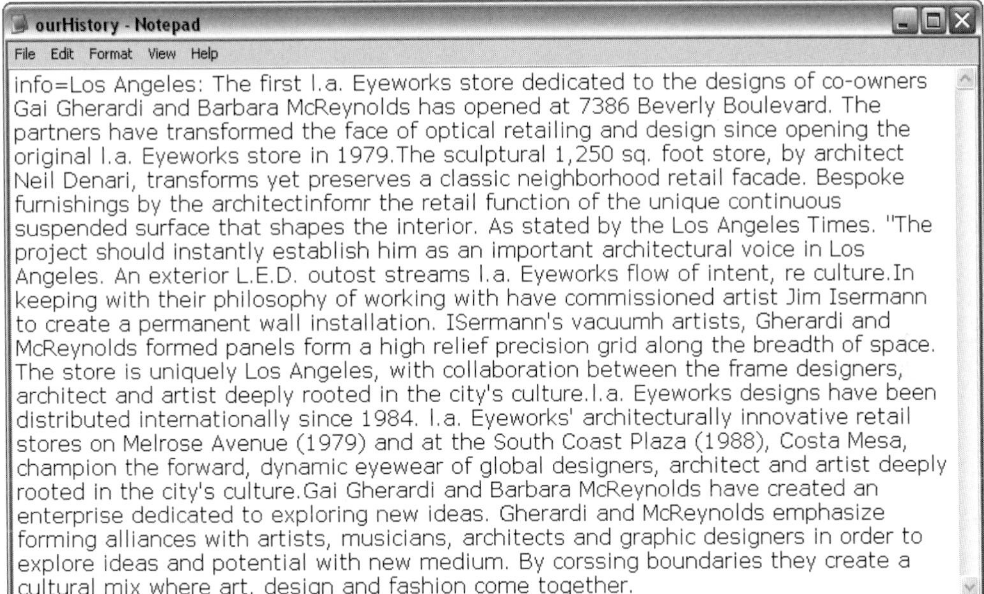

info=Los Angeles: The first l.a. Eyeworks store dedicated to the designs of co-owners Gai Gherardi and Barbara McReynolds has opened at 7386 Beverly Boulevard. The partners have transformed the face of optical retailing and design since opening the original l.a. Eyeworks store in 1979.The sculptural 1,250 sq. foot store, by architect Neil Denari, transforms yet preserves a classic neighborhood retail facade. Bespoke furnishings by the architectinfomr the retail function of the unique continuous suspended surface that shapes the interior. As stated by the Los Angeles Times. "The project should instantly establish him as an important architectural voice in Los Angeles. An exterior L.E.D. outost streams l.a. Eyeworks flow of intent, re culture.In keeping with their philosophy of working with have commissioned artist Jim Isermann to create a permanent wall installation. ISermann's vacuumh artists, Gherardi and McReynolds formed panels form a high relief precision grid along the breadth of space. The store is uniquely Los Angeles, with collaboration between the frame designers, architect and artist deeply rooted in the city's culture.l.a. Eyeworks designs have been distributed internationally since 1984. l.a. Eyeworks' architecturally innovative retail stores on Melrose Avenue (1979) and at the South Coast Plaza (1988), Costa Mesa, champion the forward, dynamic eyewear of global designers, architect and artist deeply rooted in the city's culture.Gai Gherardi and Barbara McReynolds have created an enterprise dedicated to exploring new ideas. Gherardi and McReynolds emphasize forming alliances with artists, musicians, architects and graphic designers in order to explore ideas and potential with new medium. By corssing boundaries they create a cultural mix where art, design and fashion come together.

1. Hide or minimize Flash MX 2004, navigate to your **Desktop > la_eyeworks > site > vars** folder, and open the file **ourHistory.txt** in **Notepad** (Windows), **TextEdit** (Mac), **BBEdit** (Mac), or an equivalent simple text editor.

*This is the same text file, **ourHistory.txt**, that you opened in the previous chapter and added the **info** variable to. Now, you're going to add some HTML tags to this text file to slightly style the text. First, you're going to create a few line breaks in the text so that when the viewer is scrolling through the text, it doesn't appear as one, huge block of type.*

*To create a paragraph break, one might initially think to use the paragraph tag, **<p>**. However, in Flash MX 2004, the **<p>** tag functions slightly differently than it does in a Web browser. In Flash MX 2004, the **<p>** tag* defines *a new paragraph, but does not create a paragraph* break. *In Flash MX 2004, paragraph tags are used to specify text alignment (**<p align="right">**) and to assign CSS style classes (**<p class="body">**). To create a visual paragraph break in the text, use two **
** tags.*

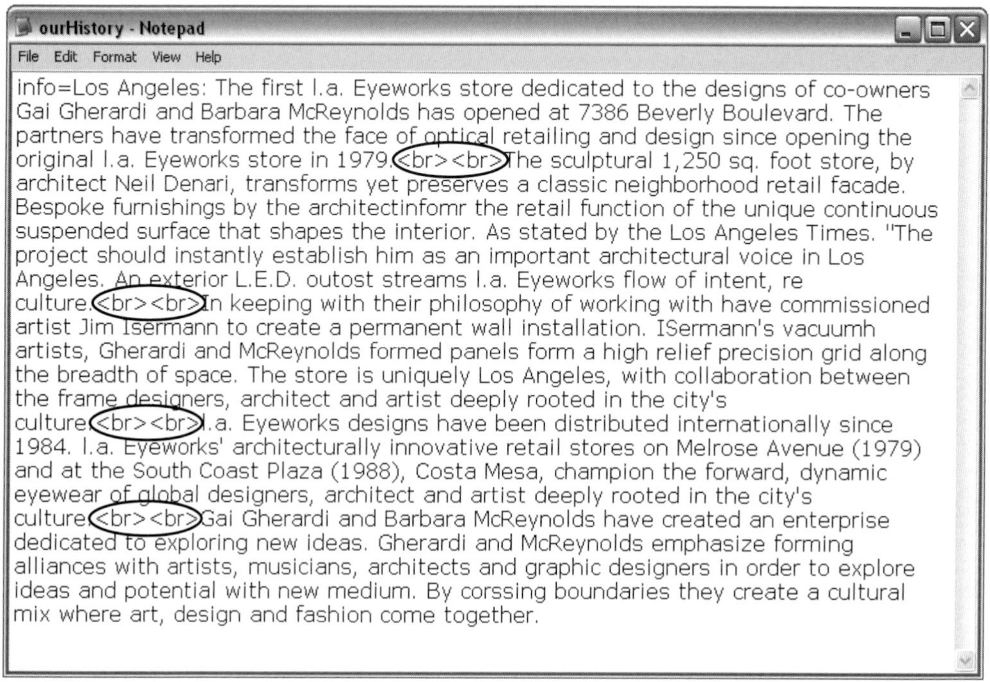

2. Type two break tags, **

**, before the following sentences: "The sculptural 1,250 sq. foot store..."; "In keeping with their philosophy..."; "l.a. Eyeworks designs have been distributed..."; and "Gai Gherardi and Barbara McReynolds have created...". To help you find those places easier, they're circled in the screen shot above.

---

3. Save the **ourHistory.txt** text file, and bring Flash MX 2004 back into the foreground. Then, make sure **about_us.fla** is the FLA currently in the foreground.

Even though (if you remember) back in the previous chapter you specified that the text that loads into the text field be HTML formatted text (by typing the action **`htmlText`***), that's only half the job. You also need to turn on the* ***Render Text as HTML*** *option for the about us text field to tell Flash MX 2004 to use (and not display) the HTML tags you're entering.*

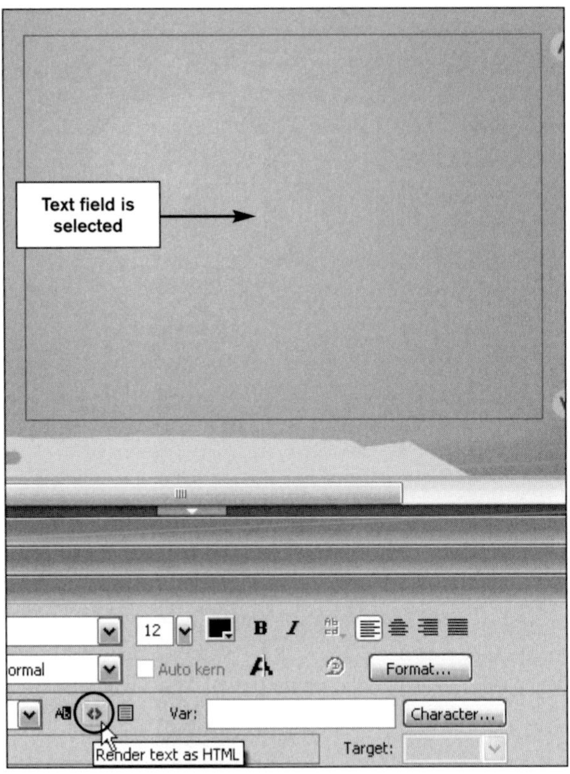

4. Make sure you're in the **about_us.fla** and that you have the **loadedInfo** text field selected, and then click the **Render text as HTML** button in the **Properties inspector**. Now, any text that loads into that text field will utilize its HTML tags for formatting, alignment, and so forth. If you did not select the **Render text as HTML** button, the HTML tags would actually be *displayed* (rather than utilized) along with the text. That, obviously, would be a bad thing.

*Since you've made changes to the **about_us.fla**, you need to save your changes and publish a new SWF.*

---

5. Save the changes you made to the **about_us.fla** file by choosing **File > Save**. Then, publish a new SWF by choosing **File > Publish**.

*Now that you've published a new **about_us.swf** file, you can preview the work you've done thus far by returning to the **master.fla** file and testing your movie.*

---

6. Bring the **master.fla** file into the foreground. If you accidentally closed it, you can open it again by hiding or minimizing Flash MX 2004 and navigating to your **Desktop > la_eyeworks > site** folder and double-clicking the **master.fla** file. (You can also open **master.fla** by choosing it from the **File > Open Recent** menu.) Then, test the movie by choosing **Control > Test Movie**.

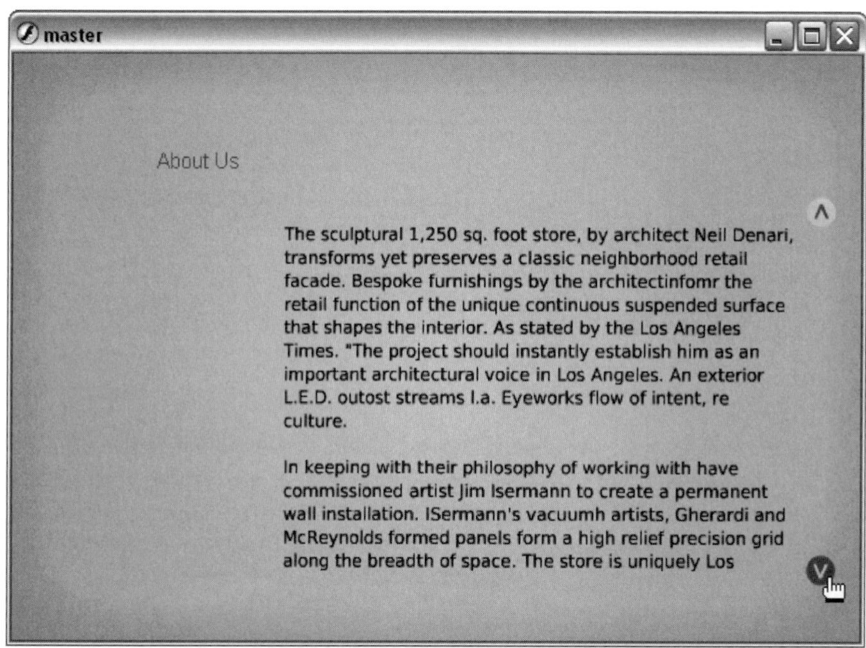

*When the **master.swf** preview window appears, the about us module loads, and the our history text is loaded. Then, you should see your line breaks. Scroll through the text to view the line breaks you added with HTML! Again, one of the great things about using HTML markup tags to style your dynamically loaded text is that it makes it very easy for you, or your client, or both to style the text to your liking without opening Flash MX 2004.*

Next, you're going to add another HTML tag, this time to create a hyperlink with a portion of the text!

7. Close the **master.swf Preview** window, hide or minimize Flash MX 2004, and open the **ourHistory.txt** file again.

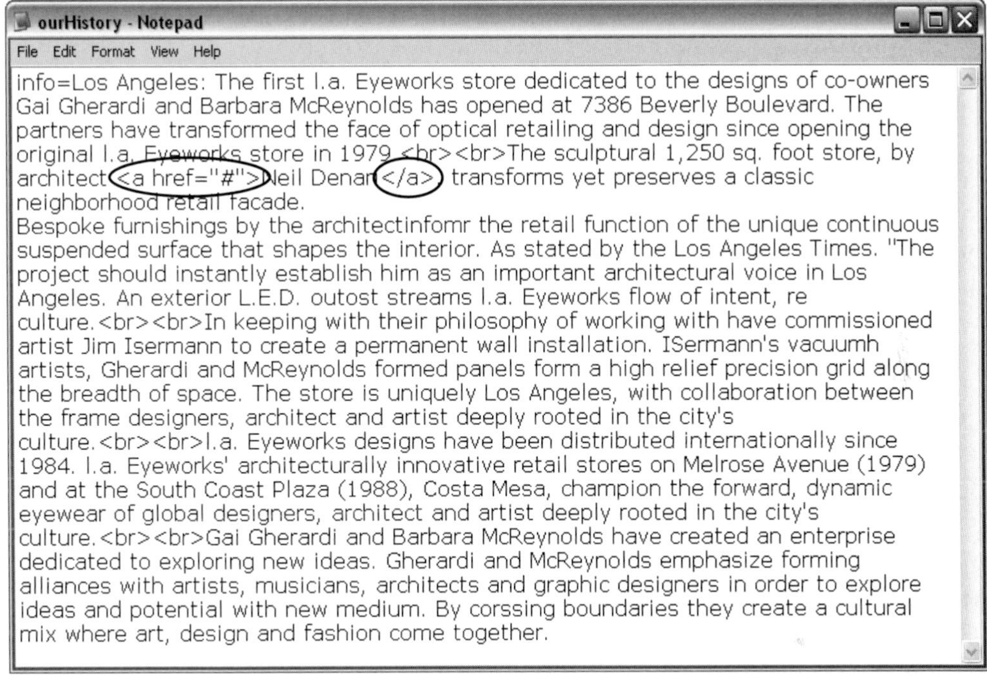

info=Los Angeles: The first l.a. Eyeworks store dedicated to the designs of co-owners Gai Gherardi and Barbara McReynolds has opened at 7386 Beverly Boulevard. The partners have transformed the face of optical retailing and design since opening the original l.a. Eyeworks store in 1979.

The sculptural 1,250 sq. foot store, by architect<a href="#">Neil Denari</a> transforms yet preserves a classic neighborhood retail facade.
Bespoke furnishings by the architectinfomr the retail function of the unique continuous suspended surface that shapes the interior. As stated by the Los Angeles Times. "The project should instantly establish him as an important architectural voice in Los Angeles. An exterior L.E.D. outost streams l.a. Eyeworks flow of intent, re culture.

In keeping with their philosophy of working with have commissioned artist Jim Isermann to create a permanent wall installation. ISermann's vacuumh artists, Gherardi and McReynolds formed panels form a high relief precision grid along the breadth of space. The store is uniquely Los Angeles, with collaboration between the frame designers, architect and artist deeply rooted in the city's culture.

l.a. Eyeworks designs have been distributed internationally since 1984. l.a. Eyeworks' architecturally innovative retail stores on Melrose Avenue (1979) and at the South Coast Plaza (1988), Costa Mesa, champion the forward, dynamic eyewear of global designers, architect and artist deeply rooted in the city's culture.

Gai Gherardi and Barbara McReynolds have created an enterprise dedicated to exploring new ideas. Gherardi and McReynolds emphasize forming alliances with artists, musicians, architects and graphic designers in order to explore ideas and potential with new medium. By corssing boundaries they create a cultural mix where art, design and fashion come together.

8. In the **ourHistory.txt** file, before the words "Neil Denari", type the following:

<a href="#">

And, after the words "Neil Denari", type:

</a>

*The **<a>** tag is called an **anchor** tag. An anchor tag allows you to create a hyperlink on a bit of text (just like in an HTML-based Web page). The **</a>** tag is the **closed anchor** tag. Just like when you're writing ActionScript functions and **if** statements, Flash MX 2004 needs to know where the anchor starts and where it stops. The text between the anchor tag (**<a>**) and the closed anchor tag (**</a>**) ("Neil Denari" in this example) is the hyperlink. The text between the quotation marks after **href=** is the URL where you want the visitor to be taken to when they click the hyperlink. In this case, you're using a "placeholder" URL–signified by the # symbol–because Mr. Denari doesn't have a Web page of his own to link to.*

Wouldn't it be nice to also be able to specify your own leading (the amount of space between each line) for this text as well? Thankfully, it's very easy to do.

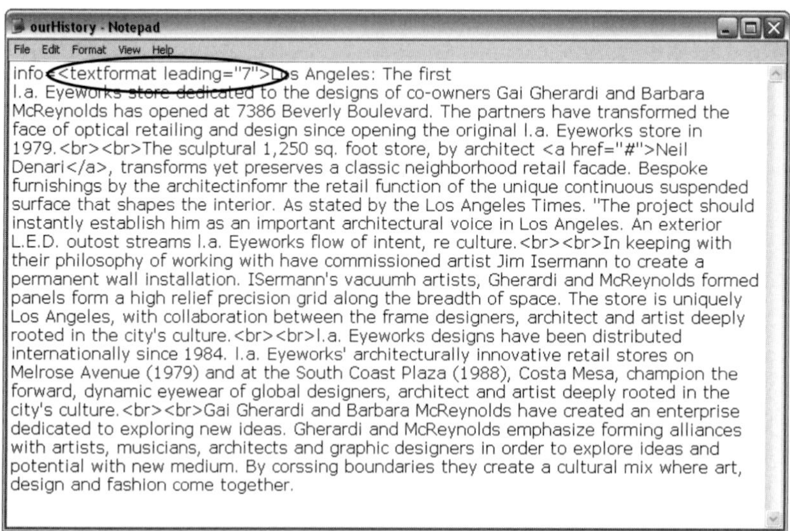

9. Click immediately after **info=** (located towards the beginning of the text file), and then use the **textformat** tag to add 7 points of leading by typing the following:

<textformat leading="7">

Just like with the other HTML tags, you also need to specify where the **textformat** tag ends.

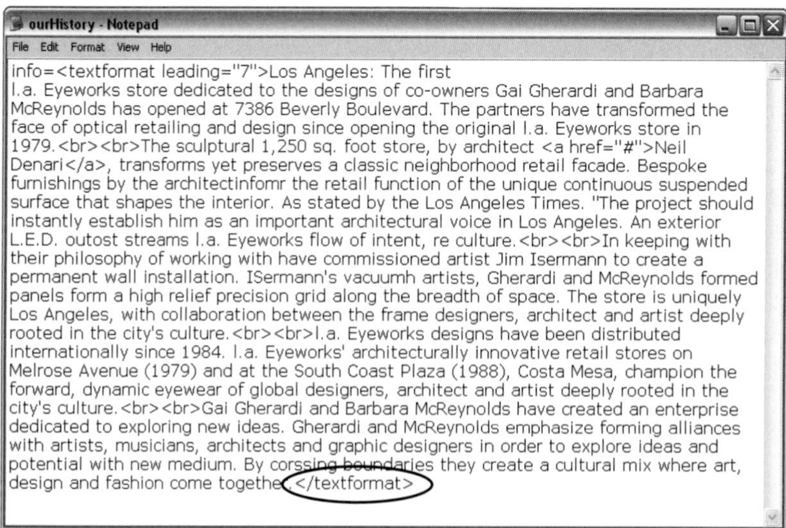

10. Click at the very end of the text file and close the **textformat** tag by typing the following:

</textformat>

By putting the opening ***`textformat`*** *tag at the very beginning of the text and the closing* ***`textformat`*** *tag at the very end, that applies the* ***`textformating`*** *property of* ***`leading="7"`*** *to all of the our history text.*

Now that you know that your Flash MX 2004 files are all set up to accept HTML tags in loaded text files, you don't even need to return to Flash MX 2004 to preview the changes!

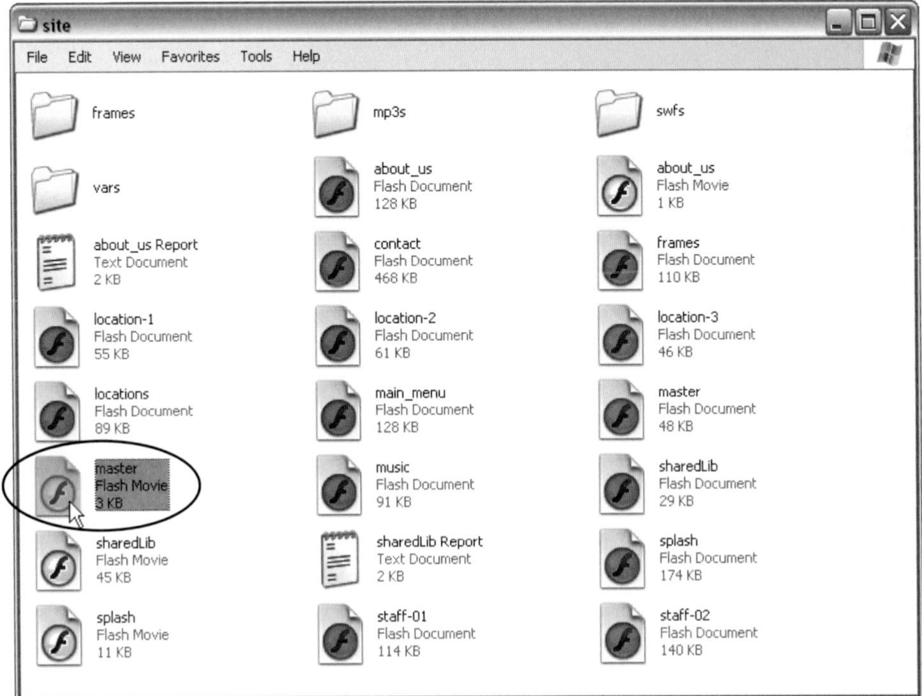

11. Save the changes you've made to the **ourHistory.txt** file, navigate to your **Desktop > la_eyeworks > site** folder, and double-click the **master.swf** file to open it in the standalone Macromedia Flash Player 7.

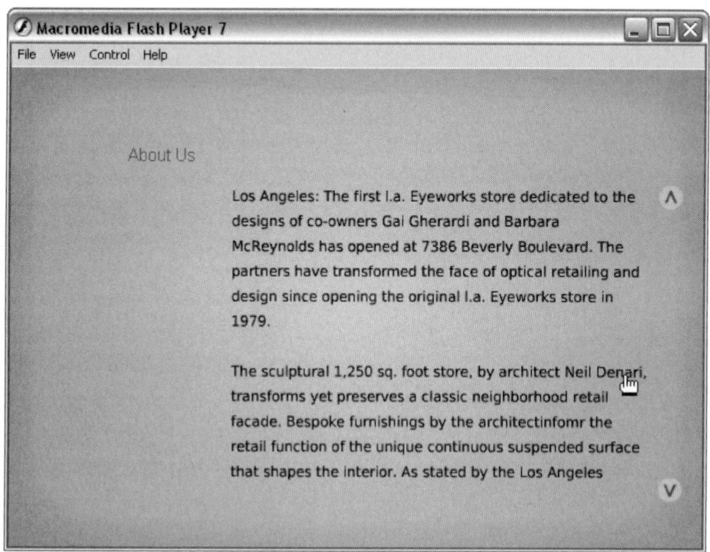

12. After you've double-clicked the **master.swf** file, you'll see the loaded text, with your custom-specified leading of 7 pixels applied to it! Within that however, the text "Neil Denari" won't look like an average hyperlink does on a Web page. This is because Flash MX 2004, by default, renders a hyperlink differently than a Web browser does. However, if you hover your mouse cursor over the text "Neil Denari", you'll notice that the arrow cursor turns into a hand cursor.

Even though the "Neil Denari" text doesn't look *like a hyperlink, it still acts as one. If you were to enter a real URL in the* ***ourHistory.txt*** *file in place of the URL placeholder, #, clicking the "Neil Denari" text in this SWF file would open your specified URL in a Web browser. You can even call JavaScript from these hyperlinks as well (*`"javascript:myMethod('param');"` *or* `"asfunction:myMethod('param');"`*)!*

---

13. Once you have finished looking at the work you've done thus far, **close** the Macromedia Flash Player window and return to Flash MX 2004.

In the next exercise, you will–among other things–make that hyperlink look and act *like a "traditional" hyperlink does in a Web browser.*

So there you have it. In this exercise, you used HTML tags to add line breaks and a hyperlink to the dynamically loaded text! Although you may not realize it yet, this is a fantastically powerful feature because it allows you to easily style dynamic text. Or more appealingly, the client can do it (or maybe not...depending on the client). ;-) For more information about the HTML tags that Flash MX 2004 supports, open the ***Help*** *panel (****F1****), and from the help "books" on the left side of the Help panel, choose* ***ActionScript Reference Guide > Working with Text > Using HTML-formatted Text > Supported HTML tags****.*

About CSS and Flash MX 2004

New to Flash MX 2004, you can use Cascading Style Sheets (CSS) to modify the styling of text. Similar to HTML tag support, Flash MX 2004's supported CSS properties are also substantially less than what a Web browser supports. For most uses, however, Flash MX 2004's supported CSS properties should be sufficient. For detailed, up-to-date information about the CSS properties that Flash MX 2004 supports, open the **Help** panel (**F1**). In the Help panel, from the Help "books" on the left-side, choose **ActionScript Reference Guide > Working with Text > Formatting Text with Cascading Style Sheets > Supported CSS properties**.

When you want to use CSS to modify the style of dynamic text in your Flash MX 2004 project, there are essentially two ways to go about doing it. You can either create and write the CSS styles directly into the Flash MX 2004 project via the Actions window. Or, you can write the CSS styles in a separate CSS file (much like you have a separate **ourHistory.txt** file to contain the our history text) and then dynamically *load* the CSS file and apply it to a text field when you need it. Even though creating a separate CSS file to contain the CSS styles, and then dynamically loading and applying those CSS styles, takes more effort (and ActionScript elbow grease), it has clear advantages over writing your CSS styles directly into the Flash MX 2004 project.

For example, if you're loading a separate CSS file, when you want to make changes to the CSS styles, you simply have to open the CSS file with any simple text editor, or a CSS-editing program such as Macromedia Dreamweaver MX 2004, Bradsoft's Top Style, or others and make the required changes. (For more CSS-editing program recommendations, see Appendix B, "Online Resources" at the end of this book.) Next time the SWF file is played, those CSS changes are automatically loaded and applied to the dynamic text. Conversely, if the CSS styles were written directly into your Flash MX 2004 movie, the only way to edit those styles would be to open the FLA in Flash MX 2004, make the required changes, and then republish a new SWF file from that FLA. By dynamically loading and applying an external CSS file, you can also use the *same* CSS file that you use for the HTML portions of a Web site. This significantly cuts down on production time because you don't have to use separate CSS files for the Flash MX 2004 and HTML portions of a Web site, and by making changes to the CSS file, you're updating not only the HTML content, but the Flash MX 2004 content as well! As you can see, even though it may require a little extra effort to dynamically load and apply an external CSS file, it is a *much* better way to approach CSS integration into your Flash MX 2004 projects.

When loading external CSS files and applying them to a text field, those styles need to be loaded and applied *before* the text is loaded into the same text field. If the text gets loaded into a text field first and *then* the styles are applied to that text field, the text will *not* utilize the CSS styles until new text loads into the same text field. So when you load external CSS files, you need to ensure that the CSS styles are applied to the text field *first*. Because of that reason, you *won't* be placing the ActionScript that performs the dynamic CSS loading/applying within the **master.fla**, as you have with the other scripts that are used by multiple SWFs (such as the **MovieClipLoader** and **LoadVars** scripts). This is because the scripts placed on the first keyframe in the **master.fla** file get executed all at the *same time* (roughly). If you put the script that loads and applies the CSS file on the first keyframe of **master.fla** with the other scripts, the **LoadVars** script (which loads the text from the external text file and inserts it into the text field) would get executed at the same time as the CSS-loading script. This means that there would be the potential for the text to load into the text field *before* the CSS styles are applied to the field. As I mentioned previously, this would cause the loaded text to *not* utilize the CSS styles. Because of this potential problem, you will be writing the CSS-loading script directly into the SWF file that needs it. Although this goes against my preaching of keeping commonly used scripts centralized, from an intermediate Flash MX 2004 perspective, it's the best way around the potential problems I just outlined.

3. Using CSS

In this exercise, you will learn how to use ActionScript to load–and apply–an external CSS file to a text field. As part of that, you will also learn how to use CSS to apply styles to text (giving you the ability to change such things as text color, font face, font size, and so forth) and to style the way a hyperlink looks and behaves.

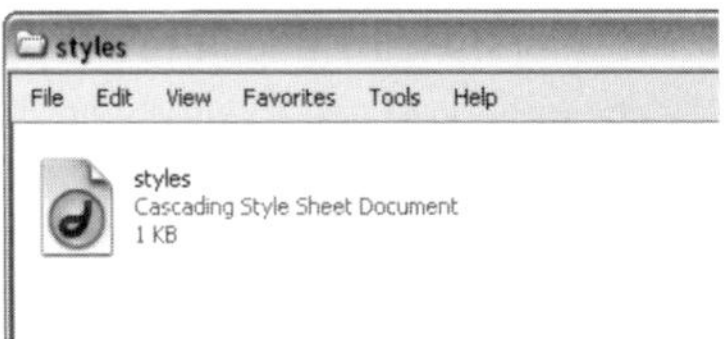

1. Hide or minimize Flash MX 2004, and then navigate to your **Desktop > la_eyeworks > site > styles** folder. In there, you'll find a file called **styles.css**. (Again, on some operating systems, the file might not display its three-letter .css extension.) Once you've located it, open the **styles.css** file.

Note: *If you have Macromedia Dreamweaver installed, the document will open Macromedia Dreamweaver when you double-click it. If you don't have Macromedia Dreamweaver installed, you can open the* ***styles.css*** *file in a simple text editor such as Notepad (Windows), TextEdit (Mac), or BBEdit (Mac).*

---

styles - Notepad

File Edit Format View Help

```
p {
		font-family: "Bitstream Vera Sans";
		font-size: 11px;
}
a:link {
		color: #CC0000;
		text-decoration: underline;
}
a:hover {
		color: #3F7FBE;
		text-decoration: none;
}
.hilight {
		font-weight: bold;
}
.alignRight {
		text-align: right;
}
.colorBlue {
		color: #3F7FBE;
}
```

2. Once you've opened the file, you'll see that it contains CSS style information. Now, because this book isn't about working with Cascading Style Sheets, I won't be going over all the nitty-gritty details about working with and editing CSS. That's a whole topic unto itself. Following this exercise is a table that gives you a quick breakdown of the CSS tags used in this **styles.css** document and what they all mean.

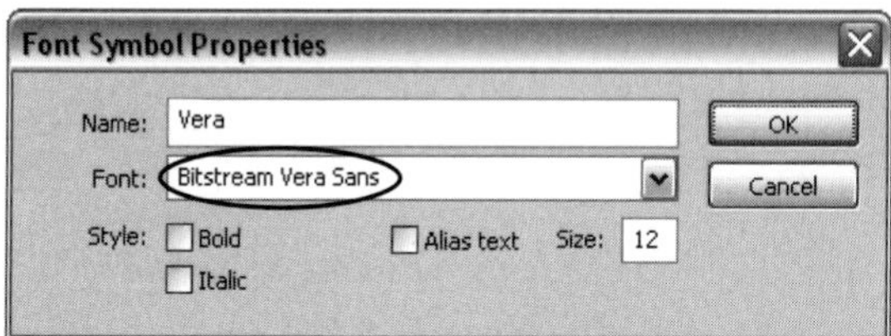

***Note:** When defining font-families in a CSS document, if you want to use fonts from the Shared Library–as this example does–you need to specify the font name as you see it within the **Font Symbol Properties** dialog box in the shared library,* not as *the linkage identifier name that you assigned to the font symbol.*

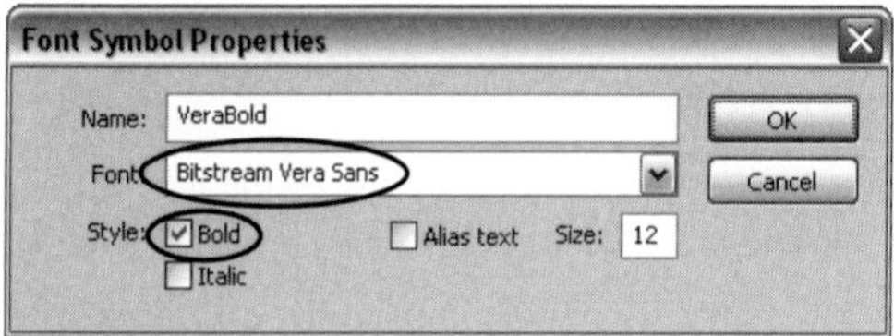

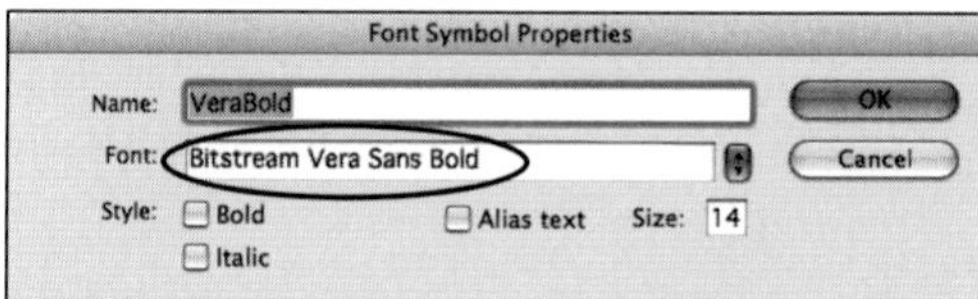

(Windows) *(Macintosh)*

***Warning:** Here's where there's a glaring cross-platform difference that, for the most part, stems from how the Mac and Windows operating systems treat installed fonts. Fonts installed under the Windows operating system are grouped by their font face. In other words, the Bitstream Vera font that you installed earlier was comprised of a series of faces–Vera Sans, Vera Sans Bold, Vera Sans Italic, and so forth. Under the Windows OS, those separate faces are only listed as one face, Vera Sans, that has various* styles *(bold, italic, and so forth) that represent the individual (grouped) font faces. The Macintosh operating system, however, does* not *group the separate font faces together as the Windows OS does. This is a very important detail because it will affect how you specify which font face to use in the CSS file you will be loading in this exercise.*

*The **styles.css** file you currently have open is the proper **styles.css** file for the Windows operating system–you don't need to make any changes to it if you're running Windows. But notice how, under the CSS class **`.hilight`**, when the* bold *style of Bitstream Vera Sans is needed, the CSS file just sets the font-weight to bold. Because the **`.hilight`** class will be applied to selective bits of text within the CSS redefined **<p>** tag, the **`.hilight`** class will inherit the styles applied to the **<p>** tag, namely the font face (Bitstream Vera Sans), font size, and font color. (That is why they're called* Cascading *Style Sheets, because the styles* cascade*). So, under the Windows OS, because the font faces are grouped, to change the font face to Bitstream Vera Sans Bold, you just have to change the font-weight (a.k.a. font style) to bold.*

Macintosh Users Read This!

Under the Macintosh OS, where the fonts *are not* grouped together as they are under Windows, instead of **`font-weight: bold`** under the **`.hilight`** CSS class, you would instead need to use the font face you want the text to be displayed in. So if you're currently running the Macintosh OS, and you created the shared library with the shared Bitstream fonts under the Mac OS, you would need to delete **`font-weight: bold;`** and replace it with **`font-family: "Bitstream Vera Sans Bold";`**.

```
p {
        font-family: "Bitstream Vera Sans";
        font-size: 11px;
}
a:link {
        color: #CC0000;
        text-decoration: underline;
}
a:hover {
        color: #3F7FBE;
        text-decoration: none;
}
.hilight {
        font-weight: bold;
}
.alignRight {
        text-align: right;
}
.colorBlue {
        color: #3F7FBE;
}
```

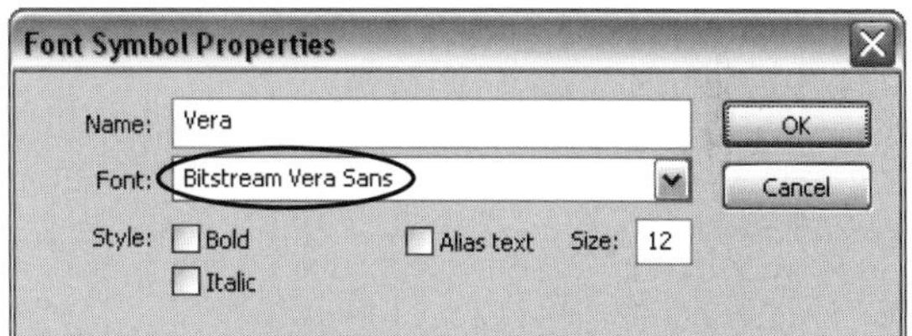

In essence, when specifying a font face in a CSS file in conjunction with a shared font in a shared library (as you are in the construction of the L.A. Eyeworks Web site), you need to use the same CSS *font-family* name *that the font uses in the shared library under your operating system. This has* ***no*** *effect on what the viewer sees when he or she visits the L.A. Eyeworks Web site. You don't need to create separate CSS files for Macintosh and Windows operating systems. If you want a CSS-styled text field to use one of your shared fonts, you need to ensure that the font-family name you specify in the CSS file matches the font name displayed in the* ***Font*** *field in the* ***Font Symbol Properties*** *dialog box. In other words, this is only an author-time issue, not a run-time issue.*

Now that you've seen the CSS styles, you need to specify where those styles will be applied in the ***ourHistory.txt*** *file.*

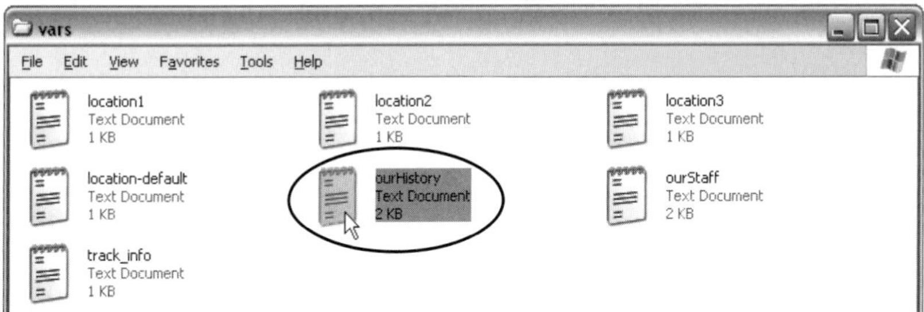

3. Navigate to your **Desktop > la_eyeworks > site > vars** folder, and open the **ourHistory.txt** file (or bring it to the foreground if you still have it open from the previous exercise) in a simple text editor such as Notepad (Windows), TextEdit (Mac), or BBEdit (Mac).

Within the ***ourHistory.txt*** *file, you want all the text to be styled using the CSS redefined paragraph tag* **<p>**. *If you recall, the* ***styles.css*** *file redefined the* **<p>** *tag so that whatever was within the* **<p></p>** *tags would be styled with the Bitstream Vera Font, at 11 px. You also want the first two words of the our history text, "Los Angeles," to be bold. Luckily, a CSS class for just this purpose was created for you, in the* ***styles.css*** *file, called* ***`.hilight`***.

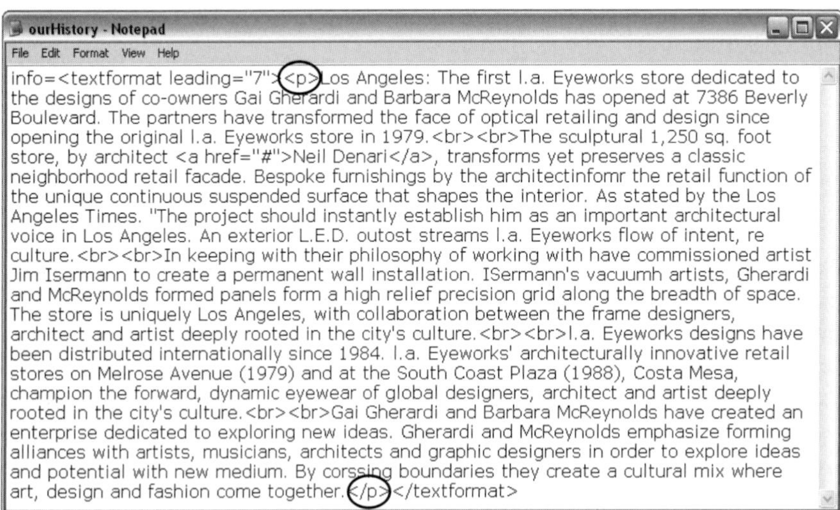
ourHistory - Notepad

File Edit Format View Help

info=<textformat leading="7"><p>Los Angeles: The first l.a. Eyeworks store dedicated to the designs of co-owners Gai Gherardi and Barbara McReynolds has opened at 7386 Beverly Boulevard. The partners have transformed the face of optical retailing and design since opening the original l.a. Eyeworks store in 1979.

The sculptural 1,250 sq. foot store, by architect <a href="#">Neil Denari</a>, transforms yet preserves a classic neighborhood retail facade. Bespoke furnishings by the architectinfomr the retail function of the unique continuous suspended surface that shapes the interior. As stated by the Los Angeles Times. "The project should instantly establish him as an important architectural voice in Los Angeles. An exterior L.E.D. outost streams l.a. Eyeworks flow of intent, re culture.

In keeping with their philosophy of working with have commissioned artist Jim Isermann to create a permanent wall installation. ISermann's vacuumh artists, Gherardi and McReynolds formed panels form a high relief precision grid along the breadth of space. The store is uniquely Los Angeles, with collaboration between the frame designers, architect and artist deeply rooted in the city's culture.

l.a. Eyeworks designs have been distributed internationally since 1984. l.a. Eyeworks' architecturally innovative retail stores on Melrose Avenue (1979) and at the South Coast Plaza (1988), Costa Mesa, champion the forward, dynamic eyewear of global designers, architect and artist deeply rooted in the city's culture.

Gai Gherardi and Barbara McReynolds have created an enterprise dedicated to exploring new ideas. Gherardi and McReynolds emphasize forming alliances with artists, musicians, architects and graphic designers in order to explore ideas and potential with new medium. By corssing boundaries they create a cultural mix where art, design and fashion come together.</p></textformat>

4. In the **ourHistory.txt** file, add a paragraph tag **<p>** between the words "Los Angeles" and the **`<textformat leading="7">`** tag. Then, add an end paragraph tag **</p>** at the end of the text file, immediately after the last period, but before the **`</textformat>`** tag. Since you used CSS to style everything within the paragraph tags, all the text within this document will have those styles applied to it.

Next, the text "Los Angeles" needs to be bolded. To do this, you will apply the CSS class to the ***<span>*** *tag.*

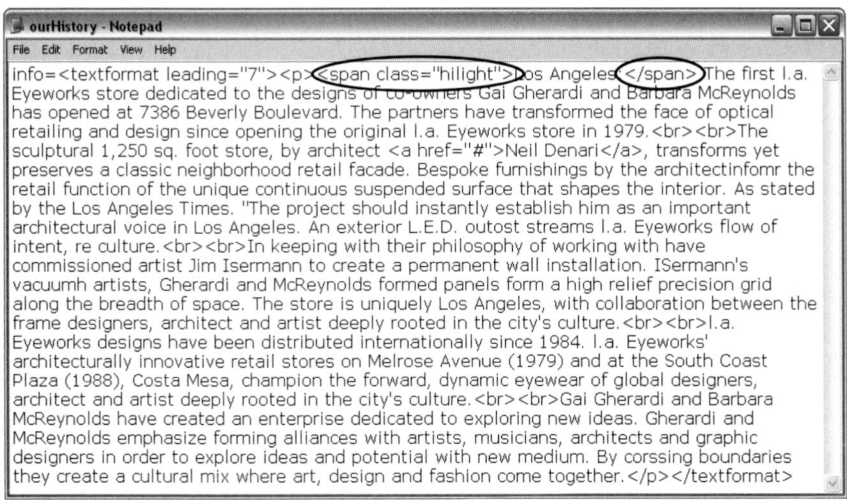

```
info=<textformat leading="7"><p><span class="hilight">Los Angeles:</span>The first l.a.
Eyeworks store dedicated to the designs of co-owners Gai Gherardi and Barbara McReynolds
has opened at 7386 Beverly Boulevard. The partners have transformed the face of optical
retailing and design since opening the original l.a. Eyeworks store in 1979.<br><br>The
sculptural 1,250 sq. foot store, by architect <a href="#">Neil Denari</a>, transforms yet
preserves a classic neighborhood retail facade. Bespoke furnishings by the architectinfomr the
retail function of the unique continuous suspended surface that shapes the interior. As stated
by the Los Angeles Times. "The project should instantly establish him as an important
architectural voice in Los Angeles. An exterior L.E.D. outost streams l.a. Eyeworks flow of
intent, re culture.<br><br>In keeping with their philosophy of working with have
commissioned artist Jim Isermann to create a permanent wall installation. ISermann's
vacuumh artists, Gherardi and McReynolds formed panels form a high relief precision grid
along the breadth of space. The store is uniquely Los Angeles, with collaboration between the
frame designers, architect and artist deeply rooted in the city's culture.<br><br>l.a.
Eyeworks designs have been distributed internationally since 1984. l.a. Eyeworks'
architecturally innovative retail stores on Melrose Avenue (1979) and at the South Coast
Plaza (1988), Costa Mesa, champion the forward, dynamic eyewear of global designers,
architect and artist deeply rooted in the city's culture.<br><br>Gai Gherardi and Barbara
McReynolds have created an enterprise dedicated to exploring new ideas. Gherardi and
McReynolds emphasize forming alliances with artists, musicians, architects and graphic
designers in order to explore ideas and potential with new medium. By corssing boundaries
they create a cultural mix where art, design and fashion come together.</p></textformat>
```

5. Click between the paragraph tag **<p>** and the words "Los Angeles:", and type the following:

```
<span class="hilight">
```

Then you need to specify where that span ends. Click *after* the words "Los Angeles:", and type the following:

```
</span>
```

6. Save the **ourHistory.txt** file by choosing **File > Save**.

*Great! Now that you've gotten a peek at what's going on "behind the scenes" in the **styles.css** file, and you've set the style tags in the **ourHistory.txt** file, you next need to write the script that dynamically loads that **styles.css** file into your **about_us.fla** movie and applies it to the `loadedInfo` text field where the dynamically loaded text (such as **ourHistory.txt**) is displayed.*

---

7. Close the **styles.css** and **ourHistory.txt** files, and bring Flash MX 2004 back to the foreground. Once you're back in Flash MX 2004, make sure the **about_us.fla** file is in the foreground. If you accidentally closed **about_us.fla**, you can easily open it again by navigating to your **Desktop > la_eyeworks > site** folder and double-clicking the **about_us.fla** file.

---

8. Select the first keyframe in the **a** layer and open the **Actions** panel (**F9**).

```
//-------------<load CSS>--------------\\

//-------------</load CSS>--------------\\

_level0.myLV.load("vars/ourHistory.txt");
```

9. In the **Actions** panel, move the very top action, **`_level0.myLV.load("vars/ourHistory.txt");`** down two lines by clicking to the left of the line and by pressing **Enter** (Windows) or **Return** (Mac) twice. Then, click the very top line in the **Actions** panel, and type the first comment:

```
//------------<load CSS>------------\\
```

After you've typed that comment, press **Enter** (Windows) or **Return** (Mac) twice to create two line breaks (and to give yourself an empty line to start writing actions), and then type the closing comment:

```
//------------</load CSS>------------\\
```

Now that the commenting is in place, you can start writing the script that loads and applies the external CSS file.

```
//-------------<load CSS>--------------\\
var cssStyles:TextField.StyleSheet = new TextField.StyleSheet ();
//-------------</load CSS>--------------\\
```

10. Click between the two comments you just added in the previous step and create a new **`TextField.StyleSheet`** object by typing the action:

```
var cssStyles:TextField.StyleSheet = new TextField.StyleSheet ();
```

*Much like you've seen with the **`MovieClipLoader`** and **`LoadVars`** objects, this action just creates a new **`TextField.StyleSheet`** object within the **cssStyles** variable and strict types the data type of the variable to **`TextField.StyleSheet`**. Before CSS styles can be loaded and applied to a text field, this line–which creates a new **`TextField.StyleSheet`** object–must be created first. Then, you can tell the **`TextField.StyleSheet`** object which CSS file you want to load.*

```
//-------------<load CSS>--------------\\
var cssStyles:TextField.StyleSheet = new TextField.StyleSheet ();
cssStyles.load("styles/styles.css");
//-------------</load CSS>--------------\\
```

11. Click at the end of the **`var cssStyles:TextField.StyleSheet = new TextField.StyleSheet ();`** line, press **Enter** (Windows) or **Return** (Mac) to create a line break, and write the action that will load the **styles.css** file by typing the following:

`cssStyles.load ("styles/styles.css");`

*Just like with the **`MovieClipLoader`** and **`LoadVars`** actions, when you're telling those objects to load a file, you first type the variable name (in this case, **`cssStyles`**) you assigned to that object and then type **`.load`** and the name/location of the file you want to load. You'll also notice that the CSS file you're directing the **`cssStyles TextField.StyleSheet`** object to load is **styles/styles.css**. You might also be wondering what the forward slash (/) is in there for. If you remember, the **styles.css** file containing the CSS style information you want to load is* not *located in the same directory as the **about_us.fla** file. Instead, it's located in a folder–within the folder where the **about_us.fla** file is–titled **styles**. If you're referencing an asset that is located in a different directory, you need to specify the directory path to the target file, as you have just done here. Next, you need to tell the **`TextField.StyleSheet`** object what to do when the **styles.css** file has been completely downloaded. This will be done* exactly *the same way it was done in the **`LoadVars`** script–which you wrote in the previous chapter–by creating an **`onLoad`** function.*

```
//-------------<load CSS>--------------\\
var cssStyles:TextField.StyleSheet = new TextField.StyleSheet ();
cssStyles.load("styles/styles.css");
cssStyles.onLoad = function (success) {
//-------------</load CSS>--------------\\
```

12. Click at the end of the **`cssStyles.load ("styles/styles.css");`** line, press **Enter** (Windows) or **Return** (Mac) to create a line break, and create the beginning of the **onLoad** function by typing the following:

`cssStyles.onLoad = function (success) {`

*Exactly like you wrote when you authored the **`LoadVars`** script in the **master.fla** file, this **`onLoad`** function will get automatically executed when the targeted file (**styles.css**, in this case) is completely downloaded. So, what should happen after the CSS file has been downloaded? There are actually two things that need to happen: 1) the CSS styles need to be applied to the **`loadedInfo`** dynamic text field, and 2) the text needs to load into the text field. As mentioned before, the CSS styles need to be applied to the text field* before *the text is loaded into the same text field. That way, the text inherits the CSS styles as it is loaded into the field. If the CSS styles are applied to the text field* after *the text is inserted into the field, the text will* not *inherit the CSS styles.*

```
//-------------<load CSS>--------------\\
var cssStyles:TextField.StyleSheet = new TextField.StyleSheet ();
cssStyles.load("styles/styles.css");
cssStyles.onLoad = function (success) {
    if (success) {
//-------------</load CSS>--------------\\
```

13. Click at the end of the **`cssStyles.onLoad = function (success) {`** line, press **Enter** (Windows) or **Return** (Mac) to create a line break, and type the following:

`if (success) {`

*At this point, you're probably saying to yourself, "Gee...this seems rather...familiar." Again, the structure of this script is nearly identical to the **LoadVars** script you wrote earlier in this chapter. You're creating this conditional **if** statement within the **onLoad** function because you want to determine* if *the **styles.css** file was loaded and parsed correctly. Within this **if** statement, you will script what you want to happen* if *the styles are loaded correctly. As with the earlier **LoadVars** script, you will also specify what you want to happen if the **styles.css** file was* not *loaded and parsed correctly.*

```
//-------------<load CSS>--------------\\
var cssStyles:TextField.StyleSheet = new TextField.StyleSheet ();
cssStyles.load("styles/styles.css");
cssStyles.onLoad = function (success) {
    if (success) {
        loadedInfo.styleSheet = cssStyles;
//-------------</load CSS>--------------\\
```

14. Click at the end of the **`if (success) {`** line, press **Enter** (Windows) or **Return** (Mac) to create a line break, and attach your CSS styles to the **`loadedInfo`** text field by typing the following:

`loadedInfo.styleSheet = cssStyles;`

*What this line essentially says is to attach a style sheet to the **loadedInfo** text field and that the style sheet to attach is the **cssStyles TextField.StyleSheet** object (the object that you loaded the **styles.css** file into). Now that the text field has CSS styles applied to it, you can safely load the text into that field.*

```
//-------------<load CSS>--------------\\
var cssStyles:TextField.StyleSheet = new TextField.StyleSheet ();
cssStyles.load("styles/styles.css");
cssStyles.onLoad = function (success) {
    if (success) {
        loadedInfo.styleSheet = cssStyles;

//-------------</load CSS>--------------\\

_level0.myLV.load("vars/ourHistory.txt");
```

15. Click at the end of the **`loadedInfo.styleSheet = cssStyles;`** line and press **Enter** (Windows) or **Return** (Mac) to create a line break. Underneath the **`TextField.StyleSheet`** object script that you're currently writing is the action–which you wrote earlier in this chapter–that loads the **ourHistory.txt** file using the **`myLV loadVars`** object located in the **master.fla** file. This is the action that you want to be executed after the CSS styles have been applied to the **`loadedInfo`** text field. So, simply select this action by dragging over it, and then drag it to the new line break you just created under the **`loadedInfo.styleSheet = cssStyles;`** line.

*Now you just need to close the **`if`** statement and then script what should happen if the **styles.css** file did not load and get parsed correctly for one reason or another. Just like the **`LoadVars`** script that you authored earlier, you're going to specify that an error message be inserted into the **`loadedInfo`** text field should an error occur.*

```
//-------------<load CSS>--------------\\
var cssStyles:TextField.StyleSheet = new TextField.StyleSheet ();
cssStyles.load("styles/styles.css");
cssStyles.onLoad = function (success) {
    if (success) {
        loadedInfo.styleSheet = cssStyles;
        _level0.myLV.load("vars/ourHistory.txt");
    } else {
//-------------</load CSS>--------------\\
```

16. Click at the end of the **`_level0.myLV.load("vars/ourHistory.txt");`** line, press **Enter** (Windows) or **Return** (Mac) to create a line break, and close the **`if`** statement and add an **`else`** by typing the following:

```
} else {
```

*Here you can specify what should happen if the **styles.css** file was not downloaded and parsed successfully. The if/else relationship essentially reads in plain English, "If such-and-such happens, do this. Otherwise (else), do this other thing."*

*For this, you're going to specify that the exact same thing happens as was specified in the **`LoadVars`** script. Essentially, an error message gets inserted into the **`loadedInfo`** text field.*

```
//-------------<load CSS>--------------\\
var cssStyles:TextField.StyleSheet = new TextField.StyleSheet ();
cssStyles.load ("styles/styles.css");
cssStyles.onLoad = function (success) {
    if (success) {
        loadedInfo.styleSheet = cssStyles;
        _level0.myLV.load("vars/ourHistory.txt");
    } else {
        loadedInfo.text = "There has been an error loading the requested information.  Please
contact the Webmaster and report your error.";
```

17. Click at the end of the **} else {** line, press **Enter** (Windows) or **Return** (Mac) to create a line break, and then write the action that will insert the error text into the **loadedInfo** text field by typing the following:

loadedInfo.text = "There has been an error loading the requested information. Please contact the Webmaster and report your error.";

*There you have it. The error message in all of its stunning glory. That also completes the major sections of the **TextField.StyleSheet** object script. All that's left to do now is to close the **else** and **onLoad** function actions by inserting a couple of closed curly braces (**}**).*

```
//-------------<load CSS>--------------\\
var cssStyles:TextField.StyleSheet = new TextField.StyleSheet ();
cssStyles.load ("styles/styles.css");
cssStyles.onLoad = function (success) {
    if (success) {
        loadedInfo.styleSheet = cssStyles;
        _level0.myLV.load("vars/ourHistory.txt");
    } else {
        loadedInfo.text = "There has been an error loading the requested information.  Please
contact the Webmaster and report your error.";
    }
}
//-------------</load CSS>--------------\\
```

18. Click at the end of the **loadedInfo.text = "There has been..";** line, press **Enter** (Windows) or **Return** (Mac) to create a line break, and close the **else** statement by typing a closed curly brace (**}**). Press **Enter** (Windows) or **Return** (Mac) again to create another line break, and then close the **onLoad** function by typing another closed curly brace (**}**).

*You've just completed the **TextField.StyleSheet** script. That's quite an accomplishment, which is clearly recognizable when you sit back and look at the script you just composed. Congratulations! But before you start clapping your hands in glee and prancing around the living room, you should save and test your work to make sure that everything is functioning as you expect it to.*

---

19. Save the **about_us.fla** by choosing **File > Save**. Then, since you've made changes to the **about_us.fla** file, you need to publish a new SWF file that incorporates those changes. You'll then preview the **about_us.swf** module through the **master.swf** file.

Note: *The reason why you constantly need to publish a SWF file from the* ***about_us.fla*** *(and from the other modules, as well, once you get to that point) whenever you make any changes to that file is because of the way the content is structured. Keep in mind that much of the necessary actions are located within the* ***master.fla*** *Timeline. Because of that, the site modules that are loaded into the* ***master.swf*** *file (about us, frames, locations, and so forth) need to be viewed* through *the* ***master.swf*** *file. Later in this book, you'll learn how to make each module* modular *so that it can easily be a fully functional, stand-alone module.*

---

20. Publish a new SWF from the **about_us.fla** file by choosing **File > Publish**. This will publish an updated **about_us.swf** file in the **site** folder (where the **about_us.fla** file is located).

---

21. Hide or minimize Flash MX 2004, navigate to your **Desktop > la_eyeworks > site** folder, and double-click the **master.swf** file to preview your work in the Macromedia Flash Player.

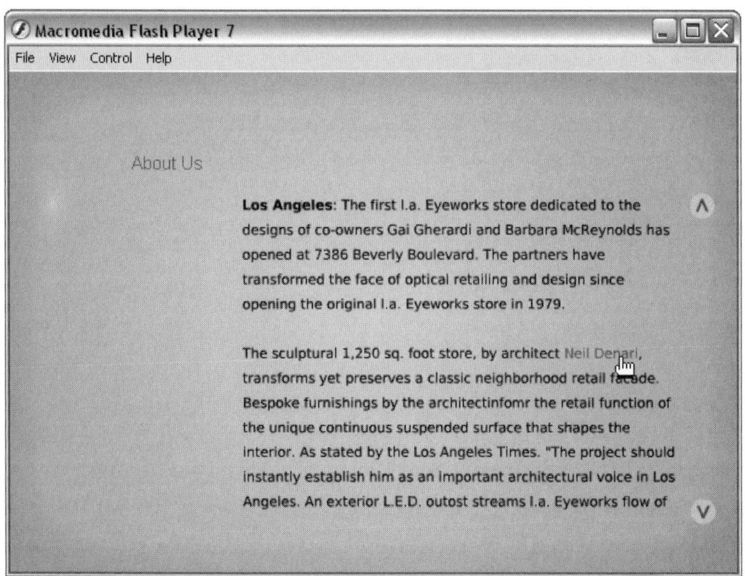

Awesome! There's the our history text, dynamically loaded and styled using a dynamically loaded style sheet! As you can see, the text "Los Angeles" is bolded thanks to the ***`hilight`*** *CSS class, and the "Neil Denari" hyperlink looks exactly like a hyperlink you normally see on HTML-based Web pages. Not only that, but if you hover your mouse over the hyperlink, it will perform the* ***a:hover*** *CSS style and display the hyperlink with no underline and a different color!*

Not only have you just styled the dynamic our history text, but you also have made those style changes by using a combination of HTML and a dynamically loaded CSS file. As I mentioned previously, a huge *advantage to this setup is now, whenever you want to modify the font style, font color, or font size, you don't even need to open Flash MX 2004 to do it! You can just open the* ***styles.css*** *file in a simple text editor and make your changes there. Next time the* ***about_us.swf*** *file is displayed, it will automatically incorporate your changes. Über cool. Give yourself a big pat on the back!*

You'd be a slack Flash MX 2004 designer/developer if you didn't make one last check. Remember that you wrote in the ***onLoad*** *error handling for the CSS file? You specified that an error message should be displayed in the* ***loadedInfo*** *text field if the* ***styles.css*** *file was* not *successfully loaded. The viewer would see this error message if there was a problem locating or loading the* ***styles.css*** *file for some reason. To test this error management, all you need to do is rename the* ***styles.css*** *file. Then, Flash MX 2004 won't be able to load the file (because it's looking for a file with the* exact *name of* ***styles.css****) and will display the error message.*

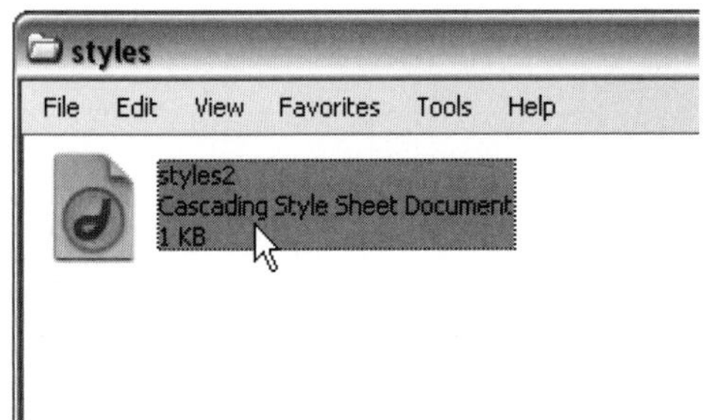

22. Navigate to your **Desktop > la_eyeworks > site > styles** folder, and change the name of the **styles.css** file to something else, like **styles2.css**.

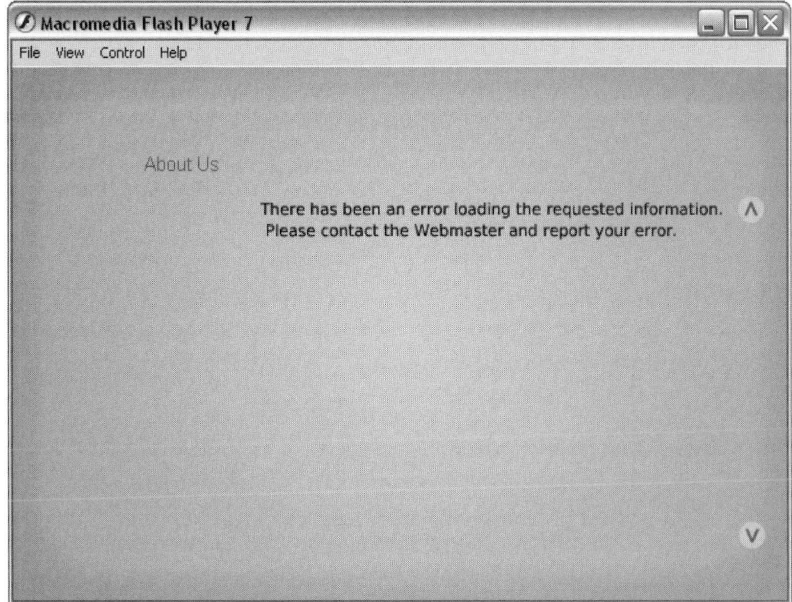

23. Navigate to your **Desktop > la_eyeworks > site** folder, and test your `TextField.StyleSheet` error management by double-clicking the **master.swf** file to play it in the Macromedia Flash Player. You should see the error message appear in place of the text! This is because, back in the `TextField.StyleSheet` script, you specified within the `onLoad` function that if the **styles.css** file did *not* load correctly to instead (else) display this error message.

Now that you've verified that the error message works properly, you need to change the ***styles2.css*** *file back to its proper name.*

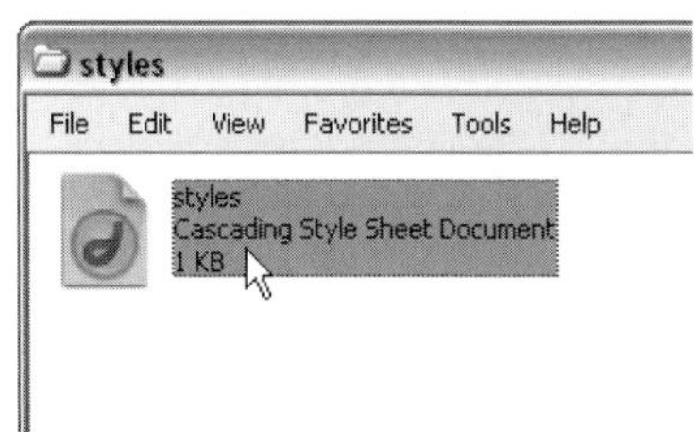

24. Close the standalone Macromedia Flash Player 7 window, and then navigate to your **Desktop > la_eyeworks > site > styles** folder and rename the **styles2.css** file to its proper name, **styles.css**. If you were to double-click the **master.swf** file again to play it, you'd notice that your text is back to "normal" and displays correctly.

The following table outlines and describes the various CSS properties used in the styles.css file that you worked with in this last exercise.

styles.css Properties Description	
CSS Property	**Description**
p	Defines the styling information of the HTML paragraph tag, **<p>**. Whatever properties you assign to this style will affect every place you've used the **<p>** tag. For example, this is useful when you want to specify the base styling of all the text in a text field. (In this case, any text within the HTML tags **<p> </p>** will be styled with the font Bitstream Vera Sans, and set at 11 px.)
a:link	Defines the styling information of any hyperlinks (hyperlinks use the HTML tag **<a>**) in the text. In this case, all hyperlinks will have the hex color #CC0000 (red) and an underline applied to it.
a:hover	Defines the styling information of any hyperlinks that the viewer's mouse is hovering over. In this case, the **a:hover** style specifies that when the viewer hovers over a hyperlink, the link will change from its a:link styling to a style where the text is colored using the hex color #3F7FBE (blue). There is no underline under the hyperlink.
.hilight	Defines the styling information of whatever you assign this class to. In this case, when you assign the **.hilight** class to an HTML tag (such as **<span>**), the displayed font will change to be set to a font weight of bold. This will, essentially, just make the text this class is applied to appear bold. Because this class will be applied selectively within the CSS redefined **<p>** tag, it will inherit any styles applied to that **<p>** tag, namely the font face, color, and size. Under Windows OS, when this class is applied to a bit of text, it will only change the font to the bold style of Bitstream Vera Sans. Under the Macintosh OS, you would need to specify, instead of **font-weight: bold**, the name of the font face, Bitstream Vera Sans Bold, to achieve the same results.
.alignRight	Defines the styling information of whatever you assign this class to. In this case, when you assign this class to an HTML tag, the text will be aligned to the right side of the text field it is displayed within.
.colorBlue	Defines the styling information of whatever you assign this class to. In this case, when you assign this class to an HTML tag, the text will be colored using the hex color #3F7FBE (blue).

You learned some great new actions and techniques in this chapter! Not only did you learn how to modify the layout of dynamically loaded text using HTML tags, but you also learned how to style that text using Cascading Style Sheets and how to dynamically load an external CSS file that contains all of your CSS style information. After you begin to use these actions and techniques in your own Flash MX 2004 projects, you'll probably start to wonder how you ever developed Web sites without them!

In the next chapter, you will learn to use the **`TextFormat`** *class to create a very, very cool interactive submenu for the About Us module. You will also learn a new feature of Flash MX 2004: nesting inline SWF files in your dynamic text! I know, I know. I'm excited, too! ;-)*

6.

TextFormat Class

la_eyeworks

Macromedia Flash MX 2004
Beyond the Basics

In this chapter, you will learn how to use the **`TextFormat`** class to create a nifty, completely ActionScript-driven, interactive submenu for the **About Us** section. Once you create the submenu, you will use it to dynamically load the text for the **our staff** subsection. In the **our staff** subsection, you will also learn a new feature of Flash MX 2004: how to add inline (in line with the text) SWF files to the scrollable **our staff** text! Keep reading–it only gets better.

I. What You Are Building

In this exercise, you will get to preview exactly *what* it is you are building *before* you start building it. That way, as you're working through the exercises in this chapter, you'll have a better idea of how some of these abstract ActionScript concepts fit together to create a functional piece of the L.A. Eyeworks Web site.

1. Open your preferred Web browser and navigate to this URL:

http://www.lynda.com/flashbtb/laeyeworks/

2. Once the L.A. Eyeworks Web site finishes loading, click the **about us** option in the navigation menu.

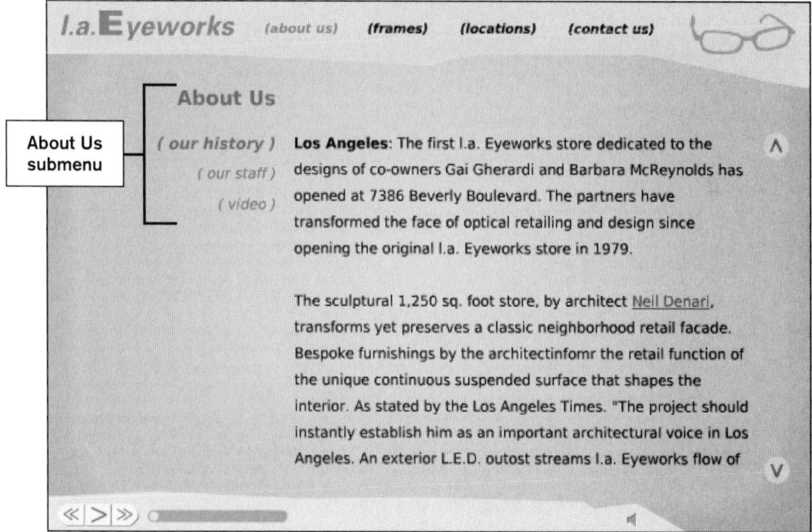

Notice how the our history text loads by default. That's the part you finished constructing in Chapter 4, "LoadVars Class." *But also notice, in the submenu, how the* ***our history*** *option is a point size bigger and bold.*

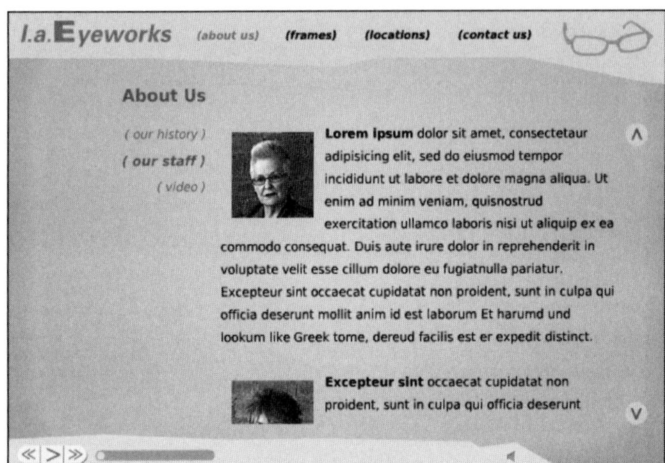

3. Click the submenu option **our staff**. When you click the **our staff** option, notice that the **our history** option reduces a point size and becomes unbolded but that the **our staff** option then becomes one point size larger and bolded. Seeing a pattern here?

Essentially, the submenu behaves in the following manner:

- *Whichever section the viewer is currently looking at, the submenu option that corresponds to that active section becomes "disabled." The text increases in size by one point, and the text becomes bolded.*
- *When the viewer clicks another submenu option, the submenu option that was disabled becomes "enabled." It reduces by one point size and is no longer bolded.*
- *Whichever section displays by default when the about us module first loads (in this case, the our history section), that submenu option automatically is disabled.*
- *When a submenu option becomes disabled, the viewer cannot interact with it. They will not see the finger cursor when they move their mouse over it, and nothing will happen when they click it.*
- *When a submenu option becomes re-enabled, the viewer can then interact with it. They will see the text rollover effect, and clicking that option will trigger the loading of the corresponding section.*

Although initially, you may have taken that little submenu for granted and had not really given it a second thought, I hope now that you'll appreciate it a little more. There's actually quite a lot of interactivity going on in that submenu, and Flash MX 2004 doesn't build it all for you. It's going to take quite a bit of ActionScript, as well as learning some new actions, to build the submenu functionality. So go grab a cup of coffee, a cushion for your chair, and get started with the construction!

---

4. Close your Web browser.

What Is the TextFormat Class?

In essence, the **TextFormat** class allows you to use ActionScript to alter the text formatting of the text within dynamic or input text fields. When you want to modify text formatting by using the **TextFormat** class, you first have to create an instance (object) of the **TextFormat** class. One way to do that is by simply typing the following:

```
var myFormat:TextFormat = new TextFormat();
```

Then, you can "attach" text formatting styles to the **myFormat** variable that you assigned the **TextFormat** object to by typing the following, for example:

```
myFormat.font = "Bitstream Vera Sans";
myFormat.color = 0xFF0000;
myFormat.bold = true;
myFormat.size = 13;
```

Then, once you've defined the styling of the **myFormat TextFormat** object, you can easily apply those styles to text in a text field by typing the following, for example:

```
this.myTextField.setTextFormat(myFormat);
```

The text in the text field immediately takes on the text styles you defined in the **TextFormat** object.

In addition to specifying the **TextFormat** class styles in the format I just outlined, you can also specify the **TextFormat** class styles in one line, as parameters of the **TextFormat** class constructor. Essentially, this allows you to cut down on the amount of code it would require to specify text styles. For example, to specify the same text styles created in the example above, you could set the same text font, size, color, and bolding by typing it in one line:

```
var myFormat:TextFormat = new TextFormat("Bitstream Vera Sans", 13, 0xFF0000, true);
```

This method takes up far fewer lines of ActionScript code than does the previous method. However, when specifying the **TextFormat** properties in this manner, the parameters need to be specified in a specific order:

```
new TextFormat(font, size, color, bold, italic, underline, url, target, align,
leftMargin, rightMargin, indent, leading);
```

When using this method, if you want to set the font, size, and bold, but leave the color (between size and bold) alone, you still would have to set the parameter to *null*. For example:

```
new TextFormat("Bitstream Vera Sans", 13, null, true);
```

So, as I'm sure you're coming to understand, the **TextFormat** class can be a fantastic and powerful way to modify the styling of the text within a text field through ActionScript. Based on the viewers' feedback (moving their mouse, clicking things, and so forth), you can specify–using ActionScript–how the text in your movies changes according to the viewers' input.

You will use the **TextFormat** class in Exercise 2 to modify the text styling of the submenu text options. A table that describes the various **TextFormat** class properties follows the exercise.

2. Adding the Submenu

In this exercise, you will build the submenu that will allow the viewer to navigate within the about us module. Eventually, there will be a total of three submenu options: our history, our staff, and video. Although you will build the interactivity for the video submenu option in the exercises in this chapter, you won't actually be creating the video section until Chapter 11, *"Building a Video Player."*

1. First, make sure that Flash MX 2004 is in the foreground and that the **about_us.fla** file is also in the foreground. If you accidentally closed the **about_us.fla** file, you can open it again by navigating to your **Desktop > la_eyeworks > site** folder and double-clicking **about_us.fla**.

The first thing you need to do is set the ***About Us*** *title text so that it is using the appropriate Bitstream Vera Sans font.*

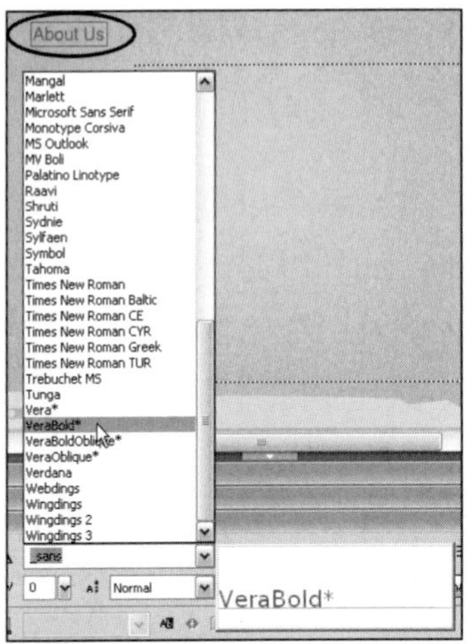

2. Single-click the **About Us** static text box on the **Stage** to select it, and in the **Properties inspector**, click the **Font** pull-down menu and choose the font **VeraBold***.

You'll also notice that there are three other fonts with asterisks (*) next to their names: Vera, VeraBoldOblique*, and VeraOblique*. The four font faces with asterisks next to their names are the shared fonts from the* ***sharedLib.fla*** *file. Whenever you have a font symbol in your library, those fonts will have asterisks next to their name in the Font pull-down menu. The names that appear in the Font pull-down menu are the names that the fonts' symbols were given when they were created in the shared library.*

Note: *Because of the way that the Windows operating system groups font styles (as was mentioned earlier), you'll need to perform one extra step to get this shared VeraBold font to display correctly.*

3. If you're running Windows, after you've selected the **VeraBold*** font from the **Font** pull-down menu, you'll also need to click the **Bold Style** button in the **Properties inspector** to have the shared font display its bold style. Macintosh users *do not* need to perform this step.

To help you get started creating the submenu options, I've provided the dynamic text fields, nested within movie clips. You may be thinking, "Text fields nested in movie clips?" The reason you'll be using dynamic text fields nested within movie clips is because, as you saw in the submenu tour at the beginning of this exercise, the submenu options will visually change depending on the currently loaded section. To accomplish that, you're going to be using ActionScript to dynamically modify the appearance of the text depending on which section is active. Because you can't control static text, or even text inside of a button symbol with ActionScript in this manner, you'll instead be using dynamic text fields nested within movie clips.

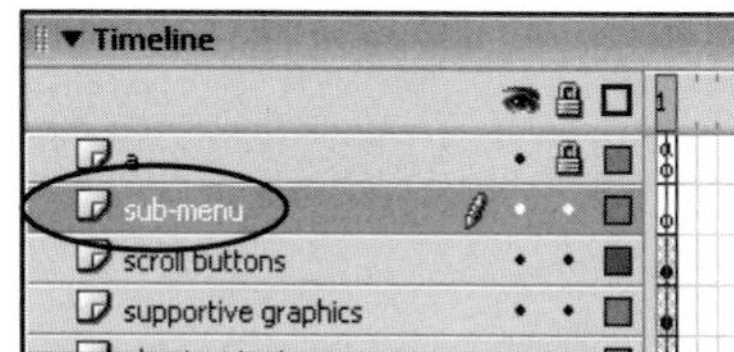

4. Select the layer underneath the **a** layer, and create a new layer. Rename this new layer **sub-menu**.

5. Open the **Library** window (**Ctrl+L** [Windows] or **Cmd+L** [Mac]).

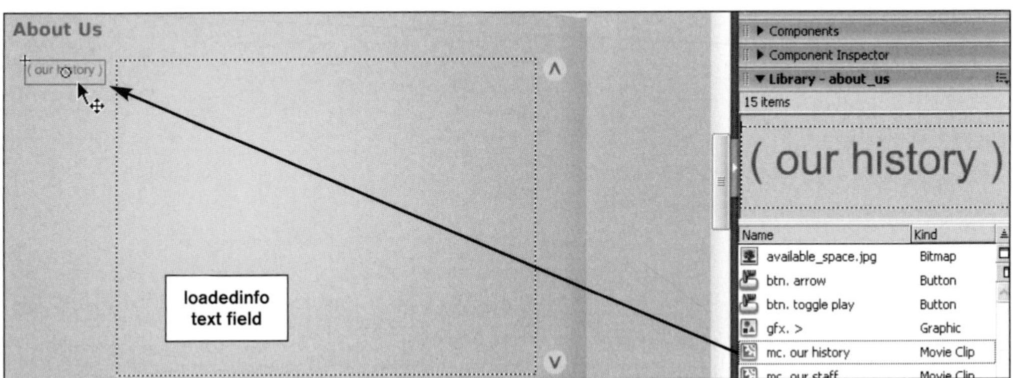

6. With the **sub-menu** layer selected, drag the symbol **mc. our history** from the **Library** window and position it aligned to the top-left side of the **`loadedInfo`** text field.

Next, you should set up the our history submenu option so it is set at its "default" (that is, non-highlighted) style.

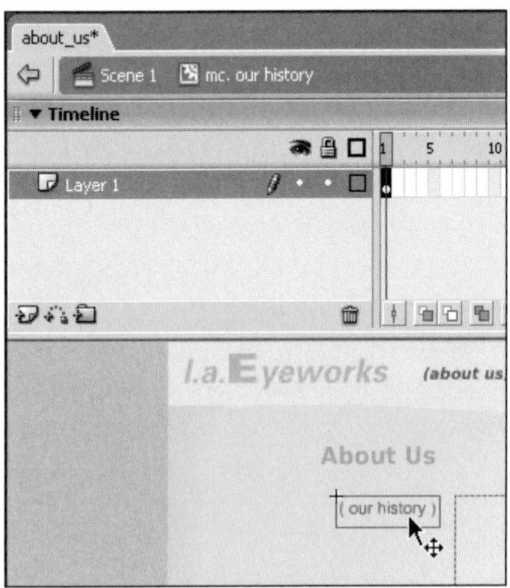

7. Open the **our history** movie clip by double-clicking its instance on the **Stage**. Once you're inside the **mc. our history** movie clip, select the text field on the **Stage** by clicking it once.

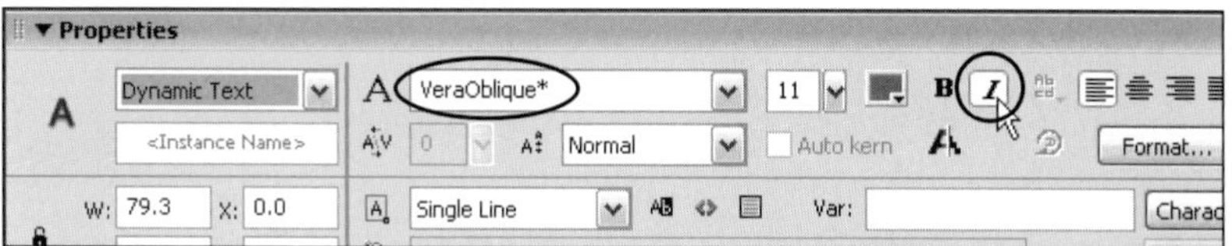

8. From the **Font** pull-down menu in the **Properties inspector**, choose **VeraOblique***. If you're running Windows, you'll also need to click the **Italic Style** button. The other options were already set for you when the text field was created, but if you accidentally changed the settings, you'll want to make sure it's a **Dynamic Text** field, the **Font Size** is **11**, and the **Color** is the hex value **#3F7FBE** (**Blue**). Although you will be specifying these same text formatting styles later using ActionScript, you're still setting these options here because it gives you a good idea of what the text will look like when it will be formatted using the `TextFormat` object. If you didn't specify these settings and just left the text at its default settings (to be styled by the `TextFormat` object upon playback), it would be difficult to approximate the final look/feel, positioning, and alignment as you position the text in this layout.

Note:** When you change the font face from **_sans** to **VeraOblique, you will notice the text resize slightly and become larger. It might even appear to overlap the `loadedInfo` dynamic text field you can see on Scene 1. Later in this exercise you will realign the text, so don't worry about repositioning it just yet.*

Because you'll be using ActionScript to modify many aspects of this text field (font face, font size, alignment, and so forth), you also must *give this dynamic text field an instance name. Without an instance name, you would not be able to target this text field with ActionScript, and therefore would not be able to modify it.*

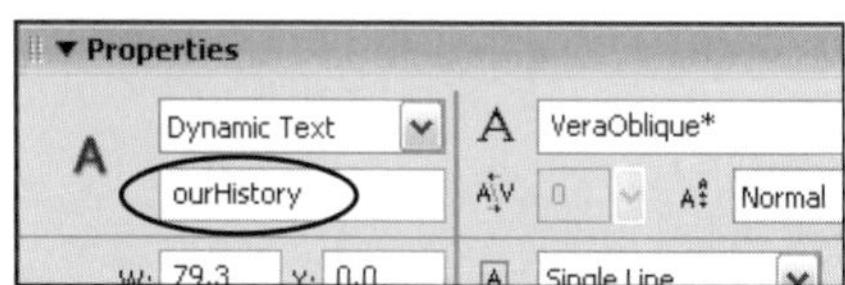

9. In the **Properties inspector**, type **ourHistory** in the **Instance Name** field. Now, when you want to target this text field with ActionScript, you can use the name **ourHistory**.

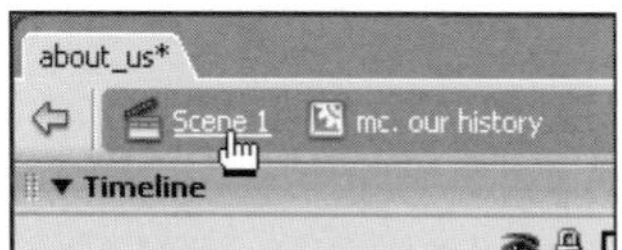

10. Return to Scene 1 by clicking its tab at the top left of the **Timeline**.

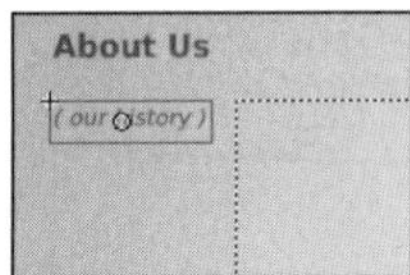

11. Since you changed the font face and style, once you're back in Scene 1 you might need to readjust the alignment of the **our history** movie clip. You can do this easily and precisely using the arrow keys on the keyboard to nudge the **our history** movie clip into place.

Since you'll be targeting the ***ourHistory*** *text field inside of the* ***mc. our history*** *movie clip, you need to give the instance of this movie clip an instance name as well. If you don't give this movie clip instance a name, you can't access the text field inside of it.*

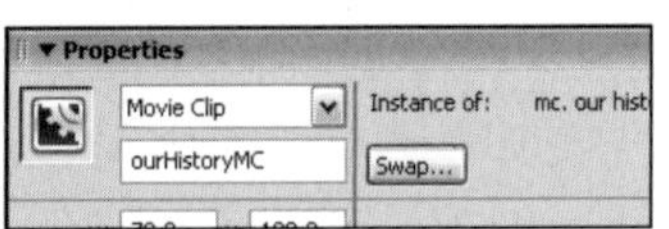

12. With the instance of the **mc. our history** movie clip still selected, give this movie clip instance a name by typing **ourHistoryMC** in the **Instance Name** field of the **Properties inspector**. Now, when you want to target the **ourHistory** text field inside this movie clip with ActionScript, you can simply refer to it by typing **ourHistoryMC.ourHistory**.

Now you just need to repeat that process for the remaining two submenu options: ***our staff*** *and* ***video***.

13. Repeat Steps 6 through 12 to integrate the movie clips **mc. our staff** and **mc. video** into the submenu. When repeating those steps, here's some specific information you'll need. The **our staff** dynamic text field should have an instance name of (yup, you guessed it) **ourStaff**, and the **mc. our staff** movie clip instance that contains the **ourStaff** text field should be given an instance name of **ourStaffMC**. The **video** dynamic text field should have an instance name of **ourVideo**, and the **mc. video** movie clip instance that contains the **ourVideo** text field should be given an instance name of **ourVideoMC**.

When you're finished, the three submenu options should be all nicely aligned to their right sides and spaced evenly, slightly apart. Ahh...there's something to be said for a nicely ordered submenu. ;-)

---

14. Once you've completed setting up the submenu options, save your changes to the **about_us.fla** file by choosing **File > Save**.

Next, you need to set up the ActionScript objects that will change the text styles when the viewer interacts with the submenu options.

---

15. Select the first keyframe in the **a** layer and open the **Actions** panel (**F9**).

```
//-------------</scroll buttons>--------------\\

// create TextFormat Objects that define the states of the sub-menu options
```

16. Click after the closing scroll buttons comment line, `//---------------</scroll buttons-----------------\\`, press **Enter** (Windows) or **Return** (Mac) twice to create a couple line breaks, and type the following comment all on one line:

```
// create TextFormat Objects that define the states of the sub-menu options
```

*Underneath this comment is where you will build the **TextFormat** ActionScript objects that will handle the changing of the text styles. These objects will get executed when the viewer interacts with the submenu options (for example, when the viewer moves his or her mouse over the our history option, the **TextFormat** object that defines the **rollOver** appearance will be executed). Because you will be specifying a font face to use, this process will differ depending on whether you're using Windows or Macintosh operating systems. This goes back to what was mentioned previously about how Windows groups font styles together, whereas the Macintosh does not. The steps that differ will be clearly marked.*

*First, you will create the **TextFormat** object that will handle how the submenu text options will appear when they're "disabled." A submenu option will become disabled under one of these two circumstances:*

- *When a subsection (our history, our staff, and so forth) is loaded, the corresponding sub-menu option will appear "disabled."*
- *When the viewer moves his or her mouse over an active (that is, nondisabled) submenu option, the option will display the disabled style. Moving his or her mouse off of the submenu option will cause the text to revert back to the "enabled" style.*

```
// create TextFormat Objects that define the states of the sub-menu options
var btnDisable:TextFormat = new TextFormat();
```

17. Click after the comment that you typed in Step 16, press **Enter** (Windows) or **Return** (Mac) to create a line break, and begin to create the **btnDisable TextFormat** object by typing the following:

```
var btnDisable:TextFormat = new TextFormat();
```

*This line creates a new **TextFormat** object and assigns it to the variable **btnDisable**. Now, you just need to specify how the submenu text options will appear when they meet one of the two circumstances outlined previously. To refresh your memory, the submenu text options appear as Bitstream Vera Sans Oblique at 11 pt by default. When a submenu text option appears disabled when its corresponding subsection is loaded, or when the viewer rolls his or her mouse over it, you want the style to change to Bitstream Vera Sans* Bold *Oblique at 12 pt. Essentially, the font changes to* bold *oblique (instead of just oblique) and increases one point size.*

```
// create TextFormat Objects that define the states of the sub-menu options
var btnDisable:TextFormat = new TextFormat("Bitstream Vera Sans", 12, null, true, true);
```

(Windows)

---

18. If you're running Windows, click between the parentheses after **TextFormat** and type the following:

"Bitstream Vera Sans", 12, null, true, true

As detailed in the "What is the TextFormat class?" section, this specifies that the font be set to Bitstream Vera Sans, the font size be set to 12 pt, to not modify the color (null), to enable bold, and to enable italic.

```
// create TextFormat Objects that define the states of the sub-menu options
var btnDisable:TextFormat = new TextFormat("Bitstream Vera Sans Bold Oblique", 12);
```

(Macintosh)

---

19. If you're running Macintosh, click between the parentheses after **TextFormat** and type the following:

"Bitstream Vera Sans Bold Oblique", 12

*The reason why these steps differ depending on the platform goes back to Windows' grouping of font styles. Because the Windows OS groups the Bitstream Vera Sans font styles, you cannot refer–with ActionScript–to the font (as you have on the Macintosh in this case) Bitstream Vera Sans Bold Oblique. All the Windows OS "sees" is "Bitstream Vera Sans." So on the Windows OS, if you want the Bitstream Vera Sans font face to appear both bold and italic, you need to do that by adding additional bold and italic parameters onto the **TextFormat** object. The Macintosh does* not *group the font styles, so Macintosh users can refer directly to the font face Bitstream Vera Sans Bold Oblique.*

Now that you've specified what the submenu text options will look like when they're disabled (or rolled over), you need to specify what the submenu text options will look like when they're enabled (or rolled off).

```
// create TextFormat Objects that define the states of the sub-menu options
var btnDisable:TextFormat = new TextFormat("Bitstream Vera Sans", 12, null, true, true);
var btnEnable:TextFormat = new TextFormat();
```

20. Click after the **var btnDisable:TextFormat = new TextFormat**... line that you created in Steps 17-19, press **Enter** (Windows) or **Return** (Mac) to create a line break, and begin to create the **btnEnable TextFormat** object by typing the following:

var btnEnable:TextFormat = new TextFormat();

```
// create TextFormat Objects that define the states of the sub-menu options
var btnDisable:TextFormat = new TextFormat("Bitstream Vera Sans", 12, null, true, true);
var btnEnable:TextFormat = new TextFormat("Bitstream Vera Sans", 11, null, false, true);
```

(Windows)

---

21. If you're running Windows, click between the **`TextFormat`** parentheses and type the following:

`"Bitstream Vera Sans", 11, null, false, true`

*This sets the **`btnEnable TextFormat`** style to (respectively) the Bitstream Vera Sans font, 11 pt, no color change, no bold, and italic.*

```
// create TextFormat Objects that define the states of the sub-menu options
var btnDisable:TextFormat = new TextFormat("Bitstream Vera Sans Bold Oblique", 12);
var btnEnable:TextFormat = new TextFormat("Bitstream Vera Sans Oblique", 11);
```

(Macintosh)

---

22. If you're running Macintosh, click between the **`TextFormat`** parentheses and type the following:

`"Bitstream Vera Sans Oblique", 11`

*This, of course, sets the **`btnEnable TextFormat`** style to the Bitstream Vera Sans Oblique font at 11 pt.*

*That's it! There you have your two **`TextFormat`** objects: **`btnDisable`** and **`btnEnable`**. These two **`TextFormat`** objects will be used as the user interacts with the submenu options and when content is loaded into the about us module. Next, you can test these **`TextFormat`** objects that you just created by instructing the submenu option–which corresponds to the section that automatically loads (our history)–to disable itself. Because the **our history** subsection gets automatically loaded when the about us module loads, it stands to reason that the our history submenu button should thereby be disabled. This also acts as a visual identifier to viewers to reinforce which subsection they're currently viewing.*

```
// create TextFormat Objects that define the states of the sub-menu options
var btnDisable:TextFormat = new TextFormat("Bitstream Vera Sans", 12, null, true, true);
var btnEnable:TextFormat = new TextFormat("Bitstream Vera Sans", 11, null, false, true);

// disable the sub-menu option that corresponds to the currently-loaded section
```

23. Click after the **`var btnEnable:TextFormat = new TextFormat`**... line, press **Enter** (Windows) or **Return** (Mac) twice to create a couple line breaks, and type the following comment:

`// disable the sub-menu option that corresponds to the currently-loaded section`

---

24. Click after the comment line, and press **Enter** (Windows) or **Return** (Mac) to create a line break.

When applying a ***TextFormat*** *object to alter the text style of some text, you need to make sure you apply it to the text field itself. This is why, when you dragged the submenu options onto the Stage, you gave instance names to the dynamic text fields and the movie clip instances that contained them. Fortunately, you don't have to remember the instance names you assigned the movie clips and text fields.*

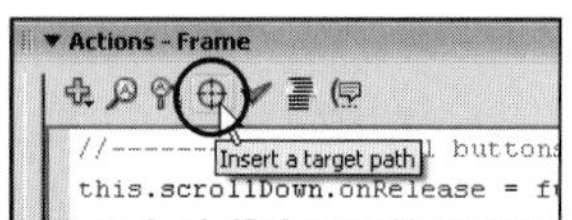

25. Click the **Insert a target path** button at the top of the **Actions** panel.

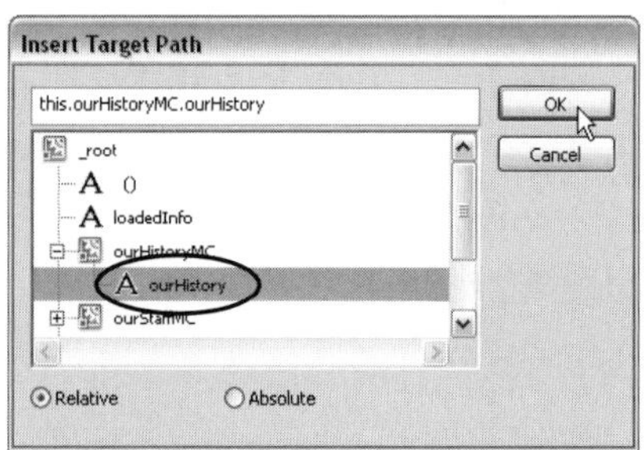

26. This will open the **Insert Target Path** dialog box. Open the **ourHistoryMC** movie clip by clicking the plus sign to its left (on the Macintosh, it's an arrow). Here you'll see the text field you gave an instance name to, **ourHistory**. Click once on **ourHistory** to select it. When you do, you'll see the target path appear at the top of the dialog box. Click **OK** to have that path inserted in the **Actions** panel.

```
// create TextFormat Objects that define the states of the sub-menu options
var btnDisable:TextFormat = new TextFormat("Bitstream Vera Sans", 12, null, true, true);
var btnEnable:TextFormat = new TextFormat("Bitstream Vera Sans", 11, null, false, true);

// disable the sub-menu option that corresponds to the currently-loaded section
this.ourHistoryMC.ourHistory.setTextFormat(btnDisable);
```

27. Click after the target path that was inserted into the **Actions** panel and apply the **`btnDisable`** **`TextFormat`** to the **`ourHistory`** text field by typing the following:

`.setTextFormat(btnDisable);`

Don't forget to add the dot (.) between ***ourHistory*** *and* ***setTextFormat****. In essence, this line says "Apply the* ***btnDisable TextFormat*** *to the* ***ourHistory*** *text field that's nested inside the* ***ourHistoryMC*** *movie clip." To apply a* ***TextFormat*** *object to a text field, you use the* ***setTextFormat*** *action (followed by, in parentheses, the name of the* ***TextFormat*** *object that you want to apply), as you saw here.*

Great! So in the past few steps, you've created two **`TextFormat`** *objects that set the style formatting of the submenu text options, and you've applied one of those objects (***`btnDisable`***) to the* **`ourHistory`** *text field. It's time to test your movie and make sure everything works as expected! (I can hear your palms sweating from here.) ;-)*

---

28. Save the changes you've made to the **about_us.fla** file by choosing **File > Save**. Then, publish an updated SWF file from this FLA by choosing **File > Publish**.

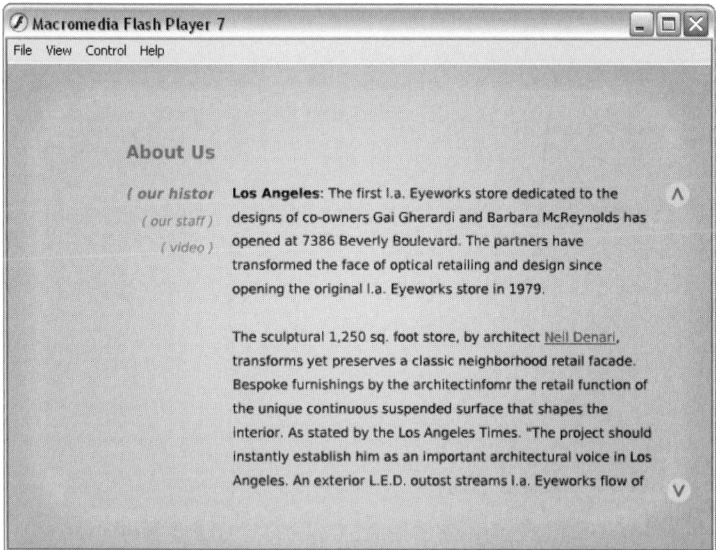

29. Hide or minimize Flash MX 2004, navigate to your **Desktop > la_eyeworks > site** folder, and double-click the **master.swf** file to preview your work in the stand-alone Macromedia Flash Player 7.

If everything works as expected, you should see something that looks exactly *like the screen shot above. You'll see the* **(our history)** *text, nicely bolded and 1 point size bigger than its submenu option cousins (thanks to the* **`btnDisable TextFormat`** *object), but if you look closely, the* **(our history)** *text is cut off! It simply says "(our histor". What has happened here is that, when the* **`btnDisable TextFormat`** *object was applied to the text field, it made the text bold and 1 point size bigger. When those two things happened, the text exceeded the size of the text field. Because the text field itself remains at the same size (it does not automatically increase in size along with the text), the text within the field appears cropped off. Not only that, but also take note* how *the text resized in the field. It resized to the right. This same thing will happen, by the way, when you add the* **`rollOver`** *ActionScript to the submenu options. Unless you tell it otherwise, when the viewer rolls over each submenu text option, the text will be styled with the* **`btnDisable TextFormat`** *object and will increase in size, thereby cropping the text just as you currently see the "(our histor" text cropped.*

To prevent this from happening, you need to add an action that tells each submenu text field to auto-size itself. If you left it at that, the text field would expand to fit the text within it (even when the **btnDisable TextFormat** *object changes the text formatting), but it would expand to the right. That wouldn't be a good thing because it would expand right into the* **loadedInfo** *text! So not only do you need to use ActionScript to tell the submenu text fields to auto-size, but you also need to tell them to auto-size to the* left.

TextFormat Class Properties

Property	Description
TextFormat.align	Allows you to specify the alignment of a paragraph. Your options are "left", "center", and "right" for left-aligned, center-aligned, and right-aligned, respectively.
TextFormat.blockIndent	Allows you to set the indentation, in points, of all the text.
TextFormat.bold	This is a Boolean value (true or false) to indicate whether you want the text to be bold (true) or not (false).
TextFormat.bullet	This is a Boolean value (true or false) to indicate whether the text is a bulleted list (true) or not (false). If **TextFormat.bullet** is set to true, the text is indented, and a bullet (•) is displayed to the left of the first line in each paragraph.
TextFormat.color	Allows you to specify the color of the text. Keep in mind that although this color value is specified as a hex value (#000000 for black, #FFFFFF for white, and so forth), it's preceded with the text "0x". So, for example, if you were using the **TextFormat** color property to set the text color to black, you would write **TextFormat.color = 0x000000;**.
TextFormat.font	Allows you to specify the font face of text. For example, if you were using the **TextFormat** font property to set the text's font face, you would write **TextFormat.font = "Bitstream Vera Sans";**. Because the font name is a string, you need to make sure to enclose the font name in quotes.
TextFormat.indent	Similar to **TextFormat.blockIndent**, but **TextFormat.indent** allows you to set the indentation, in points, of the first character in each paragraph. **blockIndent**, on the other hand, sets the indentation of *all* of the text.

continues on next page

TextFormat Class Properties *continued*	
Property	**Description**
TextFormat.italic	This is a Boolean value (true or false) to indicate whether you want the text to be italic (true) or not (false).
TextFormat.leading	Allows you to specify the leading (the space between each line of text), in points.
TextFormat.leftMargin	Allows you to specify the size of the left margin (the distance between the left edge of the text field and the text itself) of text, in points.
TextFormat.rightMargin	Allows you to specify the size of the right margin (the distance between the right edge of the text field and the text itself) of text, in points.
TextFormat.size	Allows you to specify the size of the text in points.
TextFormat.tabStops	Allows you to specify, in points, custom tab stops. Tab stops are, for example, where the text insertion point jumps to when you're typing inside an input text field and you press the Tab key.
TextFormat.target	Allows you to specify the browser window that will be targeted when the viewer clicks some text that has been assigned a URL. (See farther down in this table for the **`TextFormat.url`** description). If you're familiar with HTML programming, this is the same as the target property that you can assign to an anchor tag, **`<a href=http://www.myWebSite.com target="_blank">`**, for example. If you do not specify a **`TextFormat.target`** property, the default is **`_self`**, which means that when the viewer clicks a text link with a URL assigned to it, it will open that URL in the same browser window.
TextFormat.underline	This is a Boolean value (true or false) to indicate whether you want the text to be underlined (true) or not (false).
TextFormat.url	Allows you to specify a URL that the text will link to. Because the URL is a string, you need to make sure you enclose the URL in quotes.

3. Auto-Sizing a Text Field

In this exercise, you will create some ActionScript that will allow the submenu text fields to auto-size. This will allow those text fields to automatically expand and contract as the text within those fields is modified by the **TextFormat** class. This will also prevent the submenu text options from getting cropped–as you saw in the last exercise–when an option becomes "disabled."

1. Close the Macromedia Flash Player 7 window that you were playing the **master.swf** file within. Bring Flash MX 2004 back into the foreground, and make sure that **about_us.fla** is still the currently active movie.

2. Select the first keyframe in the **a** layer, and open the **Actions** panel (**F9**).

```
// set the alignment of the sub-menu options to autoSize right

// create TextFormat Objects that define the states of the sub-menu options
var btnDisable:TextFormat = new TextFormat("Bitstream Vera Sans", 12, null, true, true);
var btnEnable:TextFormat = new TextFormat("Bitstream Vera Sans", 11, null, false, true);

// disable the sub-menu option that corresponds to the currently-loaded section
this.ourHistoryMC.ourHistory.setTextFormat(btnDisable);
```

3. Click to the *left* of the **// create TextFormat Objects that define the states of the sub-menu options** comment line, press **Enter** (Windows) or **Return** (Mac) twice to create several line breaks (which will also move the comment and everything else underneath it down two lines), and then move your cursor up two lines. Then, create a new comment by typing the following:

```
// set the alignment of the sub-menu options to autoSize right
```

4. Click to the right of the comment you created in the previous step, and press **Enter** (Windows) or **Return** (Mac) to create a line break.

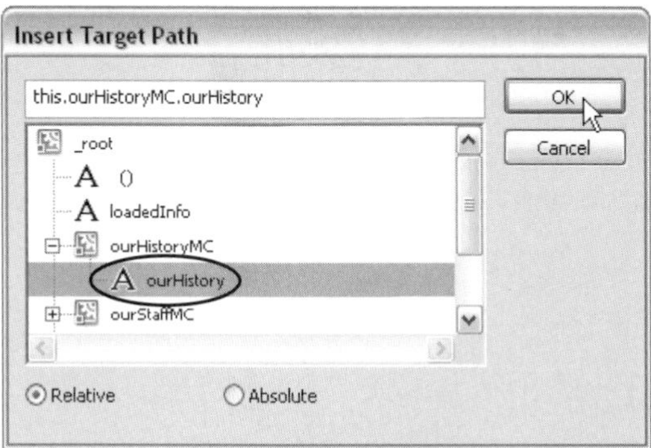

5. Click the **Insert a target path** button at the top of the **Actions** panel, and in the **Insert Target Path** dialog box, expand the **ourHistoryMC** movie clip and select **ourHistory**. When you click **ourHistory**, you'll see the path inserted at the top of the dialog box. Click **OK**.

*This will insert the path to the **ourHistory** text field in the Actions panel.*

```
// set the alignment of the sub-menu options to autoSize right
this.ourHistoryMC.ourHistory.autoSize = "right";
```

6. After **`this.ourHistoryMC.ourHistory`**, type the following:

`.autoSize = "right";`

*Don't forget the dot (.) between **ourHistory** and **autoSize**. Essentially, this action just says, "Allow the **`ourHistory`** text field to expand to fit whatever's inside of it (**`autoSize`**) but have it size from the right (so that content spreads out to the left)."*

*Now you just need to repeat those steps to set **`autoSize = "right"`** for the remaining two submenu text fields, **`ourStaff`** and **`ourVideo`**.*

```
// set the alignment of the sub-menu options to autoSize right
this.ourHistoryMC.ourHistory.autoSize = "right";
this.ourStaffMC.ourStaff.autoSize = "right";
this.ourVideoMC.ourVideo.autoSize = "right";
```

7. Repeat Steps 5 and 6 to set **`autoSize = "right"`** for the **`ourStaff`** and **`ourVideo`** text fields. Once finished, your actions should look exactly like the ones in the screen shot above.

*Fantabuloso! You've just told each text field in the submenu options to resize itself (anchored at the right so they resize out to the left) to fit whatever text is in its field. You can easily test this by publishing a new SWF from **about_us.fla**, opening **master.swf**, and observing how the our history submenu options appear.*

8. Save the changes you've made to the **about_us.fla** file by choosing **File > Save**. Then, publish an updated SWF file by choosing **File > Publish**.

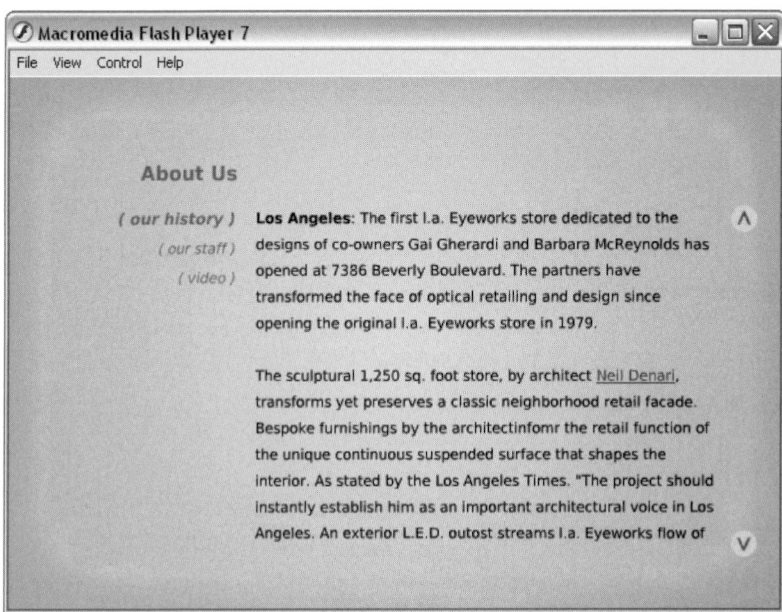

9. Once you've published a new SWF from the **about_us.fla**, hide or minimize Flash MX 2004, navigate to your **Desktop > la_eyeworks > site** folder, and double-click **master.swf** to open it in Macromedia Flash Player 7.

You'll now notice that the submenu option (our history) is no longer cropped! Thanks to the **`autoSize = "right"`** *action, the* **`ourHistory`**, **`ourStaff`**, *and* **`ourVideo`** *text fields will now automatically resize to make room for whatever text is displayed within their fields. Not only that, but the fields will be anchored on the* right *and will expand (or contract) out (or in) to the left if need be. Sweet!*

Creating the Roll Over/Roll Out States of the Submenu Options

In this exercise, you're going to create the ActionScript that will control the Roll Over/Roll Out states of the submenu options. As you saw in Chapter 4, "*LoadVars Class*"–when you added the functionality to the buttons that allows the viewer to scroll the **loadedInfo** text up and down–you will *not* add ActionScript directly to the submenu options themselves. Instead, in the spirit of keeping your scripts centralized, you will add the submenu option ActionScript to a *keyframe* in the **about_us.fla** *Timeline*.

1. Close the stand-alone Macromedia Flash Player 7 window that you were viewing the **master.swf** file with, bring Flash MX 2004 back to the foreground, and make sure **about_us.fla** is the currently active project.

---

2. Select the first keyframe in the **a** layer, and open the **Actions** panel (**F9**).

```
// disable the sub-menu option that corresponds to the currently-loaded section
this.ourHistoryMC.ourHistory.setTextFormat(btnDisable);

//-------------<our history option>--------------\\
```

3. Click at the end of the very bottom action in the Actions panel, **this.ourHistoryMC.ourHistory.setTextFormat(btnDisable);**. Press **Enter** (Windows) or **Return** (Mac) twice to create a couple of line breaks, and then type out the opening comment for the actions that will govern the behavior of the **our history** submenu option:

//---------------<our history option>----------------

```
//-------------<our history option>--------------\\

//-------------</our history option>--------------\\
```

4. Select the comment line you just created and copy it. Then, click after the comment line, press **Enter** (Windows) or **Return** (Mac) twice to create a couple of line breaks (to give yourself a little room between the comments to write some actions), and paste the commented line you just copied. Then, close the comment by typing a forward slash (/) before **our history**.

```
//-------------<our history option>--------------\\
this.ourHistoryMC.onRollOver = function () {
//-------------</our history option>--------------\\
```

5. Click between the two **our history** comment lines you just created and write the **rollOver** function for the our history submenu option by typing the following:

`this.ourHistoryMC.onRollOver = function () {`

This line essentially says, "When the viewer rolls his or her mouse over the ourHistoryMC movie clip that is on this *Timeline (the same Timeline this script is being authored on), perform this function..."*

*Now you just need to define what should happen when the viewer rolls his or her mouse over one of the submenu options. Ignore the fact, for now, that you've already told the our history submenu option to be "disabled" when the about us module first loads (to correspond with the fact that the our history text also loads automatically when the about us module first loads). If the viewer clicks another submenu option, the our history option will become re-enabled, and the viewer will then be able to interact with it. So what should happen when the viewer moves his or her mouse over the our history option? All that should happen is that **TextFormat btnDisable**—which you created earlier—should be applied to the **ourHistory** text field. That way, when the viewer moves his or her mouse over the our history option, the our history text will become bolded and one point size bigger.*

Note: *When you're adding ActionScript to the Timeline (as you are now) that defines what happens when certain mouse events (**onRollOver**, **onRollOut**, **onRelease**, and so forth) occur, the actions you add within a function (like the one you just created) can be thought of as being within the Timeline you just targeted if the action is preceded by the keyword **this**. In other words, in the function you just wrote, you targeted the ourHistoryMC movie clip. Any actions you place within this function and precede with **this.** can be thought of as being within the ourHistoryMC movie clip Timeline. If you leave off the **this.** keyword, the action will address the root Timeline. So when you're writing actions within a function, such as the one you just wrote, you need to be aware of how you're writing paths to variables, objects, named symbols, and the like.*

```
//-------------<our history option>--------------\\
this.ourHistoryMC.onRollOver = function () {
    this.ourHistory.setTextFormat(btnDisable);
//-------------</our history option>--------------\\
```

6. Click after the **`this.ourHistoryMC.onRollOver = function () {`** line you wrote in the last step, press **Enter** (Windows) or **Return** (Mac) once to create a line break, and instruct the **`ourHistory`** text field to set its **`TextFormat`** (which you created earlier) to **`btnDisable`** by typing the following:

`this.ourHistory.setTextFormat(btnDisable);`

You might be wondering why you didn't have to specify the full path *to the* ***ourHistory*** *text field. In other words, why didn't you write* ***this.ourHistoryMC.ourHistory.setTextFormat(btnDisable);****? Don't you have to tell Flash MX 2004 that the* ***ourHistory*** *text field is in the ourHistoryMC movie clip? This goes back to what was mentioned a few paragraphs ago. When adding actions within a mouse event function (like the one you just wrote), the action(s) within that function can be thought of as being* inside *the target of that function. Although that description may have just seemed like gibberish, it essentially breaks down like this. The line where you define the mouse event function (which you wrote in Step 5) targets the ourHistoryMC movie clip. This means that the actions placed within this function can be thought of as existing* inside *the ourHistoryMC movie clip's Timeline. So if you want to refer to something inside of that movie clip Timeline (such as, in this case, the* ***ourHistory*** *text field), you can just refer to it directly as you wrote in Step 6.*

```
//-------------<our history option>--------------\\
this.ourHistoryMC.onRollOver = function () {
    this.ourHistory.setTextFormat(btnDisable);
}
//-------------</our history option>--------------\\
```

7. Close this function by clicking after the **`this.ourHistory.setTextFormat(btnDisable);`** line you wrote in the last step, pressing **Enter** (Windows) or **Return** (Mac) once to create a line break, and typing a closed bracket (**}**).

Splentabulous! (Yes, I'm aware that's not a real word. But with so much "stiff" ActionScript going on, sometimes it feels good to just let loose with made-up words now and then.) Similar to the ***onRelease*** *functions you earlier added to the* ***loadedInfo*** *scrolling text buttons, this function governs what happens when the viewer rolls his or her mouse over the* ***our history*** *submenu option. Now, of course, you should specify what happens when the viewer rolls his or her mouse* off *(****onRollOut****) of the our history option. Luckily, from an ActionScript point of view, the* ***onRollOut*** *script will be very similar. This means that you can just copy the* ***onRollOver*** *script you just wrote, paste the copy below it, and easily change a few simple items.*

```
//-------------<our history option>--------------\\
this.ourHistoryMC.onRollOver = function () {
    this.ourHistory.setTextFormat(btnDisable);
}

//-------------</our history option>--------------\\
```

8. Click after the closing function bracket you created in the last step, and press **Enter** (Windows) or **Return** (Mac) to create a line break.

```
//-------------<our history option>--------------\\
this.ourHistoryMC.onRollOver = function () {
    this.ourHistory.setTextFormat(btnDisable);
}
this.ourHistoryMC.onRollOver = function () {
    this.ourHistory.setTextFormat(btnDisable);
}
//-------------</our history option>--------------\\
```

9. Select the three lines of ActionScript that comprise the **`this.ourHistoryMC.onRollOver`** function by dragging from the top line down to the closing bracket. Once those three lines are selected, hold down the **Ctrl** key (Windows) or **Option** key (Mac), and drag that selected script down to the line break you created in the previous step. This copies the entire **`onRollOver`** script, and now you can easily make a few minor adjustments to it to create an **`onRollOut`** function. Easy!

```
//-------------<our history option>--------------\\
this.ourHistoryMC.onRollOver = function () {
    this.ourHistory.setTextFormat(btnDisable);
}
this.ourHistoryMC.onRollOut = function () {
    this.ourHistory.setTextFormat(btnEnable);
}
//-------------</our history option>--------------\\
```

10. In the copied function, change **`onRollOver`** to **`onRollOut`**, and change **`btnDisable`** to **`btnEnable`** (the name of the **`TextFormat`** object you created earlier). That's it! This new function basically reads, "When the viewer rolls his or her mouse off of the **our history** option, change the text format of the **`ourHistory`** text field to the **`btnEnable TextFormat`** object (Bitstream Vera Sans Oblique font face at 11 pt)."

You can't test your work just yet because, by default, the our history submenu option is already disabled. But the remaining two submenu options also need to have these same (relatively) ***`onRollOver`*** *and* ***`onRollOut`*** *functions assigned to them. Just like you did in Steps 9 and 10, you can select* both *of these functions you just created, copy them, and modify a few items to make them work correctly for each of the two remaining submenu options.*

```
//-------------<our history option>--------------\\
this.ourHistoryMC.onRollOver = function () {
    this.ourHistory.setTextFormat(btnDisable);
}
this.ourHistoryMC.onRollOut = function () {
    this.ourHistory.setTextFormat(btnEnable);
}
//-------------</our history option>--------------\\
```

11. Click after the closing **`</our history option>`** comment line, and press **Enter** (Windows) or **Return** (Mac) twice to create two line breaks.

```
//-------------<our history option>--------------\\
this.ourHistoryMC.onRollOver = function () {
    this.ourHistory.setTextFormat(btnDisable);
}
this.ourHistoryMC.onRollOut = function () {
    this.ourHistory.setTextFormat(btnEnable);
}
//-------------</our history option>--------------\\
```

12. Select both **onRollOver** and **onRollOut** functions you just created for the **our history** option–making sure to also select the comments–by dragging over the entire script.

```
//-------------<our history option>--------------\\
this.ourHistoryMC.onRollOver = function () {
    this.ourHistory.setTextFormat(btnDisable);
}
this.ourHistoryMC.onRollOut = function () {
    this.ourHistory.setTextFormat(btnEnable);
}
//-------------</our history option>--------------\\
//-------------<our history option>--------------\\
this.ourHistoryMC.onRollOver = function () {
    this.ourHistory.setTextFormat(btnDisable);
}
this.ourHistoryMC.onRollOut = function () {
    this.ourHistory.setTextFormat(btnEnable);
}
//-------------</our history option>--------------\\
```

13. Hold down the **Ctrl** (Windows) or **Option** (Mac) key and drag the selected script down to the second line break you created in Step 11. This copies that entire block of actions down to where your line break is.

Because of the way the instance names of the submenu option movie clips and text fields are structured, all you essentially have to do to make this script work for the our staff option is replace each occurrence of the word "History" with the word "Staff".

```
//-------------<our staff option>--------------\\
this.ourStaffMC.onRollOver = function () {
    this.ourStaff.setTextFormat(btnDisable);
}
this.ourStaffMC.onRollOut = function () {
    this.ourStaff.setTextFormat(btnEnable);
}
//-------------</our staff option>--------------\\
```

14. In the copied script, replace each occurrence of the word "History" with the word "Staff". So, for example, instead of **this.ourHistoryMC.onRollOver = function () {**, the version of this action that will target the **ourStaffMC** would instead read **this.ourStaffMC.onRollOver = function () {**. Make sure to also replace the word "History" with "Staff" in the duplicated *comments* as well.

*You could have, of course, created the **onRollOver** and **onRollOut** scripts from scratch if you so chose. But it's much simpler to copy those functions you already created for the **our history** option and change a few items so that it applies to the **our staff** option. Because the scripts, for the most part, are nearly identical, it's much easier to copy and change than it is to rewrite from scratch.*

Now you can test the our staff submenu option script you just created.

---

15. Save the changes you've made to the **about_us.fla** by choosing **File > Save**. Then, publish an updated SWF file by choosing **File > Publish**.

---

16. Hide or minimize Flash MX 2004, navigate to your **Desktop > la_eyeworks > site** folder, and double-click **master.swf** to open it in Macromedia Flash Player 7.

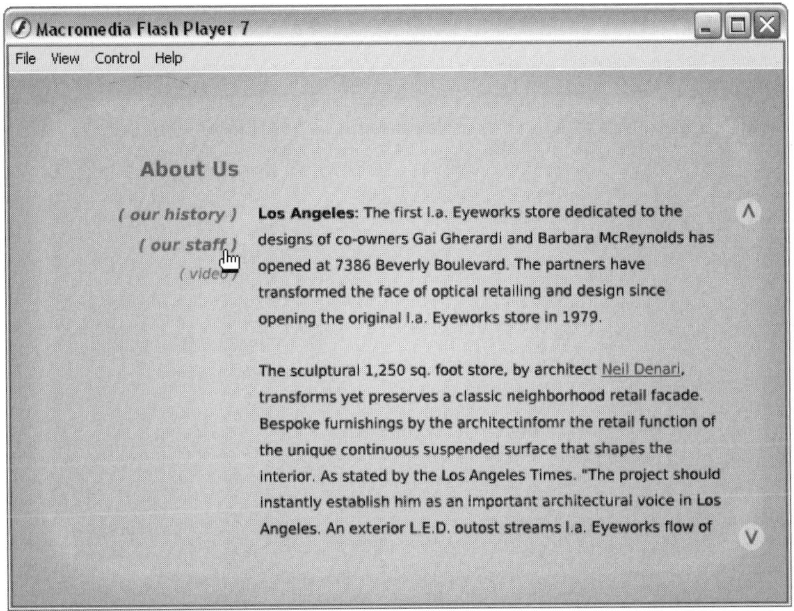

17. When the stand-alone Macromedia Flash Player 7 window opens and the **about us** module is displayed, move your mouse over and off of the **(our staff)** option. You'll notice that the text changes as you move your mouse over and off of that submenu option. Cool! You've just created a **`rollOver/rollOut`** effect, *purely* with ActionScript. Congratulations!

---

18. Keep the stand-alone Macromedia Flash Player 7 window open because you will be needing it in the next exercise.

5. Disabling Interactivity for Usability

Now that you've seen how to use the **TextFormat** class to create an interactive submenu, you need to finish what you started by "fixing" how the submenu options respond to user interaction. As you'll see in the first few steps in this exercise, sometimes you'll want to *disable* the interactivity for a particular submenu option. In this exercise, you will learn how to do just that.

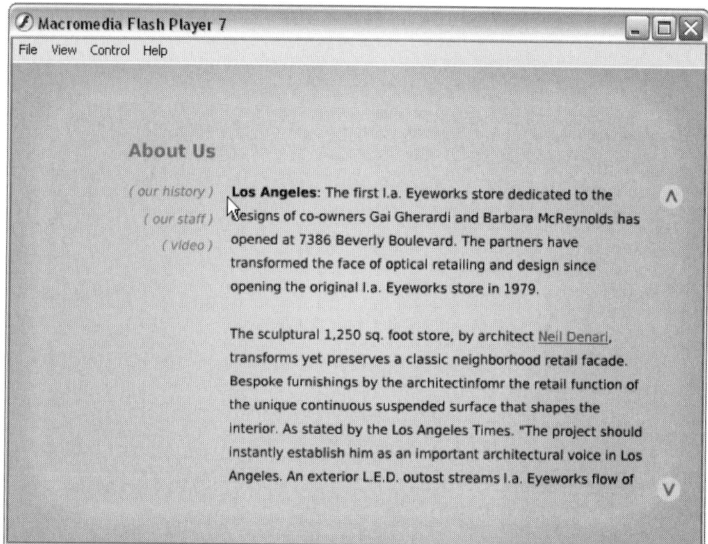

1. Now, before you start feeling all warm and fuzzy about what you accomplished in the last exercise, roll your mouse over and then off of the **(our history)** option.

Notice how, when you roll your mouse over the our history option, you see the finger cursor appear. That finger cursor (while representing something completely different if seen driving down an L.A. freeway) represents interactivity. It means, in effect, "Hey, if you click me, something's going to happen." Because the our history section is already loaded, and the our history option is therefore already "disabled," you don't want to see the finger cursor when the viewer rolls his or her mouse over that option. As a matter of fact, you don't want the viewer to see the finger cursor when he or she moves the mouse over an option whose section is already loaded. In other words, if the our staff section is loaded, and thereby the (our staff) submenu option is "disabled," you don't want the viewer to see the finger icon. Why not? Because when a section is already loaded, clicking that section's option should not do anything. What could it do? The viewer is already viewing that content. Because of that, you will (later) use ActionScript to disable the interactivity of the submenu option that corresponds to the currently loaded section. This means that when the our staff section is loaded, moving your mouse over the (our staff) submenu option will not display the finger cursor icon.

Also notice that when you roll your mouse off of the (our history) submenu option, the our history text reverts back to its "enabled" state. This is a bad thing, because now in the submenu, there is no visual representation of which subsection the viewer is currently looking at. This goes back to the idea of when the viewer should see the finger cursor icon and when they shouldn't, and luckily this is very easy to correct.

---

2. Close the stand-alone Macromedia Flash Player 7 window, and then bring Flash MX 2004 back to the foreground. Make sure that the **about_us.fla** file is the foreground project.

---

3. Select the first keyframe in the **a** layer and open the **Actions** panel (**F9**).

First, you are going to write the action that disables the interactivity of the our history submenu option when the about us module first loads.

```
// disable the sub-menu option that corresponds to the currently-loaded section
this.ourHistoryMC.ourHistory.setTextFormat(btnDisable);
this.ourHistoryMC.enabled = false;
```

4. Click after the **`this.ourHistoryMC.ourHistory.setTextFormat(btnDisable);`** line, press **Enter** (Windows) or **Return** (Mac) once to create a line break, and disable the interactivity of the **ourHistoryMC** movie clip by typing the following:

`this.ourHistoryMC.enabled = false;`

This line, in effect, reads "Set the enabled *property of the ourHistoryMC movie clip to* false.*" When you set the* enabled *property of a movie clip or button symbol to* false, *it disables any interactivity that that symbol has. It's almost like temporarily deleting the actions assigned to a symbol.*

In following with the good practice of testing work after any major changes, you should now test this addition to make sure it works.

---

5. Save your progress by choosing **File > Save**. Then publish an updated SWF by choosing **File > Publish**.

---

6. Hide or minimize Flash MX 2004, navigate to your **Desktop > la_eyeworks > site** folder, and double-click the **master.swf** file to open it in the stand-alone Macromedia Flash Player 7.

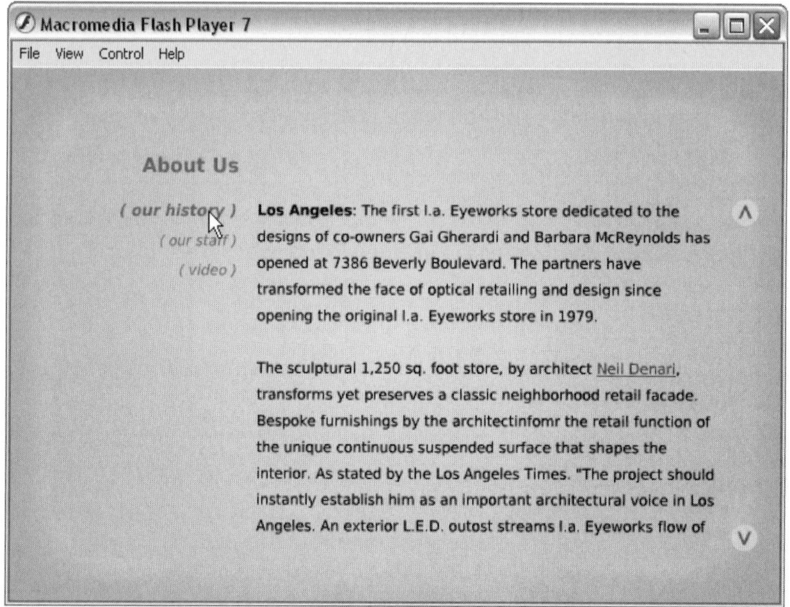

7. When the stand-alone Macromedia Flash Player 7 window opens and the **About Us** module loads, move your mouse over the **(our history)** submenu option. Notice now how you don't see the finger cursor when your mouse interacts with that option! The **`.enabled`** property just essentially disables the interactivity of a symbol. In fact, whenever the viewer clicks *any* of the other submenu options, not only will you want to set the **`TextFormat`** style of that text option to **`btnDisable`**, but you'll also want to disable the interactivity of that option with the **`.enabled`** property. In a later exercise in this chapter, you are going to do just that.

6. Copying and Pasting Functionality

Before continuing with shaping the interactivity of the submenu, you should first finish defining the **onRollOver/onRollOut** functionality of the options in the submenu by adding the ActionScript to the **video** option.

1. Close the stand-alone Macromedia Flash Player 7 window you had open in the last exercise, and bring Flash MX 2004 back to the foreground. Then, make sure the active project is **about_us.fla**.

2. Click the first keyframe in the **a** layer, and open the **Actions** panel (**F9**).

```
//-------------<our staff option>--------------\\
this.ourStaffMC.onRollOver = function () {
    this.ourStaff.setTextFormat(btnDisable);
}
this.ourStaffMC.onRollOut = function () {
    this.ourStaff.setTextFormat(btnEnable);
}
//-------------</our staff option>--------------\\
```

3. Click after the closing **</our staff option>** comment line, and press **Enter** (Windows) or **Return** (Mac) twice to create a couple of line breaks.

```
//-------------<our staff option>--------------\\
this.ourStaffMC.onRollOver = function () {
    this.ourStaff.setTextFormat(btnDisable);
}
this.ourStaffMC.onRollOut = function () {
    this.ourStaff.setTextFormat(btnEnable);
}
//-------------</our staff option>--------------\\

//-------------<our staff option>--------------\\
this.ourStaffMC.onRollOver = function () {
    this.ourStaff.setTextFormat(btnDisable);
}
this.ourStaffMC.onRollOut = function () {
    this.ourStaff.setTextFormat(btnEnable);
}
//-------------</our staff option>--------------\\
```

4. Select the entire **our staff** option script (including the opening and closing comment lines) by dragging around it. Then, while holding down the **Ctrl** key (Windows) or **Option** key (Mac), drag the selected script down to the second new line you created in Step 3. This will copy the entire **our staff** option script below the original.

```
//-------------<our video option>--------------\\
this.ourVideoMC.onRollOver = function () {
    this.ourVideo.setTextFormat(btnDisable);
}
this.ourVideoMC.onRollOut = function () {
    this.ourVideo.setTextFormat(btnEnable);
}
//-------------</our video option>--------------\\
```

5. In the script you just copied, change every occurrence of the word "Staff" to "Video". For example, change the line **`this.ourStaffMC.onRollOver = function () {`** to **`this.ourVideoMC.onRollOver = function () {`**.

*There you have it! You've just completed the **`onRollOver`** and **`onRollOut`** interactivity for the three submenu options. Congrats! Before continuing, you should probably save, publish, and check your work once more to make sure everything is in working order.*

6. Save the changes you've made to **about_us.fla** by choosing **File > Save**. Then, publish an updated SWF by choosing **File > Publish**.

7. Hide or minimize Flash MX 2004, navigate to your **Desktop > la_eyeworks > site** folder, and double-click the **master.swf** file to preview your work in the stand-alone Macromedia Flash Player 7.

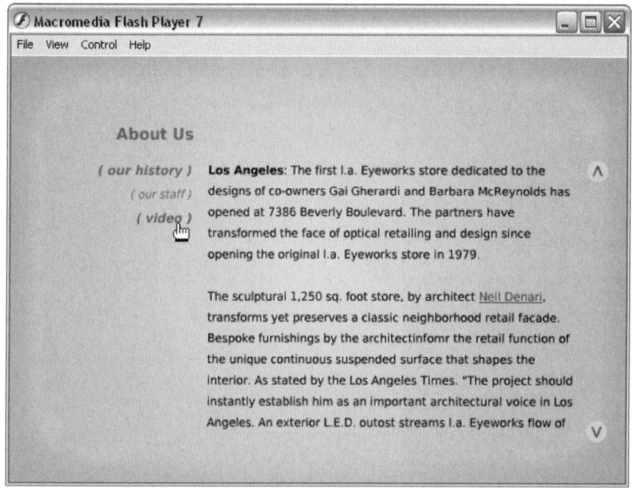

8. When the stand-alone Macromedia Flash Player 7 window opens and displays the **about us** module, make sure all the submenu options (well, except **our history**, of course) work properly when you roll your mouse over and off each text option. Neat!

7. Enabling Interactivity for Usability

Now that you've scripted what the submenu options do when the user rolls over/off each option, you need to script what should happen when the viewer *clicks* each option. In this exercise, you will write the ActionScript that specifies what happens when the viewer clicks the our history or our staff options. The video option will be scripted in Chapter 11, "*Building a Video Player*."

1. Close the Macromedia Flash Player 7 window, and then bring Flash MX 2004 back to the foreground and make sure that the active project is the **about_us.fla** file.

---

2. Select the first keyframe in the **a** layer, and open the **Actions** panel (**F9**).

Because the our history option is disabled by default, you're going to create the script that defines what happens when the viewer clicks the our staff option first.

Click after this closed curly brace, and then press Enter/Return to create a line break to type the next Action into.

```
//-------------<our staff option>--------------\\
this.ourStaffMC.onRollOver = function () {
    this.ourStaff.setTextFormat(btnDisable);
}
this.ourStaffMC.onRollOut = function () {
    this.ourStaff.setTextFormat(btnEnable);
}
this.ourStaffMC.onRelease = function () {
//-------------</our staff option>--------------\\
```

3. Within the **our staff** script, click after the closing **onRollOut** function bracket (**}**), press **Enter** (Windows) or **Return** (Mac) to create a line break, and create the **onRelease** function by typing the following:

```
this.ourStaffMC.onRelease = function () {
```

*Now, you must figure out exactly what should happen when the viewer clicks the our staff option. Later in this chapter, you'll define what content should load and how the other sub-menu options should behave when that happens, but for the here-and-now, you need to decide what the our staff option itself will do when the viewer clicks it. In essence, when the viewer clicks that option, it will become exactly what the our history option is now. It will have the **btnDisable TextFormat** applied to it (Bitstream Vera Sans Bold Oblique at 1 pt size bigger [12 pt]), and its interactivity will be disabled by setting its **enabled** property to false.*

```
//-------------<our staff option>--------------\\
this.ourStaffMC.onRollOver = function () {
    this.ourStaff.setTextFormat(btnDisable);
}
this.ourStaffMC.onRollOut = function () {
    this.ourStaff.setTextFormat(btnEnable);
}
this.ourStaffMC.onRelease = function () {
    this.ourStaff.setTextFormat(btnDisable);
    this.enabled = false;
}
//-------------</our staff option>--------------\\
```

4. Click after the **`this.ourStaffMC.onRelease = function () {`** line, press **Enter** (Windows) or **Return** (Mac) once to create a line break, and type the following:

```
this.ourStaff.setTextFormat(btnDisable);
this.enabled = false;
}
```

*You've seen these actions before, of course. But together, they say "First, set the **TextFormat** style of the **ourStaff** text field to be **btnDisable**. Then, disable the interactivity of the ourStaffMC movie clip by setting its **enabled** property to* false.*"*

5. Save the changes you've made by choosing **File > Save**. Then, publish an updated SWF by choosing **File > Publish**.

6. Hide or minimize Flash MX 2004, navigate to your **Desktop > la_eyeworks > site** folder, and double-click the **master.swf** file to open it in the stand-alone Macromedia Flash Player 7.

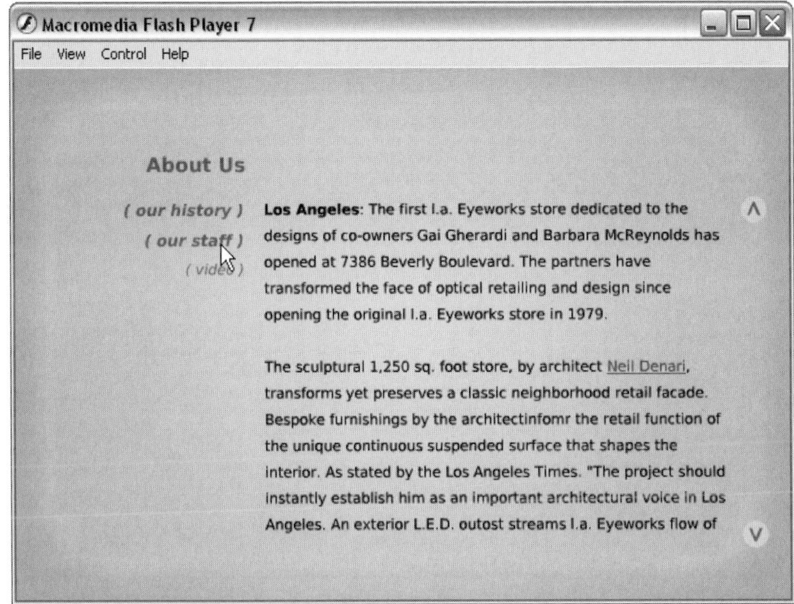

7. When the stand-alone Macromedia Flash Player 7 window opens and the about us module loads, click the **our staff** submenu option.

When you do that, you'll notice that the our staff text becomes 1 pt size bigger, the font face becomes bold, and the finger cursor is replaced with the standard cursor arrow. Great! That's exactly what you want to happen. The problem now (hehe) is that both the our history and our staff options are disabled.

What you want to happen is that when the viewer clicks the our staff option, any other option that is currently disabled should become re-enabled. The problem is, from an ActionScript point of view, it's not very easy to tell Flash MX 2004 to disable all of the other options except *the one you just clicked. So instead, you're going to take advantage of the mere milliseconds it takes Flash MX 2004 to execute the actions you tell it to execute. You're going to create a function whose sole job is to re-enable* all *of the submenu options. Then, you will trigger that function each time the viewer clicks an option. Immediately after that function is triggered, you will instruct Flash MX 2004* to then *disable the option the viewer just clicked.*

If—after that brief description—you're still lost, continue with the following steps as you learn to build the re-enable function and complete the scripting for the submenu. I'm sure, after you complete the next steps, it'll become much clearer to you.

First, you need to create the function that enables all of the submenu options. These are all actions that you've seen before; they will just be placed within a function so they can be easily executed when needed.

8. Close the stand-alone Macromedia Flash Player 7, and then bring Flash MX 2004 back to the foreground. Also make sure that the active project is the **about_us.fla** file.

---

9. Select the first keyframe in the **a** layer, and open the **Actions** panel (**F9**).

```
// disable the sub-menu option that corresponds to the currently-loaded section
this.ourHistoryMC.ourHistory.setTextFormat(btnDisable);
this.ourHistoryMC.enabled = false;



//-------------<our history option>--------------\\
this.ourHistoryMC.onRollOver = function () {
    this.ourHistory.setTextFormat(btnDisable);
}
this.ourHistoryMC.onRollOut = function () {
    this.ourHistory.setTextFormat(btnEnable);
}
//-------------</our history option>-------------\\
```

10. Click to the *left* of the **<our history option>** comment line, press **Enter** (Windows) or **Return** (Mac) twice to create two line breaks, and press the **up arrow** key on your keyboard twice to move the insertion point two lines up.

This will give you some space in the Actions panel to write the option re-enable function.

```
// re-enable the sub-menu options
function reEnableOptions () {
    this.ourHistoryMC.enabled = true;
    this.ourHistoryMC.ourHistory.setTextFormat(btnEnable);
    this.ourStaffMC.enabled = true;
    this.ourStaffMC.ourStaff.setTextFormat(btnEnable);
    this.ourVideoMC.enabled = true;
    this.ourVideoMC.ourVideo.setTextFormat(btnEnable);
}
```

11. Create the function that, when called, will enable all of the options in the submenu by typing the following:

```
// re-enable the sub-menu options
function reEnableOptions () {
    this.ourHistoryMC.enabled = true;
    this.ourHistoryMC.ourHistory.setTextFormat(btnEnable);
    this.ourStaffMC.enabled = true;
    this.ourStaffMC.ourStaff.setTextFormat(btnEnable);
    this.ourVideoMC.enabled = true;
    this.ourVideoMC.ourVideo.setTextFormat(btnEnable);
}
```

These are all actions that you have seen before; this time they are just all nested within a function called ***reEnableOptions****. As you can see by looking down the list of actions within the* ***reEnableOptions*** *function, what they do–together–is to set the* ***enabled*** *property of each submenu option to* true *and to set the text formatting of each submenu option text field to the* ***TextFormat*** *object,* ***btnEnable****. What this means is that when this function is triggered, each option in the submenu will be available to interact with.* After *this function is performed, then you will write another action that* disables *whichever option the viewer clicked.*

As you saw in Step 7, when the viewer clicked the our staff submenu option, the our staff option became disabled–as it should–but the our history option did not become re-enabled. That is what the ***reEnableOptions*** *function, which you just created, will be used for. When the viewer clicks a submenu option, all of the submenu options will become re-enabled, and then the option the viewer clicked will become disabled.*

```
//-------------<our staff option>--------------\\
this.ourStaffMC.onRollOver = function () {
    this.ourStaff.setTextFormat(btnDisable);
}
this.ourStaffMC.onRollOut = function () {
    this.ourStaff.setTextFormat(btnEnable);
}
this.ourStaffMC.onRelease = function () {
    reEnableOptions();
    this.ourStaff.setTextFormat(btnDisable);
    this.enabled = false;
}
//-------------</our staff option>--------------\\
```

12. Within the **our staff option** script, click after the **this.ourStaffMC.onRelease = function () {** line, press **Enter** (Windows) or **Return** (Mac) to create a line break, and trigger the **reEnableOptions** function by typing the following:

reEnableOptions();

That was relatively painless, wasn't it? ;-)

In this case, the ordering of the actions is very *important. Within the* ***onRelease*** *function, first comes the* ***reEnableOptions*** *function call. This action gets executed, and all of the submenu options instantly become "active" again.* Then *come the next two lines where the option the viewer clicked,* ***ourStaff****, becomes disabled. It gets the* ***btnDisable TextFormat*** *applied to it, and its* ***enabled*** *property is set to false. Voilà! Before going out and writing similar* ***onRelease*** *actions for the remaining two submenu options, you should test the modifications you've made to the* ***ourStaff*** *option first.*

---

13. Save the changes you've made by choosing **File > Save**. Then, publish an updated SWF by choosing **File > Publish**.

---

14. Hide or minimize Flash MX 2004, navigate to your **Desktop > la_eyeworks > site** folder, and double-click the **master.swf** file.

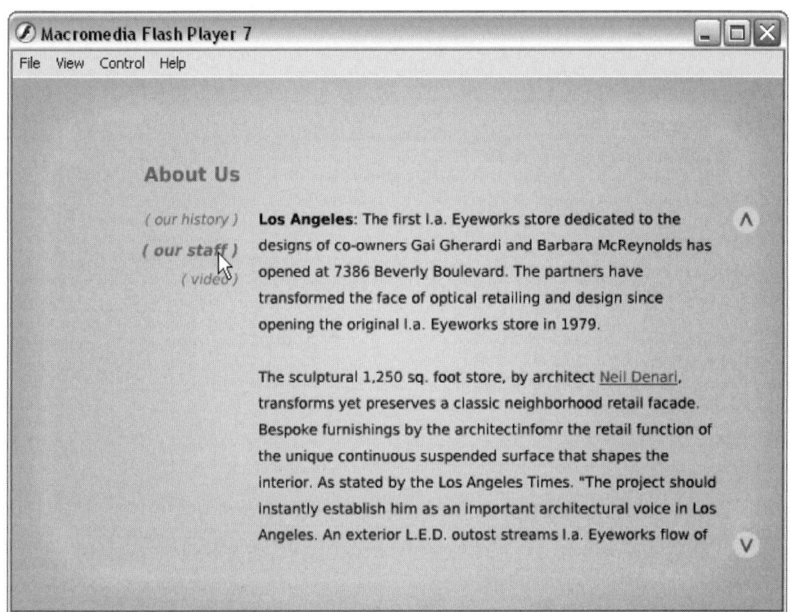

15. When the stand-alone Macromedia Flash Player 7 window opens and displays the **about us** module, click the **our staff** submenu option. When you do, **our staff** becomes disabled. (You can no longer interact with it, and it becomes bolded and 1 pt size larger). Also, the **our history** option that *was* disabled is now enabled, and you can interact with it. Huzzah!

In the next exercise, you will duplicate the same effect for the our history and video subsection options.

Finishing the Submenu

In this exercise, you will duplicate the re-enable/disable functionality that you added to the our staff submenu option in the previous exercise to create the same interactivity effect for the our history and video options.

1. Close the stand-alone Macromedia Flash Player 7, which you had open from the previous exercise, and bring Flash MX 2004 back to the foreground. Also, make sure that the active project is the **about_us.fla** file.

---

2. Select the first keyframe in the **a** layer, and open the **Actions** panel (**F9**).

*Because the **onRelease** script that you completed writing for the our staff option in the previous exercise is nearly identical to the one that will be required for the other two submenu options, why not simply copy the **onRelease** script on the our staff option and paste it for use with the remaining two options?*

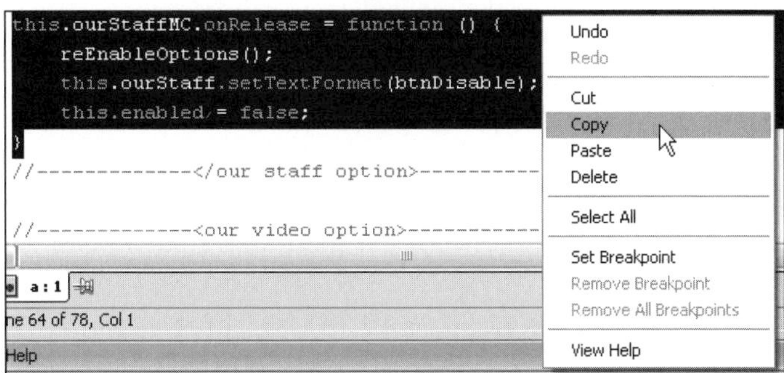

3. Select the **our staff onRelease** script, which you completed in the previous exercise, by dragging around it. Then, copy the script. You can easily copy the script by using your keyboard shortcut (**Ctrl+C** [Windows] or **Cmd+C** [Mac]), or you can **right-click** (Windows) or **Ctrl+click** (Mac) any portion of the selected script (as shown in the screen shot above), and choose **Copy** from the contextual menu that appears.

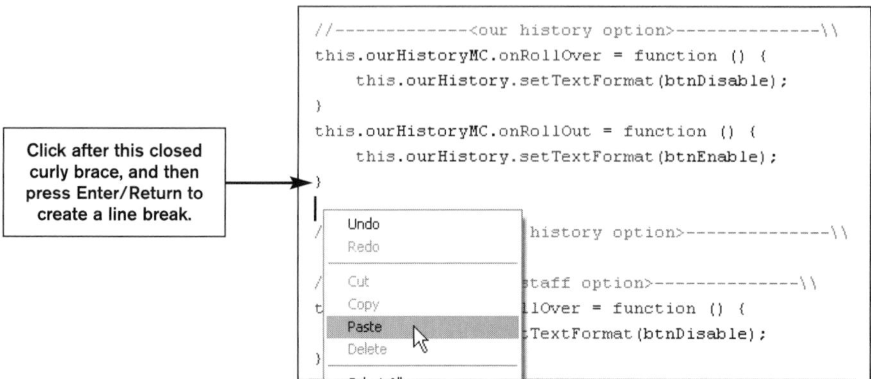

4. Then, within the **our history option** actions, click after the close function bracket (**}**) after the **onRollOut** function and press **Enter** (Windows) or **Return** (Mac) to create a line break. **Right-click** (Windows) or **Ctrl+click** (Mac) after that new line break, and choose **Paste** from the contextual menu that appears. This will paste the **onRelease** script you copied from the **our staff option**, where you can then modify it to work correctly for the **our history option**.

```
//-------------<our history option>--------------\\
this.ourHistoryMC.onRollOver = function () {
    this.ourHistory.setTextFormat(btnDisable);
}
this.ourHistoryMC.onRollOut = function () {
    this.ourHistory.setTextFormat(btnEnable);
}
this.ourHistoryMC.onRelease = function () {
    reEnableOptions();
    this.ourHistory.setTextFormat(btnDisable);
    this.enabled = false;
}
//-------------</our history option>--------------\\
```

5. Within the copied **onRelease** script, change the two occurrences of the word "Staff" to "History".

*As simple as that, this **onRelease** script will now apply to the our history option! Now, you need to perform these same steps to apply this **onRelease** script to the video option as well.*

```
//-------------<our video option>--------------\\
this.ourVideoMC.onRollOver = function () {
    this.ourVideo.setTextFormat(btnDisable);
}
this.ourVideoMC.onRollOut = function () {
    this.ourVideo.setTextFormat(btnEnable);
}
this.ourVideoMC.onRelease = function () {
    reEnableOptions();
    this.ourVideo.setTextFormat(btnDisable);
    this.enabled = false;
}
//-------------</our video option>--------------\\
```

6. Within the **our video option** script, click after the end function bracket (**}**) for the **onRollOut** function, and press **Enter** (Windows) or **Return** (Mac) once to create a line break. **Right-click** (Windows) or **Ctrl+click** (Mac) that new line break, and choose **Paste** from the contextual menu that appears. That will paste the **our staff onRelease** script, which you still have in your computer's clipboard, where you can then adjust it to work properly with the **our video option**. To make the **onRelease** script work correctly, all you have to do is replace the two occurrences of the word "Staff" with the word "Video."

Lastly, when the viewer clicks the our history submenu option, not only do you want the other options to be re-enabled and not only do you want the our history submenu option itself to become disabled, but you also want the our history section content to load. In the next exercise, you will create another of the about us module subsections: our staff. By the end of the next exercise, when you click the our staff option, the our staff content will load. You need to give the viewer the ability to re-view the our history content, if they so choose, by adding an action that loads the our history content when the viewer clicks the our history option. Nicely enough, that action has already been written. Remember how, in the last chapter, you wrote an action that loaded the our history text when the about us module first loaded? Well, you want that same action to also be performed when the viewer clicks the our history submenu option.

```
//-------------<load CSS>--------------\\
var cssStyles:TextField.StyleSheet = new TextField.StyleSheet ();
cssStyles.load ("styles/styles.css");
cssStyles.onLoad = function (success) {
    if (success) {
        loadedInfo.styleSheet = cssStyles;
        _level0.myLV.load("vars/ourHistory.txt");
    } else {
        loadedInfo.text = "There has been an err
    }
}

//-------------</load CSS>--------------\\
```

Undo
Redo
Cut
Copy
Paste
Delete

7. Scroll to the top of the **Actions** window, select the action **_level0.myLV.load("vars/ourHistory.txt");**, and copy it.

```
//------------<our history option>-------------\\
this.ourHistoryMC.onRollOver = function () {
    this.ourHistory.setTextFormat(btnDisable);
}
this.ourHistoryMC.onRollOut = function () {
    this.ourHistory.setTextFormat(btnEnable);
}
this.ourHistoryMC.onRelease = function () {
    reEnableOptions();
    this.ourHistory.setTextFormat(btnDisable);
    this.enabled = false;
    _level0.myLV.load("vars/ourHistory.txt");
}
//------------</our history option>-------------\\
```

8. Scroll down the **Actions** panel until you reach the **our history option** script. Then, within the **`onRelease`** function, click after the **`this.enabled = false;`** line, press **Enter** (Windows) or **Return** (Mac) to create a line break, and paste the copied action into the new line.

Now, when the viewer clicks the our history submenu option, the our history text will load, exactly like it does when the about us module first loads.

Before you begin the celebratory dancing and drinking (hold that off until later, mmkay? I need you sober for the last exercise in this chapter), you should save, publish, and test your work to make sure everything works as intended.

---

9. Save the changes you've made by choosing **File > Save**. Then, publish an updated SWF by choosing **File > Publish**.

---

10. Hide or minimize Flash MX 2004, navigate to your **Desktop > la_eyeworks > site** folder, and double-click the **master.swf** file to open it in the stand-alone Macromedia Flash Player 7.

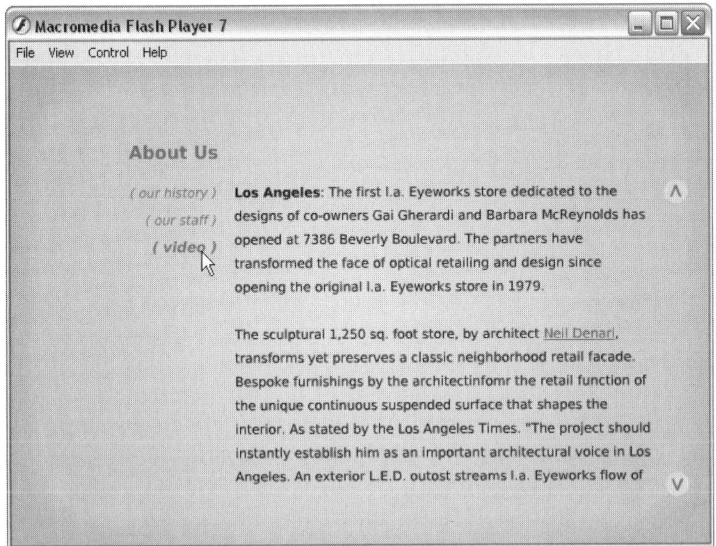

11. Whee! This is almost fun (oh, what simple pleasures we Flash MX 2004 developers have)! Click each submenu option. As you click an option, whichever option was previously disabled should become re-enabled. Click each submenu option to make sure that this occurs.

---

12. When you're finished marveling at your genius creation, close the stand-alone Macromedia Flash Player 7 window.

There you have it! Quite a few lines of code later, and you have a fully interactive submenu–all created with ActionScript! Now even though, for some of you, this exercise took all the effort you could muster, keep in mind that the benefits are well worth the effort you put into creating this menu and what you learned by doing it. If you had built this submenu using beginner-level methods, you would probably have button symbols nested within movie clip symbols, and you would then instruct the playhead within that movie clip to jump around, thereby displaying the various buttons enabled and disabled. Can you imagine, however, making any significant changes to the submenu if it was constructed in that manner? It would be very time consuming to edit or work with in any meaningful way. Conversely, with the submenu you just constructed, edits and modifications are a breeze! If you want to change the text styling of the ***rollOver*** *states, for example, all you'd have to do is modify the* ***btnDisable TextFormat*** *action, and you'd be done. That one action defines how every submenu button will look when the viewer moves his or her mouse over it. So although building a submenu in this manner certainly has a higher learning curve than a more basic method, it is well worth it in the end.*

In the next and final exercise, you will make a minor edit to the our staff option script that will allow the visitor to see the our staff information when they click the our staff submenu option. Imagine that. This submenu is actually useful *too. What a novel idea! (Note the sarcasm.) ;-)*

9. Creating the Our Staff Subsection

In this exercise, you will create the our staff subsection. Similar to the our history subsection, the our staff content is essentially text located in an external text file. This content will get loaded and displayed when the viewer clicks the our staff submenu option that you created earlier in this chapter. As you have seen in previous exercises in this book, the our staff text is styled, using HTML tags (and CSS styles, which you load using a script you created in a previous exercise) to make it more visually appealing. (Because you already learned about them, the HTML and CSS tags have already been written into the our staff text file for you.) Another new Flash feature you will learn is the integration of inline SWF files into the our staff text, where the text actually wraps around the SWFs. This is a lot like using an embedded image in an HTML-based Web page.

1. Hide or minimize Flash MX 2004 (if you have it in the foreground), navigate to your **Desktop > la_eyeworks > site > vars** folder, and open the file **ourStaff.txt** in **Notepad** (Windows), **TextEdit** (Macintosh), or **BBEdit** (Macintosh).

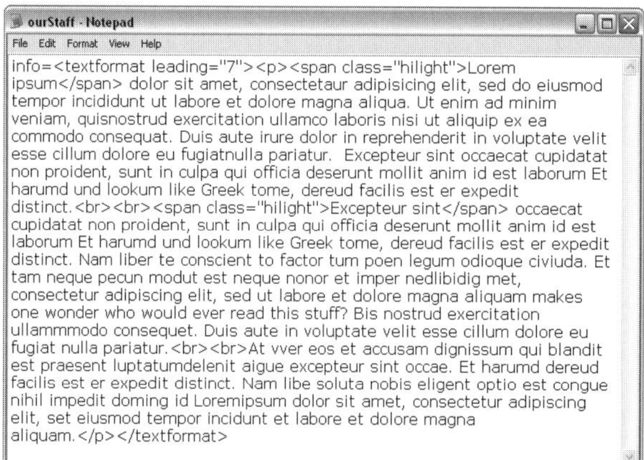


```
info=<textformat leading="7"><p><span class="hilight">Lorem
ipsum</span> dolor sit amet, consectetaur adipisicing elit, sed do eiusmod
tempor incididunt ut labore et dolore magna aliqua. Ut enim ad minim
veniam, quisnostrud exercitation ullamco laboris nisi ut aliquip ex ea
commodo consequat. Duis aute irure dolor in reprehenderit in voluptate velit
esse cillum dolore eu fugiatnulla pariatur.  Excepteur sint occaecat cupidatat
non proident, sunt in culpa qui officia deserunt mollit anim id est laborum Et
harumd und lookum like Greek tome, dereud facilis est er expedit
distinct.<br><br><span class="hilight">Excepteur sint</span> occaecat
cupidatat non proident, sunt in culpa qui officia deserunt mollit anim id est
laborum Et harumd und lookum like Greek tome, dereud facilis est er expedit
distinct. Nam liber te conscient to factor tum poen legum odioque civiuda. Et
tam neque pecun modut est neque nonor et imper nedlibidig met,
consectetur adipiscing elit, sed ut labore et dolore magna aliquam makes
one wonder who would ever read this stuff? Bis nostrud exercitation
ullammmodo consequet. Duis aute in voluptate velit esse cillum dolore eu
fugiat nulla pariatur.<br><br>At vver eos et accusam dignissum qui blandit
est praesent luptatumdelenit aigue excepteur sint occae. Et harumd dereud
facilis est er expedit distinct. Nam libe soluta nobis eligent optio est congue
nihil impedit doming id Loremipsum dolor sit amet, consectetur adipiscing
elit, set eiusmod tempor incidunt et labore et dolore magna
aliquam.</p></textformat>
```

*As you can see, this our staff section text uses greeking (gibberish text that is often used as placeholder text in design mockups) with HTML tags identical to the ones you learned how to utilize in the **ourHistory.txt** file in a previous exercise. Also notice that the variable in this text file, **info**, has the same name as the variable in the **ourHistory.txt** file. When using the **LoadVars** script–which you created in Chapter 4,* "LoadVars Class"*–to load text from an external text file, you* must *use the variable **info** within the text file. This is because the **LoadVars** script is looking for–specifically–the variable **info** and the text (the variable's value) within it to load.*

*First, you're going to add the action that loads the variables from this **ourStaff.txt** file into the **loadedInfo** text field when the viewer clicks the our staff submenu button in the about us module.*

2. Bring Flash MX 2004 to the foreground, and make sure that the active project is the **about_us.fla** file.

3. Select the first keyframe in the **a** layer, and open the **Actions** panel (**F9**).

Because of the extra effort you put into crafting the ***LoadVars*** *script, loading the variables from an external text file (such as the* ***ourStaff.txt*** *file) requires only one action.*

```
//-------------<our staff option>-------------\\
this.ourStaffMC.onRollOver = function () {
    this.ourStaff.setTextFormat(btnDisable);
}
this.ourStaffMC.onRollOut = function () {
    this.ourStaff.setTextFormat(btnEnable);
}
this.ourStaffMC.onRelease = function () {
    reEnableOptions();
    this.ourStaff.setTextFormat(btnDisable);
    this.enabled = false;
    _level0.myLV.load("vars/ourStaff.txt");
}
//-------------</our staff option>-------------\\
```

4. Locate the **our staff option** script and then, under the **onRelease** function, click after the **this.enabled = false;** line. Write the action (which is nearly identical to the action you wrote earlier in this chapter that loads the variables from the **ourHistory.txt** file) that instructs the **LoadVars** object within the **master.swf** Timeline to load the variables from the **ourStaff.txt** file by typing the following:

```
_level0.myLV.load("vars/ourStaff.txt");
```

Simply, this action says, "Tell the ***LoadVars*** *object called* ***myLV****—which is located in the* ***master.swf*** *file (*__***_level0***__*)—to load the variables from the* ***ourStaff.txt*** *file within the folder* ***vars****." The* ***LoadVars*** *script then takes over, loads the variables from the* ***ourStaff.txt*** *file, and inserts them into the text field called* ***loadedInfo*** *in* ***_level5*** *(the level that the* ***about_us.swf*** *file is loaded into).*

Before continuing, you should test what you've done so far to make sure everything's working.

5. Save the changes you've made by choosing **File > Save**. Then, publish an updated SWF by choosing **File > Publish**.

6. Hide or minimize Flash MX 2004, navigate to your **Desktop > la_eyeworks > site** folder, and double-click the **master.swf** file to open it in the stand-alone Macromedia Flash Player 7.

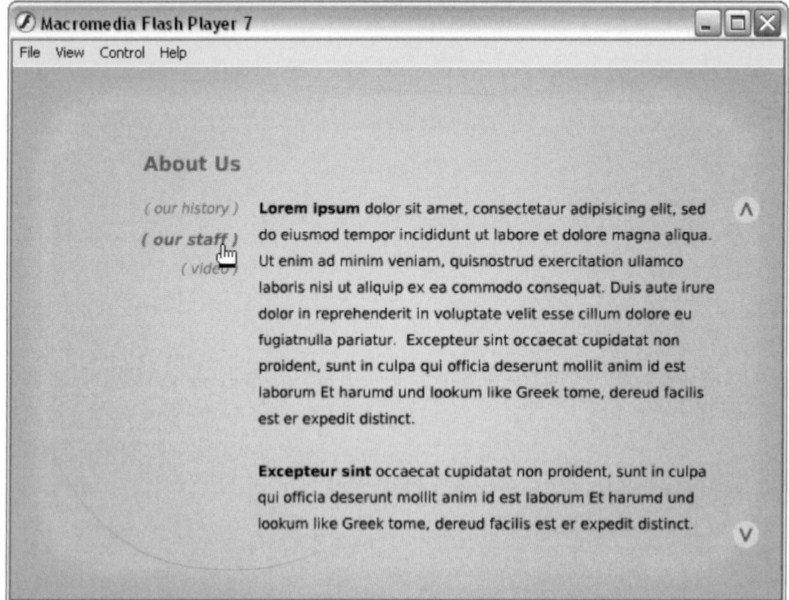

7. When the Macromedia Flash Player 7 window opens and the **about us** module loads, you'll see the **our history** information automatically load. Then, click the **our staff** submenu option. You'll notice that the **our history** information is replaced with the styled greeking text that you saw in the **ourStaff.txt** file at the beginning of this exercise. Coolio! If you click the **our history** submenu option, you'll notice that the **our staff** text will be replaced with the **our history** text. Then, if you click the **our staff** option, you'll notice that the **our history** text is replaced with the **our staff** text, Then, if you click...well...you get the idea. ;-)

---

8. Now that you've gotten the **our staff** text to load correctly, you are going to learn how to embed SWF files inline into that text. Close the stand-alone Macromedia Flash Player 7 window and then navigate to your **Desktop > la_eyeworks > site > swfs** folder.

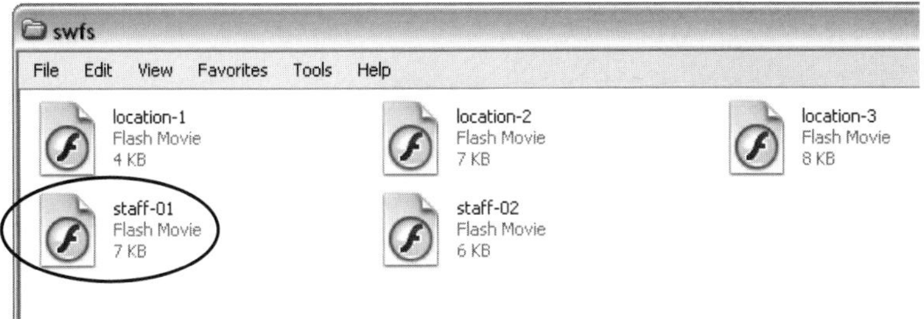

9. In the **swfs** folder, you'll notice a SWF titled **staff-01.swf**. Double-click this SWF file to open it in the stand-alone Macromedia Flash Player 7. Also, be sure to note the location of this file. Just like when you're using the **LoadVars** class to load the variables from an external TXT file, you need to know the location of this SWF file so you can write the correct path to it in the **ourStaff.txt** file.

*As you'll see when the SWF opens, it's just a series of three animated images that fade into each other. Later, if you're interested in seeing the source FLA for this SWF, navigate to your **Desktop > la_eyeworks > site** folder, and double-click the **staff-01.fla** file.*

10. Close the stand-alone Macromedia Flash Player 7 window.

*In the **swfs** folder, you'll also notice another SWF, in particular, titled **staff-02.swf**. **staff-01.swf** and **staff-02.swf** are the two SWF files that you are going to place–inline–into the **ourStaff.txt** file.*

11. Bring the **ourStaff.txt** file back to the foreground. If you accidentally closed it, you can open it again by navigating to your **Desktop > la_eyeworks > site > vars** folder and opening the **ourStaff.txt** file in your text editor.

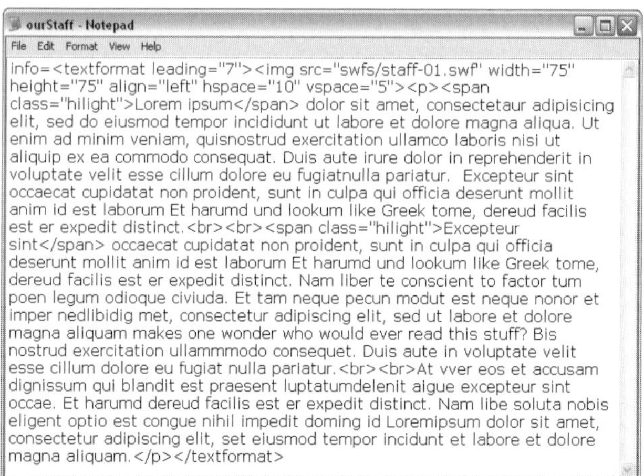


```
info=<textformat leading="7"><img src="swfs/staff-01.swf" width="75"
height="75" align="left" hspace="10" vspace="5"><p><span
class="hilight">Lorem ipsum</span> dolor sit amet, consectetaur adipisicing
elit, sed do eiusmod tempor incididunt ut labore et dolore magna aliqua. Ut
enim ad minim veniam, quisnostrud exercitation ullamco laboris nisi ut
aliquip ex ea commodo consequat. Duis aute irure dolor in reprehenderit in
voluptate velit esse cillum dolore eu fugiatnulla pariatur.  Excepteur sint
occaecat cupidatat non proident, sunt in culpa qui officia deserunt mollit
anim id est laborum Et harumd und lookum like Greek tome, dereud facilis
est er expedit distinct.<br><br><span class="hilight">Excepteur
sint</span> occaecat cupidatat non proident, sunt in culpa qui officia
deserunt mollit anim id est laborum Et harumd und lookum like Greek tome,
dereud facilis est er expedit distinct. Nam liber te conscient to factor tum
poen legum odioque civiuda. Et tam neque pecun modut est neque nonor et
imper nedlibidig met, consectetur adipiscing elit, sed ut labore et dolore
magna aliquam makes one wonder who would ever read this stuff? Bis
nostrud exercitation ullammmodo consequet. Duis aute in voluptate velit
esse cillum dolore eu fugiat nulla pariatur.<br><br>At vver eos et accusam
dignissum qui blandit est praesent luptatumdelenit aigue excepteur sint
occae. Et harumd dereud facilis est er expedit distinct. Nam libe soluta nobis
eligent optio est congue nihil impedit doming id Loremipsum dolor sit amet,
consectetur adipiscing elit, set eiusmod tempor incidunt et labore et dolore
magna aliquam.</p></textformat>
```

12. Within the **ourStaff.txt** file, add the HTML information that will place the **staff-01.swf** file inline before the opening text "Lorem ipsum." Click *before* the HTML **<p>** tag towards the beginning of the text file and type the following:

```
<img src="swfs/staff-01.swf" width="75" height="75" align="left" hspace="10" vspace="5">
```

There's quite a lot going on in that HTML tag, as you can see. The HTML tag itself, stripped of all its attributes, is **<img>** *(short for "image," of course).* **src** *(short for "source") is the path to–and the name of–the SWF (or JPG) file to place. When writing a path to the SWF/JPG file to place, one interesting tidbit to keep in mind is that the path you want to write should* not *be written relative to the text file it will be placed within. Instead, the path should be written relative to the SWF file this text will get loaded into. In other words, when writing a path to a SWF/JPG within a text file that gets loaded into another SWF (as the* ***ourStaff.txt*** *file does), write it relative to where the SWF file is located (the SWF file that the text gets loaded into,* not *the SWF that is added–inline–to the text file itself). This is somewhat counterintuitive, especially if you've built any HTML-based Web pages before. But once you remember that the text file gets loaded into a SWF, and that the path to the inline images must be written relative to that SWF, it makes a little more sense.*

The other HTML attributes are fairly self-explanatory. **width** *and* **height** *are the width and height of the SWF file in pixels.* **align** *is how the SWF/JPG file will be aligned within the text field. For* **align**, *your options are "left" and "right". If you don't specify an* **align** *attribute, the default is "left."* **hspace** *and* **vspace** *show how large of a horizontal and vertical (respectively) pixel buffer you want between the SWF/JPG and the text that surrounds it. The HTML* **<img>** *tag is one of those tags that you don't have to close (***</img>***).*

Before writing the other ***staff-02.swf*** *file into the* ***ourStaff.txt*** *file, you should test your changes thus far to make sure everything works correctly. Because these changes are all done to the* ***ourStaff.txt*** *file, you don't even need to return to Flash MX 2004 to view the changes.*

13. Save the changes you've made to the **ourStaff.txt** file by choosing **File > Save**. Then, hide or minimize your text editing program, navigate to your **Desktop > la_eyeworks > site** folder, and double-click the **master.swf** file to view it in the stand-alone Macromedia Flash Player 7.

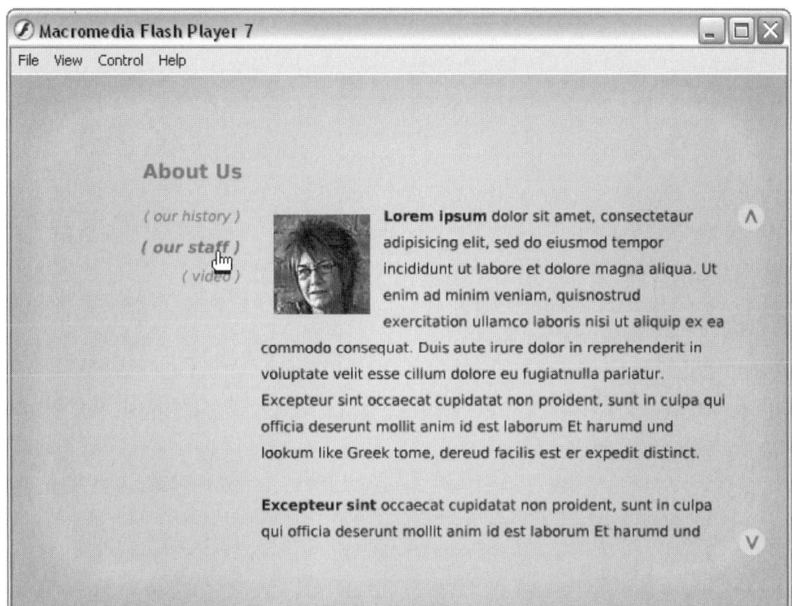

14. When the stand-alone Macromedia Flash Player 7 window opens and the **about us** module loads, click the **our staff** submenu option to load the **ourStaff.txt** file. When you do, you'll see the **staff-01.swf** file, inline (and animating) within the loaded text. Holy cripes, Batman! As simple as it may seem, this new Flash MX 2004 feature is really awesome, and it allows the designer many more design possibilities that haven't been available before. Hurray!

*Now you just need to add the HTML tag to insert the **staff-02.swf** file into the text.*

15. Close the stand-alone Macromedia Flash Player 7 window, and bring the **ourStaff.txt** file back to the foreground.

*Because both **staff-01** and **staff-02** SWF files are the same size, it's easier to copy the **img** tag (and its attributes) that you wrote in Step 12 and paste it where you need it, rather than type that long tag over from scratch again.*

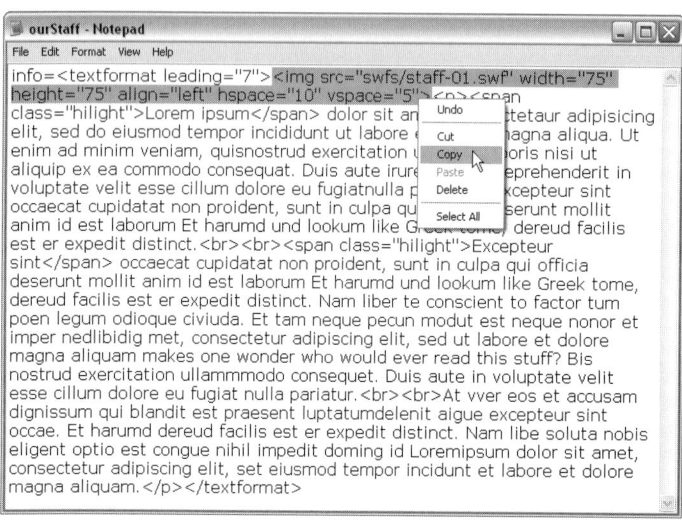

16. Select the **`<img src="swfs/staff-01.swf" width="75" height="75" align="left" hspace="10" vspace="5">`** line and copy it.

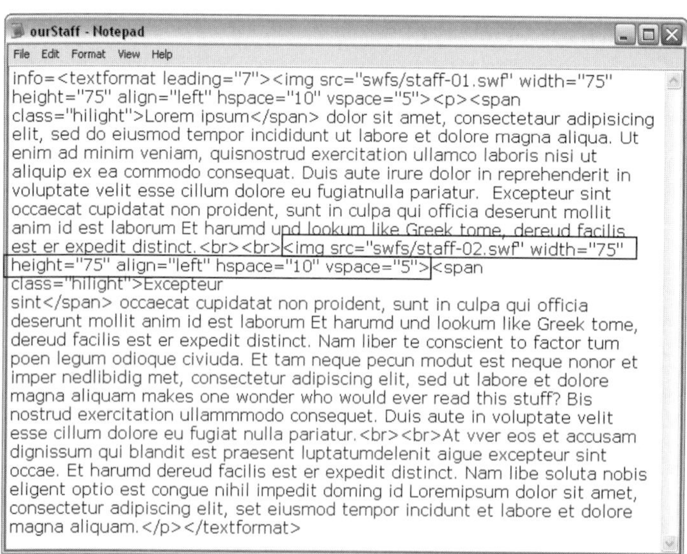

17. Towards the middle of the **ourStaff.txt** text file are two break tags (**`<br><br>`**). Click *after* those tags, and paste the **`<img>`** tag you just copied. Then, simply change the name of the SWF file from **staff-01.swf** to **staff-02.swf**.

That's it! You should verify that your changes work, one last time.

---

18. Save the changes you've made to the **ourStaff.txt** file by choosing **File > Save**. Then, hide or minimize your text editing program, navigate to your **Desktop > la_eyeworks > site** folder, and double-click the **master.swf** file to view it in the stand-alone Macromedia Flash Player 7.

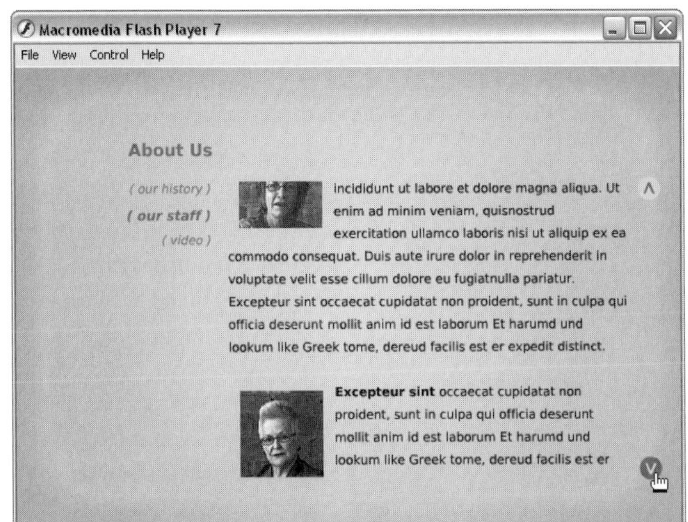

19. When the stand-alone Macromedia Flash Player 7 window opens and the **about us** module loads, click the **our staff** submenu option to load the **ourStaff.txt** file. Inline within the loaded text are the two SWF files: **staff-01.swf** and **staff-02.swf**. Awesome! Notice that you can also scroll through the loaded text, or switch back to the **our history** section and scroll through the text there as well.

I certainly hope you're pleased with your progress in this book thus far because you have definitely *come a long way. And it's only Chapter 6! In the last few chapters, you have learned* a lot *of new information while constructing the about us module. You learned how to use the* ***LoadVars*** *class to dynamically load text from an external file, how to scroll through loaded text, how to style loaded text using HTML tags written into the text file, how to further style the dynamic text by using dynamically loaded CSS files (using the* ***TextField.StyleSheet*** *class), how to build an ActionScript-controlled submenu using text options styled using the* ***TextFormat*** *class, and (as if that wasn't enough) how to embed inline SWF files into the dynamic text. You absorbed an incredible amount of content in these past few chapters, and I highly recommend taking a vacation now that you've completed this mammoth task. ;-)*

In the next chapter, you will build on what you learned in this chapter by constructing a dynamic slideshow. This slideshow will constitute the ***frames*** *module and will utilize dynamically loaded JPG images for each frame picture and dynamically loaded information about each frame (using, of course,* ***LoadVars****). You will also revisit the* ***MovieClipLoader*** *and expand on it to create a graphical preloader to display the preloading progress of your content. *Whew!* It's a lot to cover, so you'd better get started. I'll race ya there (after you've had your vacation, of course)!*

7. Building a Slideshow

la_eyeworks

Macromedia Flash MX 2004
Beyond the Basics

In this chapter, you will build the interactive slideshow that fits into the Frames section of the L.A. Eyeworks Web site. The Frames module is a simple slideshow that's comprised of the slideshow images, a few lines of descriptive text that accompanies each image, and a small dynamic text field that displays which image is currently being viewed out of the total number of images. What makes this slideshow interesting, however, is that all of the slideshow images and accompanying descriptive text will be dynamically loaded using the **MovieClipLoader** and **LoadVars** object you created in Chapter 3, "*Getting Started*," and Chapter 4, "*LoadVars Class*," respectively. The viewer will also be able to click a forward and backward button, which you will make functional by writing the ActionScript, to navigate through the dynamic slideshow. I'm ready if you are!

What You Are Building

In this exercise, you will look at the finished Web site so you can get a better idea of what it is that you will be building before you begin.

1. Open your preferred Web browser, and access the following URL:

http://www.lynda.com/flashbtb/laeyeworks/

2. When the Web site loads, click the **(frames)** option from the navigation bar at the top of the page.

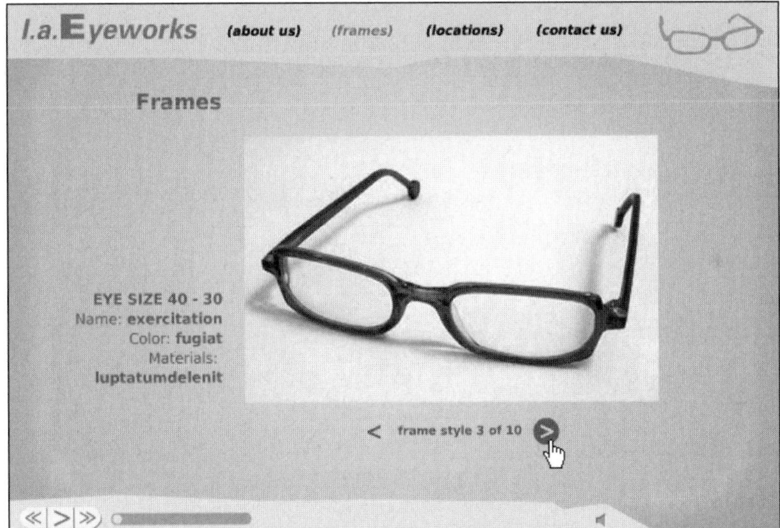

*This will load (using the **`MovieClipLoader`**) the Frames module. Immediately (or pretty immediately, depending on the speed of your Internet connection) you should see the first slide in the Frames slideshow load. That slideshow picture is actually a JPG image that is stored in a separate folder on the Web server. As you click the forward and backward buttons below the slides, the **`MovieClipLoader`** loads the next and previous (respectively) slides in sequence. As each new slideshow image appears, you'll also notice that the text to the left of the slide also updates to give descriptive information about each pair of glasses. Not only that, but below the slide image is another bit of text that displays which image is being viewed out of the total number of images.*

*In this exercise, you'll be learning how to combine many of the scripts you've constructed in previous chapters to build this slideshow. I hope you're excited because you're going to be learning some really powerful techniques as well as beginning to see–now that you've created many of the main scripts (**`MovieClipLoader`**, **`LoadVars`**, and so forth)–how easy it can be to create some fairly complex interactivity. It's not all going to be simply review, however. A major part of learning to work with Flash MX 2004 is learning how to combine actions together in various ways to achieve different types of interactivity. Even though you have dealt with certain actions in previous chapters that you will be reusing in this–and following–chapters, you will be mixing those actions together and adding on to them in different ways to create different types of functionality and interactivity.*

---

3. When you're finished viewing the **Frames** section, close your Web browser.

---

2. Setting Up

In this exercise, you will open up a prebuilt FLA and get ready to add functionality to it. You will add some instance names to movie clips and text fields used in this module, and you'll import some elements from the shared library.

1. Navigate to your **Desktop > la_eyeworks > site** folder, and double-click the file **frames.fla** to open it in Flash MX 2004.

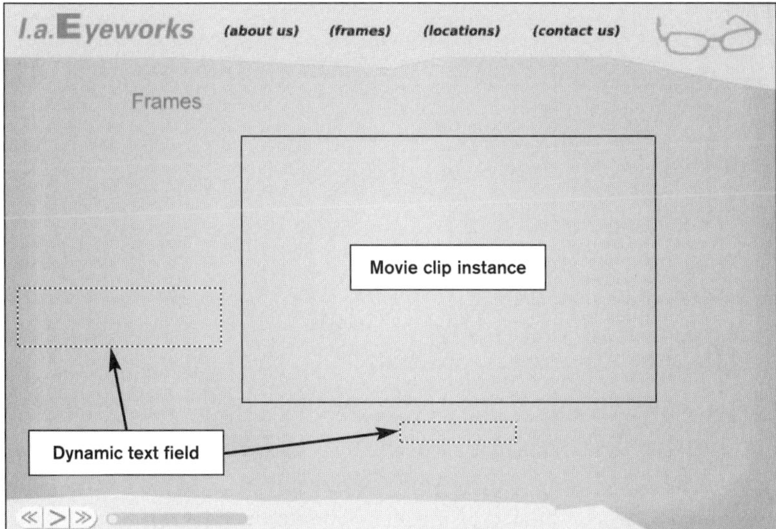

*Once you have the **frames.fla** file open, you'll notice that the FLA contains a couple dynamic text fields and a movie clip symbol with a box drawn in it. That box, by the way (which is simply just a stroke drawn inside the movie clip symbol), represents the physical size of the slideshow JPG images–320 px wide by 200 px high–and is only there to give you a visual representation of where the slideshow images will be when they are dynamically loaded into that movie clip. When you're finished creating the Frames module, you will disable that stroke so that it doesn't get published in the completed SWF.*

Because both dynamic text fields and the movie clip instance will be targeted with ActionScript, they–of course–need to have unique instance names. The far-left dynamic text field is where descriptive information will be displayed about each slideshow image. The movie clip instance is where each slide will be loaded. Lastly, the dynamic text field below the movie clip instance is where the slide number information will be displayed.

First, however, you will need to bring in some shared elements that you will be using in the construction of this module.

2. Make sure you don't have **sharedLib.fla** open. (If it *is* open, you won't be able to complete the rest of this step.) Then, choose **File > Import > Open External Library**. When the **Open as Library** dialog box opens, navigate to your **Desktop > la_eyeworks > site** folder and double-click **sharedLib.fla.** This will open only the library of the shared library, **sharedLib.fla.**

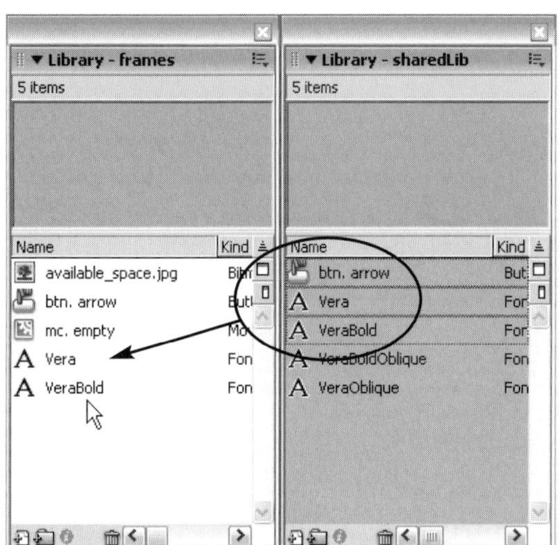

3. Undock the **Libraries** (if they aren't already) of the **frames** and **sharedLib** FLAs, and then position them side by side so you can see both of their contents. Then, select the symbols **btn. arrow**, **Vera**, and **VeraBold** in the **sharedLib Library** window. (You can select them all by **Shift+clicking** each one in turn.) Once those symbols are selected, drag them onto the **frames Library** window. As you've seen previously, this will make a link to those shared library items in the frames.fla file.

4. Close the **sharedLib Library** window. You won't need it again in this exercise.

Now that you've linked the shared fonts (wasn't that easy?), you can assign them to the two premade dynamic text fields on the ***frames.fla*** *Stage.*

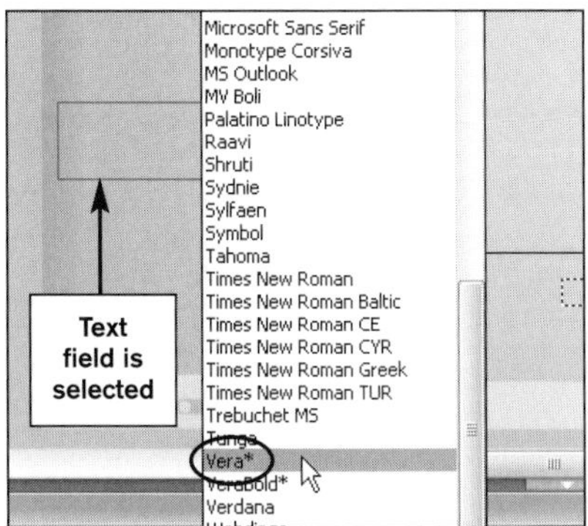

5. Select the left-most dynamic text field by single-clicking it. Then, in the **Properties inspector**, choose the shared font symbol **Vera*** from the **Font** pull-down menu.

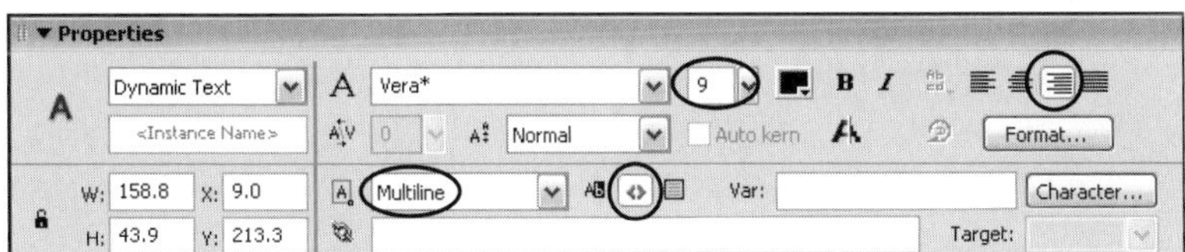

*Leave the rest of the text field options the way they are. The text field should be set to a font size of **9**, **Align right**, **Multiline** line type, and with **Render Text as HTML** enabled. Of course, to be able to specify this text field as the target to load text into, you need to give it an instance name.*

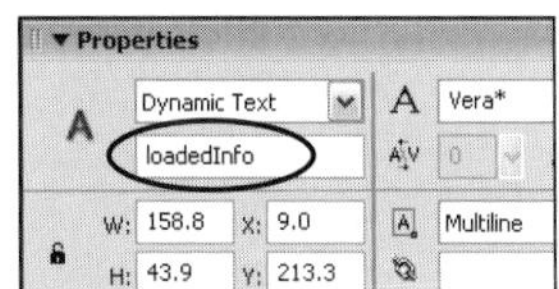

6. With the text field still selected, in the **Properties inspector**, type **loadedInfo** in the **Instance Name** field.

loadedInfo *is now the instance name of this text field, and you can use that name when you want to target that specific text field with ActionScript. If your brain isn't mush by now, you might recall the instance name* ***loadedInfo*** *from previous exercises.* ***loadedInfo*** *is the name of the text field that the* ***LoadVars*** *script (which you wrote back in Chapter 4, "LoadVars Class") will put variable values in when you load the variables from an external text file. Later, when you use the* ***LoadVars*** *script to load the slide information variable files, the values of those external variables will be inserted into this* ***loadedInfo*** *text field.*

Because the remaining text field will be targeted with ActionScript, you also need to define its settings, as well as give it an instance name.

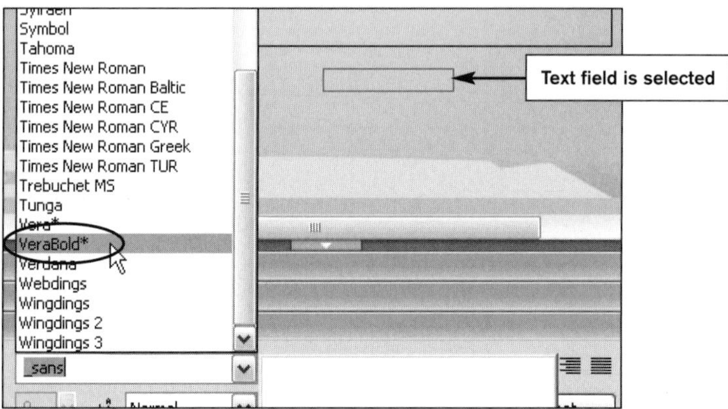

7. Click the bottom-most text field once to select it. Then, in the **Properties inspector**, choose the shared font symbol **VeraBold*** from the **Font** pull-down menu.

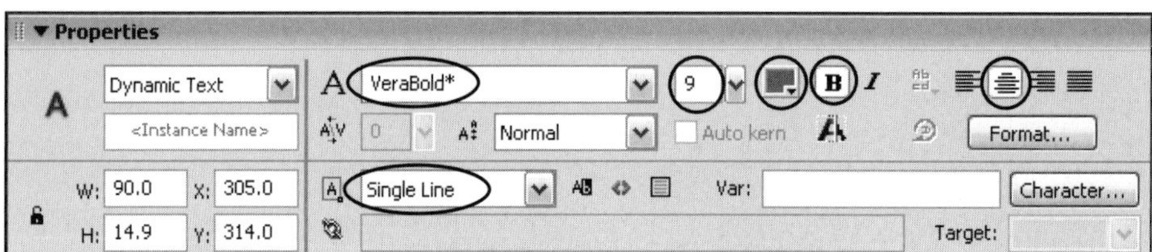

The font size should be ***9****, the text color should be* ***#3F7FBE (Blue)****,* ***Align center****,* ***Single Line*** *line type, and* ***Render Text as HTML*** *should* not *be enabled. If you're running a Windows operating system, make sure* ***Bold Style*** *is enabled (as is circled in the screen shot above). If you're running Macintosh, leave* ***Bold Style*** *disabled.*

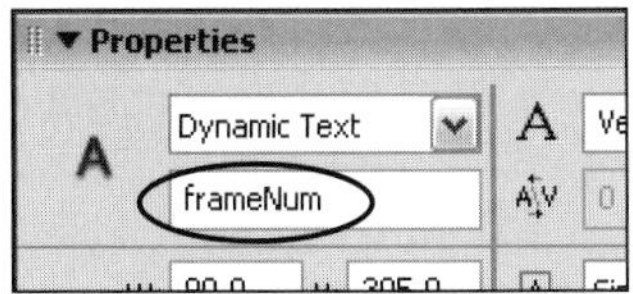

8. With the lower text field still selected, click in the **Instance Name** field in the **Properties inspector**, and give this field the instance name **frameNum**.

You also need to give an instance name to the movie clip instance where the slide JPG image will dynamically load into.

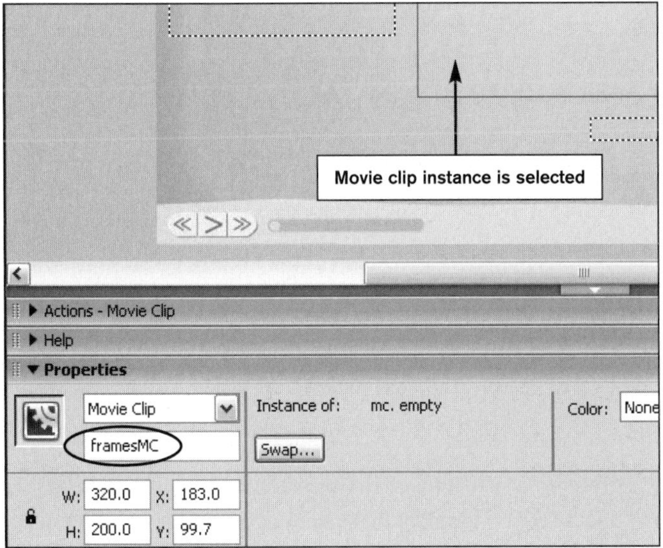

9. Single-click the movie clip instance **mc. empty** on the **Stage** to select it. (If you have difficulty selecting the movie clip instance, try single-clicking one of the sides [strokes] of the box.) Once the movie clip instance is selected, give it an instance name by opening the **Properties inspector**, and type **framesMC** in the **Instance Name** field.

Lastly, you should set the Frames title so that it uses one of the shared fonts that you linked earlier in this exercise.

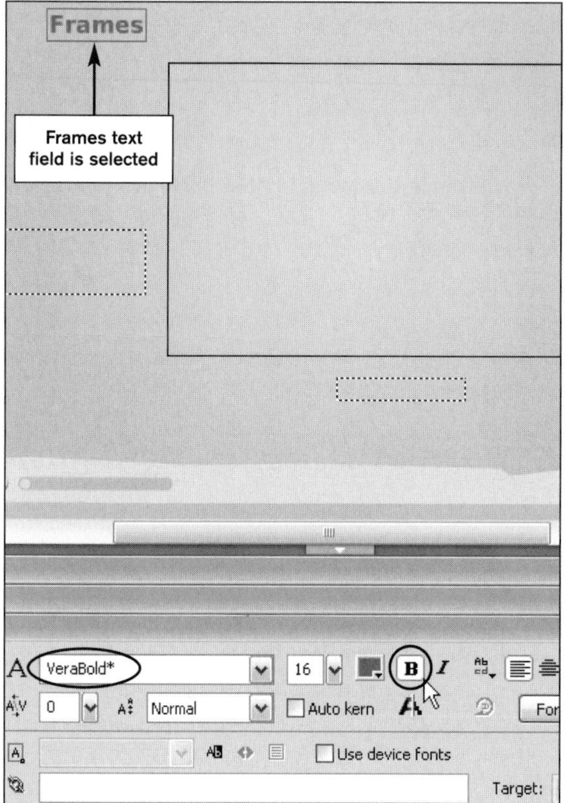

10. Single-click the "Frames" text toward the top of the **Stage** to select it. Then, in the **Properties inspector**, click the **Font** pull-down menu and choose **VeraBold***. If you're using Windows, you'll also need to remember to enable the bold styling by clicking the **Bold Style** button. The rest of the options should remain the same. The font size should be **16**, text color should be **#3F7FBE** (**Blue**), and **Align left** should be enabled.

11. Save the changes you've made to **frames.fla** by choosing **File > Save**.

*There ya have it! This Frames module is all set up and ready for you to add the slideshow interactivity. In the next exercise, you will write the scripting that will dynamically load the slideshow JPG images into the **framesMC** movie clip instance.*

What Is the "if" Statement?

In Chapter 4, "*LoadVars Class*," you were briefly introduced to the **if** statement, which allows you to create **conditional logic** in your Flash MX 2004 movie. In other words, you can create a script that is executed when certain circumstances occur in the Flash MX 2004 movie, or even have a completely different script that is executed when *different* circumstances present themselves. The **if** statement allows your movie to seemingly react as various conditions arise. For example, if you want to check to see if the content that is loading into **_level5** has finished yet, and if so, play the main Timeline, you could use an **if** statement like this:

```
if (_level5.getBytesLoaded == _level5.getBytesTotal) {
    _level0.play();
}
```

When that **if** statement is executed, it will check to see *if* **_level5** has been loaded. (The scripting within the parentheses after **if** is called the **condition**.) After the **if** statement finds a result of that condition, it will return a Boolean value: a *true* or a *false*. If the condition is true (in this case, if **_level5** has been completely loaded), the **if** statement will execute all the actions between the curly braces **{ }** (called the **statements**). So, in this example, the **if** statement simply reads, "If the bytes loaded for **_level5** are equal to **_level5**'s total bytes (meaning that **_level5** has been completely downloaded), tell the main Timeline (**_level0**) to play." Pretty straightforward, eh?

But what if you want a different action to be executed if that condition is *not* true? The way the script is currently set up, if the condition is not true, Flash MX 2004 just ignores the statement(s) within the **if** statement and continues processing any other actions available. It just moves on. But, what if you wanted some text to be inserted into a text field on the main Timeline if the condition turned out to be false (if **_level5** hadn't been completely downloaded yet)? In this situation, you would write something called an **else** into the **if** statement. An **else** is used for when you want some other action to happen if the condition turns out to be false. This is called **branching logic**. Here is what an **else** would look like integrated into the previous **if** statement:

```
if (_level5.getBytesLoaded == _level5.getBytesTotal) {
_level0.play();
} else {
    _level0.textMsg.text = "still downloading";
}
```

So as you can see, the **else** is just tacked on after the **if** statement. If the condition for the **if** statement turns out to be false, you place within curly braces whatever you want to happen after **else**. Those actions will get executed automatically if the **if** condition is false.

if statements, as you've gotten a taste of here, are *essential* for creating many kinds of powerful interactivity. They allow your movie to ask questions and to then respond appropriately based on the answer it receives. You have already used **if** statements in scripts you've written thus far, and you will continue to use them throughout other exercises in this book.

3. Loading the First Slide

In this exercise, you are going to create the ActionScript that will load the first image of the slideshow into the correct location in the Frames module. The slideshow is fairly basic. What makes this slideshow interesting, however, is that each image in the slideshow is an external JPG file. This means that **frames.swf** will be smaller in file size, and you will have the added advantage of being able to swap different images without ever opening the Flash MX 2004 project (great for clients who want to maintain the work you've done for them!). You'll start the construction of this slideshow by building simple functionality. Then, over the course of the exercises in this chapter, you will build on that to create more complex interactivity, such as providing the viewer with a way to navigate through the slideshow.

1. Before you start writing the ActionScript, you should first go see where the slideshow images are and what their filenames are. On your hard drive, navigate to your **Desktop > la_eyeworks > site** folder. This is the folder, of course, where all your site files (including **master.swf, about_us.swf, frames.swf**, and so on) are located. Notice that within the **site** folder is another folder titled **frames**. Double-click the **frames** folder to open it.

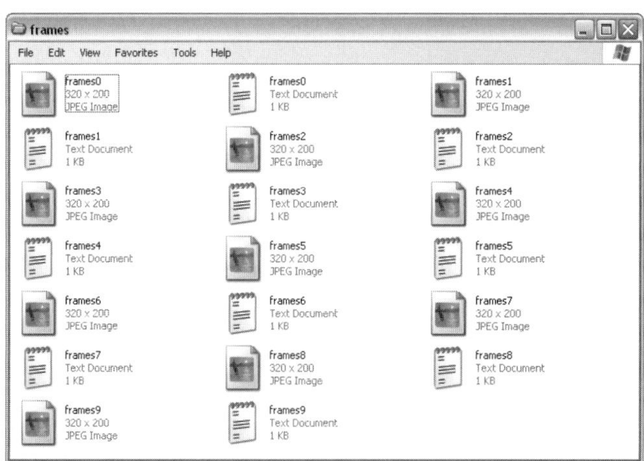

*Notice that the **frames** folder contains a series of JPG and TXT files. But also take notice of their names. If you look at the JPG images, notice how their file names all begin with **frames** and are then followed by a number–**frames0.jpg**, **frames1.jpg**, and so forth. (The screen shot above doesn't show the file extensions because that is the default behavior of Windows XP. On the other hand, if you're using a Macintosh, the Mac operating system* does *show the file extensions by default.) The associated text files also have an identical naming convention. These files were named this way (sequentially) on purpose. When you write the ActionScript to advance to the next slide, you'll simply tell Flash MX 2004 to get the file that starts with the word "frames," and then add a number onto it that is one greater than the current slide.*

2. Bring Flash MX 2004 back to the foreground.

3. Make sure you still are working in the **frames.fla** file. If you accidentally closed it, you can open it again by accessing your **Desktop > la_eyeworks > site** folder and double-clicking the **frames.fla** file. (You can also select **frames.fla** from the **Open a Recent Item** column in the **Start Page**.)

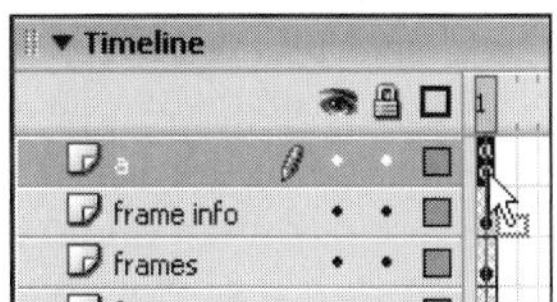

4. Single-click the first (and only) keyframe in the top-most layer **a**, and open the **Actions** panel (**F9**).

```
// -----------------<pre-built code for chapter 7>---------------- \\
/*
frameNum.autoSize = "center";
loadedInfo.autoSize = "right";
// -----------------<TextField.StyleSheet>---------------- \\
var cssStyles:TextField.StyleSheet = new TextField.StyleSheet ();
cssStyles.load ("styles/styles.css");
cssStyles.onLoad = function (success) {
    if (success) {
        loadedInfo.styleSheet = cssStyles;
        loadFrame();
    } else {
        loadedInfo.text = "There has been an error loading the requested information.  Please contact the
Webmaster and report your error.";
    }
}
// -----------------</TextField.StyleSheet>---------------- \\
*/
// -----------------</pre-built code for chapter 7>---------------- \\
```

*You'll immediately notice that there are already some prebuilt actions in the Actions panel. These actions are ones you will be utilizing later in this chapter, and they have been included with this starter file **frames.fla** because they are all actions you've already learned in this book. If you look at the included actions, you'll notice that it's simply a **`TextField.StyleSheet`** object (nearly identical to the one you created in Chapter 5, "HTML and CSS," which you used to load and apply CSS styles to the **`loadedInfo`** text field in the About Us module). You'll also find two **`autoSize`** actions, which you learned how to use in Chapter 6, "TextFormat Class," to auto-size the About Us submenu text fields. You'll also notice that the included actions have been commented out. That way, as you're working on the ActionScript in the first part of this chapter, those included actions won't interfere with the scripts you're writing. Later in this chapter, you will uncomment the prebuilt actions and utilize them in a few new ways, such as creating the dynamic descriptive slide text and the dynamic slide counter text.*

Next, you're going to write an action that will load the first slideshow image–using the ubiquitous ***MovieClipLoader****–into the* ***framesMC*** *movie clip instance on the Stage. However, you don't want to write an action that says, "Go load the image* ***frames0.jpg*** *into the* ***framesMC*** *movie clip." Why not? Because you need to keep in mind that this slideshow needs to be* dynamic. *When the viewer clicks the Next Slide button, you need to be able to tell Flash MX 2004 to take whichever slide image the viewer is currently looking at and go load the next one in the sequence. This all goes back to the specific naming of each of the slideshow images:* ***frames0***, ***frames1***, *and so forth. Remember, the word "frames" remains consistent throughout each image; only the number at the end changes. So what you need first is a way to keep track of the current image number. By default, the viewer will start by looking at image 0. When the viewer clicks the Next Slide button, Flash MX 2004 will download and display image 1.*

```
var curFrameNum:Number = 0;

// ----------------<pre-built code for chapter 7>---------------- \\
/*
frameNum.autoSize = "center";
loadedInfo.autoSize = "right";
```

5. In the **Actions** panel, click the top-most empty line-break (provided for you as well) above the prewritten actions, and type the following:

`var curFrameNum:Number = 0;`

There's nothing in that action you haven't seen before in this book. Essentially, you're simply creating a variable called ***curFrameNum****, you're strict typing it as a* ***Number****, and you're then inserting the number 0 into that variable. This variable,* ***curFrameNum*** *(short for current frame number) is, of course, going to keep track of which slide the viewer is currently looking at. But why start at the number 0? Why not just start at the number 1 instead? You can actually start at any number you'd like when building this slideshow; you would just need to incorporate that into the script you're going to write later in this chapter. However, as mentioned previously, my goal in this book is to teach you good ActionScript practices. That way, if you decide to further your ActionScript knowledge, you'll already be a step ahead and won't have to relearn the basics of more advanced methods. So you're starting with the number 0 because more advanced actions, such as array elements and XML nodes, start with the count of 0. In Flash MX 2004 ActionScript–and most other computer programming languages–0 (even though you may think of 0 as representing "nothing" and thereby simply not use it) is the first number when counting sequentially–0, 1, 2, 3, and so forth.*

In the next step, you are going to incorporate that variable into an action that instructs the ***MovieClipLoader*** *object to load the first slide (****frames0.jpg****) into the* ***framesMC*** *movie clip instance.*

```
var curFrameNum:Number = 0;

_level0.myMCL.loadClip("frames/frames" + curFrameNum + ".jpg"
```

6. Click at the end of the **`var curFrameNum:Number = 0;`** line, press **Enter** (Windows) or **Return** (Mac) twice to create a couple of line breaks, and create the first part of the slide loading action by typing the following:

`_level0.myMCL.loadClip("frames/frames" + curFrameNum + ".jpg"`

Although this action isn't finished yet, what you have written thus far should be fairly familiar to you. What is probably unfamiliar *to you are the plus signs (+) you see in this action. All the plus signs do are concatenate. Technically, it's a* symbolic operator *called* addition *(yeah, duh eh?). When you see the plus sign, you can simply think of it as tape (the sticky kind). It takes whatever comes before it and adds it onto whatever comes after it, just like if you were adding numbers like 2 + 2. The addition operator in Flash MX 2004, however, is much more powerful. In this action, it is adding* strings *("frames/frames" and ".jpg") onto an* expression *(the variable **curFrameNum**). Now, when this action gets compiled when you publish your movie, the expression **curFrameNum** will be replaced with whatever the value of that variable is. As you wrote in the last step, the value of the **curFrameNum** variable is the number 0. So when this part of the action is compiled, it will read **_level0.myMCL.loadClip ("frames/frames0.jpg"**. Of course, **frames/** is the name of the folder storing the images, and **frames0.jpg** is the name of the first JPG image to load. Cool! To complete this action—now that you've specified which asset to load (**frames/frames0.jpg**)—you need to write* where *that asset should load.*

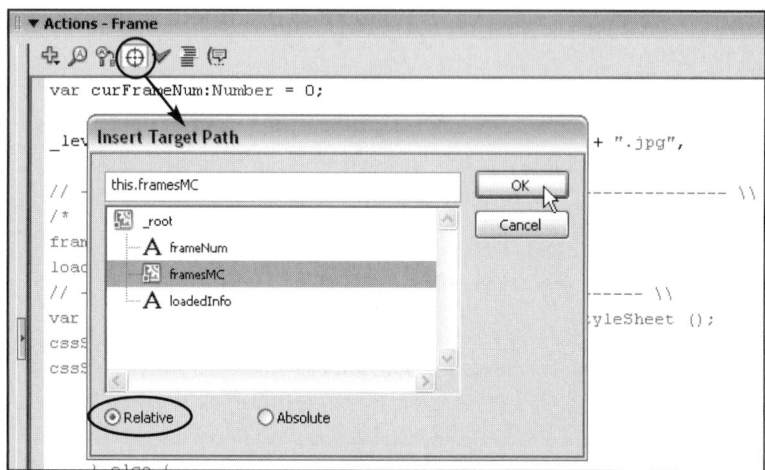

7. Click at the end of the `_level0.myMCL.loadClip("frames/frames" + curFrameNum + ".jpg"` line, and then type a comma and a space (,). Next, you need to specify the location (and the path to that location) where the slideshow image will load. Click the **Insert Target Path Button**. In the **Insert Target Path** window that appears, select the **Relative** button, click **framesMC**, and then click **OK**. **`this.framesMC`** (the path to where the slide images are to be loaded) will then be inserted into the action.

Alternatively, if you remembered the instance name and path to what you're targeting, you could simply type it in the Actions panel by hand without ever opening the Insert Target Path window. However, using the Insert Target Path window is a great way to ensure that you have set both the path and the spelling correctly when writing an action.

```
var curFrameNum:Number = 0;

_level0.myMCL.loadClip("frames/frames" + curFrameNum + ".jpg", this.framesMC);
```

8. To end the action, make sure the insertion point (the blinking bar that shows you where you're typing) is after **`this.framesMC`**, and then type a semicolon (**;**).

*Taken as a whole, this action simply reads, "Use the **`MovieClipLoader`** script (located in the **master.swf** movie [**`_level0`**]) to load the image located at **frames/frames0.jpg** into the **`framesMC`** movie clip instance."*

*Before continuing, it's always a good idea to test your work. That way, as you continue, you know you're building on ActionScript that works. Of course, to test the Frames module you first need to publish an updated SWF. Then, because the Frames module makes use of the **`MovieClipLoader`** script located in **master.fla**, you need to return to **master.fla**, add an action to load the Frames module, and test **frames.swf** as it is loaded into **master.swf**.*

9. Save the changes you've made to **frames.fla** by choosing **File > Save**. Then, publish an updated SWF by choosing **File > Publish**.

10. Bring **master.fla** into the foreground. If you accidentally closed it since you worked with it last, you can easily open it again by navigating to your **Desktop > la_eyeworks > site** folder and double-clicking **master.fla** to open it.

11. Select **Keyframe 10** in the **a** layer and open the **Actions** panel (**F9**).

```
stop();
// myMCL.loadClip("splash.swf", 5);
// myMCL.loadClip("about_us.swf", 5);
myMCL.loadClip("frames.swf", 5);
```

12. Comment out the **`myMCL.loadClip("about_us.swf", 5);`** line by adding two forward slashes (**//**) before the line. Then, click after the same line and press **Enter** (Windows) or **Return** (Mac) to create a line break. Lastly, write the action that will load the **frames.swf** file into **`_level5`** by typing the following:

```
myMCL.loadClip("frames.swf", 5);
```

13. Save the changes you've made to **master.fla** by choosing **File > Save**. Then, test **master.fla** by choosing **Control > Test Movie**.

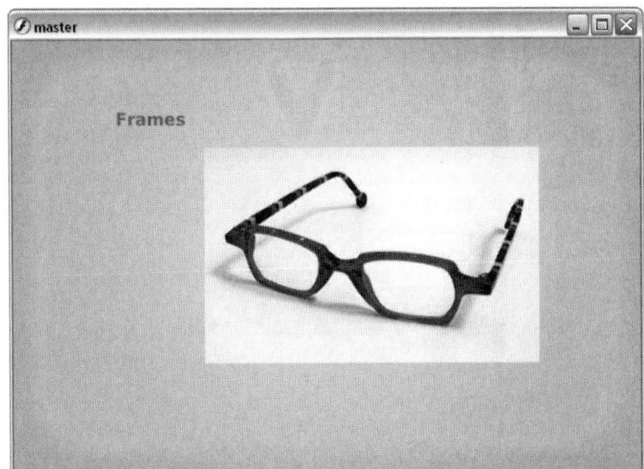

When the Frames module loads into ***master.swf****, you'll instantly see the first slideshow image appear. Awesome!*

14. Close the preview window and return to **frames.fla**.

Now that you've gotten the first slideshow image to load correctly, in the next exercise you will add script that will enable users to navigate both forward and backward through the slides.

4. Loading the Total Slides Variable

In this exercise, you will add the Next Slide/Previous Slide buttons that the viewer will use to navigate forward and backward (respectively) through the slideshow. You will also create a new **LoadVars** object to handle the loading of an external variable that keeps track of the total number of slides in the slideshow. The total number of slides variable (**totalFrames**) is important because it represents the total number of images in the slideshow. By keeping track of the total number of slides, you can (and later will) write an action that will allow the slideshow to loop as the viewer navigates through the slideshow images.

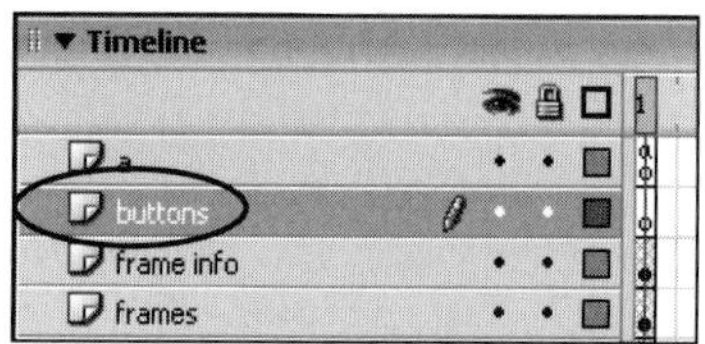

1. Single-click the layer below the **a** layer (**frame info**), and create a new layer. Rename the new layer **buttons**. This is the layer that will hold the Next Slide/Previous Slide buttons.

2. Open the **frames.fla Library** by pressing **Ctrl+L** (Windows) or **Cmd+L** (Mac).

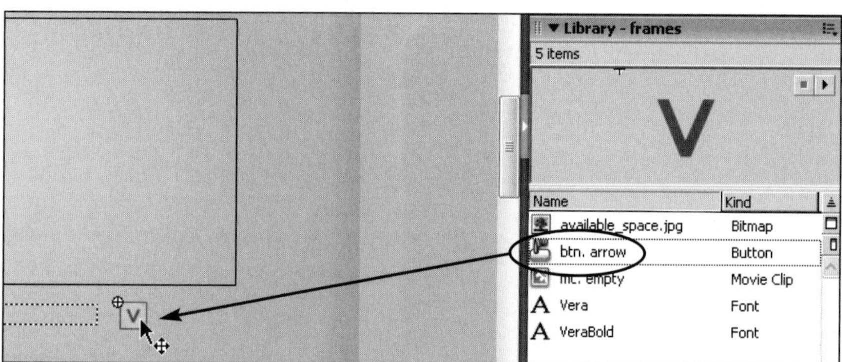

3. Drag an instance of the button symbol **btn. arrow** from the **Library** onto the **Stage**. Position the button below the **framesMC** movie clip instance and a little to the right of the **frameNum** dynamic text field.

Currently, the arrow button is pointing down. To visually make the most sense as the Next Slide button, it should really be pointing to the right.

4. With the **btn. arrow** button symbol still selected, choose **Modify > Transform > Rotate 90° CCW.** This will, as the menu option implies, rotate the arrow button so that it's facing to the right. After rotating it, you will need to use the arrow keys to nudge the arrow button back into place.

Next, you need a button that will allow the viewer to navigate backward through the slideshow.

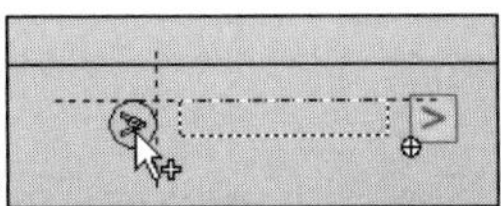

5. Hold down the **Ctrl** key (Windows) or the **Option** key (Mac) and drag the **btn. arrow** button symbol instance to the left side of the **`frameNum`** dynamic text field. This will make a copy of the **btn. arrow** button symbol.

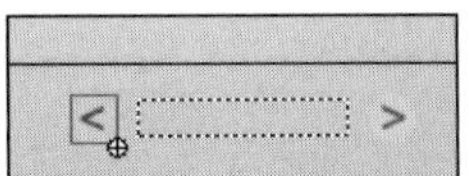

6. With the copied button symbol selected, choose **Modify > Transform > Flip Horizontal.** This will flip the copied button symbol so that it is facing to the left instead of to the right. You might need to use the arrow keys to reposition the copied button arrow after you've flipped it.

As you've seen before, if you want to assign ActionScript to those button symbols from a keyframe, you'll need to first give instance names to both button symbols.

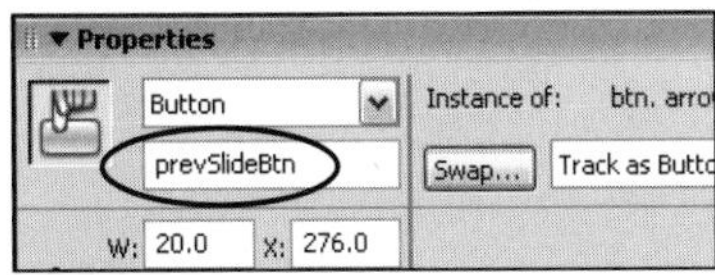

7. With the left-facing arrow button selected, click in the **Instance Name** field in the **Properties inspector** and type **prevSlideBtn**. This is now the instance name of the Previous Slide button and is the name you can use when you want to refer to that button with ActionScript.

8. Select the right-facing arrow button, and give it an **Instance Name** of **nextSlideBtn**.

*Now that you've given a unique name to each button instance, you can begin to create the script that will control the Next Slide/Previous Slide functionality. You'll start by writing the **`onRelease`** function that you will attach to the **`nextSlideBtn`** button symbol. The first part of this process is identical to when you've attached actions–from a keyframe to a symbol instance–earlier in this book.*

9. Select the first keyframe in the **a** layer, and open the **Actions** panel (**F9**).

```
var curFrameNum:Number = 0;

_level0.myMCL.loadClip("frames/frames" + curFrameNum + ".jpg", this.framesMC);

// -----------------<next slide button>---------------- \\

// -----------------</next slide button>---------------- \\
```

10. Click at the end of the action that you wrote in the previous exercise, **`_level0.myMCL.loadClip ("frames/frames" + curFrameNum + ".jpg", this.framesMC);`**, and press **Enter** (Windows) or **Return** (Mac) twice to create a couple of line breaks. Then, type out the opening comment:

```
// -----------------<next slide button>------------------ \\
```

Click at the end of that comment, press **Enter** (Windows) or **Return** (Mac) twice to create two more line breaks, and then type out the closing comment:

```
// -----------------</next slide button>------------------ \\
```

Now you have the opening and closing comments that will contain the Next Slide button ActionScript.

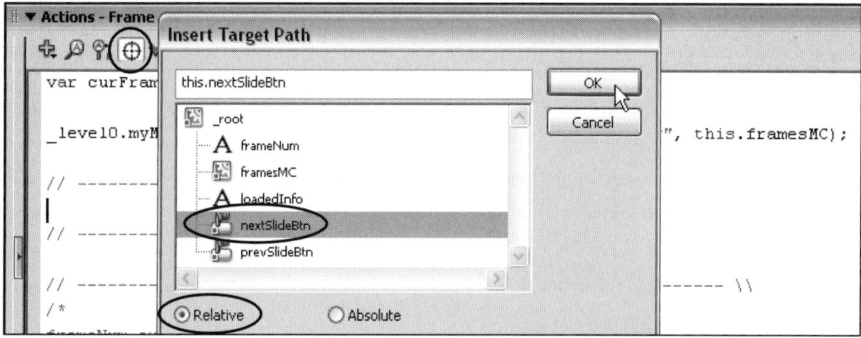

11. Click between the opening and closing **next slide button** comment lines, and then insert the path to the button symbol you want to target with ActionScript by clicking the **Insert a Target Path** button. In the **Insert Target Path** dialog box that opens, make sure that **Relative** is selected, and then click the button symbol **nextSlideBtn**. This will insert that instance name, and the path to it, in the target field. Click **OK**.

```
// -----------------<next slide button>--------------- \\
this.nextSlideBtn.onRelease = function() {
// -----------------</next slide button>--------------- \\
```

12. Click after the inserted target path, **this.nextSlideBtn**, and type the following:

.onRelease = function() {

Make sure to type the period (.) between ***nextSlideBtn*** *and* ***onRelease****. The first line in this function says, "When the viewer clicks (****onRelease****) on the* ***nextSlideBtn****, execute the following actions within this function."*

Next, you need to create the actions that will be executed when the viewer clicks the Next Slide button. So at this point, as a Flash MX 2004 designer/developer, you should be asking yourself, "OK self. What should happen when the viewer clicks the Next Slide button? Well, I want an action to be executed that tells the ***MovieClipLoader*** *to load the next JPG in sequence. Hmm. But what will happen if the viewer is already looking at the last slide in the sequence? What should happen then? I suppose that if the viewer is already looking at the last slide, and he or she then clicks the Next Slide button, the slideshow should go back to the first slide in the sequence. That way, the slideshow will continually loop as the viewer clicks through it." And if you were thinking that to yourself before you just read it here, you're exactly correct. ;-)*

The functionality you're going to start to create in this exercise (and will then finish in the following exercise) will cause the slideshow to loop back to the beginning when the viewer is looking at the last slide in the slideshow and he or she clicks the Next Slide button. So how would you start writing a script that takes all that into account? The first thing you want to find out–when the viewer clicks the Next Slide button–is whether or not he or she is currently looking at the last slide. If yes, you can then instruct your ***MovieClipLoader*** *to load the first slide in the sequence. If not, you can then tell the* ***MovieClipLoader*** *to simply load the next slide in sequence. A key piece to this script working correctly is finding out which slide is the last slide. If you want the slideshow to loop back to the first slide when the viewer has reached the end of the slideshow, you first need a way to determine which slide is the last.*

Earlier in this chapter you created a variable, ***curFrameNum****, that tracked the current slide. Now you need another variable that keeps track of the total number of slides. You could easily create this variable in the first keyframe of* ***frames.fla****. But if the client ever wanted to add or remove slides (thereby changing how many slides there are total), they would have to open* ***frames.fla*** *in a copy of Flash MX 2004 (because Flash MX 2004 FLA files can't be opened in previous versions of Flash) and have the know-how to change the number in the variable. As discussed earlier in this book, it's best to keep elements (variables, images, and so forth) the client might need to change themselves outside of the FLA. That way, if the client needs to make a change, it's much easier for them–with much less know-how (not to mention the necessary software)–to do it themselves.*

*What all this means is that instead of creating the variable–which keeps track of the total number of slides in the slideshow–in **frames.fla** itself, you're instead going to store that variable in an external text file, and use **LoadVars** to dynamically load it in. Because of the way the main **LoadVars** script that you originally wrote in **master.fla** is set up, it can only be used to load the descriptive text for each slideshow image. So in order to utilize another external variable for a different purpose, you're going to create a separate, slimmed-down **LoadVars** script that will specifically handle the loading of the variable that tracks the total number of slides. Although that may sound excessive, keep in mind that it requires only two lines of code (and two lines of code that you've seen before, at that).*

*You'll come back to this **nextSlideBtn** script later, but first you need to write the **LoadVars** script that will allow you to determine the total number of slides. You need to know that number before you can continue writing the functionality for the Next Slide/Previous Slide buttons.*

```
var slideInfoLV:LoadVars = new LoadVars();

var curFrameNum:Number = 0;

_level0.myMCL.loadClip("frames/frames" + curFrameNum + ".jpg", this.framesMC);

// -----------------<next slide button>---------------- \\
this.nextSlideBtn.onRelease = function() {
// -----------------</next slide button>---------------- \\
```

13. Click to the left of the top-most line, **var curFrameNum:Number = 0;**, and press **Enter** (Windows) or **Return** (Mac) twice to create a couple of line breaks. Then, click the top-most empty line break you just created and define a new **LoadVars** object with the instance name **slideInfoLV** by typing the following:

var slideInfoLV:LoadVars = new LoadVars();

As you saw in Chapter 4, "LoadVars Class," *this action creates a new **LoadVars** object and assigns it the instance name of **slideInfoLV**. This **LoadVars** object will load the external variable (within a text file) that will keep track of the total number of slides in the slideshow. So what about that text file? Because you've already seen what comprises a text file that contains external variables, I created the text file for you to save you some time. Before you load it into your project, however, you need to know the name of the variable in the text file, as well as* where *the text file is located.*

14. Hide or minimize Flash MX 2004, and navigate to your **Desktop > la_eyeworks > site > vars** folder.

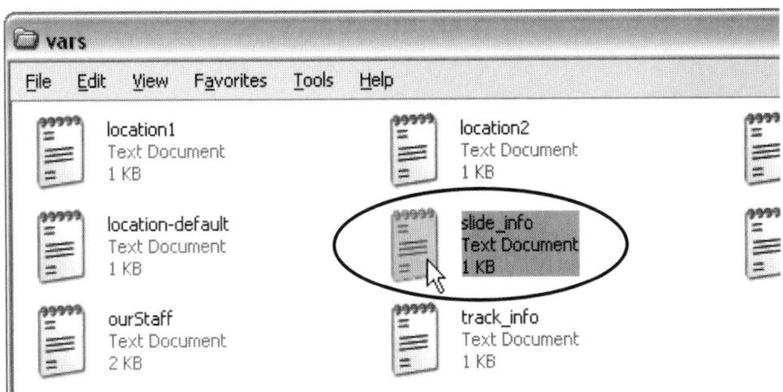

15. Within the **vars** folder is a text file titled **slide_info.txt**. Open this text file in a plain text editor such as **Notepad** (Windows), **TextEdit** (Mac), or **BBEdit** (Mac).

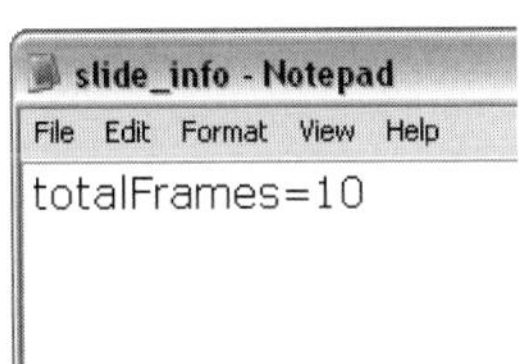

*As you can see, the contents are very basic. There's one variable, **`totalFrames`**, with a value of 10. Now, technically, there are 10 slides total. However, the last slide in the slideshow ends with the number **9** **(frames9.jpg)**. So when using the **totalFrames** variable in a script to define which slide is the* last *slide, the number **10** is actually incorrect. Later, when you use **totalFrames** in a script, you will need to make sure you take into account that while the **totalFrames** variable* does *represent the total number of slides, it* does not *represent the number of the* last *slide in the slide show (9). Again, this goes back to the fact that the slide show starts with the number 0.*

*The main reason why you have to jump through a few ActionScript hoops when dealing with **totalFrames** comes back to allowing yourself, and the client, to easily update this variable. If the client were to ever modify the total number of slides, all they would have to do is to open this text file, update the number, save the file, and upload it to the correct location on the server. Voilà! They wouldn't need to open/edit the **frames.fla** file, or even own a copy of Flash MX 2004 for that matter. Now that you've seen the contents of the text file and where it's located, you can load it and utilize it in the project.*

---

16. Close the text file and bring Flash MX 2004 back to the foreground. Make sure you still have **Keyframe 1** selected in the **a** layer of **frames.fla** and that your **Actions** panel is open.

```
var slideInfoLV:LoadVars = new LoadVars();
slideInfoLV.load("vars/slide_info.txt");

var curFrameNum:Number = 0;

_level0.myMCL.loadClip("frames/frames" + curFrameNum + ".jpg", this.framesMC);

// -----------------<next slide button>---------------- \\
this.nextSlideBtn.onRelease = function() {
// -----------------</next slide button>---------------- \\
```

17. Click at the end of the top-most action, **`var slideInfoLV:LoadVars = new LoadVars();`**, press **Enter** (Windows) or **Return** (Mac) to create a line break, and load the variables from the **slide_info.txt** file by typing the following:

```
slideInfoLV.load("vars/slide_info.txt");
```

*This action uses the **`LoadVars`** object you just created, **`slideInfoLV`** to load the variables from the **slide_info.txt** file that is in the **vars** folder.*

*You have now loaded, within the Frames module, the total number of slides in the slideshow. Whenever you need to use that number in a script, you can simply write **`slideInfoLV.totalFrames`**, where **`slideInfoLV`** is the instance name of the **`LoadVars`** object you created and **`totalFrames`** is the variable name (which contains the total number of slides [10]) located within the loaded **slide_info.txt** file. Cool!*

In the next exercise, you will finish writing the script that allows the viewer to navigate (and loop) forward through the slideshow.

5. Adding the Next Slide Functionality

In this exercise, you will continue writing the ActionScript that will allow the viewer to advance to the next image in the slideshow. You will also write actions into this script that allows the slideshow to "loop"–that is, to return to the beginning of the slideshow if the viewer is already looking at the last slideshow image when he or she clicks the Next Slide button.

```
// ----------------<next slide button>---------------- \\
this.nextSlideBtn.onRelease = function() {

    if (curFrameNum < Number(slideInfoLV.totalFrames) - 1) {
// ----------------</next slide button>---------------- \\
```

1. Within the Next Slide button script, click at the end of the **`this.nextSlideBtn.onRelease = function() {`** line, press **Enter** (Windows) or **Return** (Mac) twice to create two line breaks, and type the following:

```
if (curFrameNum < Number(slideInfoLV.totalFrames) - 1) {
```

*What this **if** action says is, "If the slide number that is currently being viewed (**curFrameNum**) is less than the total number of slides (as retrieved from the external **slide_info.txt** file) minus one..." Remember, you need to subtract one from the **totalFrames** variable because even though that variable represents the total number of slides (10), the last slide number is 9 (**frames9.jpg**).*

*However, what is probably not familiar to you in this action is the inclusion of **Number**, which is a built-in function that converts the expression within the parentheses after it to a number. The reason you're using **Number** in this action comes down to this:*

*When you use **LoadVars** to load variable/value pairs from an external text file–as you did earlier in this chapter to load the total number of slideshow images–the values are loaded into to the **LoadVars** object as strings. A string, as mentioned earlier, is a bit of text such as "Shane Rebenschied." Conversely, a **Number** is a number such as 1, 2, 3, and so forth. Normally, when you're loading a number in a text file into your Flash MX 2004 project using **LoadVars**, you can display that number in your movie and everything will work just fine. But if you want to use that number in an equation, Flash MX 2004 normally won't be able to use that number properly.*

For example, say you have a variable in an external text file called **myVariable***, and the value of that variable is the number 1. Your text file would look like this:* **myVariable=1***. You then use a* **LoadVars** *object with an instance name of* **myLV** *to load that variable into your project. Then, you'd like to add 1 to the* **myVariable** *number. So from within your movie, you write* **myLV.myVariable + 1;***. Because the value of* **myVariable** *is 1, you would expect the result of that equation to be 2. What you'd actually end up with, however, is 11. Instead of using mathematical addition to add 1 + 1, Flash MX 2004 has concatenated 1 and 1 for a result of 11 because the loaded* **myVariable** *number is treated as a string (text). So before you can use a number that you've imported into your project using* **LoadVars***, that number (which is actually a string), needs to be converted into an actual number. In Step 1, that's what* **Number(slideInfoLV.totalFrames)** *does. The* **Number** *function converts the value of the* **slideInfoLV.totalFrames** *(which, if you remember, is 10), into a number. You're converting the value of the* **slideInfoLV.totalFrames** *variable into a number because you are using it in an equation, to subtract 1 from. In more advanced ActionScript terms, this is referred to as* ***casting***.

Now, if the **if** *action you wrote in Step 1 is true (when executed), it means that the viewer is not currently looking at the last slide. If he or she isn't looking at the last slide in the slideshow when the* **nextSlideBtn** *button is clicked, the next slide–in sequence–should be loaded. How, exactly, do you go about loading the next slide in sequence? First, you need to add 1 onto the variable that is keeping track of the current slide. Once you've done that you can then tell the* **MovieClipLoader** *to load that particular slide number. First, you need to add 1 onto the current slide number (so the script can then go and load the next slide in sequence).*

```
// -----------------<next slide button>---------------- \\
this.nextSlideBtn.onRelease = function() {

    if (curFrameNum < Number(slideInfoLV.totalFrames) - 1) {
        curFrameNum++;
// -----------------</next slide button>---------------- \\
```

2. Click at the end of the **if** action, **if (curFrameNum < Number(slideInfoLV.totalFrames) - 1) {**, press **Enter** (Windows) or **Return** (Mac) once to create a line break, and add 1 onto the current slide number by typing the following:

curFrameNum++;

This simple action basically says, "Add one onto the number in the **curFrameNum** *variable." The* **curFrameNum** *variable, as you remember, is keeping track of which slide number is the current slide. The double plus sign (++) that you see in that action is called an* ***increment***. *It just adds one onto the expression. So, in this case, the* **curFrameNum** *variable resolves (when the Frames module is first played) to the number 0. When you increment that number, it changes the number to 1. The increment operator (++), in this case, simply tells Flash MX 2004 to add 1 onto the number within the* **curFrameNum** *variable. Nifty!*

*Before you write the action that actually does the loading of the slideshow images, you should first complete the **if** action by writing an **else** action that defines what should happen if the **if** action turns out to be false. In other words, what should happen if the viewer is looking at the last slide when they click the Next Slide button? Simply, to make the slideshow loop, the **curFrameNum** variable should be set back to 0.*

```
// -----------------<next slide button>---------------- \\
this.nextSlideBtn.onRelease = function() {

    if (curFrameNum < Number(slideInfoLV.totalFrames) - 1) {
        curFrameNum++;
    } else {
        curFrameNum = 0;
    }
// -----------------</next slide button>---------------- \\
```

3. Click at the end of the **curFrameNum++;** line, press **Enter** (Windows) or **Return** (Mac) once to create a line break, and add the **else** action by typing the following:

```
} else {
```

Then set the **curFrameNum** variable to equal **0**. End the **else** action by clicking at the end of the **} else {** line, pressing **Enter** (Windows) or **Return** (Mac) once, and typing the following:

```
curFrameNum = 0;
}
```

*When you're finished writing the **if** and **else** actions, they should look like those in the screen shot above.*

*What the **if** and **else** actions say when combined is, "When the viewer clicks the Next Slide button, if the current slide number is less than the total number of slides (minus one), then set the current slide to be one number greater than the current slide. Otherwise (if the viewer is looking at the last slide), just set the current slide number to 0." Those **if** and **else** actions combined is what makes the slideshow loop when the viewer gets to the end.*

*Now that you've defined what number should reside in the **curFrameNum** variable, you need to write the action that will load that particular slide number. But rather than copy the action–which you wrote earlier in this exercise–that loads the slide image into the **framesMC** movie clip instance, you're instead going to place that action within a function. (Remember, a function is just a container to hold actions.) Because the load slide action will be needed when the viewer clicks the Next Slide button or the Previous Slide button, it will be easier to just place the action within a function and then call that function whenever you need it instead of duplicating the action and attaching it to the Next Slide and Previous Slide buttons. Later, this function will also contain the action that loads the descriptive slide text. Because those actions will need to be executed from various places (from the Next Slide button and from the Previous Slide button), it's a much better workflow to place those commonly used actions in a function and simply call that function whenever it is needed.*

```
function loadFrame() {
    _level0.myMCL.loadClip("frames/frames" + curFrameNum + ".jpg", this.framesMC);
}

// ----------------<next slide button>---------------- \\
this.nextSlideBtn.onRelease = function() {

    if (curFrameNum < Number(slideInfoLV.totalFrames) - 1) {
        curFrameNum++;
    } else {
        curFrameNum = 0;
    }
// ----------------</next slide button>---------------- \\
```

4. Click at the beginning of the action that loads the current slide, **`_level0.myMCL.loadClip ("frames/frames" + curFrameNum + ".jpg", this.framesMC);`**, and press **Enter** (Windows) or **Return** (Mac) to create a new line break *above* that line. Then, create a new function by clicking the new line and typing the following:

`function loadFrame() {`

---

5. To close the function, click at the end of the **`loadClip`** action, **`_level0.myMCL.loadClip ("frames/frames" + curFrameNum + ".jpg", this.framesMC);`**, press **Enter** (Windows) or **Return** (Mac) once to create a line break, and type a closed curly braces (**}**), as shown in the screen shot above.

*The **`loadClip`** action should also be indented within the function (to follow proper ActionScript formatting), so click at the beginning of the **`_level0.myMCL.loadClip("frames/frames" + curFrameNum + ".jpg", this.framesMC);`** line and press **Tab** once to indent the action. Great! Now when you want that **`loadClip`** action (and any other actions you place within that function) to be executed, you can just call the function's name (and the path to the function, if you're calling the function from a different Timeline) by typing **`loadFrame();`**.*

*Now that you've created a function to hold the action that loads the slideshow image, you can call that **`loadFrame`** function from the **`nextSlideBtn`** function.*

```
// ----------------<next slide button>---------------- \\
this.nextSlideBtn.onRelease = function() {

    if (curFrameNum < Number(slideInfoLV.totalFrames) - 1) {
        curFrameNum++;
    } else {
        curFrameNum = 0;
    }

    loadFrame();
// ----------------</next slide button>---------------- \\
```

Click after this closed curly brace

6. Within the Next Slide button script, click after the closing **else** curly brace (as circled in the screen shot above), press **Enter** (Windows) or **Return** (Mac) twice to create a couple of line breaks, and trigger the **loadFrame** function by typing the following:

loadFrame();

*This will trigger the **loadFrame** function–thereby executing all the actions within it–when the viewer clicks the Next Slide button. Because it comes* after *the **if** and **else** actions that set what the number in the **curFrameNum** variable should be, when the **loadFrame** function is triggered, it will load whichever slide corresponds with that number. Pretty slick!*

*As yet, however, the only action within the **loadFrame** function is the action that loads the next slide JPG. Later in this chapter, you will place another action within that function that also needs to be triggered each time the viewer clicks the Next Slide and Previous Slide buttons.*

```
// -----------------<next slide button>---------------- \\
this.nextSlideBtn.onRelease = function() {

    if (curFrameNum < Number(slideInfoLV.totalFrames) - 1) {
        curFrameNum++;
    } else {
        curFrameNum = 0;
    }

    loadFrame();

}
// -----------------</next slide button>---------------- \\
```

7. Close the **nextSlideBtn** function by clicking at the end of the **loadFrame();** line, pressing **Enter** (Windows) or **Return** (Mac) twice to create a couple of line breaks, and typing a closed curly brace (**}**).

There you have it, the (nearly) completed functionality for the Next Slide button! But before you can test your movie, there's one last action you need to add. By moving the ***loadClip*** *action–which loads the current slideshow image–into a function as you did in Steps 4 and 5, it won't automatically get executed when the Frames module first loads. Translation? When the Frames module first loads, the first slideshow image will not automatically load and display. To fix this, you need to call the function so that the* ***loadClip*** *action will execute when the Frames module first loads. Later, this action will be incorporated into another action, but for now–for testing–you can just call the function outright.*

```
function loadFrame() {
    _level0.myMCL.loadClip("frames/frames" + curFrameNum + ".jpg", this.framesMC);
}
loadFrame();
```

8. Click after the closed curly brace for the **loadFrame** function, press **Enter** (Windows) or **Return** (Mac) once to create a line break, and trigger the **loadFrame** function by typing the following:

loadFrame();

When the ***frames.swf*** *file first loads, this will automatically execute the* ***loadFrame*** *function and all the actions within it. What does that mean in plain English? It means that now, when the Frames module first loads, the first slide will automatically load.*

9. Save the changes you've made to **frames.fla** by choosing **File > Save**. Then publish an updated SWF by choosing **File > Publish** (**Shift+F12**) on Mac or Windows.

10. Hide or minimize Flash MX 2004, and navigate to your **Desktop > la_eyeworks > site** folder. Then double-click **master.swf** to play it in the stand-alone Macromedia Flash Player 7.

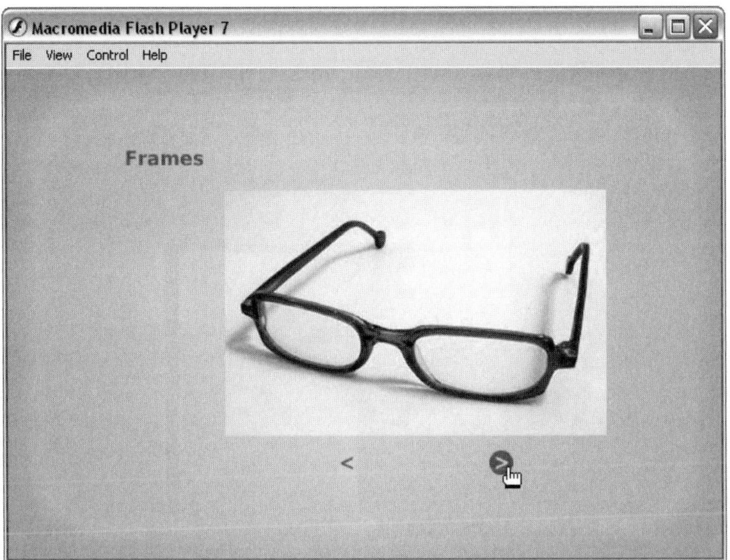

*When the Frames module first loads into **master.swf**, you should see the first slideshow image load and display, just like it did before. But now, click the Next Slide button. When you click the Next Slide button, the next image in the slideshow sequence will load and display where the first image was. Stupendous! Each time you click the Next Slide button, the next slideshow image will load. (Behind the scenes, your movie is adding 1 onto the **`curFrameNum`** variable every time you click the Next Slide button). When the last slideshow image, **frames9.jpg**, is displayed, the **`if`** action you wrote within the **`nextSlideBtn.onRelease`** function is no longer true. The **`curFrameNum`** value is no longer less than the **`totalFrames`** value minus one (9). Because the **`if`** action is no longer true, the **`else`** action you wrote takes over, sets the **`curFrameNum`** variable back to 0, and then the **`loadFrame`** function is triggered, causing the slideshow to load the first slide in sequence, **frames0.jpg**. So as you can see, you can keep clicking that Next Slide button until you grow calluses an inch thick on your finger, but the slideshow will never end. Thanks to the combination of the **`if`** and **`else`** actions, the slideshow will seamlessly loop through the slideshow.*

---

11. Close the stand-alone Macromedia Flash Player 7 window, and bring Flash MX 2004 back to the foreground. Make sure that **frames.fla** is still your foreground FLA and that you have the first keyframe in the **a** layer selected with the **Actions** panel open.

*Now, obviously, you need to add similar–but opposite–functionality to the Previous Slide button. Luckily, the ActionScript you wrote for the Next Slide button is very similar to the script needed for the Previous Slide button. What does that mean? It means in the next exercise you can duplicate the script you just wrote for the Next Slide button and slightly modify the duplicate so that it will work for the Previous Slide button. *Whew**

Adding the Previous Slide Functionality

In this exercise, you will finish what you started in the previous exercises. You will take the Next Slide button script, duplicate it, and modify it to work with the Previous Slide button. Because the functionality of the Next Slide/Previous Slide buttons are very similar, it makes sense to reuse as much of the work as possible.

```
// -----------------<next slide button>---------------- \\
this.nextSlideBtn.onRelease = function() {

    if (curFrameNum < Number(slideInfoLV.totalFrames) - 1) {
        curFrameNum++;
    } else {
        curFrameNum = 0;
    }

    loadFrame();

}
// -----------------</next slide button>---------------- \\
```

Undo
Redo
Cut
Copy
Paste
Delete
Select All
Set Breakpoint
Remove Breakpoint
Remove All Breakpoints
View Help

1. Select the entire **Next Slide** button script, even the open/closed comment lines. Then, **right-click** (Windows) or **Ctrl+click** (Mac) anywhere on that selected script. From the contextual menu that appears, choose **Copy**.

```
// -----------------<next slide button>---------------- \\
this.nextSlideBtn.onRelease = function() {

    if (curFrameNum < Number(slideInfoLV.totalFrames) - 1) {
        curFrameNum++;
    } else {
        curFrameNum = 0;
    }

    loadFrame();

}
// -----------------</next slide button>---------------- \\
```

Undo
Redo
Cut
Copy
Paste
Delete

2. Click at the end of the closing **next slide button** comment, **// --------------</next slide button---------------** \\, and press **Enter** (Windows) or **Return** (Mac) twice to create a couple of line breaks. Then **right-click** (Windows) or **Ctrl+click** (Mac) the second new line you just created, and from the contextual menu that appears, choose **Paste**. This will paste a copy of the **Next Slide** button script below the original.

```
// ----------------<previous slide button>---------------- \\
this.nextSlideBtn.onRelease = function() {

    if (curFrameNum < Number(slideInfoLV.totalFrames) - 1) {
        curFrameNum++;
    } else {
        curFrameNum = 0;
    }

    loadFrame();

}
// ----------------</previous slide button>---------------- \\
```

3. In the copied script, start by changing the comments. Change the word "next" in the opening comment to "previous." Do the same for the closing comment. Make sure that you're making these changes to the copied script and not to the original **Next Slide** button script.

*This script applies to the Previous Slide button, so you also need to make sure you change the target of the **onRelease** function.*

```
// ----------------<previous slide button>---------------- \\
this.prevSlideBtn.onRelease = function() {

    if (curFrameNum < Number(slideInfoLV.totalFrames) - 1) {
        curFrameNum++;
    } else {
        curFrameNum = 0;
    }

    loadFrame();

}
// ----------------</previous slide button>---------------- \\
```

4. Change the targeted button symbol **nextSlideBtn** to target the **Previous Slide** button, **prevSlideBtn**.

*When navigating through the slideshow backward, you obviously don't need the **if** action to check if you're not viewing the last slideshow image. When going backward, you want the **if** action to check if the viewer is looking at the first slide when he or she clicks the Previous Slide button. Because if he or she is already looking at the first slide, then you want the slideshow to jump to the last slide in the sequence. This is the same concept as the Next Slide button, just in reverse.*

```
// ----------------<previous slide button>---------------- \\
this.prevSlideBtn.onRelease = function() {

     if (curFrameNum == 0) {
          curFrameNum++;
     } else {
          curFrameNum = 0;
     }

     loadFrame();

}
// ----------------</previous slide button>---------------- \\
```

5. Within the parentheses after the **`if`** statement, change the condition **`curFrameNum < Number (slideInfoLV.totalFrames) - 1`** to instead read **`curFrameNum == 0`**. Again, since the viewer is navigating backward, you need to determine whether he or she is viewing the first image in the slideshow when he or she clicks the **Previous Slide** button. If he or she clicks the **Previous Slide** button, you need to tell the slideshow to jump to the *end* and display the last image (thereby, making the slideshow "loop").

But before continuing writing this script, you probably want to know what's with the double equals signs (==) after ***`curFrameNum`****. Up until this point, you've only seen a single equals sign used in an action. The single equals sign is called an* ***assignment operator****. As you've seen in this script, it simply* assigns *the value to the right of the equals sign to what is on the left of the equals sign. In the previous script, you wrote* ***`curFrameNum = 0`****. This action* assigns *the number 0 to the variable* ***`curFrameNum`****. But what if—when writing an action—you wanted to check for* equality*? What if you wanted to check if the content to the left of the equals sign was* equal *to what was on the right? In the modification you just made to the* ***`if`*** *action in the previous step, you wrote* ***`if (curFrameNum == 0)`****. Instead of assigning a value to an expression (as a single equals sign does), this* ***`if`*** *action will check to see whether the value of the variable* ***`curFrameNum`*** *is* equal *to the number 0. The double equals sign is called an* ***equality operator****. It simply tests for equality between what's on the left of the equals sign and what's on the right.*

So what should happen if *the slideshow image the viewer is looking at is the first slide when he or she clicks the Previous Slide button? Simply, the slideshow should jump to the last image. That way, the slideshow will loop, even as the viewer continually clicks the Previous Slide button (just like what happens—but in reverse—when the viewer continually clicks the Next Slide button).*

```
// -----------------<previous slide button>---------------- \\
this.prevSlideBtn.onRelease = function() {

    if (curFrameNum == 0) {
        curFrameNum = Number(slideInfoLV.totalFrames) - 1;
    } else {
        curFrameNum = 0;
    }

    loadFrame();

}
// -----------------</previous slide button>---------------- \\
```

6. Change the line **curFrameNum++;** to instead read as follows:

curFrameNum = Number(slideInfoLV.totalFrames) - 1;

This action reads, "Set the current frame number to be whatever the total number of frames is, minus one." The ***slideInfoLV.totalFrames*** *should be familiar–you used it in the Next Slide button script for the same purpose (to retrieve the total number of slides in the slideshow). In this case, you're using that same variable to set the current slide number variable (****curFrameNum****) to equal the total number of slideshow frames if the user clicks the Previous Slide button while viewing the first slide in the slideshow. But just like before, you're subtracting one from the* ***totalFrames*** *variable to arrive at the number that represents the last slide in the slideshow,* ***9****. Because the* ***totalFrames*** *variable represents the total number of slides in the slideshow but not the* number *in the last slide of the slideshow, you need to subtract one to get the correct number–that's* ***9****–to use in this script.*

Now that you've specified what should happen if the viewer clicks the Previous Slide button when the slideshow is already on the first image, you need to specify what should happen when the viewer clicks the Previous Slide button when the slideshow is not *on the first slide image. Well, simply enough, the slideshow should just go to the* preceding *image.*

```
// -----------------<previous slide button>---------------- \\
this.prevSlideBtn.onRelease = function() {

    if (curFrameNum == 0) {
        curFrameNum = Number(slideInfoLV.totalFrames) - 1;
    } else {
        curFrameNum--;
    }

    loadFrame();

}
// -----------------</previous slide button>---------------- \\
```

7. Within the **else** action, change the line **curFrameNum = 0;** to instead read this:

curFrameNum--;

*In the Next Slide button script, you used the action **curFrameNum++;** to add 1 onto the value of the **curFrameNum** variable. This action (as I'm sure you've guessed) simply does the opposite and* sub-tracts *1 from the value of the **curFrameNum** variable. The double minus signs are called a **decrement operator**. The double minus signs merely subtract 1 from the expression to its left. In this case, they subtract 1 from the **curFrameNum** variable.*

*Taken all together, this Previous Slide button script reads, "When the viewer clicks the Previous Slide button, if the current slide image is 0, tell the **MovieClipLoader** script to load and display the* last *slide in the slideshow. Otherwise, just load the previous image in the slideshow."*

Congratulations! You've finished adding the slideshow functionality to the Next Slide/Previous Slide buttons! But, of course, you should test your changes to make sure everything is working as it should.

8. Save the changes you've made to **frames.fla** by choosing **File > Save**. Then publish an updated SWF by choosing **File > Publish**.

9. Hide or minimize Flash MX 2004, navigate to your **Desktop > la_eyeworks > site** folder, and double-click **master.swf** to view it in the stand-alone Macromedia Flash Player 7.

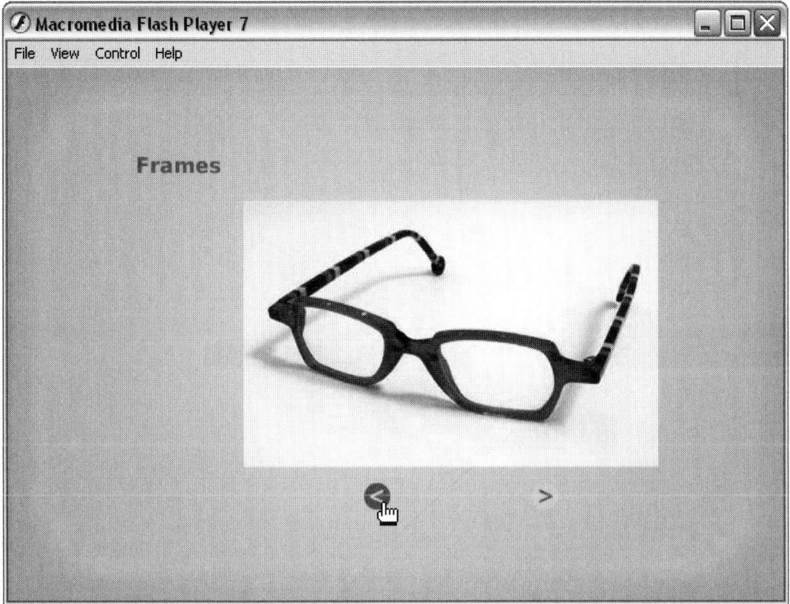

As you click through the Next Slide and Previous Slide buttons, notice how the slideshow continually loops both forward and backward. Very nice! You should give yourself a big pat on the back. You just created a slideshow that not only loops forward and backward but also dynamically loads each slide image from an external JPG file.

---

10. When you're finished, close the stand-alone Macromedia Flash Player 7 window, and bring Flash MX 2004 back to the foreground. Make sure that **frames.fla** is still the foreground FLA and that you have the first keyframe in the **a** layer selected with the **Actions** panel open.

Adding the Slideshow Descriptive Text

In this exercise, you are going to utilize the prebuilt **TextField.StyleSheet** object–which was included with the **frames.fla** file–to load and display the dynamic descriptive text that accompanies each slide in the slideshow. Accompanying each slide (if you remember from Exercise 1) are a few lines of descriptive text that update along with the slideshow images.

1. In **frames.fla**, with the first keyframe in the **a** layer selected and the **Actions** panel open, scroll down toward the bottom of the actions.

```
// -----------------<pre-built code for chapter 7>---------------- \\
/*
frameNum.autoSize = "center";
loadedInfo.autoSize = "right";
// -----------------<TextField.StyleSheet>---------------- \\
var cssStyles:TextField.StyleSheet = new TextField.StyleSheet ();
cssStyles.load ("styles/styles.css");
cssStyles.onLoad = function (success) {
    if (success) {
        loadedInfo.styleSheet = cssStyles;
```

2. Select the following two comment lines and delete them:

```
// -----------------<pre-built code for chapter 7>----------------- \\
/*
```

```
frameNum.autoSize = "center";
loadedInfo.autoSize = "right";
// -----------------<TextField.StyleSheet>---------------- \\
var cssStyles:TextField.StyleSheet = new TextField.StyleSheet ();
cssStyles.load ("styles/styles.css");
cssStyles.onLoad = function (success) {
    if (success) {
        loadedInfo.styleSheet = cssStyles;
        loadFrame();
    } else {
        loadedInfo.text = "There has been an error loading the requested information.  Please
contact the Webmaster and report your error.";
    }
}
// -----------------</TextField.StyleSheet>---------------- \\
*/
// -----------------</pre-built code for chapter 7>---------------- \\
```

3. Then select and delete the bottom two comment lines:

```
*/
// -----------------</pre-built code for chapter 7>----------------- \\
```

As mentioned earlier, the block of actions you just uncommented are pretty straightforward. The top two lines

```
frameNum.autoSize = "center";
loadedInfo.autoSize = "right";
```

simply set the text fields **frameNum** *and* **loadedInfo** *to allow them to resize as big as need be, and to align center and align right, respectively.*

The block of actions commented as **TextField.StyleSheet** *is nearly identical to the* **TextField.StyleSheet** *object you authored in Chapter 5,* "HTML and CSS." *This* **TextField.StyleSheet** *script loads the CSS style sheet* **styles.css** *located in the* **styles** *folder, and if the loading is successful, applies those styles to the* **loadedInfo** *text field on the Stage and executes the* **loadFrame** *function you created earlier in this chapter. If the loading of the* **styles.css** *file is* not *successful for one reason or another, an error message will appear in the* **loadedInfo** *dynamic text field.*

This **TextField.StyleSheet** *script is here inside* **frames.fla** *so that the descriptive text that accompanies each slide can be styled using an external style sheet. That way any changes that need to be made to the styling of the descriptive text can be made quickly and easily by modifying the* **styles.css** *file.*

Now as of yet, an action that will load the descriptive slide text into the **loadedInfo** *dynamic text field hasn't been written. But before you start writing that action, you need to know* where *that action should be located. Because the descriptive text accompanies each slide in the slideshow, it should be written alongside the action that loads each JPG in the slideshow. If you remember, earlier in this chapter you wrote a function called* **loadFrame** *and placed the slide-loading action within that function. As the viewer clicks the Next Slide/Previous Slide buttons, the* **loadFrame** *function gets executed and the next or previous slide loads. The action that loads the text that accompanies each slide will also be placed within the* **loadFrame** *function so that it gets executed at the same time.*

```
function loadFrame() {
    _level0.myMCL.loadClip("frames/frames" + curFrameNum + ".jpg", this.framesMC);
    _level0.myLV.load("frames/frames" + curFrameNum + ".txt");
}
```

4. Within the **loadFrame** function, click at the end of the `_level0.myMCL.loadClip("frames/frames" + curFrameNum + ".jpg", this.framesMC);` line, press **Enter** (Windows) or **Return** (Mac) once to create a line break, and type the following:

```
_level0.myLV.load("frames/frames" + curFrameNum + ".txt");
```

This action instructs the ***myLV LoadVars*** *object (which you created in* **master.fla** *back in Chapter 4,* "LoadVars Class"*) to load the variables from the text file that corresponds with the current slide number. In Exercise 3, you saw that the descriptive slideshow TXT files were located in the same folder as the slideshow images, and even had the same naming convention as the images–**frames0.txt**, **frames1.txt**, and so forth. This action simply utilizes the **curFrameNum** number to load the variables from the appropriate text file.*

*As you can see in the action you just wrote, there are many similarities to the action above it that does the loading of the slideshow JPG image. Simply, the action you just wrote says, "Tell the **myLV LoadVars** object located in* **master.swf** *to load the variables from a text file." Just like the **loadClip** action above, the name of the text file to load the variables from is dependent on whatever number is currently in the **curFrameNum** variable. When* **frames.swf** *is first loaded, **curFrameNum** equals 0. This action, when first compiled, would then read **_level0.myLV.load("frames/frames0.txt");**. But every time the reader clicks the Next Slide or Previous Slide button, the **curFrameNum** number will shift one number up or down, respectively. At the same time, the **loadFrames** function–and the actions within it–will get executed.*

*Back in Exercise 5, you added an action that triggers the **loadFrame** function when* **frames.swf** *first loads. But now that the action that loads the descriptive text is also within the **loadFrame** function, you don't want it to be executed right when* **frames.swf** *is first loaded. This goes back to what was mentioned in Chapter 5,* "HTML and CSS"*: when applying CSS styles to a text field, for the text within that field to utilize the CSS tags, the text has to load in the text field* after *the styles have been applied to the same field. Simply, it means load and apply the CSS styles first, and* then *load the text. Because of that, you want the **loadFrame** function executed only* after *the styles have finished downloading.*

```
// ------------------<TextField.StyleSheet>---------------- \\
var cssStyles:TextField.StyleSheet = new TextField.StyleSheet ();
cssStyles.load ("styles/styles.css");
cssStyles.onLoad = function (success) {
    if (success) {
        loadedInfo.styleSheet = cssStyles;
        loadFrame ();
    } else {
        loadedInfo.text = "There has been an error loading the requested information.  Please
contact the Webmaster and report your error.";
    }
}
// ------------------</TextField.StyleSheet>---------------- \\
```

*Because the action that triggers the **loadFrame** function has already been written into the **TextField.StyleSheet** script (see above), all you need to do is delete the same **loadFrame();** action you added out "in the open" in Exercise 5.*

```
function loadFrame() {
    _level0.myMCL.loadClip("frames/frames" + curFrameNum + ".jpg", this.framesMC);
    _level0.myLV.load("frames/frames" + curFrameNum + ".txt");
}
loadFrame();
```

5. Scroll up in the **Actions** panel. Underneath the **loadFrame** function is the action that executes that function, **loadFrame();**. Select **loadFrame();** and delete it.

*Now the **loadFrame** function, which loads the current slide and accompanying descriptive text, will only be executed after the **styles.css** file has been completely downloaded and applied to the **loadedInfo** text field, or when the Next Slide/Previous Slide buttons are clicked.*

6. Save **frames.fla** by choosing **File > Save** (**Ctrl+S** [Windows] or **Cmd+S** [Mac]), and publish an updated SWF by choosing **File > Publish** (**Shift+F12**).

7. Hide or minimize Flash MX 2004, and navigate to your **Desktop > la_eyeworks > site** folder. Double-click **master.swf** to open and view it in the stand-alone Macromedia Flash Player 7.

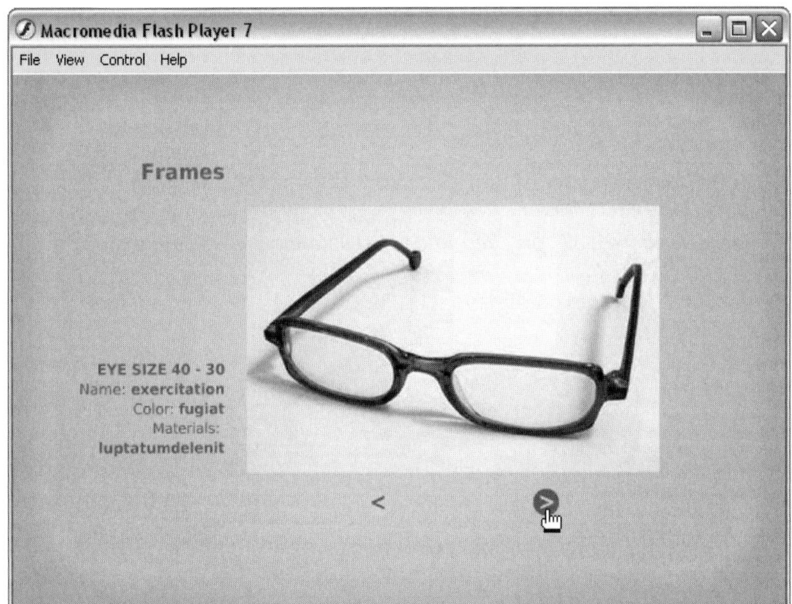

This time, when the Frames module loads, you'll see a block of styled, descriptive text load next to each slideshow image. As you click the Next Slide/Previous Slide buttons, not only will the next and previous slides appear, but the descriptive text will also update accordingly!

Of course, the great thing about that descriptive text is that not only is the text all located in individual text files (for easy editing by you or the client), but the text is also styled *using an external* ***styles.css*** *style sheet. To change the styling of the text, you can simply open the* ***styles.css*** *file, make your changes, and save the file. Keep in mind, however, that the same* ***styles.css*** *file is also used in other modules. So any changes you make to the* ***styles.css*** *file will also be incorporated into the rest of the L.A. Eyeworks Web site. If you want to modify the styling of* just *the descriptive slide text, you can either create new style classes in the* ***styles.css*** *file that you apply solely to the descriptive text, or you can create a separate CSS file that is loaded specifically for use in the slideshow.*

8. When you're finished, close the stand-alone Macromedia Flash Player 7 window, and bring Flash MX 2004 back to the foreground. Make sure that **frames.fla** is still the foreground FLA and that you have the first keyframe in the **a** layer selected with the **Actions** panel open.

8. Adding the Current Slide Counter

In this exercise you will create a counter that keeps track of which slide the viewer is looking at. You will insert that number, along with a little bit of text and the total number of slides, into the **frameNum** dynamic text field that sits between the Next Slide and Previous Slide buttons.

There are two numbers that you need to create this counter. You need the current slide number that the viewer is looking at, and you need the total number of slides. Thankfully, you already have been keeping track of those variables. The first variable you created in this chapter, **curFrameNum**, is the variable that keeps track of which slide number is currently being viewed. The variable that keeps track of the total number of slides is one that you imported from an external TXT file earlier in this chapter. The variable name is **totalFrames**, but because it was it was loaded into your project using **LoadVars**, it has to be referenced inside of the **LoadVars** object. So when referring to the **totalFrames** variable, you need to write **slideInfoLV.totalFrames**.

The action you're about to create, which inserts the slide counter text into the **frameNum** text field, is an action that you want to happen when any of the following occur:

- The **frames.swf** file first loads.
- The viewer clicks the Next Slide button.
- The viewer clicks the Previous Slide button.

Because this action will be utilized in multiple places, it will be best to place it within a function. Then you can simply call that function whenever you need the action to be executed. The function **loadFrame** that you created earlier in this chapter would be a perfect place to insert the counter action you're about to create. The **loadFrame** function also gets called when **frames.swf** first loads, and when the viewer clicks the Next Slide or Previous Slide buttons. However, because the slide counter action uses a variable located in an external TXT file (**totalFrames**), you only want the action to be performed once that variable has been completely downloaded. If you simply stuck the slide counter action wherever, there would be a chance that the counter text would be inserted into the **frameNum** text field before the **totalFrames** variable had been completely downloaded. If that happened, the slide counter text would not display correctly.

So to get the slide counter action to be executed only when the **totalFrames** variable has been completely downloaded, it will need to be in a separate function. That function will then get executed from an **onLoad** event handler within the **LoadVars** object. Sound like I'm talking gibberish again? It will become clearer as you work through the steps in this exercise.

1. Make sure you're in **frames.fla**, you have the first keyframe in the **a** layer selected, and you have the **Actions** panel open.

Click after this curly brace

```
function loadFrame() {
    _level0.myMCL.loadClip("frames/frames" + curFrameNum + ".jpg", this.framesMC);
    _level0.myLV.load("frames/frames" + curFrameNum + ".txt");
}

function slideCounter() {

}
```

2. Click after the closed curly brace for the **loadFrame** function (circled in the screen shot above), press **Enter** (Windows) or **Return** (Mac) twice to create a couple of line breaks, and create and close a new function by typing the following:

```
function slideCounter() {
}
```

Note: *Don't forget to add a line break between the* ***function slideCounter() {*** *line and the closed curly brace (***}***). This will give you space where you can begin typing the next action.*

```
function slideCounter() {
    frameNum.text = ("frame style " + (curFrameNum + 1) + " of " + Number(slideInfoLV.totalFrames));
}
```

3. Click in the empty line break between the **slideCounter** function and the closed curly brace, and write the action that will display the slide counter text in the **frameNum** text field by typing the following all on one line without any line breaks:

```
frameNum.text = ("frame style " + (curFrameNum + 1) + " of " +
Number(slideInfoLV.totalFrames));
```

By now, you're probably saying to yourself, "What is all that...stuff?!" Since there's quite a lot going on in this action–some of which you probably recognize, some of which you probably don't–here's a breakdown of the pieces of this action (from left to right):

- ***frameNum.text =*** *You will recognize as the command to insert some text into a dynamic text field with an instance name of* ***frameNum****. As mentioned previously,* ***frameNum*** *is the name of the dynamic text field on the Stage that sits between the Next Slide and Previous Slide buttons. Everything after the equals sign is the text that is to be inserted into that text field.*
- ***"frame style "*** *This tells Flash MX 2004 that you want to insert the string "frame style" into the text field. (Notice the space after the word "style" and before the end quote.)*
- **+** *You will recognize the plus sign, used throughout this action, from previous exercises. It allows you to add (concatenate) more text after the first string, "frame style ".*

- ***(curFrameNum + 1)*** *This takes the **curFrameNum** variable (whatever number it happens to be at that time; when **frames.swf** first loads, it's 0) and adds 1 to it. Why would you want to add 1 onto it? If you recall, the **curFrameNum** variable, to adhere to good ActionScript practices, initially equals 0. Although it makes sense to use the number 0 as the starting number of the slideshow, a visitor to the L.A. Eyeworks Web site would most likely get confused if they saw the slide counter text read "frame style 0 of 9." So to create a more logical message, you're going to add 1 onto the **curFrameNum** and **slideInfoLV.totalFrames** variables when they are placed into the **frameNum** text field. That way, the slide counter text will read something that makes much more sense to the viewer, "frame style 1 of 10."*

You'll also notice that it is in parentheses. You've also probably noticed parentheses used throughout this action. Whenever you see a set of parentheses, it simply tells Flash MX 2004 to execute whatever is inside the parentheses before *executing whatever is outside of the parentheses. By enclosing **curFrameNum + 1** within parentheses, you're telling Flash MX 2004 to first get the value of the **curFrameNum** variable, add that number to 1, and then go on to perform whatever is outside of those parentheses. By using parentheses you can control how parameters are applied to each other and can prevent other parameters from being inadvertently applied to others.*

- ***" of "*** *This, like **"frame style "**, simply instructs Flash MX 2004 to insert the string " of ". (Notice the space before and after the word "of.")*

- ***Number(slideInfoLV.totalFrames)*** *As you saw in Exercise 5 earlier in this chapter, this simply instructs Flash MX 2004 to retrieve the value of the loaded variable **slideInfoLV.totalFrames** and change that data type to a number.*

*Next, you need to instruct the function **slideCounter** to be executed when the **totalFrames** variable within the **slide_info.txt** file has been completely downloaded. To do that, you can add an **onLoad** event handler to the **slideInfoLV LoadVars** object you created earlier in this chapter.*

```
var slideInfoLV:LoadVars = new LoadVars();

slideInfoLV.onLoad = function (success) {
slideInfoLV.load("vars/slide_info.txt");
```

4. Click at the end of the **var slideInfoLV:LoadVars = new LoadVars();** line (at the top of the **Actions** panel), press **Enter** (Windows) or **Return** (Mac) twice to create a couple of line breaks, and type the following:

slideInfoLV.onLoad = function (success) {

*This creates the **onLoad** event handler for the **slideInfoLV LoadVars** object. Next, you need to define what should occur **if** (hint, hint) the variables within **slide_info.txt** have been completely downloaded and, conversely, what should occur if there is an error accessing **slide_info.txt**.*

```
slideInfoLV.onLoad = function (success) {
    if (success) {
        slideCounter();
    } else {
        frameNum.text = "error";
    }
}
```

5. Complete the **onLoad** event handler by clicking at the end of the **slideInfoLV.onLoad = function (success) {** line, pressing **Enter** (Windows) or **Return** (Mac) once to create a line break, and typing the following:

```
if (success) {
    slideCounter();
} else {
    frameNum.text = "error";
    }
}
```

As you saw in Chapter 4, "LoadVars Class," *when you wrote the **myLV LoadVars** object in the **master.fla** Timeline, this series of actions said, "If the variables within the **slide_info.txt** file are downloaded successfully, execute the **slideCounter** function. Otherwise (**else**), insert the text "error" into the **frameNum** text field."*

Learning to write ActionScript is akin to learning how to read phonetically. When learning to read, you might look at a long word such as "fantastically" and initially give up because it looks so daunting. But if you phonetically break it down, fan-tas-tic-ally, it will make much more sense. ActionsScript can be very similar in that if you look at a large block of ActionScript, you might say to yourself, "Geez. There's no way I'll understand what's going on there." But if you break it down piece by piece, line by line (as you have and will continue to do throughout this book), it will become much more clear.

Although you're not yet finished, you have enough to test the changes you've made thus far.

---

6. Save the changes to **frames.fla** by choosing **File > Save** (**Ctrl+S** [Windows] or **Cmd+S** [Mac]), and publish an updated SWF by choosing **File > Publish** (**Shift+F12**).

---

7. Hide or minimize Flash MX 2004, navigate to your **Desktop > la_eyeworks > site** folder, and double-click **master.swf** to open and view it in the stand-alone Macromedia Flash Player 7.

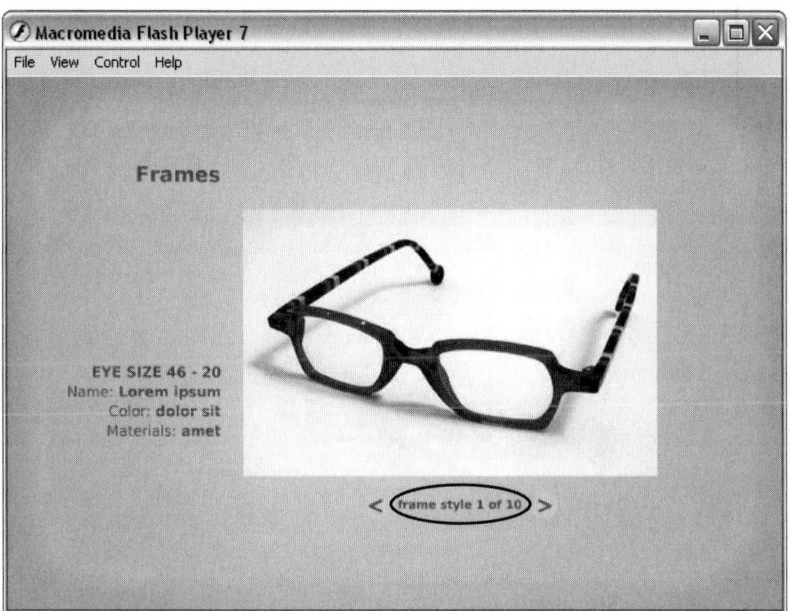

When the Frames module loads, you'll see the text "frame style 1 of 10" between the Next Slide and Previous Slide buttons. Hooray! However, you'll notice that if you click either the Next Slide or Previous Slide buttons, the text never changes. You're going to fix that next by triggering the **`slideCounter`** *function each time the viewer clicks the slideshow navigation buttons.*

8. When you're finished, close the stand-alone Macromedia Flash Player 7 window and bring Flash MX 2004 back to the foreground. Make sure that **frames.fla** is still the foreground FLA and that you have the first keyframe in the **a** layer selected with the **Actions** panel open.

```
// -----------------<next slide button>---------------- \\
this.nextSlideBtn.onRelease = function() {

    if (curFrameNum < Number(slideInfoLV.totalFrames) - 1) {
        curFrameNum++;
    } else {
        curFrameNum = 0;
    }

    loadFrame();
    slideCounter();

}
// -----------------</next slide button>---------------- \\
```

9. Scroll down to the **Next Slide** button script, click at the end of the `loadFrame();` line, press **Enter** (Windows) or **Return** (Mac) once to create a line break, and type the following:

`slideCounter();`

*This will execute the **`slideCounter`** function and the action within it. Within it is, of course, the action that inserts the slide counter text into the **`frameNum`** text field. When this action is executed again, it will retrieve the current values of the variables, and the **`frameNum`** text field on the Stage will update.*

Next, you need to repeat this process for the Previous Slide button.

```
// -----------------<previous slide button>---------------- \\
this.prevSlideBtn.onRelease = function() {

    if (curFrameNum == 0) {
        curFrameNum = Number(slideInfoLV.totalFrames);
    } else {
        curFrameNum--;
    }

    loadFrame();
    slideCounter();

}
// -----------------</previous slide button>---------------- \\
```

10. Scroll down to the **Previous Slide** button script, click at the end of the `loadFrame();` line, press **Enter** (Windows) or **Return** (Mac) once to create a line break, and type the following:

`slideCounter();`

*And there you have it. The **`slideCounter`** function is now triggered when the variables within **slide_info.txt** have been completely downloaded and when the viewer clicks either the Next Slide or Previous Slide buttons. This will cause the **`frameNum`** text to update as the viewer navigates through the slideshow.*

Before you start booking yourself on Leno or Letterman to tout your achievements, you should test your changes one last time to make sure everything is working as it should.

11. Save the changes to **frames.fla** by choosing **File > Save** (**Ctrl+S** [Windows] or **Cmd+S** [Mac]), and publish an updated SWF by choosing **File > Publish** (**Shift+F12**).

12. Hide or minimize Flash MX 2004, navigate to your **Desktop > la_eyeworks > site** folder, and double-click **master.swf** to open and view it in the stand-alone Macromedia Flash Player 7.

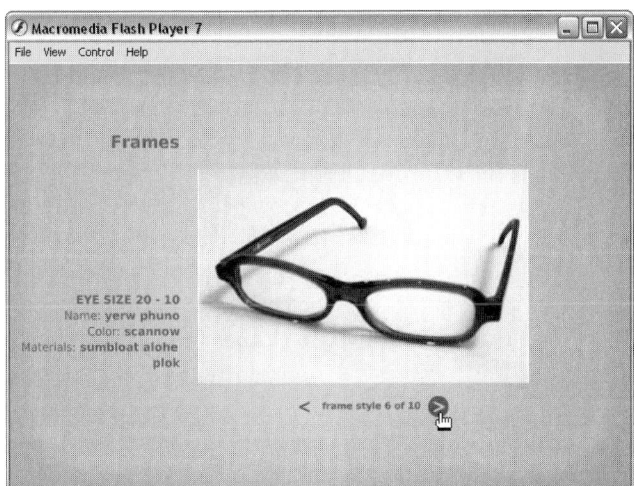

13. When the slideshow appears, click the Next Slide and Previous Slide buttons. As you do, you'll notice that the text between the slideshow navigation buttons updates. Congratulations!

14. When you're finished, close the stand-alone Macromedia Flash Player 7 window, bring Flash MX 2004 back to the foreground, and close **frames.fla**.

In this chapter, you learned how to create a seamlessly looping slideshow accompanied by dynamic descriptive text and a slide counter that gave you feedback about whatever slide you were currently viewing. As mentioned previously, one of the awesome things about this slideshow is that nearly everything is dynamic and external to the Flash MX 2004 movie. The slideshow images are external JPG files that were brought in using the ***myMCL MovieClipLoader*** *object in* ***master.swf****, the descriptive text is comprised of external TXT files that are loaded using the* ***myLV LoadVars*** *object (and styled with an external style sheet) also located in* ***master.swf****, and the slide counter text is dynamically created using variables involved in the functionality of the slideshow itself. By keeping the content external to the FLA, you make it much easier for yourself or the client to update the individual pieces.*

As you worked through the exercises in this chapter, I hope you were able to realize how much faster it was to create a slideshow with this level of dynamics with relatively minimal effort, thanks to the ***MovieClipLoader*** *and* ***LoadVars*** *scripts that you created–and are now repurposing for a different use–in earlier chapters.*

Building a Preloader

| What You Are Building | Getting Started |
| onLoadProgress |

la_eyeworks

Macromedia Flash MX 2004
Beyond the Basics

In this chapter, you will learn how to build a preloader. Preloaders are constructed in a variety of different sizes, shapes, and designs, but their basic function remains the same. A **preloader** is essentially a graphic or small amount of text that gives the viewer feedback about the progress of whatever is currently being loaded into the Flash MX 2004 movie. Some preloaders display how many bytes or kilobytes have been downloaded, while others just show progress bars or simply an animated "loading" graphic. When the downloading asset has completed downloading, the preloader usually disappears, and the downloaded content is displayed. In this chapter, you will write the ActionScript that will make a graphical preloader appear and function when the **MovieClipLoader** is activated to download a SWF or JPG asset. If you've built a preloader before, you'll be pleasantly surprised at how simple a preloader is to build, using the new **MovieClipLoader** class.

I. What You Are Building

In this exercise, you will look at the finished L.A. Eyeworks Web site so you can see how the preloader looks and works *before* you start building it. That way, as you work through some of the more abstract ActionScript concepts in this chapter, you'll have a better idea of how they apply to the finished piece.

1. Open your preferred Web browser, and access the following URL:

http://www.lynda.com/flashbtb/laeyeworks/

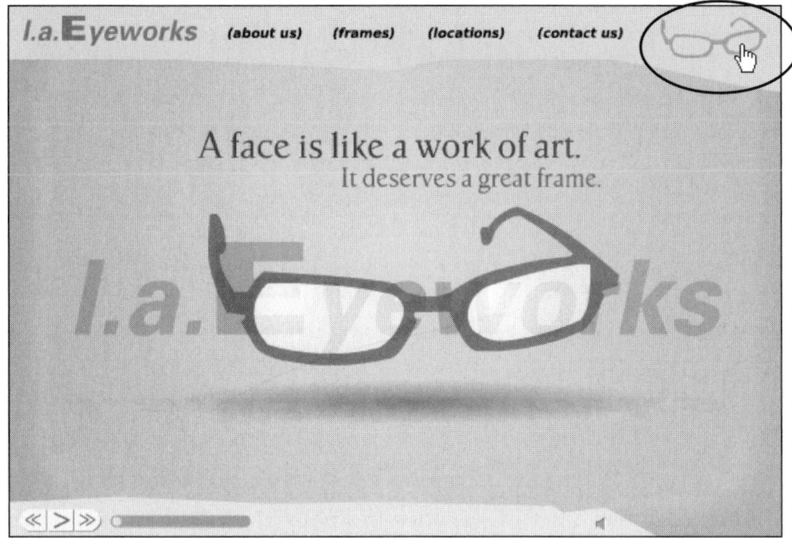

2. When the Web site finishes loading, click on the **glasses** graphic at the top-right corner of the menu bar.

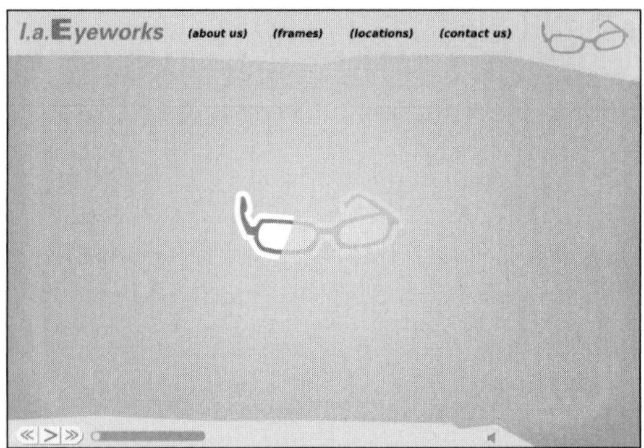

This will trigger a SWF file with a large JPG inside it to start downloading. Because the SWF file is being downloaded into **`_level5`**–*the same level where the splash graphic resides–the splash graphic will disappear. In its place, a graphic of a faded pair of frames will appear. As the content is downloading, you'll see an identical graphic of glasses frames "wipe" in over the faded pair. Depending on the speed of your Internet connection, the downloading–and thereby, the animated "revealing" of the glasses–may move quickly, or it may take a few minutes. As more of the SWF file is downloaded, more of the glasses are revealed. When the glasses have been completely revealed, the preloader will disappear and the downloaded SWF file will appear in its place. During the course of this book, you won't add functionality to the glasses graphic on the menu bar that downloads a large SWF file (as you just saw). This functionality was added to the completed L.A. Eyeworks site at* ***www.lynda.com/flashbtb/laeyeworks/*** *so you can easily and clearly see the preloader in action. Because it would be extremely difficult to observe the preloader as it gave feedback on the downloading progress of the small files on the L.A. Eyeworks site, this was added to the completed site so the preloader can be clearly seen.*

If a preloader didn't exist, the viewer would see a blank page while the large SWF file was downloading. Depending on the experience (or lack of) of the viewer, he or she might think the site is broken–since it would appear that nothing is happening–and leave the site. One of the primary roles of the preloader is to provide feedback to viewers so they know that 1) Something is happening; 2) The requested content is being downloaded; and 3) By looking at the preloader progress, they know how much longer they have to wait.

In this chapter, you will write the ActionScript that makes this preloader work. Although the preloader graphics *have already been built for you, you still need to build their functionality. Making use of the new, fantastically awesome* **`MovieClipLoader`** *class (which you created an object from back in* Chapter 3, "Getting Started"*), you will utilize the* **`onLoadProgress`** *listener to create the preloader. If you've had any experience with building a preloader before, I'm sure you'll be pleasantly surprised with how much easier this one is to build. Because the preloader will make use of the* **`onLoadProgress`** *listener that is built into the* **`MovieClipLoader`**, *any time the* **`MovieClipLoader`** *is asked to load a SWF or JPG file, the preloader will automatically be activated.*

---

3. When you're finished checking out the preloader, close your Web browser.

2. Getting Started

Before you get started writing the preloader ActionScript, you should look at the preloader animation itself so you understand the specifics of how it was created.

1. Hide or minimize Flash MX 2004 if you have it open. Then navigate to the **Desktop > la_eyeworks > site** folder on your hard drive and double-click **preloader.fla** to open it in Flash MX 2004.

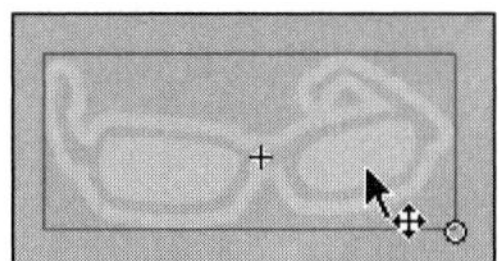

2. In the middle of the **Stage**, you'll notice a graphic of faded-back glasses. Single-click on the glasses graphic to select it and open the **Properties inspector** (**Ctrl+F3** [Windows] or **Cmd+F3** [Mac]).

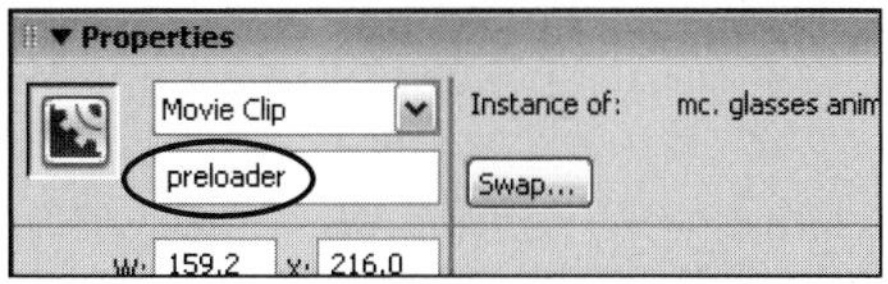

3. In the **Properties inspector**, notice how the faded-back glasses graphic is actually an instance of a movie clip, and it has an instance name of **preloader**. That instance name is important because as you begin to write the preloader ActionScript, you will need to instruct this movie clip instance to move its playhead. As you're aware of by now, whenever you want to use ActionScript to manipulate a symbol instance (button or movie clip), it *must* have an instance name first. That way, Flash MX 2004 understands which symbol instance you're referring to.

4. Double-click the **preloader** movie clip instance on the **Stage** to open it.

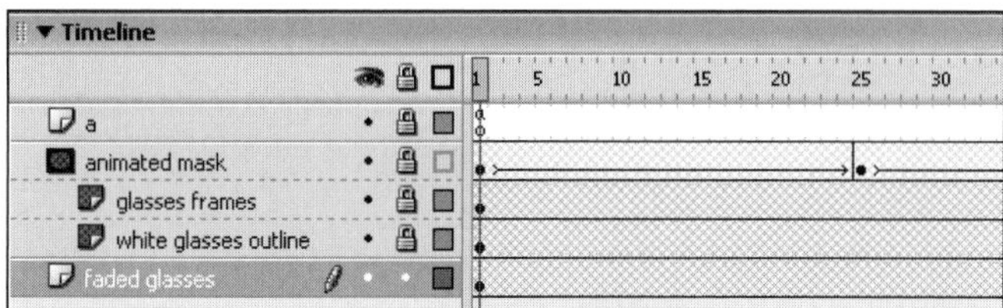

Within the Timeline of the ***mc. glasses anim*** *movie clip symbol, you'll immediately notice that the Timeline contains a shape tweened animated mask, a few masked layers, and a few normal layers. One of those normal layers,* ***a****, is the layer that contains the ActionScript. If you were to select the first keyframe in the* ***a*** *layer and open the* ***Actions*** *panel, you'd notice that a* **`stop();`** *action has been applied there. This means that the shape tween animation you see in the layer beneath* ***a*** *will* not *automatically play. This animation will instead be paused on the first frame. The ActionScript that you will write in the next exercise will determine when and where the animation will play.*

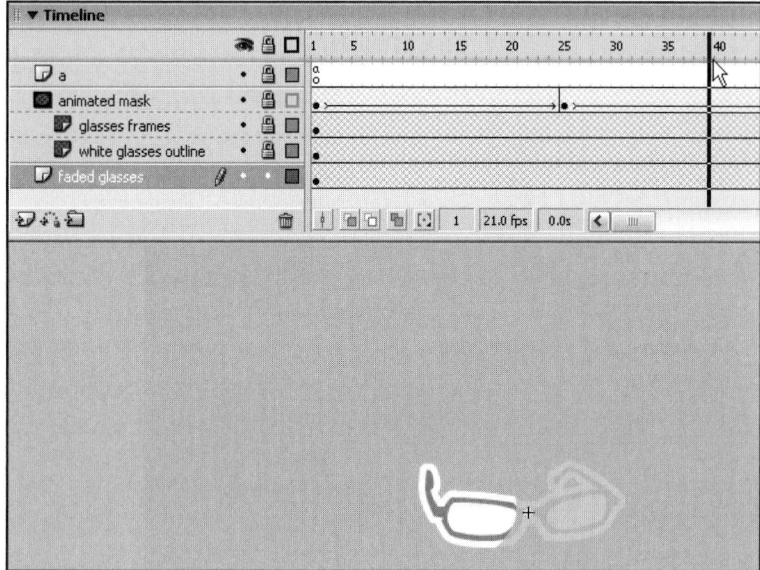

5. Drag the playhead down the **mc. glasses anim Timeline**. As you do, you'll notice a nearly identical glasses graphic (except this one is not faded back) animate over the faded-back glasses image. This is done, as you can see in the **Timeline**, with a simple shape tween that's acting as a mask. As the mask animates, it reveals the glasses.

Instead of the more common linear progress bar, the L.A. Eyeworks site will make use of this "themed" progress bar to act as the visible side of the preloader.

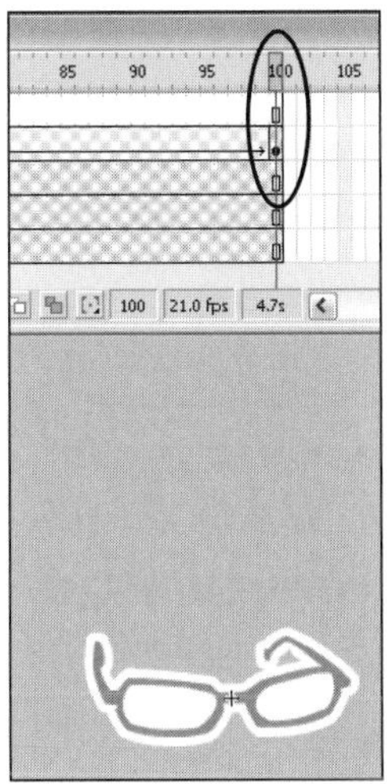

6. Drag the playhead to the end of the shape tweened mask animation. You'll notice that the mask animation ends on **Frame 100**. It ends, purposefully, on **Frame 100** for the following reason:

A progress bar, much like you see on your computer when you download a file off of the Internet, is actually showing you the percentage of the file that has been downloaded. Percentages, of course, go from 0 (none downloaded) to 100 (completely downloaded). In the next exercise, when you begin writing the ActionScript to create the preloader, you will–using a little math–find out what percentage of the file has been downloaded up until that point. Once you know the percentage, you can simply tell this animated preloader mask to move the playhead to the corresponding number. Voilà! So yes, the preloader "reveal" animation starting on Frame 1 and ending on Frame 100 is done that way for a reason: each frame of the preloader animation corresponds with a percentage downloaded of the SWF or JPG file.

Because you'll want the preloader to appear above all the other assets in the L.A. Eyeworks site (what good does the preloader do ya if it appears underneath *the slideshow, eh?), you'll need to use the **myMCL MovieClipLoader** object to load the preloader in a level* above *the rest of the L.A. Eyeworks content. Of course, before you can use the **MovieClipLoader** to load the preloader, you need to publish a **preloader.swf** file.*

---

7. Choose **File > Publish**, or better yet, press the keyboard shortcut **Shift+F12**. This will publish a SWF file, **preloader.swf**, into the **site** folder where the rest of the L.A. Eyeworks site files are located.

---

8. Close **preloader.fla**–you won't be needing it again in this chapter. If you're prompted to save your changes, click **No** (Windows) or **Don't Save** (Mac).

*In the next exercise, you will write the **onLoadProgress** listener into the **MovieClipLoader** object. You will also complete the preloader by writing a few actions that control various aspects of how the preloader behaves.*

3. onLoadProgress

In this exercise, you will write the ActionScript that will make the preloader fully functional. Because the **MovieClipLoader** class has a built-in event model specifically for creating preloaders and monitoring the downloading progress of SWF and JPG files, it makes your job as the Flash MX 2004 designer/developer much easier than in previous versions of Flash.

Before you can start manipulating the preloader with ActionScript, you need to use the **myMCL MovieClipLoader** object you created in Chapter 3, "*Getting Started*," to load the **preloader.swf** file into a level *above* all the other loaded SWF and JPG files.

1. Open **master.fla**. You can select it from the **Start Page**, from **File > Open Recent**, or by navigating to your **Desktop > la_eyeworks > site** folder and double-clicking **master.fla**.

2. Select the first keyframe in the **a** layer and open the **Actions** panel (**F9**).

```
// trigger the MCL to load these assets:
myMCL.loadClip("trigger.swf", 5);
myMCL.loadClip("preloader.swf", 50);
```

3. Click at the end of the **myMCL.loadClip("trigger.swf", 5);** line, press **Enter** (Windows) or **Return** (Mac) once to create a line break, and load **preloader.swf** into **level 50** by typing the following:

```
myMCL.loadClip("preloader.swf", 50);
```

*As you have seen before, this will load **preloader.swf** into level 50. Loading **preloader.swf** into a high level like 50 just ensures that it is above all the other assets and that there is plenty of room underneath it to load other assets.*

*Now that you've loaded **preloader.swf** into level 50, you can begin to author the ActionScript that makes the preloader work. To start, you're going to create the **onLoadProgress** listener.*

```
var myMCL:MovieClipLoader = new MovieClipLoader();
var myListener:Object = new Object();

myMCL.addListener(myListener);

myListener.onLoadProgress = function () {

}
```

4. Click at the end of the **myMCL.addListener(myListener);** line, press **Enter** (Windows) or **Return** (Mac) twice to create a couple of line breaks, and create the **onLoadProgress** listener by typing the following:

```
myListener.onLoadProgress = function () {
}
```

Note: *Be sure to include an extra line break between the open curly brace (**{**) and the closed curly brace (**}**). This will give you a line break within the **onLoadProgress** function where you can begin to write the preloader ActionScript.*

If you can stretch your brain cells all the way back to Chapter 3, "Getting Started," *you'd remember that the **onLoadProgress** listener (and the actions you created within it) are executed* every time *content is downloaded to your hard drive using the **MovieClipLoader** class. In other words, when a SWF or JPG file is told to download using the **MovieClipLoader** class, every time content is written to disk, the **onLoadProgress** listener–and the actions you write within it–are executed.*

*Prior to Flash MX 2004, building a preloader involved creating a way to continually loop through the preloader ActionScript code. Usually this involved creating some sort of ActionScript-based loop such as a **setInterval** or an **onClipEvent(enterFrame)** loop. However, now that Flash MX 2004 introduced the **MovieClipLoader** class, and within that the **onLoadProgress** listener, it essentially removes the extra step(s) of having to write an ActionScript loop. All you have to do now is create the **onLoadProgress** listener, as you just did, and Flash MX 2004 will automatically execute the actions you place within it every time downloaded content is written to disk. I can't even begin to tell you how much of a leap ahead that is from previous methods of constructing preloaders.*

Now, to build a progress-bar-based preloader, as you will in this chapter, you need to know two essential things about the currently downloading SWF or JPG file. You need to know how many bytes have been downloaded and how many bytes there are total. Once you know those two numbers, you can perform a little math to arrive at the percentage *of the asset that has been downloaded up to that point. And finally, once you have the percentage, you can tell the preloader shape tween animation which frame its playhead should go to.*

In Chapter 4, "LoadVars Class," *when you wrote the* ***LoadVars*** *script, you learned that certain parameters are automatically passed from the* ***LoadVars*** *object. Specifically, you learned that the* ***LoadVars*** *object sends out either a true or false Boolean value for the* **success** *parameter, depending on whether or not the variables have been downloaded correctly. The* ***MovieClipLoader*** *class* also *automatically sends out parameters when various events occur. Nicely enough, the* ***MovieClipLoader*** *class broadcasts* ***loadedBytes*** *and* ***totalBytes*** *parameters that the* ***onLoadProgress*** *listener can receive and utilize to build a preloader. How easy is that?*

```
myListener.onLoadProgress = function (target_mc, loadedBytes, totalBytes) {

}
```

5. Click between the parentheses after **myListener.onLoadProgress = function** (as shown above), and enter the **onLoadProgress** function parameters by typing the following:

target_mc, loadedBytes, totalBytes

loadedBytes *and* ***totalBytes*** *are, as I mentioned previously, parameters passed from the* ***MovieClipLoader*** *object. Those parameters will give you the loaded bytes of the currently downloading SWF or JPG file, and the total bytes of the downloading asset, respectively. You will utilize those two parameters when writing the preloader ActionScript in the next steps.* ***target_mc****, another parameter passed from the* ***MovieClipLoader*** *object, will give you the name of the SWF or JPG asset the* ***MovieClipLoader*** *object is currently downloading. Although you won't be using that name in the construction of this preloader, you still have to enter it as a parameter of the* ***onLoadProgress*** *function, or the preloader won't work. This is because (in case you wanted to know) the SWF or JPG that is being targeted is always the first parameter passed from the event. Without that first parameter being received by the* ***onLoadProgress*** *listener, the* ***loadedBytes*** *and* ***totalBytes*** *parameters will not be received either.*

Now that you have the ***onLoadProgress*** *listener set up correctly, you can begin to write the ActionScript to make the preloader show the progress of the currently downloading asset.*

```
myListener.onLoadProgress = function (target_mc, loadedBytes, totalBytes) {
    var preloadPercent:Number = Math.round((loadedBytes / totalBytes) * 100);
}
```

6. Click in the empty line break between the open curly brace **{** and the closed curly brace **}** (as pictured above), and type, all in one line with no line breaks, the following :

`var preloadPercent:Number = Math.round((loadedBytes / totalBytes) * 100);`

- *The first part of this action,* ***var preloadPercent:Number****, should be familiar to you. You're simply creating a local variable called* ***preloadPercent*** *and strict typing it so that its data type is a number. That way, you ensure that the value of the variable (everything to the right of the equals sign) is a number and not another data type, such as a string, which might break your script.*
- ***Math.round*** *simply rounds the value that results from the expression in the parentheses that follows it. In this case, that's* ***loadedBytes*** *divided by* ***totalBytes*** *and multiplied by 100. That way, if the number turns out to be 24.3,* ***Math.round*** *rounds it down to 24. If the number turns out to be 24.6, however,* ***Math.round*** *will round it* up *to 25.* ***Math.round*** *rounds the value to the nearest whole number. You need a whole number in this action because you're going to be using that number to tell the preloader animation which frame to go to.*
- ***(loadedBytes / totalBytes)*** *merely divides* ***loadedBytes*** *and* ***totalBytes****. Remember, in place of these parameters, the* ***MovieClipLoader*** *object will insert the relative numbers for whatever SWF or JPG file it is currently downloading at that time. Because these parameters are in parentheses, they will be calculated* first*, and then everything outside of the parentheses will be executed following that.*
- **** 100****. The asterisk (*) is a multiplication operator. Just like in basic math, it multiplies the value to its left with the value to its right.*

When completely executed, the number inserted into the ***preloadPercent*** *variable is the percentage of the currently downloading SWF or JPG file that has been downloaded up until the time this action is executed. As you can see, the math involved to calculate the percentage downloaded is fairly straightforward. You simply divide the* ***loadedBytes*** *into the* ***totalBytes*** *and then multiply that value by 100.*

Now that you have the percentage progress of the downloading SWF or JPG file, you can use that number to instruct the preloader animation which frame it should go to.

```
myListener.onLoadProgress = function (target_mc, loadedBytes, totalBytes) {
    var preloadPercent:Number = Math.round((loadedBytes / totalBytes) * 100);
    _level50.preloader.gotoAndStop(preloadPercent);
}
```

7. Click at the end of the **`var preloadPercent:Number = Math.round((loadedBytes / totalBytes) * 100);`** line, press **Enter** (Windows) or **Return** (Mac) once to create a line break, and type the following:

`_level50.preloader.gotoAndStop(preloadPercent);`

*This action instructs **`_level50`** (the level that **preloader.swf** is loaded into) to move the playhead in the **preloader** movie clip instance to the number that's in the **`preloadPercent`** variable you created in the last step. So, in essence, whatever percentage (0 to 100) the downloading SWF or JPG file has completed downloading, the **preloader** movie clip in **preloader.swf** will move its playhead to the equivalent frame.*

And that's the preloader! Again, if you've written a preloader before, I'm sure you're elated at how simple and straightforward the construction of this preloader is.

*However, now comes the "bad" news. Due to a bug in the current (as of this writing) release of Flash MX 2004 (7.0.1), the **`onLoadProgress`** listener will not execute in the Flash MX 2004 API. What this means is that now that you have your preloader script written and you want to see if it works correctly by choosing **Control > Test Movie**, you will* not *see the preloader work. This doesn't mean that the preloader is broken or will not work at all; it just simply means that you can't preview it from within Flash MX 2004 itself. To preview a preloader built with the **`onLoadProgress`** listener, you must first upload the relevant site files to a remote Web server, and then test your site through a Web browser. For those of you with a Web presence provider and the know-how, feel free to upload your site files to your remote server and test your work through your Web browser. For those of you without a Web site or the know-how, Appendix C has some Web presence provider suggestions for where you can buy a Web presence and upload your Web site. For now, though, you're just going to have to trust me that the preloader works as it should. ;-)*

*To complete the preloader, you still need to specify when the preloader should be visible and when it shouldn't. If you don't specify this, when an asset has been completely downloaded, the preloader will remain visible on the Stage. To hide the preloader once an asset has been fully downloaded, you will utilize another **`MovieClipLoader`** listener called **`onLoadComplete`**.*

```
myListener.onLoadProgress = function (target_mc, loadedBytes, totalBytes) {
    var preloadPercent:Number = Math.round((loadedBytes / totalBytes) * 100);
    _level50.preloader.gotoAndStop(preloadPercent);
}

myListener.onLoadComplete = function (target_mc) {
    _level50._visible = false;
}
```

Click after this closed curly brace

8. Click after the closed curly brace that closes the **onLoadProgress** function, press **Enter** (Windows) or **Return** (Mac) twice to create a couple of line breaks, and type the following:

```
myListener.onLoadComplete = function (target_mc) {
    _level50._visible = false;
}
```

*Although you probably understand the majority of what this script is doing, you are probably not familiar with the **onLoadComplete MovieClipLoader** listener. As its name implies, the **onLoadComplete** listener is executed when the downloading SWF or JPG file has been* completely *downloaded. Within the **onLoadComplete** function, the action **_level50._visible = false;** instructs level 50–the level that the preloader is loaded into–to turn its visibility off. This, of course, makes it invisible. So, when taken together, this script reads, "When the currently downloading SWF or JPG file has been* completely *downloaded, hide the preloader."*

Now that you've specified when the preloader should hide itself, you also need to specify when it should be visible. If you don't, once the preloader hides itself the first time, you will never see it again. That type of functionality may work well for the in-laws, but it's not a very good practice to follow when constructing a preloader.

```
myListener.onLoadProgress = function (target_mc, loadedBytes, totalBytes) {
    _level50._visible = true;
    var preloadPercent:Number = Math.round((loadedBytes / totalBytes) * 100);
    _level50.preloader.gotoAndStop(preloadPercent);
}

myListener.onLoadComplete = function (target_mc) {
    _level50._visible = false;
}
```

9. Click at the end of the **onLoadProgress** function, **myListener.onLoadProgress = function (target_mc, loadedBytes, totalBytes) {**, press **Enter** (Windows) or **Return** (Mac) once to create a line break, and type the following:

_level50._visible = true;

*Similar–but opposite–to the action you wrote in Step 8, this action instructs **preloader.swf** (loaded in level 50) to become visible.*

*So when the preloader ActionScript is taken all together, it reads, "Every time data is downloaded from a SWF or JPG file that was downloaded using the **MovieClipLoader** class, 1) Make the preloader visible; 2) Figure out the percent of the asset that has been downloaded; and 3) Move the preloader playhead to that same frame. Then, when the asset has been completely downloaded, hide the preloader."*

---

10. Save the changes you've made to **master.fla** by choosing **File > Save** (**Ctrl+S** [Windows] or **Cmd+S** [Mac]).

*There you have it. A completely working, functional preloader! No extra actions are needed to allow this preloader to work for all the modules in the entire L.A. Eyeworks site. Any time any SWF or JPG file is downloaded using the **myMCL MovieClipLoader** object, this preloader will automatically do its thing. It's a thing of beauty I tell ya... ;-)*

MOVIE | Adding More Information to the Preloader

Located on the **H•O•T CD-ROM**, in the **movies** folder, is a QuickTime movie titled **detailed_preloader.mov**. In this movie, I will show you how to construct a preloader that provides more feedback about the currently downloading movie. You will learn not only how to show the downloading progress of the asset by percentage, but also how to show how many kilobytes have been downloaded out of the total kilobytes to be downloaded. If you want to learn how to build a preloader that provides more feedback to the viewer about the downloading asset, you definitely need to watch this movie.

I hope you had a nice rest in this relatively simple chapter, because you're about to jump back into ActionScript to learn how to build and script a feedback form...head first! Come on in–the water is fine!

9. Building a Form

| What You Are Building | Setting Up |
| Simple Form Validation | Using LoadVars to Send the Form |
| Styling the Form |

la_eyeworks

Macromedia Flash MX 2004
Beyond the Basics

In this chapter, you will build a form where the visitor can leave you feedback, and you build it completely within Flash MX 2004. Building the form will involve the use of the **`TextArea`** and **`TextInput`** components and some ActionScript elbow grease. In this chapter, not only will you build the feedback form, but you will also learn what it takes to send the form results to a CGI script (more on what a CGI script is later) to be processed. Although you won't actually be uploading the L.A. Eyeworks site to a remote Web server during the course of this book, I *will* address in Appendix C how a Flash MX 2004–built form interfaces with a CGI script and where you can find CGI scripts online that you can use in conjunction with your own Web presence provider to process your Flash MX 2004 form results.

I. What You Are Building

Before you get started with constructing the feedback form, it will help you to better understand exactly *what* you are building if you look at the final result first. In this exercise, you're going to look at the finished feedback form so that as you learn about some of these more abstract concepts, the form will make more sense to you because you'll already understand how it all fits together to create the final, working piece.

1. Open your preferred Web browser, and access the following URL:

http://www.lynda.com/flashbtb/laeyeworks/

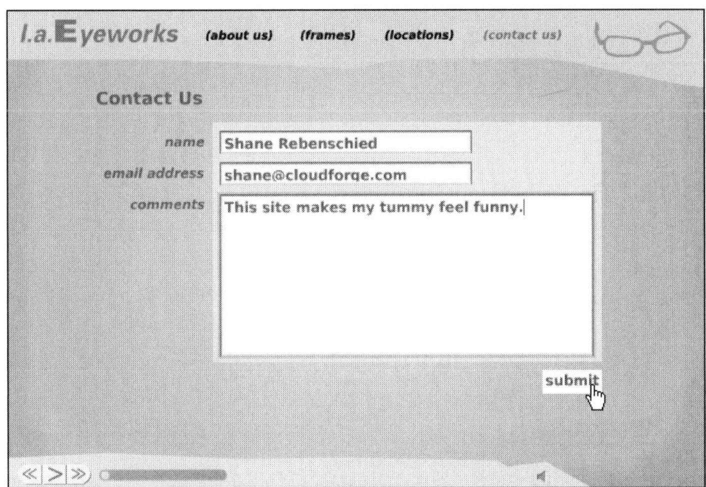

2. When the Web site finishes loading, click the **(contact us)** button in the menu bar. This will load the **Contact Us** module, which contains a feedback form. Fill out each field in the form and click **submit**.

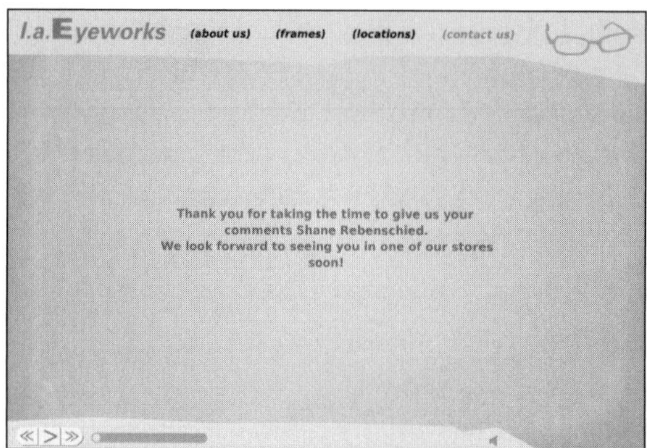

3. After you click **submit**, you'll see some text appear on the **Stage**. If you read through the first sentence, you'll notice that your name–or whatever you entered in the **name** field–has been inserted into the text. This is a nice way to personalize a "thank you" message like this one, and it also lets the viewer know that his or her feedback was received.

*When you clicked the **submit** button, the **Contact Us** module–behind the scenes–nicely packaged up your information, passed it to a CGI script on the remote Web server, which then arranged your comments in an email, and then sent it to me. Pretty slick! When you build the contact form, if you choose to connect it to your own CGI script on your Web server, you'll be able to define which email address the viewer's comments will be sent to.*

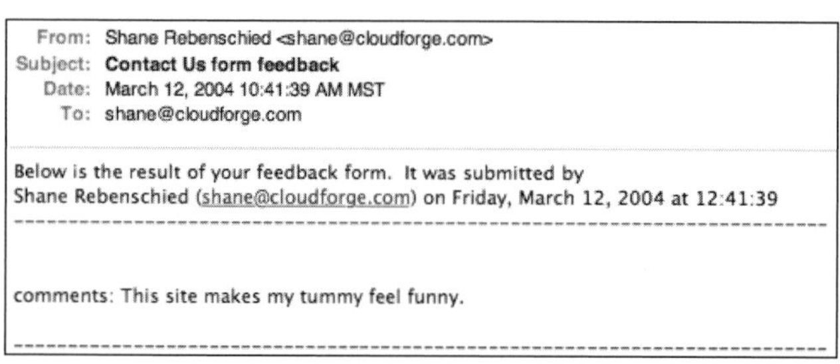

From: Shane Rebenschied <shane@cloudforge.com>
Subject: **Contact Us form feedback**
Date: March 12, 2004 10:41:39 AM MST
To: shane@cloudforge.com

Below is the result of your feedback form. It was submitted by
Shane Rebenschied (shane@cloudforge.com) on Friday, March 12, 2004 at 12:41:39

comments: This site makes my tummy feel funny.

***Note:** If I were to check my email at this point, the email you see in the screen shot above would be waiting in my Inbox. The CGI script that processed the form results collected the form information and laid it out nicely in an email for me. Nifty! If you choose to connect the feedback form to your own CGI script on your Web server, depending on the CGI script/server combination, your email might be organized/laid out differently than what you see above.*

4. Return to the feedback form. (You can do this by clicking another option in the main menu and then, after that section loads, clicking again on the **(contact us)** main menu option.) This will reload the **Contact Us** module.

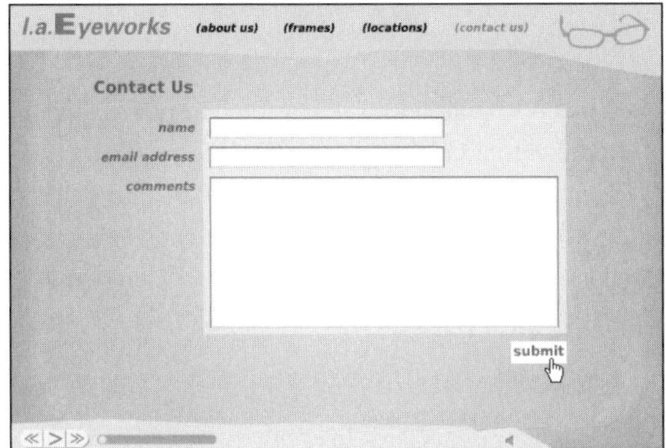

5. This time, *do not* enter any information in the form. Instead, just click the **submit** button.

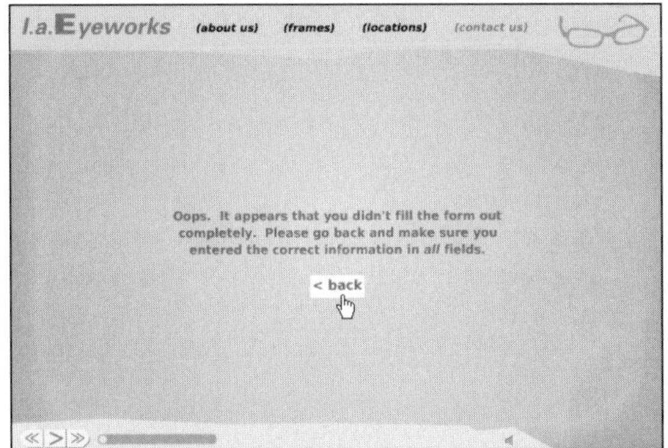

This time you'll notice that a different *message appears on the Stage. This message reads "Oops. It appears that you didn't fill the form out completely. Please go back and make sure you entered the correct information in* all *fields." Below the message is also a* **back** *button that, when clicked, will return you to the feedback form so you can fill out all the fields in the form again.*

In this chapter, you will write the ActionScript that creates this functionality. In essence, when the viewer clicks the **submit** *button, an action is executed that checks to make sure that viewers entered information in* every *field. If they didn't, then upon clicking the* **submit** *button they are presented with this error message. However, if viewers* did *enter information in* every *field, then they will see the message you saw in Step 3.*

All in all, this chapter is fairly straightforward. You'll be learning how to utilize a few components to create a feedback form, how to create simple form validation (checking to see if the viewer entered text in every form field), how to define tab order, and how to use a **LoadVars** *object to package and send the feedback form text to a CGI script for processing. So go splash some cold water on your face and do some jumping jacks because there's a lot to cover in the following exercises!*

2. Setting Up

In this exercise, you will begin to gather all the necessary elements and pieces together to create the feedback form. Since you've already learned a few of the techniques that make the feedback form fully functional, to save time I've included a prebuilt starter file, **contact.fla**, to give you a head-start. You'll start by dragging some components onto the Stage to act as the fields in the form, and you'll then give unique instance names to those components–as well as a few other symbols–so you can reference them with ActionScript.

1. Close any other FLAs you currently have open in Flash MX 2004. This will help to prevent confusion as you're opening and closing the **contact.fla Library**.

---

2. Hide or minimize Flash MX 2004. In your operating system, navigate to your **Desktop > la_eyeworks > site** folder and double-click **contact.fla**.

This is a prebuilt FLA, complete with some assets to get you started with the construction of the feedback form.

First, you need to import the two shared fonts that will be used in this FLA, Bitstream Vera Sans Bold, and Bitstream Vera Sans Bold Italic.

---

3. Choose **File > Import > Open External Library**. From the **Open as Library** dialog box that opens, navigate to your **Desktop > la_eyeworks > site** folder, and double-click **sharedLib.fla**. This will open only the **Library** of **sharedLib.fla**.

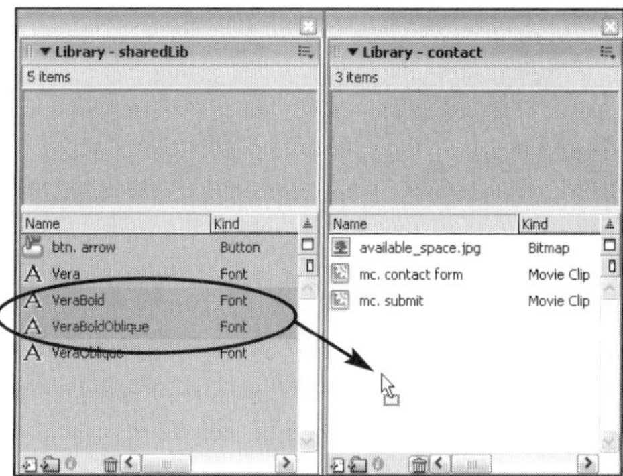

4. Undock the **sharedLib** and **contact Library** windows and position them so they're next to each other. Then in the **sharedLib Library**, select the two shared font symbols **VeraBold** and **VeraBoldOblique** and drag them into the **contact** Library window.

*As you have seen before in this book, this will import those two shared font symbols into **contact.fla**, where they can be used without adding to the file size of the published **contact.swf** file.*

---

5. Close the **sharedLib Library** window–you won't need it again in this chapter. To save space if need be, you can also redock the **contact Library** window with the rest of your open panels.

Next, you will use those two shared font symbols to define the font faces of some various text blocks. Later, you will use those same font symbols when specifying the font face for the feedback form components.

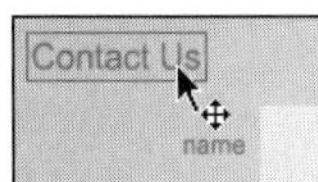

6. On the **Stage** of **contact.fla** is the module title **Contact Us**. Single-click it to select it.

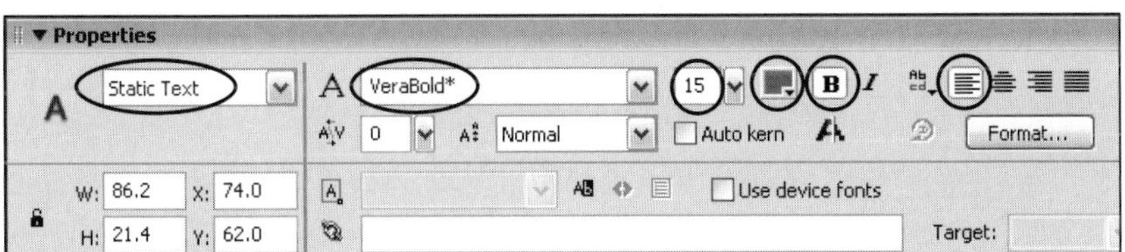

7. With the **Contact Us** text block selected, open the **Properties inspector** (**Ctrl+F3** [Windows] or **Cmd+F3** [Mac]). Most of the text options have been predefined for you, but you still need to set up a few options. Click the **Font** pull-down menu, and from the font list choose **VeraBold***. This is one of the shared fonts you imported earlier in this exercise. Then, if you're running the Windows operating system, click the **Bold Style** button. If you're running the Macintosh OS, *do not* click the **Bold Style** button. Lastly, simply verify that the remainder of your settings are the same as those in the screen shot above.

To keep it self-contained and easy to move around later, the feedback form is going to be constructed within a movie clip.

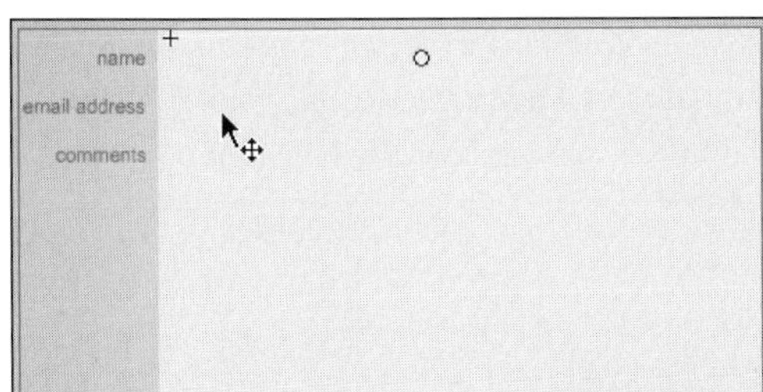

8. Single-click the light-blue box on the **Stage**. If you look at your **Properties inspector**, you'll notice that it is an instance of a movie clip symbol **mc. contact form**. Along with that light-blue box, the text **name**, **email address**, and **comments**–which act as labels for the soon-to-be three components that comprise the feedback form–are also nested within the **mc. contact form** movie clip.

9. Double-click the **mc. contact form** movie clip instance to open it.

*Within this movie clip instance are two prebuilt layers, **bg** and **text**. The **bg** layer contains the light-blue background (to make it easier to see, its layer outline mode is enabled), and the **text** layer contains the text **name, email address**, and **comments**.*

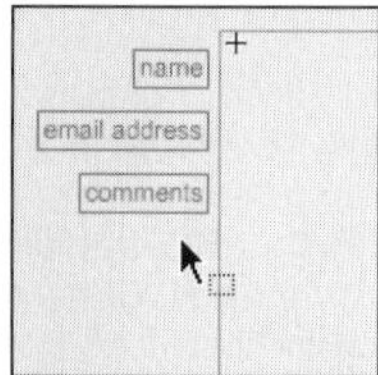

10. Select the three blocks of text: **name**, **email address**, and **comments**.

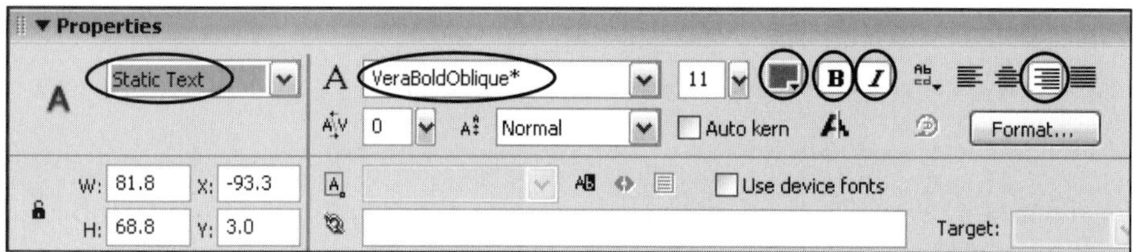

11. With the three text blocks selected, open the **Properties inspector** (**Ctrl+F3** [Windows] or **Cmd+F3** [Mac]). Most of the text options have been predefined for you, but you still need to set up a few options. Click the **Font** pull-down menu, and from the font list choose **VeraBoldOblique***. This is one of the shared fonts that you imported earlier in this exercise. Then, if you're running the Windows operating system, click the **Bold Style** and **Italic Style** buttons. If you're running the Macintosh OS, *do not* click the **Bold Style** or **Italic Style** buttons. Lastly, simply verify that the remainder of your settings are the same as those in the screen shot above.

Now you just need to drag the components that will comprise the feedback form onto the Stage and give each of them an instance name, and you'll be ready to start writing the ActionScript to breathe interactive life into the form.

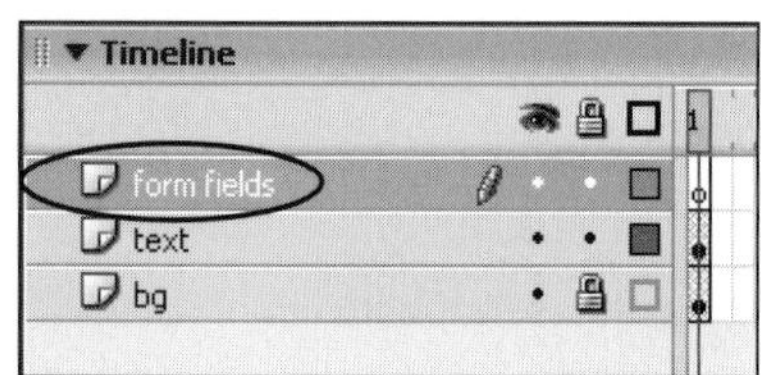

12. Create a new layer. Rename the new layer **form fields**.

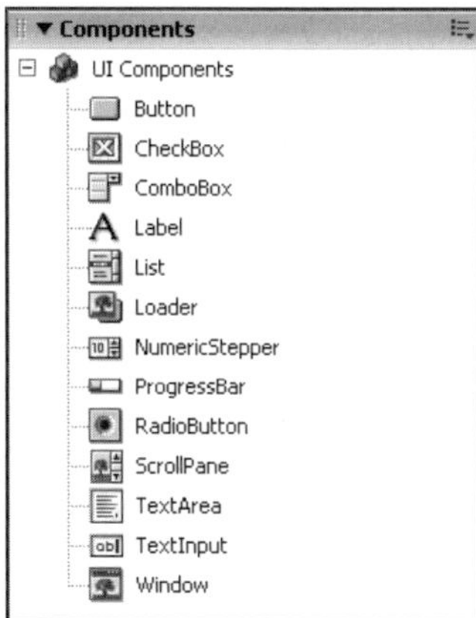

13. Open the **Components** panel (**Ctrl+F7** [Windows] or **Cmd+F7** [Mac]).

Note: *The components available in the Components panel will differ depending on whether you're using Flash MX 2004 or Flash MX Professional 2004. In both versions of Flash, however, there is a **UI Components** group.*

---

14. Expand the **UI Components** group by clicking the **plus sign** (Windows) or **right-facing arrow** (Mac) to the left of the group. This will reveal all the user interface components.

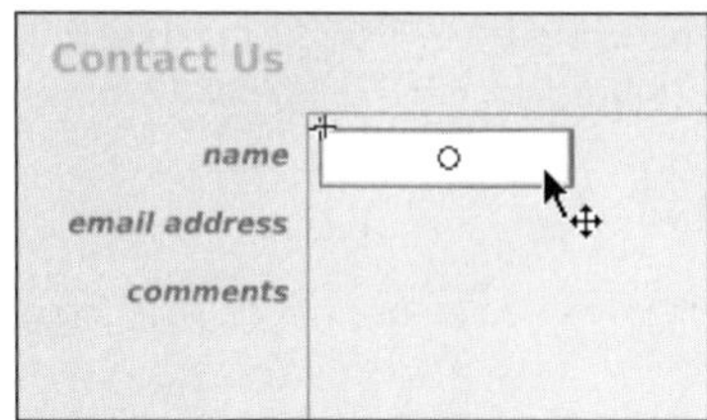

15. Drag the component **`TextInput`** from the **Components** panel and place it to the right of the text block **name**, but just within the yellow box (which is just the vector outline of the light-blue box you saw earlier on the **Stage**).

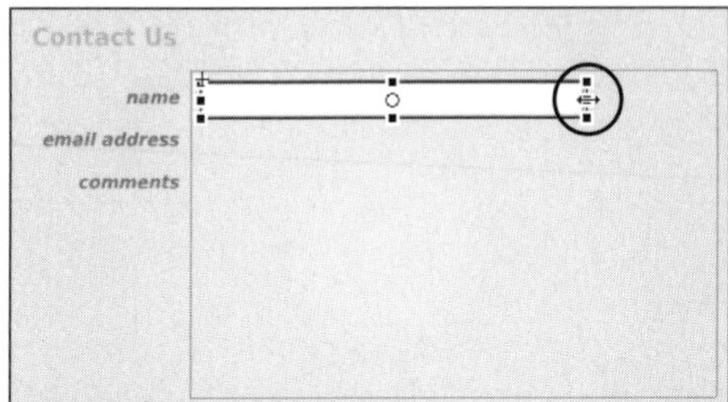

16. With the `TextInput` component on the **Stage** still selected, select the **Free Transform** tool (**Q**). Then, expand the width of the `TextInput` component by clicking the center, right-most resize handle and dragging it to the right.

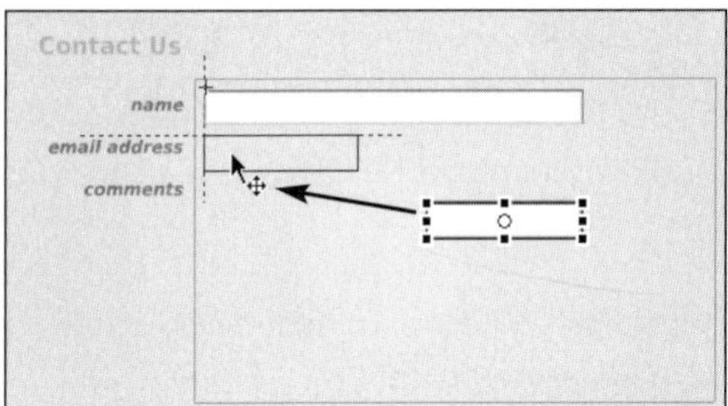

17. Drag another instance of the `TextInput` component from the **Components** panel onto the **contact.fla Stage**. Place it to the right of the text block **email address**, but just underneath the `TextInput` component to the right of **name**. You can also utilize the new **auto-align** feature, pictured in the screen shot above, to assist you with achieving precise alignment.

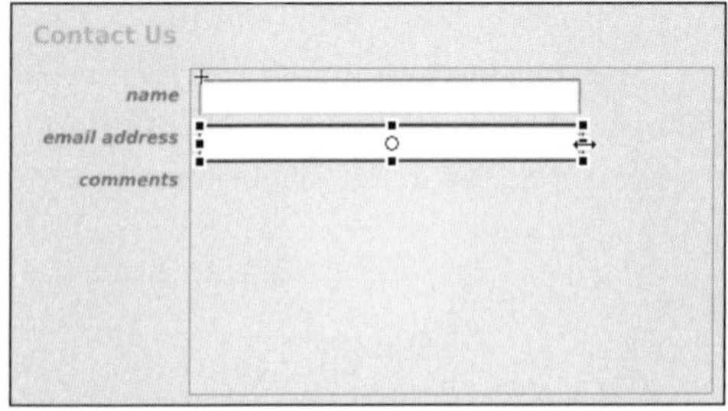

18. Using the **Free Transform** tool again, drag the center, right-most resize handle to the right until it is the same width as the `TextInput` component that's to the right of the **name** text block.

Note: *If you prefer, you can use the* ***Info*** *panel, instead of the* ***Free Transform*** *tool, to make sure the components are the same size and aligned on the same* ***x*** *coordinates.*

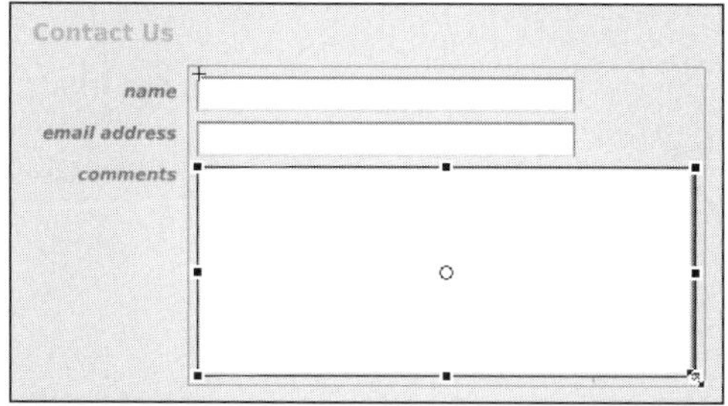

19. From the **Components** panel again, drag an instance of the **`TextArea`** component and place it on the **Stage** to the right of the **comments** text block. (**Note:** Drag out an instance of the **`TextArea`** component, *not* the **`TextInput`** component you utilized in the previous steps.) Then, using the **Free Transform** tool, resize the **`TextArea`** component so that it matches what you see in the screen shot above.

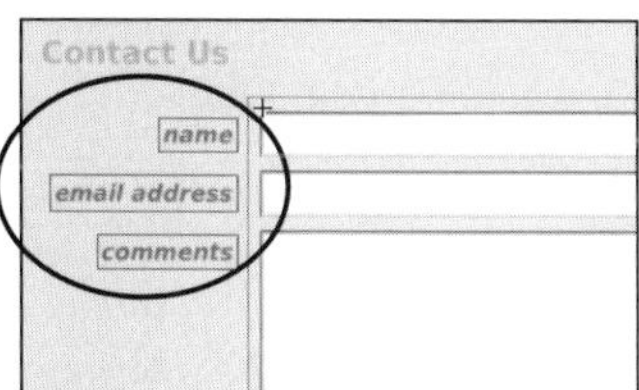

*Depending on your operating system, you may need to slightly adjust the position of the text blocks **name**, **email address**, and **comments** so they are better aligned with the components you just placed on the Stage.*

The components you just dragged onto the Stage will be the input fields where viewers will enter their name, email address, and comments, respectively. But before you can continue, you need to give each component an instance name. Once each component has a unique instance name, you'll be able to target each one with ActionScript.

20. With the **Selection** tool selected (**V**), single-click the **`TextInput`** component that's to the right of the **name** text block.

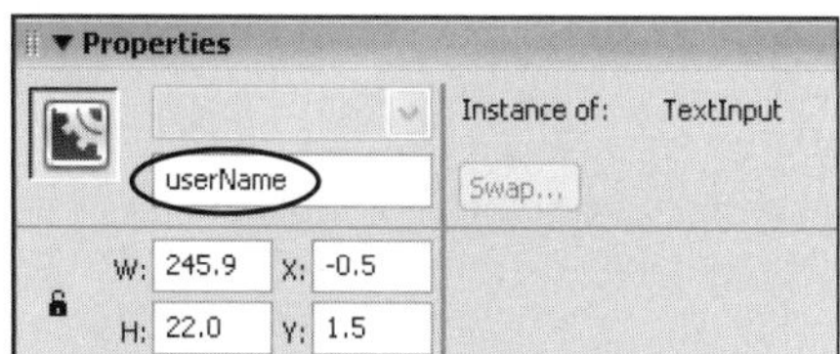

21. Open the **Properties inspector** (**Ctrl+F3** [Windows] or **Cmd+F3** [Mac]), and in the **Instance Name** field, type **userName**.

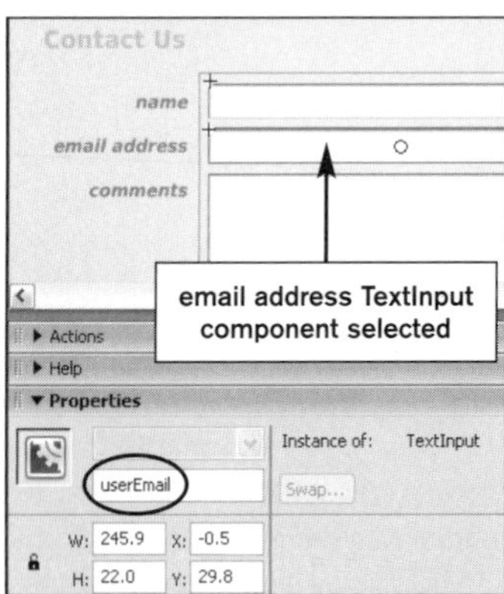

22. Single-click the `TextInput` component that sits to the right of the **email address** text block, and in the **Properties inspector**, type **userEmail** in the **Instance Name** field.

Note: *By this point, you're probably wondering where these instance names come from that you're assigning to the components. Well, like variables, these instance names can be whatever you'd like. However, you still have to follow the same naming conventions when assigning instance names: no spaces, no special characters (!*&), and so forth. Later, you will write some actions that collect the information the viewer has typed into the component fields, package them up, and send them to a CGI script to be processed.*

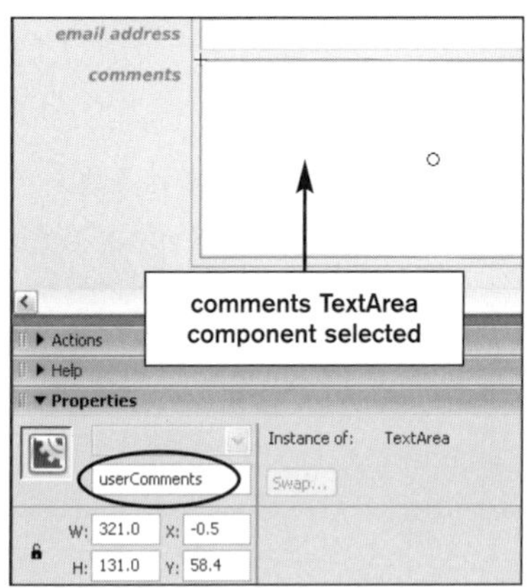

23. Single-click the `TextArea` component that sits to the right of the **comments** text block. In the **Properties inspector**, type **userComments** in the **Instance Name** field.

Great! Now that you've given instance names to each of the form components, you can target them with ActionScript. Before you start writing the ActionScript, however, there are still a few more things you need first. After viewers have filled out the feedback form, they'll need something to click to send their comments to you.

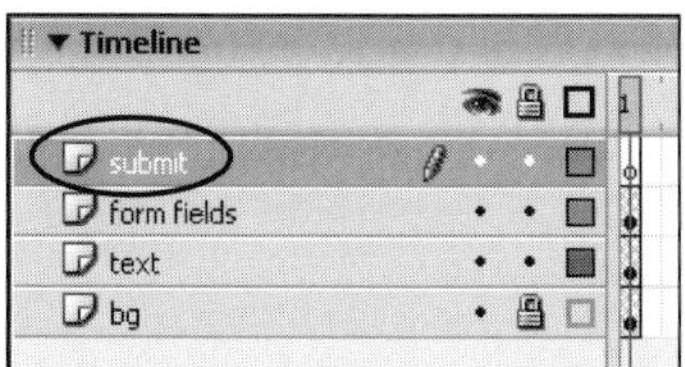

24. Create a new layer. Rename the new layer **submit**. This layer will contain the submit movie clip instance that the viewer will click to submit the feedback form to a CGI script for processing.

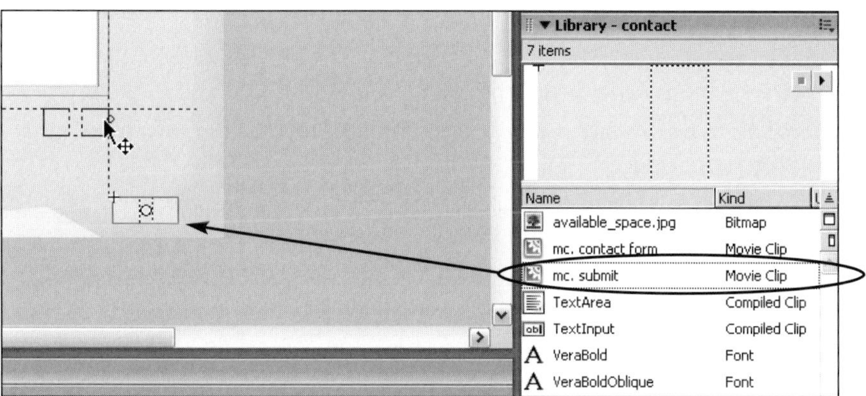

25. Open the **contact.fla Library** (**Ctrl+L** [Windows] or **Cmd+L** [Mac]) and drag an instance of **mc. submit** onto the **Stage**. Then, reposition it so that it's underneath the yellow-outlined box and aligned to its right-hand side.

Note: *You'll notice that the* ***mc. submit*** *movie clip instance you just dragged onto the Stage has a dynamic text field nested within it. (That's what the dashed outline is.) If you were to double-click this movie clip instance, you'd also notice that there are two frames within this symbol. On the first frame, the background rectangle is a light blue, and on the second frame it's white. These two frames make up the rollover effect you will trigger later with ActionScript. The dynamic text field within the movie clip is where you will insert text, also using ActionScript. This allows you to use this generic movie clip for a variety of uses and gives you the ability to change the text in the movie clip depending on how and where it is being used.*

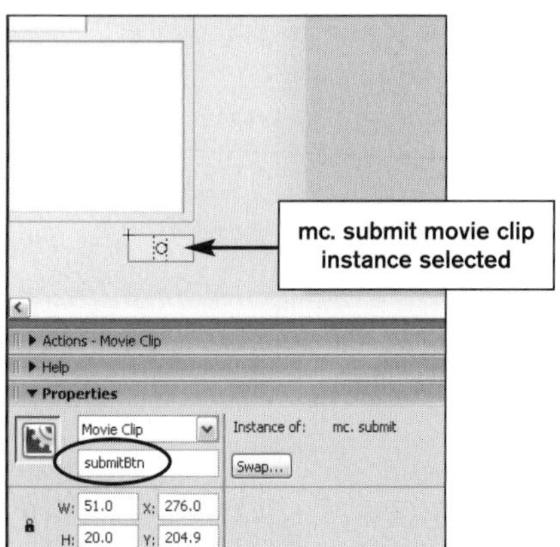

26. With the **mc. submit** movie clip instance still selected, open the **Properties inspector** and type **submitBtn** in the **Instance Name** field.

Now that you've created the form fields using components and have the submit button ready to go, the last "setting up" step is to give the movie clip these elements are all nested within, ***mc. contact form****, an instance name as well. Remember, if you want to target elements that are nested within a symbol using ActionScript, the parent symbol instance itself also needs to have a unique instance name.*

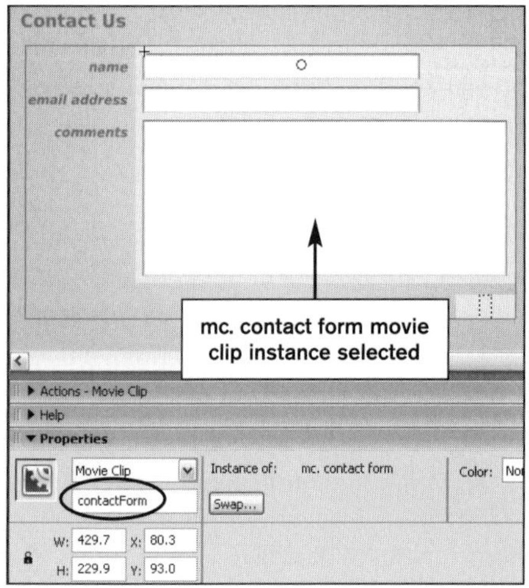

27. Return to the **Scene 1** Timeline by clicking its icon above the **Timeline**. Select the **mc. contact form** movie clip instance by single-clicking it. Then, open the **Properties inspector** and type **contactForm** in the **Instance Name** field.

Now, whenever you want–for example–to use ActionScript to target the ***userName*** *component that resides in the* ***mc. contact form*** *movie clip instance, you can type (from the main, Scene 1 Timeline):* **`contactForm.userName`**. *Easy!*

---

28. Save the changes you've made to **contact.fla** by choosing **File > Save** (**Ctrl+S** [Windows] or **Cmd+S** [Mac]).

29. Test the work you've done thus far by choosing **Control > Test Movie** (**Ctrl+Enter** [Windows] or **Cmd+Return** [Mac]).

Granted, the feedback form is somewhat minimalist at the moment, but keep in mind that this form will be loaded into ***master.swf****–and thereby the rest of the L.A. Eyeworks site–when the viewer clicks the* ***(contact us)*** *link in the navigational menu bar. If you type in the fields, you'll notice that the text is displayed with a standard* ***_sans*** *device font, and the text color is set to black. In a later exercise in this chapter, you will learn how to specify a different font face for the form text to be displayed with, as well as how to change the size of the text and its color.*

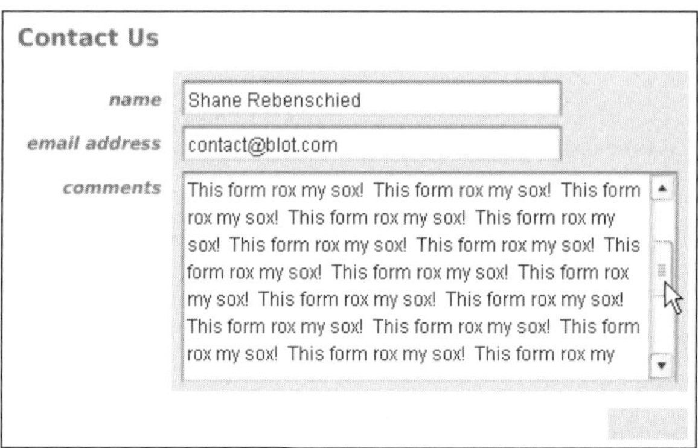

*You might also be wondering, at this point, why you're using **TextInput** and **TextArea** components for the form fields instead of a simple **Input Text** field. Still previewing **contact.swf**, if you were to type a large amount of text within the **comments** field, you would immediately see one reason why. When using the **TextArea** component in a form, if the viewer types enough text so that it exceeds the size of the field, scroll bars will automatically appear. By dragging the scroll bar or clicking the scroll arrows, you can easily scroll through the text in the **comments** field. A simple Input Text field does not have that built-in capability. Then, since you're already using the **TextArea** component, because of the way version 2 components work in Flash MX 2004, adding other components adds very little to the file size. So once you've added one component for the feedback form, it's best to continue using components in the construction of the form for consistency of appearance, functionality, and authoring the ActionScript.*

---

30. When you're finished with the feedback form, close the **Preview** window and return to **contact.fla**.

In the next exercise, you will begin to write the ActionScript that makes the form functional. You'll start by writing a simple form validation script that just checks to make sure that the viewer has typed text in each of the three form fields. If they have, a "Thank You" message will be displayed. If not, an error message will be shown instead.

3. Simple Form Validation

In this exercise, you're going to write a little bit of ActionScript that, in essence, does some simple form validation. When viewers click the **submit** symbol to send their comments to you, you want to first check that they filled out all the fields in the form. When you are building your own form–for your own uses–later, you can pick and choose which fields are required; that is, which fields the viewer *must* enter text in. For this feedback form, however, *every* field is required. If viewers don't enter information in every field, they'll be presented with an error message. Conversely, if viewers *do* enter information in every field, they'll see a "Thank You" message, and the form will be sent to a server-side CGI script for processing.

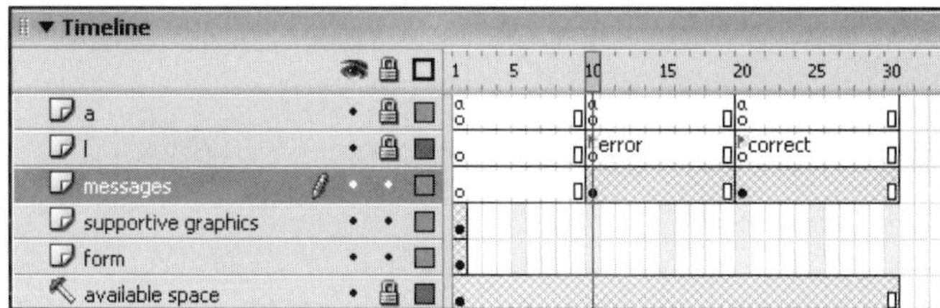

1. In the **Timeline** of **contact.fla**, move the playhead to **frame 10**.

You probably have already noticed the two labels in the ***l*** *layer,* ***error*** *and* ***correct****, on Keyframes* ***10*** *and* ***20****, respectively. These two labels represent the two possible outcomes when the viewer clicks the* ***submit*** *symbol. If the viewer enters information in every field, the playhead will jump to the* ***correct*** *label. On the other hand, if the viewer does* not *fill out every field in the feedback form, the playhead will jump to the* ***error*** *label.*

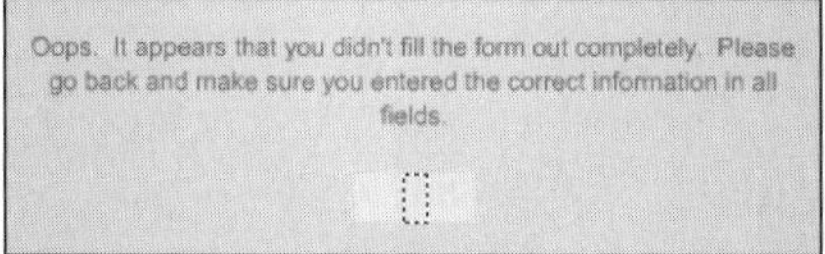

On the Stage, on Keyframe 10, is a block of static text that reads ***Oops. It appears that you didn't fill the form out completely. Please go back and make sure you entered the correct information in all fields.*** *Beneath that error message is something familiar–an instance of the* ***mc. submit*** *movie clip symbol you dragged onto the Stage earlier to act as the form submit button. In this case, however, there's some prebuilt ActionScript on the* ***a*** *layer in Keyframe 10 that instructs the dynamic text field in that movie clip instance to display the text* ***< back****. Another action specifies that if the viewer clicks that* ***mc. submit*** *movie clip instance, the playhead is to jump back to Keyframe 1. So this movie clip instance acts as a way for the viewer to go back to the feedback form so they can* completely *fill it out and attempt to submit the form again.*

Next you're going to change the font face of the error message so that it matches the fonts used in the rest of the L.A. Eyeworks site.

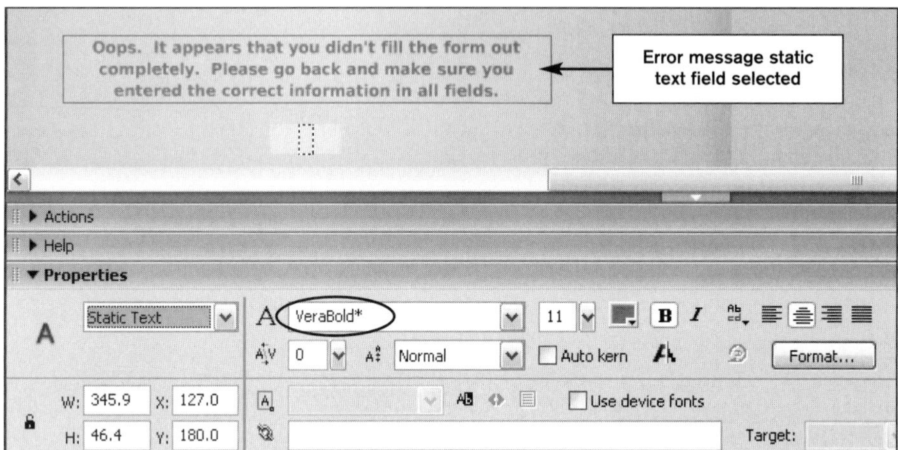

2. Single-click the error message static text field on the **Stage** to select it. Then, from the **Font** pull-down menu in the **Properties inspector**, choose the shared font symbol **VeraBold***. If you're running a Windows operating system, click the **Bold Style** button. If you're running the Macintosh OS, you should *not* click the **Bold Style** button. Lastly, simply verify that the text options in your **Properties inspector** match those in the screen shot above.

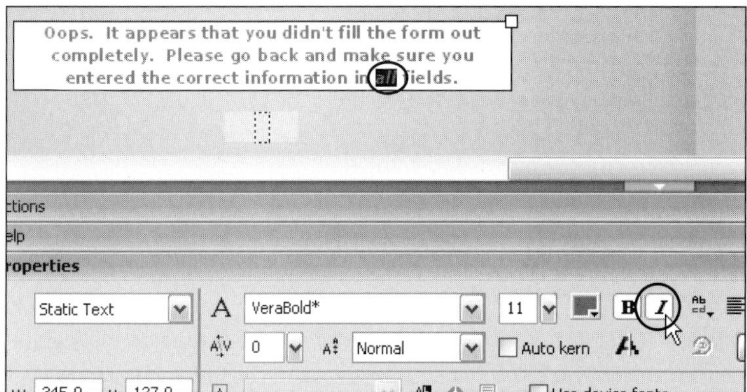

3. In the error message, make the word **all** italicized by double-clicking the text field, selecting the word **all**, and–if you're running a Windows OS–clicking the **Italic Style** button. If you're running the Mac OS, select the word **all**, and instead of clicking the **Italic Style** button, click the **Font** pull-down menu and choose the shared font symbol **VeraBoldOblique***.

The last "housekeeping" step before you begin to author the simple form validation script is to specify the font face for the ***correct*** *message as well. You've just specified the font face for the* ***error*** *message; now you need to repeat that process for the* ***correct*** *message.*

4. Move the playhead so it's over the **Timeline** label **correct** on **Keyframe 20**.

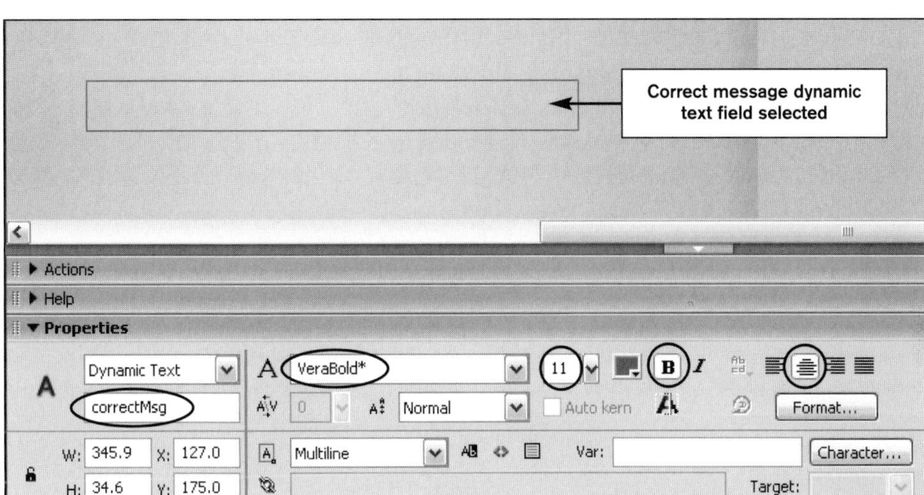

5. On the **Stage**, single-click the dynamic text field to select it. Then, in the **Properties inspector**, click the **Font** pull-down menu and choose the shared font symbol **VeraBold***. If you're currently running a Windows operating system, click the **Bold Style** button in the **Properties inspector**. If you're running the Macintosh OS, you *do not* need to click the **Bold Style** button. Last, verify that the text options in your **Properties inspector** match those in the screen shot above.

*So you've changed the font face of the **correctMsg** dynamic text field, but what text is going to be displayed in there?*

6. Click **Keyframe 20** in the **a** layer and open the **Actions** panel (**F9**).

```
//--------------------<correct message AS>---------------------\\

this.correctMsg.autoSize = "center";
this.correctMsg.text = "Thank you for taking the time to give us your comments " + gatherForm.visitor_name + ".\n
We look forward to seeing you in one of our stores soon!";

//--------------------</correct message AS>---------------------\\
```

*You'll quickly notice that some prebuilt ActionScript already exists in Keyframe 20. Like the other prebuilt ActionScripts in **contact.fla**, these actions were included because for the most part, they are actions you've already learned. The two actions you see in Keyframe 20 instruct the **corrrectMsg** dynamic text field on the Stage to automatically resize from the center, and to insert some text within that text field.*

However, there are a couple elements within the bottommost action you probably aren't familiar with:

- **gatherForm.visitor_name**: *At this point, you have no idea what* **gatherForm.visitor_name** *is. Later in this chapter, you will construct a* **LoadVars** *object to collect the text the viewer types in the feedback form. Once that text has been all collected, you will have the option of sending it to your own CGI script to be processed. Well,* **gatherForm** *is the name of the* **LoadVars** *object. One of the variable names within the* **gatherForm LoadVars** *object is* **visitor_name**. *As you'll see later in this chapter, you will write an action that instructs Flash MX 2004 to take whatever the viewer types in the* **name** *field in the feedback form and insert it into that* **visitor_name** *variable in the* **gatherForm** *object. (I'll talk about the "hows" and "whys" of doing that later in this chapter.) In the script, on Keyframe 20 in layer* **a**, **gatherForm.visitor_name** *is inserted within two strings:* ***Thank you for taking the time to give us your comments*** *and* ***.\n We look forward to seeing you in one of our stores soon!*** *If a visitor to the L.A. Eyeworks Web site were to fill out the form, type* **Shane** *in the* **name** *field, and click the* **submit** *symbol, the message would read:* ***Thank you for taking the time to give us your comments Shane. We look forward to seeing you in one of our stores soon!***

- **\n**: *The other piece you probably do not recognize is the text* **\n** *that's included at the beginning of the string* ***.\n We look forward to seeing you in one of our stores soon!****. Inserting* **\n** *in a string of text allows you to create a line break. So instead of the two strings of text being combined with the visitor's name into one long line, the* **\n** *inserts a line break. The resulting text looks like this:*

  Thank you for taking the time to give us your comments Shane.
  We look forward to seeing you in one of our stores soon!

Note: **\n** *is referred to as an "escape sequence" and, as briefly mentioned above, represents a new line. Besides* **\n**, *there are other escape sequences you can insert into strings of text. Escape sequences are useful, for example, if you wanted to insert a quotation mark within a string of text. If you were to just type a quotation mark within a string of text, you would get compile errors when you tried to publish your FLA. This is because the ActionScript compiler would interpret those quotation marks as the end or beginning of another string. Escape sequences allow you to use certain characters that cannot be represented in ActionScript otherwise. A table, listing these escape sequences, is provided following this exercise for your reference.*

Now that you've seen—and set up—the **error** *and* **correct** *messages the viewer will see if the feedback form has been filled out incorrectly or correctly (respectively), it's time to start writing some ActionScript. The actions you're about to write will perform some simple form validation. If the viewer has entered text in every form field, show the viewer the* **correct** *message. On the other hand, if the viewer has not entered text in every form field, show the viewer the* **error** *message.*

---

7. To start, select the first keyframe in layer **a** and open the **Actions** panel (**F9**).

```
stop();



// -----------------<pre-built code for chapter 9>--------------- \\
/*
//--------------------<submit button AS>---------------------\\

this.contactForm.submitBtn.btnLabel.autoSize = "center";
this.contactForm.submitBtn.btnLabel.text = "submit";

// onRollOver
this.contactForm.submitBtn.onRollOver = function() {
    contactForm.submitBtn.gotoAndStop (2);
}

// onRollOut
this.contactForm.submitBtn.onRollOut = function() {
    contactForm.submitBtn.gotoAndStop (1);
}

// onRelease
this.contactForm.submitBtn.onRelease = function() {

}

//--------------------</submit button AS>---------------------\\
*/
// -----------------</pre-built code for chapter 9>--------------- \\
```

*As you can see, there's some ActionScript in Keyframe 1 that has been created for you. Just like in previous FLAs, this ActionScript was prebuilt for you because it involves actions you learned earlier in this book. In this case, these actions apply to the **submit** button. Reading down the ActionScript, you'll notice that it's mostly comprised of roll-over and roll-out actions for the **submitBtn** movie clip instance. Toward the top are two actions. One, **this.contactForm.submitBtn.btnLabel.autoSize = "center";**, allows the text field nested within the **mc. submit** movie clip to automatically resize itself from its center. The other, **this.contactForm.submitBtn.btnLabel.text = "submit";**, then inserts the text "submit" into that dynamic text field. You'll also see, toward the bottom, that there is an empty function set up for the **onRelease** behavior of the submit button. It's within that empty **onRelease** function that you'll write the action that performs the simple form validation.*

First, you need to uncomment the provided ActionScript.

```
// --------------------<pre-built code for chapter 9>---------------- \\
/*
//--------------------<submit button AS>---------------------\\

this.contactForm.submitBtn.btnLabel.autoSize = "center";
this.contactForm.submitBtn.btnLabel.text = "submit";
```

8. Select the top two commenting lines, as shown in the screen shot above, and delete them.

```
// onRelease
this.contactForm.submitBtn.onRelease = function() {

}

//--------------------</submit button AS>---------------------\\
*/
// ------------------</pre-built code for chapter 9>--------------- \\
```

9. Then, select the bottom two commenting lines, as shown in the screen shot above, and delete those as well.

Now that those comments have been removed, the ActionScripts are ready to go.

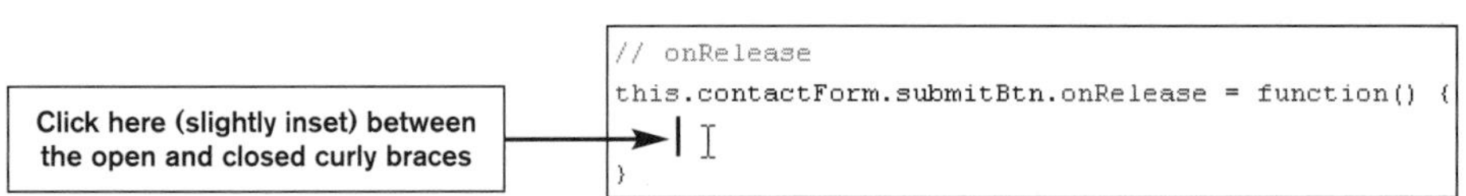
Click here (slightly inset) between the open and closed curly braces
// onRelease
this.contactForm.submitBtn.onRelease = function() {
}

10. Click between the **`this.contactForm.submitBtn.onRelease = function() {`** line and the closed curly brace (**}**). To follow correct ActionScript formatting, click slightly inset between the two lines where a tabbed space has already been inserted for you (as shown in the screen shot above).

```
// onRelease
this.contactForm.submitBtn.onRelease = function() {
    if (contactForm.userEmail.text == ""
}
```

11. Then, type the following:

`if (contactForm.userEmail.text == ""`

*This is, of course, the beginning of an **`if`** statement. In essence, it reads "If the text in the **`userEmail`** component (in the **contactForm** movie clip) is equal to nothing...." As you can see, after the double equals signs there are two quotation marks, back to back. This symbolizes the absence of text; in other words, if the viewer has not typed* anything *in the **`userEmail`** field. But remember, you need to check if the viewer typed some information in* every *field. You need an **`if`** statement that essentially says "If the viewer has* not *typed some text in the **`userEmail`** field, the **`userName`** field, or the **`userComments`** field, show the **error** message. Otherwise, show the **correct** message."*

```
// onRelease
this.contactForm.submitBtn.onRelease = function() {
    if (contactForm.userEmail.text == "" || contactForm.userName.text == "" ||
contactForm.userComments.text == "") {
}
```

12. Finish the **if** statement by typing all on one line with no line breaks (the line break you see in the action in the screen shot above is from the actions wrapping in the **Actions** panel):

|| contactForm.userName.text == "" || contactForm.userComments.text == "") {

Note: *For consistency and better readability, type a space after the action you started in Step 11, and the action that you continue in Step 12.*

*What will strike you as new as you're typing the rest of this **if** statement are the double pipes (||). The pipes, by the way, can by typed by pressing the **Shift** key and the **Backspace** key. The double pipes–in ActionScript–is called a* logical ***OR*** operator. *Very simply, it means "or." So by adding them into this **if** statement, it now reads "If the **userEmail** field is empty,* or *if the **userName** field is empty,* or *if the **userComments** field is empty...." And, obviously, the **if** statement isn't completed yet.*

*Now what should happen if the **if** statement you just wrote is false? In other words, what should happen if the viewer has* not *typed text in* every *field? Yes, as you have read before in this exercise, the **error** message should be displayed.*

```
// onRelease
this.contactForm.submitBtn.onRelease = function() {
    if (contactForm.userEmail.text == "" || contactForm.userName.text == "" ||
contactForm.userComments.text == "") {
        gotoAndStop ("error");
}
```

Click after this open curly brace and press Return/Enter to create a line break

13. Click after the open curly brace (circled in the screen shot above) you finished typing at the end of Step 12, and press **Enter** (Windows) or **Return** (Mac) once to create a line break. Then, type the following:

gotoAndStop ("error");

*This, of course, tells the playhead to move to the frame label **error**.*

*Now you need to specify what should happen if that **if** statement is* not *true. In other words, what should happen if the viewer* did *type text in* every *field? Well, if the viewer did type text in every field, the **correct** message should be displayed.*

```
// onRelease
this.contactForm.submitBtn.onRelease = function() {
    if (contactForm.userEmail.text == "" || contactForm.userName.text == "" ||
contactForm.userComments.text == "") {
        gotoAndStop ("error");
    } else {
        gotoAndStop ("correct");
    }
}
```

14. Click at the end of the **gotoAndStop ("error");** line, press **Enter** (Windows) or **Return** (Mac) once to create a line break, and type the following:

```
} else {
    gotoAndStop ("correct");
}
```

*As you have seen before, this adds an **else** onto the **if** statement. Within the **else** statement, the playhead is instructed to move to the **correct** label. Taken all together, this **if** statement reads "If the viewer does* not *type anything in the **userEmail**, **userName**, or **userComments** fields, move the playhead to the **error** label. Otherwise, move the playhead to the **correct** label."*

And there you have a simple form validation script. All it's really checking for is if the viewer has typed something *in* every *text field. If the viewer has, he or she is shown a "Thank You" message. If not, he or she is instead shown an error message.*

Now you just need to save your work, test the movie, cross your fingers, and make sure everything is working as you expect it to.

---

15. Save the changes you've made to **contact.fla** by choosing **File > Save** (**Ctrl+S** [Windows] or **Cmd+S** [Mac]).

---

16. Test **contact.fla** by choosing **Control > Test Movie** (**Ctrl+Enter** [Windows] or **Cmd+Return** [Mac]).

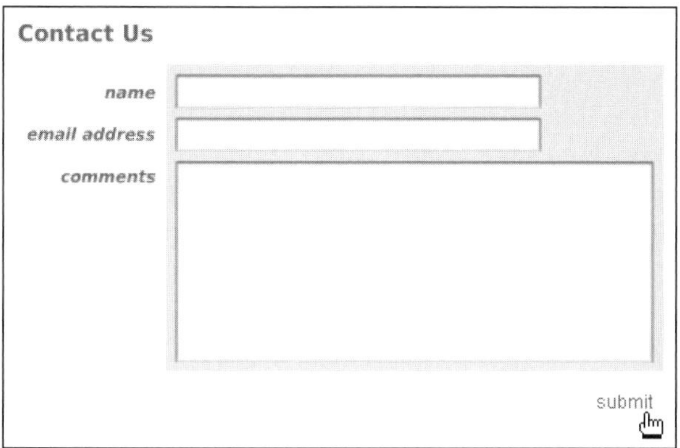

17. When the **Preview** window appears and you see your **Contact Us** form, don't type anything in any of the fields. To test that the form validation script (to use a fancy term for a simple `if` statement) is working correctly, just click **submit**.

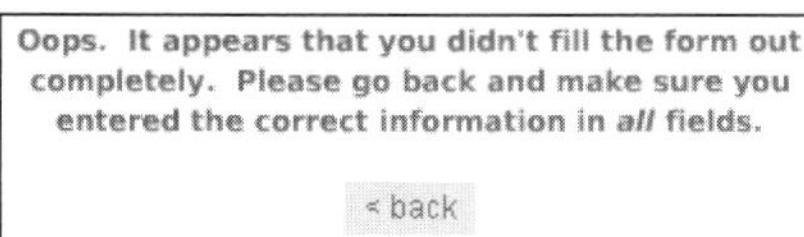

Because you didn't type text in every *field, the* ***if*** *statement works correctly and moves the playhead to the* ***error*** *frame, thereby displaying the error message. Yayy!*

18. Click **<back** to return back to the **Contact Us** form (**Keyframe 1**).

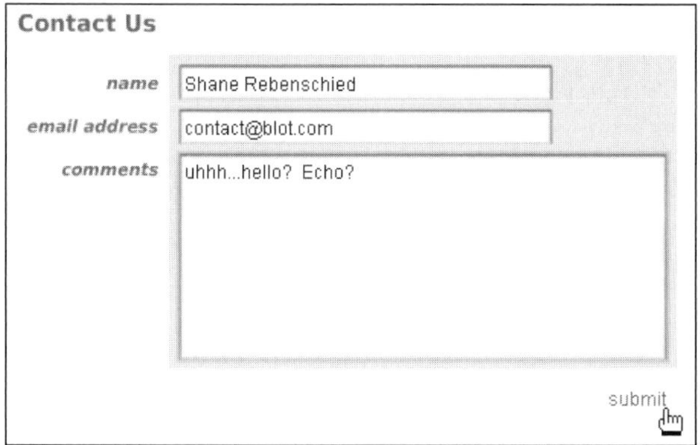

19. This time, type something in every field, and click **submit**.

Thank you for taking the time to give us your comments undefined.
We look forward to seeing you in one of our stores soon!

Now, because you typed text in every *field, the **if** statement is false, which causes the **else** statement within it to execute. This moves the playhead to the **correct** label, displaying the "Thank you" message. If you read through the "Thank you" message, you'll notice that in place of where your name should be (or whatever you typed in the **name** field), it instead says "undefined". Unless you actually typed "undefined" in the **name** field, you'll realize that it's not actually working as intended. This is because the action used to retrieve the text that was entered in the **name** field references a **LoadVars** script you haven't created yet. Until then, you'll just have to take my word that it will work (honest) later in this chapter.*

But, as you can see, the form validation script worked—yet again—and displayed the "Thank you" message when every *field had text entered into it.*

To be a good little Flash MX 2004 designer/developer, you should also make sure that the form validation script works as intended when only one or two fields have text in them.

---

20. With the **Preview** window still open, press **Ctrl+Enter** (Windows) or **Cmd+Return** (Mac) *twice*. This will reload the **contact.swf** file, and the form will be displayed again.

21. This time, type some text in only one or two of the fields, but not all. Then, click **submit**.

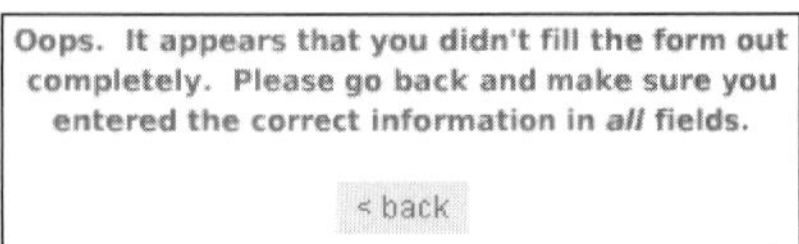

*You'll then be presented, once again, with the **error** message.*

*When the viewer fills out the form and clicks the submit button, a simple **if** statement is executed that checks to make sure that text has been entered in* every *field. Based on the results of that check, either an "Oops" or "Thank you" message will be displayed.*

---

22. When you're finished previewing **contact.swf**, close the **Preview** window and return to **contact.fla**.

*Congratulations! Your **Contact Us** feedback form is a raging success, and now you can boast to your friends and coworkers about how you "constructed a feedback form validation script last night." Take it from me, they'll be sooo impressed. You'll be the most popular kid on your block...again!*

Escape Sequences

Escape Sequence	Character
\b	Backspace character
\f	Form-feed character
\n	Line-feed character
\r	Carriage-return character
\t	Tab character
\"	Double quotation mark
\'	Single quotation mark
\\	Backslash

MOVIE | Defining Tab Order

In the **movies** folder on the **H•O•T CD-ROM** is a movie titled **tab_order.mov**. In this movie, you will learn how to define which field should be the "active" field when the viewer presses the **Tab** key. As you have seen when you're filling out an HTML-based form on a Web site, when you are typing in a form field and press the **Tab** key, the "active" field status will jump to another field. Well, using the **tabIndex** action, you can specify the order in which the various form fields will become "active" as the viewer presses the **Tab** key. In this movie, you will not only learn how to define the tab order, but also how it can be *very* beneficial when dealing with complex form layouts.

Using LoadVars to Send the Form Results

In this exercise, you are going to build a **LoadVars** object whose job it will be to collect the text the viewer has typed into the form fields and store it. You will also learn how Flash MX 2004–based forms connect to a CGI script, as well as what you'll need to modify in order to take that stored text and send it to a CGI script on your own server so it can be processed. Initially, it may sound somewhat daunting, but as you'll see when you start writing the ActionScript, it's fairly straightforward.

Before you get started, I should answer a question that might be burning in your mind. What is a CGI script, and what does it have to do with the feedback form? That simple question is actually multifaceted, and I could spend pages explaining the various aspects of it. Because this is a *Macromedia Flash MX 2004* book, however, it wouldn't be prudent to ramble on about CGI scripts, middleware, and Web servers. So here is the condensed version:

CGI, an acronym for **C**ommon **G**ateway **I**nterface, is a program that resides on a Web server. A CGI script can be written in a variety of computer programming languages such as C/C++, PERL, PHP, PYTHON, and so forth. The job of the CGI script is to act as a middleman between the Web page (in your case, the L.A. Eyeworks Contact Us form) and the Web server. The ultimate goal of the feedback form is to take what the viewer types in the form, organize it so that it's easy to read (the raw output of a form is quite difficult to read by itself), and email it. Flash MX 2004 can't do all those things by itself. Flash MX 2004 simply gathers the raw text the viewer types in the form and sends it someplace else. Flash MX 2004 cannot organize that information in an easy-to-read format, nor can it email that content to an email address. That's where the CGI script comes in. From the Contact Us form, you'll use a **LoadVars** object to take the text the viewer types in the form, arrange it in a way that makes sense to the CGI script, and then pass it off to that CGI script (yes, **LoadVars** can *send* as well as *receive* variables). The CGI script will grab the text, organize it so that it's easier to read by a human, and then shoot it off to the Web server with instructions to email it to an address. Because the CGI script is the middleman in this process, a CGI script is often called **middleware** (taken from the term **software**). The type of CGI script you can use will depend on the type of server your Web site is hosted on. Additionally, most Web presence providers these days provide some standard CGI scripts that will process form results for you. A common one is called FormMail. You will learn more about locating an appropriate server and CGI scripts in Appendix C at the end of this book.

Now that you have a little bit of an understanding of how the CGI script links up with the feedback form, you're ready to start constructing the **LoadVars** script that will send the form results to the CGI script for processing.

1. Make sure you have **contact.fla** still open, that you have **Keyframe 1** in the **a** layer selected, and that the **Actions** panel is open.

*The first thing you need to construct is the **LoadVars** object itself. You've seen this a few times before, so there aren't any surprises here.*

```
stop();

var gatherForm:LoadVars = new LoadVars();

//--------------------<submit button AS>--------------------\\
```

2. Click between the **stop();** action at the top of the **Actions** panel, and the **//--------------------<submit button AS>--------------------** comment. Then, type the following:

var gatherForm:LoadVars = new LoadVars();

*As you have seen before, this simply creates a new variable **gatherForm**, strict types it as a **LoadVars** data type, and assigns a new **LoadVars** object to that variable.*

The remainder of the actions–gathering the feedback results and sending them to the CGI script–needs to be executed only after *the **submit** button has been clicked and* after *the simple form validation script, which you wrote in the previous exercise, has validated the form results as **correct**. All this means is that because these next series of actions will need to be executed when a specific event occurs, you're going to create a function for these actions to reside within. Later, you'll trigger that function so it will execute when the form has been submitted and verified.*

```
var gatherForm:LoadVars = new LoadVars();

function sendForm() {
```

3. Click at the end of the **var gatherForm:LoadVars = new LoadVars();** line you wrote in the previous step, press **Enter** (Windows) or **Return** (Mac) twice to create a line break, and type the following:

function sendForm() {

*As you have also seen before, this simply creates a function called **sendForm**. Within this function, you will write the rest of the actions associated with preparing and sending the feedback form results to a CGI script.*

```
var gatherForm:LoadVars = new LoadVars();

function sendForm() {
    gatherForm.email_to = "contact@blot.com";
```

4. Click at the end of the **function sendForm() {** line, press **Enter** (Windows) or **Return** (Mac) once to create a line break, and type the following:

gatherForm.email_to = "contact@blot.com";

*However, in place of **contact@blot.com**, type the email address you want the form results to eventually get sent to.*

*What this action says, in essence, is "Create a property called **email_to** in the **gatherForm LoadVars** object. Then, assign the string "contact@blot.com" to that **email_to** property." As was explained way back in Chapter 3, "Getting Started," objects–like the **gatherForm LoadVars** object–are made up of properties and methods. By first typing the name of the **LoadVars** object, **gatherForm**, a dot (.) and then **email_to**, you're assigning a new property called **email_to** to the **gatherForm LoadVars** object. Last, by typing = **"contact@blot.com"**, you're assigning the string "contact@blot.com" to that **email_to** property. When this script is finished, all the properties contained within the **gatherForm** object will be sent to a CGI script to be processed. When Flash MX 2004 sends the properties in the **gatherForm** object, they are actually sent as variables that a CGI script can read and process. So **email_to**–for example–within the FLA is considered a property of the **gatherForm** object. But when it gets sent to the CGI script, it is sent and interpreted by the CGI script as a variable.*

*You know where **gatherForm** came from, but what about **email_to**? Where the heck did that come from? As you've seen mentioned previously in this chapter, a CGI script that would process these form results would be expecting to receive certain variables. Some of those variables, such as **email_to**, are required. If you do not create those required variables, a CGI script will not process the form correctly. If you already have a Web presence provider and access to a form-processing CGI script, your particular CGI script will probably be expecting* different *variables. Sometimes, the CGI script programmer will insert some comments at the top of the CGI script itself that states which variables it needs to work correctly, and sometimes a CGI script you download online comes with a README file that explains those details as well. If you're having a CGI script custom-built for your needs, make sure you find out from the CGI script programmer which variables are required. That way, you'll know which properties you* must *create within the **gatherForm** object to be sent to the CGI script. Usually, the only required variable is the one that defines the email address that the form results will be emailed to.*

*The next **gatherForm** properties you're about to create are properties that correspond with the remaining fields in the feedback form.*

```
var gatherForm:LoadVars = new LoadVars();

function sendForm() {
    gatherForm.email_to = "contact@blot.com";
    gatherForm.visitor_comments = contactForm.userComments.text;
```

5. Click at the end of the **`gatherForm.email_to = "contact@blot.com";`** line, press **Enter** (Windows) or **Return** (Mac) to create a line break, and type the following:

`gatherForm.visitor_comments = contactForm.userComments.text;`

*Similar to the action you created in Step 4, this action creates a property **`visitor_comments`** in the **`gatherForm LoadVars`** object. However,* unlike *in Step 4, this action takes the text in the **`userComments TextInput`** component in the **contactForm** movie clip symbol, and inserts that into the **`visitor_comments`** property.*

*If this sounds somewhat confusing to you, here's another way to think of it. When you go to the grocery store, pick out the things you need (milk, Ibuprofen, pasta, Ibuprofen, bread, Ibuprofen, and so forth), and head to the checkout clerk to pay for your items, they don't just throw your food back into the shopping cart. The clerk–or a bagger–will take your foodstuffs, put them in bags, and then give those to you. That way, you can easily transport all of those separate items out to your car. Applying that analogy to the actions you've written in this exercise, think of the text in the feedback fields as the separate food items, the **`gatherForm LoadVars`** object as the grocery bag, and the CGI script as the car to get those groceries (text) home. All this talk of groceries is making me hungry... ;-)*

*Now, many CGI scripts are set up in such a way that you can create as many form fields as you'd like. You just need to make sure that when you're assigning the text in a particular field to a property in the **`gatherForm LoadVars`** object–as you just did in Step 5–that the property you're assigning the text to has a unique name. Although the behavior of some CGI scripts will differ, most CGI scripts should just take those extra variables and insert them into the email it sends out.*

*Next you need to assign the text within the remaining two form fields to their own properties within the **`gatherForm LoadVars`** object.*

```
var gatherForm:LoadVars = new LoadVars();

function sendForm() {
    gatherForm.email_to = "contact@blot.com";
    gatherForm.visitor_comments = contactForm.userComments.text;
    gatherForm.visitor_name = contactForm.userName.text;
    gatherForm.visitor_email = contactForm.userEmail.text;
```

6. Click at the end of the **gatherForm.visitor_comments = contactForm.userComments.text;** line, press **Enter** (Windows) or **Return** (Mac) once, and type the following:

gatherForm.visitor_name = contactForm.userName.text;

Then press **Enter** (Windows) or **Return** (Mac) again to create another line break, and type the following:

gatherForm.visitor_email = contactForm.userEmail.text;

*And there you have it. You've now assigned the text within each of the three feedback form fields to their own unique property within the **gatherForm LoadVars** object. Now you just need to write the action that takes all the groceries out to the car...err...I mean you need to write an action that takes all the properties in the **gatherForm LoadVars** object and sends them to a CGI script for processing.*

```
var gatherForm:LoadVars = new LoadVars();

function sendForm() {
    gatherForm.email_to = "contact@blot.com";
    gatherForm.visitor_comments = contactForm.userComments.text;
    gatherForm.visitor_name = contactForm.userName.text;
    gatherForm.visitor_email = contactForm.userEmail.text;

    gatherForm.send("/cgi-sys/formmail.pl", "_blank", "POST");
```

7. Click at the end of the **gatherForm.visitor_email = contactForm.userEmail.text;** line, press **Enter** (Windows) or **Return** (Mac) twice to create a couple of line breaks, and type the following:

gatherForm.send("/cgi-sys/formmail.pl", "_blank", "POST");

*This action, in essence, reads "Send the form variables in the **gatherForm LoadVars** object to the CGI script located at **/cgi-sys/formmail.pl**. When the server responds, open its response in a new, blank window, and also send the form results using the **POST** method." Because there are a few different things going on in this action, here's a quick breakdown:*

- ***gatherForm.send()**: As was outlined in Chapter 4,* "LoadVars Class," *the **LoadVars** class has a **send** method you can use to send the variables in a **LoadVars** object to a URL. **Note:** The similar **sendAndLoad** method not only sends the variables to the CGI script, but it also loads any response that the CGI script generates.*

- ***"/cgi-sys/formmail.pl"****: This is the path on the remote server where the CGI script is located. If you're using your own CGI script on another server, the CGI script help documentation or the CGI script programmer should tell you what to enter here. On most servers, CGI scripts are located directly in a folder named* ***cgi-bin****.*
- ***"_blank"****: Depending on the CGI script being used to process the form text, it may send results from the server back to the Web browser. Usually this is just a confirmation or "thank you" message to let you know that the form results were received and understood successfully. In place of* ***_blank*** *(between the quotes), you can also specify a specific HTML frame name for the results to be returned to. Because the L.A. Eyeworks Web site doesn't make use of frames, you're using* ***"_blank"*** *to have the Web browser open a new, blank window to receive the server results. As mentioned a few paragraphs ago, you can also use the* ***sendAndLoad*** *method to send the form results and then load the corresponding CGI script response (if any). If you use* ***sendAndLoad*** *instead of specifying the HTML window or frame name you want the server response sent to, you specify the ActionScript object name where the response should be sent.*
- ***"POST"****: This specifies how Flash MX 2004 is going to format the variable/value pairs to send to a CGI script. Your two choices here are* ***POST*** *and* ***GET****. Most current scripts use* ***POST****.*

There you have it! You've just written the ActionScript that will collect all the form text together into several properties in the ***gatherForm LoadVars*** *object, and send them to a CGI script to be processed and emailed to an address of your choosing. Of course, you still need to close the* ***sendForm*** *function.*

```
var gatherForm:LoadVars = new LoadVars();

function sendForm() {
    gatherForm.email_to = "contact@blot.com";
    gatherForm.visitor_comments = contactForm.userComments.text;
    gatherForm.visitor_name = contactForm.userName.text;
    gatherForm.visitor_email = contactForm.userEmail.text;

    gatherForm.send("/cgi-sys/formmail.pl", "_blank", "POST");
}
```

8. Click at the end of the **gatherForm.send("/cgi-sys/formmail.pl", "_blank", "POST");** line, press **Enter** (Windows) or **Return** (Mac) to create a line break, then close the function by typing a closed curly brace:

}

As a last little bit of housekeeping, to better visually separate this script from the others, you should add some comments.

```
//--------------------<send form LoadVars>---------------------\\
var gatherForm:LoadVars = new LoadVars();

function sendForm() {
    gatherForm.email_to = "contact@blot.com";
    gatherForm.visitor_comments = contactForm.userComments.text;
    gatherForm.visitor_name = contactForm.userName.text;
    gatherForm.visitor_email = contactForm.userEmail.text;

    gatherForm.send("/cgi-sys/formmail.pl", "_blank", "POST");
}
//--------------------</send form LoadVars>--------------------\\
```

9. Click at the beginning of the **`var gatherForm:LoadVars = new LoadVars();`** line, press **Enter** (Windows) or **Return** (Mac) once to push that action, and all others beneath it, down one line, then click in the new empty line break you just created and type the following:

```
//------------------<send form LoadVars>------------------\\
```

Then copy that comment, click after the closed curly brace you typed in Step 8, press **Enter** (Windows) or **Return** (Mac) once to create a line break, and paste the copied comment. Slightly change the comment by adding a forward slash (/) before the word **send** (as shown in the screen shot above).

*Finally, you need to specify when the **sendForm** function should get executed, thereby sending the form results to a CGI script to be processed. The form results should get sent to a CGI script only when the viewer has filled out the feedback form, clicked **submit**, and the simple form validation script has verified that* every *field has been filled out.*

```
// onRelease
this.contactForm.submitBtn.onRelease = function() {
     if (contactForm.userEmail.text == "" || contactForm.userName.text == "" ||
contactForm.userComments.text == "") {
          gotoAndStop ("error");
     } else {
          sendForm();
          gotoAndStop ("correct");
     }
}
```

10. Within the **`if`** statement you wrote in Exercise 3 (as shown in the screen shot above), click at the end of the **`} else {`** line, press **Enter** (Windows) or **Return** (Mac) once to create a line break, and type the following:

`sendForm();`

*This action, of course, executes the **sendForm** function you just wrote, thereby causing the form text to get packaged up into the **gatherForm LoadVars** object and sent off to a CGI script for processing. Pretty nifty, eh?*

---

11. Since you've made quite a few changes to **contact.fla**, save your file by choosing **File > Save** (**Ctrl+S** [Windows] or **Cmd+S** [Mac]).

In the next exercise, you're going to learn how to modify the appearance the text viewers see when they type in the feedback form. You'll even learn how to choose a custom font for the form as well!

5. Styling the Form

By now you have a *nearly* fully functional feedback form. The viewer can enter information in the various fields and submit the form. If you have your own Web space and a form-processing CGI script to use, you can even make some slight modifications to the script in the previous exercise, enabling you to send the form results to your CGI script to be processed. However, as the viewer enters text in the form fields it will display that text using the **TextInput** and **TextArea** component default settings. The defaults are a font family of _sans (usually displayed as Arial or Helvetica on the viewer's computer), a font size of 10, and a font color of black. In this exercise, you will learn how to modify those default settings so you can use whichever font family, size, or color you'd like.

There are actually a variety of ways to go about modifying the styling of a component. You can assign styles to individual component instances, to entire classes of a component, or even to *all* components in an entire SWF file. Because in the feedback form in the L.A. Eyeworks Web site you are using three components–from two different component classes–it will be easier and less time consuming to modify the styling of *all* of the components in **contact.swf** with one action. This is done using the **_global.style** declaration.

To see a list of all the component styles you can modify, open the **Help** panel (**F1**), and from the help "books" on the left side of the **Help** panel, choose **Using Components > Customizing Components > Using styles to customize component color and text > Supported styles**.

Note: If you accidentally minimized the left side of the **Help** panel and don't know how to get it back, click the **Table of Contents** button at the top of the **Help** panel.

First, you're going to start by specifying what font family you want to use for all the components in **contact.swf**.

```
//--------------------</send form LoadVars>---------------------\\

_global.style.setStyle("fontFamily", "Bitstream Vera Sans");

//--------------------<submit button AS>----------------------\\
```

(Windows)

```
//-------------------</send form LoadVars>--------------------\\

_global.style.setStyle ("fontFamily", "Bitstream Vera Sans Bold");

//-------------------<submit button AS>--------------------\\
```

(Mac)

1. Click at the end of the comment **`//-----------------</send form LoadVars>------------------\\`**, press **Enter** (Windows) or **Return** (Mac) twice to create a couple line breaks, and *if you're running a Windows operating system*, type the following:

`_global.style.setStyle("fontFamily", "Bitstream Vera Sans");`

If you're running a *Macintosh operating system*, instead type this:

`_global.style.setStyle("fontFamily", "Bitstream Vera Sans Bold");`

The only difference between the two operating systems is that Macintosh users can refer directly to **Bitstream Vera Sans Bold**, whereas Windows users cannot. If you're running a Windows operating system, to use the **bold** style of **Bitstream Vera Sans** you will need to add an additional action.

```
_global.style.setStyle("fontFamily", "Bitstream Vera Sans");
_global.style.setStyle("fontWeight", "bold");
```

(Windows)

2. ***Windows users only***: Click at the end of the **`_global.style.setStyle("fontFamily", "Bitstream Vera Sans");`** line, press **Enter** once to create a line break, and type this:

`_global.style.setStyle("fontWeight", "bold");`

`_global` *is called the* ***global style declaration****. By using the global style declaration, as you have just done, you can easily modify the styling of* all *the components used throughout an entire SWF file. By styling all the components using the global style declaration, you can easily create a unified look and feel of all the components used in a project.*

The actions (or action if you're on a Mac) you just added instruct all *of the components in* ***contact.swf*** *to use the font Bitstream Vera Sans Bold for the text that is entered into them.*

3. Save the changes you've made by choosing **File > Save** (**Ctrl+S** [Windows] or **Cmd+S** [Mac]). Then preview the feedback form by choosing **Control > Test Movie** (**Ctrl+Enter** [Windows] or **Cmd+Return** [Mac]).

4. When the **contact.swf Preview** window appears, type some text in each of the field components.

You'll notice that now, the text entered in the component fields is using the font Bitstream Vera Sans Bold. However, if you look closely, you'll notice that the text is aliased (meaning, the edges of the text is not smoothed [called ***anti-aliased****]). And if you were to copy* ***contact.swf*** *and* ***sharedLib.swf*** *(because* ***contact.swf*** *uses the shared fonts from the shared library) onto a computer that does* not *have the Bitstream Vera Sans Bold font installed, the text would be displayed using the default _sans font* even though you have specified a shared font to use. *To have the field components use Bitstream Vera Sans Bold if the viewer does not have Bitstream Vera Sans Bold installed on his or her computer, you have to add another action that instructs Flash MX 2004 to embed the font you've chosen for the components.*

5. Close the **Preview** window and return to **contact.fla**. Then, make sure you have **Keyframe 1** in layer **a** still selected and the **Actions** panel open.

```
_global.style.setStyle("fontFamily", "Bitstream Vera Sans");
_global.style.setStyle("fontWeight", "bold");
_global.style.setStyle("embedFonts", true);
```

(Windows)

```
_global.style.setStyle("fontFamily", "Bitstream Vera Sans Bold");
_global.style.setStyle("embedFonts", true);
```

(Macintosh)

6. Click at the end of the `_global.style.setStyle("fontWeight", "bold");` line (Windows) or the `_global.style.setStyle("fontFamily", "Bitstream Vera Sans Bold");` (Mac), press **Enter** (Windows) or **Return** (Mac) once to create a line break, and type the following:

```
_global.style.setStyle("embedFonts", true);
```

Some of you, upon reading that last step, might be wondering why you have to instruct Flash MX 2004 to embed fonts. You might be thinking "What is the purpose of the shared fonts in the shared library if you are embedding the font outlines in ***contact.swf*** *as well?"*

You'll be happy to know that because you're using shared fonts in a shared library, by writing an action that instructs Flash MX 2004 to embed the font outlines, Flash MX 2004 will not *embed the font outlines a second time. Instead–because you have chosen a font that you have previously specified as a shared font–**contact.swf** will simply use that shared font. Setting the global style declaration of **embedFonts** to **true**–as you have just done–will not only allow visitors who don't have the Bitstream Vera Sans Bold font installed on their computers to see that exact font in the component fields, but it also has the added benefit of anti-aliasing (smoothing) the text displayed in those fields as well.*

7. Save the changes you've made by choosing **File > Save** (**Ctrl+S** [Windows] or **Cmd+S** [Mac]). Then preview the feedback form by choosing **Control > Test Movie** (**Ctrl+Enter** [Windows] or **Cmd+Return** [Mac]).

8. When the **contact.swf Preview** window appears, type some text in each of the field components.

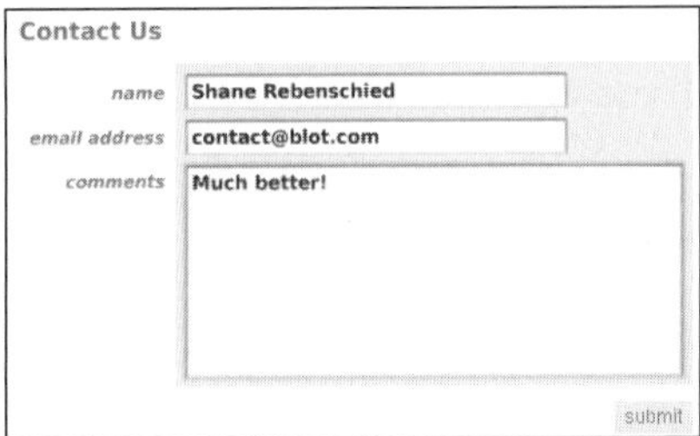

Now you'll notice that when you start typing in the field components, the text is displayed using Bitstream Vera Sans Bold (even for viewers who don't have Bitstream Vera Sans Bold installed on their computers) and is anti-aliased (smoothed) as well. Fantastic!

Next you're going to specify the font size and font color for the text in the field components.

---

9. Close the **Preview** window and return to **contact.fla**. Then, make sure you have **Keyframe 1** in layer **a** still selected and the **Actions** panel open.

```
_global.style.setStyle("fontFamily", "Bitstream Vera Sans");
_global.style.setStyle("fontWeight", "bold");
_global.style.setStyle("embedFonts", true);
_global.style.setStyle("fontSize", 12);
_global.style.setStyle("color", 0x3F7FBE);
```

(Windows)

```
_global.style.setStyle("fontFamily", "Bitstream Vera Sans Bold");
_global.style.setStyle("embedFonts", true);
_global.style.setStyle("fontSize", 12);
_global.style.setStyle("color", 0x3F7FBE);
```

(Macintosh)

---

10. Click at the end of the **`_global.style.setStyle("embedFonts", true);`** line, press **Enter** (Windows) or **Return** (Mac) once to create a line break, and type the following:

```
_global.style.setStyle("fontSize", 12);
```

Then press **Enter** (Windows) or **Return** (Mac) to again to create another line break, and type this:

```
_global.style.setStyle("color", 0x3F7FBE);
```

*The **`fontSize`** style is fairly self-explanatory. It allows you to specify the size of the font displayed in the components. However, you might be a little confused about how colors are defined using the **`color`** style. Luckily, it's quite easy to understand. The color you specified in this step, **`0x3F7FBE`**, is essentially a hexadecimal number preceded by "0x". So when you want to choose a color to use, you can simply use the built-in Flash MX 2004 **Color Mixer** panel to find the hexadecimal value of the color you want, add a "**0x**" in front of it, and there's your color.*

NOTE | Themes

Flash MX 2004 components also have built-in "themes" you can choose from. You've probably noticed that as you click in one of the component fields and press **Tab** to advance to the next field in sequence, a green "halo" appears around the outside of the field to show you that it has focus. That green halo is the default component theme called, appropriately, **haloGreen**. By using the **_global** style declaration you can change that default theme from **haloGreen** to others like **haloBlue** or **haloOrange** (there are only those three *default* themes to choose from). To change a theme for all of your components–to maintain a consistent appearance–you can simply type the following:

```
_global.style.setStyle("themeColor", "haloBlue");
```

You can even set your own halo theme color by typing this:

```
_global.style.setStyle("themeColor", 0xFF0000);
```

This would give you a bright red halo around all of the components in a SWF.

Before continuing, you should save and test your work.

11. Save the changes you've made by choosing **File > Save** (**Ctrl+S** [Windows] or **Cmd+S** [Mac]). Then preview the feedback form by choosing **Control > Test Movie** (**Ctrl+Enter** [Windows] or **Cmd+Return** [Mac]).

12. *When the* **contact.swf Preview** *window appears, type some text in each of the field components.*

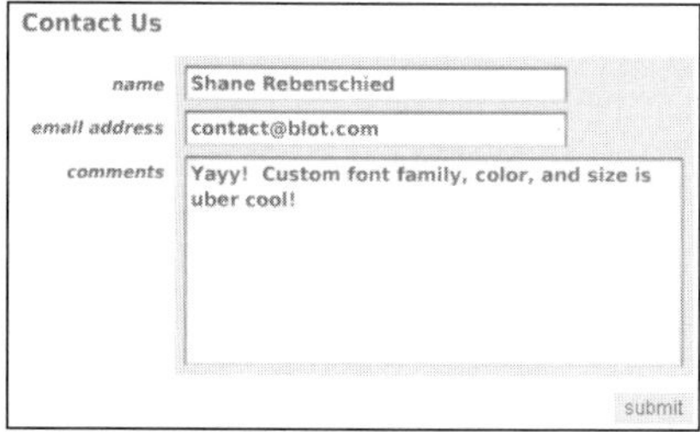

*You'll immediately notice, as you start typing in the field components, that not only is the text a slightly different size, but it's now a different color as well. Congratulations! You've successfully used the **_global** style declaration to modify the font family, size, and color of the text within component fields. And the font family you're using is pulled from the shared library as well so you're–yet again–not adding to the file size of the finished SWF by using a custom font face.*

As the last housekeeping task to perform before you close the book (bad pun intended) on this chapter, you should specify the font face for the **submit** *symbol.*

13. Close the **Preview** window and return to **contact.fla**.

14. On the **Stage**, double-click the **contactForm** movie clip instance (the same movie clip that is holding the feedback form) to open it.

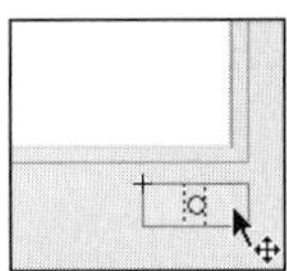

15. Then, double-click the **submitBtn** movie clip instance to open it.

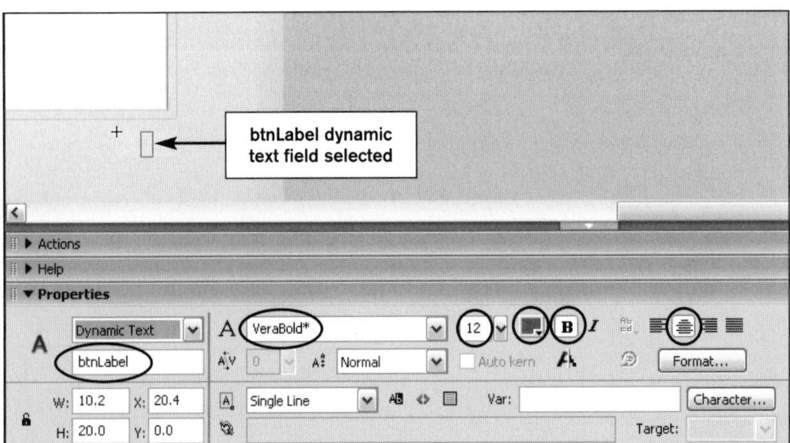

16. Single-click the **btnLabel** dynamic text field to select it and open the **Properties inspector** (**Ctrl+F3** [Windows] or **Cmd+F3** [Mac]). Most of the text options have been predefined for you, but you still need to set up a few options. Click the **Font** pull-down menu and choose **VeraBold***. This is one of the shared fonts you imported earlier in this exercise. Then, if you're running the Windows operating system, click the **Bold Style** button. If you're running the Macintosh OS, *do not* click the **Bold Style** button. Last, simply verify that the remainder of your settings are the same as those in the screen shot above.

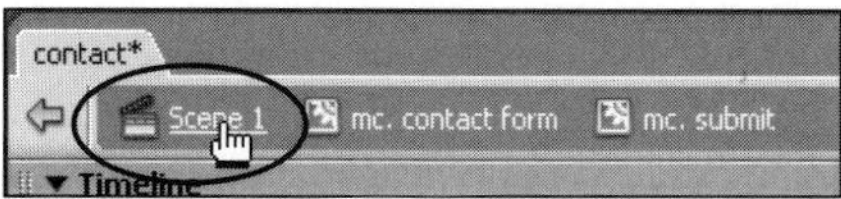

17. Return to the **Scene 1 Timeline** by clicking its tab above the top-left of the **Timeline**.

---

18. Save the changes you've made by choosing **File > Save** (**Ctrl+S** [Windows] or **Cmd+S** [Mac]). Then preview the feedback form by choosing **Control > Test Movie** (**Ctrl+Enter** [Windows] or **Cmd+Return** [Mac]).

And there you have it! A nifty, functional, customized feedback form.

In the next exciting chapter, you will learn how to use the Sound class to create an MP3 jukebox complete with a preloader, playback progress bar, and adjustable volume. See you there!

10.

MP3 Player

la_eyeworks

Macromedia Flash MX 2004
Beyond the Basics

In this chapter you will learn how to build a nifty, multitrack MP3 player that will play MP3s as it progressively downloads them. You'll build a small interface that will allow the viewer to stop or play the MP3 as well as skip to the next or previous tracks. This MP3 player will also display the artist and track name of the currently playing MP3 using the ID3 tags that are built into the MP3s themselves. Last, you will build a slider that displays the progress of the currently playing MP3, and you'll integrate a preloader into the progress bar as well. As you're probably beginning to realize, you'll be building and learning many new things in this chapter. If you haven't taken a break in a while, now would probably be a good time. ;-)

I. What You Are Building

In this exercise, you will preview and interact with the finished piece you will be building in this chapter. By first having a good understanding of what you will be building, it will help you to better understand some of the more abstract ActionScript topics as you learn them.

1. Open your preferred Web browser, and access the following URL:

http://www.lynda.com/flashbtb/laeyeworks/

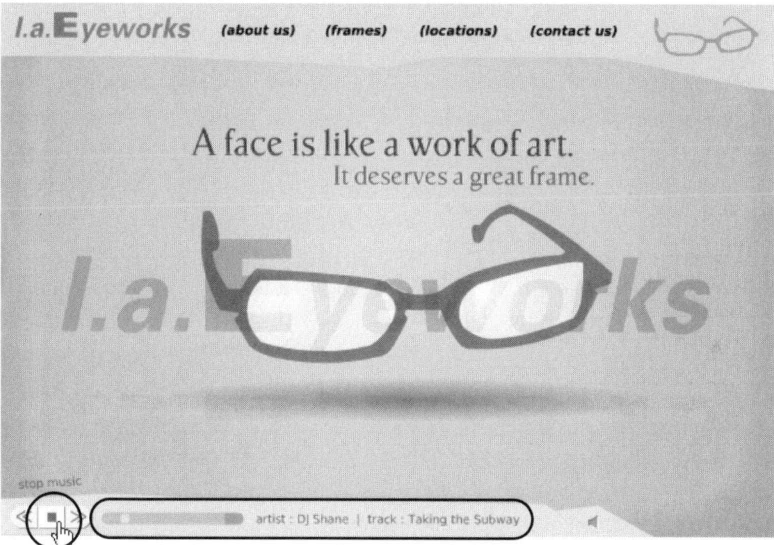

2. When the Web site finishes loading, click the **Play** button at the bottom left of the page. This will automatically begin downloading an MP3 music file from the Web server. You'll also notice, when you click the **Play** button, that it turns into a **Stop** button. This is often called a "toggle button" because it toggles back and forth between two different functionalities. It's a great way of conserving space and is something that you see repeated in many other programs.

As soon as a small amount of the MP3 has downloaded to your computer, you'll see two things happen. First, you'll see a light-blue bar animate across the dark-blue bar that sits to the right of the Previous Track/Play/Next Track buttons. This animating, light-blue bar represents how much of the MP3 has been downloaded to your computer. When the light-blue bar reaches the end of the dark-blue bar, the entire MP3 has been downloaded. This is a preloader, much like the preloader you constructed in Chapter 8, "Building a Preloader"*, except this preloader was constructed specifically for the music player. On top of the blue bar is a lighter-blue "dot" that is initially resting on the left side of the bar. But when enough of the MP3 has downloaded to your computer, the music will automatically start playing and the dot will start moving. This dot represents the playback progress of the music, much like the playhead does in Flash MX 2004, Windows Media Player, QuickTime, and so forth. When the dot gets to the right side of the blue bar, the music track has finished playing.*

*Second, after a small amount of the MP3 has been downloaded to your computer, you'll see some text appear to the right of the blue bar. This text states the artist name as well as the track name (in this case, it's me. *grin*) As was mentioned in the introduction to this chapter, the artist and track information is dynamically grabbed from the ID3 tags (more on those later) from the MP3s themselves.*

If you wait until the first track is finished, you'll notice that it will automatically begin downloading another–different–MP3. The preloader will start animating again, and once the music starts playing, the dot will start animating as well. The ID3 track information will also update to display information about the new track. Pretty nifty! The other way to advance to the next track, besides waiting for the current track to play all the way through, is to click the ***Next Track*** *button. Clicking the* ***Previous Track*** *button will, of course, play the previous track in sequence.*

The MP3 player is constructed dynamically in this manner, and streams external MP3 files, because it makes it extremely *easy to update. Whenever you want to add, remove, or change MP3s, you simply make sure they're named appropriately and their ID3 tags are set correctly, drop them in the* ***mp3s*** *folder, change some variables in an external text file, and you're done.*

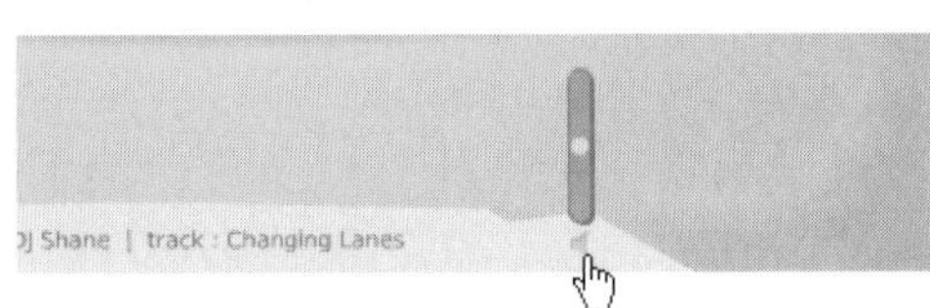

3. Last, click the **speaker** icon toward the bottom-right side. When you do, you'll notice a small, green slider appear above it.

If you click the light-green dot in the slider, you'll hear the volume of the music change as you drag the slider up and down. Also, to the right of the dot will appear a number that follows the dot as you drag it. That number represents the percentage of the volume level. As you drag the dot up and down, you'll also notice that the text's alpha changes. The louder the volume, the more opaque the volume text. The quieter the volume, the more transparent the text becomes. When you release your mouse button, the percent number will disappear.

So as you can see, there's a lot *of functionality crammed into the bottom portion of the L.A. Eyeworks Web site. In this chapter, you will learn how to build all of that functionality using some actions that you've already learned as well as some that you haven't.*

What Is Progressive Download, and What Is Streaming?

The MP3s that the MP3 player will download off of the Web server will start playing *as they are downloading*. Flash MX 2004 SWF files perform this same way. If you have a longish SWF file, when the viewer comes to your Web site to view your movie, the SWF file will start playing as soon as the first frame has been downloaded. Flash MX 2004 downloads its content–SWFs, MP3s, FLVs (**Fl**ash **V**ideo), JPGs, and so forth–using something called "progressive downloading." As it sounds, a *progressively* downloading file will download and play progressively from the beginning of the file to the end. Once an entire SWF, MP3, or FLV file has been downloaded to the viewer's computer, you are able to "seek" (fast-forward and rewind) through that content with no difficulties. However, if you want to seek to a point in an MP3 file–for example–that hasn't downloaded yet, you're out of luck.

An alternate way of delivering your content to the Flash Player 7 is by using something called "streaming." This is referred to as RTMP Streaming (**R**eal **T**ime **M**essaging **P**rotocol). When content is *streamed* off of the Web server, it is *not* saved to the viewer's computer hard drive. This means that less memory and hard drive space is required to play the content (MP3s, FLVs, and so forth), and because the content is not saved to the viewer's computer, it is considered to be fairly *secure* as well (meaning that it would be difficult for average computer users to take the content that they just watched and use it for their own purposes). With streaming content, such as an MP3 or FLV file for example, you can even "jump" to a portion of the content that hasn't downloaded yet–a feature that a progressively downloading asset doesn't have. However, to truly *stream* content you need special server software called the **F**lash **C**ommunication **S**erver (FCS). You can purchase and read more information about the FCS on Macromedia's Web site:

http://www.macromedia.com/software/flashcom/

The FCS offers a number of advantages over "traditional" *progressive* downloading, such as being able to dynamically serve different FLV files based on the viewer's Internet connection speed. If you're in charge of serving *lots* of video streams to *many* viewers, you should look into the FCS because it offers the most features and flexibility. In Appendix C, "*Getting Your Work Online/Using CGIs*," I will list some Web presence providers that offer the FCS for use.

However, because of the specialized nature and relative complexity of the FCS, this book will cover accessing content using progressive download, which *does not* require any special server software or configuration.

Sound Compression for Streaming

In the MP3 player that you will be building in this chapter, the MP3 sound files will reside–external to the SWF file that will eventually control them–on the remote Web server. You will write some ActionScript that loads and plays one of the MP3 tracks when an event occurs. But how did those music tracks become MP3s? How were the MP3s compressed, and how should one compress MP3s that are going to be progressively downloaded from a Web server?

MP3s can be created using many different programs. In Appendix B, "*Macromedia Flash MX 2004 Resources*," I will address the common programs that you can use to convert a sound file–such as WAV, AIFF, and so forth–into an MP3. For now, however, if you need a good, free, cross-platform program that can play and compress MP3 files, try using Apple Computer's iTunes. It's available for free at **http://www.apple.com/itunes/** and works on both Mac and Windows computers.

As was mentioned in Chapter 2, "*Where Do I Start?*," the target audience is really going to be the defining factor that will determine what level of MP3 compression you should use and even how heavily the video should be compressed, as you'll see in the next chapter. As was discussed in Chapter 2, the target audience for the L.A. Eyeworks Web site is likely to have a broadband Internet connection. Because of that, you can be a little liberal with how the sound files are compressed. In other words, you are able to sacrifice file size–to a point–in exchange for good sound fidelity. However, if most of your target audience still accessed the Internet using a slow dial-up connection, you would instead want to lower the sound quality (which means, to increase the MP3 compression) in exchange for a smaller file size. In essence, the larger the file size of the MP3, the better the audio will sound, but it will take longer to download. Conversely, the smaller the file size of the MP3, the worse the audio will sound, but it will take less time to download. Again, determining the target audience for the Web site (or widget) that you are constructing is *crucial* to deciding what type of MP3 compression to apply to your sounds. Without getting into the nitty-gritty details of MP3 sound compression, bit rates, sample rates, and so forth, here is a short list of MP3 tips that you should be aware of:

- When you have your original music file (WAV, AIFF, and so forth), make sure–in whichever sound-editing program you're using–that the **sample rate** is in an increment of **11 kHz** (11, 22, 44, and so forth). If you use a sample rate that is *not* in an increment of 11, Flash MX 2004 will resample them when played. This might cause the MP3 to play/behave unexpectedly. Normally, sound files have an 11 kHz incremental sample rate, so this isn't an issue to worry much about. However, if you are integrating audio into your Flash MX 2004 project, and the audio starts sounding like it's in a different pitch, or you notice other strange anomalies, check the audio sample rate to make sure that it's in an increment of 11 kHz.

- When choosing an MP3 **bit rate** to encode your sound file to, keep in mind that the bit rate corresponds to the minimum bandwidth throughput that the viewer will need to download the MP3 at a fast enough rate so that the playing of the sound doesn't overtake the downloading of the sound. In other words, if you encode your sound file with a **bit rate** of 126 kbit/sec, the viewer downloading that MP3 will need to have an Internet connection of *at least* 12.6 k/sec or greater to download the sound as fast or faster than it is playing. As long as the viewer has a connection speed that is equal to or greater than the bit rate of the MP3, the sound will not stop or "stutter" as it is downloading. The MP3s you will be using for the L.A. Eyeworks Web site are encoded using a **v**ariable **b**it **r**ate (VBR), which means that the bit rate will increase or decrease to accommodate how dynamic the sound is. Averaged out, the bit rates are approximately 103 kbit/sec, meaning that the MP3s will stream uninterrupted over a Internet connection of at least 10.3 k/sec. (The average dial-up modem speed is 5.6 k/sec. Broadband is usually *at least* 10 times that amount.) However, Flash MX 2004 has an action that will allow you to specify how much of an MP3 it should buffer (download and cache) before it begins playing the sound file. This will help to decrease the possibility of the sound playing faster than it can download, which results in the sound stopping before it reaches the end. You will learn about that action later in this chapter.

- When assigning or modifying the ID3 tags on your MP3s, use only ID3 v2.3 or v2.4 tags. v2.2 tags *are not supported* and ID3 v1 tags are inserted at the *end* of the MP3 file (which means they cannot be accessed or used until the MP3 has been *completely* downloaded). ID3 v2.3 or v2.4 tags are stored at the *beginning* of the MP3 file and can therefore be accessed as soon as the MP3 starts downloading. You'll learn more about ID3 tags later in this book, and a list of programs that can view and edit MP3 ID3 tags are listed in Appendix B, "*Macromedia Flash MX 2004 Resources*."

Note: If you'd like to read more about how Fraunhofer MP3 (the MP3 compression scheme that Flash MX 2004 supports) compression works, you can read more about it here:

http://www.iis.fraunhofer.de/amm/techinf/layer3/index.html

2. Setting Up

In this exercise, you will make a few modifications to the prebuilt starter **music.fla** file that you will be working with for the remainder of this chapter. Just like the previous chapters, this chapter includes an FLA that has some prebuilt elements and ActionScript to allow you to jump right into the new exercises and steps, bypassing the material you've already learned. In this exercise, you will also get a brief tour of what has been included with the provided FLA so that you have a good understanding of what you will be building on.

1. Navigate to your **Desktop > la_eyeworks > site** folder and double-click **music.fla** to open it in Flash MX 2004.

2. Once the FLA opens, look at the **Timeline**. You might need to expand the Timeline view a little to see all the layers.

*As you can see, there's quite a lot of provided content in this FLA. You'll also notice–besides the usual **bg** layer–that two layers (**volume** and **progress**) are specified as guide layers, and are locked and hidden. These layers are set like this so they will not be visible while you're working and will not be exported when you test your movie. This is because these layers are there for you to use when watching the included movies **volume_slider.mov** and **music_progress.mov**, which you'll read about later in this chapter. Until then, however, these layers are essentially disabled so they'll stay out of your way while you work on the other exercises.*

3. Click **keyframe 1** in layer **a**, and open the **Actions** panel (**F9**).

```
/*
//----------------<pre-built ActionScript for Chapter 10>------------------\\

//----------------<sound initialization>------------------\\
var curTrackNum:Number = 0;

// autosize some text fields
this.helpBubble.autoSize = "center";
this.trackInfo.autoSize = "left";

// load the track info vars
var myMusicLv:LoadVars = new LoadVars();
myMusicLv.load("vars/track_info.txt");

//----------------</sound initialization>------------------\\

//----------------<volume control>------------------\\
```

***Note:** Not all of the ActionScript provided with **music.fla** is pictured in the code above. Because of the large amount of included ActionScript, it would be impractical to picture it all here.*

Just like a few of the previous prebuilt FLAs, you'll notice that this FLA comes with quite a lot of ActionScript, already written into the first keyframe. The included actions are a testament to how much you've learned so far in this book, because the actions you see in that first keyframe are all actions you already know. If you scroll down the Actions panel, you should see lots of familiar actions there. Although you probably do not immediately understand what they're all doing, you'll be pulling some of those actions out of the commented area to use in various exercises throughout the remainder of this chapter.

4. Minimize the **Actions** panel by pressing **F9** again.

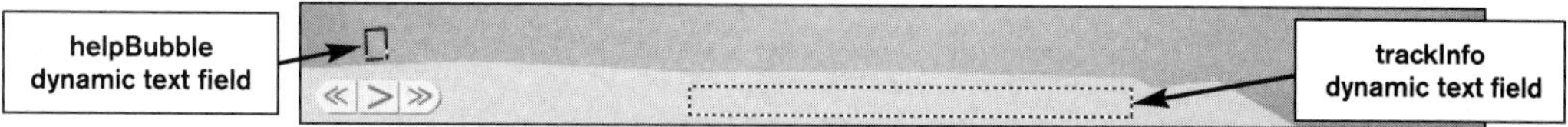

*At the bottom of the Stage, you'll notice two dynamic text fields. The small one above the Play/Stop, Next Track, and Previous Track buttons is where a small amount of descriptive text will appear when the viewer rolls his or her mouse over the buttons beneath it. This dynamic text field already has an instance name of **helpBubble** applied to it. The larger dynamic text field toward the bottom-middle of the Stage is where the MP3 ID3 information will be displayed. This field already has an instance name of **trackInfo** applied to it. As with many of the other prebuilt FLAs you've worked with in this book, in the next few steps you will import a shared font and apply it to those text fields.*

5. First, make sure you *do not* have **sharedLib.fla** open. If it is open, the next few steps will not work correctly.

6. Choose **File > Import > Open External Library**.

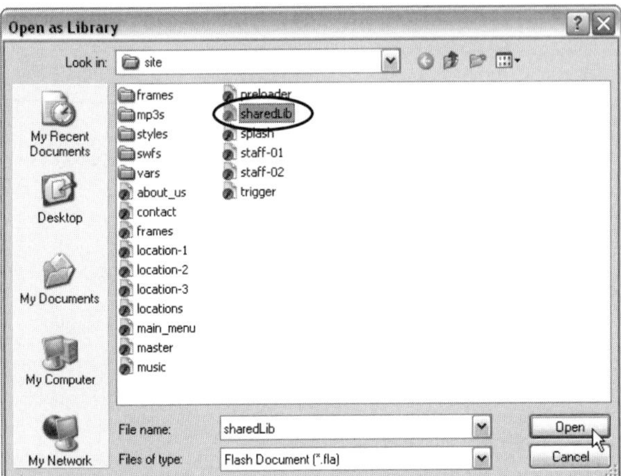

7. In the **Open as Library** window, navigate to your **Desktop > la_eyeworks > site** folder and single-click **sharedLib.fla** to select it. Click **Open** to open only the **Library** of **sharedLib.fla**.

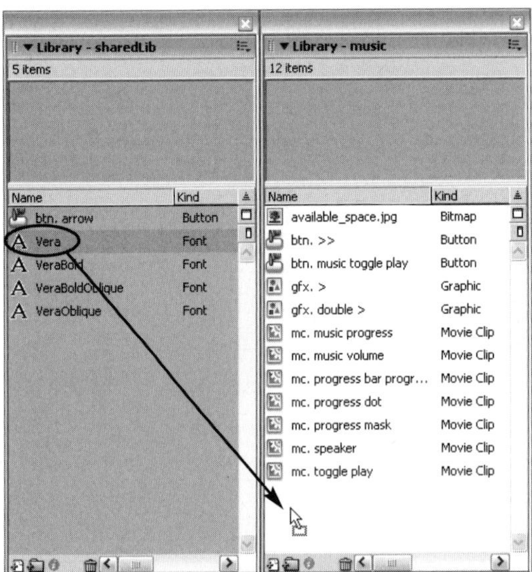

8. Open the **music.fla Library** window (**Ctrl+L** [Windows] or **Cmd+L** [Mac]) and position the **sharedLib Library** and the **music Library** windows next to each other so they can both be seen simultaneously. Then, drag the shared font **Vera** from the **sharedLib Library** window onto the **music Library** window.

*As you have done a few times before in this book, you just made a link to the shared font **Bitstream Vera Sans** in **music.fla**. You don't need to drag over any other shared fonts because Vera is the only font that will be used in the construction of the MP3 player.*

9. Close the **sharedLib Library** window and redock the **music Library** window if need be.

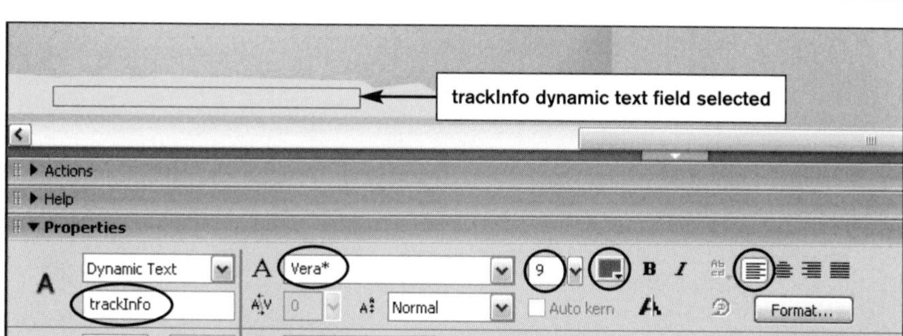

10. Next, single-click the large dynamic text field on the Stage, `trackInfo`. Then, in the **Properties inspector**, click the **Font** pull-down menu and choose the shared font **Vera***. The remaining options have already been set for you, but quickly double-check that what you see in your **Properties inspector** is the same as the selected options in the screen shot above.

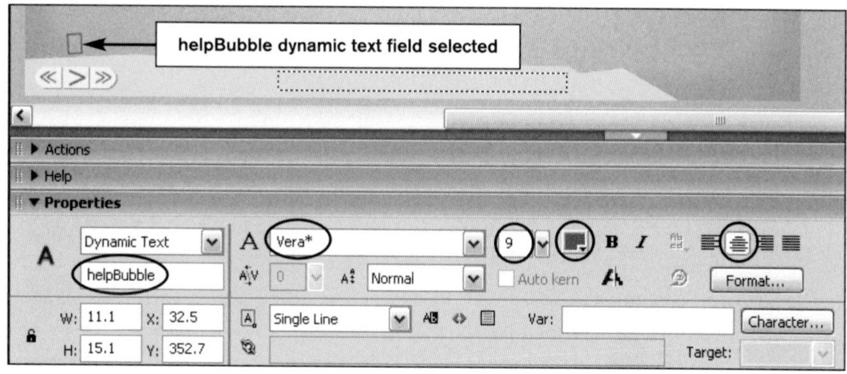

11. Repeat Step 10, but this time make sure you have the small, bottom-left dynamic text field (`helpBubble`) selected first. Once again, verify that the settings you see in the **Properties inspector** match those in the screen shot above.

That's it! The symbols that you see on the Stage–and even those that are on the locked and hidden guide layers–already have instance names applied to them to save you time and energy. Don't worry, you'll be using that saved energy later in this chapter as you write the ActionScript to construct this über cool MP3 player.

In the next exercise, you will write the ActionScript that dynamically loads and plays the first MP3.

3. Loading the MP3

In this exercise, you will write the ActionScript that will load and play the first external MP3. As you work through the steps in this exercise, you'll see many similarities between how this ActionScript is written and constructed and how some previous actions have been authored. In the following exercises in this chapter, you will learn how to give the viewer the ability to change the currently playing MP3 track, stop or play the music, observe the download and playing progress of an MP3, and change the volume of the music. This is simply the first–but critical–step in building the entire, fully functional MP3 player.

1. Hide or minimize Flash MX 2004. On your hard drive, navigate to your **Desktop > la_eyeworks > site** folder.

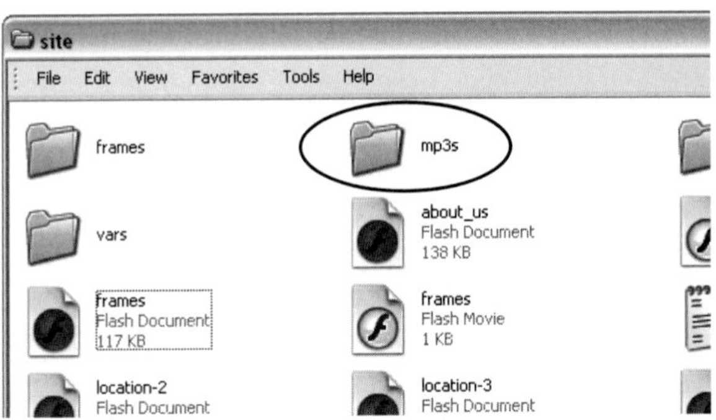

2. In the **site** folder you'll see–among other things–a folder called **mp3s**. Double-click that folder to open it.

In the ***mp3s*** *folder, you'll see two MP3s,* ***mp3-0.mp3*** *and* ***mp3-1.mp3****. These are the two MP3 tracks that you will be loading and controlling in this chapter. Now that you know what they're named and where they're located in relation to the rest of your site files, you can write the ActionScript to load and manipulate them using the* ***Sound*** *object.*

3. Close the **mp3s** folder and return to Flash MX 2004. Make sure **music.fla** is still the foreground FLA.

4. Select **keyframe 1** in the **a** layer and open the **Actions** panel (**F9**).

The first step is to create a ***Sound*** *object to handle the music that you will load and later control. The sound object, as you are about to see, is very similar in construction to the* ***MovieClipLoader*** *and* ***LoadVars*** *scripts you've built in previous chapters.*

```
//----------------<sound setup>------------------\\
var bgMusak:Sound = new Sound();
//----------------</sound setup>------------------\\

/*
//----------------<pre-built ActionScript for Chapter 10>------------------\\

//----------------<sound initialization>------------------\\
var curTrackNum:Number = 0;
```

5. Click the empty line break–already provided for you–at the top of the **Actions** panel above the prebuilt actions. Then, create a new sound object by typing the following:

```
//----------------<sound setup>----------------\\
var bgMusak:Sound = new Sound();
//----------------</sound setup>----------------\\
```

As you have already seen before with the ***MovieClipLoader*** *and* ***LoadVars*** *objects, the action you just wrote simply creates a new* ***Sound*** *object named* ***bgMusak*** *under a commented line.*

Much like the slideshow you constructed in Chapter 7, "Building a Slideshow," *the viewer will be able to advance forward and backward through the available MP3 tracks. However, where the slideshow had 10 images, the MP3 player in this chapter will use only two tracks. As you'll see as you write the ActionScript for the MP3 player, it's very easy to add or remove MP3 tracks at a later time. Because the MP3 player will allow the viewer to switch between tracks, you need to create a variable to keep track of which MP3 track is currently playing, just like you did with the* ***curFrameNum*** *variable you created for the slideshow.*

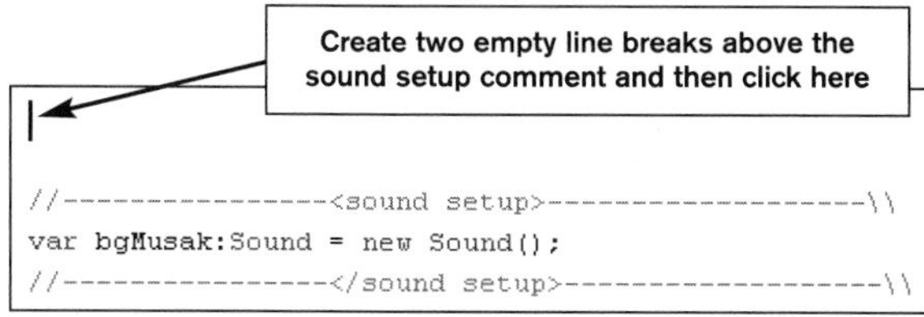
Create two empty line breaks above the sound setup comment and then click here
//----------------<sound setup>------------------\\
var bgMusak:Sound = new Sound();
//----------------</sound setup>------------------\\

6. Click at the beginning of the **//----------------<sound setup>----------------** comment line and press **Enter** (Windows) or **Return** (Mac) twice to push all the actions in **Keyframe 1** down two lines. Then, click at the new, empty line at the top of the **Actions** panel.

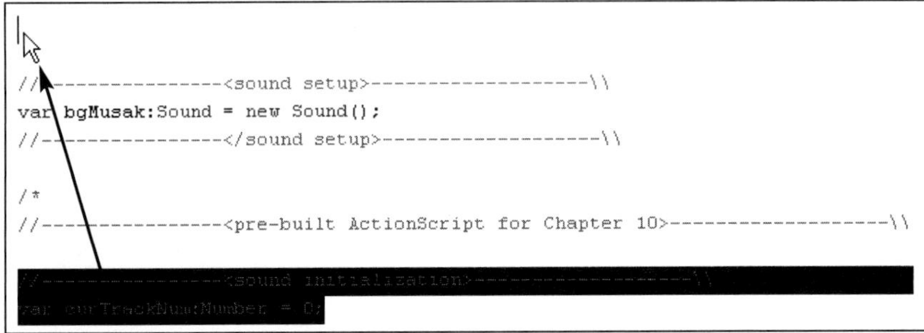
//----------------<sound setup>-------------------\\
var bgMusak:Sound = new Sound();
//----------------</sound setup>-------------------\\
/*
//----------------<pre-built ActionScript for Chapter 10>------------------\\

7. Select the following two lines of actions:

```
//----------------<sound initialization>----------------\\
var curTrackNum:Number = 0;
```

Drag them to the topmost empty line break you created in Step 6. This moves the action and comment line out of the commented-out prebuilt actions that were included with the FLA, thereby making them "active."

*Although the comment line is self-explanatory, you probably want to know what the **var curTrackNum:Number = 0;** action is for. Again, just like you used the variable **curFrameNum** in the slideshow FLA to keep track of the current slide number, this **curTrackNum** variable will keep track of the currently playing MP3. Because you will script the capability of the MP3 player to change tracks, you need to be able to keep track of* which *track is currently playing. Later, you will use the number within that variable **(0)** to specify which MP3 track should be loaded.*

```
//----------------<sound initialization>-------------------\\
var curTrackNum:Number = 0;

//----------------<sound setup>-------------------\\
var bgMusak:Sound = new Sound();
bgMusak.loadSound("mp3s/mp3-" + curTrackNum + ".mp3", true);
//----------------</sound setup>-------------------\\
```

8. Click at the end of the **var bgMusak:Sound = new Sound();** line, press **Enter** (Windows) or **Return** (Mac) once to create a line break, and type the following:

```
bgMusak.loadSound("mp3s/mp3-" + curTrackNum + ".mp3", true);
```

*Although you may initially be somewhat confused as to what this action is doing, keep in mind that this action is very similar to the action you set up in Chapter 7, "Building a Slideshow," Exercise 3, Step 6, that allowed you to load a JPG file into the slideshow. This action you just wrote loads an MP3 using the **Sound** object **loadSound** event handler. The name of the MP3 that it loads starts with the string "mp3s/mp3-" (because the MP3 name starts with "mp3-" and is in a folder titled **mp3s** in your **Desktop > la_eyeworks > site** folder). After that string, the script takes the number in the **curTrackNum** variable, **0**, sticks it onto the "mp3s/mp3-" string that came before it and the ".mp3" string that comes after it. The final result of that action is **mp3s/mp3-0.mp3**. This is, of course, the path to–and the name of–the first MP3 that will load and play.*

*You'll also notice that this action has **true** written into it. This Boolean value specifies whether the loading MP3 should be considered a **streaming** sound (**true**), or not (**false**). A streaming sound, as this MP3 player uses, will start playing as soon as enough of the sound has been downloaded and will continue to play as the remainder of it is downloaded. A nonstreaming sound is considered to be an **Event** sound and will not begin playing until the entire sound has been downloaded to the viewer's computer.*

Since you have now written enough ActionScript to create a wee bit of functionality, you can test your movie!

---

9. Save the changes you've made to **music.fla** by choosing **File > Save** (**Ctrl+S** [Window] or **Cmd+S** [Mac]).

---

10. Test your movie by choosing **Control > Test Movie** (**Ctrl+Enter** [Windows] or **Cmd+Return** [Mac]).

*When the Preview window opens, you won't see a whole lot, but you'll hear the first MP3 (**mp3-0.mp3**) immediately start playing. When the track finishes playing, it will stop. In Exercise 5 in this chapter, you will write a script that will automatically instruct the MP3 player to load and play the next MP3 in sequence when the current MP3 finishes playing. Congratulations! You've just loaded and streamed an external MP3.*

Last, you should write a small script that shows the viewer an error message if an error is encountered when loading an MP3.

---

11. Close the **music.swf Preview** window and return to **music.fla**. Make sure you have **Keyframe 1** selected in layer **a**, and make sure the **Actions** panel is open.

Insert a line break here

```
//----------------<sound setup>-------------------\\
var bgMusak:Sound = new Sound();

bgMusak.loadSound("mp3s/mp3-" + curTrackNum + ".mp3", true);
//----------------</sound setup>-------------------\\
```

12. Click at the end of the action **`var bgMusak:Sound = new Sound();`** and press **Enter** (Windows) or **Return** (Mac) to create a line break. This is where you will write a script that will insert an error message into the **`trackInfo`** dynamic text field if there's an error when attempting to load an MP3.

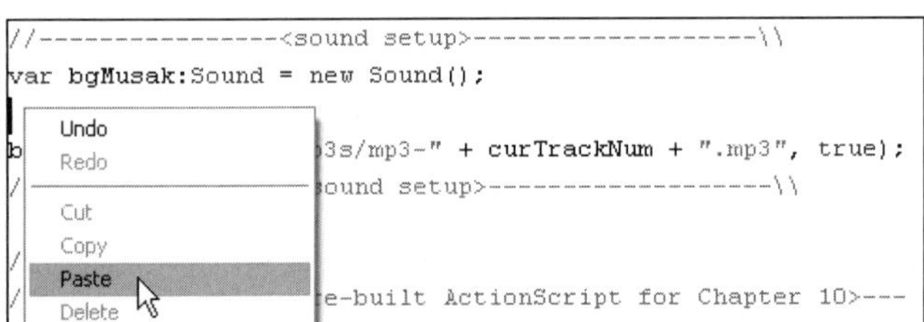

//----------------</volume control>-------------------\\
bgMusak.onLoad = function(success) {
if (!success) {
trackInfo.text = "Failed to load track.";
}
};
//----------------<next track>-------------------\\
Undo
Redo
Cut
Copy
Paste
Delete

13. Scroll a little over halfway down the **Actions** panel until you get to the script you see selected in the screen shot above. The script resides between the **`//----------------</volume control>----------------\\`** comment and then **`//----------------<next track>----------------\\`** comment. Select the script and cut it out of the **Actions** panel by **right-clicking** (Windows) or **Ctrl+clicking** (Mac) anywhere on that selected script, and choosing **Cut** from the contextual menu.

```
//----------------<sound setup>-------------------\\
var bgMusak:Sound = new Sound();

b                3s/mp3-" + curTrackNum + ".mp3", true);
/                ound setup>-------------------\\

/
/                e-built ActionScript for Chapter 10>---
```

Undo
Redo
Cut
Copy
Paste
Delete

14. Scroll back to the top of the **Actions** panel, and **right-click** (Windows) or **Ctrl+click** (Mac) in the empty line break you created in Step 12. From the contextual menu that appears, choose **Paste.** This will paste the script–which you cut in Step 13–so that it comes immediately after the **`var bgMusak:Sound = new Sound();`** action.

*It's important that this pasted script comes before the **`bgMusak.loadSound("mp3s/mp3-" + curTrackNum + ".mp3", true);`** action. In this case, the error message won't display unless the **`bgMusak.onLoad`** action comes before the **`bgMusak.loadSound`** action.*

*The **bgMusak.onLoad** script you just cut and pasted was included for you in the provided **music.fla** because it is nearly identical to–and has the same functionality–as the **myLV.onLoad** script that you wrote in Chapter 4, "LoadVars Class," Exercise 3, Steps 8 – 14. Where the **myLV.onLoad** script showed an error message to the viewer if the variables could not be loaded from an external text file, the **bgMusak.onLoad** script shows the viewer an error message if an external MP3 cannot be loaded. The **bgMusak.onLoad** script essentially reads, "When the MP3 loads, if it was not successful (**!success**) in its loading, insert the text 'Failed to load track.' in the **trackInfo** dynamic text field on the Stage."*

Of course, you would be a slack Flash developer if you didn't test that error handling to make sure it works correctly.

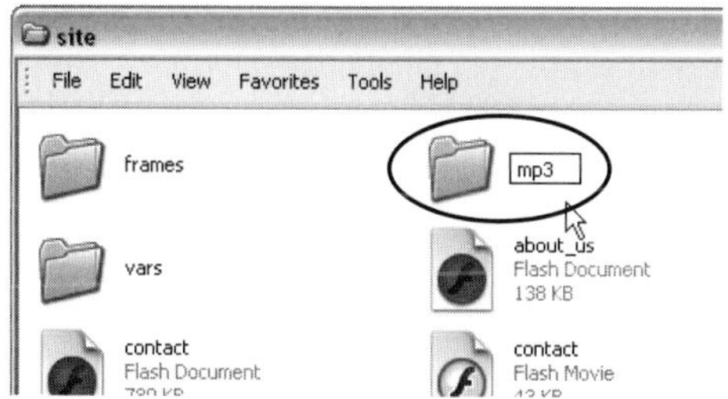

15. Hide or minimize Flash MX 2004. On your hard drive, navigate to your **Desktop > la_eyeworks > site** folder. Then, rename the **mp3s** folder to **mp3**. (You're just temporarily removing the **s** at the end in order to test your script.)

16. Then, return to Flash MX 2004 and make sure **music.fla** is still your foreground FLA.

17. Save the changes you've made to **music.fla** by choosing **File > Save** (**Ctrl+S** [Window] or **Cmd+S** [Mac]).

18. Test your movie by choosing **Control > Test Movie** (**Ctrl+Enter** [Windows] or **Cmd+Return** [Mac]).

*When **music.swf** opens in the Preview window, not only will you see the output window open with an error message (close the output window when it opens), but you'll also see the error message "Failed to load track" appear in the **trackInfo** text field that sits on the MP3 player bar at the bottom of the Stage. Who would've thought you'd be happy to see an error message, eh?*

*Now that you know the MP3 loads and plays correctly, and that the error message appears if there's a problem loading the MP3, you can rename the **mp3** folder back to its* correct *name of **mp3s**.*

19. Close the **Preview** window and hide or minimize Flash MX 2004.

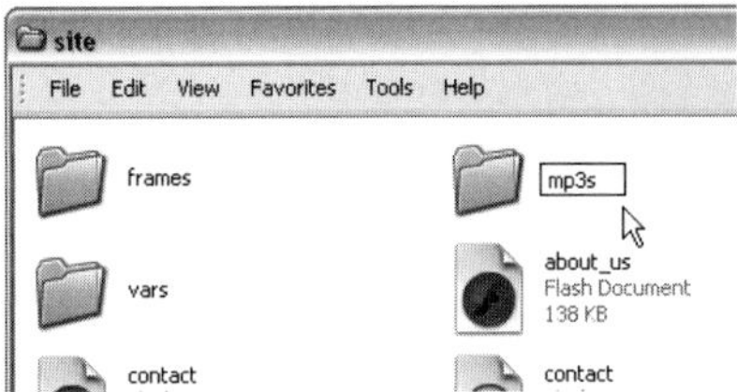

20. On your hard drive, navigate to your **Desktop > la_eyeworks > site** folder and rename the folder **mp3** to its correct name, **mp3s**.

---

21. Return to Flash MX 2004 and make sure that **music.fla** is the foreground FLA.

Give yourself a big pat on the back (and maybe a stiff drink) because you just completed the loading, streaming, playing, and error handling of the first MP3.

In the next exercise, you will learn how to stop and play the music. Take a quick break and I'll meet you back here in five minutes!

What Is the Sound Class?

The **LoadVars** class loads and sends variables, the **MovieClipLoader** class loads SWFs and JPGs, and now you have the **Sound** class, which loads sounds. The **Sound** class can either load sounds that are external to the SWF by using the **Sound.loadSound()** method–which you just learned in the last exercise–or it can even control a sound file (with linkage turned on) in a FLA's Library using the **Sound.attachSound()** method. By using the **Sound** class, you can do the following:

- Dynamically load sounds that are external to the SWF itself.
- Monitor the downloading progress of an external sound file.
- Change the volume and pan of a sound.
- Start and stop a sound.
- Read the ID3 tags of an MP3.

The **Sound** class can work with AIFF, WAV, and MP3 file formats. For the most part, however, you'll probably be working mostly with MP3 sound files because they offer a smaller file size with comparable quality. **Note:** The smaller the file size of the media you're working with, the less RAM is consumed on both the author and viewer's computer.

For your reference, here is a table listing the **Sound** class methods, properties, and event handlers. You can read more about the **Sound** class by opening the **Help** panel (**F1**), and in the left section of the **Help** panel choosing **ActionScript Dictionary > S > Sound class**. As you work through the exercises in this chapter, you'll get to use some of these in the construction of the L.A. Eyeworks MP3 player:

Methods, Properties, and Event Handlers of the Sound Class

METHODS

Method	Description
attachSound()	Allows you to specify the linkage name of a sound in the Library that you want to attach to a **Sound** object.
getBytesLoaded()	When this action is executed, it returns the number of bytes that have been downloaded up to that point from the currently loading sound.
getBytesTotal()	When this action is executed, it returns the total number of bytes of the sound that is currently being downloaded.
getPan()	When the sound pan is set using **setPan()**, the **getPan()** method will return what the last value set using **setPan()**.
getTransform()	Similar to **getPan()**, except **getTransform()** returns the last value set using **setTransform()**.
getVolume()	Similar to **getPan()** and **getTransform()**, **getVolume()** returns the last value set using **setVolume()**.
loadSound()	Allows you to load an external MP3. The **loadSound()** method allows you to specify the path to the MP3 you want to load as well as whether it should play while downloading (streaming sound) or not (event sound).
setPan()	Allows you to specify the pan (left and right balance) of a sound attached or loaded into a **Sound** object.
setTransform()	Somewhat of a combination between **setPan()** and **setVolume()**, the **setTransform()** method not only allows you to simultaneously manipulate the panning *and* volume of a playing sound, but also the level of the sound in each ear. This allows you to achieve some fairly complex panning and volume effects with your sounds.
setVolume()	Allows you to specify the volume of a sound attached or loaded into a **Sound** object.
start()	Allows you to start playing a sound. The **start()** method also allows you to specify a few parameters such as how many seconds into the sound it should start playing, as well how many times you want the sound to loop.
stop()	If you just use the **stop()** method with no parameters, all sounds will stop playing. But you can also specify the linkage ID name like so: **stop("myLinkedSymbol")**, which stops the playback of a single sound.

continues on next page

Methods, Properties, and Event Handlers of the Sound Class *continued*

PROPERTIES

Property	Description
duration	Returns the duration of a sound in milliseconds. **Warning:** If you use the **duration** property to find out the duration of a linked sound, it will return the actual duration of the sound. However, if you use the **duration** property to find out the duration of a sound that is currently being streamed, it will return only the duration of the sound that has been downloaded *up to that point.*
id3	Allows you to access the ID3 information of an MP3 file. You will learn more about this property in Exercise 4.
position	Returns the number of milliseconds that a sound has been playing. You can use this property in conjunction with the **duration** property to create a playback progress bar.

EVENT HANDLERS

Event Handler	Description
onID3	Each time new ID3 information is available, this event handler (and any actions you place within it) is executed. This is useful for triggering the population of a text field with MP3 ID3 information.
onLoad	Executed when a sound loads. You used this in the last exercise to display an error message if the MP3 is unable to load correctly.
onSoundComplete	Executed when the MP3 has stopped playing. You will use this event handler in Exercise 5 to tell the Flash Player 7 to automatically load the next MP3 track in sequence when the currently playing MP3 reaches the end.

Similar to the **LoadVars** and **MovieClipLoader** classes, the **Sound** class offers a variety of ways to load, monitor, and control sounds. You'll be using a few of these methods, properties, and event handlers throughout this chapter.

4. Stopping and Playing the Music

There's nary a more irritating set of circumstances than when you visit a Flash MX 2004–based Web site, the music starts playing, and you can't turn it off. This shameful act doesn't seem to occur as much as it used to two to four years ago, but every now and then I stumble across a Web site where the forgetful (or just straight-up reckless!) designer declined to give the viewer a way to turn off the looping bit of music. In this exercise, you will show pity on the poor Internet surfer and build a way for him or her to turn your music off should it become too distracting. In case viewers change their minds once the music has been turned off, you're also going to provide them with a way to turn it back on again. Tallyho!

At this point in the construction of your MP3 player, the MP3 starts playing automatically. However, in a new area of politeness, more and more Flash MX 2004 designers and developers are opting to have the music *off* by default. That way, viewers are not aurally bombarded when they first enter your site. Then, if viewers feel that some music would go well with what they're looking at, they can click the Play button to begin playing the music. With your current MP3, the music starts automatically playing because the **bgMusak** sound object actions that control the playing of the music are all sitting out in "the open" in Keyframe 1. An easy way to prevent those actions from being automatically executed when **music.swf** first loads is to enclose them in a function. That way, the actions within the function will be executed only when the function is explicitly called.

So the first step in this process is to create a new function and move the **bgMusak** sound object actions into their new function home.

```
//----------------<sound setup>-------------------\\
function playMusak() {
var bgMusak:Sound = new Sound();
bgMusak.onLoad = function(success) {
    if (!success) {
        trackInfo.text = "Failed to load track.";
    }
};
bgMusak.loadSound("mp3s/mp3-" + curTrackNum + ".mp3", true);
//----------------</sound setup>------------------\\
```

1. Click at the end of the comment **//----------------<sound setup>----------------** line, press **Enter** (Windows) or **Return** (Mac) once to create a line break, and type the following:

function playMusak() {

*As you have seen before, this is the opening action to create a new function called **playMusak**. Next, you need to specify where the function ends.*

```
//----------------<sound setup>-------------------\\
function playMusak() {
var bgMusak:Sound = new Sound();
bgMusak.onLoad = function(success) {
    if (!success) {
        trackInfo.text = "Failed to load track.";
    }
};
bgMusak.loadSound("mp3s/mp3-" + curTrackNum + ".mp3", true);
};
//----------------</sound setup>-------------------\\
```

2. Click at the end of the **bgMusak.loadSound("mp3s/mp3-" + curTrackNum + ".mp3", true);** line, press **Enter** (Windows) or **Return** (Mac) once to create a line break, and type the following:

};

*This closed curly brace marks the end of the **playMusak** function. All the actions between the **function playMusak() {** line and the closed curly brace you just typed are now part of the **playMusak** function. Now, a few of you might be wondering what the action **var bgMusak:Sound = new Sound();** is doing contained within the function. After all, that action doesn't start the music playing. It just simply creates a new **Sound** object called **bgMusak**. The reason why the action that creates the **bgMusak** sound object is contained within the **playMusak** function is because every time the viewer clicks the **Next Track** or **Previous Track** buttons, or when the track ends and advances to the next track in sequence, you want the **bgMusak** sound object to be re-created again from scratch. By leaving the action that creates the **bgMusak** sound object in the **playMusak** function, each time the function is executed the **Sound** object will be created anew. If you* did not *do this, whenever the MP3 player switched to another track, some of the **bgMusak** sound object's properties–such as **duration** and **position**–would get confused. In their little world, they're buzzing happily along, tracking the duration of the MP3 and the current millisecond position that its played so far, when the duration of the MP3 suddenly changes! If you were using the **duration** and **position** properties to script a playback progress slider (as you will be building later in this chapter), since those values suddenly changed with the switching of the MP3, the playback slider is all messed up now, too. Drat!*

*By re-creating this **Sound** object each time another track is loaded, it will prevent that aforementioned confusion and all the properties associated with that **Sound** object will be cleared as well.*

*In an attempt to follow correct ActionScript formatting, the actions within the **playMusak** function should be indented.*

```
//----------------<sound setup>-------------------\\
function playMusak() {
    var bgMusak:Sound = new Sound();
    bgMusak.onLoad = function(success) {
        if (!success) {
            trackInfo.text = "Failed to load track.";
        }
    };
    bgMusak.loadSound("mp3s/mp3-" + curTrackNum + ".mp3", true);
};
//----------------</sound setup>-------------------\\
```

3. Select all the actions between the **function playMusak() {** line and the curly brace that ends that function (**}**). Once all those actions are selected, press **Tab** to indent those actions.

*However, there's a slight problem with the way that script is currently set up. In Step 5 of the previous exercise, you created a new **Sound** object by typing **var bgMusak:Sound = new Sound();**. Then, in Steps 1 and 2 in this exercise, you moved that action, and a few others, into a function. What this means is that the **bgMusak** variable that you're attaching a new **Sound** object to resides within the function **playMusak** and can therefore* only be accessed *from within that same function. Why is this a bad thing? Because if you are writing a script, and that script originates from* outside *of the **playMusak** function, you can't get access to the **bgMusak** sound object.*

*To get around this, what you need to do is first create the **bgMusak** variable from* outside *the **playMusak** function, and then from within the function you can assign that variable to the **Sound** object. That way, when you need to refer to the **bgMusak** variable that the **Sound** object is attached to (to tell the sound to stop, get its duration, and so forth) from outside of the **playMusak** function, you can easily do so. This is called* initializing a variable.

```
//----------------<sound setup>-------------------\\
function playMusak() {
    bgMusak = new Sound();
    bgMusak.onLoad = function(success) {
        if (!success) {
            trackInfo.text = "Failed to load track.";
        }
    };
    bgMusak.loadSound("mp3s/mp3-" + curTrackNum + ".mp3", true);
};
//----------------</sound setup>-------------------\\
```

4. Within the **playMusak** function, change the action **var bgMusak:Sound = new Sound();** so that it instead reads as follows:

bgMusak = new Sound();

*However, because you still want to set the data type of the **bgMusak** variable to a **Sound** object using strict typing, in the next step you're going to initialize that variable* outside *of the function. As covered previously, if you used **var bgMusak:Sound** to strict type the **bgMusak** variable from* within *the function, **bgMusak** would then reside* within *the function and would be inaccessible from* outside *of it.*

```
//----------------<sound initialization>------------------\\
var curTrackNum:Number = 0;
var bgMusak:Sound;

//----------------<sound setup>------------------\\
function playMusak() {
    bgMusak = new Sound();
    bgMusak.onLoad = function(success) {
        if (!success) {
            trackInfo.text = "Failed to load track.";
        }
    };
    bgMusak.loadSound("mp3s/mp3-" + curTrackNum + ".mp3", true);
};
//----------------</sound setup>------------------\\
```

5. Click at the end of the **`var curTrackNum:Number = 0;`** line toward the top of the **Actions** panel, press **Enter** (Windows) or **Return** (Mac) once to create a line break, and type the following:

`var bgMusak:Sound;`

*This action creates a new variable called **bgMusak** and strict types it to a **Sound** object. So now, the **bgMusak** variable resides on **_root**, outside of the **playMusak** function. The action within the function, **bgMusak = new Sound();**, now just assigns a new **Sound** object to the **bgMusak** variable that is on **_root**. What this means is that now, when you want to refer to the **bgMusak** sound object, you can easily do so by writing **_root.bgMusak**, or–if the action you're authoring also resides on **_root**–by typing **bgMusak**.*

Now that the first MP3 won't automatically start downloading and playing–because you inserted that ActionScript into a function–you can start writing the actions that will play and download the music when the viewer clicks the Play button, and stop the music when he or she clicks the Stop button.

6. On the **Stage**, double-click the instance of the **mc. toggle play** movie clip symbol. This movie clip symbol contains both the **Play** and **Stop** buttons and acts as a toggle button. (When you click the **Play** button, it advances to the next frame to show the **Stop** button. When you click the **Stop** button, it goes back to the **Play** button.)

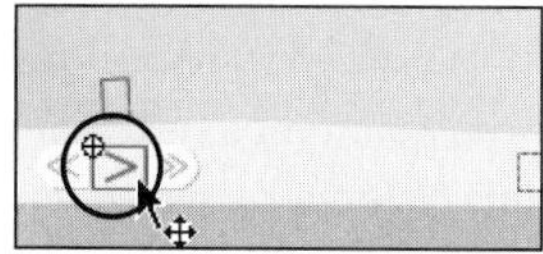

7. Once you've opened the **mc. toggle play** movie clip symbol, single-click the **Play** button on the **Stage** and open the **Actions** panel (**F9**).

At this point, some of you might be wondering–after all that talk of centralizing *ActionScript code by putting it on the first keyframe–why you're selecting a button symbol and opening the* ***Actions*** *panel? Sacrilegious! The reason is, in this case, to retain simplicity. To save valued space on the Stage, the Play and Stop buttons were made into a toggle button. Just like the controllers for QuickTime and Windows Media Player, when you click the Play button, and the media begins to play, the Play button toggles to a Stop button. Clicking the Stop button stops the media and then toggles back to a Play button.*

There are a few different ways to create toggle buttons; putting some buttons in a movie clip symbol is only one of those ways. When using the technique of adding mouse events to button and movie clip symbols from a keyframe–what you've been using exclusively up until this point–it unfortunately breaks down when it comes to a movie clip–based toggle button. ActionScript can't instruct a symbol to do something if that symbol does not exist yet. In the case of this toggle button, the Play button is initially visible, but the Stop button is not. Simply, this messes up the way you've been writing your ActionScript up until now. Sure, there are ways of making it work, using different techniques, while still keeping your ActionScript centralized, but in this case it's easier to go low-tech than it is to go high-tech. Rather than try to stuff more new techniques and ActionScript down your throat just to create a simple toggle button, I felt that it would be best to go simple in this case. You've already got enough new material to learn in this chapter. :-)

```
on (rollOver) {
     _root.helpBubble.text = "play music";
}

on (rollOut) {
     _root.helpBubble.text = "";
}

on (release) {
     nextFrame();
}
```

*Upon opening the **Actions** panel, you'll notice that this Play button already has some ActionScript assigned to it. All that these actions are really saying is, "When the viewer rolls his or her mouse over the Play button, put the text 'play music' in the **helpBubble** dynamic text field on the Stage. When the viewer rolls his or her mouse off of the Play button, clear the text in the **helpBubble** field. Last, when the viewer clicks the Play button, move the playhead in this movie clip symbol to the next keyframe, thereby displaying the Stop button." The Stop button also has ActionScript already assigned to it that essentially does the opposite of what the Play button does.*

Now, what you need to add is the action that says, "When the viewer clicks the Play button, play the music."

```
on (rollOver) {
     _root.helpBubble.text = "play music";
}

on (rollOut) {
     _root.helpBubble.text = "";
}

on (release) {
     _root.playMusak();
     nextFrame();
}
```

8. Click at the end of the **on (release) {** line, press **Enter** (Windows) or **Return** (Mac) once to create a line break, and type the following:

_root.playMusak();

*This action tells the **playMusak** function–that you moved all the sound-related actions into back in Steps 1 and 2–on **_root** to execute. When that function is executed, the first MP3 track will start downloading and playing.*

Once the music has started playing, you of course want to give the viewer a way to turn it off. However, just telling the music to stop playing won't actually do the trick. The problem with simply telling the music to stop is that if one of the MP3s is currently downloading when the viewer clicks the Stop button, even though you could write an action that told the music to stop–and it would–the MP3 would still continue to download. This means that until that track finishes its downloading, most of the visitor's available bandwidth would be consumed. This will slow down everything else the visitor tries to access/download on your Web site until that downloading file completes. So instead of simply telling the music to stop, you're going to write a quick action that deletes the entire ***bgMusak*** *sound object. By deleting the* ***bgMusak*** *sound object, not only will the sound stop playing, but if an MP3 track is currently in the process of downloading, the download will stop as well!*

At this point, some of you might be saying, "Delete the ***Sound*** *object? Uhh...don't we need that to play the MP3s?" As a matter of fact, you do need the* ***bgMusak*** *sound object to play the music. But remember, with the way the MP3 player is currently written, the* ***bgMusak*** *sound object is created anew every time the Play button is clicked and every time–as you will see later–the Next Track and Previous Track buttons are clicked.*

In the next few steps, you will create a function on the Scene 1 Timeline (_root) that deletes the ***bgMusak*** *sound object. You're putting this sole action within a function because it will be used by the Stop button as well as the Next Track and Previous Track buttons.*

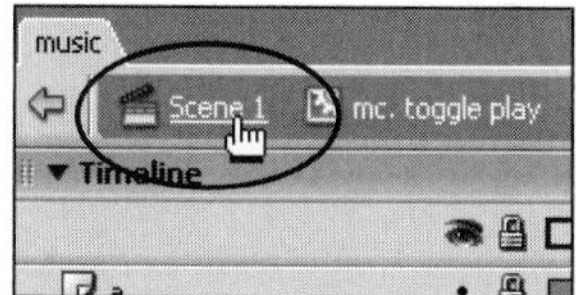

9. Return to **Scene 1** by clicking its tab above the top left of the **Timeline**.

10. Click **Keyframe 1** in layer **a** and open the **Actions** panel (**F9**).

```
//----------------<sound setup>------------------\\
function stopMusak() {
function playMusak() {
    bgMusak = new Sound();
```

11. Toward the top of the **Actions** panel, click after the comment **//----------------<sound setup>----------------** line, press **Enter** (Windows) or **Return** (Mac) once to create a line break, and type the first line of the function:

```
function stopMusak() {
```

```
//----------------<sound setup>-------------------\\
function stopMusak() {
    delete bgMusak;
};
function playMusak() {
```

12. Click at the end of the action you typed in the previous step, press **Enter** (Windows) or **Return** (Mac) once to create another line break, and type the following:

```
delete bgMusak;
};
```

And again, even though you have to type in the line breaks, Flash MX 2004 will automatically handle the formatting (indentation) of the ActionScript for you.

*Now you have a function called **stopMusak** that, when called, will delete the **bgMusak** sound object. Not only will this cause the playing music to stop, but it will also halt any downloads that the **bgMusak** sound object is performing.*

***Warning:** Because of a bug in the current version (current as of this writing is 1.2) of the Web browser **Safari** that runs in Mac OS X, once you trigger the progressive downloading of an MP3, there is **no way to stop it**. Deleting the **Sound** object–as you just scripted–will not stop the downloading file. It will just keep downloading regardless of whether you stop the sound, load another sound into the same object, or even delete the entire sound object itself. The only confirmed way to stop the progressive downloading of an MP3 when using Safari is to close the browser window. Unfortunately, that's not really a "realistic" bug workaround, so you'll sadly just have to accept it as a bug and hope that Apple fixes this bug in a future release of Safari. What this means to the viewer who is running Safari is that when he or she clicks the Play button to initiate the progressive downloading and playing of the external MP3 file, if he or she decides halfway through the download to stop the music or to listen to the next track by clicking the Stop or Next Track buttons, respectively, the MP3 track will continue to download. This means that until that track finishes its downloading, most of his or her available bandwidth will be consumed. This will slow down everything else the visitor tries to access/download on your Web site until that downloading file completes. Although this is certainly unfortunate, it's even more of an impetus to try to keep the file sizes of your media down to their–realistically–smallest possible sizes. All other browsers on Mac OS X or Windows are not affected by this issue.*

*Next, you need to call the **stopMusak** function from the Stop button so the music stops when it's clicked.*

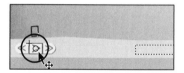

13. On the **Stage**, double-click the instance of the **mc. toggle play** movie clip symbol.

14. Move the playhead to **Frame 2**. Then, on the **Stage**, single-click the **Stop** button to select it, and open the **Actions** panel (**F9**) if it isn't already open.

```
on (rollOver) {
    _root.helpBubble.text = "stop music";
}

on (rollOut) {
    _root.helpBubble.text = "";
}

on (release) {
    _root.stopMusak();
    prevFrame();
}
```

15. Click at the end of the **`on (release) {`** line, press **Enter** (Windows) or **Return** (Mac) once to create a line break, and type the following:

`_root.stopMusak();`

This action executes the ***stopMusak*** *function on* ***_root*** *(the Scene 1 Timeline). That function deletes the* ***bgMusak*** *sound object, which causes the playing sound to stop playing and any MP3 downloading into that* ***Sound*** *object to* stop *downloading.*

Last, you need to test the changes you've made to make sure that everything is working as it should.

16. Save the changes you've made to **music.fla** by choosing **File > Save** (**Ctrl+S** [Window] or **Cmd+S** [Mac]).

17. Test your movie by choosing **Control > Test Movie** (**Ctrl+Enter** [Windows] or **Cmd+Return** [Mac]).

18. When **music.swf** opens in the **Preview** window, you won't hear the music start playing by itself, as it did last time you tested the movie. To start the music playing, click the **Play** button.

19. Once you click the **Play** button, the music will start playing, and the **Play** button will change into a **Stop** button. While the music is playing, if you click the **Stop** button, the music will stop!

So, congratulations! You've just given the viewer the ability to start and stop the background music.

However, while you were testing your movie you probably noticed something strange. When you moved your mouse over the Play and Stop buttons, you probably noticed a small bit of text appear above the buttons. If you remember, the prebuilt ActionScript that was already applied to those buttons told a dynamic text field–on the Stage–with an instance name of ***helpBubble*** *to display the text "play music" and "stop music." Well, the* ***helpBubble*** *dynamic text field hasn't yet been told to automatically resize itself to fit whatever text is displayed inside of it. So that small bit of text you're seeing is only the first letter or two of "play music" and "stop music." In the next step, you're going to use the* ***autoSize*** *action–which you've used previously–to instruct the* ***helpBubble*** *text field to resize itself when necessary.*

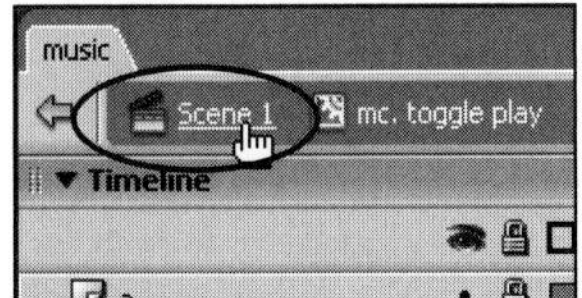

20. Close the **Preview** window to return to **music.fla**. Then, return to **Scene 1** by clicking its tab above the top left of the **Timeline**.

21. Click **Keyframe 1** in layer **a** and open the **Actions** panel (**F9**).

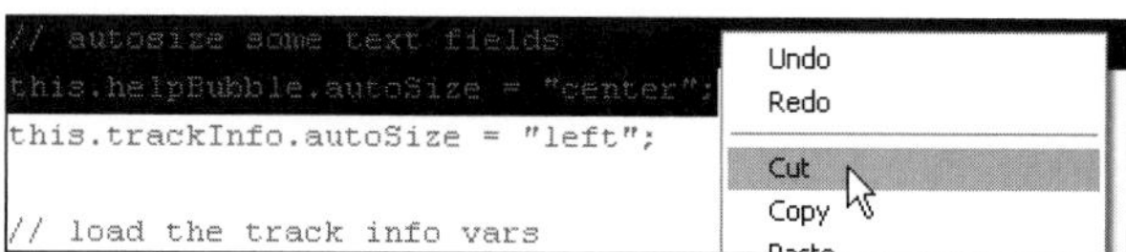

22. In the **Actions** panel, scroll down a little until you reach the commented-out, prebuilt actions for Chapter 10. Select the following actions–toward the top of the prebuilt actions:

```
// autosize some text fields
this.helpBubble.autoSize = "center";
```

23. Then, **right-click** (Windows) or **Ctrl+click** (Mac) anywhere on those selected actions. From the contextual menu that appears, choose **Cut.**

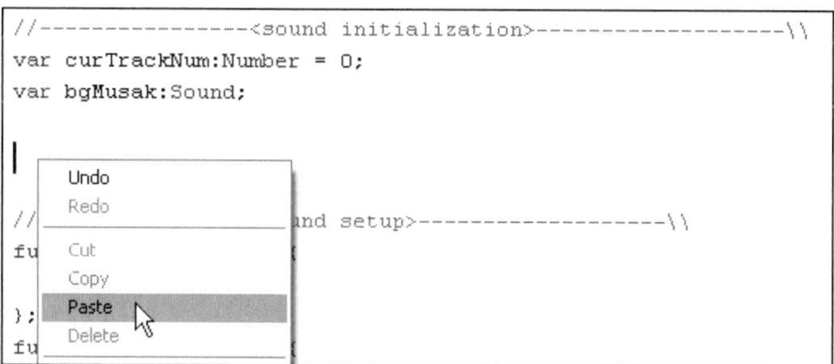

24. Scroll up to the top of the **Actions** palette and click at the end of the **`var bgMusak:Sound;`** action. Press **Enter** (Windows) or **Return** (Mac) twice to create a couple line breaks, and then **right-click** (Windows) or **Ctrl+click** (Mac) that second empty line break you just created. From the contextual menu that appears, choose **Paste**.

This will paste the actions that you just cut from the prebuilt action set.

```
//----------------<sound initialization>-------------------\\
var curTrackNum:Number = 0;
var bgMusak:Sound;

// autosize some text fields
this.helpBubble.autoSize = "center";

//----------------<sound setup>-------------------\\
```

*Now you have an action–just like you've created in earlier chapters–that tells the **`helpBubble`** dynamic text field to automatically resize itself to accommodate any text that gets inserted into it.*

25. Save the changes you've made to **music.fla** by choosing **File > Save** (**Ctrl+S** [Window] or **Cmd+S** [Mac]).

26. Test your movie by choosing **Control > Test Movie** (**Ctrl+Enter** [Windows] or **Cmd+Return** [Mac]).

27. When the **music.swf Preview** window opens, move your mouse over the **Play** button. When you do, you'll notice that–above the buttons–the text "play music" appears. Click the **Play** button to play the music and to toggle the **Play** button to show the **Stop** button. When your mouse is over the **Stop** button, the text should then read "stop music."

28. When you're finished checking out the rollover text, close the **music.swf Preview** window.

And voila! You've just completed the construction of the music Play and Stop buttons, as well as some descriptive text that gets inserted into a text field when the viewer rolls over those same buttons.

In the next exercise, you will write a little ActionScript that will pull the ID3 information from the currently playing MP3 and insert it into a text field on the Stage. Just when you thought it couldn't get more exciting... ;-)

5. Displaying the ID3 Information

Most of you are probably aware that the "digital music revolution" is well underway. With MP3-playing software such as Apple iTunes for your computer, portable MP3 devices such as the Apple iPod, and now boom boxes and car stereos that play MP3s, it's quickly becoming a technology that is being integrated into our daily lives. If you've ever played an MP3 on your computer, or on a portable MP3-playing device like an Apple iPod, have you ever wondered how it knew that you were listening to "Windowlicker" by Aphex Twin? Or which order the album tracks are supposed to be in, or even which album the songs came from? This information is actually written into each MP3 track, and the various bits of information are called **ID3 tags**. The ID3 tags keep track of a wide variety of information about each MP3 such as the name of the artist, the name of the album, the track name, the year the song was released, which track number it is out of the total number of tracks, the genre, and more.

Starting with Flash MX, you could use a little ActionScript to have the Flash Player grab some of those ID3 version 1 (v1) tags and display them. This is useful for when you want to have an MP3 player, for example, and display some dynamic information about the currently playing track without having to manually type it all out in your FLA. However, the problem with ID3 v1 tags and building an MP3 player that progressively downloaded its MP3 tracks off of a remote server was that ID3 v1 tags are stored at *the end* of the MP3 file. This meant that you couldn't access those ID3 tags until the MP3 had been *completely* downloaded. Obviously, when attempting to create a streaming MP3 player, having the ID3 tags at the end of the file doesn't help you out very much. With the introduction of Flash MX 2004, the Flash Player 7 now supports ID3 v2.3 and 2.4 tags. The great thing about ID3 v2.3 and 2.4 tags is that they're stored at *the beginning* of the MP3 file and can therefore be accessed as soon as the MP3 file starts to download. So if you're building an MP3 player that progressively downloads its tracks–as you are doing in this chapter–you can display those ID3 tags right from the get-go.

In this exercise, you're going to write some ActionScript that will grab a few of those ID3 tags and display them in the **`trackInfo`** dynamic text field on the Stage.

1. First, make sure that **music.fla** is the current foreground FLA, that you have **Keyframe 1** in layer **a** selected, and that you have the **Actions** panel open (**F9**).

*The ID3 tags will be displayed in the long, horizontal dynamic text field at the bottom of the Stage. If you remember, that text field has an instance name of **`trackInfo`** already applied to it. When you use ActionScript to insert some text in that field, it will* not *automatically resize itself to fit the text that gets inserted into it. Just like you did in the previous exercise, you need an action to do that for you.*

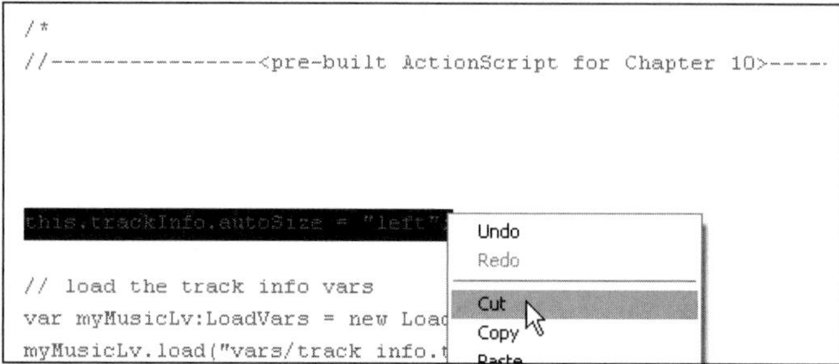

2. Scroll down in the **Actions** panel a bit until you come to the action **`this.trackInfo.autoSize = "left";`**. Once you've located that action, select it and then **right-click** (Windows) or **Ctrl+click** (Mac) it. From the contextual menu that appears, choose **Cut.**

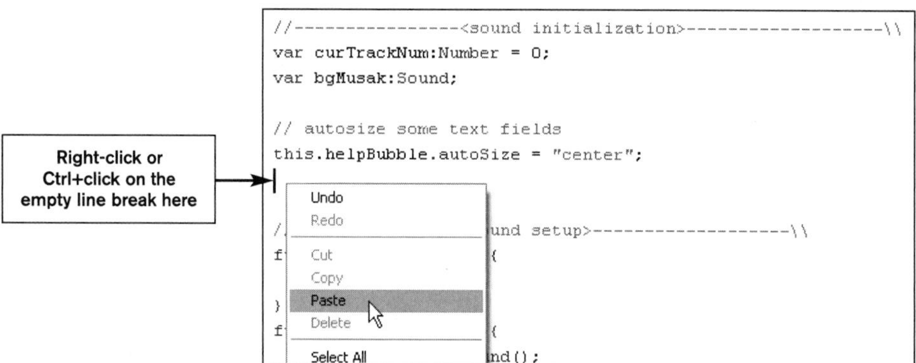

3. Scroll back toward the top of the **Actions** panel, click at the end of the **`this.helpBubble.autoSize = "center";`** line, and press **Enter** (Windows) or **Return** (Mac) once to create a line break. Then, **right-click** (Windows) or **Ctrl+click** (Mac) that new, empty line break. From the contextual menu that appears, choose **Paste.**

```
// autosize some text fields
this.helpBubble.autoSize = "center";
this.trackInfo.autoSize = "left";
```

As you have seen a few times before, you now have an action that sets the ***trackInfo*** *dynamic text field so that it will automatically resize as needed, while keeping the text within it aligned to the left side of the field.*

If your brain isn't jello yet, you might recall that right before Exercise 4 is a table called "Methods, Properties, and Event Handlers of the Sound Class." In that table is a ***Sound*** *class event handler called* ***onID3****. The* ***onID3*** *event handler is fired every time the ID3 tags change of whichever sound is being loaded using the* ***bgMusak*** *sound object. That sounds like just the thing you need to populate a dynamic text field with the MP3's ID3 tags! In fact, that's exactly what you're going to use in these next steps.*

```
//----------------<sound setup>-------------------\\
function stopMusak() {
    delete bgMusak;
};
function playMusak() {
    bgMusak = new Sound();
    bgMusak.onID3 = function() {
    bgMusak.onLoad = function(success) {
        if (!success) {
            trackInfo.text = "Failed to load track.";
        }
    };
    bgMusak.loadSound("mp3s/mp3-" + curTrackNum + ".mp3", true);
};
//----------------</sound setup>-------------------\\
```

4. In the **Actions** panel, locate the actions contained within the **<sound setup>** comments. Then, click after the **bgMusak = new Sound();** line, press **Enter** (Windows) or **Return** (Mac) once to create a line break, and type the opening action for this event handler:

bgMusak.onID3 = function() {

Just like the other ***Sound*** *class event handlers–such as* ***onLoad****, which you wrote in Exercise 3–the* ***onID3*** *event handler needs to be assigned to a function. The actions you place within this function will be executed each time the* ***onID3*** *event handler is fired.*

```
//----------------<sound setup>-------------------\\
function playMusak() {
    bgMusak = new Sound();
    bgMusak.onID3 = function() {
        trackInfo.text = "artist : " + bgMusak.id3.TCOM + " | track : " + bgMusak.id3.TIT2;
    bgMusak.onLoad = function(success) {
        if (!success) {
            trackInfo.text = "Failed to load track.";
        }
    };
    bgMusak.loadSound("mp3s/mp3-" + curTrackNum + ".mp3", true);
};
```

5. Click at the end of the **`bgMusak.onID3 = function() {`** line, press **Enter** (Windows) or **Return** (Mac) once to create a line break, and then type–all on one line with no line breaks–the following:

`trackInfo.text = "artist : " + bgMusak.id3.TCOM + " | track : " + bgMusak.id3.TIT2;`

In plain English, this action reads, "Insert some text into the ***trackInfo*** *dynamic text field. The text to insert should be 'artist :' then the ID3 tag TCOM (which is the composer/artist), the text '| track :' and then the ID3 tag TIT2 (which is the track title)." So if the currently loading/playing MP3 is "Windowlicker" by Aphex Twin, the final result of this action–and thereby the text to be inserted into the* ***trackInfo*** *text field–would be "artist : Aphex Twin | track : Windowlicker".*

Note: *To see a full list of the ID3 tags that Flash MX 2004 can access, open the* ***Help*** *panel* ***(F1)****, and from the Help "books" on the left, open* ***ActionScript Dictionary > S > Sound.id3.***

```
//----------------<sound setup>-------------------\\
function stopMusak() {
    delete bgMusak;
};
function playMusak() {
    bgMusak = new Sound();
    bgMusak.onID3 = function() {
        trackInfo.text = "artist : " + bgMusak.id3.TCOM + " | track : " + bgMusak.id3.TIT2;
    };
    bgMusak.onLoad = function(success) {
        if (!success) {
            trackInfo.text = "Failed to load track.";
        }
    };
    bgMusak.loadSound("mp3s/mp3-" + curTrackNum + ".mp3", true);
};
//----------------</sound setup>-------------------\\
```

6. Close the **`bgMusak.onID3`** function by clicking at the end of the action that you wrote in the last step, pressing **Enter** (Windows) or **Return** (Mac) to create a line break, and typing the following:

`};`

And that's it! All that this action is doing is every time the ID3 information changes for the sound being targeted by the **bgMusak** *sound object, the* **onID3** *event handler is triggered and some text, along with some ID3 tags, are inserted into the* **trackInfo** *text field. As you saw when writing this action, when you want to get access to the ID3 tags for the MP3 that is being downloaded/played, you first type the name of the* **Sound** *object that the MP3 is loading into (***bgMusak** *in this case),* **id3**, *and then the name of the ID3 tag that you want to grab the value of. So if you wanted to get access to any comments that had been inserted into the ID3 comment tag of an MP3, you could simply type* **bgMusak.id3.COMM**.

There are also quite a few programs that allow you to edit the ID3 tags of MP3 files. In Appendix B, "Macromedia Flash MX 2004 Resources," *you'll find some recommended ID3 editing programs for both Windows and Mac.*

Before congratulating yourself, you should test your movie to make sure everything is working.

---

7. Save the changes you've made to **music.fla** by choosing **File > Save** (**Ctrl+S** [Window] or **Cmd+S** [Mac]).

---

8. Test your movie by choosing **Control > Test Movie** (**Ctrl+Enter** [Windows] or **Cmd+Return** [Mac]).

9. When **music.swf** appears in the **Preview** window, click the **Play** button. As you have already seen before, this will start playing the music. But when it starts playing, you'll also see some text appear in the **trackInfo** text field. It will say "artist : DJ Shane | track : Taking the Subway." The text "artist :", the pipe (|), and "track :": were all manually specified in the action you wrote in Step 5, but the text "DJ Shane" and "Taking the Subway" is the content of the ID3 tags TCOM and TIT2, respectively. Pretty darn cool!

As has been mentioned previously, any time you can use dynamic content, go for it. By incorporating the ID3 tags into the track information that is displayed in the **trackInfo** *dynamic text field, it makes the MP3 player so much easier to update in the future. Whenever you want to add or remove MP3s, either you or the client simply have to verify that the correct ID3 tags have been set, upload the MP3s to the server, and you're done!*

At this point, you might be looking at the large, blank space between the last track, the Play/Stop button, the Next Track button, and where the ID3 information is, and wondering why its there. Later in this chapter, you will be referred to watch the movie **music_progress.mov** *where you will learn how to script a MP3 preloader and a playback progress slider. This will sit in that empty space.*

---

10. When you're finished checking out the ID3 text, close the **Preview** window and return to **music.fla**.

In the next exercise, you're going to script a way for the viewer to skip to the next track or go back to the previous track. You will also script the capability for the MP3 player to automatically advance to the next MP3 track in sequence when the currently playing song reaches its end.

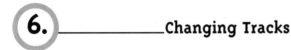

6. Changing Tracks

What would an MP3 player jukebox be if you couldn't switch tracks, eh? In this exercise, you will add some ActionScript that will allow the viewer to advance to the next MP3 track in sequence, go to the previous MP3 track, or just wait for the currently playing MP3 to end, and let the MP3 player switch to the next track automatically. Well, what are you waiting for? ;-)

Similar to the slideshow, the MP3 player will loop through the MP3 tracks. When Track 1 is finished playing, the MP3 player will advance to Track 2. When Track 2 has finished playing, the MP3 player will go back to Track 1. (There are only two MP3 tracks total.) So, for the script to know if the MP3 it is currently playing is the *last* MP3 track in the sequence, you need a way to keep track of the total number of MP3 tracks. When constructing the slideshow, you used the variable **`totalFrames`** to keep track of the total number of slides. In this exercise, you're going to create a variable named **`totalTracks`** to keep track of the total number of MP3 tracks. But just like you did with the slideshow, you're going to keep that variable in an external text file, and use a **`LoadVars`** object to load that variable into your SWF. This allows you or the client to easily add or remove MP3 tracks to the MP3 player and make the required changes without even having to open Flash MX 2004. So the first step is to load that **`totalTracks`** variable.

1. Hide or minimize Flash MX 2004, and on your hard drive navigate to your **Desktop > la_eyeworks > site > vars** folder.

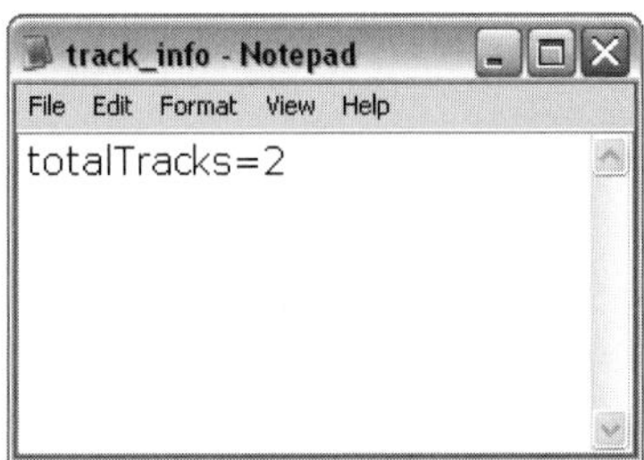

2. In the **vars** folder, open the text file **track_info.txt** in a simple text program such as **Notepad** (Windows), **TextEdit** (Mac), or **BBEdit** (Mac). In that text file, you'll see one variable, **`totalTracks`**, with a value of **2**. If you–or the client–were to ever add or remove MP3 tracks, you'd simply have to change that number accordingly.

*Now that you've seen where the text file is, what it is named, and what's inside of it, you can write the **`LoadVars`** script to load it into **music.swf**.*

3. Close the text file and return to Flash MX 2004. Then, make sure **music.fla** is the foreground FLA, that you have **Keyframe 1** selected in the **a** layer, and that you have the **Actions** panel open.

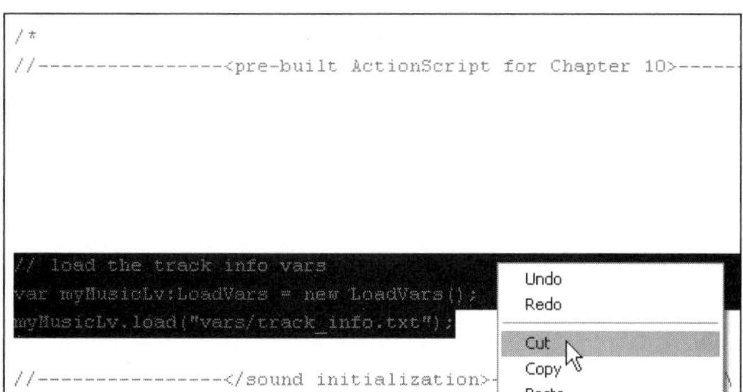

4. Scroll down in the **Actions** panel until you reach the following script:

```
// load the track info vars
var myMusicLv:LoadVars = new LoadVars();
myMusicLv.load("vars/track_info.txt");
```

Then, select those three lines, and **right-click** (Windows) or **Ctrl+click** (Mac) anywhere on that selected script. From the contextual menu that appears, choose **Cut**.

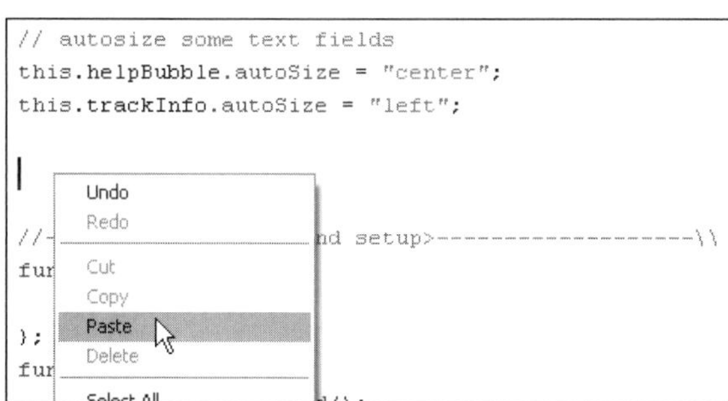

5. Scroll to the top of the **Actions** panel, click at the end of the `this.trackInfo.autoSize = "left";` line, and press **Enter** (Windows) or **Return** (Mac) twice to create a couple line breaks. Then, **right-click** (Windows) or **Ctrl+click** (Mac) that second empty line break you just created. From the contextual menu that appears, choose **Paste**.

```
// autosize some text fields
this.helpBubble.autoSize = "center";
this.trackInfo.autoSize = "left";

// load the track info vars
var myMusicLv:LoadVars = new LoadVars();
myMusicLv.load("vars/track_info.txt");
```

*Presto! You now have a **LoadVars** object called **myMusicLv** that you're using to load the variables from the file **track_info.txt** located in the **vars** folder. As you saw earlier, this text file contains the variable **totalTracks** with a value of **2**. So whenever you're writing an action, and you need to get access to that variable/value, you can simply type **myMusicLv.totalTracks**.*

Now that you know how many tracks there are total, you can use that number in a script to get the MP3 player to loop through all the music tracks. In the next few steps, you're going to write a script that instructs the MP3 player to advance to the next track in sequence when the currently playing track finishes. If the last track is the currently playing track, when it finishes playing, the script will automatically instruct the MP3 player to load and play the first track.

*Because you will later write a script that changes the track when the current track finishes playing, you need to have a way to detect when a playing track reaches its end. Fortunately, just like **onLoad** and **onID3**, Flash MX 2004 has an event handler to fill this need as well. In the next few steps, you're going to use the **onSoundComplete** event handler to detect when the current track has finished playing and to then advance to the next track in sequence.*

```
//----------------<sound setup>-------------------\\
function stopMusak() {
    delete bgMusak;
};
function playMusak() {
    bgMusak = new Sound();
    bgMusak.onSoundComplete = function() {
    bgMusak.onID3 = function() {
        trackInfo.text = "artist : " + bgMusak.id3.TCOM + " | track : " + bgMusak.id3.TIT2;
    };
    bgMusak.onLoad = function(success) {
        if (!success) {
            trackInfo.text = "Failed to load track.";
        }
    };
    bgMusak.loadSound("mp3s/mp3-" + curTrackNum + ".mp3", true);
};
//----------------</sound setup>-------------------\\
```

6. Within the **<sound setup>** comments, click at the end of the **bgMusak = new Sound();** line, press **Enter** (Windows) or **Return** (Mac) once to create a line break, and type the following:

bgMusak.onSoundComplete = function() {

*Similar to the **onLoad** and **onID3** event handlers that you wrote earlier in this chapter, this line is the first step in creating the **onSoundComplete** event handler. Where the **onLoad** event handler was triggered when the sound was loaded, and the **onID3** event handler was triggered when the sound's ID3 information changed, the **onSoundComplete** event handler is triggered when the currently playing sound finishes (complete). So now you just need to specify what should occur when that happens.*

The first thing you need to find out is if the currently playing track is the last *track in sequence. Because if it is the last track that just finished playing, you need to tell the MP3 player to load and play the* first *track.*

```
//----------------<sound setup>-------------------\\
function stopMusak() {
    delete bgMusak;
};
function playMusak() {
    bgMusak = new Sound();
    bgMusak.onSoundComplete = function() {
        if (curTrackNum == (myMusicLv.totalTracks - 1)) {
```

7. Click at the end of the **bgMusak.onSoundComplete = function() {** line, press **Enter** (Windows) or **Return** (Mac) once to create a line break, and type the following:

```
if (curTrackNum == (myMusicLv.totalTracks - 1)) {
```

*Simply, the beginning of this **if** statement reads, "If the track number (the number of the currently playing MP3) is equal to the total number of tracks minus one..."*

*"Why the total number of tracks minus 1?" some of you might be asking. Remember, the MP3s start with the number **0** (for reasons stated in the slideshow chapter) as in **mp3-0.mp3**, **mp3-1.mp3**, and so forth. So even though there are two tracks total, the last MP3 in sequence ends with **1**. Therefore, when you need to determine if the last MP3 track is playing, you need to subtract one from the **totalTracks** variable. Some of you, upon hearing that explanation, might be thinking "Well why not just put **1** in the **totalTracks** variable instead of **2**? Then you'd avoid having to do that silly subtraction stuff." And even though that would surely work, do you really want to explain to the client in charge of updating the **track_info.txt** file to subtract one from the total number of MP3 tracks? Because I don't exactly relish explaining details like that to the client (who has other things to worry about), it's much easier to just subtract one from the **totalTracks** variable in the code.*

*The **if** statement you just wrote essentially asks if the currently playing track is the last track in sequence. If this statement results in the Boolean **true**, when this track finishes playing (**onSoundComplete**), the **curTrackNum** value should be set back to **0**. As you'll see later, after the **curTrackNum** number has been set to whichever track should play next, you'll simply call the **playMusak** function, which will then play whichever MP3 track number is specified in that **curTrackNum** variable.*

```
//----------------<sound setup>-------------------\\
function stopMusak() {
    delete bgMusak;
};
function playMusak() {
    bgMusak = new Sound();
    bgMusak.onSoundComplete = function() {
        if (curTrackNum == (myMusicLv.totalTracks - 1)) {
            curTrackNum = 0;
        } else {
            curTrackNum ++;
        }
```

8. Click at the end of the action you wrote in the last step, press **Enter** (Windows) or **Return** (Mac) once to create a line break, and type the following:

```
curTrackNum = 0;
} else {
curTrackNum ++;
}
```

Note: *Although you will need to create the line breaks just like you see it in the code above, Flash MX 2004 will automatically handle the indentation of the actions for you.*

*Taken along with the **if** statement you started writing in Step 7, this script reads, "If the currently playing track number is equal to the total number of available MP3 tracks (meaning, that there aren't any more new tracks to play), set the current track number back to 0 (the beginning). Otherwise, set the current track number to whichever number comes next." So now you've set that **curTrackNum** to whichever track number should be playing when the current track finishes, but you haven't (yet) instructed the MP3 player to actually* play *that specific MP3 track.*

```
//----------------<sound setup>-------------------\\
function stopMusak() {
    delete bgMusak;
};
function playMusak() {
    bgMusak = new Sound();
    bgMusak.onSoundComplete = function() {
        if (curTrackNum == (myMusicLv.totalTracks - 1)) {
            curTrackNum = 0;
        } else {
            curTrackNum ++;
        }
        playMusak();
    };
```

9. Press **Enter** (Windows) or **Return** (Mac) to create a new line break under the last closed curly brace you typed in Step 8, and type the following:

```
playMusak();
};
```

This instructs the MP3 player to execute the ***playMusak*** *function you built earlier, which, of course, starts playing whichever track number is specified in the* ***curTrackNum*** *variable. The last line (* ***};*** *) closes the* ***bgMusak.onSoundComplete*** *function, and you now have an MP3 player that will automatically and continually loop through all the MP3 tracks that it has available.*

Now, you just need to cross your fingers, whisper a small prayer, put on your tin foil hat, and test your movie!

10. Save the changes you've made to **music.fla** by choosing **File > Save** (**Ctrl+S** [Window] or **Cmd+S** [Mac]).

11. Test your movie by choosing **Control > Test Movie** (**Ctrl+Enter** [Windows] or **Cmd+Return** [Mac]).

12. When **music.swf** appears in the **Preview** window, click the **Play** button to start playing the music. Now you just need to kick back and wait for the track to reach the end to hear it automatically advance to the next track in sequence. Coolio!

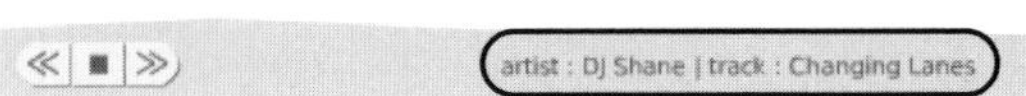

When the track automatically changes to the next track, you'll see the ID3 text automatically change as well. This is because the ***onID3*** *event handler received the message that the ID3 information for the music had changed, and then executed all the actions within the function it is attached to. The actions within the* ***onID3*** *event handler function grabbed the new ID3 information from the new MP3 and displayed it in the* ***trackInfo*** *dynamic text field. It's like a well-oiled machine!*

Because the script you just wrote essentially instructs the MP3 player to play the next MP3 track in sequence–even jumping back to the first track if it needs to–the MP3 player will play continual music until the cows come home.

But what if the viewer doesn't want to wait for the currently playing track to end before she can listen to the next track? Maybe the viewer thinks the current track is boring, and wants to hear what the next track sounds like. In that case, the viewer will click the Next Track or Previous Track buttons, that you've kindly given them, to jump one track ahead or one track behind in sequence. In the next steps, you're going to bring all the ActionScript together to make that functionality work. Thankfully, the ActionScript to add that functionality onto the Next Track and Previous Track buttons will be nearly identical to the script you just wrote.

13. Close the **Preview** window and return to **music.fla**. Make sure you have **Keyframe 1** selected in layer **a** and that you have the **Actions** panel open.

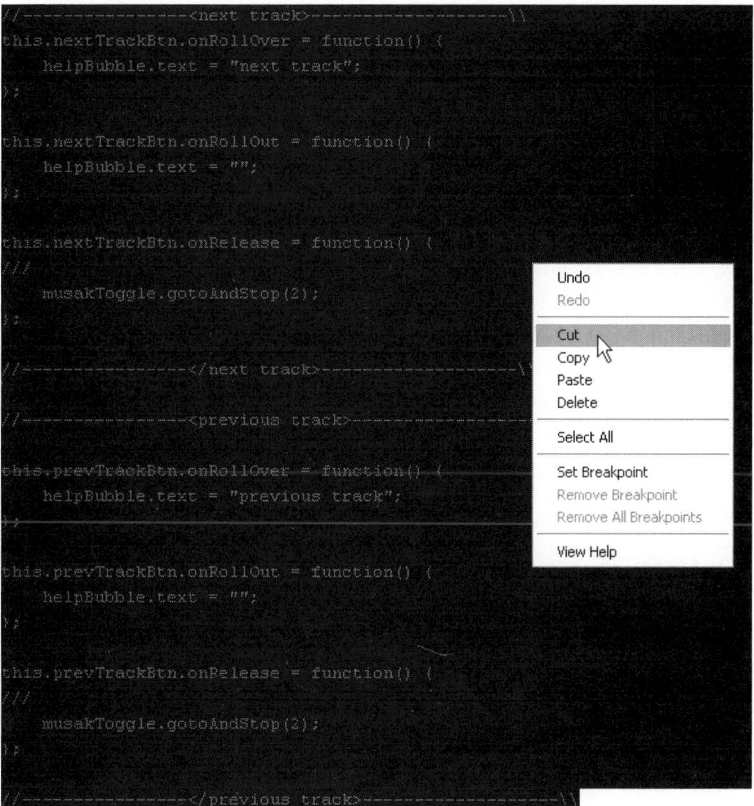

14. Scroll down toward the bottom of the **Actions** panel, and select the giant block of code that starts with the comment `//----------------<next track>----------------\\` and ends with `//----------------</previous track>----------------\\` as you can see in the screen shot above. Then, **right-click** (Windows) or **Ctrl+click** (Mac) anywhere on that selected script. From the contextual menu that appears, choose **Cut**.

Although it may initially look daunting, the ActionScript you just cut is just a series of simple ***onRollOver***, ***onRollOut***, *and* ***onRelease*** *mouse event commands for the Next Track and Previous Track buttons. After you paste this ActionScript into the correct place in the next step, you will add to that script to make it functional for the Next Track and Previous Track buttons.*

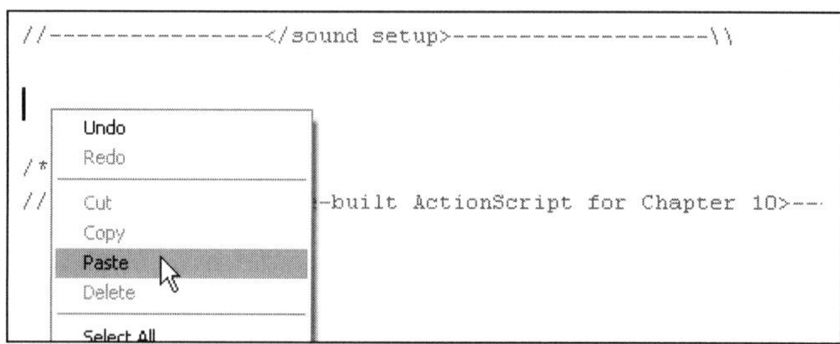

15. Scroll up in the **Actions** panel a little, click at the end of the **//---------------</sound setup>----------------** line, and press **Enter** (Windows) or **Return** (Mac) twice to create a couple line breaks. Then, **right-click** (Windows) or **Ctrl+click** (Mac) that second empty line break you just created. From the contextual menu that appears, choose **Paste.**

This will paste all that ActionScript you just cut from the prebuilt actions area. Again, this code was provided for you because it's all stuff you've already learned. If you read through the code, you'll see that it's just a series of simple mouse events for the Next Track and Previous Track buttons. What you need to do now, however, is to modify the ***onRelease*** *mouse events for both the Next Track and Previous Track buttons so that when the viewer clicks one those buttons, it changes the currently playing track. As was mentioned previously, the ActionScript to create that functionality will be nearly identical to the ActionScript you already wrote that changes the track when the currently playing song finishes. So to save yourself some time and energy, you're just going to copy some ActionScript that you've already written and paste it into the* ***onRelease*** *states of the Next Track and Previous Track buttons.*

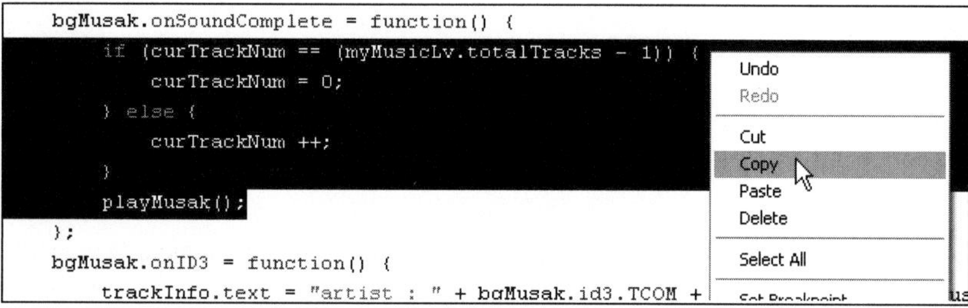

16. Underneath the **bgMusak.onSoundComplete = function() {** line, select all the ActionScript that you wrote in Steps 7 through 9, as you can see in the screen shot above. Then **right-click** (Windows) or **Ctrl+click** (Mac) anywhere on that selected script. From the contextual menu that appears, choose **Copy**.

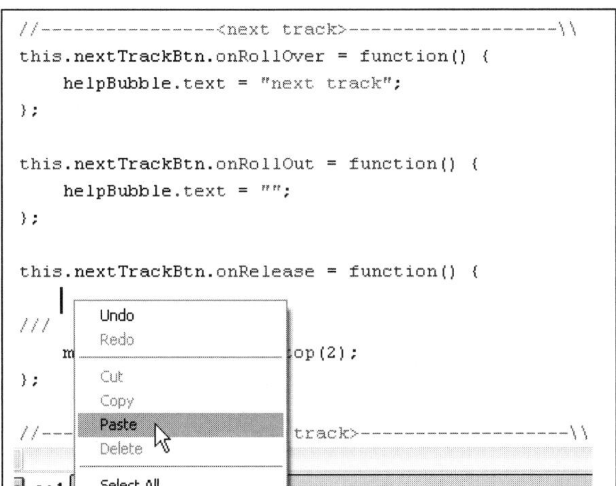

17. Scroll down a little in the **Actions** panel until you come to the **<next track>** comment lines. **Note:** The actions within the **<next track>** and **</next track>** comments are actions that apply to the **Next Track** button on the **Stage**. Then, click at the end of the **`this.nextTrackBtn.onRelease = function() {`** and press **Enter** (Windows) or **Return** (Mac) to create a line break. **Right-click** (Windows) or **Ctrl+click** (Mac) that new line break you just made, and from the contextual menu that appears, choose **Paste**.

```
this.nextTrackBtn.onRelease = function() {
            if (curTrackNum == (myMusicLv.totalTracks - 1)) {
            curTrackNum = 0;
        } else {
            curTrackNum ++;
        }
        playMusak();
///
    musakToggle.gotoAndStop(2);
};
```

*This will paste the **`if`** statement you copied from the **`bgMusak.onSoundComplete`** function. Now, within the **`nextTrackBtn.onRelease`** mouse event, the script essentially reads like this, "When the viewer clicks the Next Track button, if the currently playing track number is equal to the total number of tracks, set the track number back to 0. Otherwise, set the current track number to be one greater than whatever it currently is. After you've set the track number to be whatever it should be, tell the music to play."*

```
this.nextTrackBtn.onRelease = function() {
        if (curTrackNum == (myMusicLv.totalTracks - 1)) {
            curTrackNum = 0;
        } else {
            curTrackNum ++;
        }
```

Note: *Depending on how you copied and pasted that* ***if*** *statement, the first line of that* ***if*** *action might be indented one tabbed space too much. If this happens to you, simply click right before the* ***if****, and press* **Delete** *or* **Backspace** *to remove that extra tab space. When you're finished, the* ***if*** *should be aligned with the* **}** *before* ***else*** *and the* **}** *under* ***curTrackNum ++;****.*

However, if a viewer comes to the L.A. Eyeworks Web site, clicks the Play button to start playing some music, decides that she doesn't like the music—that's still downloading to her computer—and clicks the Next Track button, the next track will start downloading, but the previous track does not stop downloading. It continues to download, using up unnecessary bandwidth until it finishes its download. This would be horrible because unless the viewer is on a high-speed broadband Internet connection that has bandwidth to spare, his or her poor Internet connection is now trying to download two *large MP3 files* simultaneously. *Just like you did with the Stop button, you need to tell the* ***bgMusak*** *music to stop downloading whichever MP3 track it's currently downloading* before *it starts downloading another. Fortunately, you've already created the* ***stopMusak*** *function to do just that.*

```
this.nextTrackBtn.onRelease = function() {
        if (curTrackNum == (myMusicLv.totalTracks - 1)) {
            curTrackNum = 0;
        } else {
            curTrackNum ++;
        }
        stopMusak();
        playMusak();
///
    musakToggle.gotoAndStop(2);
};
```

18. Click at beginning of the **playMusak();** line and press **Enter** (Windows) or **Return** (Mac) to create a line break. Then, click the new line break you just created above **playMusak();** and type the following:

stopMusak();

As you used on the Stop button earlier in this chapter, the ***stopMusak*** *function deletes the* ***bgMusak*** *sound object. By deleting the* ***bgMusak*** *sound object, not only does it stop the currently playing sound, but it will also stop any sound that is currently being downloaded into that* ***Sound*** *object as well. Then, after that has occurred, the next action* ***playMusak*** *triggers the next sound to start playing.*

*Next, you need to write similar functionality for the Previous Track button. However, where the **`if`** statement for the Next Track button was* identical *to the **`if`** statement you wrote earlier into the **`bgMusak.onSoundComplete`** event handler, the **`if`** statement for the Previous Track button will need to be changed to accommodate for going* backwards *in sequence.*

*Currently, the **`if`** statement added to the Next Track button first checks to see if the currently playing track is the last available track. However, when going backwards through the MP3 player, you're not really interested if you're on the* last *track. You're more interested if you're on the* first *track. That way, if you* are *on the first track when the viewer clicks the Previous Track button, you can instruct the MP3 player to load the last track.*

```
//----------------<previous track>-------------------\\

this.prevTrackBtn.onRollOver = function() {
    helpBubble.text = "previous track";
};

this.prevTrackBtn.onRollOut = function() {
    helpBubble.text = "";
};

this.prevTrackBtn.onRelease = function() {
    |
///
    musakToggle.gotoAndStop(2);
};

//----------------</previous track>-------------------\\
```

19. Scroll down a little in the **Actions** panel until you come to the **<previous track>** comment lines. These actions within the **<previous track>** and **</previous track>** comments are actions that apply to the **Previous Track** button on the **Stage**. Then, click at the end of the **`this.prevTrackBtn.onRelease = function() {`** and press **Enter** (Windows) or **Return** (Mac) to create a line break.

```
this.prevTrackBtn.onRelease = function() {
    if (curTrackNum == 0) {
        curTrackNum = (myMusicLv.totalTracks - 1);
    } else {
        curTrackNum --;
    }
///
    musakToggle.gotoAndStop(2);
};
```

20. Click the new line break you created in the last step and type the following:

```
if (curTrackNum == 0) {
curTrackNum = (myMusicLv.totalTracks - 1);
} else {
curTrackNum --;
}
```

As usual, besides the line breaks you see in the code sample and in the screen shot above, Flash MX 2004 will automatically format the ActionScript for you as you type it. So you don't need to worry about adding or removing tab spaces–Flash MX 2004 will do it all for you.

*Although this **if** statement script is similar to the one you added to the Next Track button, it's a wee bit different. Taken along with the **prevTrackBtn.onRelease** mouse event, this **if** statement reads in plain English, "When the viewer clicks the Previous Track button, if the currently playing track is the first track, set the current track number to be whatever the total number of tracks is. Otherwise, just set the current track number to be one number lower than whatever it currently is." In essence, the **if** statements handle the MP3 player in the same way that the slideshow behaved. With the slideshow, it would continually loop through the 10 available slides as the viewer clicked the Next Slide and Previous Slide buttons. The MP3 player does the same thing, except with MP3s instead of JPGs.*

*To finish, you still need to write the action that deletes the **bgMusak** sound object and another action that starts playing the correct track.*

```
this.prevTrackBtn.onRelease = function() {
    if (curTrackNum == 0) {
        curTrackNum = (myMusicLv.totalTracks - 1);
    } else {
        curTrackNum --;
    }
    stopMusak();
    playMusak();
///
    musakToggle.gotoAndStop(2);
};
```

21. Click after the closed curly brace that you ended with in the last step, and press **Enter** (Windows) or **Return** (Mac) to create a line break. Then, type the following:

stopMusak();
playMusak();

And–drum roll please–there you have it! Of course, the last step is to save and test your work to make sure everything is working as it should.

---

22. Save the changes you've made to **music.fla** by choosing **File > Save** (**Ctrl+S** [Window] or **Cmd+S** [Mac]).

---

23. Test your movie by choosing **Control > Test Movie** (**Ctrl+Enter** [Windows] or **Cmd+Return** [Mac]).

24. When **music.swf** opens in the **Preview** window, click the **Play** button to start playing the music.

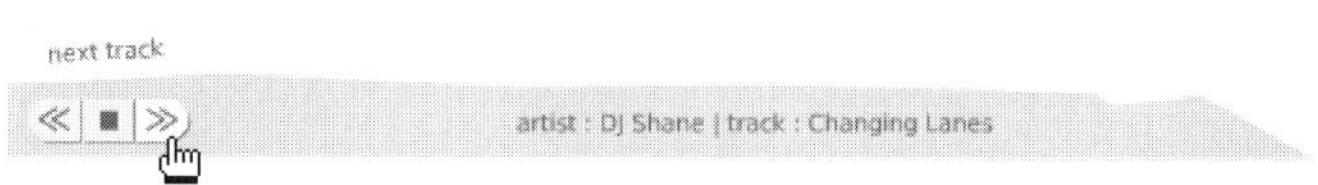

25. When the music starts playing, click the **Next Track** button. You'll notice that the MP3 player will start playing the next track, and the ID3 information will update as well.

26. Once you've verified that the **Next Track** button works correctly, click the **Previous Track** button. You'll notice that the MP3 player will play the previous track in sequence. Although, with only two MP3 tracks, it's hard to tell if it went back a track or went forward a track. I suppose you'll just have to take my word for it. ;-)

If you continually click the Previous Track or Next Track buttons, you'll notice that the MP3 player loops continually through the available tracks.

Hooray! You've constructed a working, fully functional MP3 player complete with Stop, Play, Next Track, and Previous Track buttons, as well as a dynamic text field that is updated with ID3 tags pulled from the MP3 files themselves. Break out the champagne—or at least a spritzer—because that's quite an accomplishment you've achieved in this chapter.

MOVIE | Creating an MP3 Preloader and Displaying the Playback Progress

Located on the **H•O•T CD-ROM** in the **movies** folder are four QuickTime movies titled **music_progress.mov**, **music_progress_part2.mov**, **music_progress_part3.mov**, and **music_progress_part4.mov**.

In these movies, you will learn how to build a few different pieces of functionality that fit into one graphic. You will learn how to build a preloader (different from the **MovieClipLoader**-based preloader that you constructed in Chapter 8, "*Building a Preloader*") that monitors and displays the downloading progress of the MP3s. Built into that, you will also construct the ActionScript that animates a small slider across that same graphic. This slider represents the playback progress of the currently playing MP3.

You can see the results of these QuickTime movies by pointing your Web browser to **http://www.lynda.com/flashbtb/laeyeworks/**, clicking the **Play** button on the MP3 player, and watching the graphic (highlighted in the screen shot above) to the right of the Play/Stop, Next Track, and Previous Track buttons.

MOVIE | Changing the Volume

Located on the **H•O•T CD-ROM** in the **movies** folder are three QuickTime movies titled **volume_slider.mov**, **volume_slider_part2.mov**, and **volume_slider_part3.mov**.

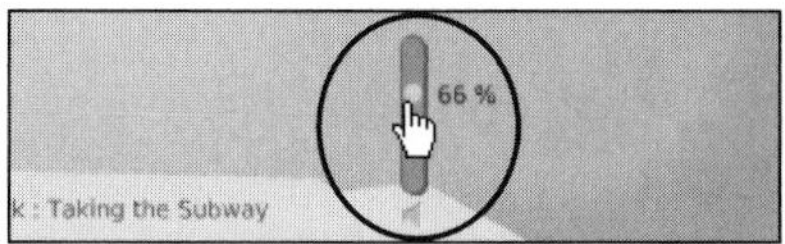

In these QuickTimes movies, you will learn how to adjust the volume of the music by creating a draggable slider. As you drag the slider up and down, the volume of the music will adjust accordingly.

You can see what you will be building in these movies, by pointing your Web browser to **http://www.lynda.com/flashbtb/laeyeworks/**, clicking the **Play** button on the MP3 player, clicking the small speaker icon toward the right side of the MP3 player bar, and dragging the light-green slider. You'll also notice that as you drag the slider, displayed to right of the slider is the volume listed as a percentage. When you stop dragging the slider, the percentage text disappears. Clicking the **speaker** icon again will hide the volume slider.

*I'd highly recommend watching, and following along with, the **music_progress.mov** and **volume_slider.mov** series of movies. Not only do they teach some new and interesting ActionScript concepts, but you'll also get to add some great functionality to the MP3 player. Treat the movies just as you would exercises in the book.*

*In the next chapter, you will learn how to create a video player. In building the video player, you'll learn how to use the `NetStream` class to progressively download a FLV (**Fl**ash **V**ideo) file off of a remote server, as well as how to stop and play that video. There's lots of new topics in the next chapter, so go rest up and I'll meet you there!*

Building a Video Player

la_eyeworks

Macromedia Flash MX 2004
Beyond the Basics

In this chapter, you will learn how to build a video player. Much like the MP3 player, this video player will progressively download an external FLV (**Fl**ash **V**ideo) file into the **About Us** section that you worked on in Chapters 4, 5, and 6. By creating a video player that progressively downloads its video content, you can use higher quality video; there's no limit–besides the viewer's free hard drive space–to the length of video you can use, and there's no performance degradation as there was when using video in Flash MX. There's lots of great new stuff to learn in this chapter, so strap yourself to your chair, close the curtains, lock the door, and let's get to it!

I. What You Are Building

In this exercise, you will get to preview exactly *what* it is you are building *before* you start building it. That way, as you're working through the exercises in this chapter, you'll have a better idea of how some of these abstract ActionScript concepts fit together to create a functional piece of the L.A. Eyeworks Web site.

1. Open your preferred Web browser and navigate to this URL:

http://www.lynda.com/flashbtb/laeyeworks/

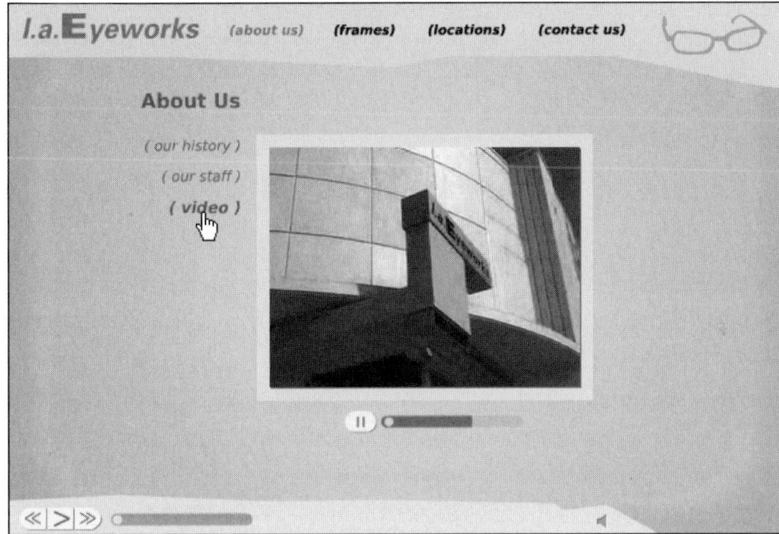

2. Once the L.A. Eyeworks Web site finishes loading, click the **about us** option in the navigation menu.

3. When the **About Us** section loads, click the **(video)** subsection option. This will make the video automatically begin downloading from the remote server. As soon as five seconds of video have been downloaded, the video will automatically start playing.

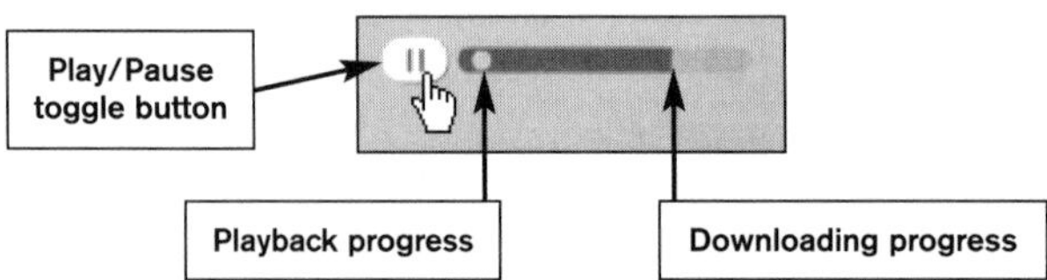

You'll also notice that as the video is downloading, a darker blue bar will animate from left to right across a lighter blue bar. That dark blue bar represents the downloading progress of the Flash MX 2004 video file (FLV). When enough of the video has been downloaded and the video starts playing, you'll see a lighter blue circle animate from left to right across the darker blue bar. That blue circle represents the playback progress of the video. Once the circle gets to the farthest point on the right side of the bar, the video ends. At any time during the playback progress, you can click the Play/Pause toggle button to pause or play the video.

Last, when the video has finished playing, you'll notice that the playback progress circle jumps back to the beginning, and the Play/Pause toggle button switches back to the Play button. This allows viewers to click it to begin playing the video again if they'd like.

---

4. When you're finished checking out the video section, close your browser window.

In this chapter, you will build all of that functionality–everything from the progressive downloading of the FLV file, to the Play/Pause toggle button, to the video preloader, to the playback progress slider. There's a lot to learn, so keep reading!

Note: *Flash MX Professional 2004 ships with media components that allow you to easily and quickly create a video player similar to the one you will be building in this chapter. However, because not everyone reading this book will have access to Flash MX Professional 2004 and because I believe it is initially better to learn how to build most things from scratch, this chapter will not cover how to use those media components. But if you're an owner of Flash MX Professional 2004 and you're looking for a quick and easy way to add FLV playback to a project you're working on, give the media components a try.*

2. Setting Up

In this exercise, you will collect all the pieces you need to build the video player. You will also assign instance names to a few symbols so that as you begin to write the ActionScript that makes this whole thing work, you'll be all set to start scripting.

1. On your hard drive, navigate to your **Desktop > la_eyeworks > site** folder and double-click **about_us.fla**.

As was discussed in Chapter 6, "TextFormat Class," *the video player is going to be integrated into the About Us section. If you can think all the way back to Chapter 6, when you were constructing the submenu, you built and scripted an option for* ***(video)****. When the viewer clicks the video option, the video will be downloaded and played directly in the About Us section.*

Once ***about_us.fla*** *finishes opening, the first thing you need is a new layer where you can place the video content.*

2. Single-click the **sub-menu** layer to select it, click the **Insert Layer** button to create a new layer, and rename the new layer **video**.

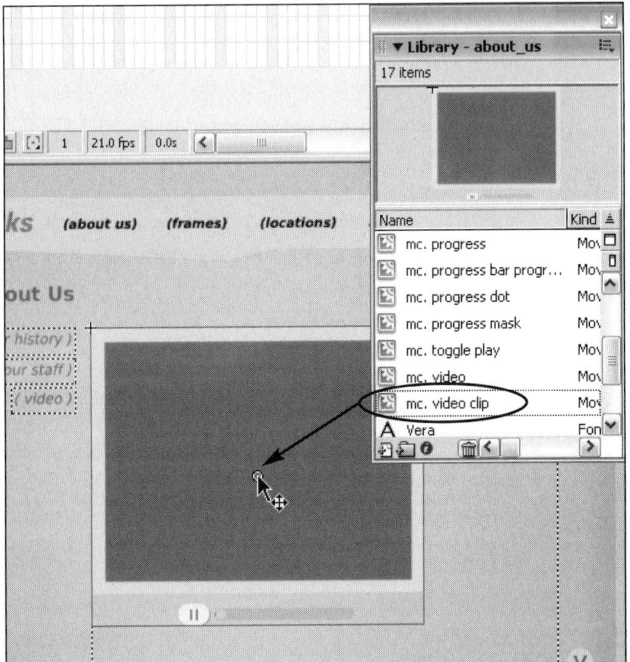

3. With the **video** layer selected, open the **about_us.fla Library** (**Ctrl+L** [Windows] or **Cmd+L** [Mac]). Then, locate the movie clip symbol **mc. video clip** and drag it onto the **Stage**.

This movie clip was already created to get you started. Inside the ***mc. video clip*** *movie clip symbol is space for the video to be displayed, the Play/Pause toggle button, and the preloader/playback progress slider. Although these elements have been provided for you, they lack the ActionScript to make them functional. You will write that ActionScript during the course of this chapter.*

All of the elements that make up the video player are housed in this one movie clip. The reason why this one movie clip contains all those items is twofold: One, instead of cluttering up the Scene 1 Timeline with a bunch of layers relating to the video section, it's all nicely contained within this one movie clip symbol. Two, as the viewer navigates to and from the video section, you're going to write some ActionScript that shows and hides the video and all of its related graphics. By keeping all of those video items within one movie clip, you can easily use one action to hide and reveal that movie clip–and the elements within it–whenever you need to.

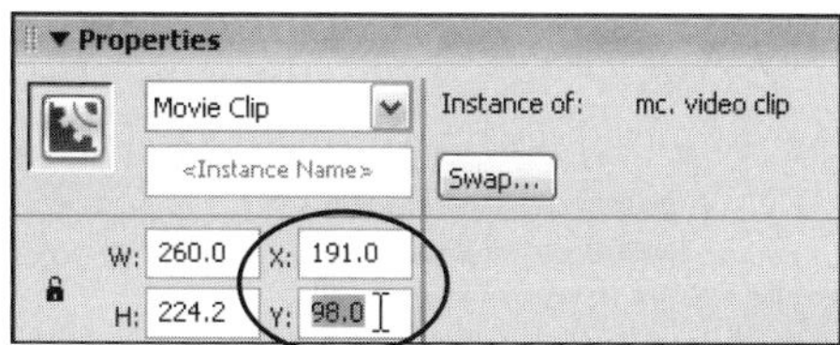

4. With the instance of **mc. video clip** still selected on the **Stage**, open the **Properties inspector** (**Ctrl+F3** [Windows] or **Cmd+F3** [Mac]). In the **Properties inspector**, set the **X** and **Y** position of the **mc. video clip** instance to **191.0** and **98.0**, respectively. This will align the top left of the **mc. video clip** symbol instance with the top left of the dynamic text field where the **our history** and **our staff** text is displayed.

Now, because you will be targeting this movie clip and the items inside it with ActionScript, you need to give this movie clip instance an instance name.

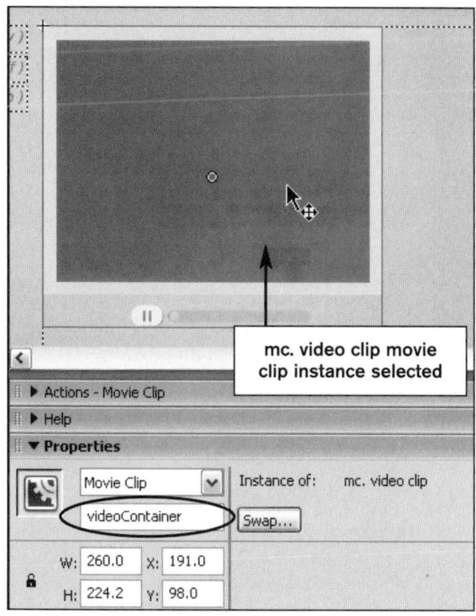

5. With the **mc. video clip** movie clip instance selected on the **Stage**, type **videoContainer** in the **Instance Name** field in the **Properties inspector**. Now that this movie clip instance has a unique instance name, you can target it–and control it–with ActionScript.

For the FLV to be displayed when it begins downloading, it needs to be attached to a video object on the Stage. In the next few steps, you'll create a new video object and use ActionScript to attach the downloading FLV to it.

6. Double-click the **videoContainer** movie clip instance on the **Stage** to open it.

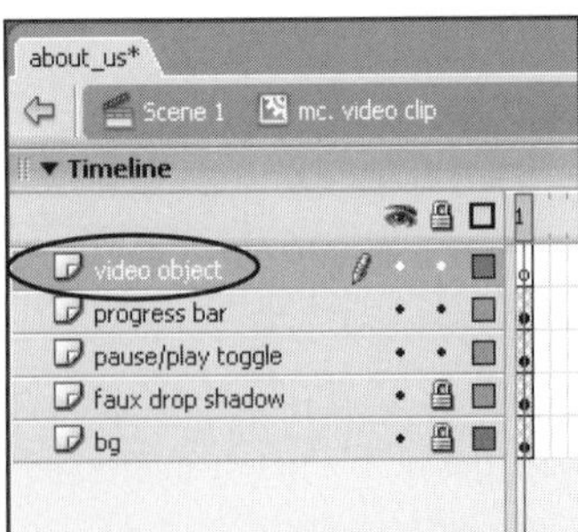

7. Single-click the top-most layer, **progress bar**, to select it. Then, create a new layer by clicking the **Insert Layer** button. Rename the new layer **video object**.

8. Open the **about_us.fla Library** (**Ctrl+L** [Windows] or **Cmd+L** [Mac]).

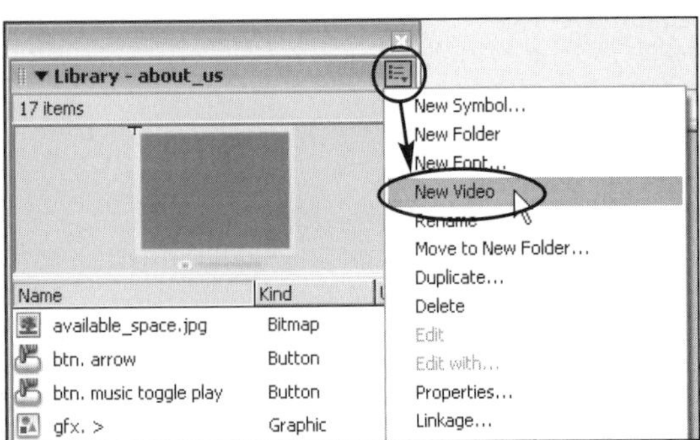

9. Choose **New Video** from the **Library** options menu located in the top-right corner of the panel.

*This will insert a new item in your library called **Embedded Video 1**. You might also notice that it has a little video camera icon to symbolize that it is a video object.*

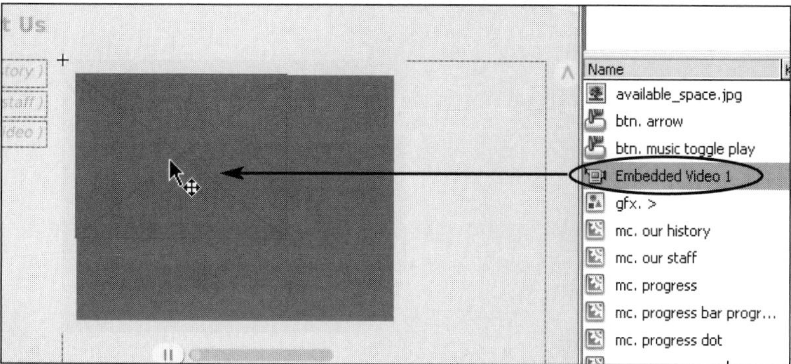

10. With the new layer **video object** still selected, drag an instance of the **Embedded Video 1** video object onto the **Stage**.

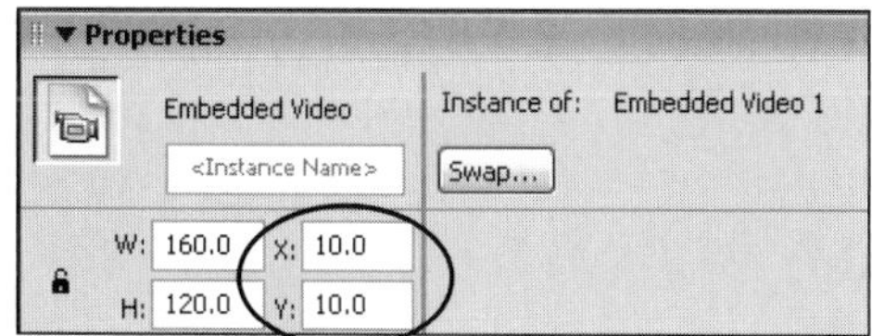

11. In the **Properties inspector**, set the **X** and **Y** coordinates to **10** and **10**, respectively. This will align the video object so that it's one pixel up and to the left of the dark blue background in the **faux drop shadow** layer. When the progressively downloaded video is played in the video object, it will appear as if it has a slight drop shadow because of that one-pixel offset from the dark blue background.

However, if you want the video to be played back at the same size as the source video, you need to make sure the video object and the source video have the same sizes. Currently–and by default–the video object is 160 pixels wide by 120 pixels tall. The source video, which you haven't seen yet, is actually 240 pixels wide by 180 pixels tall. If you don't resize the video object to match, the video will be scaled to be the same size as the video object when it is downloaded and played. If the video is scaled–especially if it's not scaled at the same aspect ratio as the original content–it is not going to look as good as it would if it were played back at a 1 to 1 ratio. Also, if Flash MX 2004 has to scale the video while it is playing, it will decrease the performance of the project slightly. Any time that Flash MX 2004 has to scale content, it requires Flash to perform calculations that it wouldn't have to perform if the content was not scaled. Because of those extra calculations, it can theoretically slow down the playback performance of your content.

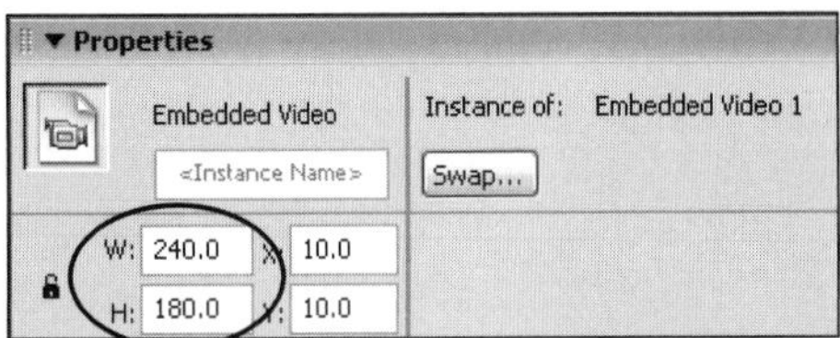

12. With the video object on the **Stage** still selected, open the **Properties inspector** and type **240** in the **W** field and **180** in the **H** field. This will set the physical dimensions of the video object to be the same size as the source FLV video itself.

Note: *If you click the* ***Lock*** *icon to the left of the* ***W*** *and* ***H*** *fields in the* ***Properties inspector****, this will lock the aspect ratio of your content. In other words, if you first click the* ***Lock*** *icon when you scale your selected content by typing a value in just the* ***W*** *or* ***H*** *field, it will scale the other value proportionately.*

Last, you need to give the video object an instance name so that you can use ActionScript to assign the progressively downloading FLV to it.

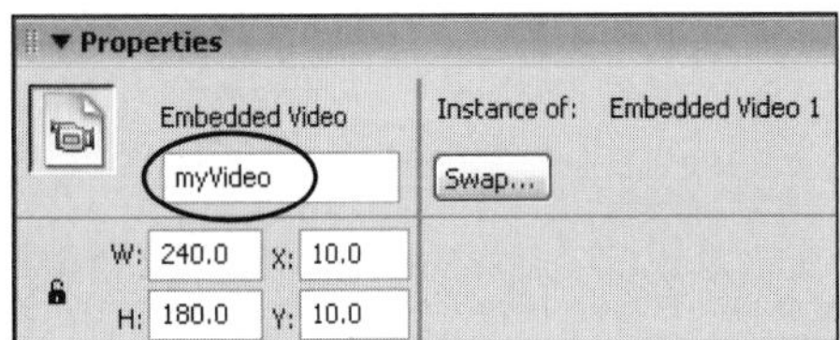

13. Type **myVideo** (paying close attention that you have the spelling and capitalization correct) in the **Instance Name** field in the **Properties inspector**.

And there you have it! Your video now has a place to be displayed. All the other items you will be targeting with ActionScript in this chapter already have their own instance names, including the Play/Pause toggle button and the playback/download progress bar, which have instance names of ***`togglePlay`*** *and* ***`vidProgBar`****, respectively.*

14. Save your changes by choosing **File > Save** or by pressing the keyboard shortcut **Ctrl+S** (Windows) or **Cmd+S** (Mac).

In the next exercise, you will start writing some ActionScript. You will begin to write the scripts that show and hide the ***`videoContainer`*** *movie clip instance–where the video and all the related graphics are embedded–as the viewer navigates to and from the video section.*

How to Create an FLV

In this chapter, you will be using ActionScript to progressively download a video clip into the **about_us.swf** file. The video clip is in a format called **Flash Video**, but is usually referred to by its acronym, **FLV**. By this point, you're probably wondering where the heck FLVs come from. The original video content can come directly from a video camera, or from a video editing program such as Apple Final Cut Pro, Apple iMovie, Adobe Premiere, Adobe After Effects, or other programs that create video content. The objective is to take your video footage and convert it to the FLV format.

There are essentially three ways you can create an FLV, each with their own strengths and weaknesses: Flash MX 2004's built-in video compressor, the Flash video exporter plug-in that ships with Flash MX Professional 2004, and a third-party program called Sorenson Squeeze. What these three methods have in common is the codec they use to compress the video. *Codec* (an acronym for **co**mpression/**dec**ompression) is the method by which the video is compressed. Flash MX 2004 only supports video that has been compressed with the Sorenson Spark codec. So even though all three of these methods compress their video using the same Sorenson Spark codec, the quality of the *engine* that actually does the compressing differs between the three. The FLV that you will be using in this chapter was compressed using Sorenson Squeeze.

Macromedia Flash MX 2004

Import a video into a blank FLA in Flash MX 2004 (standard or Professional). If you have QuickTime 4 or later installed on your system, you can import AVI, DV, MPG/MPEG, and MOV video file formats on both Windows and Mac. If you're running Windows and you have DirectX 7 or later installed, you can also import WMV and ASF video formats as well. Once you've imported the video file, go through the Video Import wizard, choose your compression settings, and let Flash MX 2004 compress the video. Once the video has finished compressing, it will appear in your library window. **Right-click** (Windows) or **Ctrl+click** (Mac) on that video in the library, and from the contextual menu, choose **Properties.** From the Properties window, you can click the **Export** button to export that compressed video file as an FLV. For more information about the supported video formats you can import into Flash MX 2004, open the **Help** panel (**F1**), and from the **Table of Contents** on the left side of the **Help** panel, choose **Using Flash > Working with Video > About file formats for imported video.**

- **Pros:** You don't need any additional software. You can use your existing copy of Flash MX 2004 to both compress the video and export it as an FLV.
- **Cons:** This method yields the worst video quality and highest file sizes of the three possible options. That's not to say that the FLV output is completely unworkable; it just means that this method doesn't yield an FLV with quality comparable to the other two options. Another drawback is the lack of 2-pass compression (more on that later).

Flash Video Exporter Plug-In

If you own Flash MX Professional 2004, you can use the Flash Video Exporter that came with the Flash installer. The Flash Video Exporter is a plug-in that will "plug into" a variety of video-editing and video-encoding applications on both Windows and Macintosh. If you have Flash MX Professional 2004 (the plug-in won't work if you have the standard version of Flash MX 2004), and if you've installed the plug-in, you can open one of the compatible applications and export your video as an FLV directly from that application. You can read more information about which applications are supported, as well as how to go about exporting an FLV from one of those applications, by opening the **Help** panel (**F1**) and from the **Table of Contents** choosing **Using Flash > Working with Video > Exporting FLV files from video-editing applications**.

- **Pros:**

  The Flash Video Exporter plug-in allows you to export your video using Variable Bitrate Encoding (VBR). Although VBR doesn't help to improve the quality of the video, because the bit rate of the video is variable (the amount of data the video is given to display itself can fluctuate up and down as the video needs it), it will usually yield an FLV with a smaller file size than an FLV that was *not* compressed using VBR.

  The Flash Video Exporter plug-in also provides you with more options when compressing the video than does compressing the FLV solely through Flash MX 2004.

  Additionally, the Flash Video Exporter offers 2-pass compression, which can provide better-looking video with a smaller file size. Overall, the video compression engine in the Flash Video Exporter plug-in is better than the video compression engine in Flash MX 2004 and even comparable in quality to Sorenson Squeeze which you'll read about next.

- **Cons:** The Flash Video Exporter plug-in only comes with the professional version of Flash MX 2004.

You can read more about the Flash Video Exporter and incorporating video into Flash projects here:

http://www.macromedia.com/devnet/mx/flash/video.html

Before using the Flash Video Exporter, it's always a good idea to check for updates first. To see if the Flash Video Exporter has been updated, check this URL:

http://www.macromedia.com/support/flash/downloads.html

Sorenson Squeeze

The third way to create FLV files is by using a third-party application by Sorenson Media called Sorenson Squeeze. Sorenson Squeeze (either the Sorenson Squeeze Compression Suite or Sorenson Squeeze for Flash MX) also allows you to compress your original video as an FLV file.

- **Pros:**

  Sorenson Squeeze allows you to compress video using 2-pass compression, which usually yields better-looking video with a smaller file size.

  Sorenson Squeeze, being an application whose sole purpose in this universe is to compress video, has a great compression engine. Video compressed with Sorenson Squeeze looks better than video compressed with Flash MX 2004 and is comparable in quality to the Flash Video Exporter plug-in.

  Sorenson Squeeze gives you a *ton* of options when compressing video–from allowing you to capture DV (**D**igital **V**ideo) directly into Squeeze to batch processing. If you are in charge of getting lots of video clips into your Flash projects, or if you just want good, high-quality video in your SWF files, definitely check out Sorenson Squeeze. If you look on the **software** folder on the **H•O•T CD-ROM**, you'll find a demo version of Sorenson Squeeze that you can try out for 30 days. This may sound like a sales pitch, but I can assure you that I don't get anything out of recommending Sorenson Squeeze to you other than that nice warm feeling in my tummy that one gets when he knows he's just improved other peoples lives. ;-)

- **Cons:**

  You have to pay for it. After you plopped down that chunk of change for Flash MX 2004, you may not be willing to drop more money to buy *another* program to compress your video

  Using Sorenson Squeeze also adds another step to your production process. With the other two options, you can go from your video-editing program directly into Flash MX 2004. But Squeeze's great options and quality come at a price. You have to add another step by going from your video editing application to Sorenson Squeeze and *then* to Flash MX 2004.

You can read more about Sorenson Squeeze here:

http://www.sorenson.com/

To Embed or Not to Embed

When wanting to integrate video into your Flash project, you essentially have two choices. You can either embed the video in the SWF file, or keep the video (FLV) external and progressively download it *into* the SWF file. In this chapter, you will be using the latter option. You will be progressively downloading an external FLV for the following reasons:

- Progressively downloading and playing external FLV files is less memory intensive. Video files that are embedded into the SWF are loaded into memory all at once, whereas external FLV files are played using cached memory and only use small amounts of memory at a time.
- The aforementioned memory issue that embedded video suffers from also affects performance. If you have a long video clip that is being entirely loaded into the viewer's memory, this can greatly reduce playback performance. Because external FLV files aren't constrained by that limitation, you can easily incorporate long video files into your Flash MX 2004 project without that same performance degradation.
- Video files that are embedded into a SWF *must play back at the same frame rate as that SWF.* However, external FLVs can play at a different frame rate than the SWFs they're appearing in. A SWF can have a frame rate of 21 frames per second (fps), but the FLV displayed within that SWF can be played back at a different frame rate such as 30 fps. Normally, when you shoot some video with a digital video camera (a.k.a. DV cam), it is shot at 29.97 fps. Films that you see at the movie theater, on the other hand, are shot at 24 fps. However, in terms of a frame rate for a Flash MX 2004 project, a frame rate of 30 fps is quite high (more on frame rates in the Note on the next page).

  With an external FLV, you can have the best of both worlds. You can have your SWF file play back at one frame rate–like 21 fps–and your FLV play back at its "native" 29.97 fps. Keep in mind, however, that the higher the frame rate of your FLV, the *more frames there are per second.* The more frames there are per second, the larger the file size of the FLV since there are more frames to store. When compressing your video as an FLV, a good, general guideline to use is half the rate of the original source footage. So if you're starting with footage from a DV cam–which records at 29.97 fps–create an FLV at 15 fps. If you're starting with footage from film–which records at 24 fps–create an FLV at 12 fps.

NOTE | Frame Rates

The following is excerpted from the book *Macromedia Flash MX 2004 Hands-On-Training*, by Rosanna Yeung:

When you set a frame rate in Flash MX 2004, you've set the maximum frame rate for your movie, or how quickly the movie "tries" to play. The actual playback frame rate depends upon several factors, including download speed and the processor speed of the computer viewing the movie. If the frame rate is set higher than the computer can display, the movie will play as fast as its processor will allow. So if you set your frame rate to 200 (which is really high), the average computer will not display the movie at that rate. Also, frames that have more objects, colors, or transparency than others take more time for the computer to render. Thus, the actual frame rate can vary during playback due to the rendering requirements from one frame to another.

Based on all this information, it is recommended that you use a frame rate of at least 12 fps and not more than 25 fps, so that the average computer can display your movie as you intended. A frame rate of 20 to 22 fps seems to work well most of the time. This rate is very similar to that used in motion pictures, which typically play at a frame rate of 24 frames per second.

- Keeping the FLV external allows you to load it in *only* when necessary. By using ActionScript to open an individual connection to download the FLV and then closing that connection when the user leaves that section, you minimize the amount of unnecessary downloading that wastes bandwidth. Even saving a little bandwidth can lower the bandwidth costs for larger corporations.

It's because of these reasons that you're using an external FLV file in this chapter. Unless you're using a simple, short video clip, I would highly recommend *always* progressively downloading external FLV files whenever you need to integrate video content into your Flash MX 2004 projects.

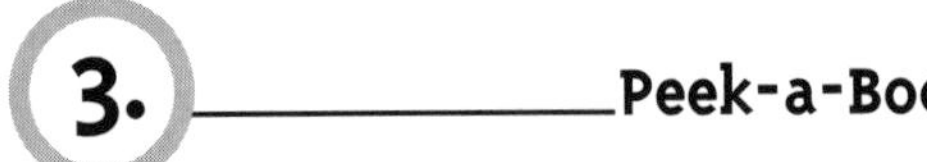

3. Peek-a-Boo

Now that you're finished setting up the **videoContainer** movie clip where the video will appear and be controlled, you need to specify when it should and shouldn't be visible. Currently, if you were to preview your changes, you'd notice that the **videoContainer** movie clip sits directly on top of the **our history** and **our staff** content. Obviously, having a video clip sitting on top of the other subsections would interfere with the viewer reading that content. In this exercise, you will write some ActionScript that controls when the **videoContainer** movie clip instance will and won't be visible.

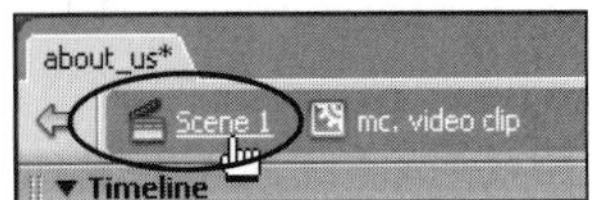

1. Return to **Scene 1** by clicking its tab above the top-left corner of the Timeline.

---

2. Single-click **Keyframe 1** in layer **a** and open the **Actions** panel (**F9**).

*The first step is to write an action that tells the **videoContainer** movie clip–where the video and all of its related graphics are nested–to initially be hidden. When the viewer first arrives at the About Us section, you don't want the video content to be visible. The viewer is going to have to click the **(video)** submenu option to make it appear.*

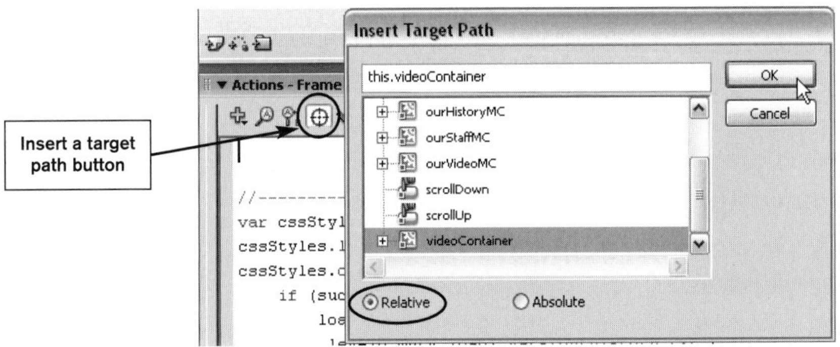

3. Scroll to the very top of the Actions panel, and click at the very beginning of the topmost line, `//----------------<load CSS>----------------\\`. Press **Enter** (Windows) or **Return** (Mac) twice to create two line breaks. Then, click the new, topmost empty line break and click the **Insert a target path** button. In the **Insert Target Path** window that appears, scroll down until you find **videoContainer**, and click it to select it. Last, make sure the **Relative** radio button is selected and click **OK**.

*This will insert the path to videoContainer, **`this.videoContainer`**. Next, you need to tell the videoContainer movie clip instance to turn its visibility off.*

```
this.videoContainer._visible = false;

//-------------<load CSS>--------------\\
var cssStyles:TextField.StyleSheet = new TextField.StyleSheet ();
cssStyles.load ("styles/styles.css");
```

4. After **this.videoContainer**, type the following:

._visible = false;

*As you have seen before, **_visible** is a property that you can set for text fields, buttons, movie clips, and even entire levels. In this case, you're simple instructing the **_visible** property of the **videoContainer** movie clip instance to be **false** (not visible).*

***Note:** Don't forget to add the period (.) after **videoContainer** and before **_visible**.*

Before you continue, you need to check the changes you've made up to this point to make sure that everything is working properly.

---

5. Save your changes by choosing **File > Save** or by using the keyboard shortcut **Ctrl+S** (Windows) or **Cmd+S** (Mac).

*Now, because the About Us section relies on **LoadVars** and **MovieClipLoader** objects that reside in **master.swf**, you need to preview **about_us.swf** from within **master.swf**.*

---

6. Publish a SWF from **about_us.fla** by pressing the keyboard shortcut **Shift+F12** (on both Windows and Mac).

---

7. Choose **File > Open Recent**. If you see **master** in the open recent list, select it to have Flash MX 2004 open it for you. Otherwise, choose **File > Open**, and in the **Open** dialog box, navigate to your **Desktop > la_eyeworks > site** folder and double-click **master.fla** to open it.

*The last time you modified **master.fla** was in Chapter 8,* "Building a Preloader," *when you added ActionScript to the **myMCL MovieClipLoader** object that managed the preloading of SWF and JPG files. Prior to that, you modified some ActionScript on **Keyframe 10** in **master.fla** so that **frames.swf** initially loads. In doing that, you commented out an action that loads **about_us.swf**. So that **about_us.swf** will load, you need to comment out the action that loads **frames.swf** and uncomment the action that loads **about_us.swf**.*

---

8. In **master.fla**, single-click **Keyframe 10** in layer **a** to select it, and open the **Actions** panel.

```
stop();
// myMCL.loadClip("splash.swf", 5);
myMCL.loadClip("about_us.swf", 5);
// myMCL.loadClip("frames.swf", 5);
```

9. Add two forward slashes at the beginning of the `myMCL.loadClip("frames.swf", 5);` line and *remove* the two forward slashes at the beginning of the `myMCL.loadClip("about_us.swf", 5);` line.

*As you have seen quite a few times before, by adding two forward slashes before the action that loads **frames.swf**, it prevents that action from being compiled, and thereby executed, when **master.swf** is played. By* removing *the two forward slashes before the action that loads **about_us.swf**, it* allows *that action to be compiled and executed when **master.swf** runs.*

---

10. Save the changes you've made to **master.fla** by pressing the keyboard shortcut **Ctrl+S** (Windows) or **Cmd+S** (Mac).

---

11. Preview **master.fla** by typing the keyboard shortcut **Ctrl+Enter** (Windows) or **Cmd+Return** (Mac).

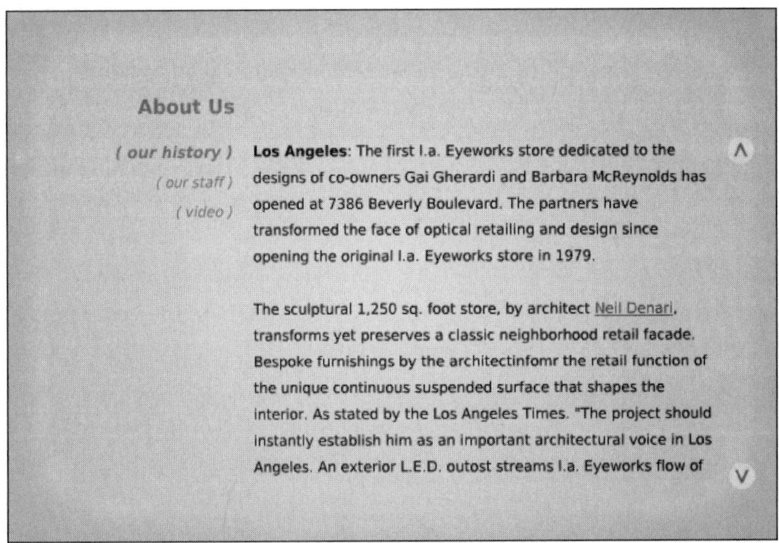

*When **about_us.swf** loads into **master.swf**, you'll know you've done everything right if the **videoContainer** movie clip instance does* not *appear. However, if you click the **(video)** option in the submenu, you'll quickly notice that nothing happens.*

In the rest of this exercise, you will create one function that shows *the **videoContainer** movie clip instance and another function to* hide *it. These two functions will be executed when the viewer enters and leaves the video subsection in the **About Us** section.*

---

12. Close the **Preview** window and close **master.fla**. You won't need to access **master.fla** again in this chapter. In **about_us.fla**, make sure you still have **Keyframe 1** selected in layer **a** and that you still have the **Actions** panel open.

The first step is to create the two functions you will need to reveal and hide the ***videoContainer*** *movie clip instance. Why a function? Because you want a set of actions to be executed only when a certain event happens–like when the viewer clicks the* ***(video)*** *submenu option or another submenu option. By putting those actions within a function, those actions will not be executed until you call the function. Also, you're going to want to perform a group of actions multiple times. When the viewer clicks* ***(our history)*** *or* ***(our staff)****, you're going to want the same set of actions to be executed. By putting all those actions within a function, you can keep all the necessary actions in one place without having to duplicate or repeat those actions for every place you need to use them.*

```
    this.ourVideo.setTextFormat(btnDisable);
    this.enabled = false;
}
//-------------</our video option>--------------\\
```

13. Scroll down to the bottom of the **Actions** panel. Click at the end of the comment line **//---------------</our video option>----------------** and press **Enter** (Windows) or **Return** (Mac) twice to create two line breaks. Then, click that bottommost line break.

```
}
//-------------</our video option>--------------\\

//-------------<video activate>--------------\\

function videoActivate() {

}

//-------------</video activate>--------------\\
```

14. Create the first function by typing the following four lines:

```
//-------------<video activate>-------------\\
function videoActivate() {
}
//-------------</video activate>-------------\\
```

*When typing the ActionScript, make sure to type an additional line break between each of the lines. That way, there's some space between the comment lines and the function, as well as between the function curly braces (***{ }***).*

Next, create the function that will eventually deactivate *(hide) the video player.*

15. Select the actions you created in Step 14, **right-click** (Windows) or **Ctrl+click** (Mac) those actions, and from the contextual menu that appears, choose **Copy**.

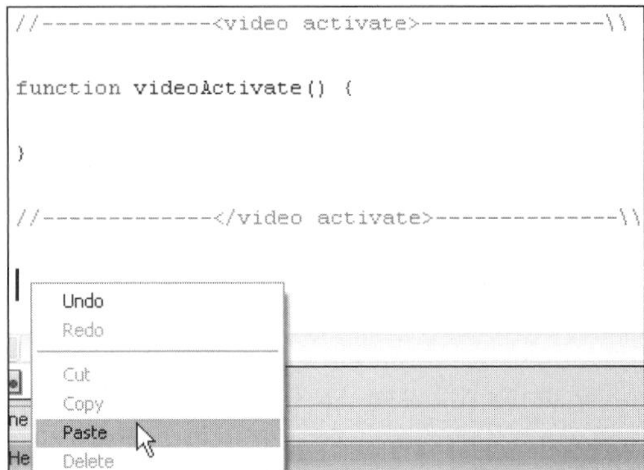

16. Click at the end of the **`//-------------</video activate>-------------\\`** line, and press **Enter** (Windows) or **Return** (Mac) twice to create two line breaks. Then, **right-click** (Windows) or **Ctrl+click** (Mac) that second line break you just created. From the contextual menu that appears, choose **Paste**. This will paste a copy of the **`videoActivate`** function–and its associated comments–two lines below the original.

```
//-------------<video activate>--------------\\

function videoActivate() {

}

//-------------</video activate>--------------\\

//-------------<video deactivate>--------------\\

function videoDeactivate() {

}

//-------------</video deactivate>--------------\\
```

17. In the copied **videoActivate** script, change the word "activate" in the open and closed comment lines to "deactivate". Also, make sure to change the function name to **videoDeactivate**.

Now that you have the functions set up, you can start filling them with the appropriate actions.

Before you can start writing the actions, however, you need to figure out what you want to happen when viewers click the ***(video)*** *submenu option and what should happen when they click another submenu option such as* ***(our history)*** *or* ***(our staff)****. When viewers click the video submenu option, they want to see the video, and therefore the following should happen: 1) The Scroll Down and Scroll Up buttons–which allow the viewer to scroll through the* ***our history*** *and* ***our staff*** *information–should disappear. 2) Any text that is currently being displayed in the* ***loadedInfo*** *text field should be cleared. 3) The video content (****videoContainer****) should become visible. Later, you will also add actions to create additional functionality, such as the video to start playing, but for now, this will enable the video content to display while the content for the other subsections becomes hidden.*

Essentially, the opposite should happen when viewers click one of the other submenu options. If they click ***(our history)*** *or* ***(our staff)****, the video content should disappear, the Scroll Down and Scroll Up buttons should reappear, and the requested content should load.*

First, start by writing the four actions that will be executed when the viewer requests the video.

```
//-------------<video activate>-------------\\

function videoActivate() {
    scrollDown._visible = false;
    scrollUp._visible = false;
    loadedInfo.text = "";
    videoContainer._visible = true;
}

//-------------</video activate>-------------\\
```

18. Click the empty line break between the **`function videoActivate() {`** line and the closed curly brace (**}**). Then, write four actions by typing the following:

```
scrollDown._visible = false;
scrollUp._visible = false;
loadedInfo.text = "";
videoContainer._visible = true;
```

*As you can see, the actions are fairly straightforward. The two actions **`scrollDown._visible = false;`** and **`scrollUp._visible = false;`** just tell the Scroll Down and Scroll Up buttons to hide. **`loadedInfo.text = "";`** inserts nothing into the **`loadedInfo`** text field, where the **our history** and **our staff** text is displayed. By inserting nothing into the text field, it will clear any text that is currently in that field. Last, **`videoContainer._visible = true;`** simply instructs the **`videoContainer`** movie clip instance, where the video content is nested, to display itself. This is the "opposite" action to the one you created in Steps 3 and 4 in this exercise.*

*Now that you've specified what should happen when the viewer requests the video content, you should also specify what should happen when the viewer clicks one of the other submenu options such as **our history** or **our staff**.*

```
//-------------<video deactivate>-------------\\

function videoDeactivate() {
    loadedInfo.scroll = 0;
    scrollDown._visible = true;
    scrollUp._visible = true;
    videoContainer._visible = false;
}

//-------------</video deactivate>-------------\\
```

19. Click the empty line break between the **`function videoDeactivate() {`** line and the closed curly brace (**}**). Then, write four actions by typing the following:

```
loadedInfo.scroll = 0;
scrollDown._visible = true;
scrollUp._visible = true;
videoContainer._visible = false;
```

*Three of those four actions are essentially opposites of what you just wrote in Step 18. When the viewer wants to leave the video subsection and navigate to another subsection such as **our history** or **our staff**, the Scroll Down and Scroll Up buttons both reappear, and the **videoContainer** movie clip then disappears. The remaining action, `loadedInfo.scroll = 0;`, instructs the `loadedInfo` text field on the Stage to set its `scroll` property back to **0**. This action is here because if the viewer–for example–scrolls through the **our history** subsection, clicks the **video** subsection option, and then goes back to another subsection such as **our history** or **our staff**, the text that loads into the `loadedInfo` text field would inherit that last scroll position. In other words, if the viewer scrolls halfway down a block of text in the **our history** subsection, goes to the **video** section, and then returns to any other subsection that inserted text into the `loadedInfo` text field, that text would automatically scroll itself to the point where the reader left off. `loadedInfo.scroll = 0;` sets the `scroll` property of the `loadedInfo` text field back to **0**, so if the reader returns to either **our history** or **our staff**, the text will load and display with the first line visible at the top of the field.*

If you were to preview your movie at this point, you would see...nothing. There would be no changes from when you previewed it last. Remember, the `videoActivate` and `videoDeactivate` functions you just so lovingly crafted won't automatically execute themselves. They need to be told when *they should perform. Well, the `videoActivate` function, which, *ahem*, activates the video, should be executed when the viewer requests the video; when he or she clicks the **(video)** submenu option. The `videoDeactivate` function, on the other hand, should be executed when the viewer* leaves *the video subsection. So when the viewer clicks the **(our history)** or **(our staff)** submenu options, the video content should "deactivate."*

*You might also be wondering what happens if the viewer clicks one of the main menu options such as **frames**, **locations**, and so forth. "Shouldn't we specify what happens then?," you might be wondering. If you think back to how the separate sections are displayed, you might remember that each section–**about us**, **video**, **locations**, and so forth–are all loaded into **master.swf** into `_level5`. So when the viewer clicks another main menu button, the entire **About Us** section is cleared, and a new section loads into its vacated place. So no, you don't need to specify what happens when the viewer clicks one of the main menu options.*

In the next few steps, you are going to write the actions that specify which function gets executed and from where.

```
//-------------<our video option>--------------\\
this.ourVideoMC.onRollOver = function () {
    this.ourVideo.setTextFormat(btnDisable);
}
this.ourVideoMC.onRollOut = function () {
    this.ourVideo.setTextFormat(btnEnable);
}
this.ourVideoMC.onRelease = function () {
    reEnableOptions();
    this.ourVideo.setTextFormat(btnDisable);
    this.enabled = false;
    videoActivate();
}
//-------------</our video option>--------------\\
```

20. Within the **this.ourVideoMC.onRelease** function (shown in the code above), click at the end of the **this.enabled = false;** action, press **Enter** (Windows) or **Return** (Mac) once to create a line break, and type the following:

videoActivate();

*This action simply says that when the viewer clicks the **(video)** submenu option, execute the **videoActivate** function. The **videoActivate** function, of course, displays the video content and hides the other subsection content.*

```
//-------------<our staff option>--------------\\
this.ourStaffMC.onRollOver = function () {
    this.ourStaff.setTextFormat(btnDisable);
}
this.ourStaffMC.onRollOut = function () {
    this.ourStaff.setTextFormat(btnEnable);
}
this.ourStaffMC.onRelease = function () {
    reEnableOptions();
    this.ourStaff.setTextFormat(btnDisable);
    this.enabled = false;
    _level0.myLV.load("vars/ourStaff.txt");
    videoDeactivate();
}
//-------------</our staff option>--------------\\
```

21. For the **(our staff)** submenu option, click at the end of the **_level0.myLV.load("vars/ourStaff.txt");** action, press **Enter** (Windows) or **Return** (Mac) to create a line break, and execute the **videoDeactivate** function by typing the following:

videoDeactivate();

*So when the viewer clicks the **(our staff)** submenu option, the video content is hidden, the Scroll Down and Scroll Up buttons reappear, the scroll property gets reset for the **loadedInfo** text field, and the **our staff** information is loaded.*

*The last step is to execute the **videoDeactivate** function when the viewer clicks the **(our history)** submenu option as well.*

```
//-------------<our history option>--------------\\
this.ourHistoryMC.onRollOver = function () {
    this.ourHistory.setTextFormat(btnDisable);
}
this.ourHistoryMC.onRollOut = function () {
    this.ourHistory.setTextFormat(btnEnable);
}
this.ourHistoryMC.onRelease = function () {
    reEnableOptions();
    this.ourHistory.setTextFormat(btnDisable);
    this.enabled = false;
    _level0.myLV.load("vars/ourHistory.txt");
    videoDeactivate();
}
//-------------</our history option>--------------\\
```

22. For the **(our history)** submenu option, click at the end of the **_level0.myLV.load("vars/ourHistory.txt");** action, press **Enter** (Windows) or **Return** (Mac) once to create a line break, and type the following:

videoDeactivate();

Now that you've specified when and where the video content should and shouldn't be visible, it's time to test your changes.

23. Save the changes you've made to **about_us.fla** by pressing the keyboard shortcut **Ctrl+S** (Windows) or **Cmd+S** (Mac).

24. Publish an updated SWF by pressing **Shift+F12** (on both Windows and Mac).

25. Hide or Minimize Flash MX 2004. Then on your hard drive, navigate to your **Desktop > la_eyeworks > site** folder and double-click **master.swf** to open it in the stand-alone Flash Player 7.

26. When the Flash Player 7 window opens and the **About Us** section appears, click the **(video)** submenu option.

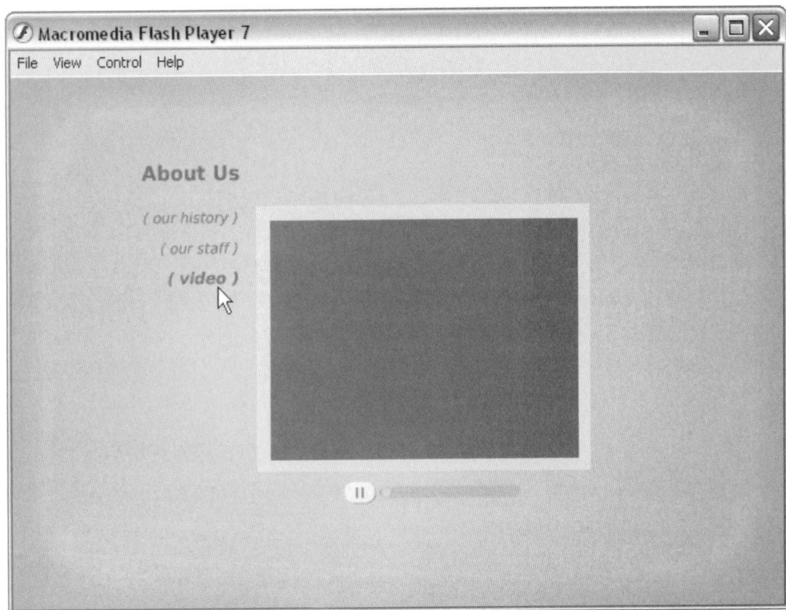

When you click the ***(video)*** *submenu option, you'll see that the default* ***our history*** *text, the Scroll Up button, and the Scroll Down button all disappear. In their place will appear the* ***videoContainer*** *movie clip instance! Of course, the video doesn't play yet because you still have to write all the ActionScript to get it to work. But the first part of just getting the video content to display while hiding the other* ***About Us*** *content works like a champ!*

Now you need to make sure that the video content disappears when the viewer clicks one of the other submenu options.

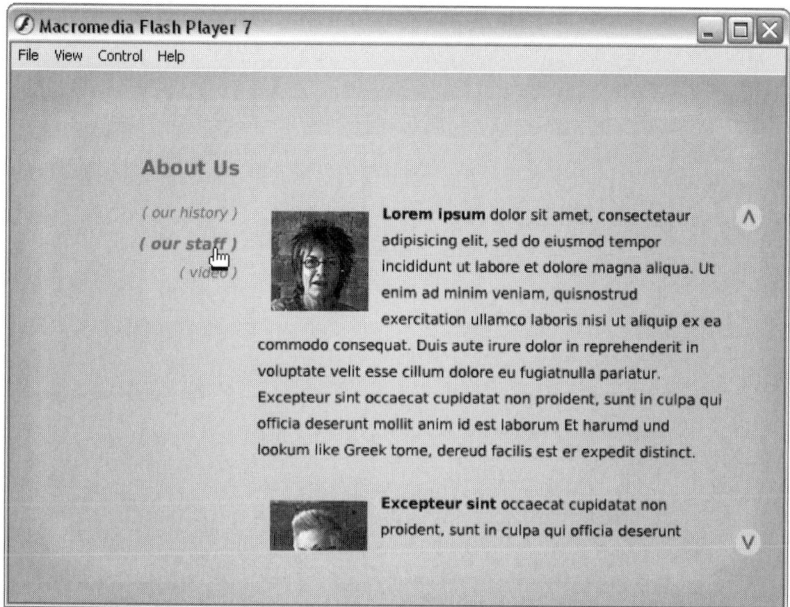

27. Click the **(our staff)** submenu option. When you do, you'll notice the video content disappear and the **our staff** content appear in its place. Fabuloso!

You now have a working video subsection that displays the appropriate content when the viewer clicks the video subsection option and hides the appropriate content when the viewer navigates to another subsection.

---

28. When you're finished verifying that your changes work as intended, close the stand-alone Flash Player 7 window and return to **about_us.fla** in Flash MX 2004.

Now that the video content appears when requested, in the next exercise you're going to write the ActionScript that progressively downloads and plays the video when the ***video*** *section is displayed.*

4. Loading and Playing the Video

In this exercise, you will learn to use the **NetConnection** and **NetStream** classes to progressively download and play an external FLV file. Buckle up because you've gone too far to stop now! ;-)

Because you don't want the actions that load and play the external FLV to automatically be executed when **about_us.swf** first loads, you're going to put them in a function.

```
    videoContainer._visible = false;
}

//-------------</video deactivate>-------------\\

//-------------<video>-------------\\

function initializeVideo() {

}

//-------------</video>-------------\\
```

1. Click at the end of the very bottom line, **//-------------</video deactivate>-------------**, press **Enter** (Windows) or **Return** (Mac) twice to create two line breaks, and type the following:

```
//-------------<video>-------------\\

function initializeVideo() {

}

//-------------</video>-------------\\
```

Be sure to include an additional line break between each action and comment. This will not only give you some visual space between the actions to make them easier to read, but it will also give you an empty line break within the function where you can begin to type actions.

You will be creating three separate objects within this function: a ***NetConnection*** *object to provide a connection to download the FLV, a* ***NetStream*** *object to control the playback of the FLV (the* ***NetStream*** *object is to FLVs what the* ***Sound*** *object is to MP3s), and a* ***LoadVars*** *object to load the variable TXT file that stores the total running time of the FLV. Because you will be using objects within a function, you will first need to instantiate (create) the objects outside of the function so you can target them with ActionScript. This is the identical concept you learned in Chapter 10, "MP3 Player," when you instantiated the* ***bgMusak*** *sound object outside of the* ***playMusak*** *function.*

//-------------<video>--------------\\
var myNetConn:NetConnection;
var myNetStream:NetStream;
var videoLV:LoadVars;
function initializeVideo() {
}
//-------------</video>--------------\\

2. Click at the end of the opening **video** comment line, **//-------------<video>-------------**, press **Enter** (Windows) or **Return** (Mac) twice to create two line breaks, and instantiate the three objects by typing the following:

```
var myNetConn:NetConnection;
var myNetStream:NetStream;
var videoLV:LoadVars;
```

These three actions, from top to bottom, create a new ***NetConnection*** *object with an instance name of* ***myNetConn****, a new* ***NetStream*** *object with an instance name of* ***myNetStream****, and a new* ***LoadVars*** *object with an instance name of* ***videoLV****. In the* ***initializeVideo*** *function, you will use all three of those objects to create the script that will progressively download the FLV.*

Although there are approximately 10 actions involved in the progressive downloading of the external FLV and in the loading of an external variable to track the total running time of the FLV, the actions and their order are fairly formulaic. In other words, after you've written these actions once, you can easily copy and paste them to a completely different project and have them work with only a few minor changes.

```
//-------------<video>--------------\\

var myNetConn:NetConnection;
var myNetStream:NetStream;
var videoLV:LoadVars;

function initializeVideo() {
    myNetConn = new NetConnection();
}

//-------------</video>--------------\\
```

3. Click the empty line break between the **`function initializeVideo() {`** line and the closed curly brace (**}**), and create a new **`NetConnection`** object by typing the following:

`myNetConn = new NetConnection();`

*As its name implies, a **`NetConnection`** object instructs Flash MX 2004 to open a new network connection. Although it sounds like you can do a lot with it, the **`NetConnection`** object is a specific connection for progressively downloading an FLV locally (off of your hard drive or removable media), over an HTTP connection (off of a Web server), or streamed off of a Flash Communication Server. The **`NetConnection`** object was also available in Flash MX, but it only allowed you to make a connection to the Flash Communication Server for streaming video. But now in Flash MX 2004, you can use the **`NetConnection`** and **`NetStream`** objects to progressively download FLV files locally or over HTTP without needing the Flash Communication Server.*

*Once you've created a **`NetConnection`** object, the next step is to use the **`connect`** constructor to open a connection.*

```
//-------------<video>--------------\\

var myNetConn:NetConnection;
var myNetStream:NetStream;
var videoLV:LoadVars;

function initializeVideo() {
    myNetConn = new NetConnection();
    myNetConn.connect(null);
}

//-------------</video>--------------\\
```

4. Click at the end of the **`myNetConn = new NetConnection();`** line, press **Enter** (Windows) or **Return** (Mac) once to create a line break, and type the following:

`myNetConn.connect(null);`

*This action simply opens up a local connection for you to progressively download a local or remote FLV. The **null** parameter that you see is a required parameter. You must pass the **null** parameter for the **connect** constructor to work correctly. When used in conjunction with the Flash Communication Server, instead of the **null** parameter, you would pass the hostname and server address as a parameter (such as **rtmp://myApplicationInstance**).*

*Now that you've created and set up a new **NetConnection** object, you need to create a new **NetStream** object. As was briefly mentioned earlier in this exercise, the **NetStream** object is to FLVs what the **Sound** object is to MP3s. The **NetStream** object allows you to monitor and control various aspects of a progressively downloading or streaming FLV such as pause, play, tracking of the downloading progress, and so forth. The **NetStream** object, which you've already assigned the instance name of **myNetStream**, uses the **NetConnection** object to download or stream FLVs through.*

*The first step is to create a new NetStream object that you pass the instance name of a **NetConnection** object to.*

```
//-------------<video>--------------\\

var myNetConn:NetConnection;
var myNetStream:NetStream;
var videoLV:LoadVars;

function initializeVideo() {
    myNetConn = new NetConnection();
    myNetConn.connect(null);
    myNetStream = new NetStream(myNetConn);
}

//-------------</video>--------------\\
```

5. Click at the end of the **myNetConn.connect(null);** line, press **Enter** (Windows) or **Return** (Mac) to create a line break, and type the following:

myNetStream = new NetStream(myNetConn);

*Now, whenever you want to find out what your FLV is up to, or to tell it to do something, you can refer to it by its **NetStream** object instance name, **myNetStream**.*

*Next, you need to tell the **Video** object that you created in Exercise 2, **myVideo**, to receive the video source from the **myNetStream** object.*

```
//-------------<video>--------------\\

var myNetConn:NetConnection;
var myNetStream:NetStream;
var videoLV:LoadVars;

function initializeVideo() {
    myNetConn = new NetConnection();
    myNetConn.connect(null);
    myNetStream = new NetStream(myNetConn);
    videoContainer.myVideo.attachVideo(myNetStream);
}

//-------------</video>--------------\\
```

6. Click at the end of the **`myNetStream = new NetStream(myNetConn);`** line, press **Enter** (Windows) or **Return** (Mac) once to create a line break, and type the following:

`videoContainer.myVideo.attachVideo(myNetStream);`

*This action instructs the **Video** object **myVideo**, which is embedded within the **videoContainer** movie clip instance, to receive the video from the **myNetStream** object.*

*And there you have, in its barest essence, the nearly completed script to progressively download an FLV into the **myVideo** video object. The only action left that's needed to actually begin the progressive download of an FLV is the action that instructs the **NetStream** object* which *FLV to download. Before you write that action, however, there are a few other actions that you need to incorporate into this script.*

*When an FLV file begins to progressively download into the **myVideo** video object, it will start playing as soon as one-tenth of a second of video has been downloaded. For broadband users, this is a great thing because it means that they can watch the video as it is downloading. They don't have to wait for the whole video to download before they can start watching it. However, for a viewer on a slow Internet connection such as a 56k modem, even though the video will start playing as soon as one-tenth of a second of it has been downloaded, it will stop playing shortly thereafter. The problem is that a viewer with a slow Internet connection is watching the video faster than it can be downloaded. This means that when the video catches up to what has been downloaded, it will stop and wait for another one-tenth of a second to download, and then it will start playing again. Start. Stop. Start. You get the idea.*

Luckily, Flash has provided a method that allows you to specify how many seconds of video the Flash Player 7 should buffer (pre-download) before it begins to play. Although this buffer time is one that I suggest you modify to suit your own needs, for the L.A. Eyeworks site you are going to initially set the buffer to five seconds. This means that the viewer has to wait until five seconds of video have been downloaded before it begins playing. By modifying the buffer to fit the specifics of your video for your own projects, you can minimize the stopping and starting that slow Internet users experience when viewing video content.

```
function initializeVideo() {
    myNetConn = new NetConnection();
    myNetConn.connect(null);
    myNetStream = new NetStream(myNetConn);
    videoContainer.myVideo.attachVideo(myNetStream);
    myNetStream.setBufferTime(5);
}

//-------------</video>--------------\\
```

7. Click at the end of the **videoContainer.myVideo.attachVideo(myNetStream);** line, press **Enter** (Windows) or **Return** (Mac) to create a line break, and type the following:

myNetStream.setBufferTime(5);

*This action–as you can probably guess–instructs the **myNetStream** object to set its buffer time to five seconds.*

At this point, you could write the simple action that loads the FLV file and call it a night. However, in Exercise 6 you will be building a playback slider that animates across a bar as the video is playing. When the slider gets to the end of the bar, the video is over. To be able to construct a playback slider like that, you need to know two things. You need to know how much of the FLV has played up until that point, and you need to know the total running time of the FLV. When you have those two numbers, you can figure out everything else that you need.

*As you saw in the **music_progress.mov** movie in Chapter 10, "MP3 Player," you used the **duration** property of the **Sound** object, and a little math, to calculate the total running time of the progressively downloading MP3. However, the **NetStream** object does not have an equivalent **duration** property. When progressively downloading an FLV file, there's no way to calculate the total running time of the FLV unless the FLV was compressed using the Flash Video Exporter, and unless you're receiving that video with the latest version of the Media Components in Flash MX Professional 2004. Because of that, in this chapter you will be loading the total running time from an external TXT file using a **LoadVars** object. Then, once you have that number, you can use it to animate the playback progress slider, which you will build in Exercise 6.*

*First, you need to create a new **LoadVars** object to handle the loading of the external TXT file. Because you will want this **LoadVars** object to perform a custom action when the variable has completed loading, you cannot use the **LoadVars** object on **master.swf**. Instead, you will create a bare-bones **LoadVars** object in **about_us.fla** to handle the loading.*

```
//-------------<video>-------------\\

var myNetConn:NetConnection;
var myNetStream:NetStream;
var videoLV:LoadVars;

function initializeVideo() {
    myNetConn = new NetConnection();
    myNetConn.connect(null);
    myNetStream = new NetStream(myNetConn);
    videoContainer.myVideo.attachVideo(myNetStream);
    myNetStream.setBufferTime(5);

    videoLV = new LoadVars();
    videoLV.onLoad = function (success) {
        if (success) {
            videoActivate();
        }
    }
}

//-------------</video>-------------\\
```

8. Click at the end of the **myNetStream.setBufferTime(5);** action, press **Enter** (Windows) or **Return** (Mac) twice to create two line breaks, and type the following:

```
videoLV = new LoadVars();
videoLV.onLoad = function (success) {
    if (success) {
        videoActivate();
    }
}
```

*As you have seen quite a few times before, this creates a new variable with an instance name of **videoLV**, which you instantiated and strict typed outside of the **initializeVideo** function earlier, and assigns an **onLoad** event handler, which executes the **videoActivate** function if the variables are successfully downloaded.*

*Earlier, you added the action that triggers the **videoActivate** action when the viewer clicks the **(video)** submenu option. However, you don't actually want the video to immediately start playing when the viewer clicks the **video** submenu option. Instead, you want the video to wait until the variable TXT file, which contains the total running time for the FLV, has been completely downloaded before playing. That way, when the FLV starts playing, it has the total running time number it needs to animate the playback progress slider. So yes, you will need to change the action assigned to the **video** submenu option so the **initializeVideo** function is executed instead of the **videoActivate** function. As you just scripted, the **initializeVideo** function will automatically trigger the **videoActivate** function when the variable file has been completely downloaded.*

*Before you change the action assigned to the **video** submenu option, you should first finish writing the **LoadVars** script. As yet, you haven't specified the TXT file from which you'll retrieve the variables. In the next few steps, you're going to see where that TXT file is located and what is inside of it.*

9. Save the changes you've made to **about_us.fla** by choosing **File > Save** (**Ctrl+S** [Windows] or **Cmd+S** [Mac]).

10. Hide or minimize Flash MX 2004, and on your hard drive navigate to your **Desktop > la_eyeworks > site > vars** folder.

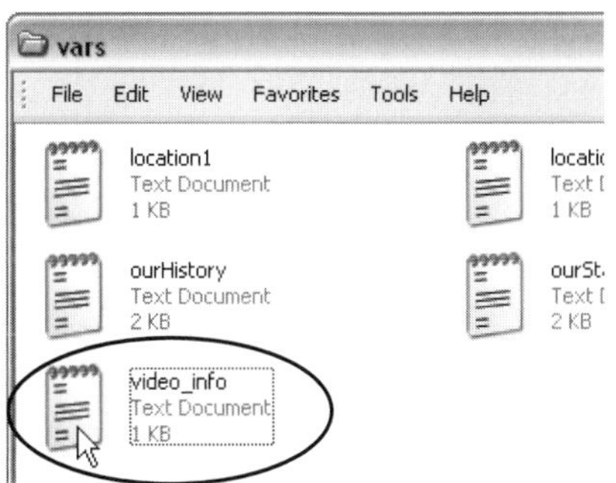

11. In the **vars** folder is a text file titled **video_info.txt**. Open it in a simple text editor such as **Notepad** (Windows), **BBEdit** (Mac), or **TextEdit** (Mac).

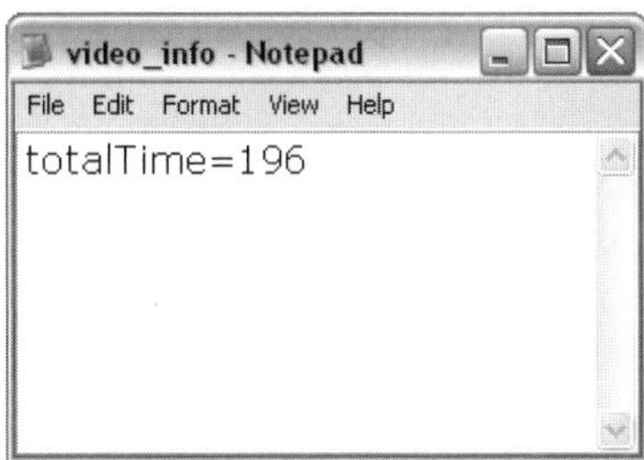

12. Inside the **video_info.txt** text file, you'll notice that there's just one variable in there, **`totalTime`**, with a value of **196**, which is the total running time, in seconds, of the FLV that you will be progressively downloading. Although you are loading this variable now, you won't actually be utilizing it until Exercise 6.

13. Close your text editor and return to **about_us.fla** in Flash MX 2004. Then, make sure you have **Keyframe 1** selected in layer **a** and that you have the **Actions** panel open.

```
//-------------<video>--------------\\

var myNetConn:NetConnection;
var myNetStream:NetStream;
var videoLV:LoadVars;

function initializeVideo() {
    myNetConn = new NetConnection();
    myNetConn.connect(null);
    myNetStream = new NetStream(myNetConn);
    videoContainer.myVideo.attachVideo(myNetStream);
    myNetStream.setBufferTime(5);

    videoLV = new LoadVars();
    videoLV.onLoad = function (success) {
        if (success) {
            videoActivate();
        }
    }
    videoLV.load("vars/video_info.txt");
}

//-------------</video>--------------\\
```

Click after this closed curly brace and press Enter (Windows) or Return (Mac) once

14. Click after the closed curly brace that ends the **videoLV.onLoad** event handler (highlighted in the code above), press **Enter** (Windows) or **Return** (Mac) once to create a line break, and type the following:

videoLV.load("vars/video_info.txt");

*This action, as you have seen before, loads the variables in the **video_info.txt** file into the **videoLV LoadVars** object.*

*Next, you need to alter one of the actions assigned to the **(video)** submenu option so that, when clicked, it executes the **initializeVideo** function instead of the **videoActivate** function.*

```
//-------------<our video option>--------------\\
this.ourVideoMC.onRollOver = function () {
    this.ourVideo.setTextFormat(btnDisable);
}
this.ourVideoMC.onRollOut = function () {
    this.ourVideo.setTextFormat(btnEnable);
}
this.ourVideoMC.onRelease = function () {
    reEnableOptions();
    this.ourVideo.setTextFormat(btnDisable);
    this.enabled = false;
    initializeVideo();
}
//-------------</our video option>--------------\\
```

15. In the **Actions** panel, scroll up until you reach the **ourVideoMC** mouse event actions. Then, under the **this.ourVideoMC.onRelease** function, change the action **videoActivate();** to instead read **initializeVideo();**.

*So now, when the viewer clicks the **(video)** submenu option, instead of the video just immediately starting to download and play, it will execute the **initializeVideo** function. The **initializeVideo** function sets up the required **NetConnection** and **NetStream** objects, downloads the variable that stores the FLV's total running time, and then once that variable has been* completely *downloaded, it triggers the **videoActivate** function, which shows the video content. When the video content is displayed, this is also the same time that you want to trigger the downloading and playing of the FLV.*

First, before you load the FLV, you should have a good idea of where *the FLV is located.*

16. Hide or minimize Flash MX 2004, and on your hard drive navigate to your **Desktop > la_eyeworks > resources > video** folder.

*In the **video** folder, you'll notice there are two files, **la_eyeworks_video.flv** and **LAEyeworks_480.mov**. If you'd like, you can open the MOV file in the QuickTime Player to watch the original 480 x 360 video. But the file you're really interested in is the one that you will be progressively downloading into **about_us.swf**, the **la_eyeworks_video.flv** file. As you can see in the screen shot above, its file size weighs in at a fairly hefty 4.2 MB. But considering that this video–even though it was scaled down in size when it was compressed to an FLV–is three minutes and sixteen seconds long, that's not a bad file size.*

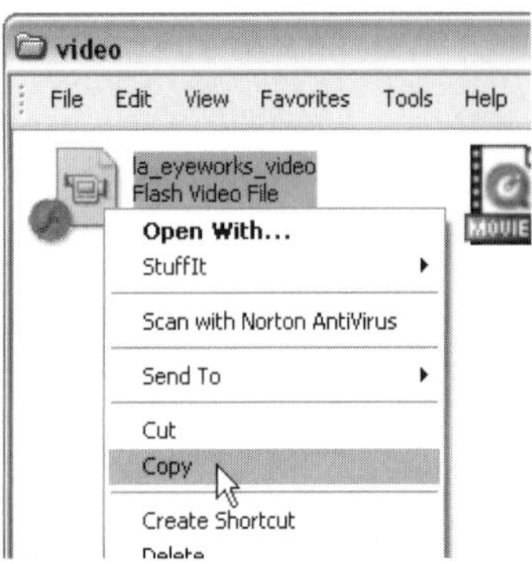

17. On Windows, **right-click** the **la_eyeworks_video** file, and from the contextual menu choose **Copy**. On Mac OS X, **Ctrl+click** the **la_eyeworks_video.flv** file, and from the contextual menu choose **Copy "la_eyeworks_video.flv"**.

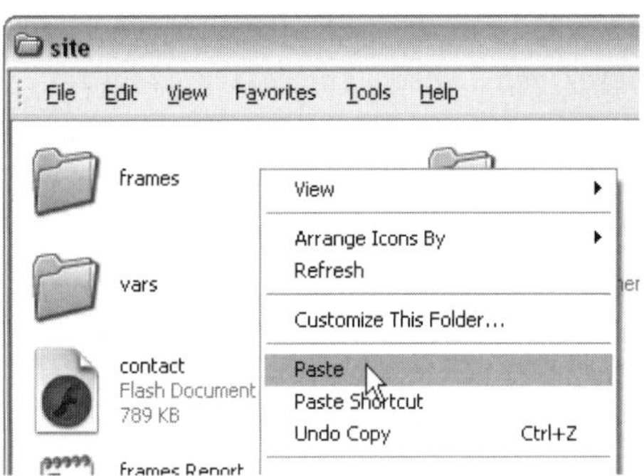

18. Then, on the hard drive, navigate to your **Desktop > la_eyeworks > site** folder. On Windows, **right-click** an empty space in the **site** folder. From the contextual menu that appears, choose **Paste**. On Mac OS X, **Ctrl+click** an empty space in the **site** folder, and from the contextual menu choose **Paste item**.

*This will copy the **la_eyeworks_video.flv** file into the **site** folder where the rest of the site files are.*

---

19. Return to **about_us.fla** in Flash MX 2004. Make sure you have **Keyframe 1** selected in layer **a** and that you have the **Actions** panel open.

```
//------------<video activate>-------------\\

function videoActivate() {
    scrollDown._visible = false;
    scrollUp._visible = false;
    loadedInfo.text = "";
    videoContainer._visible = true;
    myNetStream.play("la_eyeworks_video.flv");
}

//------------</video activate>-------------\\
```

20. In the **Actions** panel, scroll until you find the **videoActivate** function. Then, click at the end of the **videoContainer._visible = true;** action, press **Enter** (Windows) or **Return** (Mac) to create a line break, and type the following:

myNetStream.play("la_eyeworks_video.flv");

*When the **videoActivate** function is executed, this action will instruct the **myNetStream** object that you created earlier in this exercise to begin progressively downloading and playing the FLV file **la_eyeworks_video.flv**. Because that FLV resides in the same directory as the rest of your site SWF files, you don't need to specify a path to the FLV; you can just type its name to load and play it. If you were building a site that utilized several FLVs, it would help to keep your site files organized by creating a separate folder to store them.*

Whew*. Congratulations! You've just finished writing the ActionScript required to progressively download and play an external FLV. You also wrote a **LoadVars object into your **initializeVideo** function that loads the total running time of the FLV. In Exercise 6, you will use that number to construct the playback progress slider.*

Before you continue to the next exercise, however, you should save and test your work to make sure everything is working correctly.

---

21. Save the changes you've made to **about_us.fla** by choosing **File > Save** (**Ctrl+S** [Windows] or **Cmd+S** [Mac]).

---

22. Publish an updated SWF by pressing **Shift+F12** (on both Windows and Mac).

---

23. Hide or minimize Flash MX 2004, and on your hard drive, navigate to your **Desktop > la_eyeworks > site** folder. Double-click **master.swf** to open it in the stand-alone Flash Player 7.

---

24. When the **About Us** section appears, click the **(video)** submenu option.

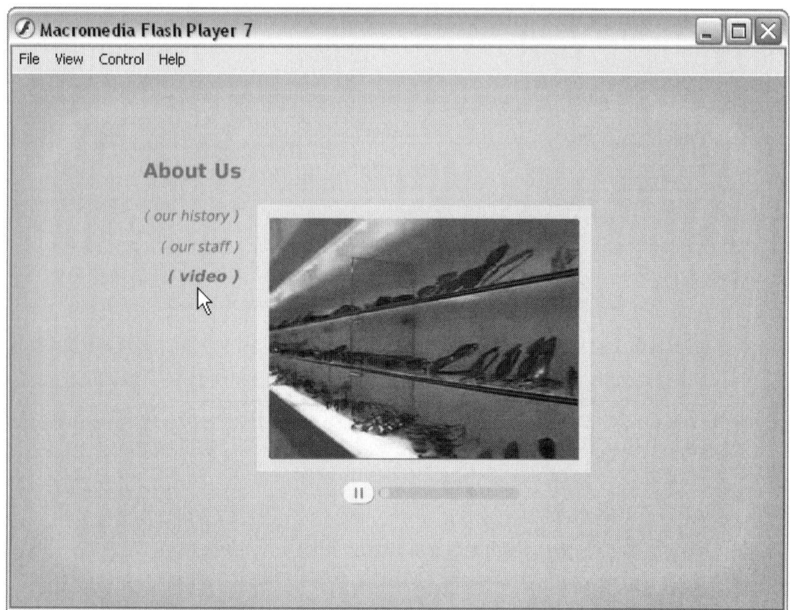

*When you click **(video)**, you'll notice that a video is now playing where there was once just a dark blue box! Thanks to a bit of ActionScript and some sweat, you've just successfully loaded an external FLV—using a `NetConnection` and `NetStream` object—into the `myVideo` video object. Like before, you'll also notice that if you click one of the other submenu options, that subsection will load and the **video** section will disappear. Clicking back on the **video** subsection will make the other subsection content disappear, the **video** content will reappear, and the video will start playing again.*

Pretty darn nifty! You're now reaping the benefits that an external FLV provides. Congratulations, once again.

---

25. When you're finished ooh-ing and ahh-ing at your magnificent creation, close the stand-alone Flash Player 7 window, and return to **about_us.fla** in Flash MX 2004.

In the next exercise, you will write a little ActionScript that will enable the viewer to pause and play the video when the Pause/Play toggle button is clicked.

5. Play/Pause Toggle

In this exercise, you will allow the user to pause and play the FLV. You will do this by adding a small amount of ActionScript to the Play and Pause buttons that, when clicked, will play or pause the progressively downloading FLV.

Just like you saw in Chapter 10, "*MP3 Player*," when adding actions to a toggle button–like this Play/Pause toggle button–you need to add the ActionScript *directly* to the button instances themselves. As you remember, the method of attaching ActionScript to a button or movie clip symbol via actions on a keyframe will not work correctly with these kinds of toggle buttons. So instead, you must attach the ActionScript directly to the button instances.

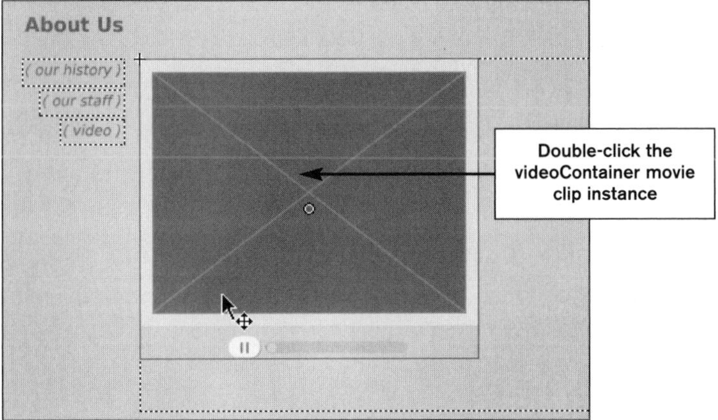

1. On the **Stage**, double-click the **videoContainer** movie clip instance to open it.

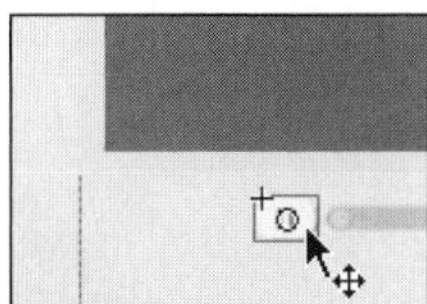

2. Then, double-click the **togglePlay** movie clip instance, where the Play and Pause buttons reside, to open it.

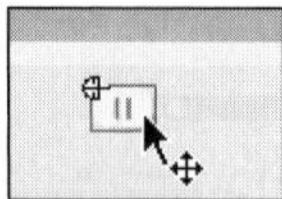

3. Single-click the **musakPauseBtn** button instance on the **Stage**, and open the **Actions** panel (**F9**).

```
on (release) {
    nextFrame();
}
```

You'll notice that there are already a few, simple actions assigned to the Pause button. These actions simply move the playhead to the next frame when the viewer clicks the Pause button. In a few steps, you'll see that the Play button has an action that moves the playhead back to Frame 1 when the viewer clicks it. This is what makes it a "toggle" button. Now, you just need to add an action to the Pause and Play buttons that instructs the FLV to pause and unpause when clicked.

```
on (release) {
    _root.myNetStream.pause();
    nextFrame();
}
```

4. Click at the end of the **`on (release) {`** line, press **Enter** (Windows) or **Return** (Mac) once to create a line break, and type the following:

`_root.myNetStream.pause();`

*This action instructs the **`myNetStream`** object back on Scene 1 (**`_root`**) to pause the FLV. **`pause()`** is a method of the **`NetStream`** class. You can pass a **true** or **false** (Boolean) parameter to the **`NetStream`** object in the **`pause`** method. If you put **true** in the parentheses after **pause**, the FLV will pause. If you pass **false**, the FLV will resume playing. However, if you don't pass any parameters in the **`pause`** method, as you were doing in the action in Step 4, it acts as a toggle pause. Each time you send the **`pause()`** method to the **`NetStream`** class, it will either pause or play the FLV. Because of that, you can easily copy this action and apply it to the Play button without any changes. Yayy. Something simple for a change!*

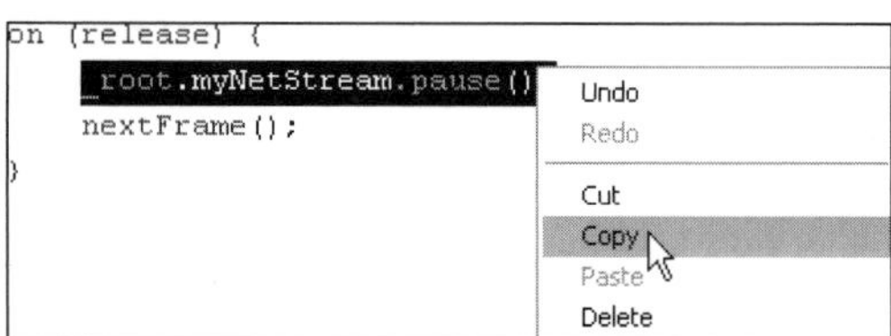

5. Select and copy the **`_root.myNetStream.pause();`** action you just wrote, and copy it.

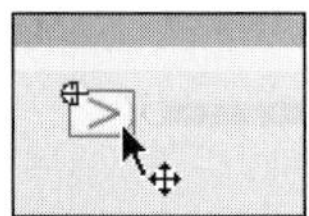

6. Move the playhead to **Frame 2**. On the **Stage**, single-click the **musakPlayBtn** button instance to select it and open the **Actions** panel (**F9**).

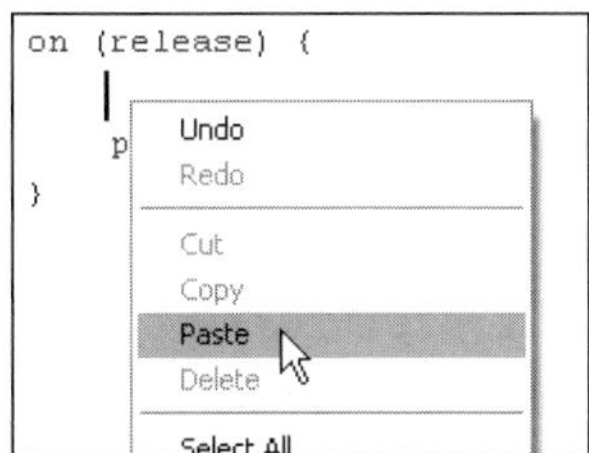

7. Click at the end of the **`on (release) {`** line, and press **Enter** (Windows) or **Return** (Mac) to create a line break. Then, **right-click** (Windows) or **Ctrl+click** (Mac) that new line break, and from the contextual menu that appears, choose **Paste**.

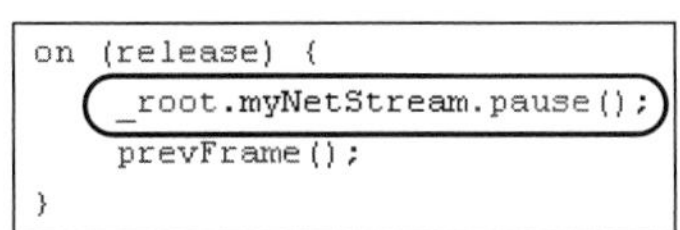

This pastes the action that you created in Step 4 onto the ***musakPlayBtn*** *toggle button.*

The Pause button on Frame 1 pauses the FLV when clicked and advances the playhead to Frame 2, where the Play button is. The Play button unpauses the FLV—by simply executing the ***pause()*** *method of the* ***NetStream*** *object again—and moves the playhead back to Frame 1 where the Pause button is. Pretty straightforward, yes?*

Now you just need to test the Pause and Play toggle buttons to make sure they work correctly.

8. Save the changes you've made to **about_us.fla** by choosing **File > Save** (**Ctrl+S** [Windows] or **Cmd+S** [Mac]).

9. Publish an updated SWF by pressing the keyboard shortcut **Shift+F12** (same on both Windows and Mac).

10. Hide or minimize Flash MX 2004, and on your hard drive navigate to your **Desktop > la_eyeworks > site** folder. Double-click **master.swf** to open it in the stand-alone Flash Player 7.

11. When the **About Us** section appears, click the **(video)** submenu option to display the video content.

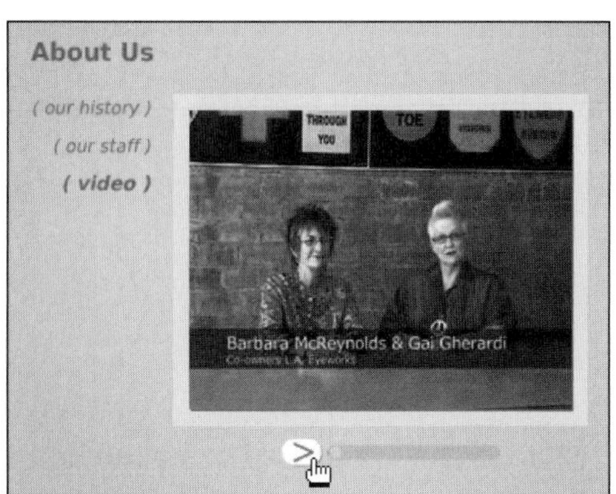

12. When the video starts playing, click the **Pause** button. When you do, the FLV will pause, and the **Pause** button will be replaced by the **Play** button.

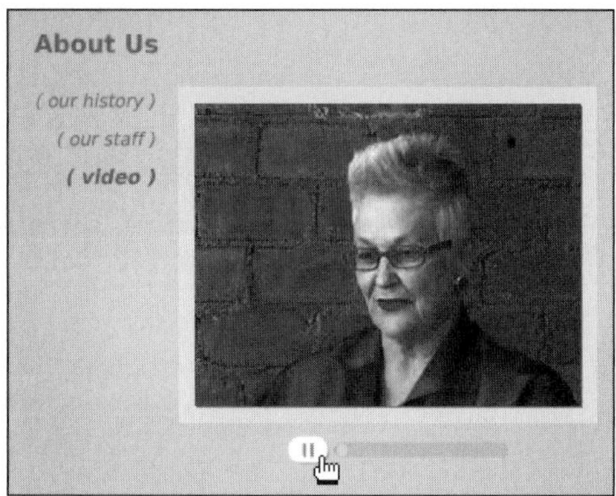

13. Click the **Play** button, and the FLV resumes playing.

You now have a working Play/Pause toggle button! Pretty darn nifty.

14. Close the stand-alone Flash Player 7 window, and return to **about_us.fla** in Flash MX 2004.

In the next exercise, you will write some ActionScript that will make that small, light blue "dot" animate across the progress bar as the FLV plays. That dot, as you saw when building a similar one for the MP3 player in the **music_progress.mov** movie in Chapter 10, "*MP3 Player*," represents the playback progress of the FLV.

What Is the NetStream Class?

As was mentioned earlier in this chapter, the **NetStream** class is to FLV files what the **Sound** class is to MP3 files. The **NetStream** class provides methods and properties for controlling an FLV and for finding out what an FLV is up to. By using a **NetStream** object, you can determine or specify the following:

- Whether the FLV should be paused or playing.
- How many seconds of the FLV should be preloaded before it begins playing.
- How many bytes of the FLV have been downloaded and the total number of bytes in the FLV.
- How many seconds of the FLV have been played.

The **NetStream** object can be used for quite a bit more, too. For more information about the **NetStream** class, open the **Help** panel (**F1**), and from the **Table of Contents** on the left side choose **ActionScript Dictionary > N > NetStream class**. For your immediate reference, here is a table that lists the **NetStream** methods, properties, and event handlers:

Methods, Properties, and Event Handlers of the NetStream Class

METHODS

Method	Description
close()	Stops playing the FLV, resets the **time** property to **0**, and allows the **NetStream** object to be used to load another FLV. This method also deletes the copy of the FLV on the viewer's computer that was being downloaded using HTTP (off of a remote Web server).
pause()	Pauses or resumes the playback of an FLV. The first time you call this method, it pauses the FLV. If you call it again, it resumes playing the FLV. You can also pass a Boolean (true or false) parameter to the **NetStream** object in this method. **pause(true)** pauses the FLV, and **pause(false)** resumes playback.
seek()	As its name implies, this allows you to "seek," or move, the playback point of the FLV to a new point in time. You can write **NetStream.seek(30);** to move your FLV to 30 seconds from the beginning (replacing "NetStream" with the name of your **NetStream** object, of course). This is akin to creating an action to fast-forward or rewind an FLV.
setBufferTime()	Allows you to specify how many seconds of video need to be buffered (preloaded) before the FLV begins to play. To use, simply call this method and pass the buffer time amount, in seconds, like so: **NetStream.setBufferTime(15);**

continues on next page

Methods, Properties, and Event Handlers of the NetStream Class *continued*

Properties

Property	Description
bufferLength	Returns the number of seconds of video currently in the buffer.
bufferTime	Returns the number of seconds that has been assigned to the buffer. Unless modified with the **setBufferTime** method, the default buffer amount is one-tenth of a second (.1).
bytesLoaded	Returns how many bytes of the FLV have been downloaded. You can use **bytesLoaded** in conjunction with **bytesTotal** to create a preloader.
bytesTotal	Returns the total number of bytes of the FLV that is currently downloading.
currentFps	Returns the current value of how many frames per second the FLV is playing at. Monitoring this property when testing your project on different computers will help you to fine-tune your FLV optimization so that you can achieve acceptable frame rates on slower computers.
time	Returns how many seconds of the FLV have been played.

Event Handlers

Event Handler	Description
onStatus	This event handler is triggered when the status of the FLV changes, such as when FLV playback starts or stops, or when there's an error accessing the FLV. A **NetStream** object will pass strings of text to the **Information** object when certain events occur, such as the starting and stopping of an FLV, when the requested FLV can't be found, and when the buffer is empty or full. The strings describing the event that occurred, which are passed to an **Information** object, are called *code properties*. The status of the code properties, either **Status** or **Error**, is called a *level property*. For your reference, an additional table follows this one, describing the various **onStatus** event code properties. You will be using the **NetStream.Play.Stop** code property later in this chapter to reset the FLV when it has finished playing.

NetStream onStatus Events		
Code property	**Level property**	**Description**
NetStream.Buffer.Empty	**Status**	The buffer is empty. Once the buffer is empty, there is no more video to play, and the FLV will therefore stop playing. As the FLV continues downloading, it fills the buffer. Once the buffer has been completely filled, the **NetStream.Buffer.Full** message will be sent, and the FLV will continue playing.
NetStream.Buffer.Full	**Status**	The buffer is full, and the FLV will begin playing.
NetStream.Play.Start	**Status**	FLV playback has started.
NetStream.Play.Stop	**Status**	FLV playback has stopped.
NetStream.Play.StreamNotFound	**Error**	The requested FLV could not be found.

Although the **NetStream** class doesn't give you *quite* as much feedback about a progressively downloading FLV as the **Sound** class provides about a downloading MP3, it still gives you enough information to do most of what you need to do when constructing a video player.

6. Building the Playback Progress Slider

In this exercise, you will construct the playback progress slider. The progress slider is a small, light blue circle that animates across the progress bar as the FLV plays. Just like the playhead in other video applications such as QuickTime and Windows Media Player, this progress slider represents how much of the video has been played and how much there is still left to play. When the slider reaches the farthest right-hand point on the bar, the video is finished. However, due to the extra ActionScript and additional complications that would be involved, you *will not* add the functionality of a draggable progress slider like QuickTime and the Windows Media Player have.

Building this playback slider is relatively simple and is also very similar to the playback slider that you built in the previous chapter. All you need to know are how many seconds of the video have been played and the total running time. Once you have that information, you'll need to script a way for Flash MX 2004 to continually loop through and recalculate those numbers, moving the slider to the appropriate position each time.

First, you're going to start by creating an ActionScript loop. You're going to build this loop so that it's triggered at the same time that the FLV begins playing. If you remember, the action that starts the playing of the FLV resides in the **videoActivate** function.

1. Make sure that you're back in **Scene 1** by clicking its tab at the top-left corner, above the **Timeline**.

---

2. Select **Keyframe 1** in layer **a** and open the **Actions** panel (**F9**).

*In the next few steps, you're going to build a way for Flash MX 2004 to continually loop through some ActionScript. But how exactly do you go about building a loop? There are actually a few different ways. In earlier versions of Flash, Flash developers used to build a "keyframe loop" where the **gotoAndPlay** action would be employed to make the Timeline playhead continually play a series of frames. Each time the playhead looped, a series of actions would be performed. However, now that ActionScript has matured into a more robust form, there are better ways of looping through a series of actions.*

There are really two main methods of looping through ActionScript. You can either use the **`setInterval()`** *function to instruct another function to be continually executed at specific time intervals, or you can use the more "old school"* **`onEnterFrame`** *event handler to loop through some ActionScript that is attached to a movie clip. Although* **`setInterval`** *is a little more "involved" to set up, it gives you very good control over how often the loop should be performed. Conversely, an* **`onEnterFrame`** *loop is a little easier to set up, but you don't have control over how often the loop is performed. (It loops at the same rate as the SWF frame rate.)*

In this exercise, you're going to use the **`onEnterFrame`** *loop event handler to create your ActionScript loop because 1) It's easier to set up, and 2) You don't need specific and ultimate control over how often the ActionScript loops. Twenty-one frames per second–the same frame rate as* **about_us.swf**–*is plenty fast enough for what you're trying to accomplish.*

```
//-------------<video activate>--------------\\

function videoActivate() {
    scrollDown._visible = false;
    scrollUp._visible = false;
    loadedInfo.text = "";
    videoContainer._visible = true;
    myNetStream.play("la_eyeworks_video.flv");

    videoContainer.vidProgBar.onEnterFrame = function() {

    }
}

//-------------</video activate>--------------\\
```

3. Scroll through the **Actions** panel until you located the **<video activate>** actions. Then, click at the end of the **`myNetStream.play("la_eyeworks_video.flv");`** line, press **Enter** (Windows) or **Return** (Mac) twice to create two line breaks, and type the following:

```
videoContainer.vidProgBar.onEnterFrame = function() {

}
```

Make sure to type a line break between the **`videoContainer.vidProgBar.onEnterFrame = function() {`** *line and the closed curly brace below it. This will give you a line break where you can start typing some actions within the* **`onEnterFrame`** *function.*

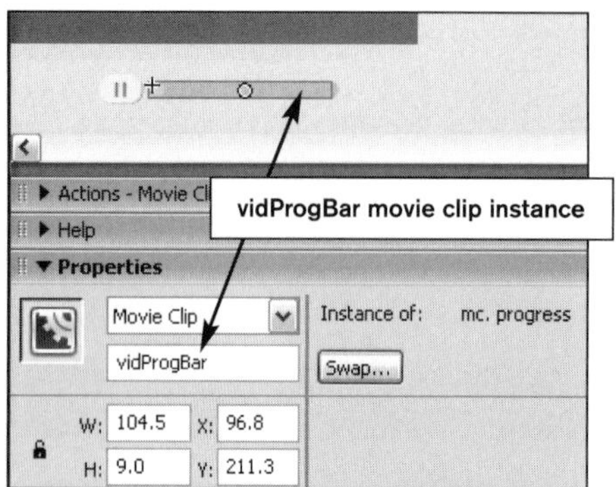

*The **videoContainer.vidProgBar** part of the action is the path to the **vidProgBar** movie clip instance. This is the movie clip where the progress bar, progress slider, and the preloader mask are contained. When assigning the **onEnterFrame** event handler to a movie clip, it's best to assign it to the movie clip that contains the items that you will be targeting with ActionScript.*

*Just like when you are assigning mouse events–**onRelease**, **onRollOver**, and so forth–to a button symbol, the **onEnterFrame** event handler also needs to be attached to a function. The actions within this function, which you will be writing next, will get executed when **onEnterFrame** is triggered.*

*So, when the viewer clicks the **(video)** submenu option in the **About Us** section, the **videoActivate** function is triggered, which thereby triggers this **onEnterFrame** loop to start. What actions do you want to be executed 21 times a second? Well, you want a few things to happen. You want Flash MX 2004 to find out what percentage of the FLV has been played. Just like what you learned in Chapter 10, "MP3 Player," in the **music_progress.mov** movies (if you didn't watch those movies, I highly recommend that you go watch them now), to get the percentage of the FLV played, you need to divide how much time has been played up to that point by the total amount of time. Once you have that number, you multiply it by 100, and that gives you the percentage played number. The percentage played number is the number you will use to move the playback slider to its appropriate position. Again, just like the **music_progress.mov** movies that you watched in Chapter 10, the progress bar is 100 pixels wide (actually, it's a little over 100 if you consider the rounded caps at the end, but where the slider will move within that bar is 100 pixels wide). Each pixel that the progress slider moves represents a percent of the FLV that has been played.*

The first step is figuring out the percentage of the FLV that has been played.

```
//-------------<video activate>-------------\\

function videoActivate() {
    scrollDown._visible = false;
    scrollUp._visible = false;
    loadedInfo.text = "";
    videoContainer._visible = true;
    myNetStream.play("la_eyeworks_video.flv");

    videoContainer.vidProgBar.onEnterFrame = function() {
       var progPos:Number = Math.round((myNetStream.time/videoLV.totalTime) * 100);
    }
}

//-------------</video activate>-------------\\
```

4. Click the empty line break, which you added in Step 3, between the **videoContainer.vidProgBar.onEnterFrame = function() {** line and the closed curly brace beneath it, and type the following:

var progPos:Number = Math.round((myNetStream.time/videoLV.totalTime) * 100);

*Most of this script should already be familiar to you since you wrote an action nearly identical to it in the **music_progress.mov** movie in Chapter 10,* "MP3 Player." *But to reiterate, in this action you're creating a local variable called **progPos**, strict typing it to the **Number** data type, and then inserting a number into that variable. The number is derived from a small equation. Get how many seconds of the FLV have been played (**myNetStream.time**), divide that number by the total running time of the FLV (**videoLV.totalTime**), multiply that result by 100, and then round that to the closest whole number (**Math.round**).*

***Note:** You might also be wondering why you're creating the variable **progPos** and strict typing it within the **onEnterFrame** function when, in the past, you've instantiated the variables outside of a function. The reason why you take the extra step of instantiating a variable outside of a function is so that you can refer to that variable from other actions that are also outside of the function. When you use **var** to create a variable within a function, it becomes a local variable that can only be referenced from within the same function. In this case, because the variable **progPos** is not going to be referenced from anywhere else except from within the function itself, it doesn't need to be instantiated from outside of the function first.*

***Note:** Local variables (variables created within a function and preceded by the **var** statement) are removed from memory after they are no longer referenced, which makes your programs or Web sites run more efficiently in the long run.*

Next, you need to instruct the playback slider to move to whatever percentage of the FLV has been played.

```
//-------------<video activate>--------------\\

function videoActivate() {
    scrollDown._visible = false;
    scrollUp._visible = false;
    loadedInfo.text = "";
    videoContainer._visible = true;
    myNetStream.play("la_eyeworks_video.flv");

    videoContainer.vidProgBar.onEnterFrame = function() {
        var progPos:Number = Math.round((myNetStream.time/videoLV.totalTime) * 100);
        videoContainer.vidProgBar.vidProg._x = progPos;
    }
}

//-------------</video activate>--------------\\
```

5. Click at the end of the action you just wrote in Step 4, press **Enter** (Windows) or **Return** (Mac) to create a line break, and type the following:

videoContainer.vidProgBar.vidProg._x = progPos;

*This action instructs the movie clip instance **vidProg** that's located within the **vidProgBar** movie clip, which is located within the **videoContainer** movie clip instance, to set its x position (x is left and right, and y is up and down) to be the same as the value of the **progPos** variable. The value of the **progPos** variable is, of course, the percentage of the FLV that has been played up to that point.*

*And that's it! That's all you need to move the playback slider to the position that represents what percentage of the FLV has been played. Remember, because the two actions you wrote on Steps 4 and 5 are contained within the **onEnterFrame** function, they're continually executed, for as long as the video content is visible, at 21 times per second. So as Flash MX 2004 continually recalculates what percentage of the FLV has been played, it also moves the playback slider to that same percentage value.*

6. Save the changes you've made to **about_us.fla** by choosing **File > Save** (**Ctrl+S** [Windows] or **Cmd+S** [Mac]).

7. Publish an updated SWF by pressing **Shift+F12** (same on both Windows and Mac).

8. Hide or minimize Flash MX 2004, and on your hard drive navigate to your **Desktop > la_eyeworks > site** folder. Then, double-click **master.swf** to open it in the stand-alone Flash Player 7.

9. When the **About Us** section is displayed, click the **(video)** submenu option to display the video content.

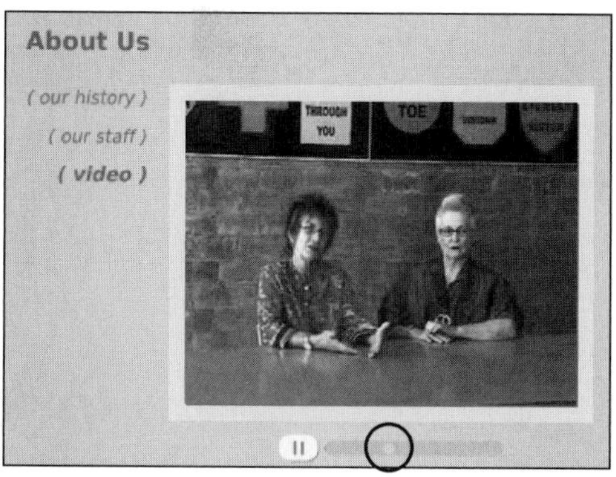

As the FLV plays, you'll notice that the playback progress slider slowly moves across the progress bar underneath it.

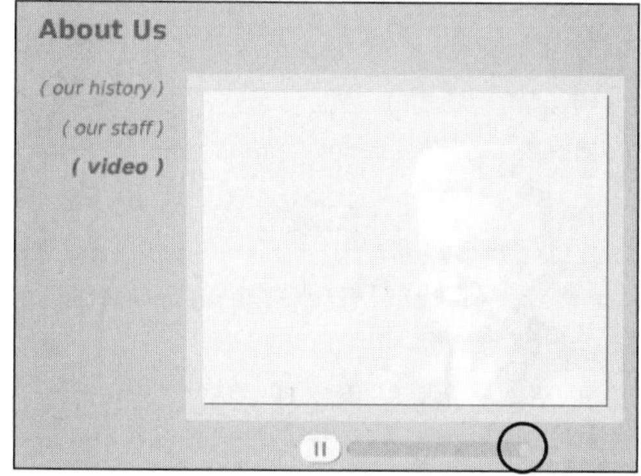

When the slider gets all the way to the right side of the progress bar, you'll notice that the video has finished. Awesome!

10. When you're finished watching the progress slider do its thing, close the stand-alone Flash Player 7 window and return to **about_us.fla** in Flash MX 2004.

The next few steps are going to be nearly identical to the steps you followed to create the MP3 download progress in the ***music_progress.mov*** *movies in Chapter 10,* "MP3 Player."

11. Make sure you have **Keyframe 1** in layer **a** selected and that you have your **Actions** panel open (**F9**).

12. Scroll through the **Actions** panel until you locate the actions that you were working on earlier in this exercise; the ones between the **<video activate>** comments.

```
//-------------<video activate>--------------\\

function videoActivate() {
    scrollDown._visible = false;
    scrollUp._visible = false;
    loadedInfo.text = "";
    videoContainer._visible = true;
    myNetStream.play("la_eyeworks_video.flv");

    videoContainer.vidProgBar.onEnterFrame = function() {
        var progPos:Number = Math.round((myNetStream.time/videoLV.totalTime) * 100);
        videoContainer.vidProgBar.vidProg._x = progPos;
        var vidDlPercent:Number = Math.round((_root.myNetStream.bytesLoaded/_root.myNetStream.bytesTotal) * 100);
    }
}
```

13. Click at the end of the **`videoContainer.vidProgBar.vidProg._x = progPos;`** line, press **Enter** (Windows) or **Return** (Mac) once to create a line break, and type the following all on one line, with no line breaks:

`var vidDlPercent:Number = Math.round((_root.myNetStream.bytesLoaded/_root.myNetStream.bytesTotal) * 100);`

*As you've seen previously, this action creates a local variable titled **`vidDlPercent`** and strict types it to the **`Number`** data type. Then, it divides how many bytes of the FLV (**`_root.myNetStream.bytesLoaded`**) have been downloaded up to that point by the total number of bytes for the FLV (**`_root.myNetStream.bytesTotal`**). To translate that number into a percentage, you then multiply that result by 100. Last, so you have a nice even number to work with, you use **`Math.round`** to round that result to the nearest whole number.*

*Now, just like you constructed in **music_progress.mov**, you just need to instruct the progress bar mask to set its **`width`** property to be the same as the percentage. As the mask width expands, it reveals another bar–carefully positioned on top of the first one–of a different color. This gives the appearance of a progress bar.*

```
//-------------<video activate>--------------\\

function videoActivate() {
    scrollDown._visible = false;
    scrollUp._visible = false;
    loadedInfo.text = "";
    videoContainer._visible = true;
    myNetStream.play("la_eyeworks_video.flv");

    videoContainer.vidProgBar.onEnterFrame = function() {
        var progPos:Number = Math.round((myNetStream.time/videoLV.totalTime) * 100);
        videoContainer.vidProgBar.vidProg._x = progPos;
        var vidDlPercent:Number = Math.round((_root.myNetStream.bytesLoaded/_root.myNetStream.bytesTotal) * 100);
        videoContainer.vidProgBar.progMaskContainer.progMask._width = vidDlPercent + 10;
    }
}

//-------------</video activate>--------------\\
```

14. Click at the end of the action you just wrote in Step 13, press **Enter** (Windows) or **Return** (Mac) to create a line break, and type the following all on one line, with no line breaks:

`videoContainer.vidProgBar.progMaskContainer.progMask._width = vidDlPercent + 10;`

*This action simply tells the movie clip with the mask in it, **progMask**, to set its **width** property to be the same number as the percentage of the FLV that has been downloaded up to that point. Keep in mind that, just like the progress slider, these actions within the **onEnterFrame** function will be continually executed–while the video content is visible–at 21 frames per second. So as the FLV is downloading, Flash MX 2004 is constantly recalculating how much of the FLV has been downloaded and adjusting the download progress mask accordingly.*

With those two lines, you have just created a progress bar that will display the downloading progress of the FLV. Pretty nifty if I do say so myself! ;-)

*Now for the bad news: Because the FLV is external, you unfortunately can't test the preloader in the Flash authoring environment. This means that when you preview your movie in Flash MX 2004–even if you choose the **Simulate Download** option–the progress bar won't appear to show the downloading progress of the FLV. Because the FLV is currently stored locally on your hard drive, and will therefore load instantly, the progress bar will just immediately jump to its finished point. While this is the same sort of problem you had with not being able to test the **MovieClipLoader**-driven progress bar in the Flash MX 2004 API, they are actually two different bugs.*

So unless you currently have access to a Web presence provider and can upload your work there and test it using your Web browser, you'll just have to trust me that it works correctly. :-)

---

15. Save the changes you've made to **about_us.fla** by choosing **File > Save** (**Ctrl+S** [Windows] or **Cmd+S** [Mac]).

*In the next exercise, you will utilize the **NetStream** class's **onStatus** event handler to "reset" the FLV when it has finished playing. Currently, the viewer is unable to replay the FLV after it has finished playing. In the next exercise, you will write a little script that will fix that.*

7. Using the onStatus Event Handler

In this exercise, you're going to use the **NetStream** class's **onStatus** event handler to detect when the FLV has finished playing. Once you've detected that the FLV has finished playing, you will write a few actions that will "reset" the FLV so that it can be replayed by the viewer if they choose.

The **onStatus** event handler works somewhat differently from the other event handlers you've seen thus far. When the **onStatus** event handler detects a change in the status of the FLV, such as the FLV starting or stopping, it sends two strings of text to two properties in the **Information** object. When you want to find out the status changes of the FLV, you use an **if** statement to ask the **Information** object questions.

The first step is to create the **onStatus** event handler and assign it to a function.

1. Scroll through the **Actions** panel until you find the section marked by the **<video>** comments.

```
function initializeVideo() {
    myNetConn = new NetConnection();
    myNetConn.connect(null);
    myNetStream = new NetStream(myNetConn);
    videoContainer.myVideo.attachVideo(myNetStream);
    myNetStream.setBufferTime(5);

    myNetStream.onStatus = function(info) {

    }

    videoLV = new LoadVars();
    videoLV.onLoad = function (success) {
        if (success) {
            videoActivate();
        }
    }
```

2. Within the **initializeVideo** function, click at the end of the **myNetStream.setBufferTime(5);** line, press **Enter** (Windows) or **Return** (Mac) twice to create two line breaks, and type the following:

```
myNetStream.onStatus = function(info) {

}
```

*Make sure to type a line break between the **myNetStream.onStatus = function(info) {** line and the closed curly brace below it. This will give you a line break where you can start typing some actions.*

*Like the other event handlers, if you want to do anything with the **onStatus** event handler, you need to assign it to a function. The actions within the function are executed when the event handler is invoked. Because the **onStatus** event handler is passing its events to the **Information** object, you need to declare the **info** parameter for the **onStatus** function.*

*Now you need to add branching logic (an **if** statement) to the **onStatus** event to query the **Information** object's properties. This will enable you to specify what should happen when the **onStatus** event is fired.*

```
function initializeVideo() {
    myNetConn = new NetConnection();
    myNetConn.connect(null);
    myNetStream = new NetStream(myNetConn);
    videoContainer.myVideo.attachVideo(myNetStream);
    myNetStream.setBufferTime(5);

    myNetStream.onStatus = function(info) {
        if (info.code == "NetStream.Play.Stop" && info.level == "status") {

        }
    }

    videoLV = new LoadVars();
    videoLV.onLoad = function (success) {
        if (success) {
            videoActivate();
        }
    }
```

3. Click at the end of the **myNetStream.onStatus = function(info) {** line, press **Enter** (Windows) or **Return** (Mac) once to create a line break, and type the following:

```
if (info.code == "NetStream.Play.Stop" && info.level == "status") {

}
```

*Make sure to type a line break between the **if (info.code == "NetStream.Play.Stop" && info.level == "status") {** line and the closed curly brace below it. This will give you an empty line break where you can start typing some actions.*

*This **if** statement essentially says "If the **code** property in the **info** object is **'NetStream.Play.Stop'**, and if the **level** property in the **info** object is 'status'...." At this point, you're probably wondering where the heck the **code** and **level** properties came from. Well, earlier in this chapter there is a table that lists the various methods, properties, and event handlers of the **NetStream** class. Following that is an additional table that describes the **onStatus** event handlers. In that table, it lists the event handlers including the **NetStream.Play.Stop** code you just used, as well as its **status** level.*

*Again, the **onStatus** event handler passes strings (bit of text) to the **code** and **level** properties in the **Information** object when certain events occur. Because you want to find out if the FLV has stopped playing—so you can reset it—in this **if** statement you're asking the **Information** object if its **code** property is **NetStream.Play.Stop** and (&&) if its **level** property is **status**. If that **if** question results in **true**, that means the FLV file has stopped. So every time there's a status change with the FLV, the **onStatus** event handler is invoked. When it's invoked, it asks this **if** statement question each time. When finally the **if** statement is true, it will execute the actions that you're about to place within it.*

```
function initializeVideo() {
    myNetConn = new NetConnection();
    myNetConn.connect(null);
    myNetStream = new NetStream(myNetConn);
    videoContainer.myVideo.attachVideo(myNetStream);
    myNetStream.setBufferTime(5);

    myNetStream.onStatus = function(info) {
        if (info.code == "NetStream.Play.Stop" && info.level == "status") {
            videoContainer.togglePlay.gotoAndStop(2);
            myNetStream.seek(0);
            myNetStream.pause(true);
        }
    }

    videoLV = new LoadVars();
    videoLV.onLoad = function (success) {
        if (success) {
            videoActivate();
        }
    }
```

4. Click in the empty line break between the **if** statement and the closed curly brace. Then, type the following three actions:

videoContainer.togglePlay.gotoAndStop(2);
myNetStream.seek(0);
myNetStream.pause(true);

- *The first action,* ***videoContainer.togglePlay.gotoAndStop(2);****, instructs the Pause/Play toggle button in the* ***videoContainer*** *movie clip instance to go to Frame 2. On Frame 2, if you remember, is the Play button. So when the FLV finishes playing, the Pause button, which is visible when the FLV is playing, will go back to displaying the Play button.*
- ***myNetStream.seek(0);*** *uses the* ***seek*** *method to instruct the FLV to go back to 0 seconds. So when the FLV has finished playing, it will automatically return to the beginning. Now, unless you tell it otherwise, it will go back to the beginning and start playing again. Because the viewer would probably like to be the one to determine if he or she wants to watch it again, you should pause the FLV.*
- ***myNetStream.pause(true);*** *uses the* ***pause*** *method to pause the FLV.*

So taken all together, these three actions instruct the Pause/Play toggle to display the Play button, the FLV to return to the beginning, and the FLV to pause. In essence, it resets itself and allows the viewer to play it again when he or she clicks the Play button.

5. Save the changes you've made to **about_us.fla** by choosing **File > Save** (**Ctrl+S** [Windows] or **Cmd+S** [Mac]).

6. Publish an updated SWF by pressing **Shift+F12** (same on both Windows and Mac).

7. Hide or minimize Flash MX 2004, and on your hard drive navigate to your **Desktop > la_eyeworks > site** folder. Then, double-click **master.swf** to open it in the stand-alone Flash Player 7.

8. When the **About Us** section appears, click the **(video)** submenu option to display the video content.

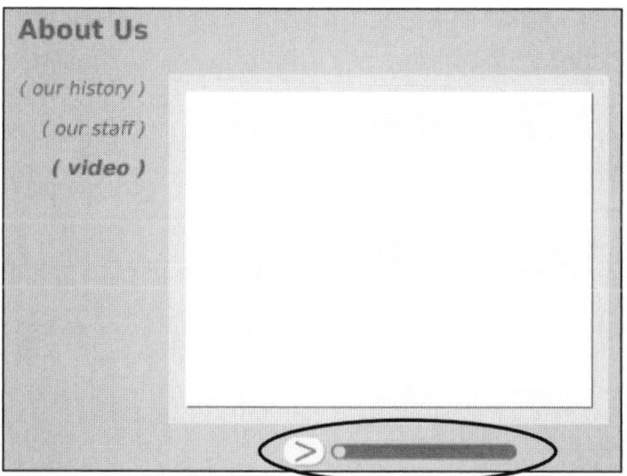

The FLV will immediately load and start playing. When the video gets to the end, you'll see the playback progress slider jump back to its starting point (because you set the playhead of the FLV back to 0 using `myNetStream.seek(0);`*), the Pause/Play toggle switch to the Play button, and the FLV will jump back to its beginning and pause there.*

Great! So when the video finishes, it now resets itself and waits for the viewer to click the Play button to watch the FLV again if he or she chooses to do so.

9. Close the stand-alone Flash Player 7 window and return to **about_us.fla** in Flash MX 2004. Then, make sure you have **Keyframe 1** selected in layer **a** and that you have the **Actions** panel open.

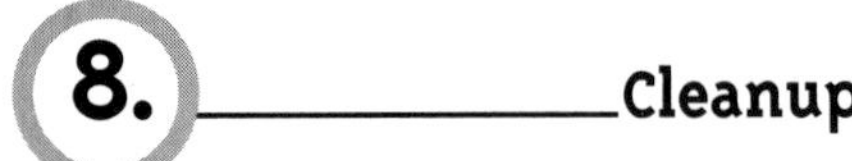

8. Cleanup

In this exercise, you're going to perform a little janitorial work and tie up some loose ends. There are still a few extra items that need to be added to the video player before it is completely finished.

The first task is to stop the **onEnterFrame** loop you created in Exercise 6. Currently, when you click the **(video)** subsection option, the FLV loads and starts playing. At that same time, the **onEnterFrame** loop starts looping through its actions, continually making calculations and using up the viewer's computer processing power. However, when the viewer leaves the **video** subsection for another subsection, that **onEnterFrame** still continues to loop through its actions, even though it's not being used. To help optimize your movie, you should stop that **onEnterFrame** loop when the viewer leaves the **video** subsection. Thankfully, you already have a function that is executed when the viewer leaves the **video** subsection: **videoDeactivate**.

1. Scroll through the **Actions** panel until you find the actions marked by the comment **<video deactivate>**.

```
//-------------<video deactivate>--------------\\

function videoDeactivate() {
    loadedInfo.scroll = 0;
    scrollDown._visible = true;
    scrollUp._visible = true;
    videoContainer._visible = false;
    delete videoContainer.vidProgBar.onEnterFrame;
}

//-------------</video deactivate>--------------\\
```

2. Click at the end of the **videoContainer._visible = false;** line, press **Enter** (Windows) or **Return** (Mac) once to create a line break, and type the following:

delete videoContainer.vidProgBar.onEnterFrame;

***delete**, as its name implies, is an operator that deletes a variable or an object. In this case, it is being used to delete the **onEnterFrame** event handler–which, technically, is a part of the movie clip object. When you delete **onEnterFrame**, the loop stops, and the memory and processing power used for this event handler is given back to the system. If you have too many **onEnterFrame** loops–or have **onEnterFrame** loops that are too complex–occurring simultaneously, it can slow down the performance of your Flash MX 2004 movie. By deleting **onEnterFrame** loops when you no longer need them, it stops those loops and calculations from occurring and thereby gives that processing power and memory back to the viewer's computer system to be used for other tasks. Now, just to waylay any fears that you're permanently deleting something that you can never use again, you can always restart an **onEnterFrame** loop simply by executing the **onEnterFrame** action again.*

Next, you need to tell the myNetStream object to stop downloading its FLV–if it is still downloading–when the viewer leaves the ***video*** *subsection. If you do not specify this, if the viewer leaves the* ***video*** *subsection while the FLV is downloading, the FLV will* still continue *to download even though the viewer has left. The action you're about to write also deletes the FLV that the viewer has downloaded to his or her computer and frees up the* ***NetStream*** *object to download a different FLV if necessary.*

```
//-------------<video deactivate>--------------\\

function videoDeactivate() {
    loadedInfo.scroll = 0;
    scrollDown._visible = true;
    scrollUp._visible = true;
    videoContainer._visible = false;
    delete videoContainer.vidProgBar.onEnterFrame;
    myNetStream.close();
}

//-------------</video deactivate>--------------\\
```

3. Click at the end of the **delete videoContainer.vidProgBar.onEnterFrame;** line, press **Enter** (Windows) or **Return** (Mac) once to create a line break, and type the following:

myNetStream.close();

Imagine this. The viewer comes to the L.A. Eyeworks Web site and clicks the Play button on the MP3 player to listen to some music while he or she cruises around through the site. The viewer visits the ***About Us*** *section and reads through the L.A. Eyeworks history as he or she happily taps his or her foot to the music. Then, the viewer clicks the* ***video*** *subsection. That's when all hell breaks loose. The audio for the video starts playing while the music is still playing as well. Obviously, that would not be a good thing. But you're a smart, forward-thinking Flash designer/developer, and you're going to nip this problem in the bud.*

As of yet, you haven't yet integrated the ***music.swf*** *and* ***about_us.swf*** *sections into* ***master.swf****. But when you do,* ***about_us.swf*** *will load into* ***_level5*** *where the rest of the content sections also load, and* ***music.swf*** *will load one level higher into* ***_level6****. So from* ***about_us.swf****, when you want to instruct the MP3 player to do something, like stop the music, you can simply refer to it as* ***_level6****.*

```
//-------------<video activate>--------------\\

function videoActivate() {
    scrollDown._visible = false;
    scrollUp._visible = false;
    loadedInfo.text = "";
    videoContainer._visible = true;
    myNetStream.play("la_eyeworks_video.flv");

    _level6.bgMusak.stop();
    _level6.musakToggle.gotoAndStop(1);

    videoContainer.vidProgBar.onEnterFrame = function() {
```

4. Scroll through the **Actions** panel until you locate the actions marked by the comment **<video activate>**. Then, click at the end of the **`myNetStream.play("la_eyeworks_video.flv");`** line, press **Enter** (Windows) or **Return** (Mac) twice to create two line breaks, and type the following two actions:

```
_level6.bgMusak.stop();
_level6.musakToggle.gotoAndStop(1);
```

*The top-most action, **`_level6.bgMusak.stop();`**, instructs the **bgMusak** sound object to stop playing the music. The second action, **`_level6.musakToggle.gotoAndStop(1);`**, instructs the music Play/Stop toggle button to display the Play button. That way, when the viewer is finished watching the video, he or she can click the music Play button to resume listening to the music.*

*Because you placed these two actions within the **videoActivate** function, when the viewer clicks the **(video)** submenu option, and the **videoActivate** function is executed, the music will automatically stop playing. Huzzah!*

It's subtleties like these that really give that extra edge to a Web site and make it look and appear professional.

---

5. Save the changes you've made to **about_us.fla** by choosing **File > Save** (**Ctrl+S** [Windows] or **Cmd+S** [Mac]).

---

6. Publish an updated SWF by pressing **Shift+F12** (same on both Windows and Mac).

---

7. Then, close **about_us.fla**–you won't be needing it in the next chapter.

Congratulations! You finished yet another chapter. In this chapter, you learned how to create a video player that progressively downloads an external FLV. You also learned how to allow the viewer to pause and play the FLV, how to add a playback progress slider, and how to create a progress bar that provides feedback about the downloading progress of the FLV. If you're understanding–or beginning to understand–the actions and exercises as you work through them, you should really be amazed at what you've learned and accomplished so far in this book. You've already learned a tremendous amount, and there's still more yet to learn. See you in the next chapter!

The Main Menu

| What You Are Building | Setting Up |

| Scripting onRollOver, onRollOut, and onRelease |

| Bringing It All Together |

la_eyeworks

Macromedia Flash MX 2004
Beyond the Basics

Now that you've constructed all of the sections of the L.A. Eyeworks Web site–minus the Locations section–you're ready to build the one piece that brings all the separate sections together: the main menu. In this chapter, you will use a few new techniques to construct the main menu, and you will get to see, for the first time, all the section modules as they peacefully coexist together in **master.swf**.

I. What You Are Building

In this exercise, you will get to preview exactly *what* it is you are building *before* you start building it. That way, as you're working through the exercises in this chapter, you'll have a better idea of how some of these abstract ActionScript concepts fit together to create a functional piece of the L.A. Eyeworks Web site.

1. Open your preferred Web browser and navigate to this URL:

http://www.lynda.com/flashbtb/laeyeworks/

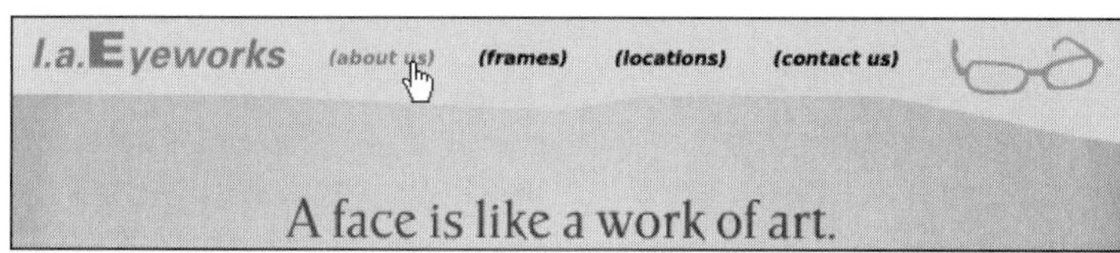

2. When the L.A. Eyeworks site finishes loading, move your mouse over the four navigation bar options. As you roll your mouse over each of the options, you'll notice that they will turn green. When you roll your mouse off of an option, it will turn back to black.

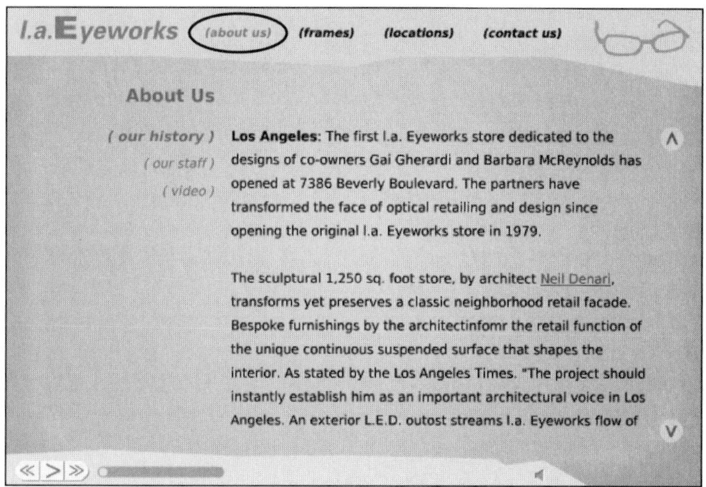

3. Click the **(about us)** option in the navigation bar. When you do, three things will happen. 1) The **(about us)** option will turn green and stay that way even if you move your mouse over other navigation menu options. 2) The **(about us)** option will become disabled, and you will not be able to interact with it. Just like you saw when constructing the submenu for the **About Us** section in Chapter 6, "*TextFormat Class*," you can use the **`enabled`** property to disable a menu option for purposes of usability. 3) The **About Us** section content will load.

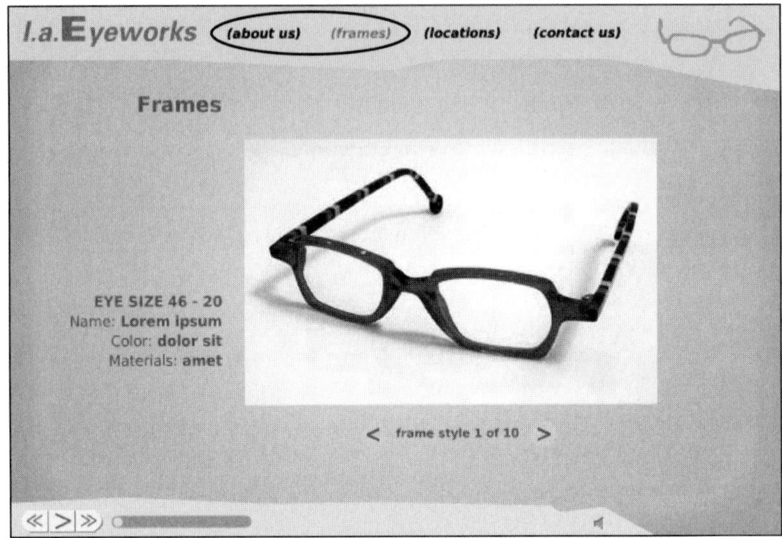

4. Click the **(frames)** option in the navigation bar. When you do, you'll notice that the **(about us)** option becomes re-enabled, the **(frames)** option becomes disabled and turns green, and the **Frames** section loads.

As you work through this chapter, you'll likely notice many similarities between the construction of the main menu and the About Us subsection menu. Because of the similarities, I've included much of the ActionScript to build the main menu in a prebuilt FLA. However, this chapter isn't all review, and you will be learning some new actions in the upcoming exercises.

---

5. Close your Web browser when you're finished checking out the main menu.

In the next exercise, you will set up the provided FLA by adding a font symbol from the shared library and linking the main menu options to that shared font.

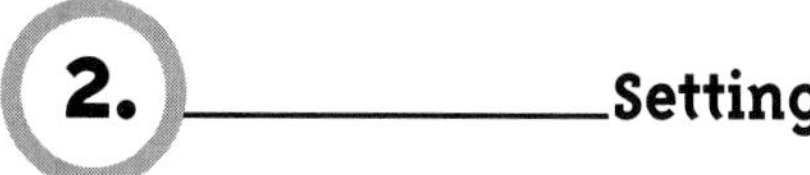

2. Setting Up

In this exercise, you will import and integrate a shared font for use in the main navigation menu options.

1. On your hard drive, navigate to your **Desktop > la_eyeworks > site** folder and double-click the file **main_menu.fla**.

This is a FLA that was provided for you so that you wouldn't need to repeat steps or ActionScript you have already learned.

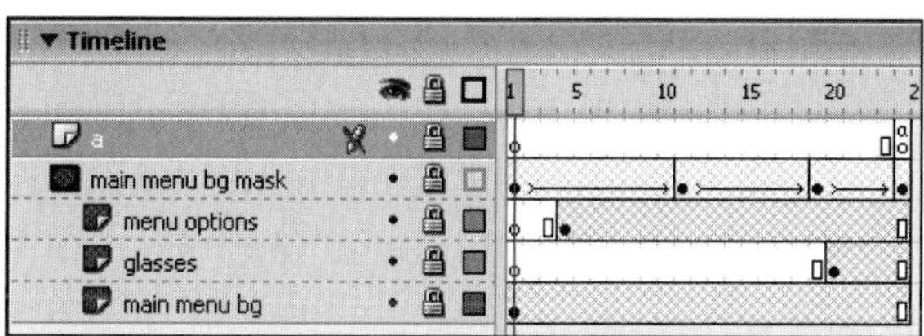

As you can see, this FLA already has some layers, a mask, a shape tween, and some actions.

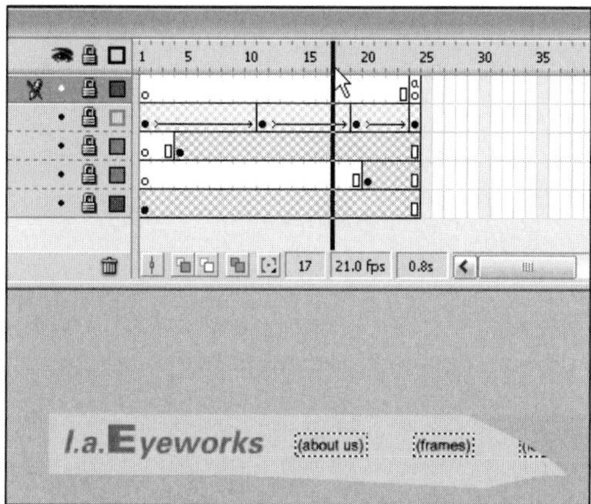

2. So that you can see what's going on in this FLA, drag the playhead down the **Timeline**. Watching the **Stage**, you'll notice that the green bar in the background is being revealed by an animated mask. That same mask also reveals the L.A. Eyeworks logo, the main menu options, and the glasses shape at the top right. At the end of the **Timeline**, you'll also notice that some actions have been assigned to a keyframe in layer **a**. Later in this chapter, you will modify these actions to add additional functionality to the main menu.

Before you can start working with ActionScript, however, you need to import a font symbol from your shared library and assign it to the text that makes up the main menu options.

3. Make sure you *do not* have **sharedLib.fla** open. If it *is* open, it will interfere with the next few steps, so make sure it is closed before continuing. Then, choose **File > Import > Open External Library**. In the **Open as Library** window, navigate to your **Desktop > la_eyeworks > site** folder and double-click the file **sharedLib.fla**.

This will open only *the Library for* ***sharedLib.fla*** *as you have seen, and done, several times before.*

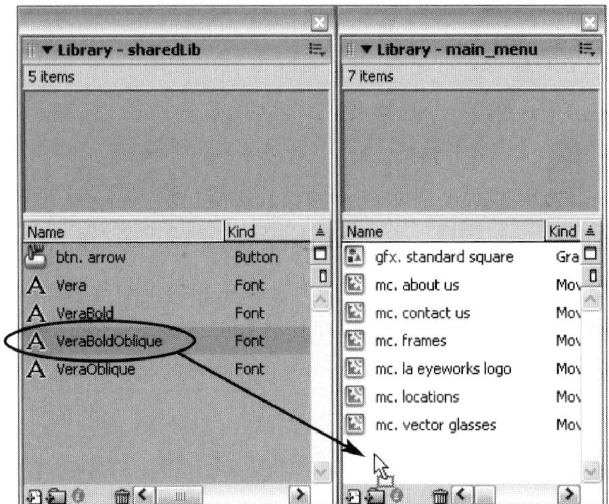

4. Open the **Library** for **main_menu.fla** (**Ctrl+L** [Windows] or **Cmd+L** [Mac]) and position it next to the **sharedLib.fla Library**. You may need to undock the **Library** windows so you can see both of them simultaneously. Then, drag the font symbol **VeraBoldOblique** from the **sharedLib Library** onto the **main_menu Library**.

5. Close the **sharedLib Library** and redock the **main_menu Library** window if you need to.

Note: *You have probably noticed, by now, that in nearly every chapter you're loading the sharedLib Library, dragging the shared elements you need into a new FLA, and then closing the sharedLib Library. In a "real-world" workflow, you could easily keep the sharedLib Library window open and pull elements from it as needed. However, to reduce confusion when working through the exercises in this book, you close the sharedLib library after each time you've used it.*

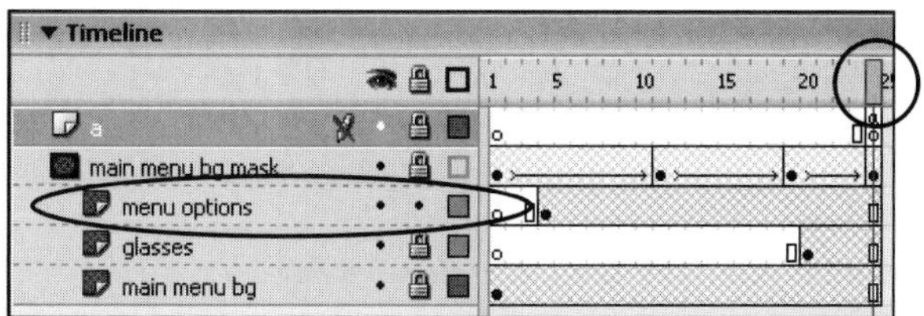

6. In the **Timeline**, move the playhead to the last frame (24) and unlock the **menu options** layer, which is the layer that houses the main menu options.

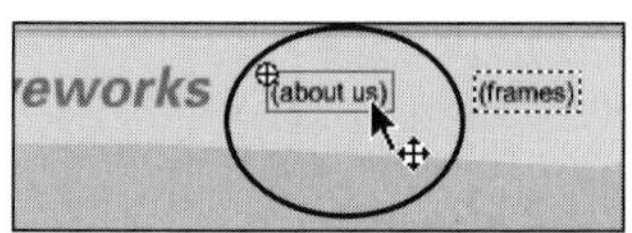

7. On the **Stage**, single-click the **(about us)** menu option and open the **Properties inspector** (**Ctrl+F3** [Windows] or **Cmd+F3** [Mac]).

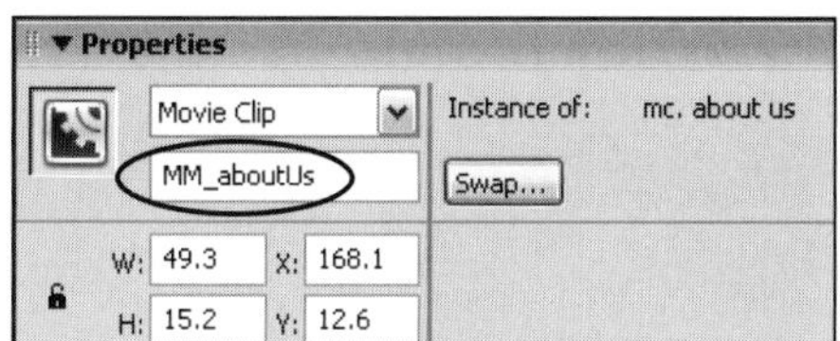

*Notice how this option is actually an instance of the **mc. about us** movie clip. It also already has an instance name of **MM_aboutUs**. The other menu options, **frames**, **locations**, and **contact us**, have instance names of **MM_frames**, **MM_locations**, and **MM_contactUs**, respectively. (The "MM" stands for **M**ain **M**enu by the way.)*

8. Double-click the **mc. about us** movie clip instance to open it.

9. Single-click the dynamic text field on the **Stage** that has the text **(about us)** inside it and open the **Properties inspector**. You'll notice that **Font** is currently set to **_sans**. However, to match the look and feel of the rest of the site, you need to change the font face.

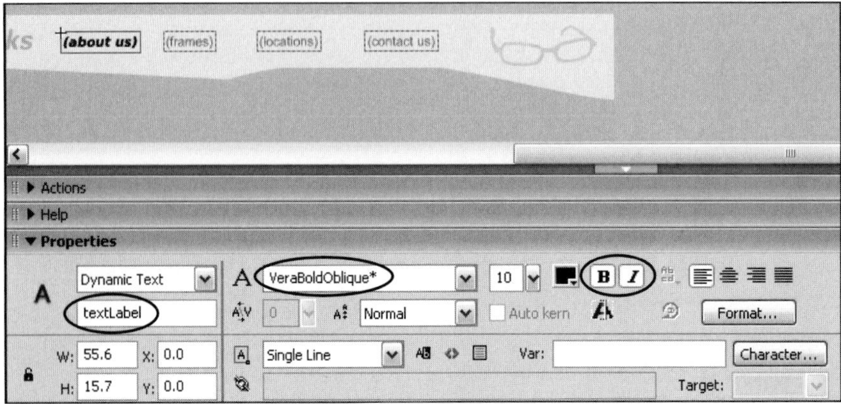

(Windows)

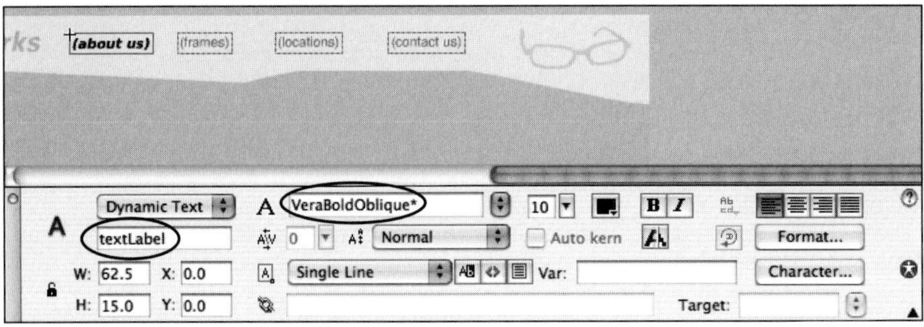

(Mac)

10. From the **Font** pull-down menu in the **Properties inspector**, choose the shared font that you imported earlier, **VeraBoldOblique***. If you're running Windows, also make sure you click the **Bold Style** and **Italic Style** buttons. If you're running on a Mac, you *do not* need to click those buttons. The remaining options can stay the same; just verify that what you see in your **Properties inspector** matches what you see in the screen shot above for your operating system.

Also note that the dynamic text field has a pre-applied instance name of **textLabel**. As you'll see when you change the font face of the other main menu options, they *all* have the same instance name of **textLabel**. Later in this chapter, when you write the ActionScript that creates the `rollOver` and `rollOut` interactivity, it streamlines the process if the text fields all have the same instance name. Because they are all inside of movie clips, the identical instance names don't cause any naming conflicts.

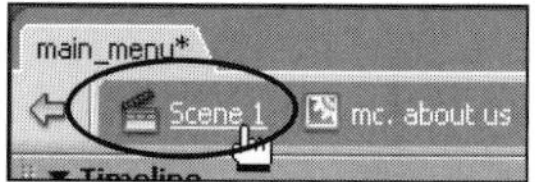

11. Return to the **Scene 1 Timeline** by clicking its tab above the top-left corner of the **Timeline**.

---

12. Repeat Steps 8 through 11 for the remaining three main menu options. All you're really doing is opening the movie clip that each option resides in, selecting the dynamic text field, and changing the font face to the shared font **VeraBoldOblique***. If you're on Windows, you need to remember to also click the **Bold Style** and **Italic Style** buttons.

---

13. When you're finished changing the font face for the main menu options, make sure you return to **Scene 1**. You will begin the next exercise there.

And with that, you're all done setting up this FLA! In the next exercise, you will write the ActionScript that will create the **`rollOver`** *and* **`rollOut`** *effects for the main menu options.*

3. Scripting onRollOver, onRollOut, and onRelease

In this exercise, you're going to write some ActionScript that creates the main menu option color rollover effects. Essentially, as the viewer rolls his or her mouse on and off the main menu options, you're just going to use a function and the **TextField** class's **textColor** property to change the text color of the **textLabel** dynamic text fields. All in all, it's fairly straightforward to set up.

The first step is to create the variables to hold the color strings that will be displayed on **onRollOver** and **onRollOut**.

1. Select **Keyframe 24** on layer **a** and open the **Actions** panel (**F9**).

```
stop();
MM_logo.enabled = false;

//----------------<define option colors>----------------\\

//----------------</define option colors>----------------\\

//----------------<re-enable menu options>-----------------\\
function reActivateBtns() {
    MM_logo.enabled = true;
    MM_aboutUs.enabled = true;
    MM_contactUs.enabled = true;
    MM_frames.enabled = true;
    MM_locations.enabled = true;
    changeOptionColor(MM_aboutUs, outColor);
    changeOptionColor(MM_frames, outColor);
    changeOptionColor(MM_locations, outColor);
    changeOptionColor(MM_contactUs, outColor);
};
//----------------</re-enable menu options>-----------------\\
```

2. Toward the top of the **Actions** panel, click after the **MM_logo.enabled = false;** line, press **Enter** (Windows) or **Return** (Mac) twice to create two line breaks, and type the following:

```
//----------------<define option colors>----------------\\

//----------------</define option colors>----------------\\
```

Note: *Make sure to include an empty line break between the two comment lines. This will give you a space where you can begin to type some actions.*

Next you're going to create a couple of variables to hold the colors (stated as a string of numbers and letters) that the menu options will change to ***onRollOver*** *and* ***onRollOut****. Later in this exercise, you will use these variables in the function that actually changes the color of the text in the* ***textLabel*** *dynamic text fields.*

```
stop();
MM_logo.enabled = false;

//----------------<define option colors>----------------\\
var overColor:Number = 0x7DBC6B;
var outColor:Number = 0x000000;
//----------------</define option colors>----------------\\
```

3. Click the empty line break between the **<define option colors>** comments, and type the following two actions:

```
var overColor:Number = 0x7DBC6B;
var outColor:Number = 0x000000;
```

*These two actions create the two variables **overColor** and **outColor** and strict type them to the **Number** data type. Then, within the variables, a color–typed in its hexadecimal format–is inserted. The hexadecimal format is simply a color's hex value–which you can get from Flash MX 2004's color picker–preceded by **0x** (that's a zero and a lowercase x). In this case, the **overColor** color is green, and the **outColor** color is black.*

*Now that you've specified the colors that the menu options will display on **onRollOver** and **onRollOut**, you can create the function that will actually do the changing of the text color. To create a single function that can be utilized by both the **onRollOver** and **onRollOut** mouse events, you will incorporate parameters into the function. When calling the function from the **onRollOver** and **onRollOut** events, you can utilize those parameters within the action that's changing the appearance of the main menu options.*

```
stop();
MM_logo.enabled = false;

//----------------<define option colors>----------------\\
var overColor:Number = 0x7DBC6B;
var outColor:Number = 0x000000;

function changeOptionColor(myOption:MovieClip, myColor:Number) {
    myOption.textLabel.textColor = myColor;
};
//----------------</define option colors>----------------\\
```

4. Click at the end of the **`var outColor:Number = 0x000000;`** line, press **Enter** (Windows) or **Return** (Mac) twice to create two line breaks, and type the following:

```
function changeOptionColor(myOption:MovieClip, myColor:Number) {
    myOption.textLabel.textColor = myColor;
};
```

*As you have seen before, this creates a function called **`changeOptionColor`**. In the parentheses after **`changeOptionColor`** are two parameters: **`myOption`** and **`myColor`**. Because the **`myOption`** and **`myColor`** parameters are essentially variable placeholders, you can–and should–strict type them just like you would any other variable. Because the **`myOption`** parameter is going to receive an instance name of a **movie clip**, it is strict typed with the **`MovieClip`** data type. **`myColor`**, being a parameter to receive a hexadecimal color value, is strict typed as a **`Number`** data type.*

Note: *If you need a "refresher" on how a function's parameters work, refer to the section titled "What Is a Function?" in Chapter 3, "Getting Started."*

*The action within the function essentially instructs a text field to change its color using the **`textColor`** text field property. The path to the text field is symbolized by the **`myOption`** parameter. Later, when you call this function, in place of the **`myOption`** parameter you will specify the name of the movie clip instance that holds the main menu option you want to modify. As you remember, within each main menu option movie clip is a dynamic text field with the instance name of **`textLabel`**. By keeping that text field instance name the same throughout the individual movie clips, it makes writing this action much easier. Last, when you call this function, the **`myColor`** parameter will be substituted with one of the color variables you created earlier, either **`overColor`** or **`outColor`**.*

Now it's time to give that function a try.

```
//----------------<about us option>-----------------\\
MM_aboutUs.onRollOver = function () {
    changeOptionColor(this, overColor);
};

MM_aboutUs.onRollOut = function () {

};

MM_aboutUs.onRelease = function () {
    reActivateBtns();
    changeOptionColor(this, overColor);
    this.enabled = false;
};
//----------------</about us option>-----------------\\
```

5. In the **Actions** panel, scroll down until you reach the actions marked by the comments **<about us option>**. Then, click the provided empty line break after the **`MM_aboutUs.onRollOver = function () {`** line, and type the following:

`changeOptionColor(this, overColor);`

*This action triggers the **`changeOptionColor`** function and passes two parameters to it when the viewer rolls his or her mouse over the **MM_aboutUs** movie clip instance. For the **`myOption`** parameter, you're passing the keyword **`this`**, which as you have seen before, is a keyword that refers to the object instance that the parent function is targeting. In this case, that's the **MM_aboutUs** movie clip instance. For the **`myColor`** parameter, you're passing the variable name that you earlier assigned to the green color: **`overColor`**. As you are seeing here, when you have a function that has more than one parameter, in the action where you call that function and define the parameters, you pass them back in the same order.*

Before you test your movie, you should also specify what should happen when the viewer rolls his or her mouse off *of the **MM_aboutUs** movie clip instance.*

```
//----------------<about us option>-----------------\\
MM_aboutUs.onRollOver = function () {
    changeOptionColor(this, overColor);
};

MM_aboutUs.onRollOut = function () {
    changeOptionColor(this, outColor);
};

MM_aboutUs.onRelease = function () {
    reActivateBtns();
    changeOptionColor(this, overColor);
    this.enabled = false;
};
//----------------</about us option>-----------------\\
```

6. Select and copy the action you just wrote in Step 5. Then, click the provided empty line break after the **MM_aboutUs.onRollOut = function () {** line, and paste the copied action. All you then have to do is simply change the parameter **overColor** to **outColor**. The rest of the action should remain the same.

This action simply states, "When the viewer rolls his or her mouse off *of the* ***(about us)*** *main menu option, tell the dynamic text field* ***textLabel*** *within the* ***MM_aboutUs*** *movie clip instance to set its color to* ***outColor*** *(black)."*

And that's all there is to scripting a ***rollOver*** *and* ***rollOut*** *color change effect. But some of you might be wondering why you're writing all this ActionScript for something that can be accomplished with a button symbol and requires* no *ActionScript. In essence, it really comes down to being able to easily update your content. If you had manually built all four of the main menu options, including the color change* ***rollOver/rollOut*** *effects as button symbols, what would happen when the client came to you, wanting to change the colors of those options? You would have to spend a good amount of time manually opening each button symbol, selecting the text within the button, and changing its color. Although that may not be too big of a hassle if you have only a few buttons, what would it be like if you had 10 buttons? 20? By defining the* ***rollOver*** *and* ***rollOut*** *states using ActionScript–as you have just done here–it takes you all of five seconds to modify those mouse event color effects. All you'd have to do is change the hexadecimal color value in the* ***overColor*** *and* ***outColor*** *variables and call it a day. Modifying those color values affects* all *of the main menu options. For those of you with HTML and CSS experience, this is analogous to a global CSS file that you refer to from all your HTML pages. Making a single change to the CSS file will affect* all *of the HTML pages that link to it.*

Better yet, you could even put those ***overColor*** *and* ***outColor*** *variables in a text file and load them into* ***main_menu.swf*** *using* ***LoadVars****. Then even the* client *could easily modify the main menu color* ***rollOver/rollOut*** *effects if he or she wanted. "Amazing," you say? Yes, I know. ;-)*

Before continuing, you should test your changes thus far so that you can make sure everything is working correctly.

---

7. Save the changes you've made to **main_menu.fla** by choosing **File > Save** (**Ctrl+S** [Windows] or **Cmd+S** [Mac]).

*Because the main menu is self-contained and doesn't rely on any ActionScript in **master.swf**, you can preview **main_menu.fla** by itself.*

---

8. Test **main_menu.fla** by pressing **Ctrl+Enter** (Windows) or **Cmd+Return** (Mac).

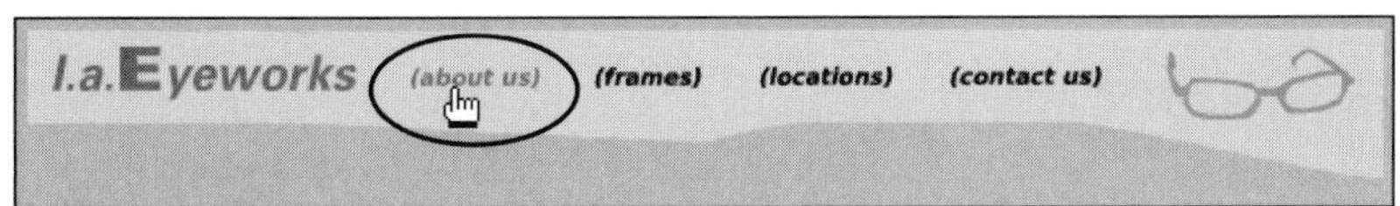

9. When the main menu is revealed, roll your mouse over and then off the **(about us)** menu option. As you do, you'll see the text change to green, and then back to black, respectively. Awesome!

---

10. Close the **Preview** window. Then, back in **main_menu.fla**, make sure **Keyframe 24** in layer **a** is still selected and you have your **Actions** panel open.

***Note:** Because creating the **onRollOver** and **onRollOut** actions for the remaining three main menu options is identical to the actions you just wrote in Steps 5 and 6, I've taken the liberty of writing the actions for you. If you're curious, you can scroll down in the **Actions** panel to see what the actions look like. In this case, setting up this functionality really does follow the adage "Seen one, seen 'em all."*

*Now that you have the **rollOver** and **rollOut** actions working correctly, what about **onRelease**?*

```
//----------------<about us option>-----------------\\
MM_aboutUs.onRollOver = function () {
    changeOptionColor(this, overColor);
};

MM_aboutUs.onRollOut = function () {
    changeOptionColor(this, outColor);
};

MM_aboutUs.onRelease = function () {
    reActivateBtns();
    changeOptionColor(this, overColor);
    this.enabled = false;
};
//----------------</about us option>-----------------\\
```

*Within the **<about us option>** comments, under the **`MM_aboutUs.onRelease`** function, you'll notice three prebuilt actions. These actions, like the others, were provided for you because you already know how to construct what they're doing. So that you have a good understanding of what's going on, however, here's a quick breakdown of what those three actions are doing and what will happen when the viewer clicks the **(about us)** main menu option:*

- ***`reActivateBtns();`** calls the prebuilt function by the same name. If you scroll your **Actions** panel toward the top, you'll notice a function called **`reActivateBtns`**. Within that function there are actions that enable the functionality of the four main menu options and the L.A. Eyeworks logo (which, when clicked, will load the splash graphic), as well as actions to set the four main menu options to display using the **`outColor`** color (black). Essentially, as its name implies, the **`reActivateBtns`** function reactivates the main menu options. In terms of functionality, this is identical to the **`reEnableOptions`** function you created in Chapter 6, "TextFormat Class."*

- ***`changeOptionColor(this, overColor);`**, as you've seen before, simply changes the **(about us)** main menu option so the text is green.*

- ***`this.enabled = false;`** disables the functionality of the **(about us)** main menu option.*

*So, when the viewer clicks the **(about us)** main menu option, the **reActivateBtns** function is executed and all of the main menu options, if they are disabled, are re-enabled. This way, if the viewer has already clicked another main menu option–thereby disabling it–it will become re-enabled when the viewer clicks a different main menu option. Once all the main menu options are re-enabled, the option the viewer clicked turns green (**`overColor`**) and becomes disabled itself. Because you know what all these actions do and how they work, I've already completed the other main menu options and assigned similar actions to them to save you some time.*

Now that you've seen how the main menu options operate when the viewer rolls over them, off of them, and clicks them, you should test the movie again so you can see it all in action.

11. Preview **main_menu.fla** again by pressing **Ctrl+Enter** (Windows) or **Cmd+Return** (Mac).

12. When the main menu appears, click **(about us)**. This will immediately disable the **(about us)** option and change its color to green.

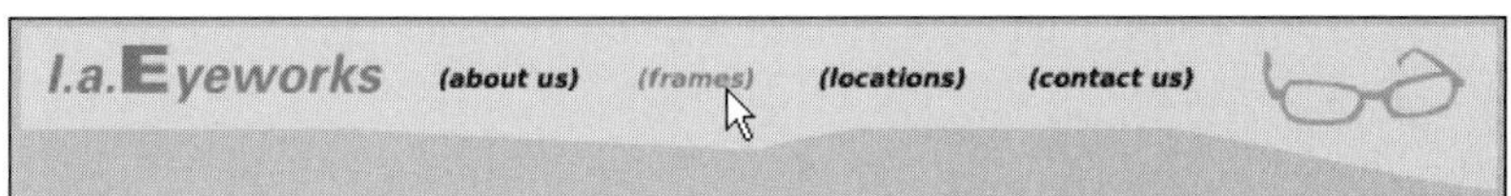

13. Click a different main menu option. When you do–thanks to the **`reActivateBtns`** function–the **(about us)** option becomes re-enabled, and the frames option becomes disabled and green. Fabulous! If you'd like, you can click the other options, but you will discover they all behave in the same way. Clicking an option disables the interactivity of that option using the **`enabled = false`** property, colors it green using the **`textColor`** property, and re-enables the other menu options using the actions in the **`reActivateBtns`** function.

14. When you're finished checking everything out, close the **Preview** window to return to **main_menu.fla**.

Now, all that's missing–of course–is to have those main menu options actually load the appropriate content. That's what you will be constructing in the next exercise. See you there!

4. Bringing It All Together

Now that you have the main menu nearly fully functional, all you have to do is add the capability for it to load in the appropriate section when the user clicks one of the options. There are multiple ways to go about building this same functionality, but in this exercise you're going to use the ubiquitous **myMCL MovieClipLoader** object in **master.swf** to do all the heavy lifting for you. All you'll have to do is write a simple one-line action that instructs the **MovieClipLoader** *which* SWF you want to load and *where* you want it to load.

1. In **main_menu.fla**, make sure you have **Keyframe 24** in layer **a** selected and that you have the **Actions** panel open.

2. Scroll down in the **Actions** panel until you locate the actions within the **<about us option>** comments.

```
//----------------<about us option>-----------------\\
MM_aboutUs.onRollOver = function () {
    changeOptionColor(this, overColor);
};

MM_aboutUs.onRollOut = function () {
    changeOptionColor(this, outColor);
};

MM_aboutUs.onRelease = function () {
    reActivateBtns();
    changeOptionColor(this, overColor);
    this.enabled = false;
    _level0.myMCL.loadClip("about_us.swf", 5);
};
//----------------</about us option>-----------------\\
```

3. Within the **onRelease** function, click at the end of the **this.enabled = false;** line, press **Enter** (Windows) or **Return** (Mac) once to create a line break, and type the following:

_level0.myMCL.loadClip("about_us.swf", 5);

*As you have seen quite a few times before, this simple action instructs the **myMCL MovieClipLoader** object in **master.swf** (**_level0**) to load **about_us.swf** into **_level5**.*

And that's it. That's all there is to loading a section SWF when the viewer clicks one of the main menu options. Because you've seen this action many times before, and because it's a very simple action, I've saved you the repetitive task of adding similar actions to the remaining three main menu options. If you scroll down in the ***Actions*** *panel, you'll notice that similar actions have already been assigned to the other menu options within their* ***onRelease*** *functions. The only change for each menu option is, of course, which SWF file is instructed to load* ***onRelease****.*

As yet, you cannot test the changes you've made thus far. Because you're utilizing the ***myMCL MovieClipLoader*** *object that resides in* ***master.swf****, you need to preview the main menu only* after *it has been loaded into* ***master.swf****. So in the next steps, you're going to modify* ***master.swf*** *to load the main menu.*

---

4. Save the changes you've made to **main_menu.fla** by choosing **File > Save** (**Ctrl+S** [Windows] or **Cmd+S** [Mac]).

---

5. Publish an updated SWF by pressing **Shift+F12** (same on both Windows and Mac).

---

6. Hide or minimize Flash MX 2004, and on your hard drive, navigate to your **Desktop > la_eyeworks > site** folder and double-click **master.fla** to open it in Flash MX 2004.

---

7. In **master.fla**, select **Keyframe 10** in layer **a** and open the **Actions** panel.

```
stop();
// myMCL.loadClip("splash.swf", 5);
myMCL.loadClip("about_us.swf", 5);
// myMCL.loadClip("frames.swf", 5);
```

You'll notice that, because you've been using Keyframe 10 in ***master.swf*** *to temporarily load SWF files for testing, there are already three other actions to load various SWF files. However, now that you have the main menu completed, it will be the method for which the viewer will access the section SWF files.*

```
stop();
myMCL.loadClip("main_menu.swf", 20);
```

8. Delete the three **myMCL.loadClip** actions in **keyframe 10**, and under the **stop();** action, type the following:

myMCL.loadClip("main_menu.swf", 20);

*As you have seen before, this action simply loads **main_menu.swf** into Level 20. Why all the way up at Level 20? Simply so that the main menu resides in a level above everything else–so it won't get accidentally blocked or obscured by another SWF–and to give you extra room in levels beneath it to load more content if you choose.*

Now it's time to see if your hard work has paid off. :-)

---

9. Save the changes you've made to **master.fla** by choosing **File > Save** (**Ctrl+S** [Windows] or **Cmd+S** [Mac).

---

10. Then, test **master.fla** by choosing **Control > Test Movie** or by pressing the keyboard shortcut **Ctrl+Enter** (Windows) or **Cmd+Return** (Mac).

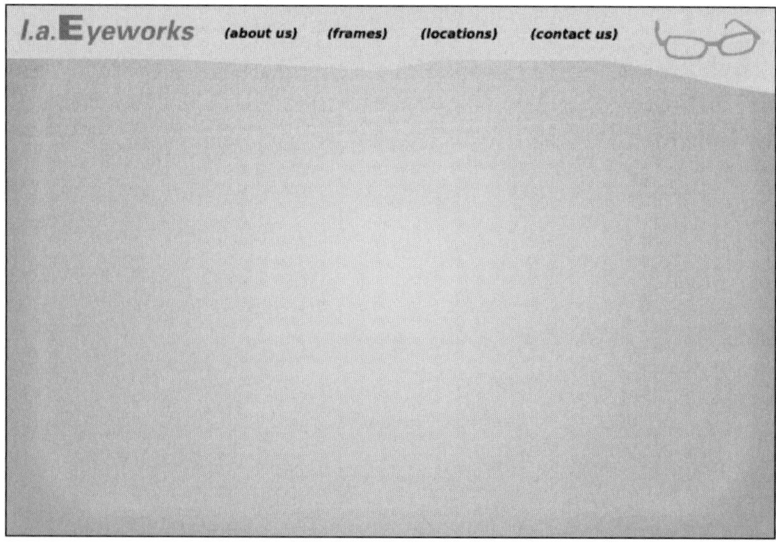

*When the **Preview** window opens, you'll see the main menu animate. Ohhhh. Ahhh.*

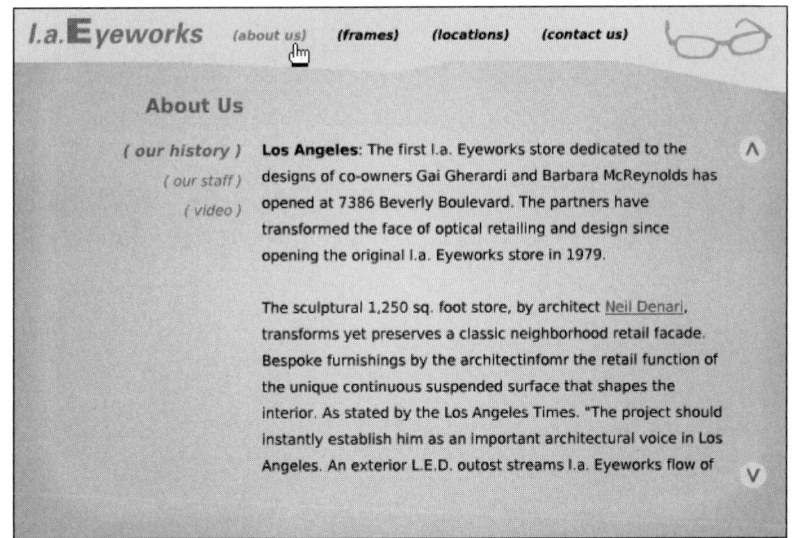

11. Click one of the main menu options. When you do, you'll notice that section's SWF load and display. You now have a working, functional navigation system!

*If you click **(locations)**, it will load and display as well. The **locations** section was not covered in this book because, although it is a necessary addition to the L.A. Eyeworks site as a whole, its construction does not demonstrate any new concepts. However, the **locations.fla** file–and the **locations.swf** file you see when you click its main menu option–are both included in the **la_eyeworks > site** folder so that you can refer to them if you'd like.*

As you click each of the main menu options, that section SWF will load in, replacing the section that was there previously. Pretty gosh darn cool if I do say so myself. ;-)

***Note:** If you click the main menu options but no content loads, chances are you forgot to complete Step 5 in this exercise. Go back to Step 5, publish an updated SWF from **main_menu.fla**, return to **master.fla**, and try testing the movie again.*

So you've gotten the main menu to load and all the sections are now loading, displaying, and functioning to perfection. But what about the animated splash page and the MP3 player? In the next few steps, you will load them as well.

12. When you're finished ogling at your main menu and congratulating yourself for building such an awesome piece of functionality, close the **Preview** window and return to **master.fla**.

13. In **master.fla**, make sure you have **Keyframe 10** in layer **a** selected and that you have your **Actions** panel open.

*When **main_menu.swf** loads, you also want to load the MP3 player and the splash page. Because they are constructed to all coexist on the Stage simultaneously, you can load them into **master.swf** all at the same time.*

```
stop();
myMCL.loadClip("main_menu.swf", 20);
myMCL.loadClip("splash.swf", 5);
myMCL.loadClip("music.swf", 6);
```

14. Click at the end of the `myMCL.loadClip("main_menu.swf", 20);` action, press **Enter** (Windows) or **Return** (Mac) once to create a line break, and type the following two actions:

```
myMCL.loadClip("splash.swf", 5);
myMCL.loadClip("music.swf", 6);
```

*These two actions load, of course, **splash.swf** into Level 5 and **music.swf** into Level 6. **Splash.swf** loads into Level 5, which is the same level that the section SWFs load into, because you want **splash.swf** to disappear when the viewer clicks one of the main menu options.*

15. Once again, save the changes you've made to **master.fla** by choosing **File > Save** (**Ctrl+S** [Windows] or **Cmd+S** [Mac]).

16. Preview the changes you've made by choosing **Control > Test Movie** or by pressing the keyboard shortcut **Ctrl+Enter** (Windows) or **Cmd+Return** (Mac).

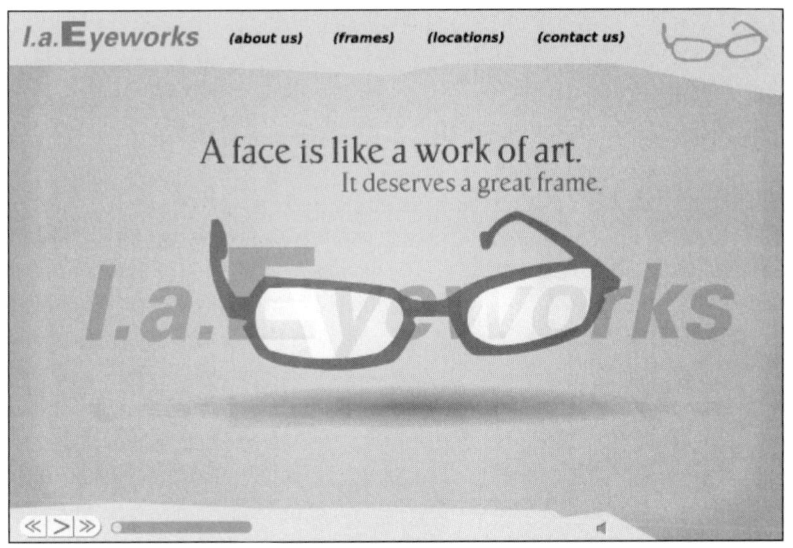

When the Preview window appears, it should bowl you over. You now have a functional navigation menu, an animated splash graphic that gets swapped out with the content sections, and a functional MP3 player. Essentially, you have a working, complete, Flash MX 2004–built Web site for L.A. Eyeworks. I hope you're proud of what you've accomplished thus far because you certainly deserve it. You've learned a tremendous amount in this book so far, and you only have yourself to thank for it. Congratulations!

---

17. Close the **Preview** window, return to Flash MX 2004, and close any FLA that you currently have open. If you're prompted by Flash MX 2004 to save your changes, click **Yes** (Windows) or **Save** (Mac).

With that, don't think that your work is over quite yet. In the next chapter, I'm going to show you how to insert your completed L.A. Eyeworks site into an HTML page using Dreamweaver MX 2004 and how to build a Flash plug-in detector as well. I'll see you in the next chapter. :-)

---

13. Getting It Ready for the World

la_eyeworks

Macromedia Flash MX 2004 Beyond the Basics

In this chapter, you will learn how to take the L.A. Eyeworks Web site you just developed and prepare it for online delivery. This will involve learning how to use Dreamweaver MX 2004 to embed the site into an HTML page to create a Flash plug-in detector. Incorporating a plug-in detector into your Web site is a critical step because it allows you to ensure that only visitors with the proper version of the Flash Player can enter and view your Flash content. Visitors to your site that *do not* have the version–or higher–of the Flash Player that you're targeting *will not* see any error messages or warnings by default. Their Flash browser plug-in will simply attempt to play back your SWF and will disregard any ActionScript it doesn't understand. Obviously, this could be a very bad thing indeed. If you, the reader, are anything like the Flash students that I've taught over the years, you're probably *very* curious about this process. So let's stop wasting valuable ink and get to it!

I. Adding Your Flash Content to an HTML Page

Once you've designed your content in Flash MX 2004, adding it to an HTML page is quite easy. However, some of you might be wondering why you even need HTML in the first place. Isn't Flash MX 2004 the end-all, be-all of Web design? Although it's true that Flash MX 2004 gives you the ability to construct some amazing things–as you have seen so far in this book–HTML still plays a part in presenting your Flash MX 2004 content to the world. Sure, you could theoretically upload your SWF file to your Web server and give out the URL directly to that SWF file, but it wouldn't look so pretty when viewers came to look at it. First, it would automatically scale itself to fit the browser window. If it scales up, any bitmap graphics you use will become pixilated and distorted. Scaling your content up can also have a detrimental effect on the performance of your movie. By placing a SWF file within an HTML page, you can specify the exact size at which a SWF displays, thereby avoiding unwanted–and unsightly–scaling. Adding a SWF file to an HTML page also allows you to specify *where* on the page the SWF file should be displayed. Top left? Bottom? Center? You can specify the positioning of the SWF when you embed it into an HTML page.

In this exercise, you will learn how to use Dreamweaver MX 2004 to embed a SWF file into an HTML page. Keep in mind, however, that you can also use other WYSIWYG (**W**hat **Y**ou **S**ee **I**s **W**hat **Y**ou **G**et) HTML editors such as Adobe GoLive to embed SWF files into an HTML page. If you know HTML markup, you can write the code yourself, or you can even let Flash MX 2004 itself create a quick-and-dirty HTML page for you with the SWF file embedded in it. So there are quite a few options when embedding a SWF file in an HTML page, but in this exercise, you will use Dreamweaver MX 2004 to do the trick.

1. Start by downloading the 30-day trial version of Macromedia Dreamweaver MX 2004 from Macromedia's Web site. You can download it by clicking on this URL and filling out a short form: **http://www.macromedia.com/cfusion/tdrc/index.cfm?product=dreamweaver**. After you've successfully downloaded Dreamweaver MX 2004, install it on your system. Last, once you've installed it, launch Dreamweaver MX 2004.

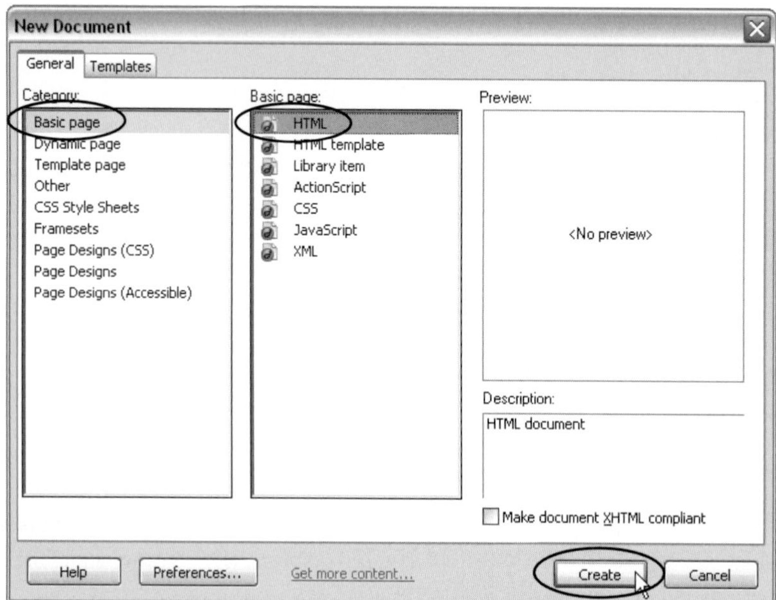

2. In Dreamweaver MX 2004, create a new, blank HTML page by choosing **File > New**. From the **New Document** window, click **Basic page** under **Category** and then **HTML** under **Basic page**. Click **Create** to create a new, blank HTML page.

Although there are a gazillion+ ways of embedding a SWF file into an HTML page, in this exercise you will embed the SWF file so that it's centered in the middle–both horizontally and vertically–of the HTML page using tables. Keep in mind, however, that one of the fantastic properties of Flash MX 2004 content is that you can put it anywhere on an HTML page. You can easily use CSS or tables to align and position the SWF file wherever you'd like, just as if you were placing a JPG or GIF on the page.

First, you need to set the margins of the HTML page so the table can be positioned all the way to the edges.

---

3. Choose **Modify > Page Properties**, or press the keyboard shortcut **Ctrl+J** (Windows) or **Cmd+J** (Mac).

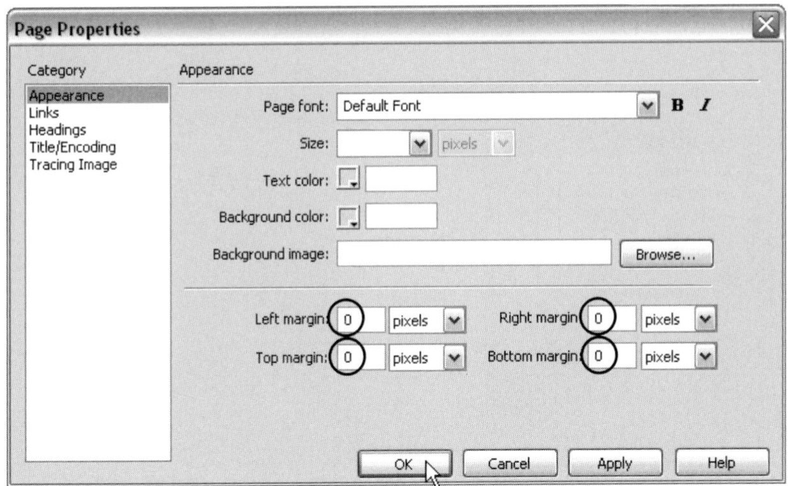

4. In the **Page Properties** window, type **0** in the **Left margin**, **Right margin**, **Top margin**, and **Bottom margin** fields. This removes the HTML page's default margin, which prevents you from pushing content all the way to the edge of the document. Click **OK**.

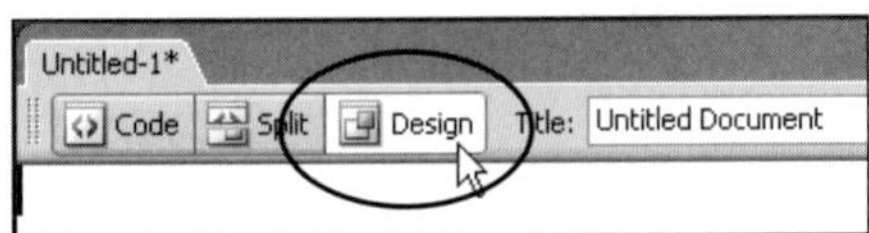

5. Make sure you're looking at the **Design** view by clicking the **Design** button at the top of the HTML page.

Note: *If you would prefer to watch the HTML code as you construct this page, you can also select the* ***Split*** *view mode. If you choose* ***Split*** *view, just make sure you make your edits and changes in the* ***Design*** *portion of the window so that you can follow along correctly with the upcoming steps.*

6. Click the HTML page and choose **Insert > Table**.

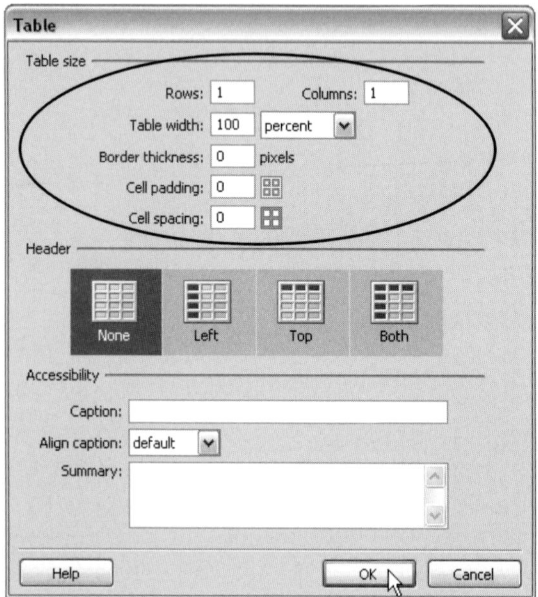

7. In the **Table** window, type **1** in both the **Rows** and **Columns** fields. Set the **Table width** to **100 percent**, the **Border thickness** to **0 pixels**, and the **Cell padding** and **Cell spacing** to **0**. Click **OK**.

This will insert a table with one row, one column, and 100% width into the page. But because you want the SWF file that will eventually reside within this table to be aligned in the center, both horizontally and vertically, *you need to set the height of the table to 100% as well.*

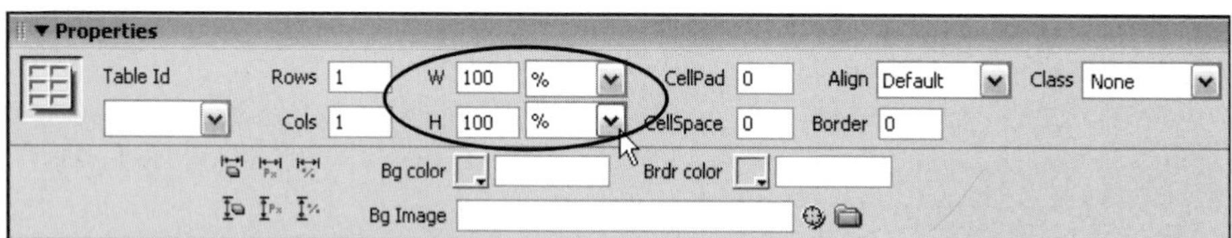

8. In the **Properties inspector** (**Ctrl+F3** [Windows] or **Cmd+F3** [Mac]), change the **H** (height) field to **100%**. This will set the width and height of the table to 100%, thereby filling the entire HTML page.

Note: *If you don't see options to change the table's width and height as you see in the screen shot above, make sure you have the table selected first.*

Because the SWF file will be embedded in the sole cell in this table, you need to set the table cell so that any content placed within it will be aligned in the center both horizontally and vertically. By default, the table cell is set to align content placed within it in the center vertically but on the left *horizontally.*

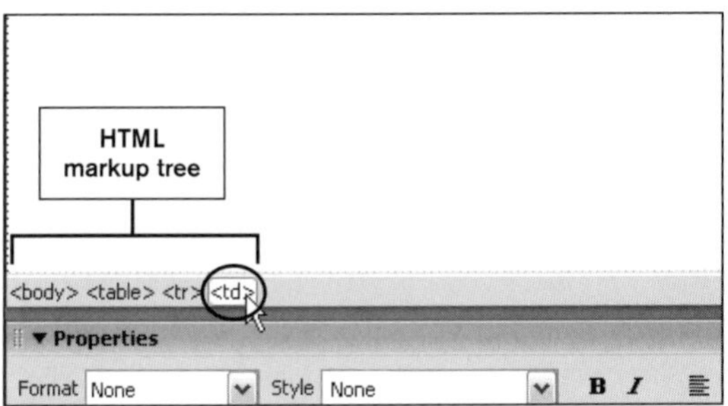

9. Click in the table cell (anywhere on the page, essentially) and then at the bottom of the HTML page window, click the **<td>** tag in the **HTML markup tree**. This will select only the cell of the table.

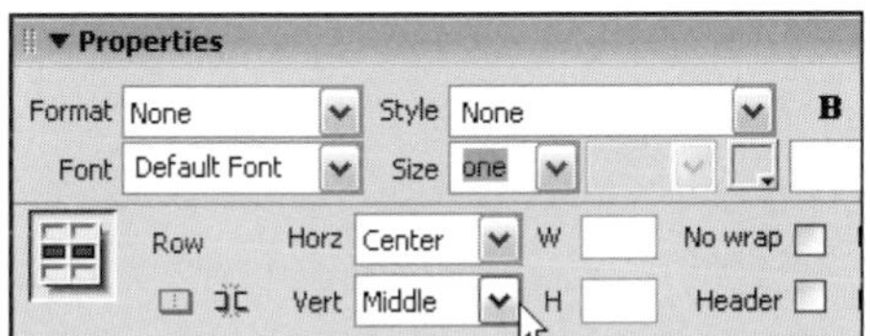

10. Open the **Properties inspector** (**Ctrl+F3** [Windows] or **Cmd+F3** [Mac]). From the **Horz** (Horizontal) pull-down menu, choose **Center**. From the **Vert** (Vertical) pull-down menu, choose **Middle**. This sets the alignment of the table cell so that content placed within it is aligned in the center horizontally and in the middle vertically (in the middle of the page essentially).

11. Click in the middle of the page. You'll notice that your blinking insertion point is now in the middle. When you place a SWF file into this cell, that's where it will be embedded.

Now, before you can place anything within this HTML page, you should save it first. Dreamweaver MX 2004 needs to know where the content you're placing in the page resides relative *to where the HTML page itself is saved. To keep your site files organized, you're going to save this HTML page in the same folder as the rest of your L.A. Eyeworks site files.*

12. Choose **File > Save** (**Ctrl+S** [Windows] or **Cmd+S** [Mac]).

13. In the **Save As** window, navigate to your **Desktop > la_eyeworks > site** folder.

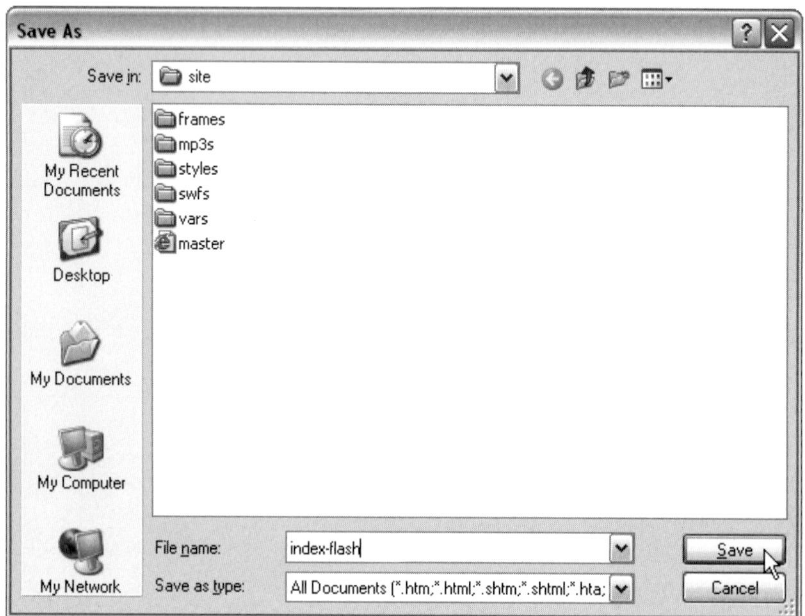

14. In the **File name** field, type **index-flash** and click **Save**. Dreamweaver MX 2004 automatically inserts an **.htm** extension on the end of the file name.

*Now that you've saved your **index-flash.htm** file into the **site** folder, you can embed the SWF file into the HTML page. But which SWF file should you embed? All in all, the L.A. Eyeworks Flash MX 2004–built Web site is constructed with approximately 15 SWF files. Out of those, which one should you embed? The SWF file you want to place in the HTML page should be whichever SWF is Level 0. The SWF that the other SWFs load into is the one you want to place in the HTML page. In the case of the L.A. Eyeworks site, that is **master.swf**. (It's not called "master" for nothing ya know.)*

---

15. First, click in the middle of the table cell so you see the blinking insertion icon there, and then choose **Insert > Media > Flash** (**Ctrl+Alt+F** [Windows] or **Cmd+Option+F** [Mac]).

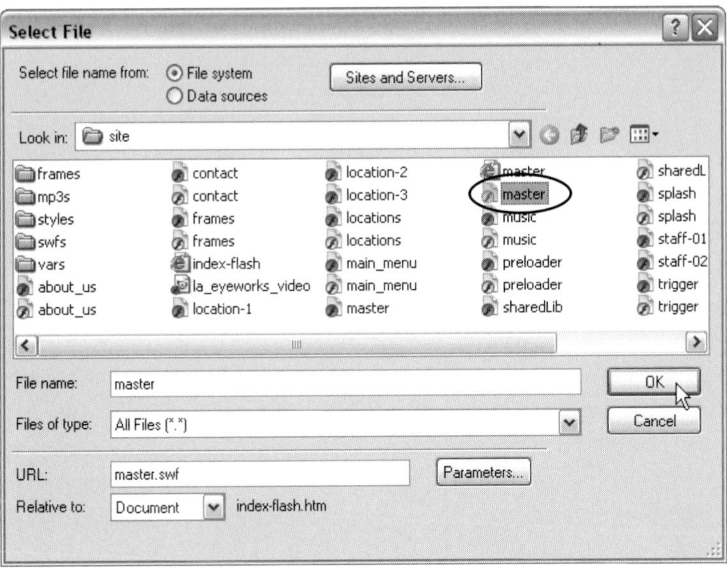

16. In the **Select File** dialog box, navigate to your **Desktop > la_eyeworks > site** folder, single-click **master.swf**, and click **OK** (Windows) or **Choose** (Mac).

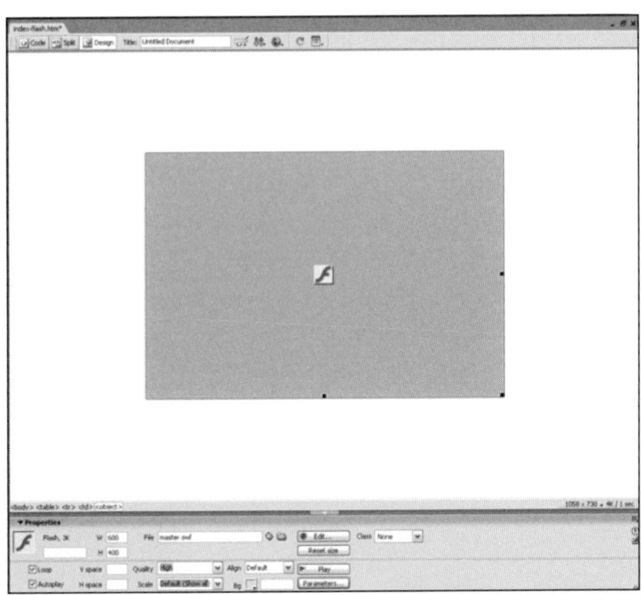

You'll notice that now, in the middle of the HTML page, is a grey box with the Flash logo in the middle. That gray box is your ***master.swf*** *file, already set at the correct size and ready to go!*

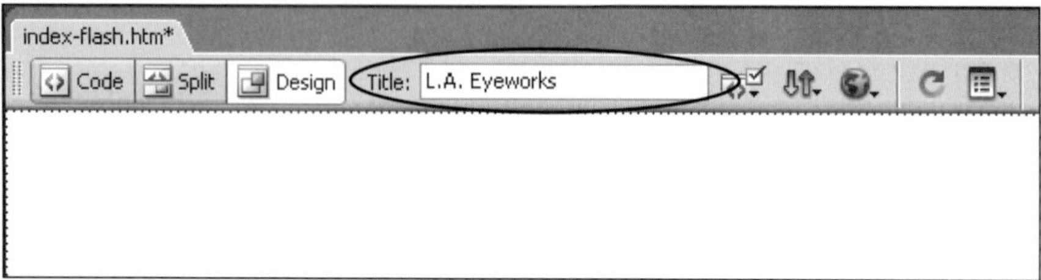

17. In the bar above the HTML page, type **L.A. Eyeworks** in the **Title** field. This is the name that will appear in the title bar of the browser window when the viewer visits this page.

18. Save your changes by choosing **File > Save** (**Ctrl+S** [Windows] or **Cmd+S** [Mac]). Then, preview your HTML page in the default browser (Internet Explorer, unless you've changed it in Dreamweaver MX 2004) by pressing **F12** (same on both Windows and Mac).

Note: *You can change the browser that Dreamweaver MX 2004 uses to preview HTML pages by clicking the* ***Preview/Debug in Browser*** *icon in the bar at the top of the HTML page and by choosing* ***Edit Browser List****. From the* ***Preferences*** *window that then opens, you can add or remove your preferred browsers. By selecting a browser in the list and clicking the* ***Primary browser*** *option, you can specify that HTML pages be opened with that particular browser when you press* ***F12****.*

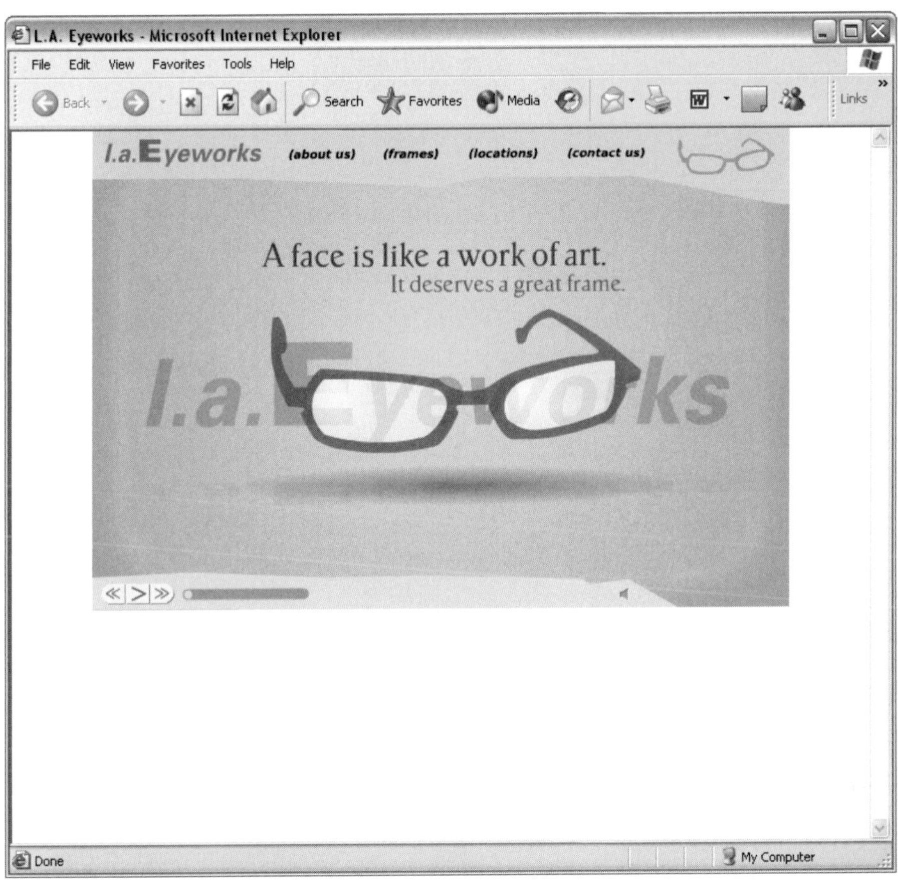

When your preferred browser opens and displays your HTML page, you'll notice that–sure enough–the L.A. Eyeworks site displays in the page and works correctly. Hooray! However, you might also notice that the SWF file isn't centered in the vertical middle of the page. It's centered in the middle horizontally, but instead of being in the center of the page, it's aligned at the top! Luckily, this is a small inconsistency with how Dreamweaver MX 2004 writes its HTML code and can be easily remedied.

***Note:** If you're running a Mac, depending on the browser you're using you might notice that the SWF file is, in fact aligned in the center of the browser window. However, to create this page so that the SWF file aligns in the center of nearly* all *browser windows on both Windows and Mac alike, you need to make a minor edit, which you will be performing next.*

---

19. Close your browser window and return to **index-flash.htm** in Dreamweaver MX 2004.

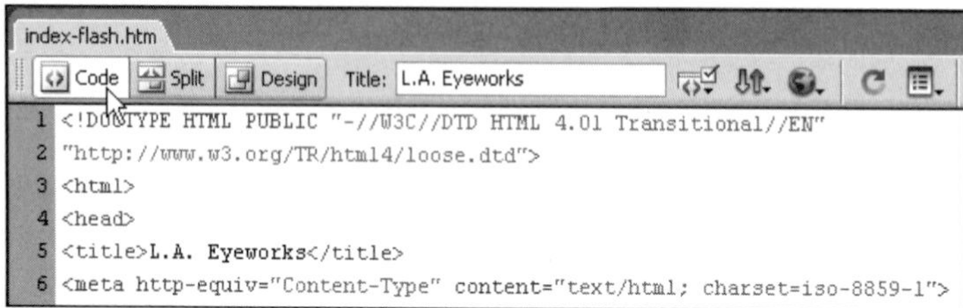

20. From the bar at the top of the HTML page, click the **Code** button to switch to **Code** view instead of **Design** view.

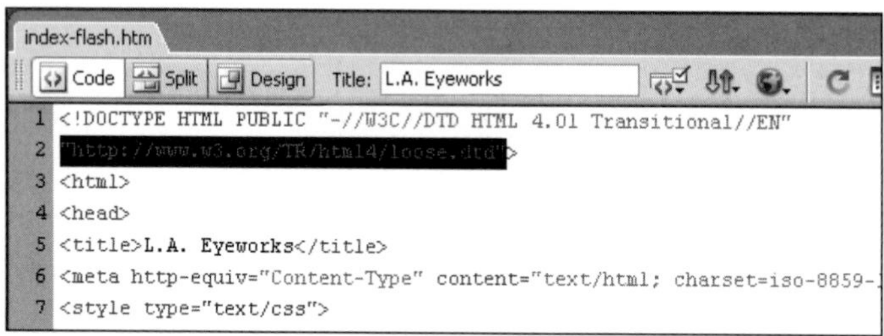

21. In **line 2**, select the code **"http://www.w3.org/TR/html4/loose.dtd"** and press **Delete** twice. This will delete that selected code and move the > symbol to the end of **line 1**.

Note: *This code is something that Dreamweaver MX 2004 inserts. If you prefer to use a different WYSIWYG HTML editor such as Adobe GoLive, you probably will not have to perform this extra step.*

```
<!DOCTYPE HTML PUBLIC "-//W3C//DTD HTML 4.01 Transitional//EN">
<html>
<head>
<title>L.A. Eyeworks</title>
<meta http-equiv="Content-Type" content="text/html; charset=iso-8859-1">
<style type="text/css">
<!--
```

When you've deleted that one line, your HTML syntax should look like the code above.

22. Save your changes by choosing **File > Save** (**Ctrl+S** [Windows] or **Cmd+S** [Mac]).

23. Preview your changes again by pressing **F12**.

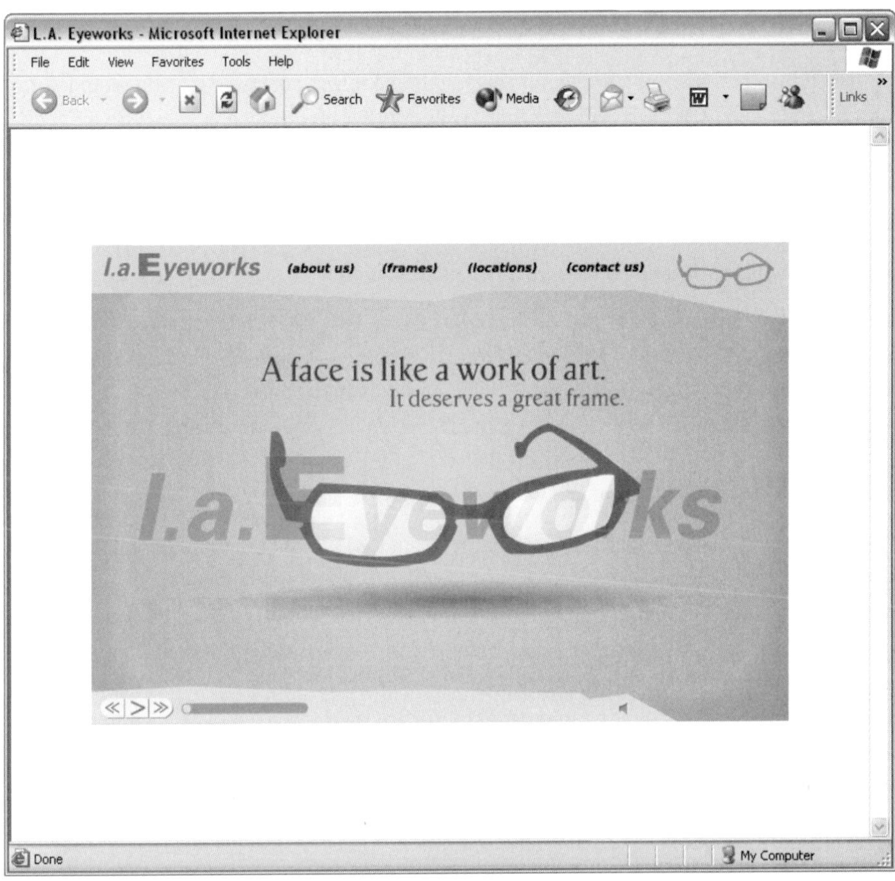

With the removal of that line, you'll now notice that the SWF file displays correctly in the center of the page, both horizontally and vertically. Huzzah!

24. Close your Web browser and return to Dreamweaver MX 2004.

25. Close **index-flash.htm** and quit Dreamweaver MX 2004. You won't need it again.

As you saw in this exercise, inserting a SWF file into an HTML page is a relatively simple task. With a few clicks of a button, you're ready to upload your content to your Web server for the whole world to see.

In the next exercise, you will construct the ever-useful, Flash plug-in detector.

Potential Upcoming Embedding Changes

To comply with the rulings of a patent infringement lawsuit, Microsoft *might* begin making changes to Internet Explorer beginning in 2004 that will alter how embedded content–such as Flash SWF files, Apple QuickTime movies, and other media that use the **<object>**, **<embed>**, or **<applet>** tags–will be treated by the browser. I say "might" because at the time of writing this, Microsoft is currently appealing the ruling, and this issue is still somewhat up in the air.

The issue in question goes something like this:

Normally, as you might have noticed in the last exercise when you saw the HTML code in the Web page you created in Dreamweaver MX 2004, Flash SWF files are embedded in an HTML page using both the **<embed>** and **<object>** tags. Internet Explorer, Apple's Safari, Netscape, Mozilla, Mozilla Firebird, and so forth all use these tags to automatically display your SWF file when the page loads. But because the legal use of these tags is in question due to the lawsuit, Internet Explorer–and most likely the other Web browsers as well–will have to change the way they display media that use those tags.

If you *do not* alter the way your SWF files are embedded into an HTML page and you continue to use the **<object>** and **<embed>** tags as you just did in the last exercise, a Web browser that has been updated to comply with the lawsuit would no longer automatically display your media. Instead, the viewer would be presented with a message, asking whether or not the visitor wants to view that content. Obviously, this change would have a detrimental effect on the "seamless" Web browsing experience that we all currently appreciate. After these changes to Internet Explorer are made, a viewer will have to confirm–*every time*–whether he or she wants to view specific types of content.

Currently–at the time that this book was written–the major players such as Microsoft, Apple, and (those most affected by this change) are working on tools that will allow a Web site designer or developer to insert their media into an HTML page *without* requiring the viewer to confirm the loading of such content. However, those tools do not exist yet. There is currently a somewhat complex manual way to update affected HTML pages, but if I showed you how to do it, it would most likely be outdated by the time this book was published anyway. Not only that, but while this book is being printed, Microsoft may win its appeal against the lawsuit and no changes to **<object>** or **<embed>** would be required, thus making this issue a moot point.

However, if you would like to read more about this issue, find tools to help make your Flash MX 2004-based Web sites compatible with these potential changes, or read instructions on updating your site using the manual way in the off chance that the appropriate tools aren't yet available by the time this book is published, you can visit the following Web sites:

http://msdn.microsoft.com/ieupdate/

http://www.macromedia.com/devnet/activecontent/faq.html

http://developer.apple.com/internet/ieembedprep.html

I will also update the support site for this book should anything new happen concerning this issue. Because this issue affects many different kinds of content across millions of Web pages, you can bet I'll be keeping a close eye on this issue. You can find the URL to the support site printed in the "*Introduction*" chapter at the beginning of this book, as well as in Appendix A at the end of this book.

Flash Plug-In Detector Options

Flash plug-in detectors come in a variety of styles. Some use pure JavaScript to do all the work, and others use a combination of JavaScript and Flash content. If you want to implement a Flash plug-in detector into your Web site, you essentially have four choices, each of which is discussed in the following sections.

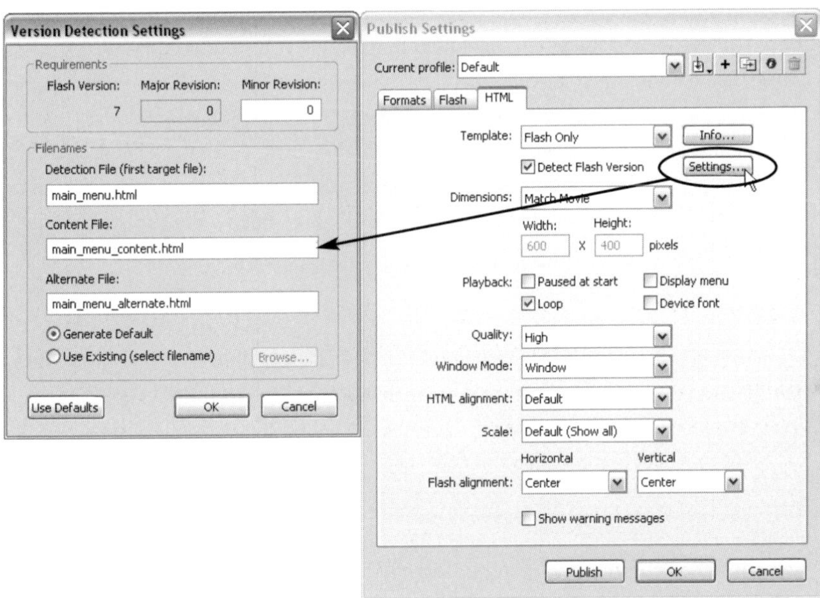

Flash MX 2004

You can use the new, built-in Flash plug-in detector. Simply enable the publishing of an HTML page from the **Publish Settings** dialog box available under **File > Publish Settings**. Then, in the **HTML** tab, click the **Detect Flash Version** check box. Clicking the **Settings** button will then give you the **Version Detection Settings** dialog box, which allows you to determine various settings about where readers should get directed to based on their plug-in version, as well as which plug-in version is the minimum one required for entry.

- **Pros:** It's built right into Flash MX 2004. You don't need any additional software, there are no extra files to edit, and it's very easy to use and configure.

- **Cons:** It doesn't let you specify your own file to use as the **Content File**–the page with the Flash MX 2004 content on it. You can specify the name to *give* the content file when Flash MX 2004 creates it, but you cannot set the content file to an HTML file that you've already built. If you try, it will simply overwrite your file with its own. Since you spent the last exercise designing your own HTML page that your SWF file resides in, this is obviously a problem. There is a way around that problem, however, as you will see in the following exercise.

Flash MX 2004 Detection Kit

Flash MX 2004 also offers a Detection Kit that comes in several flavors. If you point your Web browser to **http://www.macromedia.com/software/flash/download/detection_kit/**, you can download an "official" Flash plug-in detector directly from Macromedia. The kit contains a Flash plug-in detector that you can implement using a variety of techniques. If you're comfortable with Dreamweaver MX or later, the Detection Kit comes with a Dreamweaver extension that allows you to create the plug-in detector from within Dreamweaver itself. If you don't have Dreamweaver, or if you're more comfortable working directly with HTML code, the detection kit also has an HTML version that you can edit manually. Last, the detection kit also comes with an ActionScript-based plug-in detector that, if you feel you're most comfortable working with ActionScript, you can edit to your liking. Each of these methods of creating a Flash plug-in detector comes with its own set of instructions. Follow the provided steps, and you've got yourself a nifty plug-in detector.

- **Pros:**

  You have three options (outlined above) when creating the Flash plug-in detector. This gives you great flexibility because you can build the plug-in detector using whichever method you're most comfortable with.

  The Dreamweaver MX extension is also a great, easy, point-and-click way to create a Flash plug-in detector directly inside of Dreamweaver MX or Dreamweaver MX 2004.

- **Cons:** It requires a little more work because it's not built directly into Flash MX 2004.

Colin Moock's Flash Player Inspector (FPI)

Flash ActionScript guru and author Colin Moock has constructed his own Flash plug-in detector. Although some Flash developers swear by Macromedia's Flash Detection Kit, others swear by Colin Moock's Flash Player Inspector (FPI). If Macromedia's Flash Detection Kit isn't working out for you for one reason or another, or if you're simply feeling adventurous, feel free to give Moock's detection script a try. You can download it and read more about it here:

http://www.moock.org/webdesign/flash/detection/moockfpi/

- **Pros:** Moock's FPI is a very thorough detection script. It also gives you good control over where the viewer should be redirected to depending on which version of the Flash Player he or she has installed.

- **Cons:** You need to edit some text in an HTML file to set it up correctly. Unlike the built-in detection script that is in Flash MX 2004 and the Dreamweaver Extension, there is no easy-to-use interface to define all of the script settings. However, it should be said that Moock has made it clear which parts of the file should be edited and what they all mean.

Splash Page

You could also elect to simply forgo the Flash plug-in detector completely (as they're never 100 percent accurate) and instead create a **splash page**. This splash page, usually called **index.html**, would be the first page the viewer sees when he or she enters your site. On the splash page, you would state that your site uses Flash, and if the viewer wants to enter your site, he or she needs to have the Flash Player version 7 (or whichever version is the minimum that you're requiring) or greater to enter. You could also provide a friendly link to download the correct version of the Flash Player or another link to enter an alternate version of your Web site, an HTML version, for example. This method allows the *viewer* to determine whether or not he or she can enter your site instead of allowing a detection script to do that work for them automatically.

- **Pros:** You don't have to worry about setting up or configuring a detection script. Instead, the visitor becomes the plug-in detector, deciding whether or not he or she has the correct version of the Flash plug-in required to enter the site. This also prevents the viewer from *not* being able to enter your site in the event that a detection script fails.
- **Cons:** Not all visitors know which version of the Flash Player they have installed on their computer. If they don't know and decide to enter your Web site anyway, they could be met by a Web site that is nearly completely broken if they don't have the correct version–or higher–of the Flash Player installed.

One other thing to keep in mind when you're creating a Flash plug-in detector is that they're not fool-proof. Depending on various factors on the viewer's computer and browser, the detection script could fail, potentially leaving your visitor staring at a blank page. A *must* when you're creating a plug-in detector is to *always* add a hyperlink on the page that contains the plug-in detection script as well as the page the viewer gets redirected to if the detection script thinks he or she doesn't have the correct version of the Flash plug-in. This hyperlink would point to the front page of your Web site and/or to your Flash MX 2004 content itself. That way, if the detection script fails for some reason, the viewer won't be left stranded on a page. As a Web surfer, if there's one thing I despise when trying to view a Flash site, it's when someone's Flash detection script tells me that I *don't* have the correct version of the Flash plug-in (when I *know* I do) and then leaves me on that page without a hyperlink to allow me to enter the site anyway. Please, please, please add a hyperlink to your detection script pages–especially the page the viewer gets redirected to.

2. Building a Flash MX 2004 Plug-In Detector

Imagine this: A viewer comes to your Web site, and your Flash MX 2004-built Web page loads in his or her browser. Wanting to see where the closest L.A. Eyeworks store is located, the viewer clicks the **(locations)** option in the navigation menu. Nothing happens. No preloader, no loading, no nothing. The viewer clicks again. Nothing. The viewer, starting to wonder what's going on, clicks **(about us)**. Still, nothing happens. Disgusted with this "broken" Web site, the viewer leaves. Little did the viewer know that the reason the site was "broken" was because he or she had the Flash 6 plug-in, and your site uses the `MovieClipLoader` class in the navigation bar to load the appropriate content–a feature that the version 6 plug-in doesn't understand. Thankfully, this hypothetical scenario–which is, unfortunately, sometimes not hypothetical–is preventable.

If you take a few minutes of your time, you can install a Flash plug-in detector (sometimes called a plug-in "sniffer") that would catch a viewer attempting to enter your site with a version of the Flash plug-in that your site doesn't support. Although viewers with the *correct* version, or higher, of the Flash plug-in installed can easily–and seamlessly–enter your Web site, viewers with an *earlier* version of the plug-in can be redirected to another URL of your choosing. Unless you're constructing Flash content for projector playback, I would *highly* recommend *always* using a Flash plug-in detector.

In this exercise, you will build a Flash plug-in detector using the new **Detect Flash Version** option now available directly inside of Flash MX 2004. This allows you to quickly and easily create a Flash plug-in detector. Even though it has that slight drawback that I mentioned before this exercise, there's an easy workaround to that problem.

The first step is to open an FLA. But which one? Because you've already created the **index-flash.htm** page that **master.swf** is embedded into, it doesn't really matter which FLA you open to create the Flash plug-in detector. When Flash MX 2004 creates the plug-in detector, it will automatically create a few different files needed for the actual plug-in detection. These files are in no way linked to the FLA you use to generate them. So once you already have the HTML page with your SWF file embedded in it–which you built in the first exercise–the FLA you choose to open to create the plug-in detector is inconsequential. You could even create a new, blank FLA–if you choose–to act as the FLA that generates the plug-in detector. However, rather than clutter up your site folder with yet another FLA, you're instead going to open an existing FLA, generate the plug-in detector, and close the FLA without saving any changes. The plug-in detector for this L.A. Eyeworks site needs to be generated only once.

1. On your hard drive, navigate to your **Desktop > la_eyeworks > site** folder and double-click **master.fla** to open it in Flash MX 2004.

2. Choose **File > Publish Settings** to open the **Publish Settings** window.

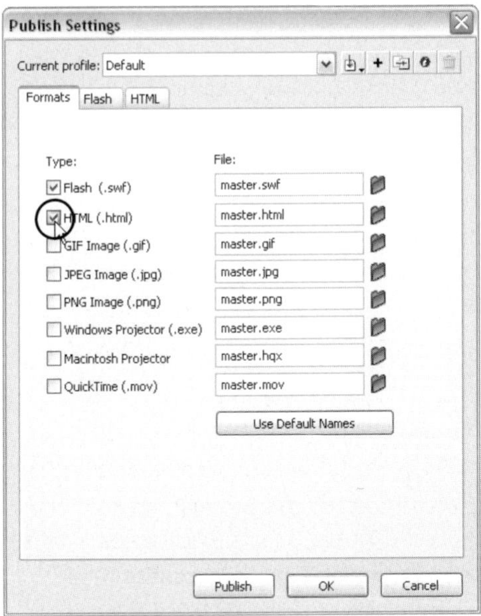

3. Under the **Formats** tab, make sure there's a checkmark in the **HTML (.html)** option.

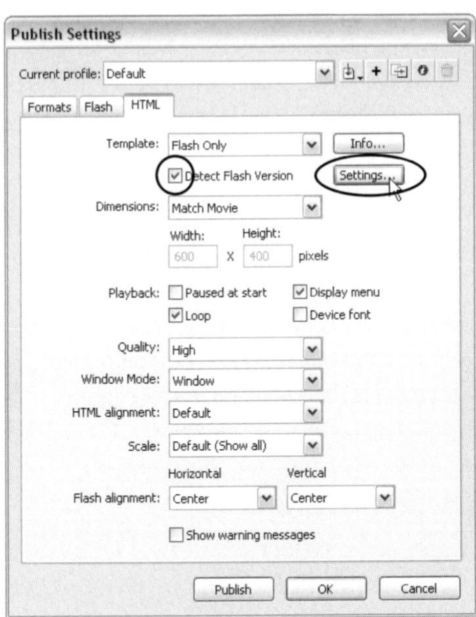

4. Click the **HTML** tab to display the HTML preferences. Then, click the **Detect Flash Version** check box, and click **Settings**.

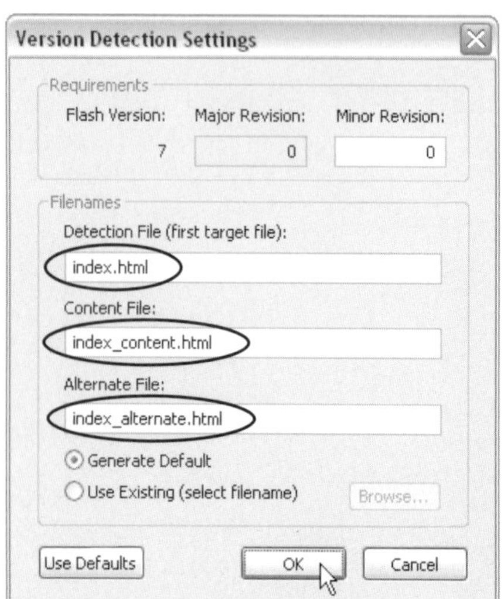

5. In the **Version Detection Settings** dialog box, change the **Detection File** to **index.html**. This is the first file the viewer will encounter when he or she wants to view your Flash MX 2004 content. As such, it is the page that will have the Flash-detection script in it. In the **Content File** field, type **index_content.html**. This is the page the viewer will get redirected to if he or she has the correct version of the Flash plug-in installed. Now, because you already constructed a page titled **index-flash.html** in Exercise 1, to prevent Flash MX 2004 from overwriting it when it creates the plug-in detector files, you're going to temporarily give the **Content File** a different file name. Last, in the **Alternate File** field, type **index_alternate.html**. This is the file the viewer will get redirected to if he or she has the *incorrect* version of the Flash plug-in version installed.

*Because you're not targeting a specific revision of the Flash version 7 plug-in, you can leave the **Minor Revision** field at the top of the window set to **0**.*

---

6. Click **OK**.

Now that you've instructed the Flash plug-in detector which file names to use for the HTML page that will contain the detection script itself; the HTML page that contains the Flash MX 2004 content; and the HTML page to redirect visitors to if they fail the detection script, you're all set to have Flash MX 2004 create all those files for you. To do that, all you have to do is publish your document.

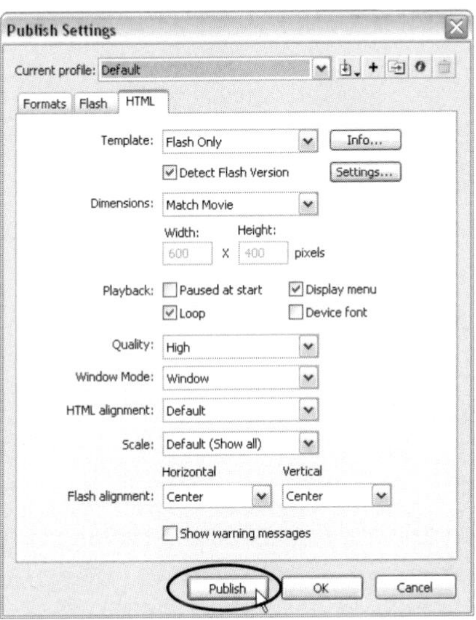

7. In the **Publish Settings** window, click **Publish**. This will publish the plug-in detector script and all the files related to it.

*Now that you've used **master.fla** to create the Flash plug-in detector, you don't need to leave the **Detect Flash Version** option enabled. Unless you change the file name of the content page, you won't need to republish the plug-in detection script. If you leave that option enabled, every time you publish **master.fla**, it will rebuild all the plug-in detection files.*

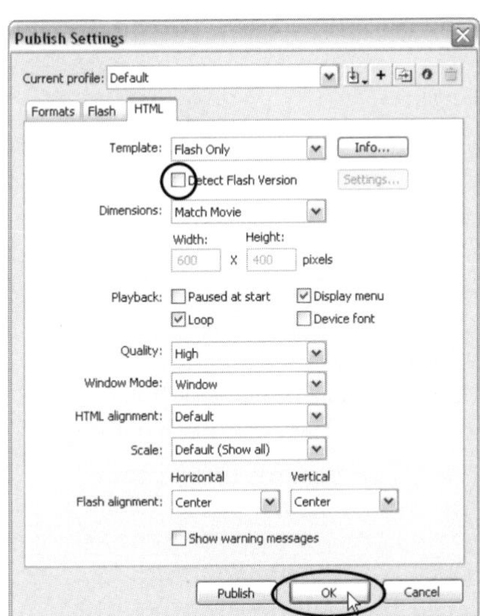

8. In the **HTML** tab, uncheck **Detect Flash Version** and click **OK**.

---

9. Hide or minimize Flash MX 2004, and on your hard drive navigate to your **Desktop > la_eyeworks > site** folder.

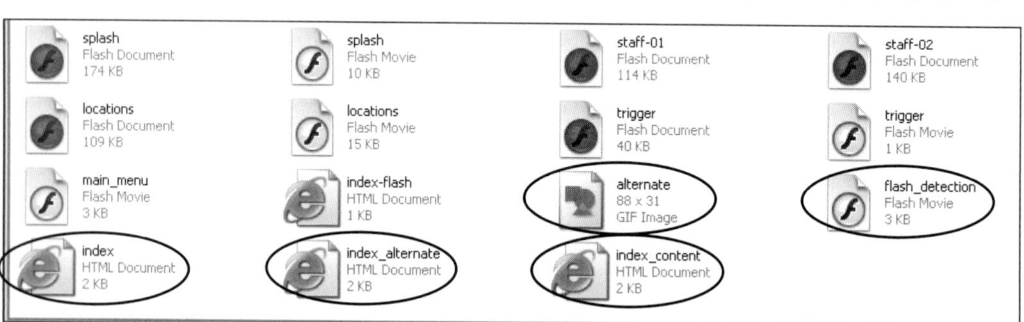

*In the **site** folder, you'll notice that Flash MX 2004 has created five new files that comprise the plug-in detector. **index.html** is the first page the viewer should hit when he or she wants to view your Flash content. That's the page that has the actual plug-in detector written into it. The **flash_detection.swf** file is embedded into **index.html** and is essentially the "engine" of the plug-in detection. **index_alternate.html** and **alternate.gif** comprise the page that the viewer will get redirected to if he or she* does not meet *the requirements of the Flash plug-in detector. **index_content.html** is the page that the viewer will see if he or she* does *have the correct version of the Flash Player and everything checks out. However, because Flash MX 2004 created that **index_content.html** file and embedded **master.swf** within it, it's not positioned and aligned like you constructed in Exercise 1 with **index-flash.htm**. **index-flash.htm** is the page that you* really *want the plug-in detector to display if the viewer meets the requirements.*

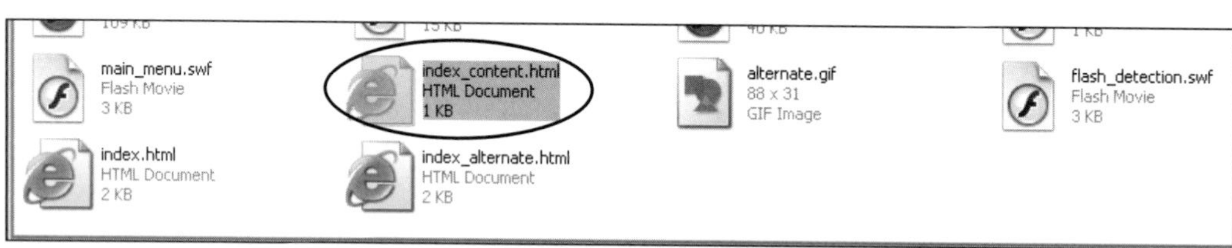

10. Delete **index_content.html**. Then, rename **index-flash.htm** to **index_content.html**.

Note: *If you're running Windows, you'll need to instruct your operating system to display the file extensions so you can change the **.htm** to **.html** (which is what the plug-in detector is targeting). There are instructions on how to show file extensions in Windows in the "*Introduction*" chapter at the beginning of this book. After you've successfully changed the file name, you can choose to hide the file extensions again if you'd like.*

Congratulations! You've just created, with the click of a few mouse buttons and the waving of a magical Flash wand, a Flash plug-in detector. You should test it just to make sure everything is working as intended.

11. Open **index.html** in your preferred Web browser. Normally, you can simply double-click the file to open it in your system's default browser.

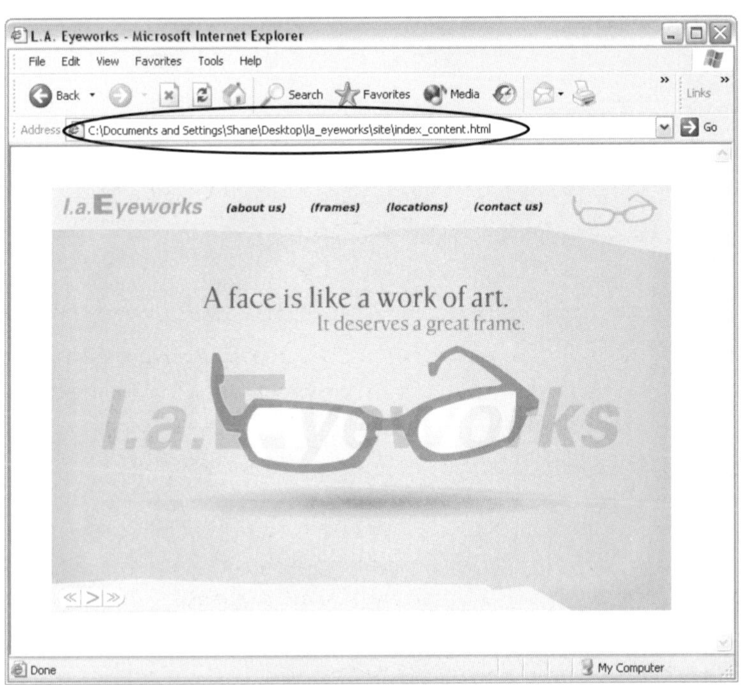

*When your browser opens **index.html**, you'll notice that your L.A. Eyeworks site successfully displays! Also, if you look in the address bar in your browser, you'll notice that even though you opened **index.html**, the HTML file you're currently looking at is **index_content.html**. This is because the Flash plug-in detector, having discovered that you're running a recent version of the Flash plug-in, redirected you to the **index_content.html** page that has the Flash content embedded in it.*

*Now unfortunately, in the Windows operating system, it's not very easy to disable or deactivate the Flash plug-in so that you can test whether the rest of the plug-in detector works. If you really, really want to fully test the functionality of the plug-in detector, you can download the Flash Player uninstaller from **http://www.macromedia.com/support/flash/ts/documents/remove_player.htm**, uninstall the Flash Player from your system, test the plug-in detector, and then reinstall the Flash Player when you're finished. If you really, really want test the plug-in detector in Mac OS X, you can move the file **Shockwave Flash NP-PPC** out of the **/Library/Internet Plug-ins/** folder (and also from your **~/Library/Internet Plug-ins/** folder if it is there as well), test the plug-in detector, and then move **Shockwave Flash NP-PPC** back to the **Internet Plug-ins** folder when you're finished. However, rather than go through all those steps, you're just going to have to trust me that the rest of it works as intended. You can, however, easily see what a viewer who does not meet the plug-in requirements will see.*

12. Close your Web browser window. On your hard drive, navigate to your **Desktop > la_eyeworks > site** folder and open **index_alternate.html** in your preferred Web browser.

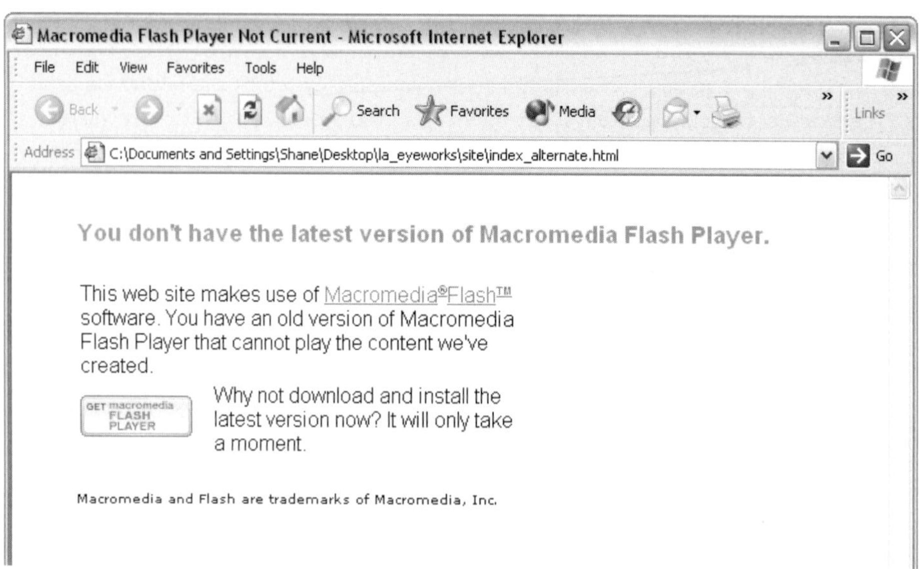

As you can see, it's just a simple page that notifies the viewer that he or she does not have the correct version of the Flash Player installed and provides a link where the viewer can download and install the latest version. Now, of course, you can edit this page to your liking and modify it so that it fits the look and feel of the rest of your site. As I mentioned previously, I would highly encourage you to add a hyperlink on this page that links to the page with the Flash content. In this case, that page is ***index_content.html****. The link could say something to the effect of, "If you know you have the correct version of the Flash Player installed and you feel this message is in error, click here to enter the Flash site." That way, if the detection script fails for one reason or another, a viewer won't get stuck on this error page.*

And that is one of several ways to create a Flash plug-in detector. With the introduction of Flash MX 2004, the capability to create a plug-in detector is now built into Flash itself. As you've seen, this makes it incredibly easy to quickly create a plug-in detector. Now you have no excuse not to add a plug-in detector to everything you build in Flash MX 2004. ;-)

Conclusion

In this chapter, you learned how to embed a SWF file into an HTML page using Dreamweaver MX 2004 and how to create a plug-in detector to prevent viewers with an older version of the Flash Player from entering your site. Your L.A. Eyeworks site is now ready to upload to a Web server so the whole world can see it! Because you've been consistently keeping your L.A. Eyeworks site-related files in the **la_eyeworks > site** folder on your **Desktop**, when you have a Web presence provider and you're ready to upload your work, all you have to do is upload all the files in the **site** folder (minus the FLA files, of course) to your Web server, and you're done!

You're also done with this book as well! A giant, humongous congratulations is in order, too. For those of you who considered yourself "ActionScript challenged" and have made it through to the end of this book, you have earned my sincere respect. This book introduced you all to a plethora of ActionScript concepts, many of them most likely new to you. From this book, you've gained the knowledge of how to use ActionScript to bring that extremely important element of *dynamics* into your Flash MX 2004 projects. By using ActionScript to build a dynamic site, you enable yourself–or your client–to easily manage and update a site by modifying only a few items.

Throughout this book you also learned how to create fun but *useful* and *practical* functionality. For example, you created an MP3 player that didn't just play MP3s, but also allowed the viewer to stop the music, skip to the next or previous track, change the volume, and even observe the playback and downloading progress of the MP3. Suffering slightly from the reputation it gained in its infancy, the general preconception of Flash is that it is used to create useless "intro animations" or other flourishes that serve no functional purpose. As you've seen in this book, nothing could be further from the truth. In these pages, I hope you've learned how to create some really fun things but, more importantly, I hope you've learned how to use Flash to say or present what you need to in a *functional* and *useful* manner.

Once again, congratulations.

:-)

Shane Rebenschied

Technical Support and Troubleshooting FAQ

| Troubleshooting | Frequently Asked Questions |
| Technical Support |

H•O•T

Macromedia Flash MX 2004
Beyond the Basics

Troubleshooting

If you run into any problems while following the exercises in this book, you might find the answer in this troubleshooting guide. This section will be maintained and updated at this book's companion Web site: **http://www.lynda.com/products/books/fl04btbhot/**.

If you don't find what you're looking for here or at the Web site, please send an email–with a *detailed* description of the problem you're experiencing *and* attach the FLA (if possible) that you're having difficulties with–to **fl04btbhot@lynda.com**.

If you have a question related to Flash MX 2004 but unrelated to a specific step in an exercise in this book, visit the Flash site at **http://www.macromedia.com/support/flash/**, or you can contact Macromedia by email at **http://www.macromedia.com/support/email/complimentary/main.cgi**.

Frequently Asked Questions

Q: I'm having ___________ (insert error here) errors. Why?

A: Before you try anything else, download the Flash MX 2004 7.0.1 updater. It resolves many issues, of which one may be the problem you're experiencing. You can download the updater at the following URL:

http://www.macromedia.com/support/flash/downloads.html

Q: On the Macintosh, why can't I see any FLA files when I choose File > Open?

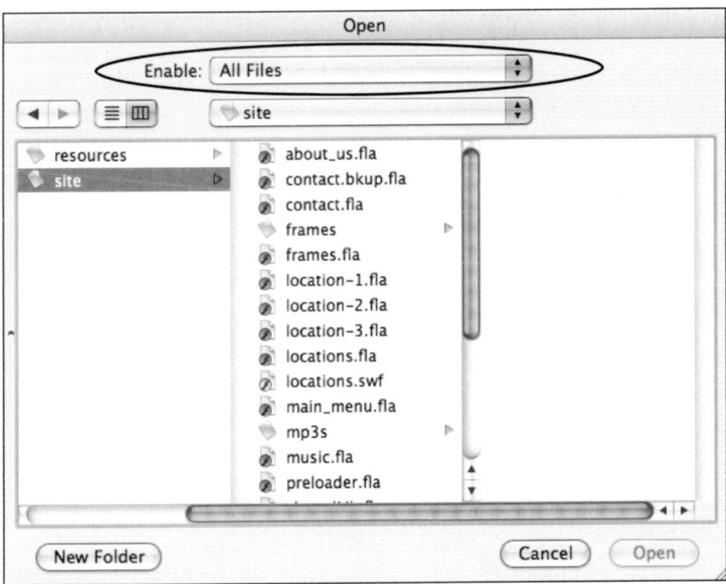

A: If the FLA file was created on a PC, you might experience a problem seeing those files when you choose **File > Open** from within Flash MX 2004 on a Macintosh. You can correct this by changing the **Enable** option to **All Files**.

Q: On the Macintosh, when I try to double-click the FLA file to open it, it will not open in Flash MX 2004. Why?

A: If the FLA file was created on a PC, you might not be able to double-click it to open the file. If this is the case, open Flash MX 2004 and choose **File > Open** to open the FLA file. If you don't see the FLA file listed when you choose **File > Open**, see the previous question. Once you save the FLA file (originally created on a PC) on your Mac, you will be able to double-click the FLA to open it.

Q: When I select the Text tool, my Properties inspector doesn't update to show me my text options. What's up with that?

A: Sometimes the **Properties inspector** will not update when you switch to the **Text** tool. To get the **Properties inspector** to display text options when you select the **Text** tool, click the **Stage**. This will cause the **Properties inspector** to update, thereby displaying the **Text** tool options. However, if clicking the **Stage** also creates a dynamic or input text field, press **Esc** and then **Backspace** or **Delete** to delete the text field.

Q: I can't get a certain action or script to work correctly. I've gone over what you said and have rebuilt the exercise a billion times, but it still won't work. Help!

A: One of the most common mistakes is often the simplest. Double-check your spelling to make sure everything–ActionScript syntax, variables, and so forth–is spelled correctly. Second, double-check that you are using capitalization consistently. In other words, if you are creating a variable `var myVar`, but are then later referring to that variable as `myvar`, it won't work. (Notice the difference in capitalization.) Flash MX 2004 is now case-sensitive, so you need to make sure you use your capitalization correctly and consistently. Last, double-check your semicolons, commas, quotation marks, and so on. ActionScript syntax uses a variety of symbols to represent various things, and it can get quite complex at times. Double-check that you're using those symbols in the same way and order that they're being displayed in the book. If you've performed all these steps and it still doesn't work, email the support address for this book–with a *detailed* description of the problem you're having and the FLA (if possible) that you're having the difficulties with–at **fl04btbhot@lynda.com**.

Q: Can I reuse the elements–graphics, audio or otherwise–in this book and on the H•O•T CD-ROM for client work or personal experimentation?

A: The assets in the book and on the **H•O•T CD-ROM** are there as tools to help you learn and understand the exercises and concepts. However, those assets *cannot* be used for client work. If you want to use them in your own experimental or personal work, feel free. But the assets *may not* be used for commercial work.

Technical Support

Macromedia Technical Support

http://www.macromedia.com/support/flash/ or
http://www.macromedia.com/support/email/complimentary/main.cgi

http://webforums.macromedia.com/flash/

If you're having problems with Flash MX 2004, please visit the first link to access the Flash Support Center. To contact Macromedia Technical Support, use the email form in the second link. They can help you with typical problems, such as when the trial version has expired on your computer, or your computer crashes when you try to launch the application. You can also try visiting the third link listed above, which is the support forums for Flash. That forum oftentimes has very helpful people who can answer your questions. Please note that lynda.com cannot help troubleshoot technical problems with Flash MX 2004.

Peachpit Press

customer_service@peachpit.com

If your book has a defective CD-ROM, please contact the customer service department at this email address. We do not have extra CDs at lynda.com, so they must be requested directly from the publisher.

lynda.com

We have created a companion Web site for this book, which can be found at **http://www.lynda.com/products/books/fl04btbhot/**

Any errors in the book will be posted to this Web site, and it's always a good idea to check there for up-to-date information. We encourage and welcome your comments and error reports at **fl04btbhot@lynda.com**. Shane will receive these emails. Please allow a 72-hour turnaround on your questions or comments, and longer on weekends or holidays.

B.

Macromedia Flash MX 2004 Resources

| Macromedia Flash MX 2004 Application Development Center |
Online Forums	Macromedia Exchange for Flash
Macromedia TechNotes	Web Sites	Flashforward	CD-ROMs
Online Training	Books	Software

H•O•T

Macromedia Flash MX 2004
Beyond the Basics

There is an incredible amount of resources and help available online for Flash MX 2004—everything from Web sites, to online forums, to email discussion groups. This appendix shares the best places I know of to get help and to discuss Flash MX 2004.

Macromedia Flash MX 2004 Application Development Center

http://www.macromedia.com/desdev/mx/flash/

Macromedia has created a section of its Web site called the Flash MX 2004 Application Development Center. This is a one-stop shop for everything Flash. For example, you can read tutorials and articles on Flash MX 2004, download sample applications, access links to other Flash MX 2004 resources, and read the white papers written on topics related to Flash MX 2004. This is the perfect link to use if you want to get more in-depth information about components, video, or other topics in Flash MX 2004.

Macromedia Online Forums

http://webforums.macromedia.com/flash/

Macromedia has set up several Web-based online forums for Flash. This is a great place to ask questions and get help from thousands of Flash users. These online forums are used by beginning to advanced Flash users, so you should have no problem finding the type of help you need, regardless of your experience with the program. The following list describes several of Macromedia's online forums.

Flash General Discussion
Online forum for general issues related to using Flash.

Flash ActionScript
This online forum is dedicated, of course, to everything ActionScript. Post your ActionScript-related questions and search for your ActionScript-related answers here.

Flash Handhelds
Online forum for technical issues related to creating Flash content for handheld devices, such as the PocketPC.

Flash Site Design
Online forum for design feedback on your Flash MX 2004 animations. This forum is dedicated to the discussion of Flash design and animation principles and practices. Other issues not specific to the Flash tools, yet important to Flash designers, can also be discussed here.

Flash Remoting
Online forum that discusses issues involved with Flash Remoting. Flash Remoting supplies the infrastructure that allows users to connect to remote services exposed by application server developers and Web services. Examples of these are message boards, shopping carts, and even up-to-the-minute stock quote graphs.

Flash Exchange Extensions
Online forum for issues relating to Flash MX 2004 extensions, including how to use them and how to troubleshoot any problems with them. (See also the "Macromedia Exchange for Flash" section on the following page.)

Flash Communication Server

Online forum to discuss issues relating to the **F**lash **C**ommunication **S**erver (FCS). The Flash Communication Server, among other things, allows video and audio to be truly streamed (RTMP streaming) to the viewer's computer.

Flash Data Integration

This online forum is dedicated to the topic of integrating data into your Flash MX 2004 movies. Want to learn, or have questions on integrating database content into your Flash movies MX 2004? Post your questions or search for your answers here.

Flash Ad Development

This online forum is dedicated to discussing "the development of rich media ad units using Flash and the Flash Ad Kit for DoubleClick DART Motif or other advertising-related Flash content."

Macromedia Exchange for Flash

http://www.macromedia.com/exchange/flash/

Macromedia has set up another section of its Web site called the Macromedia Flash Exchange. There you'll find hundreds of free extensions written by third-party users and developers that can help you build new features into your Web site. These features are not part of the Flash MX 2004 product, but they can be downloaded when you need them. Many of these extensions have features that normally would require an advanced level of ActionScript. For example, some of these behaviors enable you to create password-protected areas of your site and to create pop-up menus, scroll bars, complex text effects, and so on.

The Macromedia site is not just for developers but also for Flash MX 2004 users who want to take Flash MX 2004 to the next level. If you are a developer, this is a great place to learn how to write your own behaviors to share with the rest of the Flash community.

You can also visit **http://webforums.macromedia.com/flash/** and click the **Flash Exchange Extensions** link to access the online forum for Flash extensions.

Macromedia TechNotes

http://www.macromedia.com/support/flash/technotes.html

Macromedia has another section of its Web site that lists all of the issues that have been reported and answered by Flash staff. This can be a valuable learning resource as well.

Third-Party Web Sites

http://www.flashkit.com/

http://www.ultrashock.com/

http://virtual-fx.net/

http://www.actionscripts.org/

http://www.flzone.net/

http://flashmove.com/

http://flazoom.com/

http://www.were-here.com/

http://www.popedeflash.com/

http://www.macromedia.com/support/flash/ts/documents/flash_websites.htm

I also keep a Flash-related blog where I post interesting happenings in the Flash community, common questions and answers, FLAs of common things such as news tickers, slide shows, and so forth, as well as tips/tricks here:

http://www.blot.com/flash_questions/

Flashforward

Flashforward is an international, educational Flash conference created by Lynda Weinman of lynda.com and Stewart McBride of United Digital Artists, and sponsored by Macromedia. It's a great conference to attend once you know Flash MX 2004 and want to take your skills to a new level. The best Flash developers and designers in the world present their technical and artistic work in an educational setting. You can learn more about Flashforward and its offerings by visiting **http://www.flashforward2004.com**.

CD-ROMs from Lynda.com

http://www.lynda.com/products/videos/index.html

Learning Flash MX 2004
Learning Flash MX 2004 ActionScript
Intermediate Flash MX 2004

Online Learning Library from Lynda.com

http://movielibrary.lynda.com

Lynda.com now offers a subscription service that allows you to see over 1,600 movies on a variety of subjects, including Flash MX 2004.

Books for Further Learning About Macromedia Flash MX 2004

Macromedia Flash MX 2004 Bible
by Robert Reinhardt and Snow Dowd
John Wiley & Sons, 2003
ISBN: 0764543032

Macromedia Flash MX ActionScript Bible
by Robert Reinhardt and Joey Lott
John Wiley & Sons, 2004
ISBN: 0764543547

ActionScript: The Definitive Guide
by Colin Moock and Gary Grossman
O'Reilly & Associates, 2001
ISBN: 1565928520

Flash MX 2004 Games Most Wanted
by Kristian Besley
APress L.P., 2003
ISBN: 1590592360

Flash Web Design: The V5 Remix
by Hillman Curtis
New Riders Publishing, 2001
ISBN: 0735708967

Macromedia Flash MX 2004 Hands-On Training
by Rosanna Yeung
Peachpit Press, December, 2003
ISBN: 0321202988

MTIV: Process, Inspiration, and Practice for the New Media Designer
by Hillman Curtis
New Riders Publishing, 2002
ISBN: 0735711658

Macromedia Flash MX Video
by Kristian Besley, Hoss Gifford, Todd Marks, and Brian Monnone
Friends of Ed, 2002
ISBN: 1903450853

Macromedia Flash MX 2004 Magic
by Michelangelo Capraro, et al.
New Riders, 2004
ISBN: 0735713774

Software

CSS

The following programs allow you to easily write and edit cascading style sheets (CSS):

- Macromedia Dreamweaver MX 2004 for Windows and Mac (**http://www.macromedia.com/software/dreamweaver/**)
- Adobe GoLive CS for Windows and Mac (**http://www.adobe.com/products/golive/**)
- CSSEdit for Mac (**http://www.macrabbit.com/cssedit/**)
- Bradsoft's Top Style for Windows (**http://www.bradsoft.com/topstyle/**)

MP3 Playback/Encoding

The following programs allow you to encode audio files as MP3:

- Apple's iTunes for Windows and Mac (**http://www.apple.com/iTunes/**)
- Nullsoft's Winamp for Windows (**http://www.winamp.com**)
- Panic's Audion for Mac (**http://www.panic.com/audion/**)

ID3 Editing

The following programs allow you to edit the ID3 tags in MP3 files:

- Apple's iTunes for Windows and Mac (**http://www.apple.com/iTunes/**)
- Nullsoft's Winamp for Windows (**http://www.winamp.com**)
- Panic's Audion for Mac (**http://www.panic.com/audion/**)
- MP3 Book Helper for Windows. This is an awesome and free program for Windows that allows you to easily edit the ID3 tags of MP3s. (**http://mp3bookhelper.sourceforge.net/**)

Flowcharts

The following programs allow you to specifically create flowcharts:

- Omni Group's OmniGraffle for Mac (**http://www.omnigroup.com/applications/omnigraffle/**)
- Microsoft's Visio for Windows (**http://office.microsoft.com/**)
- Edge Diagrammer for Windows (**http://www.pacestar.com/edge/**)

C. Getting Your Work Online/Using CGIs

| Web Presence Providers | CGI Scripts |

H•O•T

Macromedia Flash MX 2004 Beyond the Basics

In Chapter 9, "*Building a Form*," you learned how to construct a feedback form in Flash MX 2004 using the **TextInput** and **TextArea** components. You also learned that when the viewer fills out the form and clicks **submit**, the form results are sent–using a **LoadVars** object–to a CGI script to be processed. The CGI script processes the form results, and in the case of a feedback form like the one you built, emails those results to whichever email address you specify. But where can you get these CGI scripts? Moreover, where can you find a Web presence provider to store those CGI scripts, and your Web site, so that everyone can see your work? In this appendix, I will share a few places where you can find CGI scripts to use in your Flash MX 2004 projects, as well as Web presence providers where you can store and display your work to the world.

Web Presence Providers

Once you've designed your Web site, you'll need a place to store it–preferably a place that has a high-speed connection to the Internet, gives you lots of disk space for your content, and offers you lots of options. The companies that provide these services for you are called "Web presence providers". There are easily thousands and thousands of Web presence providers all around the world. So which one should you choose? Which ones stretch your dollars the furthest? Listed below are a few U.S.-based Web presence providers that I've personally hosted my work on as well as some that I've heard great things about.

Web Site Hosting

The following Web presence providers offer services to host your content. All of the following presence providers offer plans that allow access to prebuilt CGI scripts as well as the ability to install your own custom CGI scripts.

- pair Networks (**http://www.pair.com/**)–This is the presence provider that hosts my personal Web site, blot.com. I've been with them for years, and they provide great, basic service with lots of disk space at a great price.
- Media Temple (**http://www.mediatemple.net/**)–This is the "hip" place to host your work on the Internet. I've also hosted my work with Media Temple in the past, and I currently have friends that host their content with them as well. The fantastic thing about Media Temple is that they also offer the use–for an additional monthly fee–of a Flash Communication Server. The Flash Communication Server, as you may remember being mentioned earlier in this book, allows you to do true streaming (RTMP) of your MP3 and FLV files. Media Temple also offers Macromedia Cold Fusion MX services, which allow you integrate database content into your Flash MX 2004 movies. If you build Flash MX 2004 content for a living and you want access to all the bells and whistles, Media Temple is the place to be.
- DreamHost (**http://www.dreamhost.net/**)–DreamHost, like pair Networks, also offers great service with great options for a great price. Although I've never hosted any of my Web sites with them before, I know others who have and who are pleased with the service.

Flash Communication Server Hosting

As discussed in Chapters 10 and 11, special server software called the **Flash Communication Server** allows you to, among other things, truly stream (RTMP) media such as MP3s and FLVs. For more information about the benefits that a Flash Communication Server provides, see the section in Chapter 10, "*MP3 Player*," titled "What Is Progressive Download, and What Is Streaming?".

The following presence providers offer Flash Communication Server accounts:

- Media Temple (**http://www.mediatemple.net/**)–See the preceding section for a description of Media Temple.
- Uvault (**http://www.uvault.com/**)–Uvault offers Flash Communication Server options similar to those offered by Media Temple, but Uvault also maintains servers in Europe. If the majority of your client base is in Europe, you should look into Uvault's services.
- NI Solutions Group (**http://www.nisgroup.com/**)–NI Solutions Group offers both Flash Communication Server services as well as ColdFusion hosting.

You can also see an up-to-date list of providers that host Flash Communication Server accounts here: **http://www.macromedia.com/partners/flashcom/**.

CGI Scripts

If you already have a Web presence provider, or if you're signing up with one of the providers that are listed here in Appendix C, check with them before searching all over the Internet for CGI scripts to use with your Flash MX 2004 project. Every Web presence provider I've seen offers pre-installed CGI scripts that come with your account. Check in the support section of your Web presence provider's home page to see which CGI scripts are already installed for your use.

When locating a CGI script to use in conjunction with your Flash MX 2004 feedback form, you're essentially looking for one that processes form results. This CGI script is often called **FormMail** or **formmail.pl**. The CGI script doesn't need to be built specifically for Flash MX 2004–based forms; in fact, most of them aren't. Usually, as long as the CGI script accepts form results from an HTML form, you can use it with your Flash MX 2004 form as well. As you learned in Chapter 9, "*Building a Form*," the FormMail CGI script accepts your Flash MX 2004 form results, processes them, and then emails them to whomever you'd like. Once you've located a CGI script that can process your Flash MX 2004 form results, you simply have to look through the instructions or README file that came with the CGI–or look on the support section of your Web presence provider's home page–to see which variables the CGI script is expecting and which are "required." Then, as you saw in Chapter 9, you simply associate those variables with the fields in your Flash MX 2004 form, and you're good to go.

But what if your Web presence provider doesn't have a **formmail.pl** script–or something similar–where can you find a free one online? Before you go looking for a form-processing CGI script, first make sure your Web presence provider gives you access to your **cgi-bin** (a special folder to store your CGI scripts) and allow you to install your own CGI scripts. Once you've verified that, here are some places where you can get free CGI scripts for your Flash MX 2004 projects:

- Matt's Script Archive (**http://www.scriptarchive.com/**)–The original free script archive on the Internet. You can find his FormMail CGI script here, complete with installation and usage instructions: **http://www.scriptarchive.com/readme/formmail.html**.
- The CGI Resource Index (**http://www.cgi-resources.com/**)–Everything CGI-related is here. The CGI Resource Index tracks scripts, books, and resources alike. So much so, that if you do a search for "Form", it returns 154 form-related CGI script results. You can see CGI scripts that process form results here: **http://cgi.resourceindex.com/Programs_and_Scripts/Perl/Form_Processing/**.

Remember, if you're having trouble installing or configuring a CGI script on your Web presence provider's servers, don't feel shy about calling technical support. After all, that's part of what you're paying for!

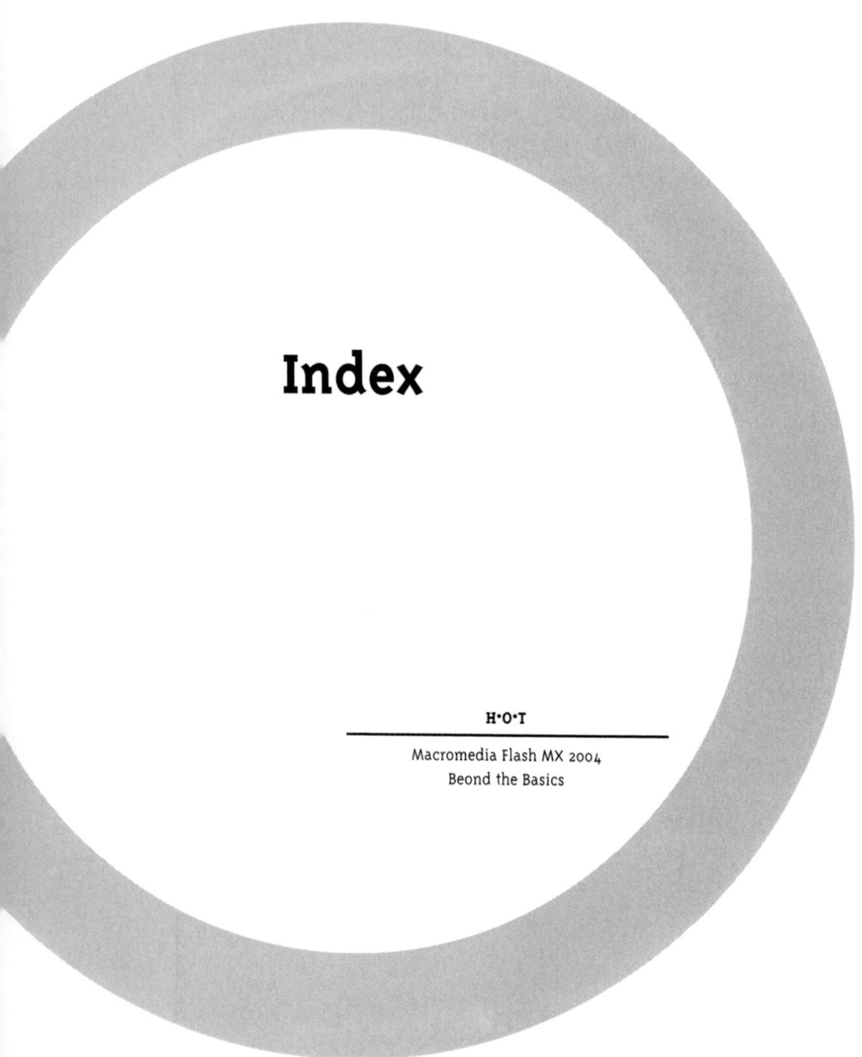

Index

H•O•T

Macromedia Flash MX 2004
Beond the Basics

A

C

D

E

J-K

L

M

N

O

P-Q

T

U

V

W-X-Y-Z

CD-ROM LICENSE AGREEMENT

THIS SOFTWARE LICENSE AGREEMENT CONSTITUTES AN AGREEMENT BETWEEN YOU AND LYNDA.COM, INC. YOU SHOULD CAREFULLY READ THE FOLLOWING TERMS AND CONDITIONS BEFORE OPENING THIS ENVELOPE. COPYING THIS SOFTWARE TO YOUR MACHINE, BREAKING THE SEAL, OR OTHERWISE REMOVING OR USING THE SOFTWARE INDICATES YOUR ACCEPTANCE OF THESE TERMS AND CONDITIONS. IF YOU DO NOT AGREE TO BE BOUND BY THE PROVISIONS OF THIS LICENSE AGREEMENT, YOU SHOULD PROMPTLY DELETE THE SOFTWARE FROM YOUR MACHINE.

TERMS AND CONDITIONS:

1. GRANT OF LICENSE. In consideration of payment of the License Fee, which was a part of the price you paid for this product, LICENSOR grants to you (the "Licensee") a non-exclusive right to use and display this copy of a Software program, along with any updates or upgrade releases of the Software for which you have paid (all parts and elements of the Software as well as the Software as a whole are hereinafter referred to as the "Software") on a single computer only (i.e., with a single CPU) at a single location, all as more particularly set forth and limited below. LICENSOR reserves all rights not expressly granted to you as Licensee in this License Agreement.

2. OWNERSHIP OF SOFTWARE. The license granted herein is not a sale of the original Software or of any copy of the Software. As Licensee, you own only the rights to use the Software as described herein and the magnetic or other physical media on which the Software is originally or subsequently recorded or fixed. LICENSOR retains title and ownership of the Software recorded on the original disk(s), as well as title and ownership of any subsequent copies of the Software irrespective of the form of media on or in which the Software is recorded or fixed. This license does not grant you any intellectual or other proprietary or other rights of any nature whatsoever in the Software.

3. USE RESTRICTIONS. As Licensee, you may use the Software only as expressly authorized in this License Agreement under the terms of paragraph 4. You may physically transfer the Software from one computer to another provided that the Software is used on only a single computer at any one time. You may not: (i) electronically transfer the Software from one computer to another over a network; (ii) make the Software available through a time-sharing service, network of computers, or other multiple user arrangement; (iii) distribute copies of the Software or related written materials to any third party, whether for sale or otherwise; (iv) modify, adapt, translate, reverse engineer, decompile, disassemble, or prepare any derivative work based on the Software or any element thereof; (v) make or distribute, whether for sale or otherwise, any hard copy or printed version of any of the Software nor any portion thereof nor any work of yours containing the Software or any component thereof; (vi) use any of the Software or any of its components in any other work.

4. THIS IS WHAT YOU CAN AND CANNOT DO WITH THE SOFTWARE. Even though in the preceding paragraph and elsewhere, LICENSOR has restricted your use of the Software, the following is the only thing you can do with the Software and the various elements of the Software: THE ARTWORK AND DATA CONTAINED ON THIS CD-ROM MAY NOT BE USED IN ANY MANNER WHATSOEVER OTHER THAN TO VIEW THE SAME ON YOUR COMPUTER, OR POST TO YOUR PERSONAL, NON-COMMERCIAL WEB SITE FOR EDUCATIONAL PURPOSES ONLY. THIS MATERIAL IS SUBJECT TO ALL OF THE RESTRICTION PROVISIONS OF THIS SOFTWARE LICENSE. SPECIFICALLY BUT NOT IN LIMITATION OF THESE RESTRICTIONS, YOU MAY NOT DISTRIBUTE, RESELL, OR TRANSFER THIS PART OF THE SOFTWARE DESIGNATED AS "CLUTS," NOR ANY OF YOUR DESIGN OR OTHER WORK CONTAINING ANY OF THE SOFTWARE OR DATA ON THIS CD-ROM, NOR ANY OF YOUR DESIGN OR OTHER WORK CONTAINING ANY DATA FROM THIS CD-ROM, ALL AS MORE PARTICULARLY RESTRICTED IN THE WITHIN SOFTWARE LICENSE.

5. COPY RESTRICTIONS. The Software and accompanying written materials are protected under United States copyright laws. Unauthorized copying and/or distribution of the Software and/or the related written materials are expressly forbidden. You may be held legally responsible for any copyright infringement that is caused, directly or indirectly, by your failure to abide by the terms of this License Agreement. Subject to the terms of this License Agreement and if the software is not otherwise copy protected, you may make one copy of the Software for backup purposes only. The copyright notice and any other proprietary notices which were included in the original Software must be reproduced and included on any such backup copy.

6. TRANSFER RESTRICTIONS. The license herein granted is personal to you, the Licensee. You may not transfer the Software nor any of its components or elements to anyone else, nor may you sell, lease, loan, sublicense, assign, or otherwise dispose of the Software nor any of its components or elements without the express written consent of LICENSOR, which consent may be granted or withheld at Licensor's sole discretion.

7. TERMINATION. The license herein granted hereby will remain in effect until terminated. This license will terminate automatically without further notice from LICENSOR in the event of the violation of any of the provisions hereof. As Licensee, you agree that upon such termination, you will promptly destroy any and all copies of the Software that remain in your possession and, upon request, will certify to such destruction in writing to LICENSOR.

8. LIMITATION AND DISCLAIMER OF WARRANTIES. a) THE SOFTWARE AND RELATED WRITTEN MATERIALS, INCLUDING ANY INSTRUCTIONS FOR USE, ARE PROVIDED ON AN "AS IS" BASIS, WITHOUT WARRANTY OF ANY KIND, EXPRESS OR IMPLIED. THIS DISCLAIMER OF WARRANTY EXPRESSLY INCLUDES, BUT IS NOT LIMITED TO, ANY IMPLIED WARRANTIES OF MERCHANTABILITY AND/OR OF FITNESS FOR A PARTICULAR PURPOSE. NO WARRANTY OF ANY KIND IS MADE AS TO WHETHER OR NOT THIS SOFTWARE INFRINGES UPON ANY RIGHTS OF ANY OTHER THIRD PARTIES. NO ORAL OR WRITTEN INFORMATION GIVEN BY LICENSOR, ITS SUPPLIERS, DISTRIBUTORS, DEALERS, EMPLOYEES, OR AGENTS, SHALL CREATE OR OTHERWISE ENLARGE THE SCOPE OF ANY WARRANTY HEREUNDER. LICENSEE ASSUMES THE ENTIRE RISK AS TO THE QUALITY AND THE PERFORMANCE OF SUCH SOFTWARE. SHOULD THE SOFTWARE PROVE DEFECTIVE, YOU, AS LICENSEE (AND NOT LICENSOR, ITS SUPPLIERS, DISTRIBUTORS, DEALERS, OR AGENTS), ASSUME THE ENTIRE COST OF ALL NECESSARY CORRECTION, SERVICING, OR REPAIR. b) LICENSOR warrants the disk(s) on which this copy of the Software is recorded or fixed to be free from defects in materials and workmanship, under normal use and service, for a period of ninety (90) days from the date of delivery, as evidenced by a copy of the applicable receipt. LICENSOR hereby limits the duration of any implied warranties with respect to the disk(s) to the duration of the express warranty. This limited warranty shall not apply if the disk(s) have been damaged by unreasonable use, accident, negligence, or by any other causes unrelated to defective materials or workmanship. c) LICENSOR does not warrant that the functions contained in the Software will be uninterrupted or error free and Licensee is encouraged to test the Software for Licensee's intended use prior to placing any reliance thereon. All risk of the use of the Software will be on you, as Licensee. d) THE LIMITED WARRANTY SET FORTH ABOVE GIVES YOU SPECIFIC LEGAL RIGHTS, AND YOU MAY ALSO HAVE OTHER RIGHTS, WHICH VARY FROM STATE TO STATE. SOME STATES DO NOT ALLOW THE LIMITATION OR EXCLUSION OF IMPLIED WARRANTIES OR OF INCIDENTAL OR CONSEQUENTIAL DAMAGES, SO THE LIMITATIONS AND EXCLUSIONS CONCERNING THE SOFTWARE AND RELATED WRITTEN MATERIALS SET FORTH ABOVE MAY NOT APPLY TO YOU.

9. LIMITATION OF REMEDIES. Licensor's entire liability and Licensee's exclusive remedy shall be the replacement of any disk(s) not meeting the limited warranty set forth in Section 8 above, which is returned to LICENSOR with a copy of the applicable receipt within the warranty period. Any replacement disk(s)will be warranted for the remainder of the original warranty period or thirty (30) days, whichever is longer.

10. LIMITATION OF LIABILITY. IN NO EVENT WILL LICENSOR OR ANYONE ELSE INVOLVED IN THE CREATION, PRODUCTION, AND/OR DELIVERY OF THIS SOFTWARE PRODUCT BE LIABLE TO LICENSEE OR ANY OTHER PERSON OR ENTITY FOR ANY DIRECT, INDIRECT, OR OTHER DAMAGES, INCLUDING, WITHOUT LIMITATION, ANY INTERRUPTION OF SERVICES, LOST PROFITS, LOST SAVINGS, LOSS OF DATA, OR ANY OTHER CONSEQUENTIAL, INCIDENTAL, SPECIAL, OR PUNITIVE DAMAGES ARISING OUT OF THE PURCHASE, USE, INABILITY TO USE, OR OPERATION OF THE SOFTWARE, EVEN IF LICENSOR OR ANY AUTHORIZED LICENSOR DEALER HAS BEEN ADVISED OF THE POSSIBILITY OF SUCH DAMAGES. BY YOUR USE OF THE SOFTWARE, YOU ACKNOWLEDGE THAT THE LIMITATION OF LIABILITY SET FORTH IN THIS LICENSE WAS THE BASIS UPON WHICH THE SOFTWARE WAS OFFERED BY LICENSOR, AND YOU ACKNOWLEDGE THAT THE PRICE OF THE SOFTWARE LICENSE WOULD BE HIGHER IN THE ABSENCE OF SUCH LIMITATION. SOME STATES DO NOT ALLOW THE LIMITATION OR EXCLUSION OF LIABILITY FOR INCIDENTAL OR CONSEQUENTIAL DAMAGES, SO THE ABOVE LIMITATIONS AND EXCLUSIONS MAY NOT APPLY TO YOU.

11. UPDATES. LICENSOR, at its sole discretion, may periodically issue updates of the Software, which you may receive upon request and payment of the applicable update fee in effect from time to time and in such event, all of the provisions of the within License Agreement shall apply to such updates.

12. EXPORT RESTRICTIONS. Licensee agrees not to export or re-export the Software and accompanying documentation (or any copies thereof) in violation of any applicable U.S. laws or regulations.

13. ENTIRE AGREEMENT. YOU, AS LICENSEE, ACKNOWLEDGE THAT: (i) YOU HAVE READ THIS ENTIRE AGREEMENT AND AGREE TO BE BOUND BY ITS TERMS AND CONDITIONS; (ii) THIS AGREEMENT IS THE COMPLETE AND EXCLUSIVE STATEMENT OF THE UNDERSTANDING BETWEEN THE PARTIES AND SUPERSEDES ANY AND ALL PRIOR ORAL OR WRITTEN COMMUNICATIONS RELATING TO THE SUBJECT MATTER HEREOF; AND (iii) THIS AGREEMENT MAY NOT BE MODIFIED, AMENDED, OR IN ANY WAY ALTERED EXCEPT BY A WRITING SIGNED BY BOTH YOURSELF AND AN OFFICER OR AUTHORIZED REPRESENTATIVE OF LICENSOR.

14. SEVERABILITY. In the event that any provision of this License Agreement is held to be illegal or otherwise unenforceable, such provision shall be deemed to have been deleted from this License Agreement while the remaining provisions of this License Agreement shall be unaffected and shall continue in full force and effect.

15. GOVERNING LAW. This License Agreement shall be governed by the laws of the State of California applicable to agreements wholly to be performed therein and of the United States of America, excluding that body of the law related to conflicts of law. This License Agreement shall not be governed by the United Nations Convention on Contracts for the International Sale of Goods, the application of which is expressly excluded. No waiver of any breach of the provisions of this License Agreement shall be deemed a waiver of any other breach of this License Agreement.

16. RESTRICTED RIGHTS LEGEND. Use, duplication, or disclosure by the Government is subject to restrictions as set forth in subparagraph (c)(1)(ii) of the Rights in Technical Data and Computer Software clause at 48 CFR § 252.227-7013 and DFARS § 252.227-7013 or subparagraphs (c) (1) and (c)(2) of the Commercial Computer Software-Restricted Rights at 48 CFR § 52.227.19, as applicable. Contractor/manufacturer: LICENSOR: LYNDA.COM, INC, c/o PEACHPIT PRESS, 1249 Eighth Street, Berkeley, CA 94710.